W9-CJN-215

KINANTHROPOMETRY AND EXERCISE PHYSIOLOGY LABORATORY MANUAL

OTHER TITLES FROM E & FN SPON

Drugs in Sport
Second edition
D. Mottram

Science and Soccer
T. Reilly

Foods, Nutrition and Sports Performance
An International Scientific Consensus organized by Mars
Edited by C. Williams and J. T. Devlin

Science and Golf II
Proceedings of the World Scientific Congress of Golf
Edited by J. A. Cochran and M. Farrally

Kinanthropometry IV
J. W. Duquet and J. A. P. Day

Physiology of Sports
Edited by T. Reilly, N. Secher, P. Snell and C. Williams

Biomechanics and Medicine in Swimming VII
J. Troup, A. P. Hollander and D. Strass

Science and Racket Sports
Edited by T. Reilly, M. Hughes and A. Lees

Writing Successfully in Science
M. O'Connor

Good Style
Writing for Science and Technology
J. Kirkman

Journal of Sports Sciences
General Editor T. Reilly

For further information about these and other titles published by E & FN Spon, please contact: The Promotions Department, Chapman & Hall, 2–6 Boundary Row, London SE1 8HN. Telephone: 0171 865 0066.

KINANTHROPOMETRY AND EXERCISE PHYSIOLOGY LABORATORY MANUAL

Tests, procedures and data

Edited by

Roger Eston

Division of Health and Human Performance, University of Wales, Bangor, UK

and

Thomas Reilly

Centre for Sport and Exercise Sciences, Liverpool John Moores University, UK

QP
303
.K56
1996

Published by
E & FN Spon, an imprint of Chapman & Hall, 2–6 Boundary Row,
London SE1 8HN, UK

Chapman & Hall, 2–6 Boundary Row, London SE1 8HN, UK

Blackie Academic & Professional, Wester Cleddens Road, Bishopbriggs, Glasgow G64 2NZ, UK

Chapman & Hall GmbH, Pappelallee 3, 69469 Weinheim, Germany

Chapman & Hall USA, 115 Fifth Avenue, New York, NY 10003, USA

Chapman & Hall Japan, ITP-Japan, Kyowa Building, 3F, 2-2-1 Hirakawacho, Chiyoda-ku, Tokyo 102, Japan

Chapman & Hall Australia, 102 Dodds Street, South Melbourne, Victoria 3205, Australia

Chapman & Hall India, R. Seshadri, 32 Second Main Road, CIT East, Madras 600 035, India

First edition 1996

© 1996 E & FN Spon

Typeset in 10/12 Palatino by Pure Tech India Ltd, Pondicherry

ISBN 0 419 17880 5

Apart from any fair dealing for the purposes of research or private study, or criticism or review, as permitted under the UK Copyright Designs and Patents Act, 1988, this publication may not be reproduced, stored, or transmitted, in any form or by any means, without the prior permission in writing of the publishers, or in the case of reprographic reproduction only in accordance with the terms of the licences issued by the Copyright Licensing Agency in the UK, or in accordance with the terms of licences issued by the appropriate Reproduction Rights Organization outside the UK. Enquiries concerning reproduction outside the terms stated here should be sent to the publishers at the London address printed on this page.

The publisher makes no representation, express or implied, with regard to the accuracy of the information contained in this book and cannot accept any legal responsibility or liability for any errors or omissions that may be made.

A catalogue record for this book is available from the British Library

Library of Congress Catalog Card Number: 95–69213

∞ Printed on permanent acid-free text paper, manufactured in accordance with ANSI/NISO Z39.48-1992 and ANSI/NISO Z39.48-1984 (Permanence of Paper).

LONGWOOD COLLEGE LIBRARY
FARMVILLE, VIRGINIA 23901

CONTENTS

List of contributors xi

Introduction 1

PART ONE: SIZE, SHAPE, PROPORTION AND GROWTH **3**

1 Human body composition **5**
M. R. Hawes
1.1 Introduction 5
1.2 Levels of approach 5
1.3 Validity 8
1.4 Body composition assessment by densitometry 8
1.5 Estimation of proportionate fatness from equations based on skinfold thickness 10
1.6 Assessment of fat-free mass by bioelectrical impedance 11
1.7 Ratios 13
1.8 Proportionate muscle mass 14
1.9 Proportionate bone mass 15
1.10 Other considerations 16
1.11 Practical 1: Densitometry 16
1.12 Practical 2: Measurement of skinfolds 19
1.13 Practical 3: Proportionate weight distribution of adipose tissue and fat-free mass 25
1.14 Practical 4: Estimation of muscle mass and regional muscularity 28
1.15 Practical 5: Estimation of skeletal mass 30
Acknowledgements 31
References 31

2 Somatotyping **35**
W. Duquet and J. E. L. Carter
2.1 History 35
2.2 The Heath–Carter somatotype method 35
2.3 Relevance of somatotyping 38
2.4 Practical 1: Calculation of anthropometric somatotypes 39
2.5 Practical 2: Comparison of somatotypes of different groups 44
2.6 Practical 3: Analysis of longitudinal somatotype series 48
References 49

3 Physical growth, maturation and performance **51**
G. Beunen
3.1 Introduction 51

LONGWOOD LIBRARY
1000279073

3.2 Standards of normal growth 53
3.3 Biological maturation: skeletal age 58
3.4 Physical fitness 63
Appendix 68
References 69

PART TWO: NEUROMUSCULAR AND GONIOMETRIC ASPECTS OF MOVEMENT 73

4 Skeletal muscle function **75**
V. Baltzopoulos
4.1 Introduction 75
4.2 Basic structure and function of skeletal muscle 75
4.3 Motor unit types and function 76
4.4 Training adaptations 76
4.5 Muscular actions 76
4.6 Force–length relationship in isolated muscle 77
4.7 Force–velocity relationship in isolated muscle 77
4.8 Muscle function during joint movement 79
4.9 Measurement of dynamic (concentric–eccentric) muscle function 80
4.10 Moment–angular velocity relationship 80
4.11 Isokinetic dynamometry applications 81
4.12 Effects of sex and age on muscle function 82
4.13 Data collection and analysis considerations 83
4.14 Practical 1: Assessment of muscle function during isokinetic knee extension and flexion 85
4.15 Practical 2: Assessment of isometric force–joint position relationship 88
References 90

5 Posture **95**
P. H. Dangerfield
5.1 Introduction 95
5.2 Curvatures and movement of the vertebral column 96
5.3 Defining and quantification of posture 97
5.4 Assessment of posture and body shape 99
5.5 Other clinically based criterion techniques of assessing posture 102
5.6 Measurements in a dynamic phase of posture (movement analysis) 106
5.7 Spinal length and diurnal variation 108
5.8 Conclusion 109
5.9 Practical 1: Measurement of posture and body shape 109
5.10 Practical 2: Assessment of sitting posture 110
5.11 Practical 3: Lateral deviations 110
5.12 Practical 4: Leg-length discrepancy 111
Acknowledgements 112
References 112

6 Flexibility **115**
J. Borms and P. Van Roy

6.1 Introduction 115
6.2 Measurement instruments 116
6.3 Practical: Flexibility measurements with goniometry 116
6.4 General discussion 141
References 143

PART THREE: AEROBIC AND ANAEROBIC CONSIDERATIONS **145**

7 Lung function **147**
R. G. Eston
7.1 Introduction 147
7.2 Evaluation of pulmonary ventilation during exercise 148
7.3 Post-exercise changes in lung function 152
7.4 Assessment of resting lung function 152
7.5 Pulmonary diffusing capacity 159
7.6 Sources of variation in lung function testing 160
7.7 Lung function in special populations 162
7.8 Prediction of lung function 163
7.9 Definition of obstructive and restrictive ventilatory defects 164
7.10 Practical exercises 164
7.11 Practical 1: Assessment of resting lung volumes 164
7.12 Practical 2: Assessment of lung volumes during exercise 167
7.13 Practical 3: Measurement of pulmonary diffusing capacity 170
References 172

8 Metabolic rate and energy balance **175**
C. B. Cooke
8.1 Basal metabolic rate 175
8.2 Measurement of energy expenditure 177
8.3 Practical 1: Estimation of body surface area and resting metabolic rate 177
8.4 Practical 2: Estimation of resting metabolic rate from fat-free mass 178
8.5 Practical 3: Measurement of oxygen uptake using the Douglas bag technique 178
8.6 Practical 4: The respiratory quotient 186
8.7 Practical 5: Estimation of RMR using the Douglas bag technique 189
8.8 Practical 6: Energy balance 190
8.9 Summary 194
References 194

9 Maximal oxygen uptake, economy and efficiency **197**
C. B. Cooke
9.1 Introduction 197
9.2 Direct determination of maximal oxygen uptake 197
9.3 Prediction of maximal oxygen uptake 201
9.4 Running economy 203
9.5 Efficiency 208
9.6 Practical 1: Direct determination of $\dot{V}O_{2\,max}$ using a discontinuous cycle ergometer protocol 211

9.7 Practical 2: Measurement of running economy 213
9.8 Practical 3: Measurement of loaded running efficiency 214
9.9 Practical 4: Measurement of the efficiency of cycling and stepping 217
References 219

10 Exercise intensity regulation **221**
J. G. Williams and R. G. Eston
10.1 Introduction 221
10.2 Methods of determining exercise intensity 221
10.3 Psychological information 226
10.4 Practical: Use of ratings of perceived exertion to determine and control the intensity of cycling exercise 229
10.5 Summary 232
References 233

11 Maximal intensity exercise **237**
E. M. Winter
11.1 Introduction 237
11.2 Terminology 237
11.3 Historical background 238
11.4 Screening 239
11.5 Cycle ergometer based tests 239
11.6 Practical 1: Wingate-type procedures 239
11.7 Practical 2: Optimization procedures 244
11.8 Practical 3: Correction procedures 249
11.9 Other procedures 251
References 253

PART FOUR: SPECIAL CONSIDERATIONS **257**

12 Thermoregulation **259**
T. Reilly and N. T. Cable
12.1 Introduction 259
12.2 Processes of heat loss/heat gain 259
12.3 Control of body temperature 260
12.4 Thermoregulation and other control systems 262
12.5 Measurements of body temperature 264
12.6 Thermoregulatory responses to exercise 265
12.7 Environmental factors 266
12.8 Anthropometry and heat exchange 269
12.9 Practical exercises 270
12.10 Practical 1: Muscular efficiency 271
12.11 Practical 2: Thermoregulatory responses to exercise 272
12.12 Practical 3: Estimation of partitional heat exchange 273
References 275

13 Assessing performance in young children 277
C. Boreham
13.1 Introduction 277
13.2 Growth maturation and performance 278
13.3 Performance testing of children 281
13.4 Anthropometric tests (body composition) 281
13.5 Aerobic endurance performance 283
13.6 Aerobic endurance testing in children 286
13.7 Determination of the anaerobic threshold 288
13.8 Field tests of aerobic endurance 289
13.9 Strength and power 289
13.10 Field test batteries for children 291
References 294

14 Statistical methods in kinanthropometry and exercise physiology 297
A. M. Nevill
14.1 Introduction 297
14.2 Organizing and describing data in kinanthropometry and exercise physiology 297
14.3 Investigating relationships in kinanthropometry and exercise physiology 303
14.4 Comparing experimental data in kinanthropometry 310
Appendix: Critical values 317
References 320

15 Scaling: adjusting for differences in body size 321
E. M. Winter and A. M. Nevill
15.1 Introduction 321
15.2 The ratio standard – the traditional method 321
15.3 Regression standards and ANCOVA 323
15.4 Allometry and power function standards 325
15.5 Practical 1: The identification of allometric relationships 326
15.6 Power function ratio standards 328
15.7 Practical 2: A worked example 329
15.8 Summary 330
Appendix A 330
Appendix B 333
References 335

Appendix: Relationships between units of energy, work, power and speed 337

Index 339

CONTRIBUTORS

V. BALTZOPOULOS
Division of Sport Science,
Alsager Faculty,
Manchester Metropolitan University, Alsager, UK.

G. BEUNEN
Centre for Physical Development Research,
Faculty of Physical Education and Physiotherapy,
K. U. Leuven, Leuven, Belgium.

C. BOREHAM
Department of Physical Education,
The Queen's University of Belfast, Belfast.

J. BORMS
Health Promotion, Human Biometry
Vrije Universiteit Brussel, Brussels, Belgium

N. T. CABLE
Centre for Sport and Exercise Sciences,
School of Human Sciences,
Liverpool John Moores University, Liverpool, UK.

J. E. L. CARTER
Department of Exercise and Nutritional Sciences,
San Diego State University, San Diego, CA, USA.

C. B. COOKE
Carnegie Physical Education and Sports Studies Group,
Leeds Metropolitan University, Leeds, UK

P. H. DANGERFIELD
Department of Human Anatomy and Cell Biology and Orthopaedic and Accident Surgery,
The University of Liverpool, Liverpool, UK.

W. DUQUET
Human Biometry,
Vrije Universiteit Brussel, Brussels, Belgium.

R. G. ESTON
Division of Health and Human Performance,
University of Wales, Bangor, Gwynedd, UK.

M. R. HAWES
Faculty of Kinesiology,
University of Calgary, Calgary, Alberta, Canada.

A. M. NEVILL
Centre for Sport and Exercise Sciences,
School of Human Sciences,
Liverpool John Moores University, Liverpool, UK.

T. REILLY
Centre for Sport and Exercise Sciences,
School of Human Sciences,
Liverpool John Moores University, Liverpool, UK.

P. VAN ROY
Experimental Anatomy,
Vrije Universiteit Brussel, Brussels, Belgium.

J. G. WILLIAMS
Department of Kinesiology,
West Chester University, West Chester, PA, USA.

E. M. WINTER
Department of Physical Education, Sport and Leisure,
De Montfort University Bedford, Bedford, UK.

INTRODUCTION

Kinanthropometry is a relatively new term although the subject area to which it refers has a rich history. It describes the relationship between structure and function of the human body, particularly within the context of movement. The subject area itself was formalized with the establishment of the International Society for Advancement of Kinanthropometry at Glasgow in 1986. The Society supports its own international conferences and publication of Proceedings linked with these events. Until now it has had no laboratory manual which would serve as a compendium of practical activities for students in this field. This text is published under the aegis of the International Society for Advancement of Kinanthropometry, in particular its working group on 'Publications and Information Exchange' in an attempt to make good the deficit.

Kinanthropometry has applications in a wide range of areas including, for example, biomechanics, ergonomics, growth and development, human sciences, medicine, nutrition, physical education and sports science. The book was motivated by the need for a suitable laboratory resource which academic staff could use in the planning and conduct of class practicals in these areas. The content was designed to cover specific teaching modules in kinanthropometry and other academic programmes, such as physiology, within which kinanthropometry is sometimes incorporated. It was intended also to include practical activities of relevance to clinicians, for example in measuring metabolic functions, muscle performance, physiological responses to exercise, posture and so on. In all cases the emphasis is placed on the anthropometric aspects of the topic.

The content is orientated towards laboratory practicals but offers much more than a prescription of a series of laboratory exercises. A comprehensive theoretical background is provided for each topic so that users of the text are not obliged to conduct extensive literature reviews in order to place the subject in context. Each chapter contains an explanation of the appropriate methodology and where possible an outline of specific laboratory-based practicals. This is not always feasible, for example in studying growth processes in child athletes. In such cases, virtually all aspects of performance testing in children are covered and special considerations with regard to data acquisition on children are outlined. Methodologies for researchers in growth and development are also described.

Many of the topics included in this text called for unique individual approaches and so it was deemed unreasonable to impose a rigid structure for each chapter on the contributors. In some cases practical laboratory activities are presented alongside the methodology as the material and ideas in the chapter are advanced. In other cases the laboratory practicals are retained until the end of that chapter as the earlier text provides the theoretical framework for their conduct. Thus, each chapter is self-standing and independent of the others; together the contributions represent a collective set of exercises for an academic programme in kinanthropometry. The self-sufficiency of each contribution also explains why relevant concepts crop up in more than one chapter, for example concepts of efficiency, metabolism, maximal oxygen uptake, scaling and so on. The last two chapters are concerned with basic statistical analysis which is designed to inform researchers and students about data handling. This should promote proper use of common statistical techniques for analysing data obtained on human subjects as well as help to avoid common abuses of basic statistical tools.

It is hoped that this text will stimulate improvement in teaching and instruction strategies in the application of laboratory techniques in kinanthropometry and related disciplines. In this way we will have made our contribution towards the education of the next generation of specialists concerned with relating human structure to its function.

Roger Eston
Thomas Reilly

PART ONE

SIZE, SHAPE, PROPORTION AND GROWTH

HUMAN BODY COMPOSITION 1

M. R. Hawes

1.1 INTRODUCTION

The quantity and proportion of various constituents of the human body are empirically linked to health, disease and quality of life. As a result, interest in body composition has grown in the past 100 years as new relationships and new technologies for measuring various constituents have emerged. Body composition is examined from the perspective of mortality and morbidity in obesity, proportionate changes during growth, functional relationships with fitness and sport performance, nutrition, cultural differences and many others.

Basic texts in human anatomy often describe the human structure in terms of increasing organizational complexity ranging from chemical (atoms and molecules) to anatomical described as a hierarchy of cell, tissue, organ, system and organism. Body composition may be described as a fundamental problem of quantitative anatomy which may be approached at any organizational level as the sum of the appropriate component parts (Figure 1.1). Knowledge of the interrelationship of constituents within a given level or between levels is important for a fundamental understanding of body composition, and may be useful for indirectly estimating the size of a particular compartment (Wang *et al.*, 1992).

1.2 LEVELS OF APPROACH

At the first level of composition are the composite masses of approximately 50 elements which comprise the **atomic level**. Total body mass is 98% determined by the combination of oxygen, carbon, hydrogen, nitrogen, calcium and phosphorus with the remaining 44 elements comprising less than 2% of total body mass. Technology is available for *in vivo* measurement of all of the major elements found in humans. Current methods usually involve exposure of the subject to ionizing radiation which places severe restrictions on the utility of this approach. An example of body composition analysis at this level would be the use of whole-body ^{40}K counting to determine total body potassium (TBK). The primary importance of the atomic level is the relationship of specific elements to other levels of organization.

The **molecular level** of organization is made up of more than 100 000 chemical compounds. These may be reduced to five main chemical groupings – lipid, water, protein, carbohydrate (mainly glycogen) and mineral. The most confusion arises with the term lipid, which may be defined as those chemicals that are insoluble in water and soluble in organic solvents such as ether. There are many forms of lipid found in the human body, but by far the most common is triglyceride (commonly, though not exclusively, referred to as fat, i.e. a particular type of lipid); triglyceride has a relatively constant density of $0.9\,g\,ml^{-1}$. Other forms of lipid comprise less than 10% of total body lipid and have varying densities; for example phospholipids $1.035\,g\,ml^{-1}$

Kinanthropometry and Exercise Physiology Laboratory Manual: Tests, procedures and data Edited by Roger Eston and Thomas Reilly. Published in 1996 by E & FN Spon. ISBN 0 419 17880 5

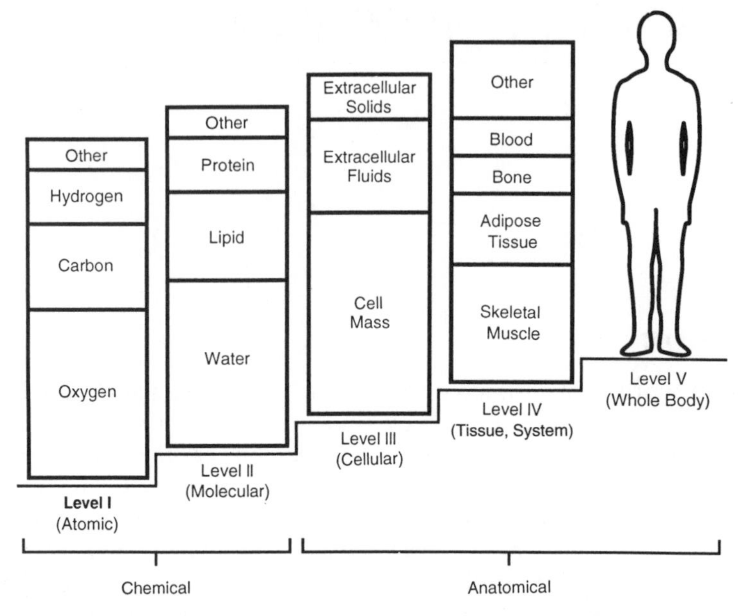

Figure 1.1 The five levels of human body composition. (Adapted from Wang *et al.*, 1992.)

and cholesterol 1.067 g ml^{-1}. Lipid is often categorized as 'essential' and 'non-essential' on the basis of function. Essential lipids are those lipids without which other structures could not function, for example lipid found in cell membranes, nervous tissue and so on and is variously estimated at 3–4% of total body mass. Although triglyceride has a physiological function (insulation and energy storage), it is considered non-essential. On this basis the fat-free mass (FFM) is composed of the mass of all body tissues with the specific exclusion of all elements soluble in organic solvents. The lean body mass (LBM), however, is the FFM with the inclusion of the essential lipids. Fat is closely linked with the notion of body composition, but it should be clearly understood that there is no means of direct *in vivo* measurement of the fat compartment. The closest that we can come is to divide the molecular components of the body into the lipid and non-lipid compartments and estimate their relative proportions from densitometry. Other molecular compartments may be estimated by isotope dilution (total body water), dual photon absorptiometry (osseous mineral) or neutron activation analysis of nitrogen (total body protein).

The **cellular** level might also be considered the first anatomical level of organization. This level of organization divides the body into total cell mass, extracellular fluid (ECF) and extracellular solids (ECS). The total cell mass is composed of many different types of cells including adipocytes, myocytes and osteocytes. A clear distinction should be drawn between lipid and adipocyte. Lipid is the organic solvent extractable component that occupies much of the cytoplasm of an adipocyte. An adipocyte is a type of connective tissue cell which includes a nucleus, organelles and a cell membrane as well as cytoplasmic lipid. There is no direct method of measuring discrete cell masses or total cell mass.

The ECF includes intravascular and extravascular plasma (interstitial fluid). This fluid is predominantly water and acts as a medium for the exchange of gases, nutrients and waste products. The ECF compartment may be estimated by isotope dilution methods.

The ECS includes organic substances such as collagen and elastin fibres in connective tissue and inorganic elements such as calcium and phosphorus which are found predominantly in bone. The ECS compartment cannot be measured directly although several components of the total compartment may be estimated by neutron activation analysis.

The fourth level of organization includes **tissues, organs** and **systems** which although of differing levels of complexity are functional arrangements of tissues. The four categories of tissue are connective, epithelial, muscular and nervous. Adipose and bone are forms of connective tissue which together with muscle tissue account for about 75% of total body mass.

Adipose tissue consists of adipocytes together with collagen and elastin fibres which support the tissue. Lipid is a component of adipose tissue. Adipose tissue is predominantly found in the subcutaneous region of the body but is also found in significant quantities surrounding organs (visceral + omental), within tissue such as muscle (interstitial) and in the bone marrow (yellow marrow). The density of adipose tissue varies according to the proportions of its constituents, the greater the proportion of fat stored the closer the density to $0.9\,g\,ml^{-1}$. The lesser the amount of fat stored relative to the other elements of adipose tissue, the greater the density of the tissue.

There is no direct method for the *in vivo* measurement of adipose tissue volume although recent advances in medical imaging technology (ultrasound, magnetic resonance imaging, computed tomography) offer great potential for accurate estimation of the quantity of adipose and other tissues. The technology permits measurement of discrete tissue areas from sectional images and serial sections may be combined by geometric modelling to predict regional and total volumes accurately. Although there are limited access and high costs associated with these techniques, they will potentially provide alternative criterion methods for the validation of more accessible and less costly methods for the assessment of body composition.

Bone is a specialized connective tissue in which the ground substance secreted by the osteocytes mixes with blood-borne minerals and becomes a hard, though dynamic tissue. The density of bone varies considerably according to such factors as age, gender and activity level. The range of bone density in cadaveric subjects has been reported as 1.18–$1.33\,g\,ml^{-1}$ by Martin *et al.* (1986) and 1.25–$1.30\,g\,ml^{-1}$ by Leusink (1972). The quantity of bone tissue may be estimated by dual photon absorptiometry (DPA) and dual energy x-ray absorptiometry (DEXA).

Muscle tissue is found in three forms, skeletal, visceral and cardiac. The density of muscle tissue is relatively constant although the quantity of interstitial adipose within the tissue will introduce some variability. Values for muscle density have been reported as $1.062\,g\,ml^{-1}$ by Mendez and Keys (1960) and $1.066\,g\,ml^{-1}$ by Forbes *et al.* (1953). Again, the quantity of muscle tissue cannot be measured directly *in vivo* although the imaging techniques mentioned with respect to adipose tissue also offer promise for measuring muscle tissue.

The other tissues, nervous and epithelial, have been regarded as less significant tissues in body composition analysis. As a result, attempts have not been made to quantify these tissues; they are usually regarded as residual tissues.

The **whole-body** or organismic level of organization considers the body as a single unit dealing with overall size, shape, surface area, density and external characteristics. Clearly these characteristics are the most readily measured and include stature, body mass and volume.

The five levels of organization of the body provide a conceptual framework within which the many approaches to body composition may be placed in context. It is evident that there must be interrelationships between levels which, if constant, may provide quantitative associations facilitating estimates of previously unknown compartments. The understanding of interrelationships between levels of complexity also guards against erroneous interpretation of data determined at different levels. As an example, body lipid is typically assessed at the molecular level whereas the quantity of muscle tissue, in a health and fitness setting, is addressed at the tissue or system level by circumference measurements and correction for skinfold thicknesses. The two methods are incompatible in the sense that they overlap by both measuring the interstitial lipid compartment.

1.3 VALIDITY

In an exercise and fitness setting the measurement of body composition focuses on the quantity and proportion of fat in the body with increasing, though peripheral, interest in estimates of muscularity and skeletal density. Any scientific method is suspect until it is proven to measure what it purports to measure; this is the notion of validity. The only direct way of validating those methods that purport to estimate the quantity of a given substance in the human body is to apply the method and compare the results to the true measure of the substance. This implies removing the substance in total by dissection and weighing its mass. Even this is not foolproof. Several valid criticisms may be raised including the observation that human tissue may degenerate and therefore change its composition after death; also a cadaver is typically an aged person who may have been bedridden for an extended period prior to death and thus may not be representative of healthy tissue proportions. Since direct validation of new methods is not practical, established relationships between tissues have been employed to make a best estimate of body composition. One indirect method in particular, densitometry, has been accorded the status of a criterion method and new methods that purport to estimate body fatness (for example, skinfold methods and bioelectric impedance) are invariably validated against it. Methods validated in this manner are described by Martin and Drinkwater (1991) as 'doubly indirect' with the potential for compounding errors of the new method with existing errors present in the criterion method. It should be evident from this discussion that assessment of body composition is not an exact science and all methods should be tempered with a sceptical examination of their validity.

1.4 BODY COMPOSITION ASSESSMENT BY DENSITOMETRY

Densitometry is an approach to estimating body fatness based on the idea that the proportion of fat to non-fat can be calculated from the known densities of the two compartments and the measured whole-body density. A simple calculation provides the relative proportion between the fat and non-fat compartments. There is no doubt that whole-body density can be measured but the constancy of the two former values is questionable.

Measurement of whole-body density is based on the relationship between density, mass and volume and Archimedes' Principle of water displacement. Mass is determined by weighing the body in air and volume is determined by the amount of water displaced when the body is fully submerged. The volume of water displaced may be measured by a manometer, by the difference in pressure acting on a force transducer inserted into the wall of the water tank, or by measuring the buoyant force acting on the submerged body (i.e. the difference between the weight of the body in air and the weight of the body when submerged). The buoyant force acting on an object is equal to the mass of the water that it displaces.

Several adjustments to the volume determined are required. Account should be taken of the residual volume of air left in the lungs after forceful exhalation, the volume of gas occupying the gastrointestinal tract, and adjustment made for the density of water at different temperatures and barometric pressure. Residual volume is typically determined by having the subject exhale maximally and then breathe within a closed system that contains a known quantity of pure oxygen. Nitrogen is an inert gas, meaning that the quantity of N_2 inhaled and exhaled as part of air does not change in response to metabolic processes. Therefore the quantity of N_2 in the lungs after maximum exhalation is representative of the residual volume. The N_2 remaining in the lungs after maximal exhalation is diluted by a known quantity of pure oxygen during several breaths of the closed circuit gas. Analysis of the resulting gas mixture from the closed circuit system reveals the dilution factor of N_2 and since N_2 occupies a constant proportion of air, the residual volume may be calculated. After determination of body volume, the following relationship is used to determine total body density.

$$\text{Density} = \text{Mass}/\text{Volume}$$

In order to divide the body into its fat and non-fat compartments three assumptions must be made:

1. the density of the fat compartment is known and is constant;
2. the density of the non-fat compartment is known and is constant;

with the implication that over a broad population

3. the components of the non-fat compartment normally exist in constant proportions.

The fat compartment of the body consists primarily of triglyceride which has a constant density of $0.9\,g\,ml^{-1}$. There are small quantities of other forms of lipid in the body located in the nervous system and within the membrane of all cells. The density of these lipids is greater than that of triglyceride but the relatively small quantity of each will have very little effect upon total density of body lipid. Thus the density of body fat may be accepted as relatively constant at $0.9\,g\,ml^{-1}$.

The second assumption that density and proportion of the lean compartment is constant is less tenable. The density and proportion of the tissues that contribute to the lean mass (predominantly muscle and bone but also including other forms of connective tissue, nervous and epithelial tissue) must be known in order to derive a single value for density. Only small differences in the density of fat-free muscle tissue have been reported (the interstitial fat is measured as part of the fat compartment); however, it is very evident that the proportion of muscle tissue will vary from individual to individual. Of more consequence is the inter- and intra-individual variance in the density of bone tissue. In a limited sample of 25 cadaveric specimens the density of bone varied between 1.18 and $1.33\,g\,ml^{-1}$ and represented a range of 16.3–25.7% of the adipose tissue free mass. It is evident from these data, which must be regarded as quite homogeneous, that the assumptions with respect to the fat-free mass cannot be accepted without severe limitations. The assignment of a value for the density of the fat-free mass must at best be considered as a mean value with a standard deviation suggested by Bakker and Struikenkamp (1977) to be in the order of $0.01\,g\,ml^{-1}$ and by Martin and Drinkwater (1991) to be as high as $0.10\,g\,ml^{-1}$. The effect of a difference between the assigned and actual density of the fat-free mass (dffm) in a given individual of as little as $\pm 0.02\,g\,ml^{-1}$ results in an error for estimated fat percentage (%Fat) in the order of $\pm 7\%$ (Figure 1.2). The resulting error from accepting these assumptions is to underestimate %Fat in individuals with a dense lean mass (typically athletes) and to overestimate in cases where the individual has a light skeletal mass (children, osteoporotics).

Adjustments have been proposed for subgroups of the general population; for example

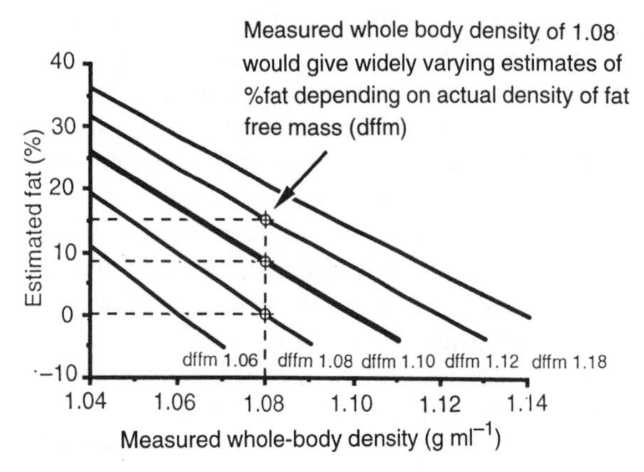

Figure 1.2 Siri's equation for estimation of %Fat plotted for different values of assumed density of fat-free mass (dffm). (Adapted from Martin and Drinkwater, 1991.)

Lohman *et al.* (1984) suggested a value of 1.063 g ml^{-1} for the density of the fat-free mass in new borns with adjustments up to 1.1 g ml^{-1} by early adulthood; Schutte *et al.* (1984) suggested a value of 1.113 g ml^{-1} for the North American Black population.

Thus, the notion of densitometry as a criterion method for evaluating body composition, or for validating other methods, requires recognition of the limitations of the method. It is clear that those pioneer researchers who first proposed the method were well aware of the limitations, but over the years they appear to have been seriously neglected.

1.5 ESTIMATION OF PROPORTIONATE FATNESS FROM EQUATIONS BASED ON SKINFOLD THICKNESS

There is some empirical logic to the idea that a representative measure of the greatest depot of body fat (i.e. subcutaneous) might provide a reasonable estimate of total body fat. This notion becomes less tenable as a greater understanding emerges with respect to various patterns of subcutaneous fat depots and different proportions of fat in the four main storage areas. The fact that well over 100 equations have been derived for estimating %Fat from skinfold thicknesses certainly raises some caution about the efficacy of this conceptual framework.

A double fold of skin and subcutaneous adipose is measured by calipers which apply a constant pressure over a range of thicknesses (Figure 1.3). Various skinfold sites have been defined and regression equations determined to predict the criterion value which inevitably has been accepted as that obtained from densitometry. Most equations have been derived from relatively small numbers of subjects which appears to limit their utility for a broader spectrum of the population.

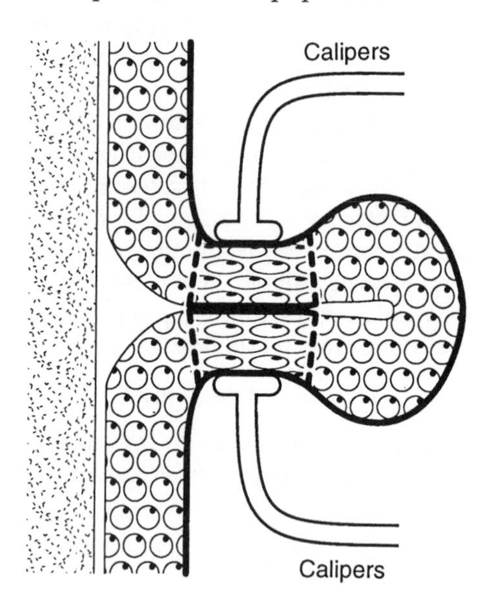

Figure 1.3 Schematic section through a skinfold at measurement site. The caliper jaws exert a constant pressure over a wide range of openings. The skinfold includes skin which varies in thickness from site to site and individual to individual; adipose tissue of variable compressibility and varying proportionate volume occupied by cell membranes, nuclei, organelles and lipid globules. (Adapted from Martin *et al.*, 1985.)

Martin *et al.* (1985) discussed the limitations of the skinfold caliper in persuasive terms. They suggested that there are several assumptions that must be tenable if caliper readings are to be used to predict total body fat. Initially, one must accept that a compressed double layer of skin and subcutaneous adipose is representative of an uncompressed single layer of adipose tissue. This implies that the skin thickness is either negligible or constant and that adipose tissue compresses in a predictable manner. Clearly skin thickness will comprise a greater proportion of a thin skinfold by comparison to a thicker skinfold and its relationship cannot be regarded as constant. In addition it has been shown that skin thickness varies from individual to individual as well as from site to site which suggests that it cannot be regarded as negligible. With respect to compression, the evidence suggests that adipose tissue compresses at different rates according to such factors as age, gender, site, tissue hydration and cell size. Martin *et al.* (1985) reported that in a sample of 14 unembalmed cadavers compressibility ranged from 38.2 to 69.3%. Compressibility is readily observed when calipers are applied to a skinfold and a rapid decline in the needle gauge occurs. The lipid content of adipose tissue must also be in a known proportion if skinfold thickness is to be indicative of total body lipid. Adipose tissue includes structures other than fat molecules; these include cell membranes, nuclei and organelles. In a relatively empty adipocyte the proportion of fat to other structures may be quite low whereas a relatively full adipocyte will occupy a proportionately greater volume. Orpin and Scott (1964) suggested that fat content of adipose tissue may range between 5.2 and 94.1% although Martin *et al.* (1992) suggested a general range of 60–85%.

The previous three assumptions relate to the measurement of a single skinfold. There remain two assumptions that must be considered with respect to the validity of skinfold thickness as a predictor of total body fat. First, the assumption that a limited number of skinfold sites in some way represents the remaining subcutaneous adipose throughout the body. Second, that a limited number of subcutaneous sites is representative of fat deposited in other storage sites (omentum, viscera, bone marrow and interstitial). It must be remembered that since skinfold equations regress to densitometric values, the derived equation essentially predicts that which is measured by the criterion, i.e. total body lipid from all storage sites in the body. It is well accepted that men and women deposit fat in different proportions in different parts of the body, including skinfolds and other storage sites. This is referred to as fat patterning and is often characterized as android (male-like) and gynoid (female-like). Fat patterning is not truly dimorphic, however, as some women tend to display a male pattern and some men tend to display a female pattern. Fat distribution at skinfold sites and in other storage depots tends to be individual in nature which compounds the issue of selection of skinfold sites for predictive equations.

An alternative and more scientifically acceptable use of skinfold measurement is the expression of the summation of a number of skinfold thicknesses as a simple anatomical entity. The sum of skinfolds expresses the directly measured thickness of skinfolds at a series of defined sites. Use of this measure avoids many of the untenable assumptions that are inherent in the calculation of the proportion of total body fat from skinfold thicknesses.

1.6 ASSESSMENT OF FAT-FREE MASS BY BIOELECTRICAL IMPEDANCE

Bioelectrical impedance (BIA) is a method of body composition analysis that has become increasingly popular for its simplicity, ease of use and attractive computer packaging. The electrical properties of living tissue, particularly that of impedance, have been used for more than 50 years to describe and measure certain tissue or organ functions. In recent years bioelectrical impedance has been used to quantify the fat-free mass (FFM) allowing the proportion of body fat to be calculated. The method is based on the electrical properties of hydrous and anhydrous tissues and their electrolyte content. Excellent reviews of the subject have been published by Van Loan (1990) and Lukaski (1987).

Nyboer *et al.* (1943) demonstrated that electrical impedance could be used to determine biological volume. In principle, a low level alternating current flows through a biological structure using the intra- and extracellular fluids as a conductor and cell membranes as capacitors (condensers). The FFM, including the non-lipid components of adipose tissue, contain virtually all of the water and conducting electrolytes of the body and thus the FFM is almost totally responsible for conductance of an electrical current. Impedance to the flow of an electrical current is a function of the resistance and reactance of the conductor although the former is the better predictor of impedance due to the relatively small magnitude of reactance. The complex geometry and bioelectrical properties of the human body are confounding factors but in principle impedance may be used to estimate the bioelectrical volume of the FFM since it is related to the length and cross-sectional area of the conductor. A bioelectrical expression of fat-free volume may in turn be used to estimate the mass of the fat and fat-free tissues.

The impedance of biological structures can be measured with a degree of accuracy by use of four polar electrodes applied to the hands and feet, an excitation current of 800 μA at 50 kHz and a bioelectrical impedance analyser (plethysmograph) that measures resistance and reactance. The resulting value (resistance is most frequently reported) must then be entered into an equation to predict the FFM regressing to a criterion value usually determined by densitometry. More than 20 equations have been published since 1985 to predict the FFM from BIA for various population subsets by age and sex (Van Loan, 1990). The most frequently occurring component in these equations is the resistance index (ht^2/R where ht is stature and R is resistance in ohms). Other variables that have been included in prediction equations include height, weight, sex, age, various limb circumferences, reactance, impedance, standing height, arm length and skeletal width. The reported r^2 or R^2 values range between 0.80–0.988 with standard error of the estimate (SEE) in the range 1.90–4.02 kg (approximately 2–3%). Slightly lower correlation values ($R^2 = 0.76$–0.92) have been reported for the prediction of %Fat and SEE of 3–4%.

Bioelectrical impedance appears to be a safe, simple method of estimating the fat and fat-free masses. However, a degree of caution must be registered about the use of BIA. The criterion method against which BIA prediction equations are validated is not error free (as discussed in the validity section) which compounds the error associated with the new method. The BIA equations tend to be population specific with generally poor characteristics of fit for a large heterogeneous population. For example, Hodgdon and Fitzgerald (1987) found that a single manufacturer's equation generally overestimated individuals with low %Fat and underestimated individuals with high %Fat. In order to improve the heterogeneity of BIA prediction equations, various anthropometric variables have been introduced. For example Segal *et al.* (1988), using a large, heterogeneous population found that prediction of %Fat improved when gender and fatness specific equations were developed. The fatness specific equations require *a priori* determination of degree of fatness (< or > 20% and 30% for males and females, respectively) by anthropometric techniques. In addition the prediction equations included height^2, weight and age as independent variables. Other cautions with the use of BIA centre on the variable state of hydration. The following recommendations for testing procedures address this concern (Heyward, 1991).

- no eating or drinking within 4 h of the test
- no exercise within 12 h of the test
- urinate within 30 min of the test
- no alcohol consumption within 48 h of the test
- no diuretics within 7 days of the test

Additionally

- inaccuracies may be introduced during the premenstrual period for women (Gleichauf and Roe, 1989)
- the changing pattern of water and mineral content of growing children suggests that a child-specific prediction equation should be used (Houtkooper *et al.*, 1989; Eston *et al.*, 1990; 1993).

1.7 RATIOS

Ratios taken as a discrete numerical value are considered by many to be an uninterpretable statistic. A change in the numerical value of a ratio raises the question whether this reflects change in the numerator, denominator or some combination of both. Analysis of the numbers that contribute to the ratio obviously provides answers to these questions but this suggests that the ratio itself is redundant. At best, ratios should be approached with caution. Many ratios have been proposed and used in kinanthropometry, but two in particular merit discussion in consideration of body composition.

1.7.1 BODY MASS INDEX

The lay person regards body weight as a reflection of degree of fatness and this perception is reinforced through the use of height–weight tables as an indicator of health risk and life expectancy by the life insurance industry. Superficially it would appear that weight per unit of height is a convenient expression that represents something about body build and about body composition. Variations of this index have been a recurring theme in anthropometry for more than one and half centuries following the pioneer work of Adolph Quetelet (1796–1874). The simple ratio of body mass/height may appear to be the most informative expression but in fact the ratio expresses a three-dimensional measure (mass) in relation to a one-dimensional (linear) measure. Since three-dimensional measures vary as the cube of a linear measure, dimensional consistency would be better served by the expression of mass to the third power of height. (This ratio is known as the **ponderal index**.) This is not the end of the discussion, however, because a further complicating factor arises when one recognizes that body shape changes as height increases (Ross *et al.*, 1987). Since the objective of the ratio is to examine mass in relative independence of height, several authors have concluded that mass/height^2 (where mass is expressed in kilograms and height in metres) is the most appropriate index. This was previously known as the **Quetelet Index** and more recently as the **Body Mass Index** (BMI). The BMI has been popularized as a ratio that says something about body composition primarily on the basis of various epidemiological studies that indicate a moderate correlation with estimates of body fat. Perhaps ironically, these same studies also show very similar correlation values between BMI and estimates of lean body mass. The BMI is influenced nearly to an equal degree by the lean and fat compartments of the body suggesting that it is as much a measure of lean tissue as it is of fat. Unfortunately, the singular correlation values between estimates of body fat and BMI have been used to promote the use of this ratio for individual counselling with respect to health status, diet, weight loss and other fitness factors. On an individual basis, people of the same height will vary with respect to frame size, tissue densities and proportion of various tissues. Persons who are heavy for their height may be heavy because of a rugged skeleton and large muscle mass, whereas others may be as heavy for their height because they carry excess adipose tissue. In a large 'normal' population there is every likelihood that there will be more of the latter which leads to the moderate correlations reported. On an individual basis, however, it would be a serious error to consider relative weight as a measure of obesity or fatness. The scientific evidence is not nearly strong enough to suggest a basis for individual decisions about health-related status (Garn *et al.*, 1986; Keys *et al.*, 1972).

1.7.2 WAIST TO HIP RATIO

It has quite recently been observed that the distribution of fat rather than the total quantity of fat might be a more significant factor in the overall health risk. Greater health risk is associated with the android pattern of trunk deposition than the gynoid pattern of hip and thigh deposits. A simple but effective subdivision of fat deposits has been made by use of a ratio between waist circumference taken at the umbilicus and hip circumference taken at the maximum gluteal girth. Bjorntorp (1984) suggested that a ratio of ≥ 1.0 in men is indicative of a rapid increase in the risk of ischaemic heart and cerebrovascular disease. The corresponding value representing increased risk for women is ≥ 0.8. This ratio appears to have some utility in the assessment of health risk although it should be used with caution.

1.8 PROPORTIONATE MUSCLE MASS

The quantity and proportion of bodily fat or adipose tissue has remained a focal point in body composition analysis because of its perceived negative relationship to health, fitness and sport performance. It is evident to many working with high performance athletes that knowledge of the changing total and regional quantity of muscle mass in an athlete is an equal or perhaps more significant variable in sport performance. Estimation of total and regional muscle mass has not received the same attention as estimation of fat mass. However, in athletes it could be argued that there is more variability in muscle mass than in body fat and therefore a greater need to study this variable. Anatomical (tissue-based) models for estimating total muscle mass have been proposed by Matiegka (1921), Heymsfield *et al.* (1982), Drinkwater *et al.* (1986) and Martin *et al.* (1990). The early approach of Matiegka (1921) was based on the recognition that total muscle mass was in large part reflected by the size of muscles on the extremities. Thus, he proposed that muscle mass could be predicted by using skinfold corrected diameters of muscle from the upper arm, forearm, thigh and calf multiplied by stature and an empirically derived constant. Drinkwater *et al.* (1986) attempted to validate Matiegka's formula using the evidence of the Brussels Cadaver Study and proposed modifications to the original mathematical constant. Martin *et al.* (1990) published equations for the estimation of muscle mass in men based on cadaver evidence. Data from six unembalmed cadavers were used to derive a regression equation to predict total muscle mass. The proposed equation was subsequently validated by predicting the known muscle masses from a separate cohort of five embalmed cadavers ($r^2 = 0.93$, SEE = 1.58 kg, approximately 0.5%) and the results compared to estimates derived from the equations of Matiegka (1921) and Heymsfield *et al.* (1982). The equation recommended by Martin *et al.* (1990) was much better able to predict muscle mass than the other two equations which substantially underestimated the muscle mass of what must be regarded as a limited sample. Martin *et al.* (1990) attempted to minimize the specificity of their equation by ensuring that the upper and lower body were represented in the three circumference terms.

Several of the above methods are based on the geometric model of extremity girths describing a circle and a single skinfold as representative of a constant subcutaneous layer overlying a circular muscle mass. A simple formula predicts the skinfold corrected geometric properties of the combined muscle and bone tissue (Figure 1.4).

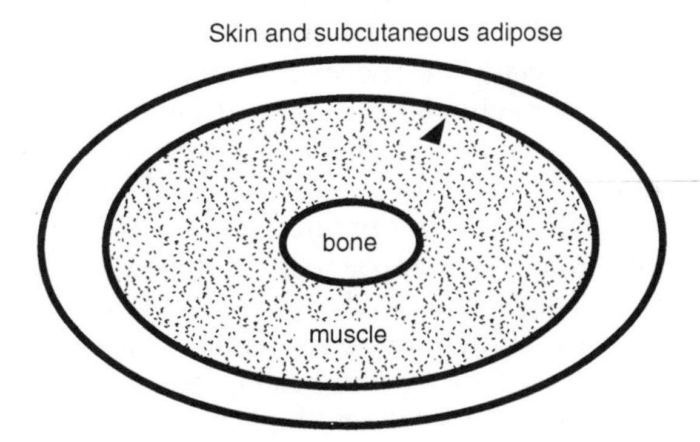

Figure 1.4 Schematic view of the derivation of estimated muscle and bone area from a measurement of external girth. There are inherent assumptions that the perimeters are circular and that a single skinfold measure is representative of the entire subcutaneous layer of the section. Muscle and bone area = $\pi\,((c/2\pi) - (\mathrm{SF}/2))^2$, where c = girth measure (cm), SF = skinfold (cm).

$$\text{muscle and bone area} = \pi\left(\frac{c}{2\pi} - \frac{SF}{2}\right)^2$$

where c is girth measure (cm) and SF is skinfold (cm)

Further, the volume of the segments of the limb have been predicted by use of the formula for a truncated cone. The anthropometric/geometric model has been found consistently to overestimate muscle area when compared to areas measured from computed tomography and magnetic resonance images (de Koning *et al.*, 1986; Baumgartner *et al.*, 1992). Nevertheless, the correlation between anthropometrically derived areas and imaged areas has been shown to be very high $r > 0.9$.

The relationship of cross-sectional area of muscle to force output is well established (Ikai and Fukunaga, 1968). Knowledge of the changing size of muscle resulting from particular training regimens is important information for a coach evaluating the effect of the programme and for the motivation of the athlete (Hawes and Sovak, 1994). Size of muscle relative to body mass may provide information on a young athlete's stage of development and readiness for certain categories of skill development; changing size of muscle may reflect the effectiveness of a particular exercise or activity; diminished size may reflect a lack of recovery time (over-training) or in-season response to changing patterns of training. In all instances regular feedback of results to the coach may provide early information for adjustment or enhancement of the training regimens.

1.9 PROPORTIONATE BONE MASS

The skeleton is a dynamic tissue responding to environmental stresses by remodelling its shape and increasing or decreasing its density. Nevertheless it is less volatile than either muscle or adipose tissue and its influence upon human performance has been largely neglected. Matiegka (1921) proposed that skeletal mass could be estimated from an equation that included stature, the maximum diameter of the humerus, wrist, femur and ankle and a mathematical constant. Drinkwater *et al.* (1986) attempted to validate the proposed equation against recent cadaver data and found that an adjustment to Matiegka's constant produced a more accurate estimate in their sample of older, cadaveric persons. Drinkwater *et al.* (1986) however, commented that the true value of the coefficient probably lies between the original and their calculated value. An estimation of bone mass within a prototypical model may provide insight into structural factors which contribute to athletic success. In a longitudinal study of high performance synchronized swimmers, Hawes and Sovak (1993) observed that the world and Olympic champion had disproportionately narrow bony diameters compared to other synchronized swimmers competing at the international level. Since positive buoyancy contributes to the ease of performing exercises above water, relatively small mass of the most dense body tissue might be construed as a morphological advantage in athletes of otherwise equal abilities.

1.10 OTHER CONSIDERATIONS

This chapter has presented an overview of the issues surrounding the notion of quantifying body composition *in vivo*. It is clear that there are many persistent problems which suggest that assessment of body composition is far from an exact science. It is also evident that recent advances in medical imaging technology offer the possibility of exciting advances in the field as the problem of validation of methods may potentially be addressed in living and healthy persons. In the interim it is noteworthy that other methods of assessing body composition have been developed and successfully used in the field. One method in particular is the 'O Scale' developed by Ross *et al.* (1986) at Simon Fraser University, Canada and marketed by Rosscraft. The method avoids the use of biological constants whose limitations have been discussed in the body of this chapter. An individual is plotted on two parallel nine-point scales for adiposity, measured by sum of skinfolds and body weight relative to normative data (> 22 000 Canadian subjects) for age and gender. The resulting graph provides separately, the individual status of body weight and adiposity relative to a normal population. Thus an individual who appears to be heavy for a given height may be shown as heavy for the reason of a high adiposity value, or may be heavy despite a low adiposity value. This is attributed to a relatively high value for adipose free tissues, particularly muscle and bone. The scales are sensitive to change over relatively short time periods and are well suited for monitoring progress within a training or fitness regimen. This method is an important departure from the traditional methods of estimating proportionate quantities of various tissues within the body. It is not included in the laboratory exercises for reasons of copyright. The following laboratory exercises are designed to provide an introduction to a variety of body composition assessment procedures.

1.11 PRACTICAL 1: DENSITOMETRY

1.11.1 PURPOSE

- To determine body composition by densitometry

1.11.2 METHODS

1. The subject should report to the laboratory several hours postprandial. A form-fitting swim suit is the most appropriate attire.
2. Height, weight and age should be recorded using the methods specified in Practical 3.
3. Determination of total body density.
   Facilities will vary from custom-built tanks to swimming pools. The following is an outline of the major procedures.
   - Determine the tare weight of the suspended seat or platform together with weight belt.
   - Record the water temperature and barometric pressure.
   - The subject should enter the tank and ensure that all air bubbles (clinging to hair or trapped in swim suit) are removed.
   - The subject should attach a weight belt of approximately 3 kg to assist in maintaining full submersion.

- The subject quietly submerses while sitting or squatting on the freely suspended platform and exhales to a maximum. Drawing the knees up to the chest will facilitate complete evacuation of the lungs. The subject remains as still as possible and the scale reading is recorded.
- This procedure is repeated up to 10 times and the mean of the three highest values accepted as the underwater weight.

4. Determination of residual volume (RV).
   - RV is the air remaining in the lungs following a maximal exhalation.
   - RV may be measured by the N_2 dilution method or estimated.
   - If the RV is to be measured, it should be completed with the subject submerged to the neck in order to approximate the pressure acting on the lungs in a fully submerged position.
   - The equipment used to determine RV will vary from laboratory to laboratory. The fundamental procedure is as follows:
   - The gas analyser should be calibrated according to manufacturer's specifications.
   - A three-way T valve is connected to a 5 litre anaesthetic bag, a pure oxygen tank and a spirometer. The system (spirometer, bag, valve and tubing) should be flushed with oxygen three times. On the fourth occasion a measured quantity (approximately 5 litres) of oxygen is introduced into the spirometer bell, the O_2 valve is closed and the T valve opened to permit the O_2 to pass into the anaesthetic bag. The bag is closed off with a spring clip and is removed from the system together with the T valve. A mouthpiece hose is attached to the T valve.
   - The subject prepares by attaching a nose clip and immersing to the neck in the tank. The mouthpiece is inserted and the valve opened so that the subject is breathing room air. When comfortable the subject exhales maximally drawing the knees to the chest in a similar posture to that adopted during underwater weighing since RV is posture dependent. At maximum exhalation the T valve is opened to the pure O_2 anaesthetic bag and the subject takes 5–6 regular inhalation–exhalation cycles. On the signal the subject again exhales maximally and the T valve to the anaesthetic bag is closed. The subject removes the mouthpiece and breathes normally. The anaesthetic bag is attached to the gas analysers and values for the CO_2 and O_2 are recorded
   - Measurement of RV should be repeated several times to ensure consistent results.

1.11.3 CALCULATION OF RESIDUAL VOLUME AND BODY DENSITY

(a) Measured residual volume (Wilmore *et al.*, 1980)

$$RV(l)=\frac{V\text{O}_2\,(l)\times FEN_2}{0.798-FEN_2}-DS\,(l)\times BTPS$$

where:

$V\text{O}_2$ is the volume of O_2 measured into the anaesthetic bag (~ 5 litres)

FEN_2 is the fraction of N_2 at the point where equilibrium of the gas analyser occurred calculated as:

$$[100\% - (\%O_2 + \%CO_2)]/100$$

DS — is the dead space of mouthpiece and breathing valve (calculated from the specific situation);

BTPS — is the body temperature pressure saturated correction factor which corrects the volume of measured gas to ambient conditions of the lung according to the following table:

Gas temp. (°C)	*Correction factor*
20.0	1.102
20.5	1.099
21.0	1.096
21.5	1.093
22.0	1.091
22.5	1.089
23.0	1.085
23.5	1.082
24.0	1.079
24.5	1.077
25.0	1.074
25.5	1.071
26.0	1.069
26.5	1.065
27.0	1.062
27.5	1.060

(b) Estimated residual volume

Men: RV = 0.0115 (age) + 0.019 (ht in cm) − 2.24 (Boren *et al.*, 1966)
Women: RV = 0.021 (age) + 0.023 (ht in cm) − 2.978 (Boren *et al.*, 1974)

Estimated RV (Boren *et al.*, 1966) has been shown to have a standard error of measurement (SEM) of 0.29 l when compared to an actual RV of 0.13 l in athletes (Morrow *et al.*, 1985). Transformed to %Fat units this represents an SEM of 1.2 %Fat. The SEM of measured RV was 0.2 %Fat.

1.11.4 BODY DENSITY CALCULATIONS

$$\text{Body density} = \frac{\text{weight in air (kg)}}{\dfrac{\text{(weight in air (kg)} - \text{(weight in } H_2O - \text{tare wt (kg)))} - \text{trapped air (l)}}{\text{water temp. correction}}}$$

where:
trapped air is the residual lung volume + tubing dead space + 100 ml (100 ml is the conventional allowance for gastrointestinal gases) and water temperature correction is according to the following table:

H_2O *temp.* (°C)	*Density of* H_2O
25.0	0.997
28.0	0.996

31.0	0.995
35.0	0.994
38.0	0.993

%Fat according to Siri (1956) = [(4.95 / body density) – 4.50] × 100
%Fat according to Brozek et al. (1963) = [(4.57 / body density) – 4.142] × 100

Interpretation

The following table is based on the normative data from Katch and McArdle (1983) and Durnin and Womersley (1974). It should be noted that 'obesity' is often defined as > 25% fat for men and > 30% fat for women.

Age (years)	*%Fat (Mean±SD)* *Men*	*%Fat (Mean±SD)* *Women*
17–30	15 ± 5	25 ± 5
30–50	23 ± 7	30 ± 6
50–70	28 ± 8	35 ± 6

1.12 PRACTICAL 2: MEASUREMENT OF SKINFOLDS

1.12.1 PURPOSE

- To develop the technique of measuring skinfolds.
- To compare various methods of computing estimates of proportionate fatness.

1.12.2 METHODS

A well organized and established set of procedures will ensure that testing sessions go smoothly and that there can be no implication of impropriety when measuring subjects. The procedures should include:

- prior preparation of equipment and recording forms
- arrangements for a suitable space which is clean, warm and quiet
- securing the assistance of an individual who will record values
- forewarning the subjects that testing will occur at a given time and place
- ensuring that girls bring a bikini style swim suit to facilitate measurement in the abdominal region and that boys wear loose fitting shorts or speed swim suit
- the measurer's technique must include recognition and respect for the notion of personal space and sensitive areas
- taking great care in the consistent location of measurement sites as defined in the following pages and the consistent application of measurement tools
- recognition that the data are very powerful in both a positive and negative sense. Young adolescents in particular are very sensitive about their body image and making public specific or implied information on body composition values may have a negative effect on an individual.

(a) Skinfolds measurements – general technique

- During measurement the subject should stand erect but relaxed through the shoulders and arms. A warm room and easy atmosphere will help the subject to relax which will help in manipulating the skinfold.
- The site should be marked with a washable felt pen.
- The objective is to raise a double fold of skin and subcutaneous adipose leaving the underlying muscle undisturbed.
- All skinfolds are measured on the right side of the body.
- The measurer takes the fold between thumb and forefinger of the left hand. This is facilitated by a slight rolling and pulling action.
- The caliper is held in the right hand and the pressure plates of the caliper are applied perpendicular to the fold and 1 cm below or to the right of the fingers depending on the direction of the raised skinfold.
- The caliper is held in position for 2 s prior to recording the measurement to the nearest 0.2 mm. The grasp is maintained throughout the measurement.
- All skinfolds should be measured three times with at least a 2 min interval to allow the tissue to restore to its uncompressed form. The median value is the accepted value.

(b) Secondary computation of proportionate fatness

It has been reported that there are over 100 equations for predicting fatness from skinfold measurements. The fact that these equations predict different and often quite diverse values for the same individual leads to the conclusion that the equations are population specific, i.e. the equation only accurately predicts the criterion value (usually densitometrically determined) for the specific population in the validation study, when applied to other populations the equation loses its validity. This diversity will be illustrated if you compute estimates of %Fat from the following frequently used equations. It should be observed that whereas interindividual comparisons of %Fat may not be valid for many of the reasons previously discussed, intra-individual comparisons of repeated measurements may provide useful information. The summation of skinfold values will also provide comparative values avoiding many of the untenable assumptions associated with estimates of proportionate fatness.

(c) %Fat equations (skinfold sites shown in Table 1.1)

Table 1.1 Summary of skinfold sites used in selected equations for the prediction of %Fat

Sum of skinfolds Population	*Parizkova Σ10 M & F*	*Jackson et al. (1980) Σ3 female*	*Jackson and Pollock (1978) Σ3 male*	*Jackson et al. (1980) Σ7 female*	*Jackson and Pollock (1978) Σ7 male*	*Durnin and Womersley (1974) Σ4 M & F*
Skinfold site						
Cheek	*					
Chin	*					
Pectoral (chest 1)	*		*	*	*	
Axilla (midaxillary)				*	*	
Chest 2	*					
Iliocristale	*					
Abdomen 1	*					

Table 1.1 (Continued)

Abdomen 2			*	*	*	
Suprailiac						*
Suprailium		*		*	*	
Subscapular	*			*	*	*
Triceps	*	*		*	*	*
Biceps						*
Patella	*					
Midthigh		*	*	*	*	
Proximal calf	*					

Parizkova (1978)–10 sites

%Fat = 39.572 log X – 61.25 (females 17–45 years)
%Fat = 22.32 log X – 29.00 (males 17–45 years)
where $X = \Sigma$ 10 skinfolds as specified (mm).

Durnin and Womersley (1974) – four sites

body density = 1.1610 – 0.0632 log $\Sigma 4$ (men)
body density = 1.1581 – 0.0720 log $\Sigma 4$ (women)
body density = 1.1533 – 0.0643 log $\Sigma 4$ (boys)
body density = 1.1369 – 0.0598 log $\Sigma 4$ (girls)

$$\%\text{Fat (Siri, 1956)} = [(4.95/\text{body density}) - 4.5] \times 100$$

where $\Sigma 4 = \Sigma 4$ skinfolds as specified (mm).

Jackson and Pollock (1978) – three sites

$$\text{body density of males} = 1.1093800 - 0.0008267\,(\Sigma \mathbf{3}_{\mathbf{M}}) + 0.0000016\,(\Sigma \mathbf{3}_{\mathbf{M}})^2 - 0.0002574\,(X2)$$

Jackson et al. (1980) – three sites

$$\text{body density of females} = 1.099421 - 0.0009929\,(\Sigma \mathbf{3}_{\mathbf{F}}) + 0.0000023\,(\Sigma \mathbf{3}_{\mathbf{F}})^2 - 0.0001392\,(\boldsymbol{X2})$$

$$\%\text{Fat (Siri, 1956)} = [(4.95/\text{body density}) - 4.5] \times 100$$

where $\Sigma 3_M = \Sigma 3$ skinfolds (mm) as specified for males
$\Sigma 3_F = \Sigma 3$ skinfolds (mm) as specified for females
$X2$ = age (years)

Jackson and Pollock (1978) – seven sites

$$\text{body density of males} = 1.112 - 0.00043499\,(\Sigma 7) + 0.00000055\,(\Sigma 7)^2 - 0.00028826\,(\boldsymbol{X2})$$

Jackson et al. (1980) – seven sites

$$\text{body density of females} = 1.097 - 0.00046971\,(\Sigma 7) + 0.00000056\,(\Sigma 7)^2 - 0.00012828\,(\boldsymbol{X2})$$

$$\%\text{Fat (Siri, 1956)} = [(4.95/\text{body density}) - 4.5] \times 100$$

where $\Sigma 7 = \Sigma 7$ skinfolds as specified (mm)

$X2$ = age (years)

(d) Locations of skinfold sites

All measurements are taken on the right side of the body

Cheek — *horizontal* skinfold raised at the midpoint of the line connecting the tragus (cartilaginous projection anterior to the external opening of the ear) and the nostrils (Figure 1.5).

Chin — *vertical* skinfold raised above the hyoid bone: the head is slightly lifted but the skin of the neck must stay loose (Figure 1.5).

Pectoral (chest 1) — *oblique* skinfold raised along the borderline of the m. pectoralis major between the anterior axillary fold and the nipple.

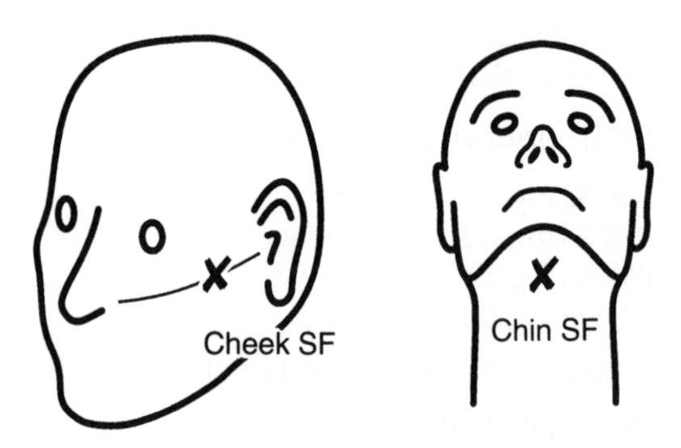

Figure 1.5 Location of the cheek and chin skinfold sites.

Females: measurement is taken at 1/3 of the distance between anterior axillary fold and nipple.
Males: measurement is taken at 1/2 of the distance between anterior axillary fold and nipple (Figure 1.6).

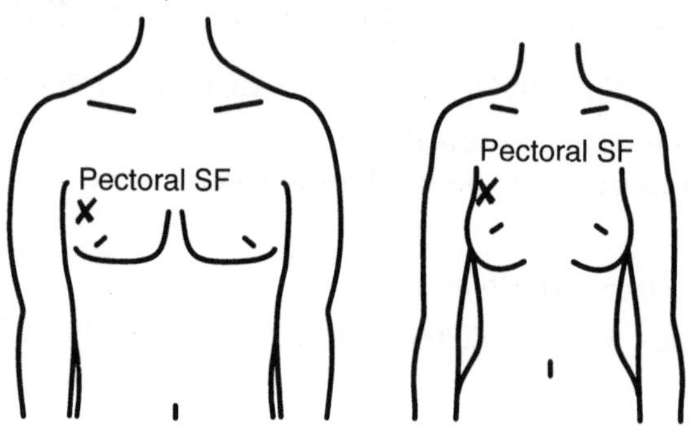

Figure 1.6 Location of the pectoral skinfold sites.

Axilla (midaxillary) — *vertical* skinfold raised at the level of the xiphosternal junction in the midaxillary line (Figure 1.7).

Chest 2 — *horizontal* skinfold raised on the chest above the 10th rib at the point of intersection with the anterior axillary line—slight angle along the ribs (Figure 1.7).

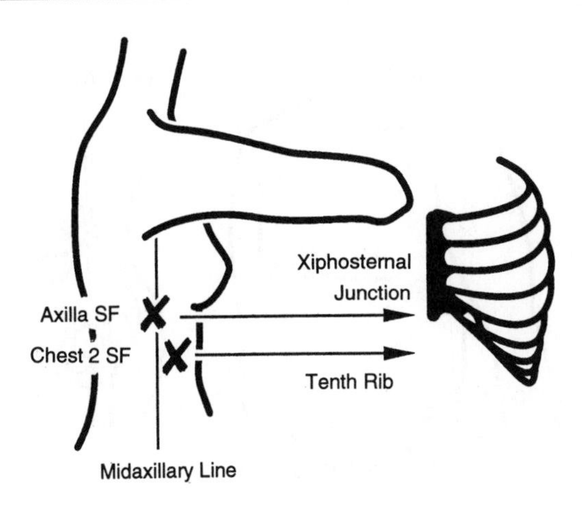

Figure 1.7 Location of the axillary and chest 2 skinfold sites.

Abdomen 1 — *horizontal* fold raised 3 cm lateral and 1 cm inferior to the umbilicus (Figure 1.8).

Abdomen 2 — *vertical* fold raised at a lateral distance of approximately 2 cm from the umbilicus (Figure 1.8).

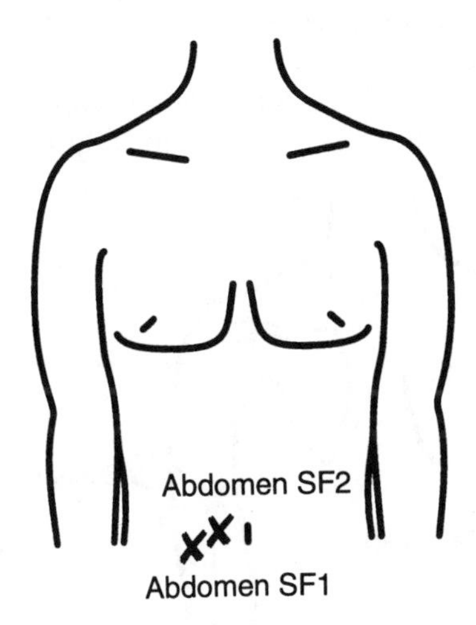

Figure 1.8 Location of the abdominal skinfold sites.

Iliocristale — *horizontal* skinfold following the natural cleavage lines of the skin. It is raised 7 cm above the anterior superior iliac spine (Figure 1.9).

Suprailiac — *diagonal* fold raised immediately above the crest of the ilium on a vertical line from the midaxilla (Figure 1.9).

Suprailium — *diagonal* fold raised immediately above the crest of the ilium on a vertical line from the anterior axillary fold (Figure 1.9).

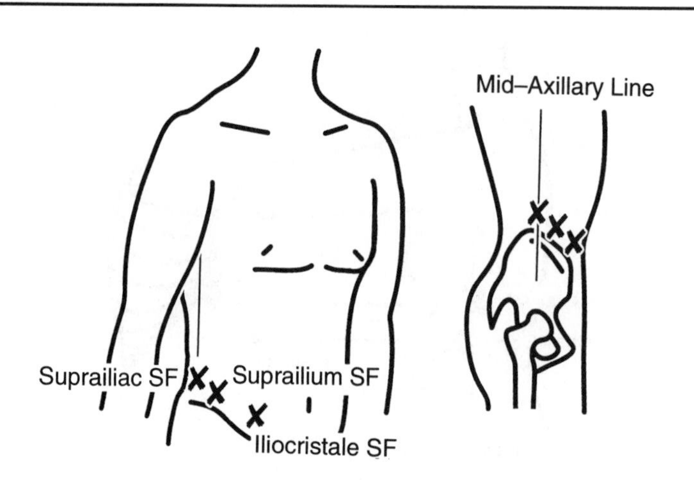

Figure 1.9 Location of the skinfold sites in the iliac crest region.

Subscapular *oblique* skinfold raised 1 cm below the inferior angle of the scapula at approximately 45° to the horizontal plane following the natural cleavage lines of the skin (Figure 1.10).

Triceps *vertical* skinfold raised on the posterior aspect of the m. triceps, exactly halfway between the olecranon process and the acromion process when the hand is supinated (Figure 1.10).

Biceps *vertical* skinfold raised on the anterior aspect of the biceps, at the same horizontal level as the triceps skinfold (Figure 1.10).

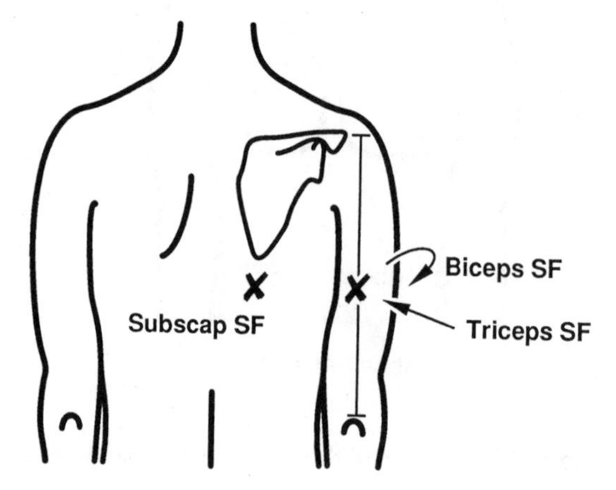

Figure 1.10 Location of the biceps, triceps and subscapular skinfold sites.

Patella *vertical* skinfold in the midsagittal plane raised 2 cm above the proximal edge of the patella. The subject should bend the knee slightly (Figure 1.11).

Mid-thigh *vertical* skinfold raised on the anterior aspect of the thigh midway between the inguinal crease and the proximal border of the patella (Figure 1.11)

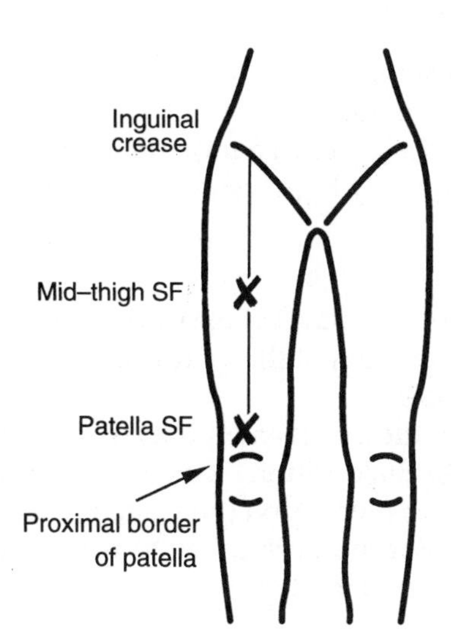

Figure 1.11 Location of the anterior thigh skinfold sites.

Proximal calf *vertical* skinfold raised on the posterior aspect of the calf in the midsagittal plane 5 cm inferior to the fossa poplitea (Figure 1.12).

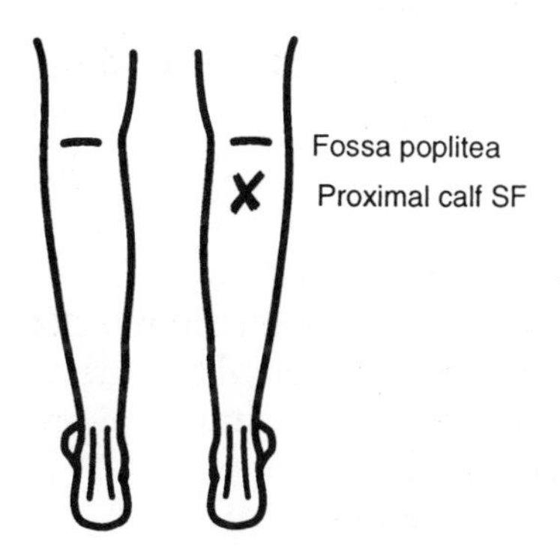

Figure 1.12 Location of the proximal calf skinfold site.

1.13 PRACTICAL 3: PROPORTIONATE WEIGHT DISTRIBUTION OF ADIPOSE TISSUE AND FAT-FREE MASS

1.13.1 PURPOSE

- To evaluate body mass index
- To evaluate waist to hip ratio as a measure of fat patterning
- To determine fat-free mass by bioelectrical impedance

1.13.2 METHOD: BODY MASS INDEX (BMI)

- BMI = body mass (kg)/stature^2(m^2)
- describes weight for height (ponderosity)
- often used in epidemiological studies as a measure of obesity
- a high BMI means proportionately high weight for height

(a) Stature

- as height is variable throughout the day, the measurement should be performed at the same time for each test session (height may still vary due to activities causing compression of the intervertebral discs, e.g. running)
- all stature measurements should be taken with the subject barefoot
- the **Frankfort Plane** refers to the position of the head when the line joining the orbitale (lower margin of eye socket) to the tragion (notch above tragus of the ear) is horizontal
- there are several techniques for measuring height which yield slightly different values. The following technique is recommended.

(b) Stature against a wall

- subject stands erect, feet together against a wall on a flat surface at a right angle to the wall mounted stadiometer
- the heels, buttocks, upper back and (if possible) cranium should touch the wall
- the subject's head should be in the Frankfort Plane, arms relaxed at sides
- the subject is instructed to inhale and stretch up
- measurer slides the headboard of the stadiometer down to the vertex and records the measurement to the nearest 0.1 cm.

(c) Body mass

- use a calibrated beam-type balance.
- subject should be weighed without shoes in minimal clothing.
- for best results, repeated measurements should be taken at the same time of day, in the same state of hydration and nourishment after voiding (preferably first thing in the morning – 12 h after ingesting food).
- measurement is recorded to the nearest 0.1 kg.

(d) Interpretation

- Values $\leqslant 19$ or $\geqslant 26$ are considered to place an individual in health risk zones according to morbidity and mortality data for males and females 20–60 years. These values should be considered within the context of the discussion presented previously.

1.13.3 METHOD: WAIST TO HIP RATIO

- W:H = waist girth/hip girth
- may be used in conjunction with trunk skinfolds to determine whether excess fat is being carried in the trunk region

- a high W:H combined with high trunk skinfolds has been shown to be associated with increased morbidity; glucose intolerance, hyperinsulinaemia, blood lipid disorders and mortality
- a high W:H with low skinfolds may be associated with high trunk muscle development

(a) Tape technique (cross-handed technique)

- the metal case is held in the right hand and stub end is controlled by the left hand
- girths are measured with the tape at right angles to the long axis of the bone
- the tape is pulled out of its case and around the body segment by the left hand, the two hands are crossed intersecting the tape at the zero mark
- the aim is to obtain the circumference of the part with the tape in contact with, but not depressing, the fleshy contour

(b) Waist girth

- subject stands erect, abdomen relaxed, arms at sides, feet together
- measurer stands facing subject and places a steel tape measure around the subject's natural waist (the obvious narrowing between the rib and the iliac crest)
- if there is no obvious waist, find the smallest horizontal circumference in this region
- measurement is taken at the end of a normal expiration to the nearest 0.1 cm

(c) Hip girth

- subject stands erect, buttocks relaxed, feet together, preferably wearing underwear or swimsuit
- measurer stands to one side of the subject and places steel tape measure around the hips at the horizontal level of greatest gluteal protuberance and the symphysis pubis
- check that the tape is not compressing the skin and record to the nearest 0.1 cm

(d) Interpretation

- Values of ≥ 0.90 (males) and ≥ 0.80 (females) are considered to place an individual in health risk zones according to morbidity and mortality data for males and females 20–70 years. These values should be considered within the context of the discussion presented previously.

1.13.4 METHOD: BIOELECTRICAL IMPEDANCE ANALYSIS (BIA)

- based on the electrical conductance characteristics of hydrous (fat free) and anhydrous (fat component) tissues
- the impedance to the flow of an electrical current is a function of resistance and reactance and is related to length and cross sectional area of the conductor (the hydrous or fat-free tissue)
- electrical resistance (Ω) is most commonly used to represent impedance

(a) Test conditions

Prior to testing the subject should:

- not have had anything to eat or drink in the previous 4 hours

- not have exercised within the previous 12 hours
- not have consumed alcohol within the previous 48 hours
- not have used diuretics within the previous 7 days
- have urinated within the previous 30 minutes

(b) Anthropometric procedures

- as defined by the manufacturer (if using the preprogrammed function of the unit) or according to the equation of choice
- the subject should lie supine on a table with the legs slightly apart and the right hand and foot bare
- four electrodes are prepared with electro-conducting gel and attached at the following sites (or as per manufacturer's instructions)
- just proximal to the dorsal surface of the third metacarpal–phalangeal joint on the right hand
- on the dorsal surface of the right wrist adjacent to the head of the ulna
- on the dorsal surface of the right foot just proximal to the second metatarsal–phalangeal joint
- on the anterior surface of the right ankle between the medial and lateral malleoli
- the subject should lie quietly while the analyser is turned on and off
- the subject should lie quietly for 5 minutes before repeating the procedure.

(c) Calculations

- as per manufacturer's instructions

or

- Females: FFM (kg) $= 4.917 + 0.821\,(ht^2/R)$ (Lukaski *et al.*, 1986)
- Males: FFM (kg) $= 5.214 + 0.827\,(ht^2/R)$ (Lukaski *et al.*, 1986)
- FFM (kg) $= 17.7868 + 0.00098\,(ht^2) + 0.3736\,(m) - 0.0238\,(R) - 4.2921\,(sex) - 0.1531\,(age)$ (Van Loan and Mayclin, 1987)

where ht = height (cm); R = resistance (Ω); m = mass (kg); sex for males = 0, females = 1; age in years.

1.14 PRACTICAL 4: ESTIMATION OF MUSCLE MASS AND REGIONAL MUSCULARITY

1.14.1 PURPOSE

- To develop the technique required to estimate total and regional muscularity

1.14.2 METHODS

Matiegka (1921) – males and females

$$\text{kg M} = [(CDU + CDF + CDT + CDC)/8]^2 \times \text{ht (cm)} \times 6.5 \times 0.001$$

$$\%\,\text{M} = (\text{kg M}/\text{body mass}) \times 100$$

where:

$$CDU = \frac{(\text{max upper arm girth})}{\pi} - \text{triceps SF (cm)}$$

$$CDF = \frac{(\text{max forearm girth})}{\pi} - \frac{(\text{forearm SF 1 (cm)} + \text{forearm SF 2 (cm)})}{2}$$

$$CDT = \frac{(\text{mid thigh girth})}{\pi} - \text{mid thigh skinfold (cm)}$$

$$CDC = \frac{(\text{max calf girth})}{\pi} - \text{mid calf skinfold (cm)}$$

- ht is stature in cm
- variables for computing corrected diameters are defined on the following pages
- CD is corrected diameter of U = upper arm, F = forearm, T = thigh, C = calf
- note that skinfolds should be expressed in cm, i.e. scale reading/10

Martin et al. (1990) – males only

$$\text{kg M} = [\text{ht} \times (0.0553\text{CTG}^2 + 0.0987\text{FG}^2 + 0.0331\text{CCG}^2) - 2445] \times 0.001$$

$$\%\ \text{M} = (\text{kg M/body mass}) \times 100$$

where:

ht is stature in cm
CTG is corrected thigh girth = thigh girth – π (front thigh SF/10)
FG is forearm girth
CCG is corrected calf girth = calf girth – π (medial calf SF/10)

1.14.3 DETERMINATION OF VARIABLES RELATED TO ESTIMATION OF MUSCLE MASS

Stature (ht) as before (Practical 3)

Maximum upper arm girth (cm)

- the girth measurement of the upper arm at the insertion of the m. deltoid
- subject stands erect with the arm abducted to the horizontal, measurer stands behind the arm of the subject, marks the insertion of the m. deltoid and measures the girth perpendicular to the long axis of the arm

Maximum forearm girth (cm)

- the maximum circumference at the proximal part of the forearm (usually within 5 cm of the elbow)
- subject stands erect with the arm extended in the horizontal plane, measurer stands behind the subject's arm and moves the tape up and down the forearm (perpendicular to the long axis) until the maximum circumference of the forearm is located

Mid thigh girth (cm)

- the girth taken at the midpoint between the trochanterion and the tibiale laterale

- subject stands erect, feet 10 cm apart and weight evenly distributed, measurer crouches to the right side, palpates and marks the trochanterion and the tibiale laterale. The midpoint is found using a tape or anthropometer
- the girth is taken at this level, perpendicular to the long axis of the thigh

Maximum calf girth (cm)
- subject stands erect, feet 10 cm apart and weight evenly distributed, measurer crouches to the right side, and moves the tape up and down the calf, perpendicular to the long axis until the greatest circumference is located

Triceps skinfold (cm)
as before (Practical 2)

Mid thigh skinfold (cm)
as before (Practical 2)

Midcalf skinfold (cm)
as before (Practical 2)

Medial calf skinfold (cm)
- a vertical skinfold taken on the medial aspect of the calf at the level of maximum calf girth, the subject stands with the right foot on a platform, flexing the knee and hip to 90°

Forearm 1 (lateralis) (cm)
- a vertical skinfold taken at the level of maximum forearm girth on the lateral aspect of the forearm with the hand supinated

Forearm 2 (volaris) (cm)
- a vertical skinfold taken at the level of maximum forearm girth taken on the anterior aspect of the forearm with the hand supinated

1.15 PRACTICAL 5: ESTIMATION OF SKELETAL MASS

- an indication of skeletal robustness that correlates highly with bone breadths at the elbow, wrist, knee and ankle

1.15.1 PURPOSE

- To develop the technique required to estimate skeletal mass by anthropometry

1.15.2 METHODS

Matiegka (1921) – males and females
$\text{kg S} = [(\text{HB} + \text{WB} + \text{FB} + \text{AB})/4]^2 \times \text{ht} \times 1.2 \times 0.001$
$\% \text{S} = (\text{kg S}/\text{ body mass}) \times 100$
where: HB is biepicondylar humerus; WB is bistyloideus; FB is biepicondylar femur; AB is bimalleolar; and ht is height in cm.

Drinkwater et al. (1986) – males and females
$kg\,S = [(HB + WB + FB + AB)/4]^2 \times ht \times 0.92 \times 0.001$
$\%\,S = (kg\,S/body\ mass) \times 100$
where variables are as defined previously.

1.15.3 DETERMINATION OF VARIABLES RELATED TO ESTIMATION OF SKELETAL MASS

- Landmarks for bone breadth measurements should be palpated with the fingers, then the anthropometer is applied firmly to the bone, compressing soft tissue when necessary.

Stature (ht) as before (Practical 3)

Biepicondylar humerus breadth
- the distance between medial and lateral epicondyles of the humerus when the shoulder and elbow are flexed
- the measurer palpates the epicondyles and applies the blades of an anthropometer or small spreading caliper at a slight upward angle while firmly pressing the blades to the bone.

Bistyloideus breadth
- the distance between the most prominent aspects of the styloid processes of the ulna and radius
- the subject flexes the elbow and the hand is pronated so that the wrist is horizontal
- the styloid processes are palpated and the anthropometer is applied firmly to the bone

Biepicondylar femur breadth
- the distance between the most medial and lateral aspects of the femoral condyles (epicondyles)
- the subject stands with the weight on the left leg and the right knee flexed (the foot may rest on a raised surface or the subject may sit with the leg hanging)
- the measurer crouches in front of the subject, palpates the femoral condyles and applies the anthropometer at a slight downward angle while firmly pressing to the bone

Bimalleolar breadth
- the maximum distance between the most medial and lateral extensions of the malleoli
- the subject stands erect with the weight evenly distributed over both feet,
- the measurer palpates the malleoli and applies the anthropometer firmly to the bone
- a horizontal distance is measured, however the plane between the malleoli is oblique

ACKNOWLEDGEMENTS

The author acknowledges the contribution of Ms Kate Plant and Dr Daniela Sovak in the preparation of the laboratory activities; Mr Steve Hudson in providing a graduate student perspective in the preparation of the text; and Mr Dale Oldham for the preparation of computer-generated illustrations

REFERENCES

Bakker, H. K. and Struikenkamp, R. S. (1977) Biological variability and lean body mass estimates. *Human Biology*, **53**, 181–225.

Baumgartner, R. N., Rhyne, R. L., Troup, C. *et al.* (1992) Appendicular skeletal muscle areas assessed by magnetic resonance imaging in older persons. *Journal of Gerontology*, **47**(3), M67–72.

Bjorntorp, P. (1984) Hazards in subgroups of human obesity. *European Journal of Clinical Investigation*, **14**, 239–41.

Black, L. F., Offord, K. and Hyatt, R. E. (1974) Variability in the maximal expiratory flow volume curve in asymptomatic smokers and nonsmokers. *American Review of Respiratory Diseases*, **110**, 282–92.

Boren, H. G., Kory, R. C. and Syner, J. C. (1966) The Veterans Administration-Army Cooperative Study on Lung Function. II The lung volume and its subdivisions in normal man. *American Journal of Medicine*, **41**, 96–114.

Brozek, J., Grande, F., Anderson, J. T. and Keys, A. (1963) Densitometric analysis of body composition: revision of some quantitative assumptions. *Annals of the New York Academy of Sciences*, **110**, 113–40.

de Koning, F. L., Binkhorst, R. A., Kauer, J. M. G. and Thijssen, H. O. M. (1986) Accuracy of an anthropometric estimate of the muscle and bone area in a transveral cross-section of the arm. *International Journal of Sports Medicine*, **7**, 246–9.

Drinkwater, D. T., Martin, A. D., Ross, W. D. and Clarys, J. P. (1986) Validation by cadaver dissection of Matiegka's equations for the anthropometric estimation of anatomical body composition in adult humans, in *The 1984 Olympic Scientific Congress Proceedings: Perspectives in Kinanthropometry* (ed. J. A. P. Day) Human Kinetics, Champaign, pp. 221–7.

Durnin, J. V. G. A. and Womersley, J. (1974) Body fat assessed from total body density and its estimation from skinfold thickness: measurements on 481 men and women aged from 16 to 72 years. *British Journal of Nutrition*, **32**, 77–97.

Eston, R. G., Kreitzman, S., Lamb, K. L. *et al.* (1990), Assessment of fat-free mass by hydrodensitometry, skinfolds, infra-red interactance and electrical impedance in boys and girls aged 11–12 years. *Journal of Sports Sciences*, **8**, 174–5.

Eston, R. G., Cruz, A., Fu, F. and Fung, L. M. (1993) Fat-free mass estimation by bioelectrical impedance and anthropometric techniques in Chinese children. *Journal of Sports Sciences*, **11**, 241–7.

Forbes, R. M., Cooper, A. R. and Mitchell, H. H. (1953) The composition of the adult human body as determined by chemical analysis. *Journal of Biological Chemistry*, **203**, 359–66.

Garn, S. M., Leonard, W. R. and Hawthorne, V. M. (1986) Three limitations of the body mass index. *American Journal of Clinical Nutrition*, **44**, 996–7.

Gleichauf, C. N. and Roe, D. A. (1989) The menstrual cycle's effect on the reliability of bioimpedance measurements for assessing body composition. *American Journal of Clinical Nutrition*, **50**, 903–7.

Hawes, M. R. and Sovak, D. (1993) Skeletal ruggedness as a factor in performance of Olympic and national calibre synchronized swimmers, in *Kinanthropometry IV* (eds W. Duquet and J. A. P. Day) E & FN Spon, London, pp. 107–13.

Hawes, M. R. and Sovak, D. (1994) Morphological prototypes, assessment and change in young athletes. *Journal of Sports Sciences*, **12**, 235–42.

Heymsfield, S. B., McManus, C., Smith, J. *et al.* (1982) Anthropometric measurement of muscle mass: revised equations for calculating bone-free arm muscle area. *American Journal of Clinical Nutrition*, **36**, 680–90.

Heyward, V. H. (1991) *Advanced Fitness Assessment and Exercise Prescription.* Human Kinetics, Champaign.

Hodgdon, J. A. and Fitzgerald, P. I. (1987) Validity of impedance predictions at various levels of fatness. *Human Biology*, **59**(2), 281–98.

Houtkooper, L. B., Lohman, T. G., Going, S. B. and Hall, M. C. (1989) Validity of bioelectrical impedance for body composition assessment in children. *Journal of Applied Physiology*, **66**, 814–21.

Ikai, M. and Fukunaga, T. (1968) Calculation of muscle strength per unit cross-sectional area of human muscle by means of ultrasonic measurement. *Internationale Zeitschrift für Angewandte Physiologie*, **26**, 26–32.

Jackson, A. S. and Pollock, M. L. (1978), Generalized equations for predicting body density of men. *British Journal of Nutrition*, **40**, 497–504.

Jackson, A. S., Pollock, M. L. and Ward, A. (1980) Generalized equations for predicting body density of women. *Medicine and Science in Sports and Exercise*, **12**, 175–82.

Katch, F. and McArdle, V. (1983) *Nutrition, Weight Control and Exercise* (2nd ed.). Lea and Febiger, Philandelphia.

Keys, A., Fidanza, F., Karvonen, M. J. *et al.* (1972) Indices of relative weight and obesity. *Journal of Chromic Disease*, **25**, 329–43.

Leusink, J. A. (1972) Fit, vet, vetrij en vrije vetzuren. Academic Thesis, State University, Utrecht, The Netherlands

Lohman, T. G., Slaughter, M. H., Boileau, R. A. *et al.* (1984) Bone mineral measurements and their relation to body density in children, youths and adults. *Human Biology*, **56**, 667–79.

Lukaski, H. C., Bolonchuk, W. W., Hall, C. B. and Siders, W. A. (1986) Validation of tetrapolar bioelectric impedance method to assess human body composition. *Journal of Applied Physiology*, **60**, 1327–32.

Lukaski, H. C. (1987) Methods for the assessment of human body composition: traditional and new. *American Journal of Clinical Nutrition*, **46**, 537–56.

Martin, A. D. and Drinkwater, D. T. (1991) Variability in the measures of body fat. *Sports Medicine*, **11**, 277–88.

Martin, A. D., Ross, W. D., Drinkwater, D. T. and Clarys, J. P. (1985) Prediction of body fat by skinfold caliper: assumptions and cadaver evidence. *International Journal of Obesity*, **9**, 31–9.

Martin, A. D., Drinkwater, D. T., Clarys, J. P. and Ross, W. D. (1986) The inconstancy of the fat-free mass: a reappraisal with applications for densitometry, in *Kinanthropometry III. Proceedings of the VII Commonwealth and International Conference on Sport, Physical Education, Dance, Recreation and Health*, (ed. T. J. Reilly, J. Watkins and J. Borms), E & FN Spon, London, pp. 92–7.

Martin, A. D., Spenst, L. F., Drinkwater, D. T. and Clarys, J. P. (1990) Anthropometric estimation of muscle mass in men. *Medicine and Science in Sports and Exercise*, **22**, 729–33.

Martin, A. D., Drinkwater, D. T., Clarys, J. P. *et al.* (1992) Effects of skin thickness and skinfold compressibility on skinfold thickness measurement. *American Journal of Human Biology*, **6**, 1–8.

Matiegka, J. (1921) The testing of physical efficiency. *American Journal of Physical Anthropology*, **4**(2), 223–30.

Mendez, J. and Keys, A. (1960) Density and composition of mammalian muscle. *Metabolism*, **9**, 184–7.

Morrow, J. R., Bradley, P. W. and Jackson, A. S. (1985) Residual volume prediction errors with trained athletes. *Medicine and Science in Sports and Exercise*, **17**, 204.

Nyboer, J., Bagno, S. and Nims, L. F. (1943) *The Electrical Impedance Plethysmograph and Electrical Volume Recorder*. National Research Council, Committee on Aviation, Washington.

Orpin, M. J. and Scott, P. J. (1964) Estimation of total body fat using skin fold caliper measurements. *New Zealand Medical Journal*, **63**, 501–7.

Parizkova, J. (1978) Lean body mass and depot fat during ontogenesis in humans, in *Nutrition, Physical Fitness and Health, International Series on Sport Sciences*, vol. 7 (eds J. Parizkova and V. A. Rogozkin), University Park Press, Baltimore, pp. 24–51.

Ross, W. D., Eiben, O. G., Ward, R. *et al.* (1986) Alternatives for conventional methods of human body composition and physique assessment, in *The 1984 Olympic Scientific Congress Proceedings Perspectives in Kinanthropometry* (ed. J. A. P. Day), Human Kinetics, Champaign, pp. 203–20.

Ross, W. D., Martin, A. D. and Ward, R. (1987) Body composition and aging: theoretical and methodological implications. *Collegium Anthropologicum*, **11**, 15–44.

Schutte, J. E., Townsend, E. J., Huff, J. *et al.* (1984) Density of lean body mass is greater in Blacks than in Whites. *Journal of Applied Physiology*, **456**, 1647–9.

Segal, K. R., van Loan, M., Fitzgerald, P. I. *et al.* (1988) Lean body mass estimation by bioelectrical impedance analysis: a four-site cross-validation study. *American Journal of Clinical Nutrition*, **47**, 7–14.

Siri, W. E. (1956) Body composition from fluid spaces and density: analysis of methods. University of California Radiation Laboratory Report UCRL no. 3349.

Van Loan, M. D. and Mayclin, P. (1987) Bioelectrical impedance analysis: is it a reliable estimator of lean body mass and total body water? *Human Biology*, **59**, 299–309.

Van Loan, M. D. (1990) Bioelectrical impedance analysis to determine fat-free mass, total body water and body fat. *Sports Medicine*, **10**, 205–17.

Wang, Z. M., Pierson Jr, R. N. and Heymsfield, S. B. (1992) The five-level model: a new approach to organizing body-composition research. *American Journal of Clinical Nutrition*, **56**, 19–28.

Wilmore, J. H., Vodak, P. A., Parr R. B. *et al.* (1980) Further simplification of a method for determination of residual lung volume. *Medicine and Science in Sports and Exercise*, **12**, 216–18.

SOMATOTYPING 2

W. Duquet and J. E. L. Carter

2.1 HISTORY

Somatotyping is a method for describing the human physique in terms of a number of traits that relate to body shape and composition. The definition of the traits, and the form of the scales that are used to describe the relative importance of the traits, vary from one body type method to another. Attempts to establish such methods date from Hippocrates, and continue to the present time. Excellent reviews of these early methods were published by Tucker and Lessa (1940a, b) and by Albonico (1970).

A classic approach, that led to the method presently most used, was introduced by Sheldon *et al.* (1940). His most important contribution to the field lies in the combination of the basic ideas of two other methods. The first was Kretschmer's (1921) classification, with three empirically determined and visually rated body build extremes, with each subject being an amalgam of the three 'poles'. The second was the analytical, anthropometrically determined body build assessment of Viola (1933), in which the ratio of trunk and limbs measures and of thoracic and abdominal trunk values are expressed proportionate to a 'normotype'. In Sheldon's method an attempt is made to describe the genotypical morphological traits of a person in terms of three components, each on a 7-point scale. This genotypic approach, the rigidity of the closed 7-point ratings, and also a lack of objectivity of the ratings, made the method unattractive to most researchers, especially in the field of kinanthropometry.

From these three principal criticisms, and in addition those of Heath (1963), emerged a new method, created by Heath and Carter (1967). It was partly influenced by ideas from Parnell (1954, 1958). A phenotypic approach was proposed with open rating scales for three components, and ratings that can be estimated from objective anthropometric measurements. The Heath–Carter somatotype method is now the universally most applied, and will be used in this laboratory manual. The most extensive description of the method, its development and applications can be found in Carter and Heath (1990). Two other original methods were introduced by Lindegård (1953) and by Conrad (1963). They are less used than the Heath–Carter method.

2.2 THE HEATH–CARTER SOMATOTYPE METHOD

2.2.1 DEFINITIONS

(a) Somatotype

A somatotype is a quantified expression/description of the present morphological conformation of a person. It consists of a three-numeral rating, e.g. 3.5–5–1. The three

Kinanthropometry and Exercise Physiology Laboratory Manual: Tests, procedures and data Edited by Roger Eston and Thomas Reilly. Published in 1996 by E & FN Spon. ISBN 0 419 17880 5

numerals are always recorded in the same order, each describing the value of a particular component of physique.

(b) Anthropometric and photoscopic somatotoypes

The principal rating of the component values is based on a visual inspection of the subject, or their photograph, preferably a front, a side and a back view, taken in minimal clothing. This rating is called the photoscopic (or anthroposcopic) somatotype rating. If the investigator cannot perform a photoscopic rating, the component values can be estimated from a combination of anthropometric measurements. The calculated three-numeral rating is then called the anthropometric somatotype. The recommended somatotyping procedure is a combination of an anthropometric followed by a photoscopic evaluation.

(c) Components

A component is an empirically defined descriptor of a particular aspect or trait of the human body build. It is expressed as a numeral on a continuous scale that theoretically starts at zero and has no upper limit. The ratings are rounded to the half-unit. In practice, no ratings lower than one-half are given (as a particular body build trait can never be absolutely absent), and a rating of more than seven is extremely high.

(d) Endomorphy

The first component, called endomorphy, describes the relative degree of fatness of the body, regardless of where or how it is distributed. It also describes corresponding physical aspects such as roundness of the body, softness of the contours, relative volume of the abdominal trunk and distally tapering of the limbs.

(e) Mesomorphy

The second component, called mesomorphy, describes the relative musculoskeletal development of the body. It also describes corresponding physical aspects such as the apparent robustness of the body in terms of muscle or bone, the relative volume of the thoracic trunk, and the possibly hidden muscle bulk.

(f) Ectomorphy

The third component, called ectomorphy, describes the relative slenderness of the body. It also describes corresponding physical aspects such as the relative 'stretchedoutness', the apparent linearity of the body or fragility of the limbs, in absence of any bulk, be it muscle, fat or other tissues.

(g) Somatotype category

Category is the more qualitative description of the individual somatotype, in terms of the dominant component or components. For example, a subject with a high rating on mesomorphy and an equally low rating on endomorphy and on ectomorphy, will be called a mesomorph or a balanced mesomorph. The complete list with possible categories and corresponding dominance variations is given in Practical 2.

2.2.2 ASSESSMENT

(a) Anthropometric somatotype

The anthropometric somatotype can be calculated from a set of 10 measurements: height, weight, four skinfolds (triceps, subscapular, supraspinale and medial calf), two biepicondylar breadths (humerus and femur) and two girths (upper arm flexed and tensed, and calf). Descriptions of measurement techniques are given later.

(b) Photoscopic somatotype

The photoscopic somatotype can only be rated objectively by persons who have trained to attain the necessary skill, and whose rating validity and reliability is established against the evaluations of an experienced rater.

This part of the procedure is therefore not included in the present text. It is, however, generally accepted that the anthropometric evaluation gives a fair estimate of the photoscopic procedure. Important deviations are only found in subjects with a high degree of dysplasia in fat or muscle tissue.

Many researchers, who do not use photographs or visual inspection, or who lack experience in rating photoscopically, report the anthropometric somatotype only. A somatotype study should therefore always mention the method used.

2.2.3 FURTHER ELABORATION

The differences or similarities in somatotypes of subjects or groups of subjects can be visualized by plotting them on a somatochart (Practical 1). A somatotype rating can be thought of as being a vector, or a point in a three-coordinate system, in which each axis carries a somatotype component scale. The somatochart is the orthogonal projection of this three-coordinate system, parallel to the bisector of the three axes, on a two-dimensional plane.

The somatotype, being an entity, should be treated as such. One possible qualitative technique is the use of somatotype categories. A quantitative technique is the use of the SAD or Somatotype Attitudinal Distance, which is the difference in component units between two somatotypes, or in terms of the somatochart, the three-dimensional distance between two points.

In time series of somatotypes of the same subject, the ongoing changes in somatotype can be expressed by adding the consecutive SADs. This sum is called the Migratory Distance (MD). These further elaborations will be covered in the Practicals.

2.2.4 MEASUREMENT TECHNIQUES

The descriptions are essentially the same as in Carter and Heath (1990). The techniques should ideally be used for subsequent calculation of the Heath–Carter anthropometric somatotype. Where the choice is possible, measures should be taken both on left and right sides, and the largest measure should be reported. In large-scale surveys, measuring on the right side is preferable.

The anthropometric equipment needed are a weighing scale for measuring the weight, a stadiometer (a height scale attached on a wall and a Broca plane) or an anthropometer for measuring the height, a skinfold caliper for the skinfolds, a small adapted sliding caliper or a spreading caliper for the breadths, and a flexible steel or fibreglass tape for the girths.

(a) Weight (Body Mass)

The subject, in minimal clothing, stands in the centre of the scale platform. Body mass is recorded to the nearest tenth of a kilogram if possible. A correction is made for clothing so that nude weight is used in subsequent calculations. Avoid measuring weight shortly after a meal.

(b) Height

The subject stands straight, against an upright wall with a stadiometer or against an anthropometer, touching the wall or the anthropometer with back, buttocks and both heels. The head is oriented in the Frankfurt plane (i.e. the lower border of the eye socket and the upper border of the ear opening should be on a horizontal line). The subject is instructed to stretch upward and take and hold a full breath. Lower the Broca plane or the ruler until it touches the vertex firmly, but without exerting extreme pressure.

(c) Skinfolds

Raise a fold of skin and subcutaneous tissue at the marked site firmly between thumb and forefinger of the left hand, and pull the fold gently away from the underlying muscle. Hold the caliper in the right hand and apply the edge of the plates on the caliper branches 1 cm below the fingers, and allow them to exert their full pressure before reading the thickness of the fold after about two seconds. The Harpenden or Slim Guide calipers are recommended.

(i) Triceps skinfold

The subject stands relaxed, with the arm hanging loosely. Raise the triceps skinfold at the midline on the back of the arm at a level halfway between the acromion and the olecranon processes.

(ii) Subscapular skinfold

The subject stands relaxed. Raise the subscapular skinfold adjacent to the inferior angle of the scapula in a direction which is obliquely downwards and outwards at 45°.

(iii) Supraspinale skinfold

The subject stands relaxed. Raise the fold 5–7 cm above the anterior superior iliac spine on a line to the anterior axillary border and in a direction downwards and inwards at 45°. (This skinfold was called suprailiac in some former texts.)

(iv) Medial calf skinfold

The subject is seated, with the legs slightly spread. The leg that is not being measured, can be bent backwards to facilitate the measurement. Raise a vertical skinfold on the medial side (aspect) of the leg, at the level of the maximum girth of the calf.

(d) Breadths

(i) Biepicondylar humerus breadth

The subject holds the shoulder and elbow flexed to 90°. Measure the width between the medial and lateral epicondyles of the humerus. In this position, the medial epicondyle is always somewhat lower than the lateral. Apply the caliper at an angle approximately bisecting the angle of the elbow. Place firm pressure on the crossbranches or the spreading branches in order to compress the subcutaneous tissue.

(ii) Biepicondylar femur breadth

The subject is seated, or standing upright with one foot on a pedestal, with knee bent at a right angle. Measure the greatest distance between the lateral and medial epicondyles of the femur. Place firm pressure on the crossbranches or the spreading branches.

(e) Girths

(i) Upper arm girth, flexed and tensed

The subject holds the upper arm horizontally and flexes the elbow 45°, clenches the hand and maximally contracts the elbow flexors and extensors. Take the measurement at the greatest girth of the arm. The tape should not be too loose, but should not indent the soft tissue either.

(ii) Standing calf girth

The subject stands with feet slightly apart. Place the tape horizontally around the calf and measure the maximum circumference. The tape should not be too loose, but should not indent the soft tissue.

2.3 RELEVANCE OF SOMATOTYPING

Why should you use somatotyping? Of what value is it in exercise and sports science? These are important and often asked questions.

The somatotype gives an overall summary of the physique as a unified whole. Its utility is in the combination of three aspects of physique into a somatotype rating. It combines the appraisal of adiposity, musculoskeletal robustness and linearity into the three-numbered rating and should conjure up in your mind a visual image of the three aspects of the physique. The adiposity is related to relative fatness or endomorphy, the relative muscle and bony robustness is related to the fat-free body or mesomorphy, and the linearity or ectomorphy gives an indication of the bulkiness or mass relative to stature in the physique. From a few simple measures, the somatotype gives a useful summary of a variety of possible measures or observations that can be made on the body.

The somatotype tells you what kind of physique you have, and how it looks. It has been used to describe and compare the physiques of athletes at all levels of competition and in a variety of sports. Somatotypes of athletes in selected sports are quite different from each other, whereas somatotypes are similar in other sports. Somatotyping has also been used to describe physique changes during growth, ageing, and training, as well as in relation to physical performance. The somatotype is a general descriptor of physique. If more precise questions are asked, such as 'What is the growth rate in upper extremity bone segments?' then different and specific measures need to be taken.

Two examples will illustrate how the somatotype gives more information than some typical measures of body composition. First, the somatotype tells you the difference between individuals with the same level of fatness. An elite male body builder, gymnast or long distance runner may all have the same estimate of body fat at 5%. All three are low in percentage body fat, but this fact alone does not tell you the important differences between the physiques of these athletes. They differ considerably in their muscle, bone and linearity. The body builder may be a 1-9-1, the gymnast a 1-6-2, and the runner a 1-3-5 somatotype. They are all rated '1' in endomorphy, but they have completely different ratings on mesomorphy and ectomorphy. The somatotype describes these differences.

As a second example, two males with the same height and weight, and therefore the same body mass index (BMI), can have physiques that look completely different. If they are both 175 cm tall and weigh 78 kg, they will have a BMI of 25.5, and a somatotype height–weight ratio of 41.0. Their somatotypes are 6-3-1 and 3-6-1. They are completely different looking physiques. Both have low linearity (1 in ectomorphy), but the BMI does not tell you anything about their specific differences in body composition as inferred from their opposite ratings of 6 (high) and 3 (low) in endomorphy or in mesomorphy.

In both the examples above, the potential performance characteristics for the subjects would be quite different because of the differences in mesomorphy and ectomorphy in the first example, and in endomorphy and mesomorphy in the second example.

2.4 PRACTICAL 1: CALCULATION OF ANTHROPOMETRIC SOMATOTYPES

2.4.1 INTRODUCTION

It is the aim of this practical to learn how to calculate anthropometric somatotypes, using the classical approach and using some fast calculation formulae, and to learn how to plot the results on a somatochart.

2.4.2 METHODS

Endomorphy is estimated from the relation between the component value and the sum of three skinfold measures, relative to the subject's height.
Mesomorphy is estimated from the deviation of two girths and two breadths from their expected values, relative to the subject's height.
Ectomorphy is estimated from the relation between the component value and the reciprocal of the ponderal index, or height over cube root of weight ratio.

(a) Steps for the manual calculation of the anthropometric somatotype

The following is a guide in 16 steps for calculating the anthropometric somatotype by means of the Heath–Carter somatotype rating form.
Endomorphy is calculated in steps 2–5, mesomorphy in steps 6–10, and ectomorphy in steps 11–14.
A worked example, in which these steps were followed, is given in Figure 2.1.

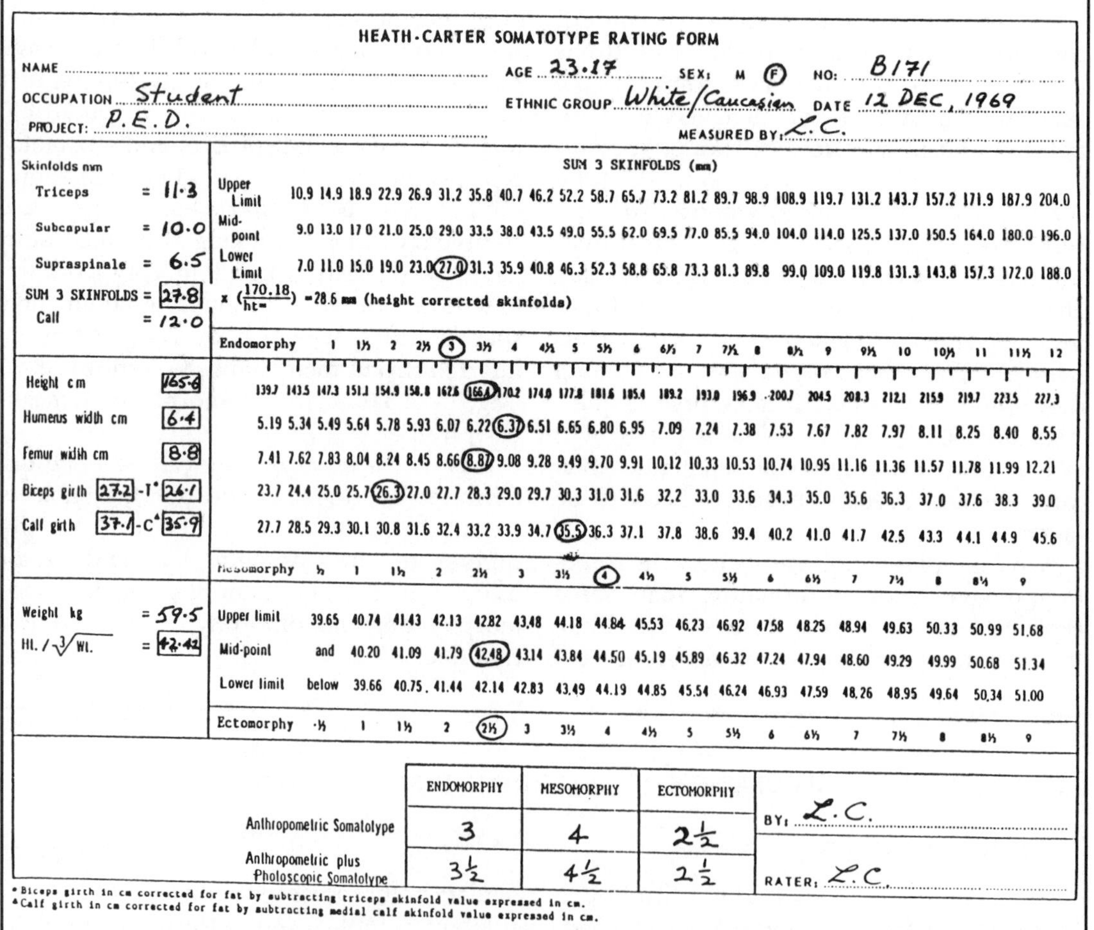

HEATH-CARTER SOMATOTYPE RATING FORM

NAME .... AGE 23.17 SEX: M (F) NO: B171
OCCUPATION Student ETHNIC GROUP White/Caucasian DATE 12 DEC, 1969
PROJECT: P.E.D. MEASURED BY: L.C.

Skinfolds mm
Triceps = 11.3
Subcapular = 10.0
Supraspinale = 6.5
SUM 3 SKINFOLDS = 27.8
Calf = 12.0

SUM 3 SKINFOLDS (mm)

Upper Limit 10.9 14.9 18.9 22.9 26.9 31.2 35.8 40.7 46.2 52.2 58.7 65.7 73.2 81.2 89.7 98.9 108.9 119.7 131.2 143.7 157.2 171.9 187.9 204.0
Mid-point 9.0 13.0 17.0 21.0 25.0 29.0 33.5 38.0 43.5 49.0 55.5 62.0 69.5 77.0 85.5 94.0 104.0 114.0 125.5 137.0 150.5 164.0 180.0 196.0
Lower Limit 7.0 11.0 15.0 19.0 23.0 (27.0) 31.3 35.9 40.8 46.3 52.3 58.8 65.8 73.3 81.3 89.8 99.0 109.0 119.8 131.3 143.8 157.3 172.0 188.0

x ($\frac{170.18}{ht=}$) =28.6 mm (height corrected skinfolds)

Endomorphy 1 1½ 2 2½ (3) 3½ 4 4½ 5 5½ 6 6½ 7 7½ 8 8½ 9 9½ 10 10½ 11 11½ 12

Height cm [165.6] 139.7 143.5 147.3 151.1 154.9 158.8 162.6 (166.4) 170.2 174.0 177.8 181.6 185.4 189.2 193.0 196.9 200.7 204.5 208.3 212.1 215.9 219.7 223.5 227.3
Humerus width cm [6.4] 5.19 5.34 5.49 5.64 5.78 5.93 6.07 6.22 (6.37) 6.51 6.65 6.80 6.95 7.09 7.24 7.38 7.53 7.67 7.82 7.97 8.11 8.25 8.40 8.55
Femur width cm [8.8] 7.41 7.62 7.83 8.04 8.24 8.45 8.66 (8.87) 9.08 9.28 9.49 9.70 9.91 10.12 10.33 10.53 10.74 10.95 11.16 11.36 11.57 11.78 11.99 12.21
Biceps girth [27.2] -T* [26.1] 23.7 24.4 25.0 25.7 (26.3) 27.0 27.7 28.3 29.0 29.7 30.3 31.0 31.6 32.2 33.0 33.6 34.3 35.0 35.6 36.3 37.0 37.6 38.3 39.0
Calf girth [37.1] -C▲ [35.9] 27.7 28.5 29.3 30.1 30.8 31.6 32.4 33.2 33.9 34.7 (35.5) 36.3 37.1 37.8 38.6 39.4 40.2 41.0 41.7 42.5 43.3 44.1 44.9 45.6

Mesomorphy ½ 1 1½ 2 2½ 3 3½ (4) 4½ 5 5½ 6 6½ 7 7½ 8 8½ 9

Weight kg = 59.5
Ht. / $\sqrt[3]{Wt.}$ = [42.42]

Upper limit 39.65 40.74 41.43 42.13 42.82 43.48 44.18 44.84 45.53 46.23 46.92 47.58 48.25 48.94 49.63 50.33 50.99 51.68
Mid-point and 40.20 41.09 41.79 (42.48) 43.14 43.84 44.50 45.19 45.89 46.32 47.24 47.94 48.60 49.29 49.99 50.68 51.34
Lower limit below 39.66 40.75 41.44 42.14 42.83 43.49 44.19 44.85 45.54 46.24 46.93 47.59 48.26 48.95 49.64 50.34 51.00

Ectomorphy ½ 1 1½ 2 (2½) 3 3½ 4 4½ 5 5½ 6 6½ 7 7½ 8 8½ 9

	ENDOMORPHY	MESOMORPHY	ECTOMORPHY	
Anthropometric Somatotype	3	4	2½	BY: L.C.
Anthropometric plus Photoscopic Somatotype	3½	4½	2½	RATER: L.C.

* Biceps girth in cm corrected for fat by subtracting triceps skinfold value expressed in cm.
▲ Calf girth in cm corrected for fat by subtracting medial calf skinfold value expressed in cm.

Figure 2.1 Example of a completed anthropometric somatotype rating.

The measurements for subject B171 were: body mass: 59.5 kg; height: 165.6 cm; triceps skinfold: 11.3 mm; subscapular skinfold: 10.0 mm; supraspinale skinfold: 6.5 mm; calf skinfold: 12.0 mm; humerus breadth: 6.4 cm; femur breadth: 8.8 cm; biceps girth: 27.2 cm; calf girth: 37.1 cm.

Step 1: Record the identification data in the top section of the rating form.

Step 2: Record the values obtained from each of the four skinfold measurements.

Step 3: Sum the values of the triceps, subscapular and supraspinale skinfolds; record this sum in the box opposite 'Sum 3 skinfolds'. Correct for height by multiplying this sum by 170.18/height (cm).

Step 4: Circle the closest value in the 'Sum 3 skinfolds' scale to the right. The scale reads vertically from low to high in columns and horizontally from left to right in rows. 'Lower limit' and 'upper limit' on the rows provide exact boundaries for each column. These values are circled if Sum 3 skinfolds is closer to the limit than to the midpoint.

Step 5: In the row 'Endomorphy' circle the value directly under the column circled in step 4.

Step 6: Record height and diameters of humerus and femur in the appropriate boxes. Make the corrections for skinfolds before recording girths of biceps and calf. (Skinfold corrections are as follows: Convert triceps and calf skinfold to cm by dividing them by 10. Subtract converted triceps skinfold from the biceps girth. Subtract converted calf skinfold from calf girth.)

Step 7: On the height scale directly to the right, circle the height nearest to the measured height of the subject.

Step 8: For each bone diameter and girth, circle the figure nearest the measured value in the appropriate row. (If the measurement falls midway between the two values, circle the lower value. This conservative procedure is used because the largest girths and diameters are recorded.)

Step 9: Deal in this step only with columns as units, not with numerical values. Check the circled deviations of the values for diameters and girths from the circled value in the height column. Count the column deviations to the right of the height column as positive deviations, with columns as units. Deviations to the left are negative deviations. Calculate the algebraic sum of the deviations (D). Use this formula: Mesomorphy = (D/8) + 4. Round the obtained value of mesomorphy to the nearest one-half rating unit.

Step 10: In the row 'Mesomorphy' circle the closest value for the mesomorphy calculated in step 9. (If the point is exactly midway between two rating points, circle the value closest to 4 on the scale. This conservative regression toward 4 guards against spuriously extreme ratings.)

Step 11: Record body mass (kg).

Step 12: Obtain height divided by cube root of weight (HWR) from a nomograph or by calculation. Record HWR in the appropriate box. Note: the HWR can be calculated easily with the help of a hand calculator. A calculator with a y to the x power (y^x) key is needed. To get the cube root, enter the base (y), press the 'y^x' key, enter 0.3333, and press the '=' key. If there is an 'INV y^x' function, or 'root of y' function ($\sqrt[x]{y}$), either may be used by entering the base, then 3 and the '=' key for the cube root.

A nomograph can be found in Carter and Heath (1990, p. 273).

Step 13: Circle the closest value in the HWR scale. Proceed with upper and lower limits as with endomorphy in step 4.

Step 14: In the row 'Ectomorphy' circle the ectomorphy value directly under the circled HWR.

Step 15: Record the circled values for each component in the row 'Anthropometric somatotype'. (If a photoscopic rating is available, the rater should record the final decision in the row 'Anthropometric and photoscopic somatotype'.)

Step 16: Investigator signs name to the right of the recorded rating.

Note: If in step 7 the recorded height is closer to the midpoint than to the two adjacent column values, place a vertical arrow between the two values, and continue to work with this half column, calculating half units for the deviations in step 9.

HEATH-CARTER SOMATOTYPE RATING FORM

NAME .... AGE .... SEX: M F NO: ....

OCCUPATION .... ETHNIC GROUP .... DATE ....

PROJECT: .... MEASURED BY: ....

Skinfolds mm

Triceps =

Subcapular =

Supraspinale =

SUM 3 SKINFOLDS = ☐

Calf =

SUM 3 SKINFOLDS (mm)

Upper Limit 10.9 14.9 18.9 22.9 26.9 31.2 35.8 40.7 46.2 52.2 58.7 65.7 73.2 81.2 89.7 98.9 108.9 119.7 131.2 143.7 157.2 171.9 187.9 204.0

Mid-point 9.0 13.0 17 0 21.0 25.0 29.0 33.5 38.0 43.5 49.0 55.5 62.0 69.5 77.0 85.5 94.0 104.0 114.0 125.5 137.0 150.5 164.0 180.0 196.0

Lower Limit 7.0 11.0 15.0 19.0 23.0 27.0 31.3 35.9 40.8 46.3 52.3 58.8 65.8 73.3 81.3 89.8 99.0 109.0 119.8 131.3 143.8 157.3 172.0 188.0

x $(\frac{170.18}{ht=})$ = mm (height corrected skinfolds)

Endomorphy 1 1½ 2 2½ 3 3½ 4 4½ 5 5½ 6 6½ 7 7½ 8 8½ 9 9½ 10 10½ 11 11½ 12

Height cm ☐ 139.7 143.5 147.3 151.1 154.9 158.8 162.6 166.4 170.2 174.0 177.8 181.6 185.4 189.2 193.0 196.9 200.7 204.5 208.3 212.1 215.9 219.7 223.5 227.3

Humerus width cm ☐ 5.19 5.34 5.49 5.64 5.78 5.93 6.07 6.22 6.37 6.51 6.65 6.80 6.95 7.09 7.24 7.38 7.53 7.67 7.82 7.97 8.11 8.25 8.40 8.55

Femur width cm ☐ 7.41 7.62 7.83 8.04 8.24 8.45 8.66 8.87 9.08 9.28 9.49 9.70 9.91 10.12 10.33 10.53 10.74 10.95 11.16 11.36 11.57 11.78 11.99 12.21

Biceps girth ☐ -T* ☐ 23.7 24.4 25.0 25.7 26.3 27.0 27.7 28.3 29.0 29.7 30.3 31.0 31.6 32.2 33.0 33.6 34.3 35.0 35.6 36.3 37.0 37.6 38.3 39.0

Calf girth ☐ -C▲ ☐ 27.7 28.5 29.3 30.1 30.8 31.6 32.4 33.2 33.9 34.7 35.5 36.3 37.1 37.8 38.6 39.4 40.2 41.0 41.7 42.5 43.3 44.1 44.9 45.6

Mesomorphy ½ 1 1½ 2 2½ 3 3½ 4 4½ 5 5½ 6 6½ 7 7½ 8 8½ 9

Weight kg =

Ht. / $\sqrt[3]{Wt.}$ = ☐

Upper limit 39.65 40.74 41.43 42.13 42.82 43.48 44.18 44.84 45.53 46.23 46.92 47.58 48.25 48.94 49.63 50.33 50.99 51.68

Mid-point and 40.20 41.09 41.79 42.48 43.14 43.84 44.50 45.19 45.89 46.32 47.24 47.94 48.60 49.29 49.99 50.68 51.34

Lower limit below 39.66 40.75 41.44 42.14 42.83 43.49 44.19 44.85 45.54 46.24 46.93 47.59 48.26 48.95 49.64 50.34 51.00

Ectomorphy ½ 1 1½ 2 2½ 3 3½ 4 4½ 5 5½ 6 6½ 7 7½ 8 8½ 9

	ENDOMORPHY	MESOMORPHY	ECTOMORPHY	
Anthropometric Somatotype				BY: ....
Anthropometric plus Photoscopic Somatotype				RATER: ....

* Biceps girth in cm corrected for fat by subtracting triceps skinfold value expressed in cm.

▲ Calf girth in cm corrected for fat by subtracting medial calf skinfold value expressed in cm.

Figure 2.2 The Heath–Carter somatotype rating form.

(b) Formulae for the calculation of the anthropometric somatotype by computer

The formulae in Table 2.1 were derived from the scales of the somatochart.

Table 2.1 Formulae for the calculation of the anthropometric Heath–Carter somatotype by calculator or computer.

Endomorphy	$= -0.7182 + 0.1451X - 0.00068X^2 + 0.0000014X^3$	
Mesomorphy	$= 0.858HB + 0.601FB + 0.188AG + 0.161CG - 0.131SH + 4.5$	
Ectomorphy	$= 0.732HWR - 28.58)$	(if $HWR > 40.74$)
	$= 0.463HWR - 17.615$	(if $39.65 < HWR \leq 40.74$)
	$= 0.5$	(if $HWR \leq 39.65$)

Symbols used: X = sum of 3 skinfolds, corrected for height; HB = humerus breadth; FB = femur breadth; AG = corrected arm girth; CG = corrected calf girth; SH = standing height; HWR = height over cube root of weight.

(c) Formulae for plotting somatotypes on the somatochart

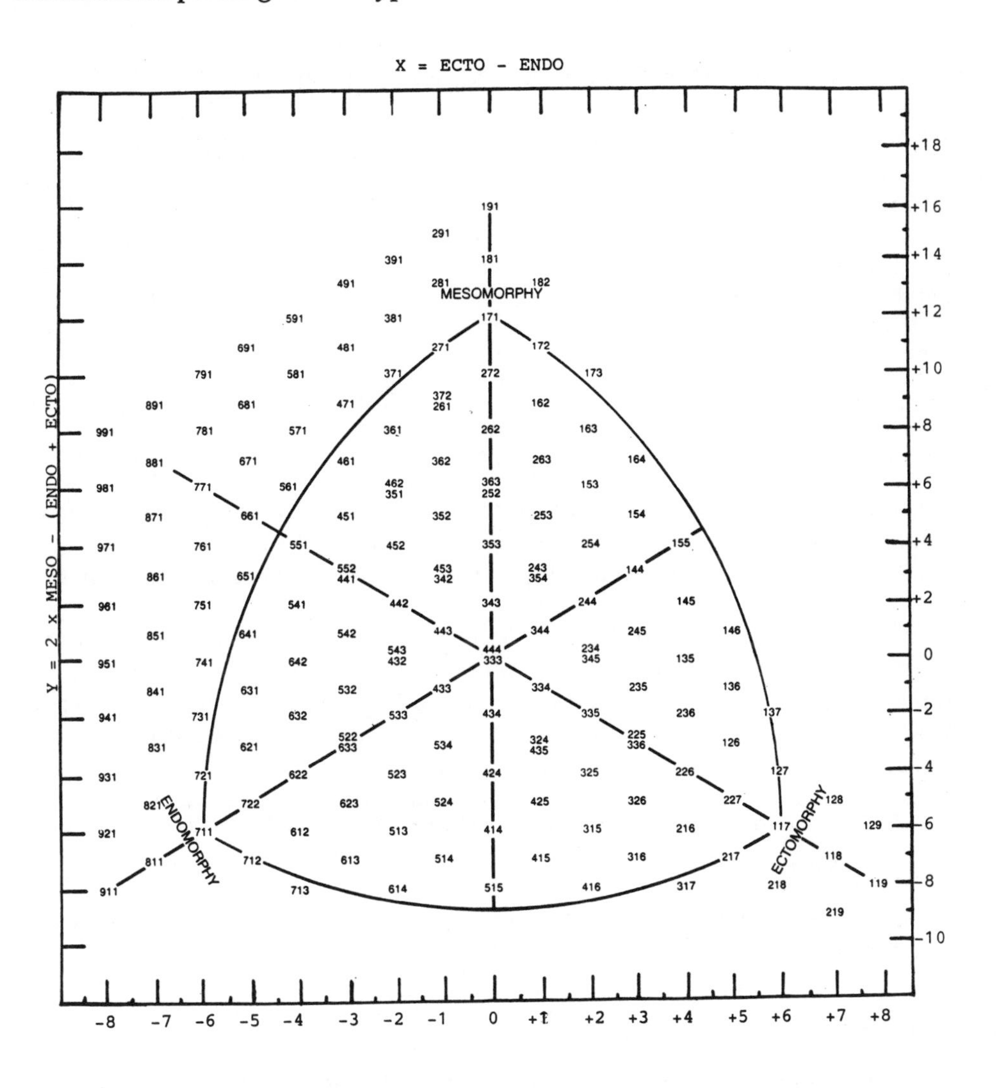

Figure 2.3 Somatochart for plotting somatotypes. (From Carter, 1980.)

The exact location of a somatotype on the somatochart (Figure 2.3) can be calculated using the formulae:

$$X = \text{ectomorphy} - \text{endomorphy}$$
$$Y = 2 \times \text{mesomorphy} - (\text{endomorphy} + \text{ectomorphy})$$

In the example in Figure 2.1 a subject with somatotype 3.0–4.0–2.5 is plotted with the following coordinates:

$$X = 2.5 - 3.0 = -0.5$$
$$Y = 2 \times 4.0 - (3.0 + 2.5) = 2.5$$

2.4.3 TASKS

A group of six adult subjects was measured. The results are shown in Table 2.2.

Table 2.2 Anthropometric measurements of six adult male subjects.

Subject	*1*	*2*	*3*	*4*	*5*	*6*
Body mass (kg)	82.0	67.7	60.5	64.4	82.4	80.8
Height (cm)	191.7	175.3	160.0	171.5	180.6	188.3
Triceps skinfold (mm)	7.0	5.0	3.0	4.2	11.2	17.1
Subscapular skinfold (mm)	6.0	7.0	5.0	5.7	8.8	12.1
Supraspinale skinfold (mm)	4.0	3.0	3.0	3.6	7.1	11.5
Medial calf skinfold (mm)	9.0	4.0	3.0	3.0	9.9	12.0
Biep. humerus breadth (cm)	7.3	7.0	6.5	6.6	7.4	6.5
Biep. femur breadth (cm)	10.1	9.4	8.9	9.7	9.2	9.1
Upper arm girth (fl. + t) (cm)	33.2	35.7	34.4	29.5	36.1	36.5
Standing calf girth (cm)	36.0	34.4	36.4	34.5	40.6	38.6

1. Calculate the anthropometric somatotype for each subject. Use copies of the somatotype rating form (Figure 2.2), and follow the example of Figure 2.1.
2. Calculate the anthropometric somatotype for each subject, using the formulae given in Table 2.1.
3. Check all calculations by rounding the second series of results to the half unit, and comparing the results with the first calculations.
4. Find the location of each subject on the somatochart, by calculating the XY-coordinates by means of the formulae above. Plot the somatotypes on a copy of the somatochart (Figure 2.3).

2.5 PRACTICAL 2: COMPARISON OF SOMATOTYPES OF DIFFERENT GROUPS

2.5.1 INTRODUCTION

It is the aim of this practical to learn how to compare anthropometric somatotypes, using the somatotype category approach and using SAD-techniques.

2.5.2 METHODS

There are many ways to analyse somatotype data. The easiest way is to consider each component separately, and to treat it like any other biological variable, using descriptive and inferential statistics. But the somatotype is more than three separate component values. Two subjects with an identical value for one of the components can nevertheless have completely different physiques, depending on the values of the two other components. For example: a somatotype 2-6-2 is completely different from a somatotype 2-2-6, but they both have the same endomorphy value. It is precisely the combination of all three component values into one expression that is the strength of the somatotype concept. Hence, techniques were developed to analyse the somatotype as a whole; among them, somatotype categories and SAD-techniques (see Duquet and Hebbelinck, 1977; Duquet, 1980; Carter *et al.*, 1983).

(a) Somatotype categories

Carter and Heath (1990) defined 13 somatotype categories, shown as areas in Figure 2.4. The exact definitions are as follows.

Central type: no component differs by more than one unit from the other two.
Balanced endomorph: endomorphy is dominant and mesomorphy and ectomorphy are equal (or do not differ by more than one-half unit).
Mesomorphic endomorph: endomorphy is dominant and mesomorphy is greater than ectomorphy.
Mesomorph–endomorph: endomorphy and mesomorphy are equal (or do not differ by more than one-half unit), and ectomorphy is smaller.
Endomorphic mesomorph: mesomorphy is dominant and endomorphy is greater than ectomorphy.
Balanced mesomorph: mesomorphy is dominant and endomorphy and ectomorphy are equal (or do not differ by more than one-half unit).
Ectomorphic mesomorph: mesomorphy is dominant and ectomorphy is greater than endomorphy.
Mesomorph–ectomorph: mesomorphy and ectomorphy are equal (or do not differ by more than one-half unit), and endomorphy is smaller.
Mesomorphic ectomorph: ectomorphy is dominant and mesomorphy is greater than endomorphy.
Balanced ectomorph: ectomorphy is dominant and endomorphy and mesomorphy are equal (or do not differ by more than one-half unit).
Endomorphic ectomorph: ectomorphy is dominant and endomorphy is greater than mesomorphy.
Endomorph–ectomorph: endomorphy and ectomorphy are equal (or do not differ by more than one-half unit), and mesomorphy is lower.
Ectomorphic endomorph: endomorphy is dominant and ectomorphy is greater than mesomorphy.

This classification can be simplified into seven larger groupings:
Central type: no component differs by more than one unit from the other two.
Endomorph: endomorphy is dominant, mesomorphy and ectomorphy are more than one-half unit lower.
Endomorph–mesomorph: endomorphy and mesomorphy are equal (or do not differ by more than one-half unit), and ectomorphy is smaller.

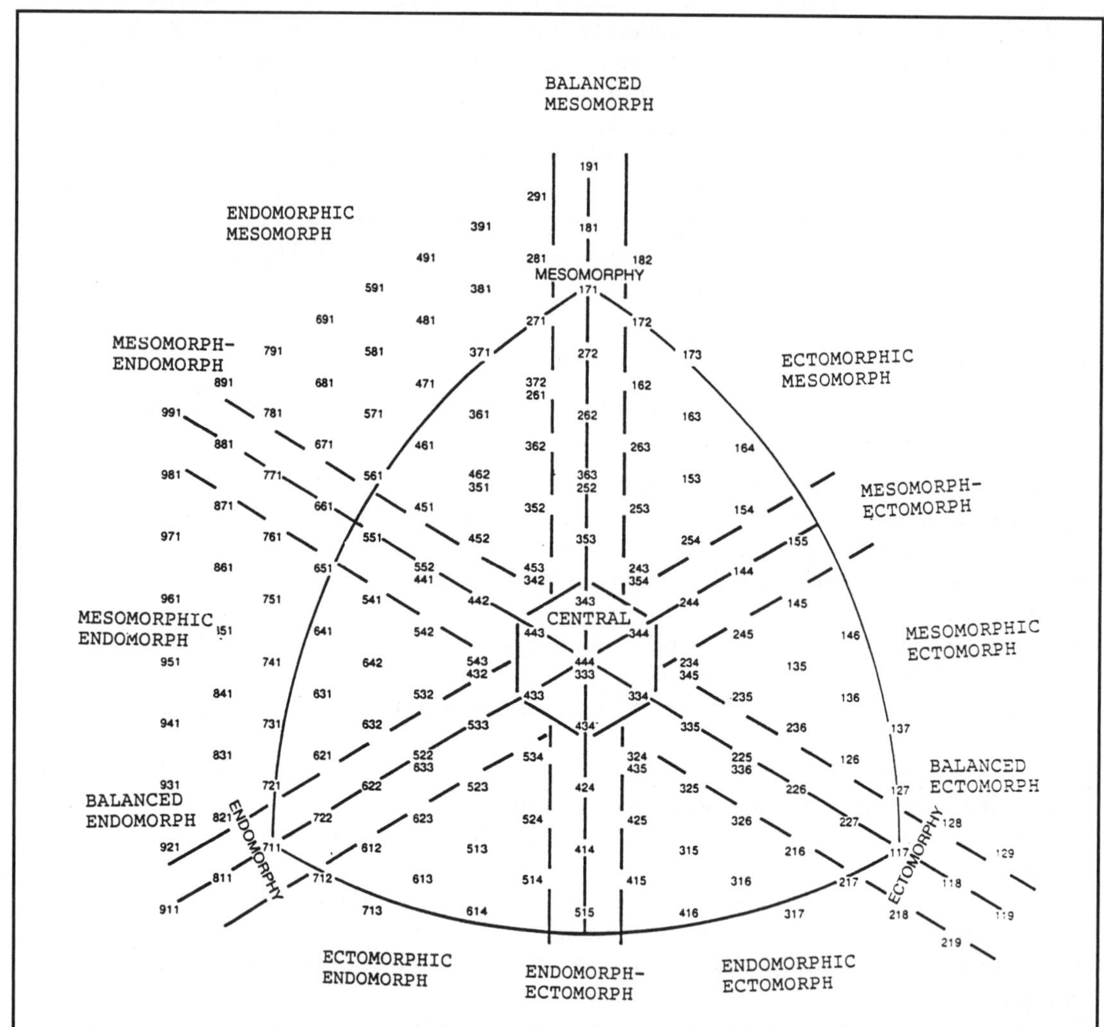

Figure 2.4 A somatochart showing the regions of the somatotype categories. (From Carter, 1980.)

Mesomorph: mesomorphy is dominant, endomorphy and ectomorphy are more than one-half unit lower.
Mesomorph–ectomorph: mesomorphy and ectomorphy are equal (or do not differ by more than one-half unit), and endomorphy is smaller.
Ectomorph: ectomorphy is dominant, endomorphy and mesomorphy are more than one-half unit lower.
Ectomorph–endomorph: endomorphy and ectomorphy are equal (or do not differ by more than one-half unit), and mesomorphy is lower.

(b) Somatotype Attitudinal Distance

The formulae for calculating the SAD are given in Table 2.3.

Table 2.3 Formulae for calculation of SAD parameters

$$SAD(A;B) = \sqrt{(end(A) - end(B))^2 + (mes(A) - mes(B))^2 + (ect(A) - ect(B))^2}$$

$$SAM(X) = \sum_i SAD(\bar{X} - X_i)/N_X$$

$$SAV(X) = \sum_i SAD(\bar{X} - X_i)^2/N_X$$

Symbols used: SAD = Somatotype Attitudinal Distance; SAM = Somatotype Attitudinal Mean; SAV = Somatotype Attitudinal Variance; end = endomorphy rating; mes = mesomorphy rating; ect = ectomorphy rating; A = an individual or a group; B = an individual or a group; X = a group; X_i = an individual member of group X; $\bar{X}$ = somatotype mean of group X; N_X = number of subjects in group X.

The SAD is the exact difference, in component units, between two somatotypes (if A and B are subjects), or between two somatotype group means (if A and B are group means), or between the group mean and an individual somatotype (if A and B are a group mean and a subject, respectively). Like other parametric statistics, the SAD can be used to calculate differences, hence mean deviations and variances. Table 2.3 also gives formulae for calculating the Somatotype Attitudinal Mean (SAM) and the Somatotype Attitudinal Variance (SAV). The SAM and the SAV describe the magnitude of the absolute scatter of a group of somatotypes around their mean. The SAD can lead to relatively simple parametric statistical treatment for calculating differences and correlations of whole somatotypes. Multivariate techniques may be more appropriate, but are also more complicated (Cressie *et al.*, 1986).

2.5.3 TASKS

Two groups of female middle distance runners were measured: international level runners and national level runners. The calculated somatotypes are shown in Table 2.4.

Table 2.4 Somatotypes of six national level and ten international level female middle distance runners (data from Day *et al.* 1977)

International	*National*
1.5–3.0–3.5	2.0–3.5–4.0
1.0–3.0–5.0	2.0–4.0–4.0
1.5–3.0–4.5	3.5–4.5–2.0
1.0–2.0–6.0	2.5–3.5–3.0
2.0–3.0–4.0	1.5–3.5–4.5
1.5–3.0–4.0	2.5–4.0–3.0
2.5–2.0–4.0	
1.0–4.0–3.0	
2.0–3.0–4.0	

1. Separate component analysis
   Calculate the means and standard deviations of each separate component for each group.
   Calculate the significance of the differences between the two groups for each component separately. Use 3 *t*-tests for independent means.
   Discuss the difference between the two groups in terms of their component differences.

2. Global somatotype analysis: location on the somatochart
   Locate and plot each somatotype on a copy of Figure 2.3 by means of the XY-coordinates. Do the same for the two somatotype means.
   Discuss this visual impression of the difference between the two samples. Is there a difference in location of the means? Is there a difference in dispersion of the individual somatotypes between the two groups?
3. Global somatotype analysis: somatotype categories
   Determine the somatotype category for each subject of the two groups.
   Construct a crosstabulation with the two groups as rows, and the different somatotype categories as columns. Discuss the difference in somatotype category frequencies between the two groups.
   Use chi-square to calculate the significance of the difference between the two groups with regard to the somatotype categories. (Note that larger cell frequencies are necessary for a meaningful interpretation of chi-square.)
4. Global somatotype analysis: SAD-techniques
   Calculate the SAV for each group, using the formulae in Table 2.3.
   Check the difference in scatter between the two groups by describing the SAM of each group, and by means of an F-test on their SAVs.
   Calculate the difference in location between the two groups, by means of the SAD between the mean somatotypes (use the formula in Table 2.3).

2.6 PRACTICAL 3: ANALYSIS OF LONGITUDINAL SOMATOTYPE SERIES

2.6.1 INTRODUCTION

It is the aim of this practical to learn how to perform an analysis of a longitudinal series of somatotypes, using the somatochart approach and using SAD-techniques.

2.6.2 METHODS

Analysis of time series in biological sciences must take into account the specific fact that the measurement series are within-subject factors. This can be achieved for illustrative purposes by connecting the consecutive plots of a particular measurement with time for the same subject. The classic way would be the evolution with time of the separate component values. The somatotype entity can be preserved by connecting the consecutive plots on the somatochart.

Quantitative analysis of the changes is possible with MANOVA techniques with a within-subject design.

A simple quantitative way to describe the total change in somatotype with time is the Migratory Distance (MD). The MD is the sum of the SADs, calculated from each consecutive pair of somatotypes of the subject:

$$MD(a;z) = SAD(a;b) + SAD(b;c) + \dots + SAD(y;z)$$

with: a = first observation; b = second observation; .... ; z = last observation; SAD(p;q) = change from somatotype p to somatotype q.

Table 2.5 Consecutive somatotypes of six children from their sixth to their seventeenth birthday (data from Duquet *et al.* 1993)

	Subject					
Age (years)	*1*	*2*	*3*	*4*	*5*	*6*
6	2.7–5.3–2.5	2.0–5.7–1.6	3.2–3.9–3.5	2.7–4.8–2.2	1.7–3.6–3.3	2.9–4.7–2.1
7	3.4–5.2–2.0	2.4–4.7–2.1	2.6–3.4–4.3	1.6–4.4–3.1	1.7–3.2–4.4	3.6–4.5–2.3
8	4.2–5.2–1.6	2.3–4.5–2.3	2.3–2.3–5.3	1.6–4.1–3.5	1.6–3.2–4.2	4.6–4.7–1.8
9	4.8–5.6–1.3	2.3–4.6–2.4	2.1–2.0–5.3	1.8–3.8–4.3	1.3–2.9–4.2	6.2–5.1–1.0
10	5.3–5.8–1.2	2.2–4.7–2.6	2.1–2.1–5.5	1.5–3.4–4.3	1.6–2.8–4.4	6.9–5.1–0.7
11	6.0–6.0–1.3	2.0–4.7–2.4	1.8–1.8–5.6	1.6–3.3–4.5	1.8–2.5–4.8	7.7–5.4–0.7
12	7.2–5.7–1.3	1.9–5.0–2.4	1.5–1.1–6.1	1.3–3.0–4.8	2.2–2.7–4.1	8.3–5.6–0.5
13	7.5–5.9–0.5	1.5–5.2–2.8	2.4–1.2–5.5	1.1–2.8–5.0	2.9–2.8–3.4	8.4–5.8–0.5
14	6.3–5.9–0.8	1.1–5.2–3.1	2.2–1.1–6.0	1.2–2.5–5.1	3.5–2.9–3.5	8.6–5.9–0.5
15	3.8–5.3–1.7	1.3–5.3–2.8	2.0–1.2–5.5	1.6–2.5–4.9	3.7–3.0–2.9	8.0–5.9–0.5
16	3.0–5.4–1.6	1.8–5.5–2.6	2.4–1.0–5.4	1.7–2.3–4.6	3.8–3.2–2.7	7.9–6.2–0.5
17	2.9–5.5–1.6	1.5–5.4–2.7	1.8–0.8–6.0	1.9–2.6–4.5	2.8–2.9–3.5	8.3–6.4–0.5

2.6.3 TASKS

A group of six year-old children was measured annually until their 17th birthday. The anthropometric somatotypes were calculated using the formulae in Table 2.1. The results are given in Table 2.5.

1. Plot the changes of each component with time. Construct diagrams with age on the horizontal axis, and the component value on the vertical axis. Prepare one complete line diagram per child, on which the evolution of each component is shown. Discuss the change in individual component values for each child with age, and also the dominance situations from age to age.
2. Calculate the XY-coordinates of each somatotype. Locate the consecutive somatotypes of each child on a copy of Figure 2.3, using the formulae given in Practical 1. Use one somatochart per child. Discuss the change in global somatotype and the change in component dominances with age for each child.
3. Calculate the Migratory Distance for each child. Use the formulae given above. Calculate also the mean MD per child. Discuss the differences in MD between the children, and compare with the somatochart profiles.

REFERENCES

Albonico, R. (1970) *Mensch–Menschen–Typen. Entwicklung und Stand der Typenforschung*, Birkhauser Verlag, Basel.

Carter, J. E. L (1980) *The Heath–Carter Somatotype Method*, San Diego State University Syllabus Service, San Diego.

Carter, J. E. L. and Heath, B. H. (1990) *Somatotyping – Development and Applications*, Cambridge University Press, Cambridge.

Carter, J. E. L., Ross, W. D., Duquet, W. and Aubry, S. P. (1983) Advances in somatotype methodology and analysis. *Yearbook of Physical Anthropology*, **26**, 193–213.

Conrad, K. (1963) *Der Konstitutionstypus. Theoretische Grundlegung und praktischer Bestimmung*, Springer, Berlin.

Cressie, N. A. C., Withers, A. T. and Craig, N. P. (1986) The statistical analysis of somatotype data. *Yearbook of Physical Anthropology*, **29**, 197–208.

Day, J. A. P., Duquet, W. and Meersseman, G. (1977) Anthropometry and physique type of female middle and long distance runners, in relation to speciality and level of performance, in *Growth and Development; Physique* (ed. O. Eiben), Akademiai Kiado, Budapest, pp. 385–97.

Duquet, W. (1980) Studie van de toepasbaarheid van de Heath & Carter–somatotypemethode op kinderen van 6 tot 13 jaar. (Applicability of the Heath–Carter somatotype method to 6 to 13 year old children.) PhD Dissertation, Vrije Universiteit Brussel, Belgium.

Duquet, W. and Hebbelinck, M. (1977) Application of the somatotype attitudinal distance to the study of group and individual somatotype status and relations, in *Growth and Development; Physique*, (ed. O. Eiben), Akademiai Kiado, Budapest, pp. 377–84.

Duquet, W., Borms, J., Hebbelinck, M. *et al.* (1993) Longitudinal study of the stability of the somatotype in boys and girls, in *Kinanthropometry IV*, (eds W. Duquet and J. A. P. Day), E & FN Spon, London, pp. 54–67.

Heath, B. H. (1963) Need for modification of somatotype methodology. *American Journal of Physical Anthropology*, **21**, 227–33.

Heath, B. H. and Carter, J. E. L. (1967) A modified somatotype method. *American Journal of Physical Anthropology*, **27**, 57–74.

Kretschmer, E. (1921) *Körperbau und Charakter*, Springer Verlag, Berlin.

Lindegård, B. (1953) Variations in human body build. *Acta Psychiatrica et Neurologica*, suppl. 86.

Parnell, R. W. (1954) Somatotyping by physical anthropometry. *American Journal of Physical Anthropology*, **12**, 209–40.

Parnell, R. W. (1958) *Behaviour and Physique*, E. Arnold, London.

Sheldon, W. H., Stevens, S. S. and Tucker, W. B. (1940) *The Varieties of Human Physique*, Harper and Brothers, New York.

Tucker, W. B and Lessa, W. A. (1940a) Man: a constitutional investigation. *Quarterly Review of Biology*, **15**, 265–89.

Tucker, W. B. and Lessa, W. A. (1940b) Man: a constitutional investigation (cont'd). *Quarterly Review of Biology*, **15**, 411–55.

Viola, G. (1933) La constituzione individuale. Cappelli, Bologna.

PHYSICAL GROWTH, MATURATION AND PERFORMANCE 3

G. Beunen

3.1 INTRODUCTION

Growth, maturation and development are three concepts that are often used together and sometimes considered as synonymous. Growth is a dominant biological activity during the first two decades of life. It starts at conception and continues until the late teens or even the early twenties for a number of individuals. Growth refers to the increase in size of the body as a whole or the size attained by the specific parts of the body. The changes in size are outcomes of (a) an increase in cell number or hyperplasia, (b) an increase in cell size or cell hypertrophy and (c) an increase in intercellular material, or accretion. These processes occur during growth but the predominance of one or another process varies with age. For example, the number of muscle cells (fibres) is already established shortly after birth. The growth of the whole body is traditionally assessed by the changes in stature measured in a standing position, or for infants, in supine position (recumbent length). To assess the growth of specific parts of the body, appropriate anthropometric techniques have been described (Weiner and Lourie, 1969; Carter, 1982; Cameron, 1984; Lohman *et al.*, 1988; Simons *et al.*, 1990).

Maturation refers to the process of becoming fully mature. It gives an indication of the distance that is travelled along the road to adulthood. In other words the tempo and timing in the progress towards the mature biological state. Biological maturation varies with the biological system that is considered. Most often the following biological systems are examined: sexual maturation, morphological maturation, dental maturation and skeletal maturation. Sexual maturation refers to the process of becoming fully sexual mature, i.e. functional reproductive capability. Morphological maturation can be estimated through the percentage of adult stature that is already attained at a given age. Skeletal and dental maturation refer respectively to a fully ossified adult skeleton or dentition (Tanner, 1962, 1989; Malina and Bouchard, 1991).

Development is a broader concept, encompassing growth, maturation, learning and experience (training). It relates to becoming competent in a variety of tasks. Thus one can speak of cognitive development, motor development and emotional development as the child's personality emerges within the context of the particular culture in which the child was born and reared. Motor development is the process by which the child acquires movement patterns and skills. It is characterized by a continuous modification based upon neuromuscular maturation, growth and maturation of the body, residual effects of prior experience and new motor

Kinanthropometry and Exercise Physiology Laboratory Manual: Tests, procedures and data Edited by Roger Eston and Thomas Reilly. Published in 1996 by E & FN Spon. ISBN 0 419 17880 5

experiences *per se* (Malina and Bouchard, 1991). The postnatal motor development is characterized by a shift from primitive reflex mechanisms towards postural reflexes and definite motor actions. It further refers to the acquisition of independent walking and competence in a variety of manipulative tasks and fundamental motor skills such as running, skipping, throwing, catching, jumping, climbing and hopping (Keogh and Sugden, 1985). From school age onwards the focus shifts towards the development of physical performance capacities traditionally studied in the context of physical fitness or motor fitness projects. Motor fitness includes cardiorespiratory endurance, anaerobic power, muscular strength and power, local muscular endurance (sometimes called functional strength), speed, flexibility and balance (Pate and Shephard, 1989; Simons *et al.*, 1969, 1990).

According to Tanner (1981) the earliest surviving statement about human growth appears in a Greek elegy of the sixth century BC. Solon the Athenian divided the growth period in hebdomads, that is, successive periods of seven years each. The infant (literally, while unable to speak) acquires deciduous teeth and sheds them before the age of seven, at the end of the next hebdomad the boy shows the signs of puberty (beginning of pubic hair), and in the last period the body enlarges and the skin becomes bearded (Tanner, 1981, p.1). Anthropometry was not born of medicine or science but of the arts. Painters and sculptors needed instructions about the relative proportions of legs and trunks, shoulders and hips, eyes and forehead and other parts of the body. The inventor of the term anthropometry was a German physician, Johan Sigismund Elshotz (1623–1688). It is noteworthy that at this time there was not very much attention given to absolute size but much more to proportions. Note also that the introduction of the 'mètre' occurred only in 1795 and even then other scales continued to be used.

The first published longitudinal growth study of which we have record was made by Count Philibert de Montbeillard (1720–1785) on request of his close friend Buffon (Tanner, 1981). The growth and the growth velocity curves of Montbeillard's son are probably the best known curves in auxology (study of human growth); they describe the growth and its velocity from birth to adulthood which have been widely studied since then in various populations (see, for example, Eveleth and Tanner, 1990). Growth velocity refers to the growth over a period of time. It is frequently used to indicate changes in stature over a period of one year.

Another significant impetus in the study of growth was given by the Belgian mathematician Adolphe Quetelet (1796–1874). He was in many ways the founder of modern statistics and was instrumental in the foundation of Statistical Society of London. Quetelet collected data on height and weight and fitted a curve to the succession of means. According to his mathematical function the growth velocity declines from birth to maturity and shows no adolescent growth spurt. This confused a number of investigators until the 1940s (Tanner, 1981, p.134). At the beginning of the nineteenth century there was an increased interest in the growing child due to the appalling conditions of the poor and their children. A new direction was given by the anthropologist Franz Boas (1858–1942). He was the first to realize the individual variation in tempo of growth and was responsible for the introduction of the concept of physiological age or biological maturation. A number of longitudinal studies were then initiated in the 1920s in the USA and later in Europe. These studies served largely as the basis of our present knowledge on physical growth and maturation (Tanner, 1981; Malina and Bouchard, 1991).

In several nations there is great interest in developing and maintaining the physical fitness levels of the citizens of all age levels, but special concern goes to the fitness of youth. Physical fitness has been defined in many ways. The American Academy of Physical Education adopted the following definition:

'Physical fitness is the ability to carry out daily tasks with vigor and alertness, without undue fatigue and with ample energy to engage in leisure time pursuits and to meet the above average physical stresses encountered in emergency situations' (Clarke, 1979). Often the distinction is made between an organic component and a motor component. The organic component is defined as the capacity to adapt to and recover from strenuous exercise, it relates to energy production and work output performance. The motor component relates to development and performance of gross motor abilities. Since the beginning of the 1980s the distinction between health-related and performance-related physical fitness has come into common use (Pate and Shephard, 1989). Health-related fitness is then viewed as a state characterized by an ability to perform daily activities with vigour, and traits and capacities that are associated with low risk of premature development of the hypokinetic diseases (i.e. those associated with physical inactivity) (Pate and Shephard, 1989, p. 4). Health-related physical fitness includes cardiorespiratory endurance, body composition, muscular strength and flexibility. Performance-related fitness refers to the abilities associated with adequate athletic performance, and encompasses components such as isometric strength, power, speed–agility, balance and arm–eye coordination.

Since Sargent (1921) proposed the vertical jump as a physical performance test for men, considerable change has taken place both in our thinking about physical performance, physical fitness and about its measurement. In the early days the expression 'general motor ability' was used to indicate one's 'general' skill. The term was similar to the general intelligence factor used at that time. Primarily under the influence of Brace (1927) and McCloy (1934), a fairly large number of studies was undertaken and a multiple motor ability concept replaced the general ability concept. There is now considerable agreement among authors and experts that the fitness concept is multidimensional and several abilities can be identified. An ability refers to a more general trait of the individual which can be inferred from response consistencies on a number of related tasks whereas skill refers to the level of proficiency on a specific task or limited group of tasks. A child possesses isometric strength since he or she performs well on a variety of isometric strength tests. Considerable attention has been devoted to fitness testing and research in the USA and Canada. The President's Council on Youth Fitness, the American Alliance for Health, Physical Education, Recreation and Dance (AAHPER, 1958, 1965; AAHPERD, 1988) and the Canadian sister organization (CAHPER, 1965) have done an outstanding job in constructing and promoting fitness testing in schools. Internationally the fundamental works of Fleishman (1964), and of the International Committee for the Standardization of Physical Fitness Tests, now the International Council for Physical Activity and Fitness Research (Larson, 1974), have received considerable attention and served, for example, as the basis for nationwide studies in Belgium (Hebbelinck and Borms, 1975; Ostyn *et al.*, 1980; Simons *et al.*, 1990). Furthermore, the fitness test battery constructed by Simons *et al.* (1969) served as the basis for studies in The Netherlands (Bovend'eerdt *et al.*, 1980) and for the construction of the Eurofit test battery (Adam *et al.*, 1988).

In the following section three laboratory practicals will be outlined focusing on standards of normal growth, biological maturity status and evaluation of physical fitness.

3.2 STANDARDS OF NORMAL GROWTH

3.2.1 METHODOLOGICAL CONSIDERATIONS

Growth data may be used in three distinct ways: (1) to serve as a screening device in order to identify individuals who might benefit from special medical or educational care; (2) to serve as control in the treatment of ill children (the paediatric use); and (3) as an index of the general health and nutritional status of the population or subpopulation (Tanner, 1989). Standards of normal growth usually include reference data for attained stature or any other anthropometric dimension and, where available, also reference values for growth velocity. Reference values for attained stature are useful for assessing the present status in other words to answer the question: 'Is the child's growth normal for his/her age and sex?' Growth velocity reference values are constructed to verify the growth process.

Reference charts of attained height, usually referred to as growth standards or curves, are constructed on the basis of cross-sectional studies. In such studies representative samples of girls and boys stemming from different birth cohorts and consequently of different age groups are measured once.

It has to be remembered that the outer percentiles such as the 3rd and 97th are subject to considerably greater sample error than the mean or the 50th percentile (Goldstein, 1986; Healy, 1986). The precision of estimates of population parameters, such as the mean, depends on the sample size and the variability in the population. If $\overline{X}$ is the sample mean then the 95% confidence values, *a* and *b*, are two values such that the probability that the true population mean lies between them is 0.95. If the distribution of the measurement is Gaussian, then for a simple random sample *a* and *b* are given by:

$$a = \overline{X} + 1.96\,\text{SE mean}$$

$$b = \overline{X} - 1.96\,\text{SE mean}$$

$$\text{in which SE mean} = \text{SD}/\sqrt{n-1}$$

From these formulae it can be seen that for a given population variance the confidence intervals decrease when the sample size increases. Major standardizing studies use samples of about 1000 subjects in each sex and age group but 500 subjects normally produce useful centiles (Eveleth and Tanner, 1990). Representative samples can be obtained in several ways, the most commonly used being simple random samples and stratified samples. In a simple random sample each subject has an equal chance of being selected in the sample and each subject in the population must be identifiable. In a stratified sample, significant strata are identified and in each stratum a sample is selected. A stratification factor is one that serves for dividing the population into strata or subdivisions of the population, such as ethnic groups or degree of urbanization. The stratification factor is selected because there is evidence that this factor affects, or is related to, the growth process.

Growth velocity standards or reference values can be obtained only from longitudinal studies. In a longitudinal study a representative sample of boys and/or girls from one birth cohort is measured repeatedly at regular intervals. The frequency of the measurements depends on the growth velocity and also on the measurement error. During periods of rapid growth it is necessary to increase the frequency of the measurements. For stature, for example, it is recommended to carry out monthly measurements during the first year of life and to measure every three months during the adolescent growth spurt. Although some recent evidence (Lampl *et al.*, 1992) suggests that there is much more variation in growth velocity, with periods of rapid change (stepwise or saltatory increase) followed by periods of no change (stasis) when growth is monitored over very short periods of time (days or weeks).

Cross-sectional standards for growth are most often presented as growth charts. Such charts are constructed from the means and standard deviations or from the centiles of the different sex and age groups. Conventionally, the 3rd, 10th, 25th, 50th, 75th, 90th and 97th centiles are displayed. The 3rd and 97th percentile delineate the outer borders of what is considered as 'normal' growth. This does not imply that on a single measurement one can decide about the 'abnormality' of the growth process. Children with statures outside the 3rd and 97th percentile need to be examined further.

Since growth is considered as a regular process over larger (years) time intervals a smooth continuous curve is fitted to the sample statistics (means, means ± 1c.SD, different percentiles). The series of sample statistics can be graphically smoothed, by eye or a mathematical function can be fitted to the data. This mathematical function is selected so that it is simple and corresponds closely to the observations. In a common procedure a smooth curve is drawn through the medians (means). This can be done by fitting non-linear regressions to narrow age groups and estimate the centre of the group. The age groups are then shifted to the next age interval, resulting in a number of overlapping intervals in which corrected (estimated) medians are identified. The next step is to estimate the other centiles taking into account the corrections that have been made to the medians in the first step. This can be done by using the residuals from the fitted 50th percentile curve within each age group to estimate the other percentiles. This procedure can be improved by setting up a general relationship between the percentiles to be estimated and the 50th percentile (Goldstein, 1984).

Longitudinal growth velocity reference values are obtained from the analysis of individual growth data. Individual growth curves are fitted to the serial measurements of each child. For many purposes graphical fits (Tanner *et al.*, 1966) are sufficient, but mathematical curves may also be employed (Goldstein, 1979; Marubini and Milani, 1986; Jolicoeur *et al.*, 1992). Most mathematical curves or models presently in use are developed for growth in stature. Some models have also been applied for a few body dimensions, such as body mass and diameters. The mathematical functions can be divided into two classes: structural models and non-structural.

In the structural models the mathematical function, usually a family of functions or mathematical model, imposes a well-defined pre-selected shape to the growth curves that are fitted to the data. If the function reflects underlying processes, then the parameters of the function may have biological meaning (Bock and Thissen, 1980). Jenss and Bayley (1937) proposed a model to describe the growth process from birth to eight years. This model includes a linear and an exponential term in which the linear part describes the growth velocity and the exponential part describes the growth deceleration. Several other functions have been used to describe the growth during the adolescent period (Deming, 1957; Marubini *et al.*, 1972; Hauspie *et al.*, 1980). More recently a number of models have also been proposed to describe the whole growth period from birth to adulthood (Preece and Baines, 1978; Bock and Thissen, 1980; Jolicoeur *et al.*, 1992).

For the non-structural approach polynomials using various fitting techniques have been applied (van't Hof *et al.*, 1976; Largo *et al.*, 1978; Gasser *et al.*, 1984). The use of increments or difference scores between observations of adjacent intervals is often not indicated. The regularity of the growth process is overlooked, two measurement errors are involved in each increment, and successive increments are negatively related (van't Hof *et al.*, 1976). The individual growth parameters obtained from the graphical or mathematical curve fitting are then combined to form the so-called mean constant growth curve and by differentiation the mean constant growth velocity curve.

For most growth studies cross-sectional standards have been published. Tanner (1989) has argued that 'tempo-conditional' standards, meaning standards that allow for differences in the tempo of growth between children, are much finer instruments to evaluate the normality of growth. Such conditional standards combine information from longitudinal and cross-sectional studies. Other conditional standards can be used such as standards for height that allow for height of parents (Tanner, 1989).

3.2.2 GROWTH EVALUATION

Depending on the number of students in the class, 30–50 secondary school girls and/or boys from the local school can be measured. Exact identification, including birth date and date of measurement, name and address and parents' heights should be asked in a small inquiry addressed to the parents. At the same time informed consent to conduct the study can be obtained. Furthermore, consent has to be obtained from the school administration. It is also advisable to obtain approval for the project by the ethics committee of the Institution.

Included here are standards for British children (Figures 3.1 and 3.2) (Tanner, 1989). If these standards are used for the evaluation of the school children, then height should be measured according to the procedures described by Tanner (1989, pp. 182–6). If local standards are available these should be used and the measuring techniques that were used in constructing these standards should be

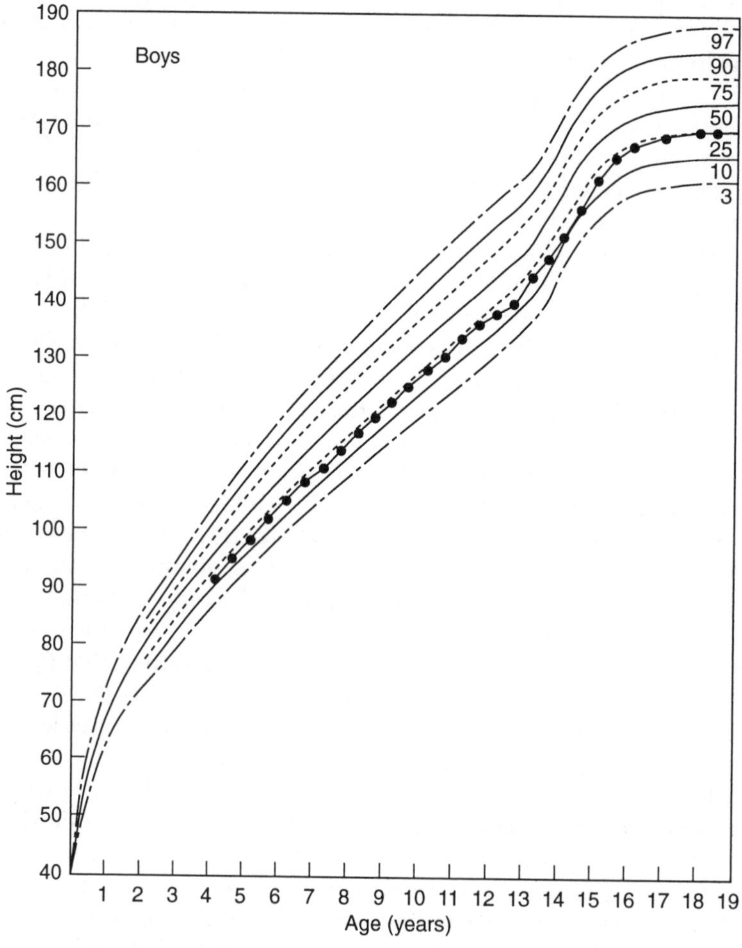

Figure 3.1 Standards of height for British boys, with normal boy plotted. M and F, parents' height centiles; vertical bar, range of expected heights of offspring of these parents.
(Reprinted by permission of the publishers from *Fetus into Man: Physical Growth from Conception to Maturity* by J. M. Tanner, Harvard University Press, Cambridge, MA, Copyright, 1978, 1989 by J. M. Tanner.)

adopted. The measuring technique is all important and each student needs to get experienced with the measuring techniques, preferably by conducting a preliminary intra- and inter-observor study with an experienced anthropometrist.

Once the data are collected each individual measurement is plotted against the reference standards. Chronological age should be converted into decimal age expressed in years and tenths of a year.

3.2.3 INTERPRETATION OF THE RESULTS

It is to be expected that the heights of the children are scattered over the growth chart. In order to evaluate the growth status, it is advisable to calculate the mid-parent percentile. This is the average of the percentile that corresponds to the height of the father and of the mother. (The sex specific growth charts are of course used to define these percentiles.) If one takes the mid-parent height percentile as the 'target', a band of ± 10 cm for boys and

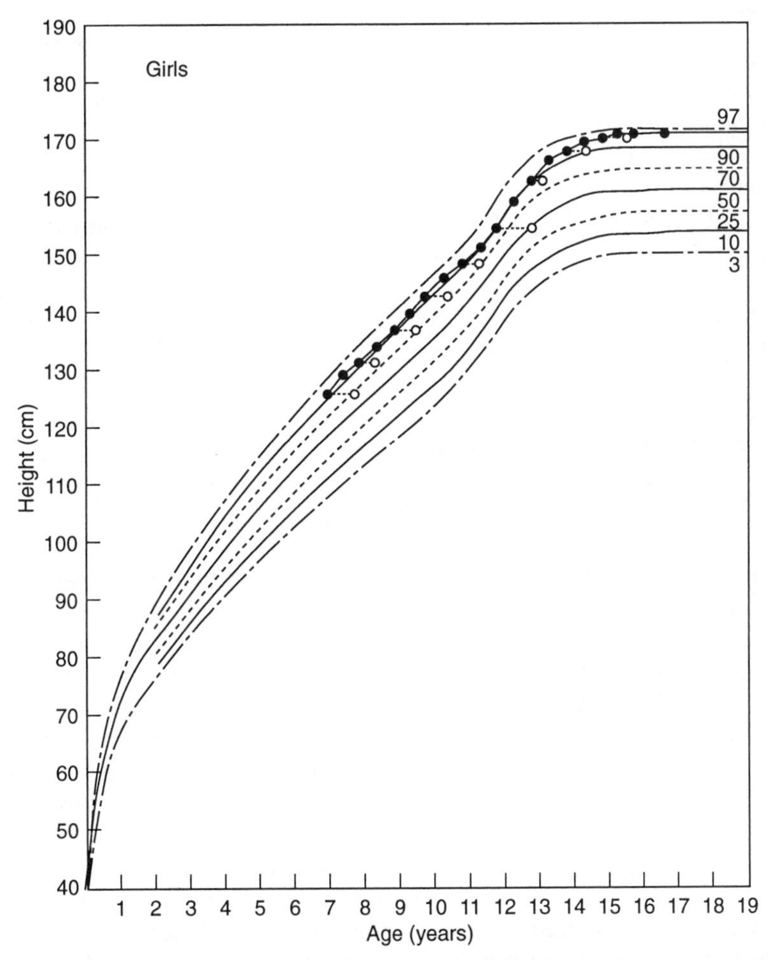

Figure 3.2 Standards of height for British girls, with normal girl plotted. M and F, parents' height centiles; vertical bar, range of expected heights of offspring of these parents.
(Reprinted by permission of the publishers from *Fetus into Man: Physical Growth from Conception to Maturity* by J. M. Tanner, Harvard University Press, Cambridge, MA, Copyright, 1978, 1989 by J. M. Tanner.)

± 9 cm for girls can be plotted (use copies of the reference chart) for each child and the observed height should fall within this band. It is unlikely that a child with two small parents, at 25th percentile, will have a stature above the 75th percentile, the upper limit of the previously mentioned growth band. On the other hand it is to be expected that a child from two tall parents, at 75th percentile, will have a stature at or even somewhat above the 97th percentile.

3.2.4 FURTHER RECOMMENDATIONS

It should be remembered that the reported parents' heights are much more subject to error than when measured. In a growth clinic it is common practice that the parents' heights will be measured.

If the height of only one parent is available, the height of the other parent can be estimated by adding, for father's height, or subtracting, for mother's height, 13 cm from the height reported by the mother or father, respectively.

If the British reference curves are used it should be kept in mind that there are large interpopulation differences and that, even within a population, differences may occur due to ethnicity, social status or degree of urbanization to name a few (see, for example, Eveleth and Tanner, 1990). The British growth charts, plotted on grids, are available from Castlemead Publications, 4a Crane Mead, Ware, Herts, SG12 9PY, UK.

3.3 BIOLOGICAL MATURATION: SKELETAL AGE

3.3.1 METHODOLOGICAL CONSIDERATIONS

It is well documented that somatic characteristics, biological maturation and physical performance are interrelated, and that young elite athletes exhibit specific maturity characteristics (Beunen, 1989; Malina and Bouchard, 1991). Young elite male athletes are generally advanced in their maturity status whereas young female athletes show late maturity status, especially in skating, gymnastics and ballet dancing. The assessment of biological maturity is thus a very important indicator of the growing child. It is therefore a valuable tool in the hands of experienced kinanthropometrists and all other professionals involved in the evaluation of the growth and development of children.

As mentioned already, several biological systems can be used to assess biological maturity status. In assessing sexual maturation the criteria described by Reynolds and Wines (1948, 1951) synthesized and popularized by Tanner (1962) are most often used. They should not be referred to as Tanner's stages since they were in use long before Tanner described them in *Growth at Adolescence*. Furthermore, there is considerable difference in the stages for pubic hair, breast or genital development, For breast, pubic hair, and genital development, five discrete stages are described (Tanner, 1962). These stages must be assigned by visual inspection of the nude subject or from somatotype photographs from which the specific areas are enlarged. Given the invasiveness of the technique, self-inspection has been proposed as an alternative but more information is needed on its reliability and validity before it can be used in epidemiological research.

Age at menarche, defined as the first menstrual flow, can be obtained retrospectively by interrogating a representative sample of sexually mature women. Note, however, the influence of error of recall. The recall data are reasonably accurate for group comparisons. The information obtained in longitudinal or prospective studies is of course much more accurate but here other problems inherent to longitudinal studies interfere. In the status quo technique representative samples of girls expected to experience menarche are interrogated. The investigator records whether or not menstrual periods have started at the time of investigation. Reference standards can be constructed using probits or logits for which the percentage of menstruating girls at each age level is plotted against chronological age, whereafter a probit or logit is fitted through the observed data. Morphological age can be assessed by means of the age at peak height velocity, i.e. the age at which the maximum growth velocity in height occurs. This requires a longitudinal study. An alternative to define morphological age is to use percentage of predicted height. The actual height is then expressed as a percentage of adult height. The problem here is to define adult height. Several techniques have been developed for the prediction of adult height. The techniques developed by Bayley (1946), Roche *et al.* (1975a) and Tanner *et al.* (1983) seem to be the most accurate and most commonly used. The predictors in these techniques are actual height, chronological age, skeletal age, and, in some techniques, parental height and/or age at menarche for girls. Until now no practical useful technique has been developed to assess 'shape age' as another indicator of morphological maturity.

Dental maturity can be estimated from the age of eruption of deciduous or permanent teeth or from the number of teeth present at a certain age (Demirjian, 1978). Eruption is, however, only one event in the ossification process and has no real biological meaning. For this reason, Demirjian *et al.* (1973) constructed scales for the assessment of dental maturity, based on the principles developed by Tanner *et al.* (1983) for the estimation of skeletal age.

Skeletal maturity is the most commonly used indicator of biological maturation. It is widely recognized as the best single biological maturity indicator (Tanner, 1962). Three main techniques are presently in use: the atlas technique, first introduced by Todd (1937) and later revised by Greulich and Pyle (1950, 1959), the bone-specific approach developed by Tanner *et al.* (1983), the bone-specific approach developed by Roche *et al.* for the knee (1975b), and for the hand (1988).

In this section the assessment of skeletal age according to the Tanner–Whitehouse method (TWII, Tanner *et al.*, 1983) will be introduced.

The TWII is a bone-specific approach which means that all the bones of a region of the body are graded on a scale and then combined to give an estimate of the skeletal maturation status of that area. The TWII system is developed for the hand and wrist. In this area 28 ossification centres of long, short and round bones are found, including primary ossification centres (round bones) and secondary ossification centres (epiphyses of the short and long bones). The primary ossification centres of the short and long bones develop before birth and form the diaphyses. The secondary centres of the short and long bones generally develop after birth and form the epiphyses. For each centre a sequence of developmental milestones is defined. Such a milestone indicates the distance that has been travelled along the road to full maturity, meaning the adult shape and fusion between epiphysis and diaphysis for short and long bones. Such a sequence of milestones is invariant, meaning that the second milestone occurs after the first but before the third. Based on careful examination of longitudinal series of normal boys and girls, stages of skeletal maturity were defined for all the bones in the hand and wrist. The stages are described in a handbook for the assessment of skeletal age (Tanner *et al.*, 1983). Each stage is indicated by a letter. Stages are converted into weighted maturity scores. These scores are defined in such a way as to minimize the overall disagreement between the scores assigned to the different bones over the total standardizing sample. Furthermore, a biological weight was assigned to the scores so that, for example, the distal epiphysis of radius and ulna are given four times more weight than the metacarpals or phalanges of the 3rd and 5th finger. Three scales are available: one for 20 bones of the hand and wrist (TWII-scale), one for the 13 short and long bones (RUS-scale, Radius, Ulna and Short bones), and one for the carpal bones (CARP-scale). Although 28 bone centres develop postnatally in the hand and wrist, only 20 bones are assessed in the total TWII-system. Since the metacarpals and phalanges, considered row-wise, show considerable agreement in their maturity status only the 1st, 3rd, and 5th fingers are estimated. Once the maturity stages are assigned to the bones, the stages are converted into maturity scores using one of the three scales. The scores are then simply added to form the overall maturity score for the hand and wrist (TWII-scale), the long and short bones (RUS-scale) or the carpals (CARP-scale). For these overall maturity scores, reference data are then constructed for a population (see e.g. Tanner *et al.*, 1983; Beunen *et al.*, 1990). Very often the maturity score is converted into skeletal age which is the corresponding chronological age at which, on the average, an overall maturity score is reached. In the Belgian population a TWII-score of 848 corresponds to a skeletal age of 13.5 years, and this is exactly the same in the British population. At other age levels, however, there are considerable differences between Belgian and British children.

3.3.2 SKELETAL AGE ASSESSMENT: TWII-SYSTEM

In assessing skeletal age radiographs have to be taken in a standard position and with standard equipment (for instructions see Tanner *et al.*, 1983). The descriptions and directions of the authors should also be carefully followed. This implies that the written criteria for the stages should be carefully studied and followed. The illustrations are only a guide for the identification of the stages. They represent the upper and lower limit of a given stage. For the assignment of stages the first criterion of the previous stage must be clearly visible and in the case of only one criterion this must be present, if there are two criteria one of the two must be present, and when three criteria are described two of the three must be visible. Depending on the scale (TWII, RUS, CARP) the corresponding scores for each sex must be given, then summed and compared to reference standards for the population.

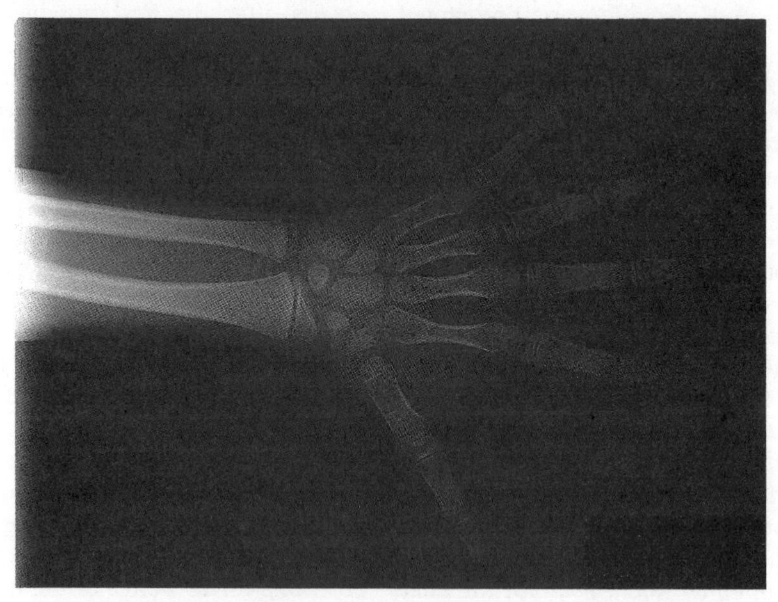

Figure 3.3 Radiograph of the hand and wrist of a Belgian boy.

In order to familiarize students with the system, three radiographs (Figures 3.3–3.5) are included for which the three maturity scores must be obtained. A scoring sheet is shown in Figure 3.6. As described above the instructions in the handbook (Tanner *et al.*, 1983) should be carefully followed and the bones are rated in the same order as indicated on the scoring sheet. The scores obtained should then be compared with those of an experienced observer. In this case the ratings can be compared with those of the author (see Appendix). His ratings show considerable agreement with those of the originators of the method (Beunen and Cameron, 1980). The differences between the students' ratings and those of the expert need to be discussed, and if time permits a second rating can be done with at least a one-week interval.

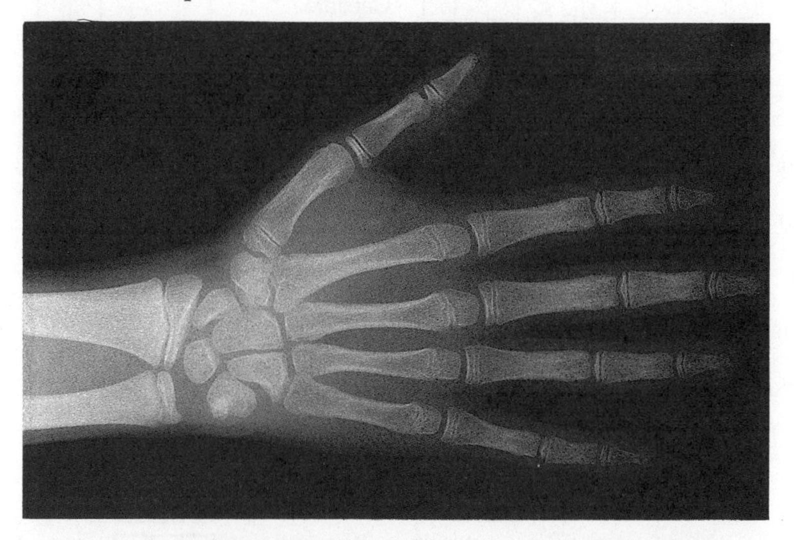

Figure 3.4 Radiograph of the hand and wrist of a Belgian boy.

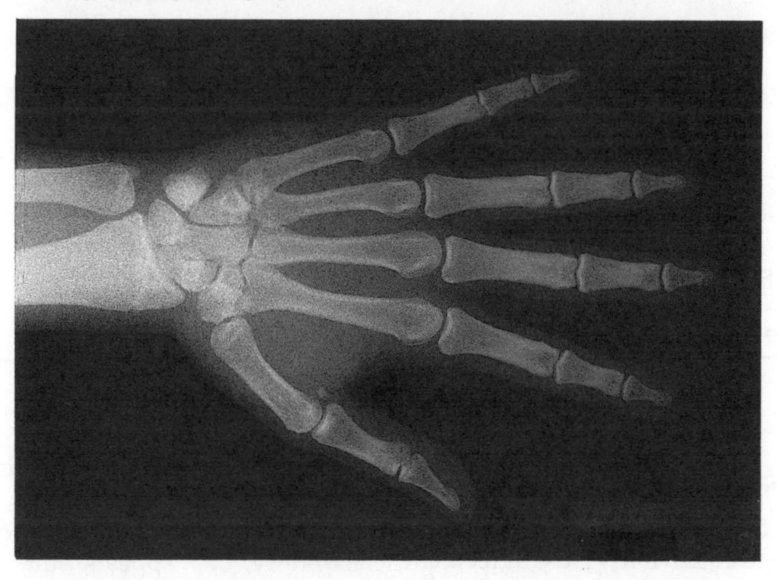

Figure 3.5 Radiograph of the hand and wrist of a Belgian boy.

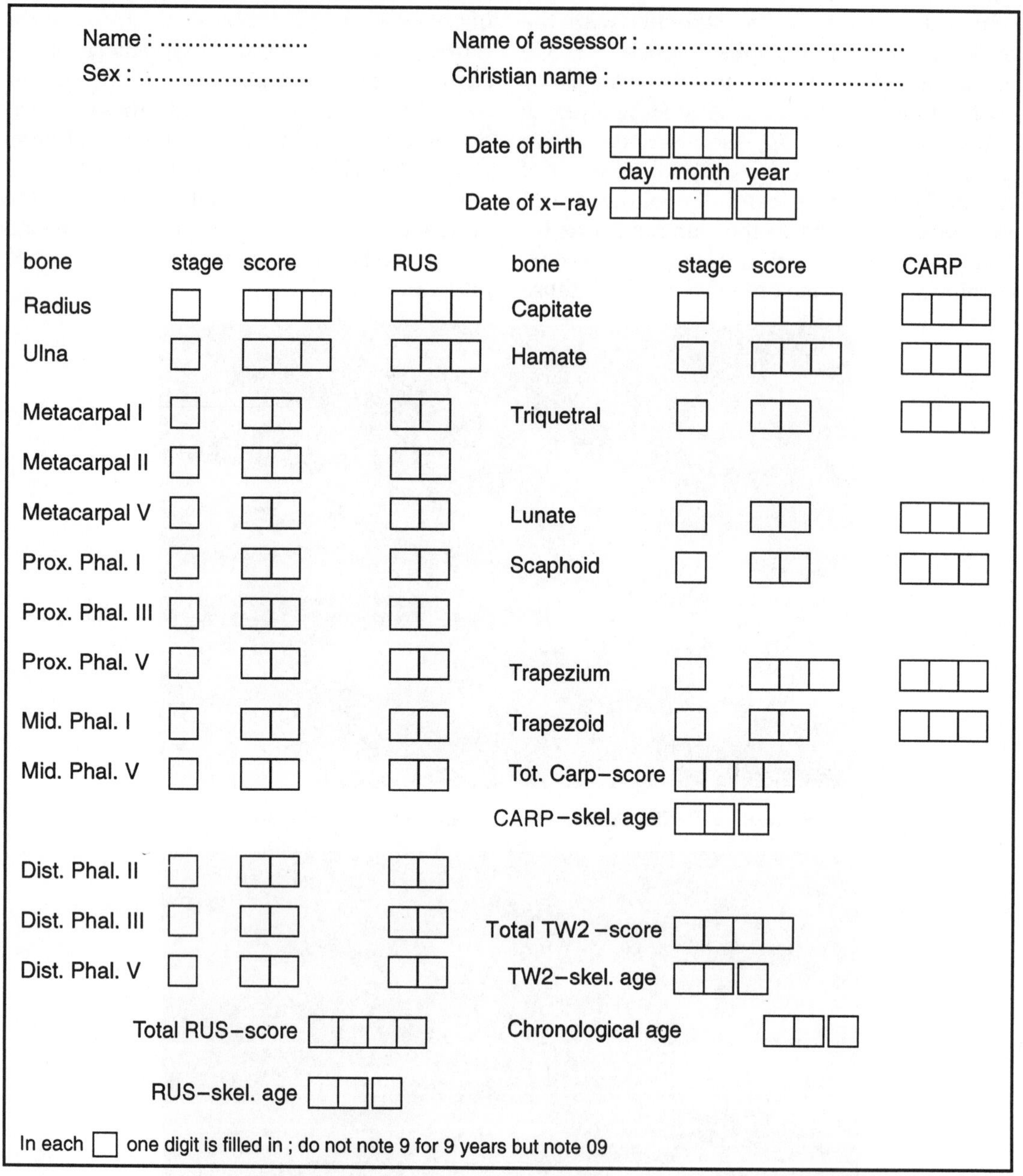

Name : ....
Sex : ....

Name of assessor : ....
Christian name : ....

Date of birth ☐☐ ☐☐ ☐☐
day month year
Date of x-ray ☐☐ ☐☐ ☐☐

bone	stage	score	RUS	bone	stage	score	CARP
Radius	☐	☐☐☐	☐☐☐	Capitate	☐	☐☐☐	☐☐☐
Ulna	☐	☐☐☐	☐☐☐	Hamate	☐	☐☐☐	☐☐☐
Metacarpal I	☐	☐☐	☐☐	Triquetral	☐	☐☐	☐☐☐
Metacarpal II	☐	☐☐	☐☐				
Metacarpal V	☐	☐☐	☐☐	Lunate	☐	☐☐	☐☐☐
Prox. Phal. I	☐	☐☐	☐☐	Scaphoid	☐	☐☐	☐☐☐
Prox. Phal. III	☐	☐☐	☐☐				
Prox. Phal. V	☐	☐☐	☐☐	Trapezium	☐	☐☐☐	☐☐☐
Mid. Phal. I	☐	☐☐	☐☐	Trapezoid	☐	☐☐	☐☐☐
Mid. Phal. V	☐	☐☐	☐☐	Tot. Carp–score ☐☐☐☐			
				CARP–skel. age ☐☐☐			
Dist. Phal. II	☐	☐☐	☐☐				
Dist. Phal. III	☐	☐☐	☐☐	Total TW2–score ☐☐☐☐			
Dist. Phal. V	☐	☐☐	☐☐	TW2–skel. age ☐☐☐			

Total RUS–score ☐☐☐☐

Chronological age ☐☐☐

RUS–skel. age ☐☐☐

In each ☐ one digit is filled in ; do not note 9 for 9 years but note 09

Figure 3.6 Scoring sheet for skeletal age assessment.

3.3.3 DISCUSSION AND COMMENTS

In most cases the student will experience that he/she is able to obtain fairly close agreement between his/her ratings and those of the expert. This does not at all imply that the student is now experienced. From intra- and interobserver studies conducted in our laboratory, it appears that before one becomes experienced about 500 radiographs have to be assessed. The assessor also needs to verify his/her own intra-observer reliability and has to compare his/her ratings with those of an expert.

As previously mentioned skeletal age is an important variable in the regression equations for predicting adult height. Given the characteristic physical structure of athletes and the role of stature in this respect it can be easily understood that the estimation of adult stature can be a useful factor in an efficient guidance of young athletes.

Finally, it should be mentioned that skeletal age is moderately to highly correlated with other indicators of biological maturity such as sexual maturity and morphological maturity. The relations with dental maturity are considerably lower. The relations are, however, never strong enough to allow individual prediction but they are strong enough to indicate the maturation status of a group of children or populations. This means that when a group of female gymnasts is markedly delayed in sexual maturity, the group is also likely to be delayed in skeletal maturity (Beunen, 1989; Malina and Bouchard, 1991).

3.4 PHYSICAL FITNESS

3.4.1 METHODOLOGICAL CONSIDERATIONS

As mentioned in the introduction the physical fitness concept and its measurement have evolved over the years and recently the distinction between health- and performance-related fitness has been introduced. Table 3.1 gives an overview of the test batteries that have been used and, more importantly, for which reference values have been constructed. For the test batteries included in Table 3.1 attempts were made to obtain tests that are objective, standardized, reliable and valid (for more information about test construction see Safrit, 1973 and Anastasi, 1988). For most of the batteries nationwide reference values were constructed. Recently attempts were made to construct criterion-referenced norms (Blair *et al.*, 1989). Within the context of the health-related fitness concept standards of required fitness levels were created by expert panels, e.g. 42 ml kg^{-1} min^{-1} for $\dot{V}O_2$ in young men and 35 ml kg^{-1} min^{-1} for young women. Very little empirical evidence is available to create such criterion-related standards for the other health-related fitness items.

From Table 3.1 it is clear that in most batteries the same components are included and that quite often the same tests are proposed. Note of course that test batteries that are intended to evaluate health-related fitness do not incorporate performance-related items. With increasing awareness about safety and risks involved in testing, some testing procedures have been adapted, e.g. sit ups were originally tested with straight legs and hands crossed behind the neck whereas in more recent procedures the arms are crossed over the chest, the knees are bent and the subject curls to a position in which the elbows touch the knees or thighs. In the latter procedure there is less risk of causing low back pain.

In order to construct reference values for a population, large representative samples of boys and girls from different age levels must be examined. The same principles apply as for the construction of growth standards discussed previously. The data obtained must be transferred into reference scales so that the individual scores can be evaluated and test results can be compared. Most often reference values are reported in percentile scales but raw scores can also be transformed into standard scales (z-scores), normalized standard scales (transformed into a normalized distribution) or age norms (motor age and motor coefficient as in the original Osereztky motor development scale). Probably none of these scales can be considered as best and much depends on the needs of the test constructed and the needs of those that intend to use the test.

Table 3.1 Fitness components and test items in selected physical fitness test batteries

FITNESS COMPONENT	TEST BATTERIES									
	AAHPER youth fitness test (1958)	*Fleishman (1964)*	*AAHPER youth fitness test (1965)*	*CAPHER (1965)*	*Simons et al. (1969)*	*ICPFT Larson (1974)*	*Fitnessgram (1987)*	*NCYFS II Ross and Pate (1987)*	*AAHPERD Physical Best (1988)*	*EUROFIT Adam et al. (1988)*
Health-related components										
Cardiorespiratory endurance	660 yard run-walk	600 yard run- walk	660 yard run-walk	300 yard	step test	600–800–1000–1 500–2000 m run	1 min walk-run for time	0.5 min run-walk 1 min run-walk	1 min run	endurance shuttle run (Léger & Lambert 1982) cycle ergometer test
body composition	–	–	–	–	triceps-subscapular-suprailiac-calf skinfolds	–	triceps-calf skinfolds	triceps-sub-scapular calf skinfold	triceps-calf-skinfolds	triceps-biceps-subscap.-suprailiac-calf skinfold
flexibility	–	turn and twist bend, twist and touch	–	–	sit and reach	forward trunk flexion or sit and reach	sit and reach	sit and reach	sit and reach	sit and reach
upper body muscular endurance & strength	pull-ups	pull-ups	pull-ups (boys) flexed arm hang (girls)	flexed arm hang	flexed arm hang	pull-ups (boys), flexed arm hang (girls and children)	pull-ups	modified pull-ups	pull-ups	flexed arm hang
abdominal muscular endurance & strength	sit-ups	leg lifts	sit-ups	sit-ups	leg lifts	sit-ups (bent knees)	sit-ups (bent knees)	sit-ups (bent knees)	sit-ups (curl to sitting position)	sit-ups (bent knees)
Performance-related components										
Static (isometric) strength	–	handgrip	–	–	arm pull	handgrip	–	–	–	handgrip
explosive strength anaerobic power	standing long jump softball throw	softball throw	standing long jump softball throw	standing long jump	vertical jump	standing long jump	–	–	–	standing long jump
running speed	50 yard dash shuttle run	100 yard shuttle run	50 yard dash shuttle run	50 yard dash 40 yard shuttle run	50 m shuttle run	50 m dash 40 m shuttle run	shuttle run (optional)	–	–	50 m shuttle run
speed of limb movement	–	–	–	–	plate tapping	–	–	–	–	plate tapping
balance	–	one foot balance	–	–	need established	–	–	–	–	flamingo balance
coordination	–	–	–	–	stick balance	–	–	–	–	–

3.4.2 PHYSICAL FITNESS TESTING

Similarly to what has been explained in the growth evaluation section (section 3.2.2), a number of secondary school children can be examined on a physical fitness test battery. In selecting a test battery it should be kept in mind that appropriate and recent reference values need to be available, and that the battery selected has been constructed according to well-established scientific procedures (see above). Furthermore, all the equipment necessary for adequate testing needs to be available.

The Eurofit test battery (Adam *et al.*, 1988) was selected for this purpose. Reference values of the Belgian population are available (Lefevre *et al.*, 1993). Table 3.1 shows that this battery includes health- and performance-related fitness items. If the Eurofit tests are examined and the reference values of 14-year-old Belgian children (Tables 3.2 and 3.3) are used, then only 14-year-old children should be tested. In the reference tables, 14 years includes 14.00 to 14.99-year-old children.

Before the test session in the secondary school all students should be familiarized with the test procedure. It is advisable first to study the test instructions and descriptions (Adam *et al.*, 1988), then to organize a demonstration session during which the tests are correctly demonstrated and then to practise the test with peers of the same class as subjects. Once the training period has finished, the session of testing in the school can be planned. As for the evaluation of growth, informed consent is needed from the parents and school, and for older children from the adolescents themselves. Care should be taken that children at risk are identified. The recommendations of the American College of Sports Medicine should be followed to identify individuals at risk (American College of Sports Medicine, 1991). Generally children that are allowed to participate in physical education classes can be tested, taking into account that some are only allowed to participate in some exercise sessions.

Obviously the general recommendations for administering the Eurofit tests should be carefully followed. The individual scores are recorded on a special sheet (Figure 3.7). Once the tests are administered the individual

Table 3.2 Profile chart of the Eurofit test for 14-year-old boys

	P3	*P10*	*P25*	*P50*	*P75*	*P90*	*P97*
Anthropometry							
Height (cm)	153.2	157.7	162.3	167.4	172.5	176.9	181.0
Body mass (kg)	38.6	42.5	47.0	52.9	60.1	68.0	77.5
Triceps skinfold (mm)		5.9	6.9	8.4	11.4	16.0	
Biceps skinfold (mm)		3.2	3.6	4.3	5.1	9.5	
Subscapular skinfold (mm)		5.1	5.7	6.3	7.9	10.9	
Suprailiac skinfold (mm)		3.8	4.2	4.8	6.9	11.2	
Calf skinfold (mm)		5.9	7.2	8.9	12.1	17.2	
Sum skinfolds (mm)		25.5	28.7	32.7	43.6	65.9	
Physical Performance							
Flamingo balance (n)		24.9	19.5	14.8	11.0	7.8	
Plate tapping (s)		14.2	13.0	11.8	10.8	10.1	
Sit and reach (cm)		11.2	16.0	21.0	25.7	29.5	
Standing long jump (cm)		164.5	179.6	194.2	208.0	221.0	
Handgrip (N)		25.3	29.0	33.4	38.0	42.6	
Sit-ups (n)		20.0	22.8	25.4	27.8	29.9	
Flexed arm hang (cm)		5.1	13.6	23.2	34.0	45.8	
Shuttle run (s)		23.3	22.2	21.2	20.4	19.7	
Endurance shuttle run (n)		4.9	6.3	7.8	9.3	10.6	

Table 3.3 Profile chart of the Eurofit test for 14-year-old girls

	P3	*P10*	*P25*	*P50*	*P75*	*P90*	*P97*
Anthropometry							
Height (cm)	149.2	153.5	157.6	162.2	166.6	170.6	174.4
Body mass (kg)	39.7	43.5	47.6	52.9	59.4	66.7	75.4
Triceps skinfold (mm)		9.0	11.0	14.2	18.7	24.4	
Biceps skinfold (mm)		4.6	5.9	8.1	11.7	16.9	
Subscapular skinfold (mm)		7.0	8.2	10.0	13.7	19.7	
Suprailiac skinfold (mm)		5.5	7.1	9.4	13.6	19.7	
Calf skinfold (mm)		9.7	12.4	16.4	22.0	29.0	
Sum skinfolds (mm)		38.3	46.4	59.1	79.4	107.2	
Physical Performance							
Flamingo balance (n)		27.6	20.7	15.4	11.3	7.5	
Plate tapping (s)		14.2	13.1	12.1	11.2	10.6	
Sit and reach (cm)		16.9	21.9	26.9	31.4	34.8	
Standing long jump (cm)		140.0	152.5	166.0	179.4	191.6	
Handgrip (N)		20.2	22.9	25.8	28.9	31.7	
Sit-ups (n)		15.9	18.6	21.0	23.4	25.8	
Flexed arm hang (cm)		0.0	2.8	7.5	14.4	23.1	
Shuttle run (s)		24.2	23.3	22.3	21.4	20.7	
Endurance shuttle run (n)		2.9	3.7	4.8	6.1	7.2	

scores are converted into reference scales. For this purpose reference scales of the Eurofit test battery for 14-year-old boys and girls are provided (Tables 3.2 and 3.3 after Lefevre *et al.*, 1993).

3.4.3 INTERPRETATION AND DISCUSSION

Each individual test score is plotted against the profiles given in Table 3.2 for boys and Table 3.3 for girls. From this profile the fitness level can be evaluated. As a guideline the test results of a Belgian 14-year-old boy (Jim) will be discussed (Table 3.4).

Jim seems to perform above average in two of the five health-related fitness items (endurance and flexibility). His skinfolds are quite high, and he performs below the median for muscular endurance and strength of the upper body and abdomen (bent arm hang and sit-ups). For his health-related condition it can be concluded that his cardiorespiratory endurance is above average for his sex and age but that given the rather high skinfolds his performance can probably be improved. To do this, Jim needs to be sufficiently active (endurance type activities) and control his energy intake (most probably excessive amounts of fat, or carbohydrates from soft drinks, sweets, snacks and so on). Furthermore, his muscular endurance and strength are weak and need to be improved. Note the negative influence of fatness (adiposity) on these items. For the performance-related items quite large variability among tests is observed. Balance is excellent, and static strength are average. Note the positive influence of fatness on static strength. Jim scores poorly on tests that require explosive actions and speed (standing long jump, shuttle run and plate tapping). Undoubtedly, these poor performance levels will have an effect on Jim's sport specific skills. He will thus profit largely from an improvement in these capacities. In conclusion, Jim needs a general conditioning programme in which the weak performance capacities are trained.

In interpreting the results, one should bear in mind that all tests and measurements are affected by measurement error. Therefore small differences in test results should be ignored. Furthermore, the selection of the

Name : .... Christian name : ....
School : .... Class : ....

Date of birth : ☐☐ ☐☐ ☐☐
day month year

Test date : ☐☐ ☐☐ ☐☐

Test	Procedure	Score	Result
Triceps skinfold*	–	mm	☐☐ ☐
Biceps skinfold*	–	mm	☐☐ ☐
Subscapular skinfold*	–	mm	☐☐ ☐
Suprailiac skinfold*	–	mm	☐☐ ☐
Calf skinfold*	–	mm	☐☐ ☐
Flamingo balance	1 trial	number min^{-1}	☐☐
Plate tapping	1 trial	time s 25 $cycle^{-1}$	☐☐ ☐
Sit and reach	2 trials	cm	☐☐
Standing long jump	2 trials	cm	☐☐ ☐
Handgrip	2 trials	kg	☐☐
Bent arm hang	1 trial	s	☐☐ ☐
Shuttle run	1 trial	s	☐☐ ☐
Endurance shuttle run	1 trial	number	☐☐

For measuring procedures follow the directions of the Eurofit manual. It is good practice to measure all the skinfolds once, repeat the measurements and verify if the difference is not larger than 10%. If so take another measurement and average the results. The test order as given on this sheet should be respected

Figure 3.7 Pro-forma for recording the Eurofit test results.

Eurofit tests was based on the factor analytic studies of Simons *et al.* (1969, 1990). In these studies it was shown that, when fitness factors are rotated to an oblique configuration, the factors showed only small intercorrelations; consequently the interrelationship between fitness items is low. This implies that it is very unlikely that a boy or girl would

Table 3.4 Individual profile of a 14-year-old Belgian boy (Jim)

	P3	*P10*	*P25*	*P50*	*P75*	*P90*	*P97*
Anthropometry							
Height (cm)	153.2	157.7	162.3	167.4	172.5	176.9	181.0
Body mass (kg)	38.6	42.5	47.0	52.9	60.1	68.0	77.5
Triceps skinfold (mm)		5.9	6.9	8.4	11.4	16.0	
Biceps skinfold (mm)		3.2	3.6	4.3	5.1	9.5	
Subscapular skinfold (mm)		5.1	5.7	6.3	7.9	10.9	
Suprailiac skinfold (mm)		3.8	4.2	4.8	6.9	11.2	
Calf skinfold (mm)		5.9	7.2	8.9	12.1	17.2	
Sum skinfolds (mm)		25.5	28.7	32.7 *	43.6	65.9	
Physical Performance							
Flamingo balance (n)		24.9	19.5	14.8	11.0 *	7.8	
Plate tapping (s)		14.2	* 13.0	11.8	10.8	10.1	
Sit and reach (cm)		11.2	16.0	21.0	* 25.7	29.5	
Standing long jump (cm)		164.5	179.6	* 194.2	208.0	221.0	
Handgrip (N)		25.3	29.0	33.4 *	38.0	42.6	
Sit-ups (n)		20.0	22.8	* 25.4	27.8	29.9	
Flexed arm hang (cm)		5.1	13.6 *	23.2	34.0	45.8	
Shuttle run (s)		23.3	22.2	* 21.2	20.4	19.7	
Endurance shuttle run (n)		4.9	6.3	7.8 *	9.3	10.6	

perform well on all items; generally there is some variation between tests. Note, however, that outstanding athletes perform above the median for most or all items. Note also that the tests correlate with somatic dimensions and biological maturity status. Static strength (handgrip) is positively correlated with height and body mass. Tests in which the subject performs against his own weight or part of it, for example tests of muscular endurance and power are negatively correlated with height and weight. From the above it is also clear that in assessing the performance capacities and especially in guiding and prescribing exercise programmes, the assessment of habitual physical activity and of nutritional status add significantly to the advice and guidance.

After a few historical notes this chapter considers growth evaluation, assessment of biological maturation and physical fitness evaluation. For each of the three sections the concept, assessment and evaluation techniques are explained and a detailed description is given of a practical. For the growth and physical fitness evaluation a small project is described in which data are collected and afterwards evaluated. For skeletal age assessment, X-rays are assessed according to the Tanner–Whitehouse technique. Each section ends with a number of recommendations and a short discussion of the evaluation and techniques that have been used. Additional details concerning the assessment of growth, maturation and performance are given in Chapter 13.

APPENDIX

Estimation according to the author of this chapter (for his intra- and inter-observor reliability see Beunen and Cameron 1980)
Estimations radiograph Figure 3.3: Boy
Radius: F, Ulna: C, MCI: D, MCIII: F, MCV: F
PPI: E, PPIII: E, PPV: E, MPIII: E, MPV: E, DPI: E, DPIII: F; DPV: E
Capitate: F, Hamate: F, Triquetral: E, Lumate: F, Schaphoid: D, Trapezium: E, Trapezoid: E
RUS-score 265, CARP-score 571, TW2-20bone-score 513
RUS-age 8.7 years, CARP-age 8.4 years, TW2-20 bone-age 8.6 years.

Estimations radiograph Figure 3.4: Boy
Radius: G, Ulna: F, MCI: E, MCIII: F, MCV: E
PPI: F, PPIII: F, PPV: F, MPIII: E, MPV: E, DPI: F, DPIII: F; DPV: F
Capitate: H, Hamate: H, Triquetral: H, Lumate: F, Schaphoid: F, Trapezium: H, Trapezoid: G
RUS-score 361, CARP-score 891, TW2-20 bone-score 775
RUS-age 12.0 years, CARP-age 12.1 years, TW2-20 bone-age 12.4 years.
Estimations radiograph Figure 3.5: Girl
All bones reached the adult stage
RUS-age: adult, CARP-age: adult, TW2-20 bone-age: adult.

REFERENCES

AAHPER (1958) *Youth Fitness Test Manual*, AAHPER, Washington.

AAHPER (1965) *Youth Fitness Test Manual*, revised edn. AAHPER, Washington.

AAHPERD (1988) *The AAHPERD Physical Best Program*, AAHEPRD, Reston, VA.

Adam, C., Klissouras, V., Ravassolo, M. *et al.* (1988) *Eurofit. Handbook for the Eurofit Test of Physical Fitness*. Council of Europe. Committee for the Development of Sport, Rome.

American College of Sports Medicine (1991) *Guidelines for Exercise Testing and Prescription*. Lea & Febiger, Philadelphia.

Anastasi, A. (1988) *Psychological Testing*, McMillan, New York.

Bayley, N. (1946) Tables for predicting adult height from skeletal age and present height. *Journal of Pediatrics*, **28**, 49–64.

Beunen, G. (1989) Biological age in pediatric exercise research, in *Advances in Pediatric Sport Sciences*, vol. 3, *Biological Issues* (ed. O. Bar-Or), Human Kinetics, Champaign, IL, pp. 1–39.

Beunen, G. and Cameron, N. (1980) The reproducibility of TW2 skeletal age assessment by a self-taught assessor. *Annals of Human Biology*, **7**, 155–62.

Beunen, G., Lefevre, J., Ostyn, M. *et al.* (1990) Skeletal maturity in Belgian youths assessed by the Tanner–Whitehouse method (TW2). *Annals of Human Biology*, **17**, 355–76.

Blair, N., Clarke, D. G., Cureton, K. J. and Powell, K. E. (1989) Exercise and fitness in childhood: implications for a lifetime of health, in *Perspectives in Exercise and Sports Medicine. Youth and Exercise and Sports*, vol. 2 (eds C. V. Gisolfi and D. R. Lamb), Benchmark Press, Indianapolis, pp. 401–30.

Bock, R. D. and Thissen, D. (1980) Statistical problems of fitting individual growth curves, in *Human Physical Growth and Maturation. Methodologies and Factors* (eds F. E. Johnston, A. F. Roche and C. Susanne), Plenum Press, New York, pp. 265–90.

Bovend'eerdt, J. H. F., Bernink, M. J. E., van Hijfte, T. *et al.* (1980) *De MOPER Fitness Test*. Onderzoeksverslag. De Vrieseborch, Haarlem.

Brace, D. K. (1927) *Measuring Motor Ability*. Barnes, New York.

CAHPER (1965) *Fitness Performance Test Manual for Boys*. CAHPER: Toronto.

Cameron, N. (1984) *The Measurement of Human Growth*, Croom Helm, London.

Carter, J. E. L. (ed.) (1982) *Physical Structure of Olympic Athletes*. Part I. *The Montreal Olympic Games Anthropological Project. Medicine and Sport 16*, Karger, Basel.

Clarke, H. H. (1979) Academy approves physical fitness definition. *Physical Fitness News-Letter*, **25**, 1.

Deming, J. (1957) Application of the Gompertz curve to the observed pattern of growth in length of 48 individual boys and girls during the adolescent cyclus of growth. *Human Biology*, **29**, 83–122.

Demirjian, A. (1978) Dentition, in *Human Growth: Postnatal Growth*, vol. 2, (eds F. Falkner and J. M. Tanner), Plenum, New York, pp. 413–44.

Demirjian, A., Goldstein, H. and Tanner, J. M. (1973) A new system for dental age assessment. *Human Biology*, **45**, 211–27.

Eveleth, P. B. and Tanner, J. M. (1990) *Worldwide Variation in Human Growth*, Cambridge University Press, Cambridge:

Fitnessgram User's Manual (1987) Institute for Aerobics Research, Dallas, TX.

Fleishman, E. A. (1964) *The Structure and Measurement of Physical Fitness*, Prentice Hall, Englewood Cliffs.

Gasser, T., Köhler, W., Müller, H.-G. *et al.* (1984). Velocity in physical changes associated with adolescence in girls. *Annals of Human Biology*, **11**, 397–411.

Goldstein, H. (1979) *The Design and Analysis of Longitudinal Studies. Their Role in the Measurement of Change*, Academic Press, London.

Goldstein, H. (1984) Current developments in the design and analysis of growth studies, in *Human*

Growth and Development (eds J. Borms, R. Hauspie, A. Sand *et al.*), Plenum Press, New York, pp. 733–52.

Goldstein, H. (1986) Sampling for growth studies, in *Human Growth: a Comprehensive Treatise*, 2nd edn, vol. 3 (eds F. Falkner and J. M. Tanner), Plenum Press, New York, pp. 59–78.

Greulich, W. W. and Pyle, I. (1950, 1959) *Radiographic Atlas of Skeletal Development of the Hand and Wrist*, Standford University Press, Standford.

Hauspie, R. C., Wachholder, A., Baron, G. *et al.* (1980) A comparative study of the fit of four different functions to longitudinal data for growth in height of Belgian boys. *Annals of Human Biology*, **7**, 347–58.

Healy, M. J. R. (1986) Statistics of growth standards, in *Human Growth: a Comprehensive Treatise* 2nd edn, vol. 3 (eds F. Falkner and J. M. Tanner), Plenum Press, New York, pp. 47–58.

Hebbelinck, M. and Borms, J. (1975) *Biometrische Studie van een Reeks Lichaamskenmerken en Lichamelijke Prestatietests van Belgische Kinderen uit het Lager Onderwijs*. Centrum voor Bevolings-en Gezinsstudiën (C.B.G.S.), Brussels.

Jenss, R. M. and Bayley, M. (1937) A mathematical method for studying the growth of a child. *Human Biology*, **9**, 556–63.

Jolicoeur, P., Pontier, J. and Abidi, H. (1992) Asymptotic models for the longitudinal growth of human stature. *American Journal of Human Biology*, **4**, 461–8.

Keogh, J. and Sugden, D. (1985) *Movement Skill Development*, Macmillan, New York.

Lampl, M., Veldhuis, J. D. and Johnson, M. L. (1992) Saltation and stasis: a model of human growth, *Science*, **258**, 801–3.

Largo, R. H., Gasser, Th., Prader, A. *et al.* (1978) Analysis of the adolescent growth spurt using smoothing spline functions. *Annals of Human Biology*, **5**, 421–34.

Larson, L. A. (ed.) (1974) *Fitness, Health, and Work Capacity: International Standards for Assessment*, Macmillan, New York.

Lefevre, J., Beunen, G., Borms, J. *et al.* (1993) *Eurofit Testbatterij. Leiddraad bij Testafneming en Referentiewaarden*. BLOSO-Jeugdsportcampagne, Brussels.

Léger, L. and Lambert, J. (1982) A maximal multistage 20 m shuttle run test to predict VO_2 max. *European Journal of Applied Physiology*, **49**, 1–12.

Lohman, T. G., Roche, A. F. and Martorell, R. (eds) (1988) *Anthropometric Standardization Reference Manual*. Human Kinetics, Champaign, Il.

Malina, R. M. and Bouchard, C. (1991) *Growth, Maturation, and Physical Activity*, Human Kinetics, Champaign, Il.

Marubini, E., Resele, L. F., Tanner, J. M. and Whitehouse, R. H. (1972) The fit of the Gompertz and logistic curves to longitudinal data during adolescence on height, sitting height, and biacromial diameter in boys and girls of the Harpenden Growth Study. *Human Biology*, **44**, 511–24.

Marubini, E. and Milani, S. (1986) Approaches to the analysis of longitudinal data, in *Human Growth: a Comprehensive Treatise*, 2nd edn, vol. 3 (eds F. Falkner and J. M. Tanner), Plenum Press, New York, pp. 33–79.

McCloy, C. H. (1934) The measurement of general motor capacity and general motor ability. *Research Quarterly*, Suppl. 5, 46–61.

Ostyn, M., Simons, J., Beunen, G. *et al.* (1980) *Somatic and Motor Development of Belgian Secondary School Boys. Norms and Standards.* Leuven University Press, Leuven.

Pate, R. and Shephard, R. (1989) Characteristics of physical fitness in youth, in *Perspectives in Exercise Science and Sports Medicine. Youth, Exercise and Sport*, vol. 2 (eds C. V. Gisolfi and D. R. Lamb), Benchmark Press, Indianapolis, pp. 1–45.

Preece, M. A. and Baines, M. J. (1978) A new family of mathematical models describing the human growth curve. *Annals of Human Biology*, **5**, 1–24.

Reynolds, E. L. and Wines, J. V. (1948) Individual differences in physical changes associated with adolescence in girls. *American Journal of Diseases of Children*, **75**, 329–50.

Reynolds, E. L. and Wines, J. V. (1951) Physical changes associated with adolescence in boys. *American Journal of Diseases of Children*, 529–47.

Roche, A. F., Wainer, H. and Thissen, D. (1975a) Predicting adult stature for individuals. *Monographs in Pediatrics*, **3**, 1–114.

Roche, A. F., Wainer, H. and Thissen, D. (1975b) *Skeletal Maturity: Knee Joint as a Biological Indicator*. Plenum Press, New York.

Roche, A. F., Chumlea, W. C. and Thissen, D. (1988) *Assessing the Skeletal Maturity of the Hand-Wrist: Fels Method*, Thomas, Springfield.

Ross, J. G. and Pate, R. R. (1987) The national children and youth fitness study II: a summary of findings. *Journal of Physical Education, Recreation and Dance*, **56**, 45–50.

Safrit, M. J. (1973) *Evaluation in Physical Education. Assessing Motor Behavior*, Prentice-Hall, Englewood Cliffs, NJ.

Sargent, D. A. (1921) The physical test of a man. *American Physical Education Review*, **26**, 188–94.

Simons, J., Beunen, G., Ostyn, M. *et al.* (1969) Construction d'une batterie de tests d'aptitude motrice pour garçons de 12 à 19 ans par le méthode de l'analyse factorielle. *Kinanthropologie*, **1**, 323–62.

Simons, J., Beunen, G. P., Renson, R. *et al.* (eds) (1990) *Growth and Fitness of Flemish Girls. The Leuven Growth Study. HKP Sport Science Monograph Series 3*. Human Kinetics, Champaign, IL.

Tanner, J. M. (1962) *Growth at Adolescence*, Blackwell Scientific Publications, Oxford.

Tanner, J. M. (1981) *A History of the Study of Human Growth*. Cambridge: Cambridge University Press.

Tanner, J. M. (1989). *Fetus into Man. Physical Growth from Conception to Maturity*, Harvard University Press, Cambridge, MA.

Tanner, J. M., Whitehouse, R. H. and Takaiski, M. (1966) Standards from birth to maturity for height, weight, height velocity and weight velocity. *Archives of Diseases of Childhood*, **41**, 454–71, 613–35.

Tanner, J. M., Whitehouse, R. H., Cameron, N. *et al.* (1983) *Assessment of Skeletal Maturity and Prediction of Adult Height (TW2 method)*, Academic Press, London.

Todd, J. W. (1937) *Atlas of Skeletal Maturation: Part 1. Hand*. Mosby, London.

van 't Hof, M. A., Roede, M. J. and Kowalski, C. J. (1976) Estimation of growth velocities from individual longitudinal data. *Growth*, **40**, 217–40.

Weiner, J. S. and Lourie, J. A. (1969) *Human Biology*, F. A. Davis, Philadelphia.

PART TWO

NEUROMUSCULAR AND GONIOMETRIC ASPECTS OF MOVEMENT

SKELETAL MUSCLE FUNCTION 4

V. Baltzopoulos

4.1 INTRODUCTION

Human movement is the result of complex interactions between environmental factors and the nervous, muscular and skeletal systems. Ideas expressed within the cerebral cortex are converted by supraspinal centre programming into neural outputs (central commands) that stimulate the muscular system to produce the required movement (Cheney, 1985; Brooks, 1986). This chapter will consider specific aspects of the structure and function of the muscular system as part of the process for producing movement. Knowledge of basic physiological and anatomical principles is assumed.

4.2 BASIC STRUCTURE AND FUNCTION OF SKELETAL MUSCLE

Skeletal muscle contains a large number of muscle fibres assembled together by collagenous connective tissue. A motoneuron and the muscle fibres it innervates represent a motor unit. The number of muscle fibres in a motor unit (innervation ratio) depends on the function of the muscle. Small muscles that are responsible for fine movements, such as the extraocular muscles, have approximately 5–15 muscle fibres per motor unit. Large muscles, such as the gastrocnemius, required for strength and power events, have innervation ratios of approximately 1: 1800. A muscle fibre comprises a number of myofibrils surrounded by an excitable membrane, the sarcolemma. The basic structural unit of a myofibril is the sarcomere which is composed of thick and thin filaments of contractile proteins. The thick filaments are mainly composed of myosin. The thin filaments are composed of actin and the regulatory proteins tropomyosin and troponin that prevent interaction of actin and myosin.

Nerve action potentials propagated along the axons of motoneurons are transmitted to the postsynaptic membrane (sarcolemma) by an electrochemical process. This generates a muscle action potential which is propagated along the sarcolemma at velocities ranging from 1 to 3 ms^{-1}. It has been reported, however, that the conduction velocity can be increased to approximately 6 ms^{-1} with resistance training (Kereshi *et al.*, 1983). The muscle action potential causes Ca^{2+} release that disinhibits the regulatory proteins of the thin filaments. This allows attachment of the myosin globular heads to binding sites on the actin filaments and forms cross-bridges. The interaction of the actin and myosin filaments causes them to slide past one another and generate force that is transmitted to the Z discs of the sarcomere. This is known as the sliding filament theory. The details of the exact mechanism responsible for the transformation of adenosine triphosphate energy from a chemical to a mechanical form in the cross-bridge cycle is not completely known (Pollack, 1983). For a detailed discussion of the electrochemical events associated with muscular contraction the reader is referred to the text by Gowitzke and Milner (1988).

Kinanthropometry and Exercise Physiology Laboratory Manual: Tests, procedures and data Edited by Roger Eston and Thomas Reilly. Published in 1996 by E & FN Spon. ISBN 0 419 17880 5

4.3 MOTOR UNIT TYPES AND FUNCTION

Motor units are usually classified according to contractile and mechanical characteristics into three types (Burke, 1981).

1. Type S: *S*low contraction time, low force level, resistant to fatigue.
2. Type FR: *F*ast contraction time, medium force level, *r*esistant to fatigue.
3. Type FF: *F*ast contraction time, high force level, *f*atiguable.

Morphological differences are also evident between the different motor unit types. For example, motoneuron size, muscle fibre cross-sectional area and innervation ratio are increased in fast compared to slow type motor units.

Another scheme classifies motor units as Type I, IIa, IIb based on myosin ATPase. Another subdivision is slow twitch oxidative (SO), fast twitch oxidative glycolytic (FOG) and fast twitch glycolytic (FG), based on myosin ATPase and anaerobic/aerobic capacity (Brooke and Kaiser, 1974). Relative distribution of different motor unit types is determined by genetic factors. Elite endurance athletes demonstrate a predominance of slow or Type I fibres. Fast twitch fibres predominate in sprint or power event athletes.

The muscle fibres in a motor unit are all of the same type, but each muscle contains a proportion of the three motor unit types (Nemeth *et al.*, 1986). Motor units are activated in a preset sequence (S–FR–FF) (orderly recruitment) that is determined mainly by the motoneuron size of the motor unit (size principle) (Henneman, 1957; Enoka and Stuart, 1984; Gustafsson and Pinter, 1985). The force exerted by a muscle depends on the number of motor units activated and the frequency of the action potentials (Harrison, 1983). The orderly recruitment theory, based on the size principle, indicates that recruitment is based on the force required, not the velocity of movement. Thus slow motor units are always activated irrespective of velocity. Most human movement is performed within the velocity range of the slow fibres (Green, 1986), although there is evidence of selective activation of muscles with a predominance of fast twitch motor units during rapid movements (Behm and Sale, 1993).

4.4 TRAINING ADAPTATIONS

Resistance training results in neural and structural adaptations which improve muscle function. Neural adaptations include improved central command that generates a greater action potential (Komi *et al.*, 1978; Sale *et al.*, 1983) and synchronization of action potential discharge in different motor units (Milner-Brown *et al.*, 1975). Structural adaptations include increases in the cross-sectional area of muscle fibres (hypertrophy) and possibly an increase in the number of muscle fibres through longitudinal fibre splitting. There is no conclusive evidence for development of new fibres (hyperplasia) in humans. The structural changes that are induced by resistance training result in an overall increase in contractile proteins and therefore muscular force capacity (MacDougall *et al.*, 1982). Adaptation of specific motor unit types depends on resistance training that stresses their specific characteristics: this is the principle of specificity. For example, during fast high-resistance training movements, slow motor units are activated, but they are not adapted because their specific characteristics are not stressed. Recent evidence suggests that limited transformation between slow and fast-twitch muscle fibres is possible with prolonged specific training (Simoneau *et al.*, 1985; Tesch and Karlsson, 1985).

4.5 MUSCULAR ACTIONS

Muscular activation involves the electrochemical processes that cause myofilament sliding, shortening of the sarcomere and exertion of force. The overall muscle length during activation is determined not only by the muscular force but also by the external load or resistance applied to the muscle. The ratio of muscular force : external load determines three distinct conditions of muscle action:

1. Concentric action: muscular force is greater than external force and consequently overall muscle length decreases (i.e. muscle shortens) during activation.
2. Isometric action: muscular force is equal to external force and muscle length remains constant.
3. Eccentric action: external force is greater than muscular force and consequently muscle length is increased (muscle lengthening) during activation.

During all three conditions, sarcomeres are stimulated and attempt to shorten by actin–myosin interaction (sarcomere contraction). The term 'contraction' = shortening should be used to describe the shortening of sarcomeres only, not changes in length of the whole muscle. During eccentric activation, for example, the muscle is lengthened and therefore terms such as 'eccentric contraction' or 'isometric contraction' are misleading (Cavanagh, 1988).

In attempting to examine whole muscle function it is important to consider the different component parts of the muscle, that is both the functional contractile (active) and the elastic (passive) components. A simplified mechanical model of muscle includes three components that simulate the mechanical properties of the different structures. The contractile component (CC) simulates the active, force-generating units (i.e. sarcomeres), the series elastic component (SEC) simulates the elastic properties of the sarcolemma and the parallel elastic component (PEC) simulates the elastic properties of the collagenous connective tissue in parallel with the contractile component (Komi, 1984, 1986; Chapman, 1985).

Muscle architecture describes the organization of muscle fibres within the muscle and affects muscle function. The angle between the muscle fibres and the line of action from origin to insertion is defined as the pennation angle. The pennation angle and the number of sarcomeres that are arranged in series or in parallel with the line of action of the muscle are important muscle architecture factors affecting muscular force.

4.6 FORCE–LENGTH RELATIONSHIP IN ISOLATED MUSCLE

In muscles isolated from the skeletal system in a laboratory preparation, the force exerted at different muscle lengths depends on the properties of the active (CC) and passive components (SEC and PEC) at different muscle lengths. Force exerted by the interaction of actin and myosin depends on the number of the available cross-bridges, which is maximum near the resting length of the muscle. The force exerted by the passive elastic elements (SEC and PEC) is increased exponentially as muscle length increases beyond resting length (Figure 4.1). The total force exerted therefore is the sum of the active and passive forces, and although at maximum length, there is no active component force because of minimum cross-bridge availability, the total force contributed by the elastic components alone may be even greater than the maximum CC force at resting length (Baratta and Solomonow, 1991).

4.7 FORCE–VELOCITY RELATIONSHIP IN ISOLATED MUSCLE

The effect of the linear velocity during muscle shortening or lengthening on the force output has been examined extensively since the pioneering work of Hill (1938). With an increase in linear concentric velocity of muscle shortening, the force exerted is decreased non-linearly because the number of cross-bridges formed, and the force they exert, are reduced (Figure 4.2). Furthermore, the distribution of different motor unit types affects the force–velocity relationship. A higher output at faster angular velocities indicates a higher percentage of FF–FR motor units (Gregor *et al.*, 1979; Froese and Houston, 1985). However, with an increase in linear eccentric velocity of muscle lengthening, the force exerted is increased (Wilkie, 1950;

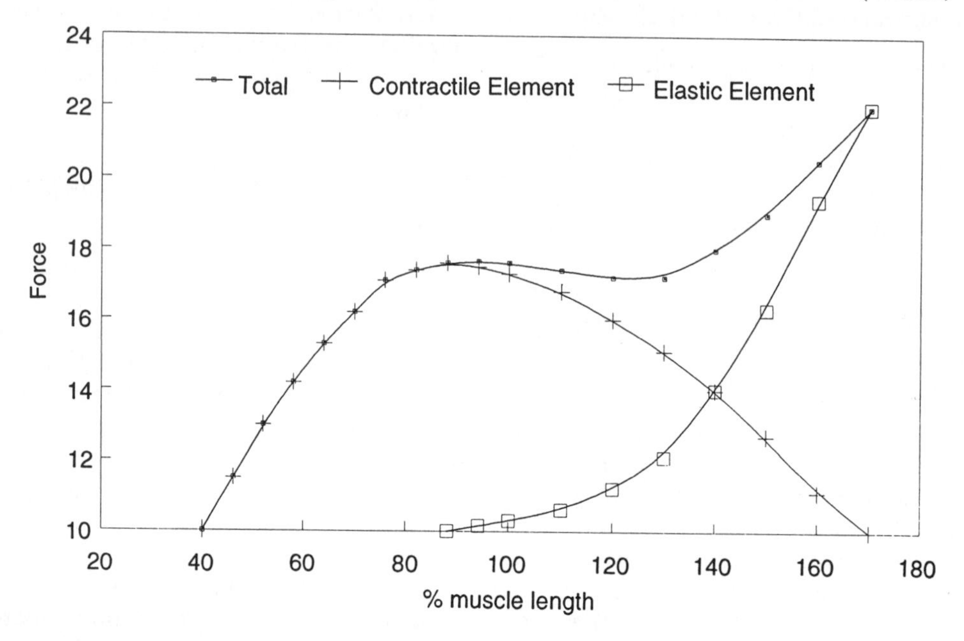

Figure 4.1 Force–length relationship in isolated muscle showing the contribution of the contractile and the elastic elements on total muscular force. Force units are arbitrary.

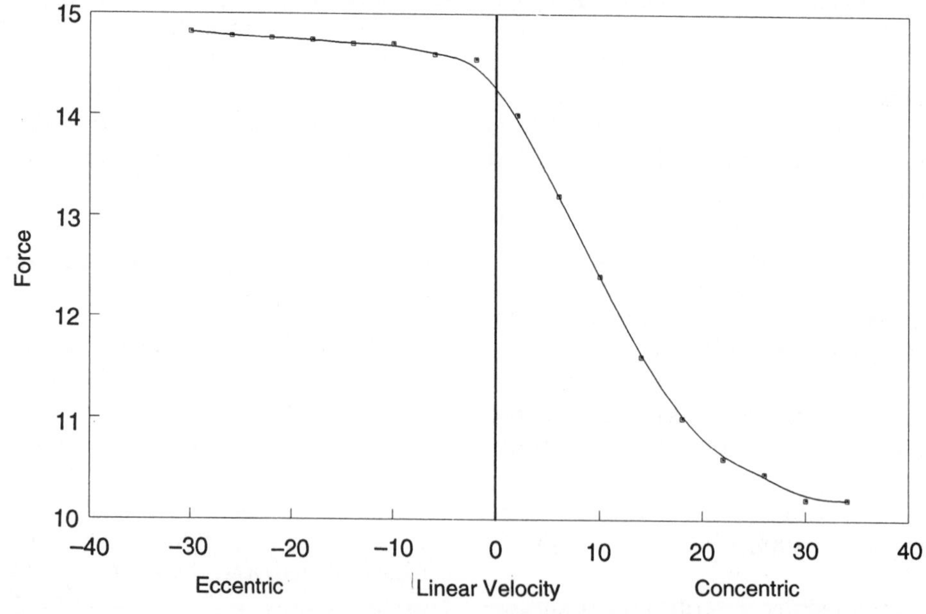

Figure 4.2 Force–velocity relationship of isolated muscle during concentric, isometric and eccentric muscle action. Force and velocity units are arbitrary and do not refer to specific muscles.

Chapman, 1976; Thorstensson *et al.*, 1976; Tihanyi *et al.*, 1987). The exact mechanism responsible for the increase in force during eccentric conditions is not known but it is suggested that detachment of cross-bridges is achieved by the external force requiring no ATP. The cross-bridge cycle is therefore reduced, increasing the rate of cross-bridge formation and the force exerted by the cross-bridges during detachment (Stauber, 1989).

4.8 MUSCLE FUNCTION DURING JOINT MOVEMENT

Examination of the mechanical properties of isolated muscle is of limited use when considering how muscles function during movements in sports or other activities. Movement of body segments results from the application of muscular force around the joint axis of rotation. It is therefore important to consider the relationship between muscle function and joint position and motion (Bouisset, 1984; Kulig *et al.*, 1984). The movement of the joint segments around the axis of rotation is proportional to the rotational effect of the muscular force or moment. This is measured in N m and is defined as the product of muscular force (in Newtons) and moment arm, i.e. the perpendicular distance (in metres) between force line and the axis of rotation of the joint (Figure 4.3). Other physiological, mechanical and structural factors that were described earlier also affect muscle function in a joint system (Figure 4.4).

Joint motion results from the action of muscle groups. Individual muscles in the group may have different origin or insertion points, they may operate over one or two joints and have different architecture. The moment arm of the muscle group is also variable over the range of motion of the joint. Assessment of dynamic muscle function therefore must consider these factors. It must be emphasized that relationships such as force–length or force–velocity refer to individual muscles whereas moment–joint position and

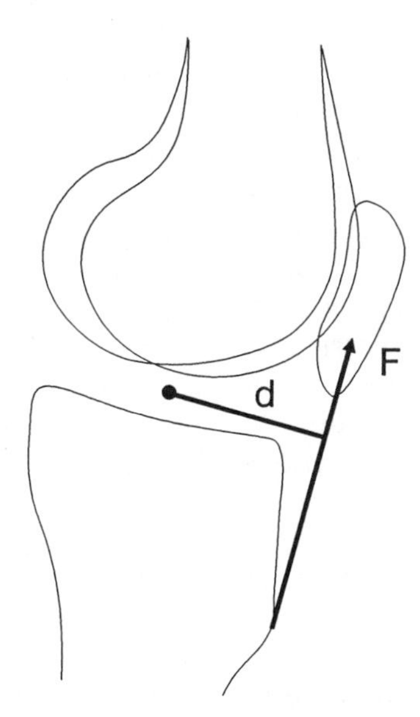

Figure 4.3 The moment arm (d) of the knee extensor group is the shortest or perpendicular distance between the patellar tendon and the joint centre. The muscular moment is the product of the force (F) along the patellar tendon and the moment arm (d).

moment–angular joint velocity relationship refer to the function of a muscle group around a joint. For example, the moment of the knee extensor group (rectus femoris, vastus lateralis, vastus medialis, vastus intermedius) at different knee joint angular velocities and positions can be examined during voluntary knee extension using appropriate instrumentation. These terms must not be confused with the force–velocity and force–length relationships of the four individual muscles. These can be examined only if the muscles were separated from a cadaveric joint in the laboratory.

4.9 MEASUREMENT OF DYNAMIC (CONCENTRIC–ECCENTRIC) MUSCLE FUNCTION

The most significant development for the study of dynamic muscle and joint function was the introduction of isokinetic dynamometry in the 1960s (Hislop and Perrine, 1967; Thistle *et al.*, 1967). Isokinetic dynamometers have hydraulic, or electromechanical mechanisms that maintain the angular velocity of a joint constant, by providing a resistive moment that is equal to the muscular moment throughout the range of movement. This is referred to as optimal loading. Passive systems (Cybex II, Akron, Merac) permit isokinetic concentric movements only, but more recently active systems (Biodex, Cybex 6000, KinCom, Lido) provide both concentric and eccentric isokinetic conditions, with maximum joint angular velocities up to 8.72 rad s^{-1} (500 deg s^{-1} for concentric actions and 4.36 rad s^{-1} (250 deg s^{-1}) for eccentric actions. It is important to note that it is the joint angular velocity that is controlled and kept constant, not the linear velocity of the active muscle group (Hinson *et al.*, 1979). Dynamometers that control the rate of change of joint angular velocity have also been developed (Westing *et al.*, 1991). Most commercial isokinetic systems have accessories that allow testing of all the major joints of the upper and lower limbs and the back. Apart from isolated joint tests, workplace manual activities such as lifting, handling materials and equipment can be simulated on adapted dynamometers using dedicated attachments. Methodological problems such as subject positioning and motivation during the test require standardized protocols. Mechanical factors such as the effect of gravitational moment or the control of the acceleration of the segment affect muscular moment measurement but appropriate correction methods have been developed and used routinely (Baltzopoulos and Brodie, 1989). Excellent test reliability and computerized assessment of muscle function permit widespread application of isokinetics for testing, training and rehabilitation.

4.10 MOMENT–ANGULAR VELOCITY RELATIONSHIP

The moment exerted during concentric actions is maximum at slow angular velocities and decreases with increasing angular velocity. Some authors have reported a constant moment output (plateau) for a range of slow angular velocities (Lesmes *et al.*, 1978; Perrine and Edgerton, 1978; Wickiewicz *et al.*, 1984; Thomas *et al.*, 1987) whereas others have found a continuous decrease from slow to fast concentric angular velocities (Thorstensson *et al.*, 1976; Coyle *et al.*, 1981; Westing *et al.*, 1988). Although the plateau has been attributed to neural inhibition during slow dynamic muscular activation, it is also affected by training level and testing protocol (Hortobagyi and Katch, 1990). The rate of decrease at higher angular velocities is affected by activity, sex and the physiological/mechanical factors discussed above. The maximum concentric moment of the knee extensors decreases by approximately 40% from 1.47 to 4.19 rad s^{-1} (60 to 240 deg s^{-1}), whereas the knee flexor moment decrease varies between 25 and 50% (Prietto and Caiozzo, 1989; Westing and Seger, 1989). The eccentric moment remains relatively constant with increasing angular velocity and approximately 20% higher than the isometric moment. There are considerable differences in muscular moment measurements at different concentric–eccentric angular velocities between the large number of studies on dynamic muscle function. These result mainly from differences in methodology, anthropometric, physiological and mechanical parameters (Cabri, 1991; Perrin, 1993).

The moment–velocity relationship is affected by the physiological principles of isolated muscular action and the mechanical factors affecting muscle function in a joint system. Figure 4.4 is a simple representation of the different mechanical and physiological factors that affect the function of a muscle group during joint movement. Direct comparisons of the moment–angular velocity relationship during isokinetic eccentric or concentric joint motion with the force–linear velocity relationship of isolated muscle is of limited use, given the number of variables affecting muscle and joint function (Bouisset, 1984; Bobbert and Harlaar, 1992).

4.11 ISOKINETIC DYNAMOMETRY APPLICATIONS

Applications of isokinetic dynamometry include assessment of bilateral and reciprocal muscle group ratios and training of specific aspects of muscle function. Bilateral differences are minimal in healthy non-athletes or in participants in sports that involve symmetrical action. However, differences of up to 15% have been reported in asymmetrical sport activities (Perrin *et al.*, 1987). Reciprocal muscle group ratios (e.g. knee flexor/extensor) indicate joint balance and possible predisposition to joint or muscle injury. Concentric knee flexion/extension moment ratios range from 0.4 to 0.6 and are mainly affected by activity, methodological measurement problems and gravitational forces in particular (Appen and Duncan, 1986; Fillyaw *et al.*, 1986; Figoni *et al.*, 1988). Studies that used moment data not

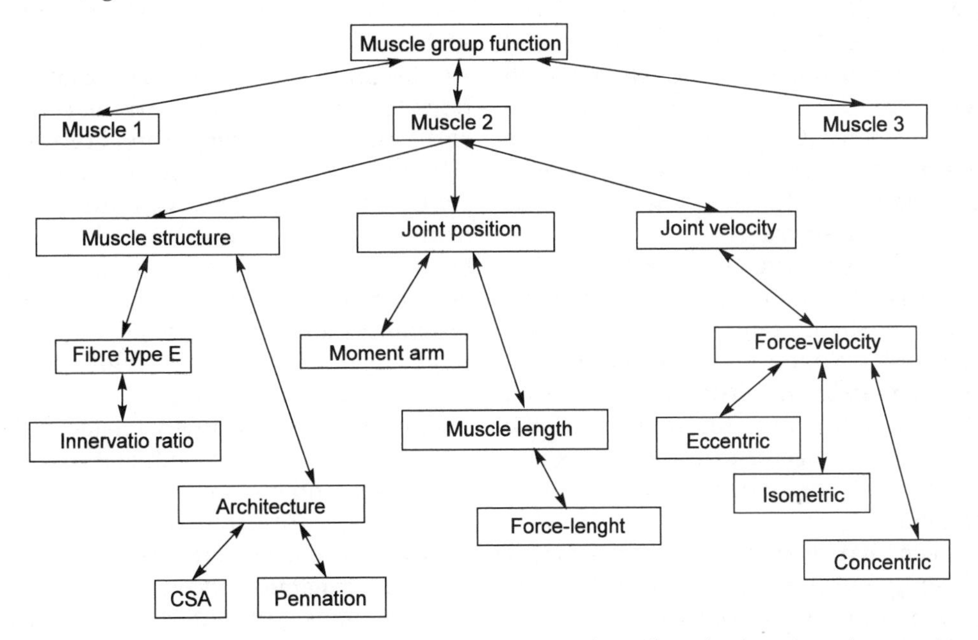

Figure 4.4 The main physiological and mechanical factors that affect the function of a muscle group. This simple model is not exhaustive and any interactions between the different factors are not indicated for simplicity.

corrected for the effect of gravitational forces demonstrate higher ratios and a significant increase with increasing angular velocity. This increase is a gravitational artefact. Gravity corrected ratios are approximately constant at different angular velocities (Appen and Duncan, 1986; Fillyaw *et al.*, 1986; Baltzopoulos *et al.*, 1991). During joint motion in sport or other activities, concentric action of agonist muscles requires eccentric action of the antagonist muscles to control the movement and ensure joint stability. For this reason, ratios of agonist concentric to antagonist eccentric action (e.g. eccentric knee flexion moment/concentric knee extension moment) are more representative of joint function during sport activities.

The most significant aspect of isokinetic training is velocity-specific adaptations and transfer of improvements to angular velocities, other than the training velocity. Training at intermediate velocities 2.09–3.14 rad s^{-1} (120–180 deg s^{-1}) produces the most significant transfer to both slower and faster angular velocities (Bell and Wenger, 1992; Behm and Sale, 1993). Eccentric training at 2.09 rad s^{-1} improves muscle function in both slower (1.05 rad s^{-1}) and faster (3.14 rad s^{-1}) angular velocities (Duncan *et al.*, 1989). There is no conclusive evidence for improvements in eccentric muscle function after concentric training and vice-versa.

Earlier studies reported no hypertrophy following isokinetic training (Lesmes *et al.*, 1978; Cote *et al.*, 1988) although more recent findings suggest isokinetic training induces increases in muscle size (Alway *et al.*, 1990). Further research is required to examine the effects of both concentric and eccentric isokinetic training programmes on muscular hypertrophy.

Isokinetic dynamometry involves isolated joint testing and not simulation of the total body motion in sport or other dynamic activities. Furthermore, the maximum joint angular velocity during isokinetic testing is limited compared to the actual joint velocities attained in many sports. These limitations suggest that isokinetic assessment must be only one of several factors used for performance prediction in different sports (Cabri, 1991; Perrin, 1993).

4.12 EFFECTS OF SEX AND AGE ON MUSCLE FUNCTION

Sex differences in muscle function parameters have been extensively examined. The absolute muscular force of the upper extremity in males is approximately 50% higher compared to females (Hoffman *et al.*, 1979; Morrow and Hosler, 1981; Heyward *et al.*, 1986). The absolute muscular force of the lower extremities is approximately 30% higher in males (Laubach, 1976; Morrow and Hosler, 1981). Because of sex differences in anthropometric parameters that affect strength such as body mass, lean body mass, muscle mass and muscle cross-sectional area, muscular performance should be relative to these parameters. Research on the relationship between body mass and maximum muscular force or moment is inconclusive with some studies indicating high significant correlations (Beam *et al.*, 1982; Clarkson *et al.*, 1982) and others no significant relationships (Hoffman *et al.*, 1979; Morrow and Hosler, 1981; Kroll *et al.*, 1990). Maximum muscular force expressed relative to body mass, lean body mass or muscle mass is similar in males and females but some studies indicate that differences are not completely eliminated in upper extremity muscles (Hoffman *et al.*, 1979; Frontera *et al.*, 1991).

Maximum force is closely related to muscle cross-sectional area in both static (Maughan *et al.*, 1983) and dynamic conditions (Schantz *et al.*, 1983). Research on maximum force relative to muscle cross-sectional area in static or dynamic conditions indicates that there is no significant difference between sexes (Schantz *et al.*, 1983; Bishop *et al.*, 1987) although higher force : cross-sectional area ratios for males have also been reported

(Maughan *et al.*, 1983; Ryushi *et al.*, 1988). However, instrumentation and procedures for measurement of different anthropometric parameters *in vivo* (for example cross-sectional area, moment arms, lean body mass, muscle mass) are often inaccurate. Measurement of cross-sectional area in pennate muscles or the elderly is inappropriate for the normalization of muscular force or moment. Muscle mass, determined from urinary creatinine excretion, is a better indicator of force generation capacity and the main determinant of age and gender-related differences in muscle function (Frontera *et al.*, 1991). The findings of muscle function studies, therefore, must always be considered relative to the inherent problems of procedures, instrumentation and *in vivo* assessment of muscle performance and anthropometric parameters.

Muscular force decreases with advancing age (Dummer *et al.*, 1985; Bemben, 1991; Frontera *et al.*, 1991). This decline has been attributed mainly to changes in muscle composition and physical activity (Bemben, 1991; Frontera *et al.*, 1991). Furthermore, the onset and rate of force decline is different in males and females and upper–lower extremity muscles (Dummer *et al.*, 1985; Aoyagi and Shephard, 1992). These differences are mainly due to reduction in steroid hormones in females after menopause and involvement in different habitual-recreational activities. Generally there is a decrease of approximately 5–8% per decade after the age of 20–30 (Shephard, 1991; Aoyagi and Shephard, 1992).

4.13 DATA COLLECTION AND ANALYSIS CONSIDERATIONS

One of the most important considerations in muscle function testing is subject positioning. The length of the muscle group, contribution of the elastic components, effective moment arm, development of angular velocity and inhibitory effects by the antagonistic muscle groups are all influenced by positioning and segment-joint stabilization during the test. For these reasons, the above factors must be standardized between tests, to allow valid comparisons.

Isokinetic isolated joint testing is not a natural movement. It therefore requires accurate instructions concerning the operation of the isokinetic dynamometers and the testing requirements together with adequate familiarization. Eccentric conditions, particularly fast angular velocities, require special attention in order to avoid injury in novices or subjects with musculoskeletal weaknesses.

Simple isometric measurements can be performed using force transducers or cable tensiometers, hand dynamometers or myometers and simple free weights or resistive exercise equipment (Watkins, 1993). The force output using these devices depends on the point of attachment on the limb, moment arm of muscle group and the joint position. It is therefore essential to express joint function in terms of moment (N·m), i.e. as the product of the force output of the measuring device (N) and the perpendicular distance (m) between the force line and the joint axis of rotation. Accurate determination of the joint centre is not possible without complicated radiographic measurements and therefore an approximation is necessary. An example is the use of the femoral epicondyle in the knee as a landmark.

Computerized, isokinetic dynamometers allow more accurate positioning of the subject, the joint tested and assessment of muscle function. However, the cost of these devices may prohibit their use as tools in teaching. The moment recorded by isokinetic dynamometers is the total (or resultant) moment exerted around the joint axis of rotation. The main component of this total joint moment is the moment exerted by the active muscle group. The contribution of other structures such as the joint capsule and ligaments to the total joint moment is minimal and therefore the moment recorded by isokinetic dynamometers is considered equal to the muscular moment. During knee extension testing, the moment exerted by the quadriceps is the product of the force exerted by the patellar tendon on the tibia and the moment arm, i.e., the perpendicular or shortest distance between the patellar tendon and the centre of the knee joint (Figure 4.3). The moment arm is variable over the range of movement (Figure 4.5), being minimum at full knee extension and flexion and maximum at approximately 0.78 rad (45 deg) of knee flexion (Baltzopoulos, 1995a). Moment arms at different joint positions are usually measured directly on the subject using radiography or derived indirectly from cadaveric studies. For example, if the knee extensor isometric moment of a subject with body weight of 800 N (body mass 81.5 kg) was 280 Nm at 0.87 rad (50 deg) of knee flexion, and assuming that the moment arm at this joint position is 0.035 m, then the muscular force exerted by the patellar tendon was 8000 N or 10 times the body weight (BW) of that subject. This method can be applied to the moment measurements from isokinetic or isometric tests in order to obtain the actual muscular force exerted. This is usually expressed relative to body weight to allow comparisons. Using a similar method, it was estimated that the maximum muscular force exerted during isokinetic knee extension ranged from 9 BW at 0.52 rad s^{-1} (30 deg s^{-1}) to 6 BW at 3.66 rad s^{-1} (210 deg s^{-1}) (Baltzopoulos, 1995b).

Another important aspect of muscle function assessment is the expression of maximum performance parameters such as moment, force and power as a ratio, relative to different anthropometric parameters (e.g. body mass, lean body mass, cross-sectional area) without considering the underlying relationship between the two parameters. This ratio is usually obtained by dividing the mean force, for example, by the mean body mass, without considering the regression line between force and body mass. A ratio relationship assumes that the regression line crosses the origin of the axes (i.e. the intercept is approximately zero). If despite a high correlation, a ratio relationship does not exist between moment and body mass then expressing the moment relative to body mass (Nm kg^{-1}) is representative of subjects with

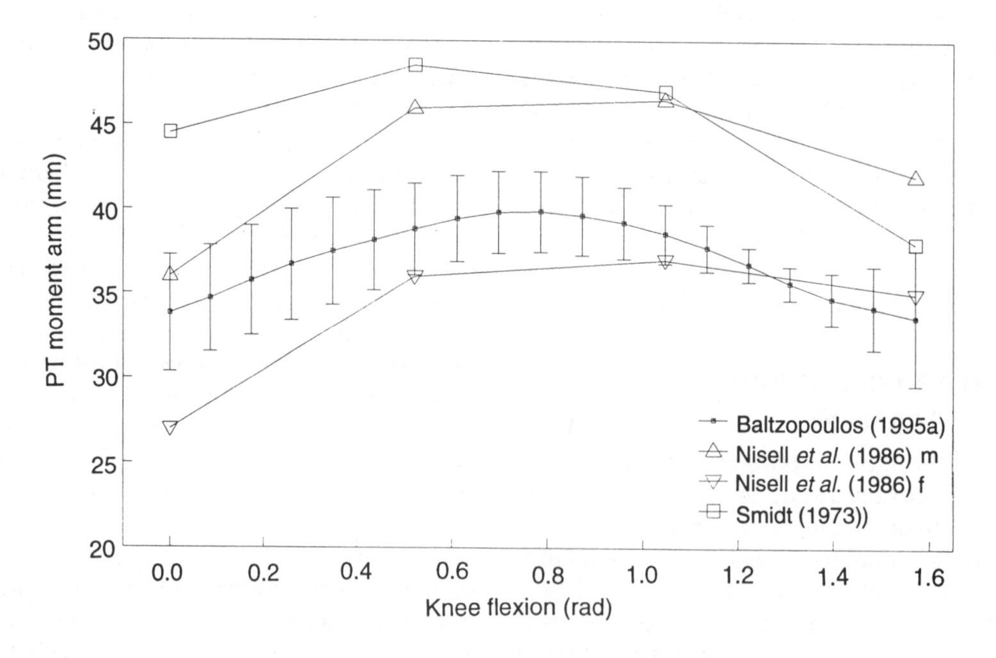

Figure 4.5 The patellar tendon moment arm during knee extension from different studies.

body mass close to the mean body mass. This, however, will over- or underestimate the moment for subjects with body mass further away from the mean body mass. Indeed the magnitude of the error in estimating the maximum moment from the ratio instead of the regression line, depends on the intercept (i.e. difference between regression and ratio lines) and the deviation of the subject's body mass from the mean body mass.

Another consideration when comparing muscle function between different groups over time is the use of an appropriate statistical technique. Analysis of covariance (ANCOVA) is necessary if the initial level of the dependent (measured) variable (e.g. maximum isokinetic moment) is different between the groups and the effects of training programmes over time are assessed. Multivariate ANOVA (MANOVA) or multivariate ANCOVA (MANCOVA) is necessary if a number of different muscle function parameters likely to affect each other, are measured and compared simultaneously.

The practical exercises in this chapter describe assessment of knee joint function at different joint angular velocities and positions. Similar parameters of muscle function during maximal voluntary activation (isokinetic or isometric) can be assessed in different groups of subjects using other muscle groups to examine the effects of age, sex and sport and the relationship of muscle function with various anthropometric parameters.

4.14 PRACTICAL 1: ASSESSMENT OF MUSCLE FUNCTION DURING ISOKINETIC KNEE EXTENSION AND FLEXION

4.14.1 PURPOSE

The purpose of this practical is to assess the maximum muscular moment (dynamic strength) of the knee extensor and flexor muscles at different concentric and eccentric knee joint angular velocities. This practical requires an isokinetic dynamometer for data collection. These devices are very expensive and may not be available in all laboratories. Data collected from a group of young female age group swimmers using a Biodex dynamometer are presented in Tables 4.1–4.3. These can be used for data analysis and discussion of the topics examined in this practical.

Table 4.1 Body mass, lean body mass and height of subjects (n =10)

Subject no.	*Body mass (kg)*	*Lean body mass (kg)*	*Height (m)*
1	51.6	39.5	1.57
2	49.4	38.1	1.57
3	58.1	41.2	1.69
4	48.1	37.0	1.62
5	62.5	46.0	1.62
6	58.7	42.9	1.55
7	54.5	38.9	1.52
8	46.5	37.2	1.62
9	68.4	54.1	1.76
10	56.2	39.4	1.53
Mean	55.4	41.4	1.60
SD	6.8	5.5	0.07

4.14.2 PROCEDURE

Record all data in the appropriate data sheet for this practical (Figure 4.6).

Table 4.2 Knee flexion moment (Nm) during isokinetic eccentric and concentric angular velocities

	Angular velocity (rad s^{-1})[a]							
	Eccentric				*Concentric*			
Subject no.	*4.19*	*3.14*	*2.09*	*1.05*	*1.05*	*2.09*	*3.14*	*4.19*
1	65	61	63	59	52	52	42	39
2	69	71	74	71	57	49	38	38
3	76	83	80	82	67	67	50	45
4	63	61	59	56	43	47	39	34
5	77	81	84	78	68	64	52	47
6	93	90	89	92	69	57	43	42
7	56	65	63	59	50	61	47	39
8	65	72	70	68	54	50	37	29
9	104	110	116	118	96	108	98	105
10	88	90	86	81	62	60	50	44

[a]1 rad s^{-1} is equal to an angular velocity of 57.296° s^{-1}.

Table 4.3 Knee extension moment (Nm) during isokinetic eccentric and concentric angular velocities

	Angular velocity (rad s^{-1})							
	Eccentric				*Concentric*			
Subject no.	*4.19*	*3.14*	*2.09*	*1.05*	*1.05*	*2.09*	*3.14*	*4.19*
1	137	140	139	132	123	105	105	101
2	128	131	134	130	122	104	78	83
3	179	183	195	186	169	141	116	105
4	152	153	151	144	132	108	82	72
5	179	184	173	169	157	115	96	87
6	180	185	187	191	168	128	98	87
7	171	169	173	166	154	119	97	84
8	159	157	161	112	131	103	82	71
9	253	249	245	238	202	162	139	121
10	159	179	175	169	152	118	98	85

1. Calibrate equipment according to the manufacturer's instructions and record date, subject name, gender, age, body mass, height and training status.
2. Measure or estimate other anthropometric parameters if required (for example lean body mass, cross-sectional area of muscle groups, segment circumference and volume, muscle mass etc.).
3. Allow the subjects general warm-up/stretching exercises. Position the subject on the dynamometer without attaching the input arm. A sitting position with the hips flexed at approximately 1.74 rad (100 deg) is recommended. A supine position may be preferable in order to increase muscular output and simulate movements where the hip angle is approximately neutral.

Side	Action	Parameter	Joint Angular Velocity (rad s^{-1})								
			Eccentric					Concentric			
			4.19	3.14	2.09	1.05	0	1.05	2.09	3.14	4.19
R	EXT	Maximum Moment (Nm)									
		Angular Position (rad))									
	FLX	Maximum Moment (Nm)									
		Angular Position (rad)									
		FLX/EXT Moment Ratio									
L	EXT	Maximum Moment (Nm)									
		Angular Position (rad)									
	FLX	Maximum Moment (Nm)									
		Angular Position (rad)									
		FLX/EXT Moment Ratio									
L/R EXT Moment Ratio											
L/R FLX Moment Ratio											

Figure 4.6 Data collection sheet (R = right, L = left, EXT = extension, FLX = flexion).

4. Align carefully the approximate joint axis of rotation with the axis of the dynamometer by modifying the subject's position and/or the dynamometer seat adjustments. For the knee test, align the lateral femoral epicondyle with the dynamometer axis and ensure that it remains in alignment throughout the test range of movement.
5. Attach the input arm of the dynamometer on the tibia above the malleoli and ensure that there is no movement of the leg relative to the input arm. Generally a rigid connection is required between the segment and the various parts of the input arm.
6. Secure all the other body parts not involved in the test with the appropriate straps. Ensure that the thigh, opposite leg, hips, chest and arms are appropriately stabilized. Make a note of the seat configuration and the joint positions in case you need to replicate the test on another occasion.
7. Provide written, clear instructions to the subject concerning the purpose of the test and the experimental procedure. Explain in detail the requirement for maximum voluntary effort throughout the test and the use of visual feedback to enhance muscular output. Allow the subject to ask any questions and be prepared to explain in detail the test requirements.
8. Familiarize the subject with the movement and allow at least five submaximal repetitions (extension–flexion throughout the range of movement) at all the test angular velocities.
9. Allow the subject to rest and, during this period, enter the appropriate data on the computer system, set the range of movement and perform the gravity correction procedure according to the instructions provided by the manufacturer of the dynamometer.

10. Start the test and allow 5–6 reciprocal repetitions (extension followed by flexion). The order of the test angular velocity should be randomized. Visual feedback and appropriate test instructions are adequate for maximum effort. If other forms of motivation are required (e.g. verbal encouragement) then make sure they are standardized and consistent between subjects.
11. After the test is completed, note the maximum moment for knee extension and flexion and the angular position where the maximum was recorded, on the data sheet for this practical. Allow 1–2 min rest and perform the test at the other angular velocities. Repeat the procedure for the other side.

4.14.3 DATA ANALYSIS

1. Plot the maximum moment of the knee extensors and flexors against the angular velocity of movement (moment–angular velocity relationship).
2. Compare the increase/decrease of the moment during the eccentric and concentric movements with previously published studies examining this relationship.
3. Discuss the physiological/mechanical explanation for these findings.
4. Calculate the flexion/extension ratio by dividing the corresponding maximum moment recorded at each speed and plot this ratio against angular velocity. What do you observe? Explain any increase or decrease at the different eccentric and concentric velocities.
5. Plot the angular position (knee flexion angle) of the maximum moment at different angular velocities. Is the maximum moment recorded at the same angular position at different angular velocities? What is the physiological/mechanical explanation for your findings?
6. If data for both sides have been collected, then calculate the bilateral moment ratio (left joint moment/right joint moment) at the different angular velocities. See if you can explain any bilateral differences.
7. Establish the relationship between maximum moment, body mass and lean body mass. Can you express the maximum moment relative to body mass or lean body mass as a ratio? Explain the rationale for your answer.

4.15 PRACTICAL 2: ASSESSMENT OF ISOMETRIC FORCE–JOINT POSITION RELATIONSHIP

4.15.1 PURPOSE

The purpose of this practical is to assess the maximum isometric moment (static strength) of the knee extensor muscles at different knee joint positions. Isometric force can be measured using relatively inexpensive instruments that are commercially available.

4.15.2 PROCEDURE

Record all data in the appropriate data sheet for this practical.

1. Record date, subject name, gender, age, body mass, height and training status.
2. Measure or estimate other anthropometric parameters if required (for example lean

body mass, cross-sectional area of muscle groups, segment circumference and volume, muscle mass etc.).

3. After some general warm-up/stretching exercises, position the subject on a bench lying on his/her side. A position with the hips flexed at approximately 1.74 rad (100 deg) is recommended. An extended position may be preferable to increase muscular output and simulate movements where the hip angle is approximately neutral.
4. Secure all the other body parts not involved in the test with appropriate straps. Ensure that the thigh, opposite leg, hips, chest and arms are appropriately stabilized.
   Make a note of the joint positions in case you need to replicate the test on another occasion. Attach the tensiometer or portable dynamometer to the limb near the malleoli. Ensure that the instrument is perpendicular to the tibia and on the sagittal plane (i.e. the plane formed by the tibia and femur). The movement must be performed on a plane parallel to the ground in order to avoid the effect of the gravitational force on the measurements. If the test is performed with the subject seated in a chair then the measurements of muscular moment are affected and must be corrected for the effect of the gravitational moment. For details of this procedure see Baltzopoulos and Brodie (1989).
5. Provide written, clear instructions to the subject concerning the purpose of the test and the experimental procedure. Explain in detail the requirement for maximum voluntary effort throughout the test and the use of feedback to enhance muscular output.
6. Familiarize the subject with the movement and allow at least two submaximal repetitions. An important aspect of isometric testing is the gradual increase of muscular force, avoiding sudden, ballistic movements. Allow the subject to ask any questions and be prepared to explain and demonstrate the test requirements.
7. Position the knee at approximately 90 deg of knee flexion, start the test and maintain maximum effort for 5–7 seconds. Verbal and/or visual feedback and appropriate test instructions are adequate for maximum effort. Ensure that feedback is standardized and consistent between subjects.
8. After the test is completed, note the maximum force recorded. Measure the distance between the point of application and the joint centre of rotation and calculate the moment for knee extension as the product of force and moment arm. Record the isometric moment and the angular position where the maximum was recorded, on the data sheet for this practical. Allow 1–2 min rest and perform the test at angular position intervals of 10 deg until full extension.

4.15.3 DATA ANALYSIS

1. Plot the maximum moment of the knee extensors against the angular joint position (moment–joint position relationship).
2. Explain the increase/decrease of the moment during the range of movement and compare these findings with previously published studies examining this relationship in other muscle groups.
3. Establish the physiological/mechanical explanation for these findings.
4. Calculate the muscular force from the equation: Moment = Force × Moment Arm. The moment arm of the knee extensors at different joint positions is presented in Figure 4.5. Is the force-position similar to the moment position relationship? What are the main

determinants of these relationships during knee extension and other joint movements such as knee and elbow flexion?

REFERENCES

Alway, S., Stray-Gundersen, J., Grumbt, W. and Gonyea, W. (1990) Muscle cross-sectional area and torque in resistance trained subjects. *Journal of Applied Physiology*, **60**, 86–90.

Aoyagi, Y. and Shephard, R. (1992) Aging and muscle function. *Sports Medicine*, **14**, 376–96.

Appen, L. and Duncan, P. (1986) Strength relationship of knee musculature: effects of gravity and sport. *Journal of Orthopaedic and Sports Physical Therapy*, **7**, 232–5.

Baltzopoulos, V. (1995a) A videofluoroscopy method for optical distortion correction and measurement of knee joint kinematics. *Clinical Biomechanics*, **10**, 85–92.

Baltzopoulos, V. (1995b) Muscular and tibio-femoral joint forces during isokinetic knee extension. *Clinical Biomechanics*, **10**, 208–14.

Baltzopoulos, V. and Brodie, D. (1989) Isokinetic dynamometry: applications and limitations. *Sports Medicine*, **8**, 101–16.

Baltzopoulos, V., Williams, J. and Brodie, D. (1991) Sources of error in isokinetic dynamometry: effects of visual feedback on maximum torque output. *Journal of Orthopaedic and Sports Physical Therapy*, **13**, 138–42.

Baratta, R. and Solomonow, M. (1991) The effects of tendon viscoelastic stiffness on the dynamic performance of isometric muscle. *Journal of Biomechanics*, **24**, 109–16.

Beam, W., Bartels, R. and Ward, R. (1982) The relationship of isokinetic torque to body weight in athletes. *Medicine and Science in Sports and Exercise*, **14**(2), 178.

Behm, D. and Sale, D. (1993) Velocity specificity of resistance training. *Sports Medicine*, **15**, 374–88.

Bell, G. and Wenger, H. (1992) Physiological adaptations to velocity-controlled resistance training. *Sports Medicine*, **13**, 234–44.

Bemben, M. (1991) Isometric muscle force production as a function of age in healthy 20 to 74 yr old men. *Medicine and Science in Sports and Exercise*, **23**, 1302–9.

Bishop, P., Cureton, K. and Collins, M. (1987) Sex differences in muscular strength in equally trained men and women. *Ergonomics*, **30**, 675–87.

Bobbert, M. and Harlaar, J. (1992) Evaluation of moment angle curves in isokinetic knee extension. *Medicine and Science in Sports and Exercise*, **25**, 251–9.

Bouisset, S. (1984) Are the classical tension–length and force–velocity relationships always valid in natural motor activities? in *Neural and Mechanical Control of Movement* (ed. M. Kumamoto), Yamaguchi Shoten, Kyoto, pp. 4–11.

Brooke, M. and Kaiser, K. (1974) The use and abuse of muscle histochemistry. *Annals of the New York Academy of Sciences*, **228**, 121–44.

Brooks, V. (1986) *The Neural Basis of Motor Control*. Oxford University Press, New York.

Burke, R. (1981) Motor units: anatomy, physiology, and functional organization, in *Handbook of Physiology* (ed. V. Brooks), American Physiological Society, Bethesola, pp. 345–422.

Cabri, J. (1991) Isokinetic strength aspects of human joints and muscles. *Critical Reviews in Biomedical Engineering*, **19**, 231–59.

Cavanagh, P. (1988) On muscle action versus muscle contraction. *Journal of Biomechanics*, **21**, 69.

Chapman, A. (1976) The relationship between length and the force–velocity curve of a single equivalent linear muscle during flexion of the elbow, in *Biomechanics IV* (ed. P. Komi), University Park Press, Baltimore, pp. 434–8.

Chapman, A. (1985) The mechanical properties of human muscle, in *Exercise and Sport Sciences Reviews* (ed. L. Terjung), Macmillan, New York, pp. 443–501.

Cheney, P. (1985) Role of cerebral cortex in voluntary movements. A review. *Physical Therapy*, **65**, 624–35.

Clarkson, P., Johnson, J., Dexradeur, D. *et al.* (1982) The relationship among isokinetic endurance, intial strength level and fibre type. *Research Quarterly for Exercise and Sport*, **53**, 15–19.

Cote, C., Simoneau, J., Lagasse, P. *et al.* (1988) Isokinetic strength training protocols: do they include skeletal muscle fibre hypertrophy? *Archives of Physical Medicine and Rehabilitation*, **69**, 281–5.

Coyle, E., Feiring, D., Rotkis, T. *et al.* (1981) Specificity of power improvements through slow and fast isokinetic training. *Journal of Applied Physiology*, **51**, 1437–42.

Dummer, G., Clark, D., Vaccano, P. *et al.* (1985) Age related differences in muscular strength and muscular endurance among female master's swimmers. *Research Quarterly for Exercise and Sport*, **56**, 97–102.

Duncan, P., Chandler, J., Cavanaugh, D. *et al.* (1989) Mode and speed specificity of eccentric and concentric exercise. *Journal of Orthopaedic and Sports Physical Therapy*, **11**, 70–5.

Enoka, R. and Stuart, D. (1984) Henneman's 'size principle': current issues. *Trends in Neurosciences*, **7**, 226–8.

Figoni, S., Christ, C. and Massey, B. (1988) Effects of speed, hip and knee angle, and gravity on hamstring to quadriceps torque ratios. *Journal of Orthopaedic and Sports Physical Therapy*, **9**, 287–91.

Fillyaw, M., Bevins, T. and Fernandez, L. (1986) Importance of correcting isokinetic peak torque for the effect of gravity when calculating knee flexor to extensor muscle ratios. *Physical Therapy*, **66**, 23–9.

Froese, E. and Houston, M. (1985) Torque–velocity characteristics and muscle fibre type in human vastus lateralis. *Journal of Applied Physiology*, **59**, 309–14.

Frontera, W., Hughes, V., Lutz, K. and Evans, W. (1991) A cross-sectional study of muscle strength and mass in 45- to 78-yr-old men and women. *Journal of Applied Physiology*, **71**, 644–50.

Gowitzhe, B. and Milner, M. (1988) *Scientific Basis of Human Movement*. Williams and Wilkins, Baltimore.

Green, H. (1986) Muscle power: fibre type recruitment metabolism and fatigue, in *Human Muscle Power* (eds N. Jones, N. McCartney and A. McComas), Human Kinetics, Champaign, pp. 65–79.

Gregor, R., Edgerton, V., Perrine, J. *et al.* (1979) Torque velocity relationships and muscle fibre composition in elite female athletes. *Journal of Applied Physiology*, **47**, 388–92.

Gustafsson, B. and Pinter, M. (1985) On factors determining orderly recruitment of motor units: a role for intrinsic membrane properties. *Trends in Neurosciences*, **8**, 431–3.

Harrison, P. (1983) The relationship between the distribution of motor unit mechanical properties and the forces due to recruitment and to rate coding for the generation of muscle force. *Brain Research*, **264**, 311–15.

Henneman, E. (1957) Relation between size of neurons and their susceptibility to discharge. *Science*, **126**, 1345–7.

Heyward, V., Johannes-Ellis, S. and Romer, J. (1986) Gender differences in strength. *Research Quarterly for Exercise and Sport*, **57**, 154–9.

Hill, A. (1938) The heat of shortening and the dynamic constants of muscle. *Proceedings of the Royal Society of London*, **126B**, 136–95.

Hinson, M., Smith, W. and Funk, S. (1979) Isokinetics: a clarification. *Research Quarterly*, **50**, 30–5.

Hislop, H. and Perrine, J. (1967) The isokinetic concept of exercise. *Physical Therapy*, **47**, 114–17.

Hoffman, T., Stauffer, R. and Jackson, A. (1979) Sex difference in strength. *American Journal of Sports Medicine*, **74**, 264–7.

Hortobagyi, T. and Katch, F. (1990) Eccentric and concentric torque–velocity relationships during arm flexion and extension. *European Journal of Applied Physiology*, **60**, 395–401.

Kereshi, S., Manzano, G. and McComas, A. (1983) Impulse conduction velocities in human biceps brachii muscles. *Experimental Neurology*, **80**, 652–62.

Komi, P. (1984) Biomechanics and neuromuscular performance. *Medicine and Science in Sports and Exercise*, **16**, 26–8.

Komi, P. (1986) The stretch-shortening cycle and human power out-put, in *Human Muscle Power* (eds N. Jones, N. McCartney and A. McComas), Human Kinetics, Champaign, IL, pp. 27–39.

Komi, P., Viitasalo, J., Rauramaa, R. and Vihko, V. (1978) Effects of isometric strength training on mechanical, electrical and metabolic aspects of muscle function. *European Journal of Applied Physiology*, **40**, 45–55.

Kroll, W., Bultman, L., Kilmer, W. and Boucher, J. (1990) Anthropometric predictors of isometric arm strength in males and females. *Clinical Kinesiology*, **44**, 5–11.

Kulig, K., Andrews, J. and Hay, J. (1984) Human strength curves, in *Exercise and Sport Sciences Reviews* (ed. R. Terjung), Macmillan, New York, pp. 417–66.

Laubach, L. (1976) Comparative muscular strength of men and women: a review of the literature. *Aviation, Space and Environmental Medicine*, **47**, 534–42.

Lesmes, G., Costill, D., Coyle, E. and Fink, W. (1978) Muscle strength and power changes during maximum isokinetic training. *Medicine and Science in Sports and Exercise*, **10**, 266–9.

MacDougall, J., Sale, D., Elder, G. and Sutton, J. (1982) Muscle ultrastructural characteristics of elite powerlifters and bodybuilders. *European Journal of Applied Physiology*, **48**, 117–26.

Maughan, R., Watson, J. and Weir, J. (1983) Strength and cross-sectional area of human skeletal muscle. *Journal of Physiology*, **388**, 37–49.

Milner-Brown, H., Stein, R. and Lee, R. (1975) Synchronization of human motor units: possible roles of exercise and supraspinal reflexes. *Electroencephalography and Clinical Neurophysiology*, **38**, 245–54.

Morrow, J. and Hosler, W. (1981) Strength comparisons in untrained men and trained women athletes. *Medicine and Science in Sports and Exercise*, **13**, 194–7.

Nemeth, P., Solanki, L., Gordon, D. *et al.* (1986) Uniformity of metabolic enzymes within individual motor units. *Journal of Neuroscience*, **6**, 892–8.

Nisell, R., Nemeth, G. and Ohlsen, H. (1986) Joint forces in extension of the knee. *Acta Orthopedica Scandinavica*, **57**, 41–6.

Perrin, D. (1993) *Isokinetic Exercise and Assessment*. Human Kinetics, Champaign, IL.

Perrin, D., Robertson, R. and Ray, R. (1987) Bilateral isokinetic peak torque, torque acceleration energy, power, and work relationships in athletes and nonathletes. *Journal of Orthopaedic and Sports Physical Therapy*, **9**, 184–9.

Perrine, J. and Edgerton, V. (1978) Muscle force–velocity and power–velocity relationships under isokinetic loading. *Medicine and Science in Sports and Exercise*, **10**, 159–66.

Pollack, G. (1983) The cross-bridge theory. *Physiological Reviews*, **63**, 1049–113.

Prietto, C. and Caiozzo, V. (1989) The in vivo force–velocity relationship of the knee flexors and extensors. *American Journal of Sports Medicine*, **17**, 607–11.

Ryushi, T., Hakkinen, K., Kauhanen, H. and Komi, P. (1988) Muscle fibre characteristics, muscle cross-sectional area and force production in strength athletes, physically active males and females. *Scandinavian Journal of Sports Sciences*, **10**, 7–15.

Sale, D., McDougall, D., Upton, A. and McComas, A. (1983) Effect of strength training upon motoneuron excitability in man. *Medicine and Science in Sports and Exercise*, **15**, 57–62.

Schantz, P., Randal-Fox, A., Hutchison, W. *et al.* (1983) Muscle fibre type distribution of muscle cross-sectional area and maximum voluntary strength in humans. *Acta Physiologica Scandinavica*, **117**, 219–26.

Shephard, R. (1991) Handgrip dynamometry, Cybex measurements and lean mass as markers of the aging of muscle function. *British Journal of Sports Medicine*, **25**, 204–8.

Simoneau, J., Lortie, G., Boulay, M. *et al.* (1985) Human skeletal muscle fibre type alteration with high-intensity intermittent training. *European Journal of Applied Physiology*, **54**, 250–3.

Smidt, G. (1973) Biomechanical analysis of knee flexion and extension. *Journal of Biomechanics*, **6**, 79–92.

Stauber, W. (1989) Eccentric action of muscles: physiology, injury and adaptations, in *Exercise and Sport Sciences Reviews* (ed. K. Pandolph), Williams and Wilkins, Baltimore, pp. 157–85.

Tesch, P. and Karlsson, P. (1985) Muscle fibre type and size in trained and untrained muscles of elite athletes. *Journal of Applied Physiology*, **59**, 1716–20.

Thistle, H., Hislop, H., Moffroid, M. and Lohman, E. (1967) Isokinetic contraction: a new concept of resistive exercise. *Archives of Physical Medicine and Rehabilitation*, **48**, 279–82.

Thomas, D., White, M., Sagar, G. and Davies, C. (1987) Electrically evoked isokinetic plantar flexor torque in males. *Journal of Applied Physiology*, **63**, 1499–502.

Thorstensson, A., Grimby, G. and Karlsson, J. (1976) Force–velocity relations and fibre composition in human knee extensor muscle. *Journal of Applied Physiology*, **40**, 12–16.

Tihanyi, J., Apor, P. and Petrekanits, M. (1987) Force–velocity–power characteristics for extensors of lower extremities, in *Biomechanics X-B* (ed. B. Johnson), Human Kinetics, Champaign, IL, pp. 707–12.

Watkins, M. (1993) Evaluation of skeletal muscle performance, in *Muscle Strength* (ed. K. Harms-Ringdahl), Churchill Livingstone, London, pp. 19–36.

Westing, S. and Seger, J. (1989) Eccentric and concentric torque–velocity characteristics, torque output comparisons, and gravity effect torque corrections for the quadriceps and hamstring muscles in females. *International Journal of Sports Medicine*, **10**, 175–80.

Westing, S., Seger, J., Karlson, E. and Ekblom, B. (1988) Eccentric and concentric torque–velocity characteristics of the quadriceps femoris in man. *European Journal of Applied Physiology*, **58**, 100–4.

Westing, S., Seger, J. and Thorstensson, A. (1991) Isoacceleration: a new concept of resistive exercise. *Medicine and Science in Sports and Exercise*, **23**, 631–5.

Wickiewicz, T., Roy, R., Powell, P., Perrine, J. and Edgerton, R. (1984) Muscle architecture and force velocity in humans. *Journal of Applied Physiology*, **57**, 435–43.

Wilkie, D. (1950) The relation between force and velocity in human muscle. *Journal of Physiology (London)*, **110**, 249–54.

POSTURE 5

P. H. Dangerfield

5.1 INTRODUCTION

The human is unique among mammals and primates in maintaining an upright posture. During human evolution, as the hindlimbs progressively assumed the role of locomotion, the vertebral column adapted from a horizontal compressed structure to a vertical weight-bearing rod. Its relationship with the pelvic girdle distally and the skull proximally also changed. The centre of gravity of primates has also evolved being shifted backwards towards the hindlimbs as the length and musculature of the hindlimbs increased. At the same time, to reduce energy expenditure in countering needless body rotation about the centre of gravity, forces for forward propulsion passed through the centre of gravity. Early changes in body form also allowed primates to adopt sitting positions with the forelimb being freed for manipulative functions. The flexibility of the vertebral column also increased as did the size of the vertebrae which, in the lumbar region, developed to cope with increased compression forces resulting from upright posture. Additionally, changes in the role of the sternum and abdominal muscles in maintaining less trunkal stiffness resulted in the wide shallow chest of humans with a reduced angulation of the ribs.

Adopting an upright posture and acquiring freedom to use the upper limb, independently of the legs, increased the dynamic demands on the vertebral column. It developed the capability to produce and accumulate moments of force while transmitting and concentrating forces from other parts of the body. These forces include dynamic compressive forces, in which the intervertebral disc acts as a flexible link, lowering the resonate frequency of the spine. This then allows the spinal musculature and ligaments to dissipate energy. As a consequence, changing to an upright posture has resulted not only in specific human functional abilities, but also unique disabilities. A considerable range of morbidity problems, in the workplace and in sport, can be attributed to the human's upright stance and to adopting a bad posture when sitting. Such conditions might include spinal curvatures of an acquired type, or the problems sometimes developed by sports participants and professional musicians due to degenerative disease of the lumbar spine and other joints. These may be accompanied by body asymmetry, which itself might adversely affect the normal posture and inertial properties of the body. This subject has been reviewed in detail by Dangerfield (1994).

Posture can be studied from a number of different aspects. These include evolution of bipedalism and the upright position, changes during development in infancy and childhood, mechanisms of physiological control and its role in health and its importance in sport, exercise and ergonomics. It is therefore important to understand the concept of posture and to examine some of the methods which have been developed to assess it, allowing investigation of the factors which

Kinanthropometry and Exercise Physiology Laboratory Manual: Tests, procedures and data Edited by Roger Eston and Thomas Reilly. Published in 1996 by E & FN Spon. ISBN 0 419 17880 5

influence it in different states, such as rest and movement.

A clear definition of posture in the context of the upright stance of the human is difficult because it is rare for an individual to remain in a static position; our daily routine is essentially dynamic and involves movement. However, posture is always the relative orientation of the constituent parts of the body in space at any moment in time. Maintaining an upright position requires constant adjustment by muscles in the trunk and limbs, under the automatic and conscious control of the central nervous system to counter the effects of gravity. Posture should therefore be regarded as a position assumed by the body before it makes its next move (Roaf, 1977).

Assessment of posture requires consideration of the human body in an upright stance, in readiness for the next movement. This may be measured using standard anthropometric equipment and methods. For example, if the working day includes sitting, sitting height should be measured. Good posture has been developed in cultures where sitting cross-legged leads to strong back muscles (Roaf, 1977).

5.2 CURVATURES AND MOVEMENT OF THE VERTEBRAL COLUMN

The normal vertebral column possesses well-marked curvatures in the sagittal plane in the cervical, thoracic, lumbar and pelvic regions. Three million years of evolution have caused rounding of the thorax and pelvis as an adaptation to bipedal gait. In infancy, functional muscle development and growth exert a major influence on the way the curvatures in the column take shape and also on changes in the proportional size of individual vertebrae, in particular in the lumbar region. The lumbar curvature becomes important for maintaining the centre of gravity of the trunk over the legs when walking commences. In addition, changes in body proportions exert a major influence on the subsequent shape of the curvatures in the column.

The cervical curvature is lordotic (Greek: I bend); that is, the curvature is convex in the anterior direction. It is the least marked vertebral curvature and extends from the atlas to the second thoracic vertebra. The thoracic curve is kyphotic (Greek: bent forwards): in other words the curvature is concave in the anterior direction (Figure 5.1). It extends from the second to the twelfth thoracic vertebrae. This curvature is caused by the increased posterior depth of the thoracic vertebral bodies. It

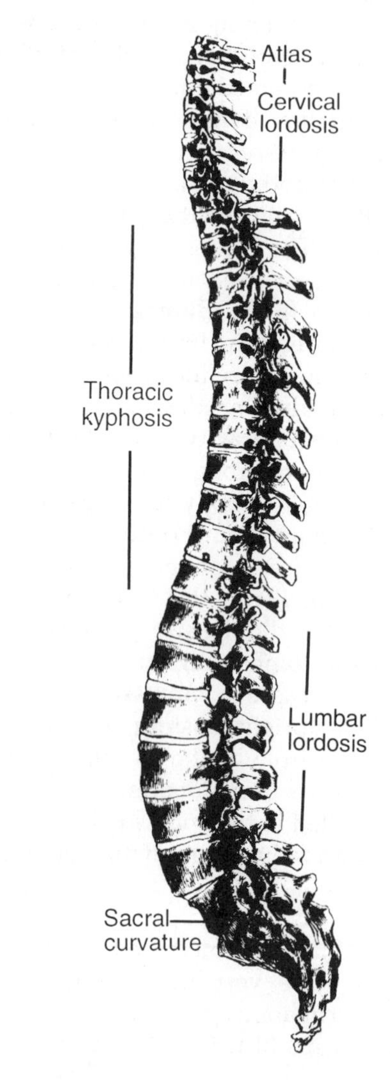

Figure 5.1 The curvatures of the vertebral column.

appears to be at its minimum during the pubertal growth spurt (Willner and Johnson, 1983). The lumbar curve is naturally lordotic and has a greater magnitude in the female. It extends from the twelfth thoracic vertebra to the lumbosacral angle, with an increased convexity of the last three segments due to greater anterior depth of intervertebral discs and some anterior wedging of the vertebral bodies. The curvature develops in response to gravitational forces, which arise as the child assumes the upright position during sitting and standing, and to the forces exerted between the psoas major and abdominal muscles and the erector spinae muscle. The lordosis increases steadily during growth (Willner and Johnson, 1983). Within the pelvis, the curve is concave anteroinferior and involves the sacrum and coccygeal vertebrae, extending from the lumbosacral joint to the apex of the coccyx.

The cervical and lumbar regions of the vertebral column are the most mobile regions, although, with the exception of the atlanto-occipital and atlanto-axial joints, little movement is possible between each adjacent vertebra. It is a summation of movement throughout the vertebral column which permits the human to enjoy a wide range of mobility. Anatomically, the movements are flexion and extension, lateral flexion to the left or right and rotation. Anatomical circumduction occurs only in the mid-thoracic region as elsewhere any lateral flexion is always accompanied by some rotation (Davis, 1959).

When physical tasks are undertaken, the body should normally be in a relaxed position which evokes the least postural stress. If forces are imposed on the body which create stress, the risk of damage to biological structures increases. This is referred to as postural strain (Weiner, 1982). Postural strain causes prolonged static loading in affected muscles.

The loading of the spine is localized in the erector spinae muscles and eventually leads to pain; for example, pain is a common result of sitting uncomfortably in a badly designed chair. The eventual result of excessive strain will be an injury. In the context of the spine, the more inappropriate the strain on the vertebral column, the greater is the likelihood of back injury. The lumbar region of the spine is the most susceptible to athletic and other injuries and can affect up to 80% of the population (Alexander, 1985). The reasons for the high risk of injury are due to the fundamental weakness of the structure itself, loading forces encountered in everyday living such as body weight, muscle contractions and external loading, and recreational and sporting activities. These all contribute to the development of postural strain and injury.

Injury itself is caused by activities that increase weight loading, rotational stresses or back arching. The result is damage to the intervertebral disc, ligaments or muscles and secondary effects which affect the sciatic and other nerves. Severe trauma might result in a fracture to the vertebral column. Symptoms of damage will include pain, stiffness and numbness or paraesthesia. It is also important to identify whether the pain was sudden in onset, such as after lifting an object, or more gradual without any obvious antecedent. Such back pain is often difficult to quantify or even prove to be a physical problem and not psychosomatic. Objective quantification is difficult (D'Orazio, 1993). As the medical problems of diagnosis, treatment and rehabilitation as well as the extensive range of biomechanical and other investigations possible in this field are beyond the scope of this chapter, the reader should consult the appropriate orthopaedic and other literature.

5.3 DEFINING AND QUANTIFICATION OF POSTURE

5.3.1 INERTIAL CHARACTERISTICS

When maintaining an erect and well-balanced position, with little muscle activity, the line of gravity of the body extends in a line from the level of the external auditory meatus, anterior to the dens of the axis, anterior to the body of the second thoracic vertebra and the body of the twelfth thoracic vertebra and the fifth lumbar vertebra to lie anterior to the sacrum (Klausen, 1965) (Figure 5.2). As a result, the vertebral bodies and intervertebral discs act as a weight-bearing pillar from the base of the skull to the sacrum. Furthermore, there is a cephalocaudal increase in the cross-sectional surface area of the discs and vertebral bodies (Pal and Routal, 1986). There is also a sexual dimorphism, with females having a lower width to depth ratio than males, due to the heavier body build of the male (Taylor and Twomey, 1984).

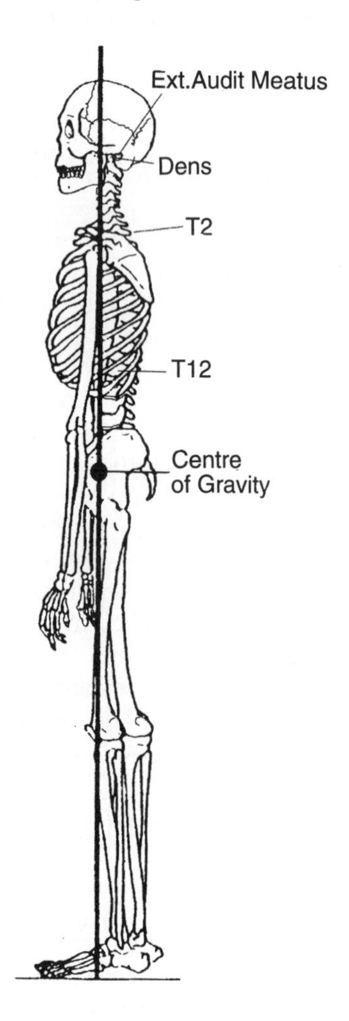

Figure 5.2 The line of centre of gravity of the body.

5.3.2 ANTHROPOMETRY AND POSTURE

Extensive literature is available which details anthropometric techniques, applied to biology, medicine and ergonomics (Weiner, and Lourie, 1969; Hrdlicka, 1972; Cameron, 1986; Pheasant, 1986; Lohman *et al.*, 1988). The actual techniques employed in each field are similar, although the definition of the measured dimensions may vary. They include direct surface measurements, employing devices for measuring length, height and mass. Indirect methods include ultrasound, x-rays (conventional radiographs and computerized tomography (CT)) and magnetic resonance imaging (MRI). By taking several readings at different places in different planes, three-dimensional descriptions of body shape may be obtained.

Biostereometrics refers to the spatial and spatiotemporal analysis of form and function based on analytical geometry. It deals with three-dimensional measurements of biological subjects which vary with time, due to forces such as growth and movement. Adapted to sport and movement science, biostereometrics enables dynamic movement and technical performance in any particular sport to be studied. Only recently have researchers come to accept this concept of dynamic movement. This is due in part to the complexity of movement and the additional difficulty in analysing data from such studies as this requires expensive and powerful computers. In consequence, assessment of body shape, particularly in biomechanics and medicine, has been governed by the illusion that the body should be examined in the anatomical position, standing still and maintaining this position like a shop dummy. This is clearly unrealistic.

It is difficult, without a clear definition of the term *Posture*, to offer precise and clear methods for measuring and thus quantifying it. As a result, methods used to quantify body shape can by inference be applied to the understanding of posture.

5.4 ASSESSMENT OF POSTURE AND BODY SHAPE

Methods employed in assessment of body shape can be considered in two groups:

1. Measurements in a static phase of posture.
2. Measurements in dynamic and changing posture.

5.4.1 MEASUREMENTS IN A STATIC PHASE OF POSTURE

These measurements involve quantification of the normal physiological curves of the vertebral column, usually in the erect position. By the adoption of a standardized position (usually an erect position), the measurement can tested for reproducibility (Ulijaszek and Lourie, 1994).

(a) Measurement of spinal length, curvature and spinal shrinkage

Clinical and biological measurement of spinal length, curvature and shrinkage is needed to understand fully the effect of posture on the human body. This applies in both sport and medical contexts.

Various techniques are available to assess posture. These range from invasive criterion techniques such as conventional radiography and computerized tomography which involve potential exposure to radiation, and magnetic resonence imaging. Other techniques involve light-based systems which negate the risks of radiation exposure. More simple and less expensive manual techniques of assessing posture are also widely used. These techniques are summarized below.

(b) Non-invasive manual techniques of assessing posture

Accurate measurement of height and length can be achieved using anthropometric equipment such as the Harpenden Stadiometer and Anthropometer (Holtain Ltd). Such equipment is portable and may be carried to field conditions allowing lengths such as biacromial diameter, tibial length, or other parameters to be measured (Figure 5.3). These instruments incorporate a counter recorder for ease of reading which reduces the likelihood of recording error.

Profile measurements which can be used to assess body angles, such as that between the spine and the vertical, may be recorded photographically. Such records are permanent and offer the opportunity to record changes in posture and position over time, such as before and after athletic events. The drawbacks are expense and time. Time constraints may be overcome by using either Polaroid instant film or electronic still cameras. Contemporary electronic cameras have the advantage of being linked directly to a personal computer via a frame grabber for

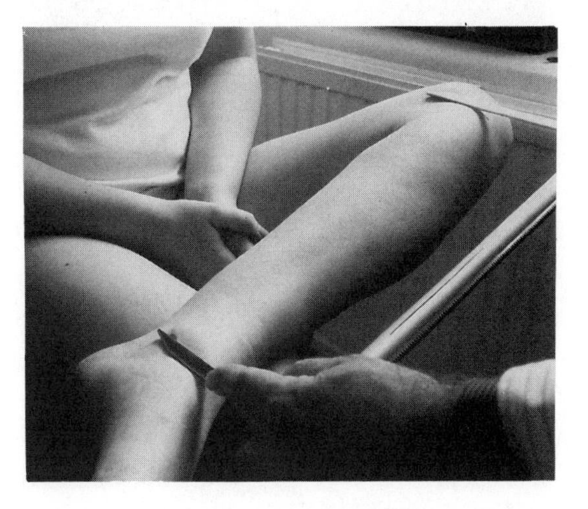

Figure 5.3 Holtain anthropometer used to measure tibial length. A counter recorder is employed which gives an instant and accurate readout of length.

quantification by means of appropriate image analysis software (Canon Ion camera). This field will develop rapidly in the future.

The most commonly assessed passive movement is spinal flexion. This is frequently done by visual inspection in the medical clinical situation, and thus is often undertaken inaccurately. Alternatively, it is also feasible to measure spinal flexion using a simple tape to measure the increase in spinal length, in different positions of flexion or extension, between skin markings made over the spinous processes.

In order to achieve accuracy in flexion measurements, goniometers and inclinometers are used. These simple instruments can measure a wide range of other spinal and pelvic angles and positions to a high degree of accuracy and reproducibility.

(c) The kyphometer

The kyphometer is a device developed to measure the angles of kyphosis and lordosis within the vertebral column (Figures 5.4 and 5.5) (Straumann Ltd, Welwyn Garden City, UK). A dial indicates the angle between the feet placed on the spine. The angle of thoracic kyphosis is estimated by placing the feet over the T1 and T12 vertebrae. This measurement is both accurate and reproducible. The angle decreases with inspiration and increases again with expiration and so care should be taken to standardize the measurement tech-

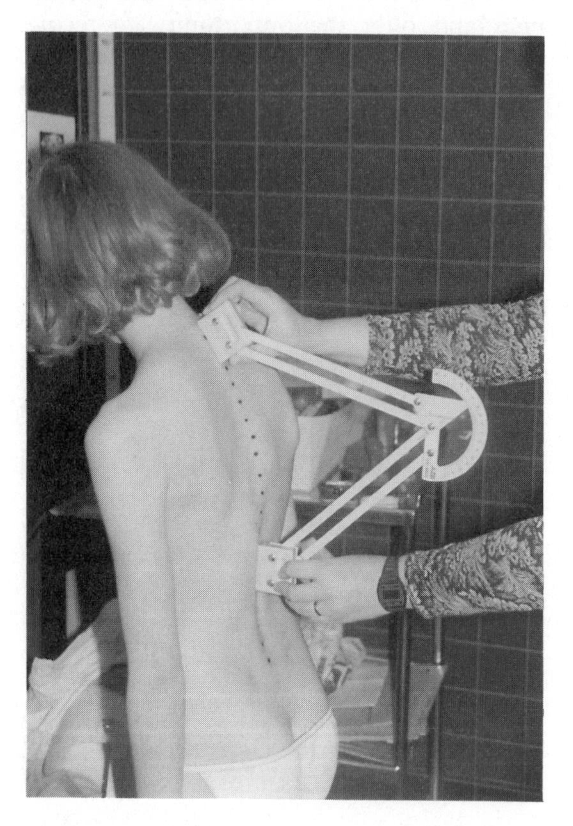

Figure 5.4 Using the kyphometer to measure thoracic kyphosis on a subject. The angle is read off the dial on the instrument.

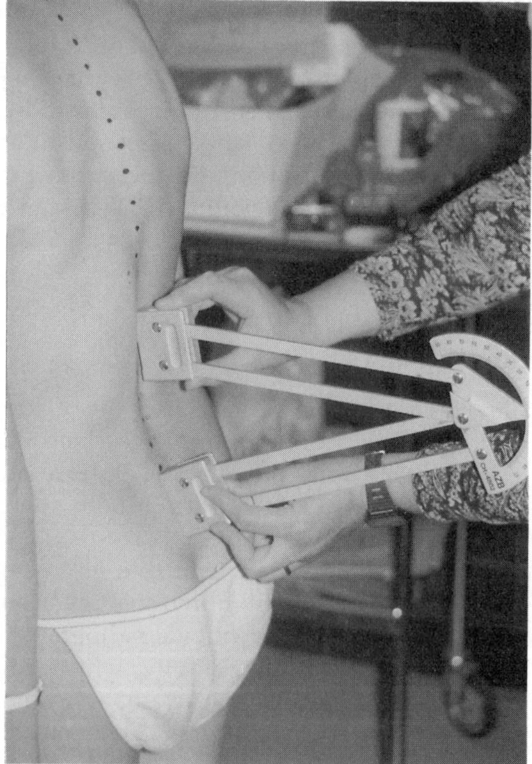

Figure 5.5 Measuring lumbar lordosis using the kyphometer.

nique with the appropriate stage of the respiratory cycle (Salisbury and Porter, 1987). Lumbar lordosis is measured between T12 and L1 vertebrae and is also affected by the respiration cycle. It is likewise affected by sexual dimorphism between the male and female subject, being larger in postpubertal females. However, experience has found that lumbar kyphosis is less easy to measure accurately than thoracic kyphosis (Dangerfield *et al.*, 1987). Both these measurements have been experimentally correlated with the same measurements undertaken on erect spinal radiographs (Dangerfield *et al.*, 1987; Hewling *et al.*, 1987; Ohlen *et al.*, 1989).

(d) Goniometers

Goniometers are used by orthopaedic surgeons and physiotherapists in measuring limb and trunk joint angles and are also used to measure flexion in the spine. They offer rapid and low cost methods of quantifying posture and spinal mobility by the measurement of angles in the spine, such as the proclive and declive angles (Figures 5.6–5.8). These angles can be expanded to measurements at each level of the vertebral column and can thus give accurate indications of the shape of the entire vertebral column. Ranges of spinal mobility may be useful in studying athletic performance but again due allowance should be made for age and sex (Tsai and Wredmark, 1993).

The same instrument may be used to assess the lateral flexibility of the spine by placing the dial over T1 vertebra and then asking the subject to flex to the right and to the left. This measurement is useful in assessing spinal movement in patients with deformity or arthritic diseases. Techniques for skin marking may also facilitate simple but accurate measurement of spinal flexion, and offer a useful measure of physical movement (MacRae and Wright, 1969; Rae *et al.*, 1984).

(e) The scoliometer

Other goniometers have been specially devised for studying the spine in scoliosis clinics. The OSI Scoliometer is used, for example, to quantify the hump deformity of scoliosis in the coronal plane (Orthopaedic Systems Inc, Hayward, CA, USA). A ball bearing in a glass tube aligns itself to the lowest point of the tube when placed across the hump-deformity, permitting a reading of the angle of trunk inclination (ATI) from a scale on the instrument (Figure 5.9). This angle is a measure of the magnitude of the rib-cage or lumbar deformity, associated with the lateral curvature of the spine.

(f) Other methods

Another method for quantifying body shape is to reproduce the outline of the structure under consideration using a rod–matrix device or a flexicurve. Contour outlines of the trunk, both in the horizontal and vertical plane, can be measured using a rod–matrix device such as the Formulator Body Contour tracer (Dangerfield and Denton, 1986) (Figure 5.10) or a flexicurve (Tillotson and Burton, 1991). Both these methods give a permanent record of shape by tracing the outline obtained onto paper but suffer from the tedium of use if more than one tracing is required. They are used in recording rib-cage shape and thoracic and lumbar lordosis and, in athletes, may be applied to assessment of lumbar movements following exercise.

These techniques are simple to employ but can be time consuming and laborious in practical use. Accuracy depends on experience of the observer and careful use of the instrument. Furthermore, reproducibility of data collection is essential. Unfortunately, in assessing movement and posture related to the spine, the technique used is often flawed, due to practical difficulties in se-

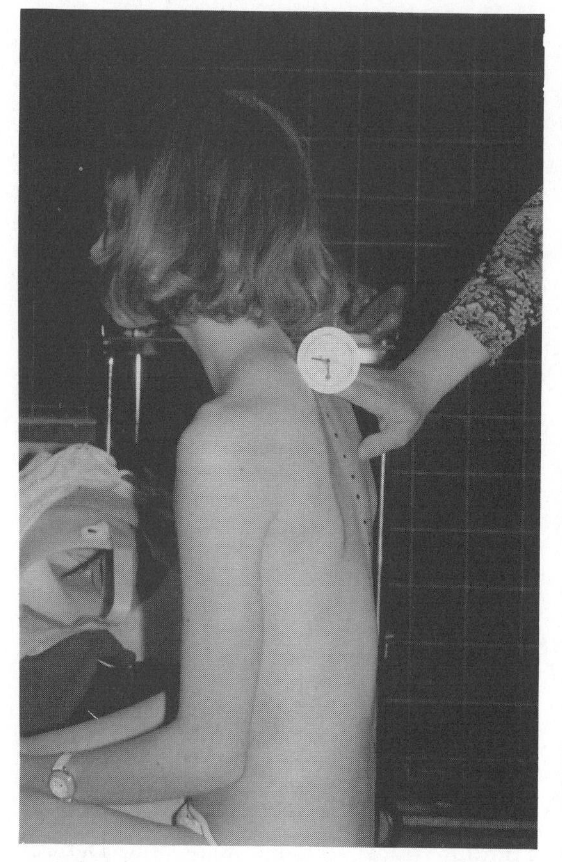

Figure 5.6 A goniometer used to measure the proclive angle, the angle between the spine and vertical at the level of the 7th cervical vertebra.

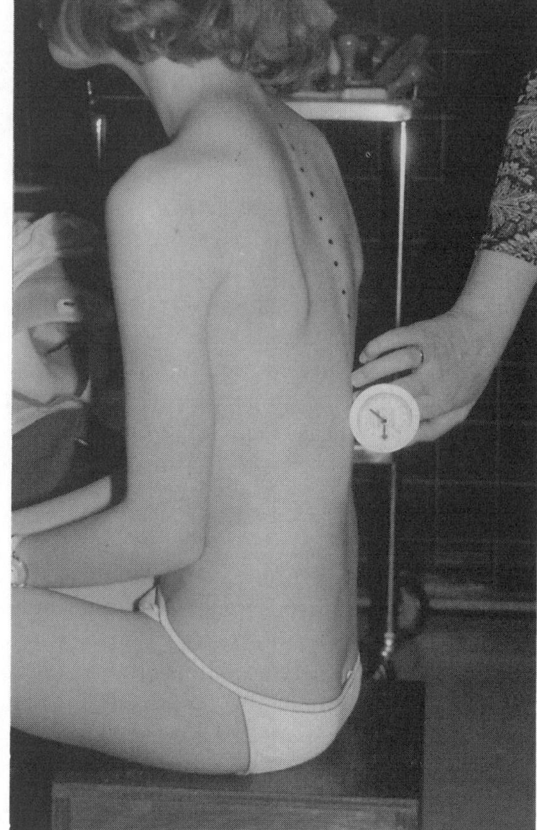

Figure 5.7 Measuring the angle at the thoracolumbar junction.

parating one particular movement from another within a complex anatomical structure.

5.5 OTHER CLINICALLY BASED CRITERION TECHNIQUES OF ASSESSING POSTURE

5.5.1 PHOTOGRAPHIC METHODS

Moiré photography employs optical interference patterns to record the three-dimensional shape of a surface. It has been used to evaluate pelvic and trunk rotation and also trunk deformity (Willner, 1979; Suzuki *et al.*, 1981; Asazuma *et al.*, 1986).

Stereophotogrammetry, originally developed for cartography, has been adopted in the evaluation of structural deformity of the trunk and for posture measurement. Two cameras are used to take overlapping pairs of photographs. These can be analysed to produce a three-dimensional contour map of the subject and can be described as points in terms of x, y and z coordinates (Sarasate and Ostman, 1986). This technique has found limited application in the study of scoliosis, a condition in which the vertebral column develops a lateral curvature and vertebral rotation, frequently leading to severe physical deformity (Figure 5.11). Scoliotic curva-

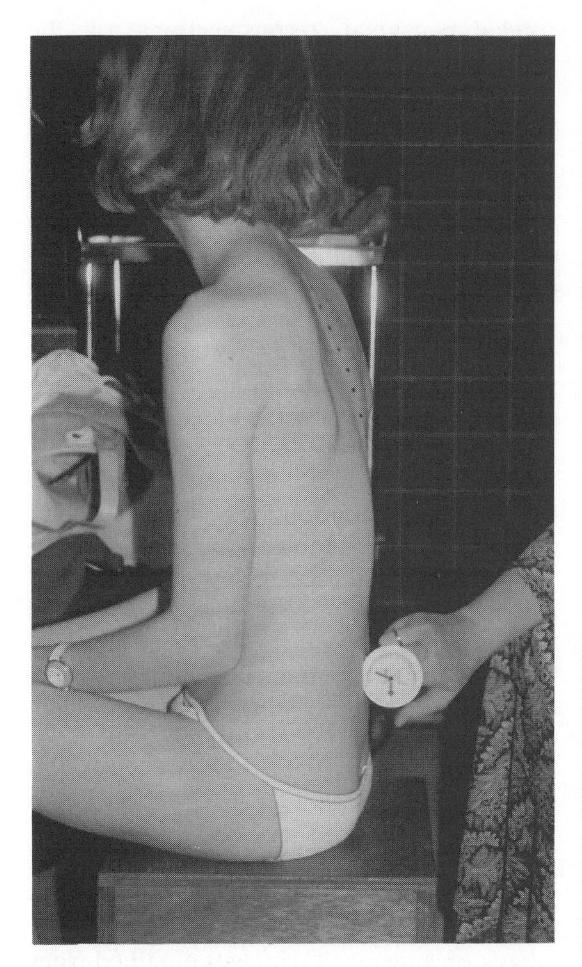

Figure 5.8 Measuring the declive angle at the lumbar–sacral junction.

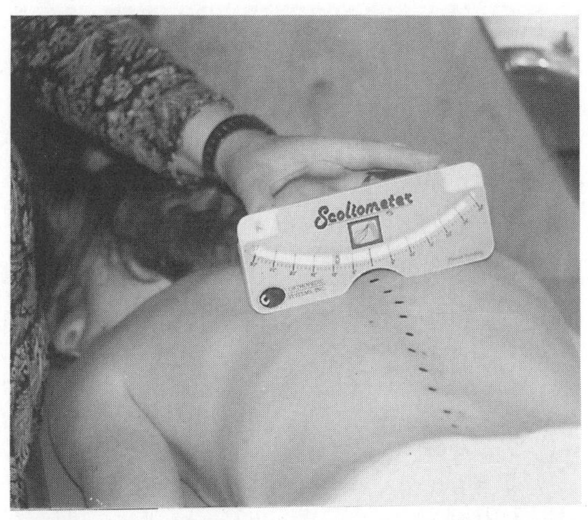

Figure 5.9 The OSI scoliometer used to measure the angle of trunk inclination (ATI) in the spine of a scoliosis subject lying prone.

tures may be due to primary pathological conditions but can also result from leg length inequality or muscle imbalance encountered in sports such as tennis, or discus and javelin throwing (Burwell and Dangerfield, 1992).

An extension of this technique is stereoradiography where two x-ray images are used instead of photographs. This technique is invasive and potentially hazardous due to the use of ionizing radiation. Consequently, it has found only limited application.

Non-invasive methods of postural assessment employ either scanning light beams or

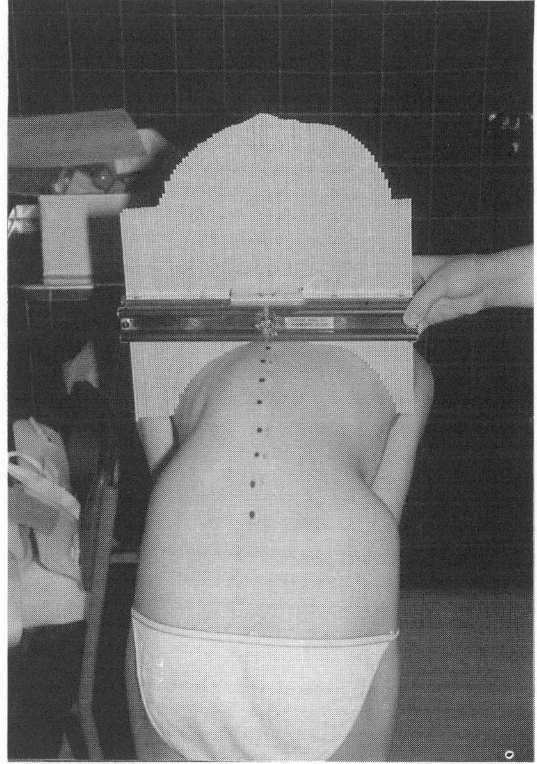

Figure 5.10 Formulator Body Contour Tracer used to record cross-sectional shape of the thorax in a patient with scoliosis (a lateral curvature of the spine causing a rib-hump deformity and asymmetry of the thorax).

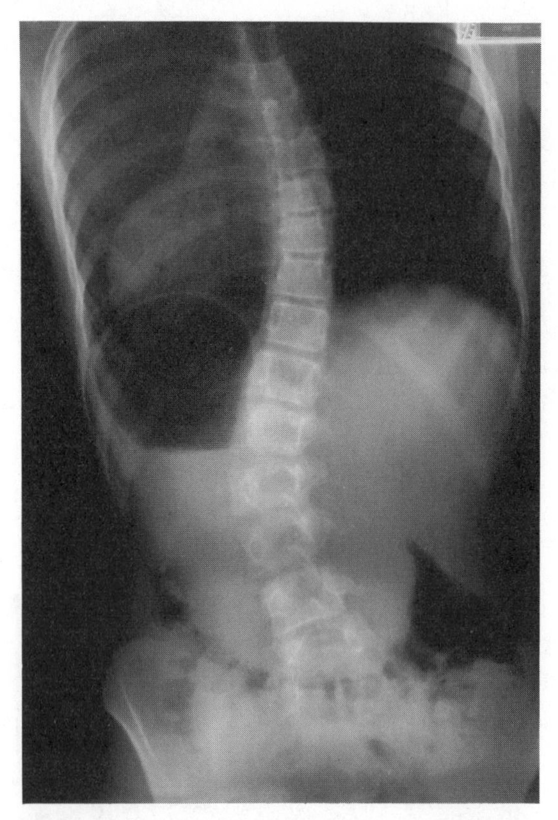

Figure 5.11 A patient with scoliosis: a condition in which the vertebral column develops a lateral curvature and vertebral rotation, frequently leading to severe physical deformity.

projection of structured light patterns onto the subject. Such methods are accurate and offer the potential of fast acquisition and analysis of results, particularly with the recent advent of high speed image processing boards within computer systems. Such techniques have been applied to the study of trunk shape, for example in scoliosis.

(a) Grating projection methods

Grating projection techniques are also well suited to research into posture, applied anatomy and body movement. These methods are subject to ongoing continual development (Hierholzer *et al.*, 1983; Dangerfield *et al.*, 1992). At present, it is possible to produce three-dimensional reconstructions of the trunk (Figure 5.12). The technique also allows automatic calculation of parameters of posture similar to those gathered using goniometers or flexicurves.

'Phase measuring profilometry' also uses grating projection. This method employs algorithms for the phase function which are defined by the geometry of the system and the shape of the object (Halioua and Liu, 1989; Halioua *et al.*, 1990). The object's shape is converted into a phase distribution as in interferometry and is analysed by digital phase measuring techniques: accuracy to less than 1 mm is possible without the need for reference plane images. This technique has been used to measure the three-dimensional shape of the trunk, face and breasts and has obvious applications in plastic surgery. It is presently expensive for routine practical use as it employs precision optical components and high-speed computer image processing.

The Loughborough anthropometric shadow scanner uses light projected onto the subject from four sources (Jones *et al.*, 1989). The subject is placed on a rotating turntable and the light is projected to fall into vertical planes on the body which pass through the centre of rotation of the turntable. Viewed by a bank of cameras, the images obtained from the rotating subject are analysed to produce accurate three-dimensional data relating to body shape and size. The shadow scanner has found application in the fields of ergonomics and clothing manufacture.

The future of static measurements lies with further developments of these light-based systems. They offer the opportunity to develop accurate and fast recording of the three-dimensional shape of the trunk and legs.

(b) Radiographic and magnetic resonance images

In order to understand the interaction of the components of skeletal anatomy, invasive criterion techniques must be employed.

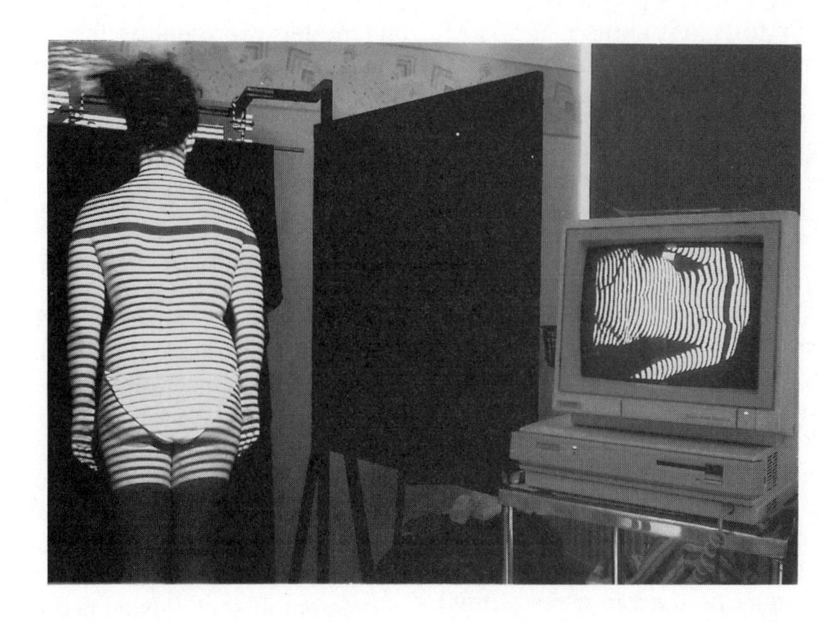

Figure 5.12 Grating projection system (SIPS: Spinal Image Processing System) used for clinical evaluation of trunk shape and scoliosis.

These include conventional radiography, computer-aided tomography (CAT) scans and magnetic resonance imaging (MRI). The radiographic approach has its attractions: it is widely employed in medical diagnostic investigations as it is relatively easy to interpret. With newer digital systems, even the dosage of radiation is reduced by a factor of at least 10 times, although the risks from ionizing radiation would raise ethical issues for anyone employing such methods in a pure research capacity. The chance to create three-dimensional reconstructions of the skeletal and soft tissue structures of the body and limbs is offered by CAT-scans which have important applications in the study of degenerative conditions. Again, the high intensity of radiation would tend to exclude its use in research other than purely medical investigations.

Magnetic resonance imaging offers a far wider range of possibilities as it can be used to obtain highly detailed images of soft tissue as well as hard tissue. It exploits the property of certain atoms, particularly hydrogen, to perform a processing movement in a magnetic field when they are disturbed from a stationary state by application of a powerful magnetic field. Magnetic Resonance Imaging is still expensive to use for research purposes; its availability is currently restricted mainly to hospitals and specialist research centres due to the expense of the magnetic coils and the low temperature required to operate them. This will inevitably change over the next few years. Procuring static and dynamic images will then become feasible. Advanced image processing methods already allow three-dimensional reconstruction of tissues in high detail. The water and other ionic contents of such tissue can be quantified using the decay times of molecular movement activated by the magnetic field (T1 and T2 images). It is expected that automation of these processes will benefit all fields of application, including acquiring geometric joint data from the spine in functional motion studies.

5.6 MEASUREMENTS IN A DYNAMIC PHASE OF POSTURE (MOVEMENT ANALYSIS)

The human rarely assumes static posture for more than a few seconds. Analysis of dynamic posture involves a study of the range of motion of the joints of the spine since the relative position of the spine constantly varies throughout movement, such as during gait or athletic events. Movement analysis refers to measurement of these changes in posture.

Quantification of movement in the lumbar spine is important when examining patients with low-back pain, a symptom frequently associated with sporting pastimes. Ranges of spinal mobility may be useful in studying athletic performance but allowance for age and sex should be made in interpreting observations.

Goniometers may be used to assess spinal range of motion. (Refer to the laboratory practical at the end of the chapter and also to Chapter 6.) These measurements are useful in assessing spinal movement in patients with deformity or arthritic diseases. Techniques for marking the skin may also facilitate simple but accurate measurement of spinal flexion, and offer a useful measure of physical movement (MacRae and Wright, 1969; Rae *et al.*, 1984). Although this technique requires only the use of a tape measure, it still has a value in assessing the contribution of lumbar flexion to body posture.

Movement analysis is complex and currently makes great demands on computer power. It is also potentially expensive and may require a dedicated laboratory in which to conduct research.

The most common form of dynamic research involves gait and movement analysis. This applies to a wide range of sports and medical problems, which can be related to posture. The tracking and analysis of human movement commenced with the early application of still photography. With the advent of movie and video cameras, cinematography has been used in the analysis of performance of occupational and sports skills, with various models representing the human body as a mechanism consisting of segments or links and joints (Vogelbach, 1990; Kippers and Parker, 1989). This approach overlooks the multi-unit nature of the vertebral column and pelvis which can exhibit many varied movement patterns. The vertebral column has 25 mobile segments, corresponding to each intervertebral joint from the base of the skull to the lumbar-sacral junction and each has its own unique movement potential. This is the concept of spinal coupling, first described by Lovett in 1905 (Panjabi *et al.*, 1989). Posture affects the range of these coupled motions. In contrast, the pelvis moves about an axis through the hip joints. By separating these units, any overall appreciation of the complex movements of trunk flexion and muscle involvement in such flexion is impossible. This is important when considering movements in the context of posture and its application either in biological, clinical or athletic terms.

Three-dimensional measurement of movement is therefore important in advancing the understanding of athletic performance. The subject is complex and only relatively recently has measurement become possible at an affordable cost. In all applications, the reproducibility and accuracy of the method must be established. Some methods have a poor record of reproducibility and offer little advantage over the use of low cost goniometers (Dillard *et al.*, 1991).

Most methods use film or video-tape to record movement and then apply computerized methods for analysis of the resulting movements. A force-plate may form a part of the laboratory equipment to record dynamic changes in lower limb forces during walking or other movements. The field of gait and movement analysis is vast, often has no direct association with studies of posture and is thus beyond the remit of this chapter.

Selspot optoelectronics and other video analysis systems have been developed for analysis of movement (Thurston and Harris,

1983; Tani and Masuda, 1985; Thorstensson *et al.*, 1985). Even today, these are usually restricted to laboratory-based research projects due to their high cost.

Electrogoniometers have been employed to monitor dynamic movements of the lumbar spine (Paquet *et al.*, 1991) with a high degree of reliability and accuracy. This approach has the advantage of being non-invasive but it is at present limited to movements in the sagittal plane.

A three-dimensional method called CODA offers the features of high degree of accuracy, rapid analysis of results and is non-invasive (Mitchelson, 1988). It consists of three rapidly rotating scanning mirrors used to view fan-shaped beams of light which sweep rapidly across the region of the subject under study. The signals detected by the scanners permit triangulation and spatial measurement of markers placed on the subject and so are used to record movement of the subject in three dimensions. The CODA-3 system has found application in clinical studies of Parkinsonian tremor, scoliosis and gait analysis programmes associated with fitting a prosthesis.

When any muscle changes its length, dynamic work is performed (Pitman and Peterson, 1989). If the movement involves a constant angular velocity, it is called isokinetic, whereas, if the muscle acts on a constant inertial mass, it is isoinertial exertion. Isotonic exertion involves maintaining constant muscle tension throughout the range of motion (Rogers and Cavanagh, 1984). These terminologies are confusing and imprecise and refer to movements which are artificial. Attempts have been made to quantify such movements using dynamometers which act to control the range of motion and/or the resistance of muscles. Such devices have been applied to measuring trunk movement and thus can be used in assessment of posture. There are many different types of dynamometer available for investigations. These include cable tensiometers and strain-gauge dynanometers for the measurement of isometric forces and isokinetic devices for dynamic movements (Mayhew and Rothstein, 1985).

The Isostation B200 lumbar dynamometer (Isotechnologies, Carrboro, North Carolina, USA) has been applied to the measurement of trunk motion, strength and velocity. Investigations have included the study of low-back pain and also normal lumbar spinal function (Dillard *et al.*, 1991; Gomez *et al.*, 1991). The use of dynamometers to study the wide range of muscle actions in the human body is a growing research field which has been extensively reviewed by Parnianpour and Tan (1993).

Three-dimensional analysis of movement using low-cost infra-red video-technology linked to image-processing boards within the PC now allows sophisticated analysis of the dynamics of athletic performance. This approach, which accommodates a variety of methods for obtaining essentially similar data, allows analysis of the effects of an individual's posture on his or her athletic performance. An ideal method, which will become possible with further advances in electronics and computers, would be to link physiological investigations or metabolic functions, electromyographic recordings of muscle activity and analysis of movements in three dimesions so as to optimize performance to prevailing conditions and produce the best athletic performance from an individual.

Electromyography (EMG) employs surface electrodes applied to suitably prepared skin over appropriate muscle groups on the body's surface. Electrical activity generated by the underlying muscles can then be recorded using appropriate amplifiers and filters to process the signals. Muscle activity can be quantified using EMG, allowing investigation of the relationship between posture or body position and exercise response. Within EMG, a subspecialty has developed, called kinesiological EMG, with the aim of analysing the function and co-ordination of muscles in different movements and postures. These measurements are frequently combined with biomechanical analysis. However, the complexity of human movement in normal daily routines, sport or disability renders it impossible to sample all the muscles within the body during the performance of motor skills (Clarys, 1987). As many sports involve dynamic postural change, massive resources would be needed to record sport specific movements using EMG and other methods.

The application of EMG to the study of sports has been reviewed by Clarys and Cabri (1993) who set down standards for the methodology and its limitations due to its partly descriptive nature. There are also many applications to rehabilitation and other fields.

Electromyographic (EMG) techniques have been applied to study the effect of posture and lifting on trunk musculature and, by inference, spinal loading (Hinz and Seidel, 1989; Mouton *et al.*, 1991). It has been demonstrated that a relationship exists between surface EMG amplitude and measured muscle movement. However, EMG investigations are complex to analyse and require an understanding of biomechanics in interpretation of findings (Clarys and Cabri, 1993). Account must also be made of muscle length, often difficult to assess in trunk and pelvic musculature. There is a large individual variation in spinal and trunk muscle activity in relation to load. Furthermore, inertial moments differ between standing and sitting positions.

The relationship between EMG activity of abdominal muscles and intra-abdominal pressures has also been studied in the context of lumbar spine support (Bartelink, 1957), lifting and diaphragm and thoracic kinetics pertaining to sporting activities (Grassino *et al.*, 1978; Grillner *et al.*, 1978). As this research has not produced consistent findings, it would appear that the changes in intra-abdominal pressure are task-specific. Their role in various sporting activities therefore requires further investigation.

Accelerometers may be used to measure the transmission of vibrations through the body, particularly over joints such as the knee and the lumbar spine in patients with low-back pain (Wosak and Voloshin, 1981). Such devices have been used in volunteers where K-wires have been inserted through the skin into the spine or pelvis or, less invasively, piezo-electric surface electrodes have been mounted on the skin. These techniques have been used in conjunction with gait analysis research. The methods can be employed to examine spinal movements relating to posture in walking and running, provided that allowance is made for skin movement.

The study of human movement is developing rapidly as costs of high-powered and fast computer hardware falls. It has the potential to increase understanding of the problems of human posture and movement in sports and other occupations.

5.7 SPINAL LENGTH AND DIURNAL VARIATION

Stature is a fundamental variable in anthropometry and ergonomics. The vertebral column comprises about 40% of the total body length as measured in stature and has within it about 30% of its length occupied by the intervertebral discs. The spinal length and thus height varies throughout the day, shrinking in the day and lengthening at night, due to compressive forces acting on the discs to eliminate fluid from the nucleus pulposus. The degree of shrinkage is related to the magnitude of the compressive load on the spine and has been used as an index of spinal loading (Corlett *et al.*, 1987). Accurate measurement of spinal shrinkage has application in evaluating sports such as weight-training, running and jumping and also in assessing procedures used to prevent back injury (Reilly *et al.*, 1991).

De Puky (1935), a pioneer investigator of spinal shrinkage, measured the change and found a daily oscillation of approximately 1% of total body height. This figure has subsequently been confirmed (Reilly *et al.*, 1991). Wing *et al.* (1992) demonstrated that 40% of the change occurred in the lumbar spine, without any change in the lordosis depth and angle, and a further 40% occurred in the thoracic spine, associated with a reduction in the kyphotic angle. Most of the shrinkage appears to occur within an hour of assuming an upright posture, whereas the loss in height is regained rapidly in the prone position. Monitoring creep over 24 hours demonstrated that 71% of height gained during the night is achieved within the first half of the night and 80% is lost again with 3 hours of arising (Reilly *et al.*, 1984). The mechanism for these changes is that fluid dynamics within the intervertebral disc and vertebral body under compression forces fluid out of the disc, leading to the length variation in the spine observed in the diurnal cycle. Quantitative T2 magnetic resonance investigations have confirmed this mechanism, with the greatest amount of fluid being lost from the nucleus pulposus of the disc (Dangerfield *et al.*, 1995).

These changes are important in sport. Disc damage is more likely if it has a high water content (Adams *et al.*, 1987). The lumbar vertebrae have the highest fluid content. Furthermore, the degree of lumbar flexion increases in the late afternoon, due to disc shrinkage. The clear message from these observations is that time of day is important to avoid straining and overloading the vertebral column. Weight training and lifting are influenced not only by the size of the forces involved but also in relation to the sleep pattern of the athlete. Avoiding such activities within the first few hours of rising reduces the risk of axial compression leading to disk damage through disc herniation and the subsequent onset of back pain.

5.8 CONCLUSION

This review has examined some of the methods currently available which might be applied to study posture. It is a very broad field and there are undoubtedly many other techniques available which might offer investigators possible approaches to the study of a particular aspect of posture. In essence, it is still important to remember the dynamic nature of the living human body and that, at present, the study of movement is both complex, potentially expensive and little understood.

5.9 PRACTICAL 1: MEASUREMENT OF POSTURE AND BODY SHAPE

5.9.1 SAGITTAL PLANE

Erect spinal curvature is the basis of acceptable static posture. Expert opinion differs as what constitutes 'good' posture, a term relating to energy economy and cosmetic acceptability. Large variations can be seen in groups of healthy subjects. Significant individual variation can be seen between slumped/erect states and deep inhalation/exhalation and it is important to standardize the position for each subject as described in the method. Both 'flat back' and excessive curvature are considered problematic, having an association with subsequent back pain. Kyphosis of 20–45° and lordosis of 40–60° have been considered to indicate normal ranges (Roaf, 1960). Fon *et al.* (1980) suggested that these figures are inappropriate for children and teenagers since spinal curvature changes with age. This is due to the reduction in elasticity of the spinal ligaments and changes in bone mineral content.

The two practical methods detailed here are regularly used in back clinics and are called kyphometry and goniometry. These experiments will yield a range of values which describe back shape.

5.9.2 EQUIPMENT

1. Debrunner's kyphometer (Straumann Ltd, Welwyn Garden City, England or Protek AG, Bern, Switzerland).

2. Goniometer, e.g. Myrin Goniometer (LIC Rehab., Solna, Sweden).

5.9.3 METHOD

The subject is instructed to stand barefoot, with the heels together, in an upright and relaxed position, looking straight ahead and breathing normally with the arms hanging loosely by the body. The shoulders should be relaxed.

Debrunner's kyphometer consists of two long arms where the angle between these arms is transmitted through parallel struts to a protractor (Figures 5.4 and 5.5). Spinal curvature with the kyphometer should be assessed both with the subject exhaling and inhaling maximally.

In order to measure thoracic kyphosis, one foot of the kyphometer should be located over T1 and T2 and the other over the T11 and T12. The kyphosis angle is read directly from the protractor.

Lumbar curvature is measured between the T11 and T12 and S1 and S2. The angle read directly from the protractor is lumbar lordosis.

A goniometer consists of a small dial that can be held to the patient's back (Figures 5.6–5.8). The difference between the back angle and the vertical is measured with a pointer which responds to gravity. The difference between the measurements at T1 and T12 indicates the degree of kyphosis and the deviation between the angles at T12 and S1 indicates the degree of lumbar lordosis. Other angles such as the proclive and declive angles can also be measured (Figure 5.6).

Use of the kyphometer or goniometer allows the quantification of the normal curvatures of the vertebral column. The angle of thoracic kyphosis and lumbar lordosis will yield useful information on individual and group posture.

5.10 PRACTICAL 2: ASSESSMENT OF SITTING POSTURE

Sitting posture may be assessed by sitting a subject on a high stool. The knees should be flexed to 90° and the thighs 90° relative to the trunk. Most weight is taken by the ischial tuberosities, acting as a fulcrum within the buttocks. If the hip angle exceeds 60°, hamstring tension increases and the spine compensates by losing the lordosis concavity of the lumbar spine. A comfortable position therefore requires consideration of the lengths of the tibia, femur and the angles of the femur relative to the pelvis and the lordosis angle of the lumbar spine (maintaining lumbar lordosis is important in avoiding lumbar postural strain). To ascertain the appropriateness of a chair for an individual, an investigation of these parameters can be easily undertaken using an anthropometer and goniometer.

The lateral flexibility of the spine can be assessed by placing the goniometer dial over T1 vertebra and then asking the subject to flex to the right and to the left.

Sagittal flexibility can be measured by goniometry but is more often quantified in field testing by the sit-and-reach test.

5.11 PRACTICAL 3: LATERAL DEVIATIONS

5.11.1 EQUIPMENT

Scoliometer, e.g. Orthopedic Systems, Inc., Hayward, California.

5.11.2 METHOD

The scoliometer is employed to quantify lateral deviations of the spine expressed as an asymmetrical trunk deformity. Used in both the thoracic and lumbar regions, it has been found to be less sensitive for the identification of lumbar scoliosis. The reason for this is unclear since lateral spinal curvature and axial trunk rotation also occur in this region. Lateral deviations are found most commonly in scoliosis. Non-structural scoliosis may be formed by disparity in leg-length and is usually non-progressive. Structural scoliosis is a serious condition with likelihood of progression throughout the growth period. If found, such cases should be referred for an urgent orthopaedic opinion.

The standing subject assumes a forward-bending posture with the trunk approximately parallel with the floor, and feet together. The subject's hands are placed palms together and held between the knees. This position has been found to offer the most consistently reproducible results in clinical studies by the author. The examiner places the scoliometer on the subject's back, with the centre of the device corresponding to the centre contour of the trunk, along the spinal column.

Starting where the neck joins the trunk, the scoliometer is moved down the spine to the sacrum. The maximum values for thoracic and lumbar areas are recorded.

Scoliometer readings in excess of 5–8° are taken to indicate significant scoliosis. The subject should be referred to a general practitioner or scoliosis specialist for radiographic examination.

5.12 PRACTICAL 4: LEG-LENGTH DISCREPANCY

The subject lies on the floor (or suitable firm surface) with the feet approximately shoulder-width apart. A steel tape-measure is used to measure the distance between the medial malleolus and the anterior superior iliac spine (this is an orthopaedic measurement of leg-length discrepancy). Although differences in leg-length are found in many normal subjects, a difference greater than 10 mm may result in postural or adaptive scoliosis.

The subject should then stand bare-footed in a normal, relaxed stance. The distance between the floor by the subject's heel and the hip is measured. Any difference in the left and right side measurements may indicate that the hip is at an angle to the horizontal, reflecting the presence of pelvic obliquity. If present, pelvic obliquity can also result in compensatory scoliosis. Pelvic obliquity can also be confirmed by placing the thumbs on each anterior superior iliac spine and 'eye-balling' their heights to check for horizontal alignment.

A specimen data collection form which could be adapted for use in a laboratory or field situation is shown in Table 5.1.

Table 5.1 A sample of a data collection form

Subject Name	M	Date	9.6.95
Date of birth	1.1.80	Sex	Male
Height	1823.0 mm		
Body mass	73.6 kg		
		Test 1	*Test 2*
Kyphometer			
Kyphosis Angle T1–T12		34.0 degrees	32.4 degrees
Lordosis Angle T12–S1		23.5 degrees	24.5 degrees
Goniometer			
Upper Proclive Angle		37.0 degrees	35.0 degrees

Table 5.1 (Continued)	*Test 1*	*Test 2*
Declive Angle	−11.0 degrees	−14.0 degrees
Lower Proclive Angle	−7.0 degrees	−10.0 degrees
Lordosis	30.0 degrees	35.0 degrees
Kyphosis	20.0 degrees	24.0 degrees
Flexibility		
Sit and Reach score	20.0 cm	20.5 cm
Scoliometer		
ATI	3.0 degrees	5.0 degrees
Lateral flexibility		
Right Side	25.0 degrees	23.0 degrees
Left Side	20.0 degrees	20.0 degrees
Leg length		
Supine		
Right leg	980.0 mm	980.0 mm
Left leg	970.0 mm	975.0 mm
Discrepancy	10.0 mm	5.0 mm
Standing		
Right leg	950.0 mm	955.0 mm
Left leg	945.0 mm	950.0 mm
Discrepancy	5.0 mm	5.0 mm

Data taken from P. H. Dangerfield (1995, unpublished data: Liverpool School Survey).

ACKNOWLEDGEMENTS

The author wishes to acknowlege assistance in preparing this chapter from Carl McEwen, Department of Movement Science, University of Liverpool.

REFERENCES

Adams, M. A., Dolan, P. and Hutton, W. C. (1987) Diurnal variations in the stresses on the lumbar spine. *Spine*, **12**, 130–7.

Alexander, M. J. (1985) Biomechanical aspects of lumbar spine injuries in athletes; a review. *Canadian Journal of Applied Sports Science*, **10**, 1–5.

Asazuma, T., Suzuki, N. and Hirabayashi, K. (1986) Analysis of human dynamic posture in normal and scoliotic patients, in *Surface Topography and Spinal Deformity* III (eds J. D. Harris and A. R. Turner-Smith), Gustav-Fischer Verlag, Stuttgart, pp. 223–34.

Bartelink, D. L. (1957) The role of abdominal pressure on the lumbar intervertebral discs. *Journal of Bone and Joint Surgery*, **39B**, 718–25.

Burwell, R. G. and Dangerfield, P. H. (1992) Pathogenesis and assessment of scoliosis, in *Surgery of the Spine* (eds G. Findlay and R. Owen), Blackwell Scientific Publications, Oxford, pp. 365–408.

Cameron, N. (1986) The methods of auxological anthropometry, in *Human Growth: A Comprehensive Treatise*, Vol. 3, 2nd edn (eds F. Faulkner and J. M. Tanner), Plenum Press, New York and London, pp. 3–46.

Clarys, J. P. (1987) Application of EMG for the evaluation of performance in different sports, in *Muscular Function in Exercise and Training* (eds P. Marconnet and P. V. Komi), Karger, Basel, pp. 200–23.

Clarys, J. P. and Cabri, J. (1993) Electromyography and the study of sports movements: a review. *Journal of Sports Sciences*, **11**, 379–448.

Corlett, E. N., Eklund, J. A. E., Reilly, T. and Troup, J. D. G. (1987) Assessment of work load from measurements of stature. *Applied Ergonomics*, **18**, 65–71.

Dangerfield, P. H. (1994) Asymmetry and growth, in *Anthropometry: The Individual and The Population* (eds S. J. Ulijaszek and C. G. N. Mascie-Taylor), Cambridge University Press, Cambridge pp. 7–29.

Dangerfield, P. H. and Denton, J. C. (1986) A longitudinal examination of the relationship between the rib-hump, spinal angle and vertebral rotation in idiopathic scoliosis, in *Proceedings of the 3rd International Symposium on Moire Fringe Topography and Spinal Deformity*, Oxford (eds J. D. Harris and A. R. Turner-Smith), Gustav Fischer Verlag, Stuttgart, pp. 213–21.

Dangerfield, P. H., Denton, J. C., Barnes, S. B. and Drake, N. D. (1987) The assessment of the rib-cage and spinal deformity in scoliosis, in *Proceedings of the 4th International Symposium on Moire Fringe Topography and Spinal Deformity*, Oxford (eds. I. A. F. Stokes, J. R. Pekelsky and M. S. Moreland) Gustav Fischer Verlag, Stuttgart, pp. 53–66.

Dangerfield, P. H., Pearson, J. D., Atkinson, J. T. *et al.* (1992) Measurement of back surface topography using an automated imaging system. *Acta Orthopaedica Belgica*, **58**, 73–9.

Dangerfield, P. H., Walker, J., Roberts, N. *et al.* (1995) Investigation of the diurnal variation in the water content of the intervertebral disc using MRI, in *Proceedings of a 2nd Symposium on 3D Deformity and Scoliosis*, Pescara, Italy (eds M. D'Amico, A. Merolli and G. C. Santambrogio), IOS Press, Amsterdam, The Netherlands, pp 447–51.

Davis, P. R. (1959) The medial inclination of the human articular facets. *Journal of Anatomy*, **93**, 68–74.

De Puky, P. (1935) The physiological oscillation of the length of the body. *Acta Orthopaedica Scandanavica*, **6**, 338–47.

Dillard, J., Trafimow, J., Andersson, G. B. J. and Cronin, K. (1991) Motion of the lumbar spine; reliability of two measurement techniques. *Spine*, **16**, 321–4.

D'Orazio, B. (ed.) (1993) *Back Pain Rehabilitation*. Andover Medical Publications, Oxford.

Fon, G. T., Pitt, M. J. and Thies, A. C. (1980) Thoracic kyphosis, range in normal subjects. *American Journal of Roentgenology*, **124**, 979–83.

Gomez, T., Beach, G., Cooke, C. *et al.* (1991) Normative database for trunk range of motion, strength, velocity and endurance with the Isostation B-200 lumbar dynamometer. *Spine*, **16**, 15–21.

Grassino, A., Goldman, M. D., Mead, J. and Sears, T. A. (1978) Mechanics of the human diaphragm during voluntary contraction. *Journal of Applied Physiology*, **44**, 829–39.

Grillner, S. J., Nilsson, J. and Thorstensson, A. (1978) Intra-abdominal pressure changes during natural movements in man. *Acta Physiologica Scandinavica*, **104**, 275–83.

Halioua, M. and Liu, H.-C. (1989) Optical three-dimensional sensing by phase measuring profilometry. *Optics and Lasers in Engineering*, **11**, 185–215.

Halioua, M., Liu, H.-C., Chin, A. and Bowings, T. S. (1990) Automated topography of the human form by phase-measuring profilometry and model analysis, in *Proceedings of the Fifth International Symposium on Surface Topography and Body Deformity* (eds H. Neugerbauer and G. Windischbauer), Gustav-Fischer Verlag, Stuttgart, pp. 91–100.

Hellsing, E., Reigo, T., McWilliam, J. and Spangfort, E. (1987) Cervical and lumbar lordosis and thoracic kyphosis in 8, 11 and 15-year-old children. *European Journal of Orthopaedics*, **9**, 129–30.

Hierholzer, E., Drerup, B. and Frobin, W. (1983) Computerized data acquisition and evaluation of moire topograms and rasterstereographs, in *Moire Fringe Topography and Spinal Deformity* (eds B. Drerup, W. Frobin and E. Hierholzer), Gustav Fisher Verlag, Stuttgart, pp. 233–40.

Hinz, B. and Seidel, H. (1989) On time relation between erector spinae muscle activity and force development during initial isometric stage of back lifts. *Clinical Biomechanics*, **4**, 5–10.

Hrdlicka, A. (1972) *Practical Anthropometry*. AMS Press, New York (reprint).

Jones, P. R. M., West, G. M., Harris, D. H. and Read, J. B. (1989) The Loughborough anthropometric shadow scanner (LASS). *Endeavor*, **13**, 162–8.

Kippers, V. and Parker, A. W. (1989) Validation of single-segment and three segment spinal models used to represent lumbar flexion. *Journal of Biomechanics*, **22**, 67–75.

Klausen, K. (1965) The form and function of the loaded human spine. *Acta Physiologica Scandinavica*, **65**, 176–90.

Lohman, T. G., Roche, A. F. and Martorell, R. (1988) *Anthropometric Standardization Reference Manual*, Human Kinetics, Champaign, IL.

MacRae, J. F. and Wright, V. (1969) Measurement of back movements. *Annals of Rheumatic Diseases*, **28**, 584–9.

Mayhew, T. P. and Rothstein, J. M. (1985) Measurement of muscle performance with instruments. *Clinics in Physical Therapy*, **7**, 57–102.

Mitchelson, D. L. (1988) Automated three dimensional movement analysis using the CODA-3 system. *Biomedical Technik*, **33**, 179–82.

Mouton, L. J., Hof, A. L., de Jongh, H. J. and Eisma, W. H. (1991) Influence of posture on the relation between surfae electromyogram amplitude and back muscle moment: consequences for the use of surface electromyogram to measure back load. *Clinical Biomechanics*, **6**, 245–51.

Ohlen, G., Sprangfort, E. and Tingwell, C. (1989) Measurement of spinal sagittal configuration and mobility with Debrunner's Kyphometer. *Spine*, **14**, 580–3.

Pal, G. P. and Routal, R. V. (1986) A study of weight transmission through the cervical and upper thoracic regions of the vertebral column in man. *Journal of Anatomy*, **148**, 245–61.

Panjabi, M., Yamamoto, I., Oxland, T. and Crisco, J. (1989) How does posture affect coupling in the lumbar spine? *Spine*, **14**, 1002–11.

Paquet, N., Malouin, F., Richards, C. L. *et al.* (1991) Validity and reliability of a new electrogoniometer for the measurement of sagittal dorsolumbar movements. *Spine*, **16**, 516–19.

Parnianpour, M. and Tan, J. C. (1993) Objective quantification of trunk performance, in *Back Pain Rehabilitation* (ed. B. D'Orazio), Andover Medical Publications, Oxford.

Pheasant, S. (1986) *Bodyspace: Anthropometry, Ergonomics and Design*. Taylor and Francis, London.

Pitman, M. I. and Peterson, L. (1989) Biomechanics of skeletal muscle, in *Basic Biomechanics of the Musculo-skeletal System* (eds M. Nordin and V Fankel), Lea & Febiger, Philadelphia, pp. 89–111.

Rae, P. S., Waddell, G. and Venner, R. M. (1984) A simple technique for measuring lumber spinal flexion. *Journal of the Royal College of Surgeons of Edinburgh*, **29**, 281–4.

Reilly, T., Tyrrell, A. and Troup, J. D. G. (1984) Circadian variation in human stature. *Chronobiology International*, **1**, 121–6.

Reilly, T., Boocock, M. G., Garbutt, G. *et al.* (1991) Changes in stature during exercise and sports training. *Applied Ergonomics*, **22**, 308–11.

Roaf, R. (1960) The basic anatomy of scoliosis. *Journal of Bone and Joint Surgery*, **488**, 40–59.

Roaf, R. (1977) *Posture*. Academic Press, London.

Rogers, M. M. and Cavanagh, P. R. (1984) A glossary of biomechanical terms, concepts and units. *Physical Therapy*, **64**, 1886–902.

Salisbury, P. J. and Porter, R. W. (1987) Measurement of lumbar sagittal mobility: a comparison of methods. *Spine*, **12**, 190–3.

Sarasate, H. and Ostman, A. (1986) Stereophotogrammetry in the evaluation of the treatment of scoliosis. *International Orthopaedics*, **10**, 63–7.

Suzuki, N., Yamaguchi, Y. and Armstrong, G. W. D. (1981) Measurement of posture using Moire topography, in *Moire Fringe Topography and Spinal Deformity* (eds M. S. Moreland, M. H. Pope and G. W. D. Armstrong), Pergamon Press, New York, pp. 122–31.

Tani, K. and Masuda, T. (1985) A kinesiologic study of erector spinae activity during trunk flexion and extension. *Ergonomics*, **28**, 883–93.

Taylor, J. R. and Twomey, L. (1984) Sexual dimorphism in human vertebral body shape. *Journal of Anatomy*, **138**, 281–6.

Thorstensson, A., Oddsson, L. and Carlson, H. (1985) Motor control of voluntary trunk movements in standing. *Acta Physiologica Scandinavica*, **125**, 309–21.

Thurston, A. J. and Harris, J. D. (1983) Normal kinetics of the lumbar spine and pelvis. *Spine*, **8**, 199–205.

Tillotson, K. M. and Burton, A. K. (1991) Noninvasive measurement of lumbar sagittal mobility. An assessment of the flexicurve technique. *Spine*, **16**, 29–33.

Tsai, L. and Wredmark, T. (1993) Spinal posture, sagittal mobility and subjective rating of back problems in former female elite gymnasts. *Spine*, **18**, 872–975.

Ulijaszek, S. J. and Lourie, J. A. (1994) Intra- and inter-observer error in anthropometric measurement, in *Anthropometry: The Individual and The Population* (eds S. J. Ulijaszek and C. G. N. Mascie-Taylor), Cambridge University Press, Cambridge, pp. 30–55.

Vogelbach, S. K. (1990) *Functional Kinetics*, Springer Verlag, Stuttgart.

Weiner, J. S. (1982) The measurement of human workload. *Ergonomics*, **25**, 953–66.

Weiner, J. S. and Lourie, J. A. (1969) Anthropometry, in *Human Biology: A Guide to Field Methods*. International Biological programme Handbook no 9. Blackwell Scientific Publications, Oxford, pp. 3–42.

Willner, S. (1979) Moire topography for the diagnosis and documentation of scoliosis. *Acta Orthopaedica Scandinavica*, **50**, 295–302.

Willner, S. and Johnson, B. (1983) Thoracic kyphosis and lumbar lordosis during the growth period in children. *Acta Pediatrica Scandinavica*, **72**, 873–8.

Wing, P., Tsang, L., Gagnon, F. *et al.* (1992) Diurnal changes in the profile, shape and range of motion of the back. *Spine*, **17**, 761–5.

Wosak, J. and Voloshin, A. (1981) Wave attenuation in skeletons of young healthy persons. *Journal of Biomechanics*, **14**, 261–7.

FLEXIBILITY 6

J. Borms and P. Van Roy

6.1 INTRODUCTION

Flexibility may be defined as the range of motion (ROM) at a single joint or a series of joints. The ROM can reflect the arthrokinematic possibilities of the joint(s) considered, but also indicate the ability of muscles and connective tissue surrounding the joint to be elongated within their structural limitations.

Measurement of flexibility has been used mainly in research and practical situations concerned with sport and physical fitness and in clinical settings. There is little doubt that good flexibility is needed particularly in sports where maximum amplitude of movement is required for an optimal execution of technique. Testing this component has therefore been common practice in training situations as a means of evaluating progress in physical conditioning and of identifying problem areas associated with poor performance or possible injury (e.g. Cureton, 1941). Ever since this quality has been considered as a component of physical fitness, a test to express and evaluate it has been included in physical fitness test batteries (e.g. Larson, 1974; AAHPERD, 1984). These so-called field tests have been widely used to measure flexibility, specifically in trunk, hip and back flexion, such as the Scott and French (1950) Bobbing Test, the Kraus and Hirschland (1954) Floor Touch Test and finally the Wells and Dillon (1952) Sit and Reach Test. The latter test has been used worldwide in practice and is still incorporated in the recently constructed Eurofit test battery for European member states (Council of Europe, 1988).

In the 'sit and reach' test, the individual sits on the floor with the legs extended forward and feet pressed flat against a box that supports the measuring device. With the back of the knees pressed flat against the floor, the individual leans forward and extends the finger tips as far as possible. The distance reached is recorded and serves as an assessment of either the subject's flexibility at the hips, back muscle or hamstrings, or of the subject's general flexibility. It remains questionable which joints and muscles are being assessed because of the complexity of the movement. The test is used so widely, perhaps because the bending movement is so popular as a synonym for being supple, and probably because many health problems associated with poor flexibility are related to the lower back.

In spite of the popularity the test enjoys, its simple instructions, its low cost, its high reproducibility, its high loading on the flexibility factor in factor analysis studies, the test has been subjected to criticism, as were other tests where linear instead of angular measurements were applied. The individual with long arms and short legs will tend to be advantaged compared to an individual with the opposite anthropometric characteristics (Broer and Galles, 1958; Borms, 1984). Another criticism relates to the specificity of the test which purports to assess the individual's

Kinanthropometry and Exercise Physiology Laboratory Manual: Tests, procedures and data Edited by Roger Eston and Thomas Reilly. Published in 1996 by E & FN Spon. ISBN 0 419 17880 5

general flexibility, whereas it is now generally considered as a specific trait. In non-performance oriented testing, however, the indirect methods involving linear measurements can be suitable approximations of flexibility.

Direct methods of measuring angular displacements have been used in research and in clinical situations, unlike the case for mass screening. Direct methods of measurement are recommended because they are not affected by body segment proportions.

6.2 MEASUREMENT INSTRUMENTS

The **protractor goniometer** is a simple but useful device consisting of two articulating arms, one of which contains a protractor made of Plexiglass or metal, constructed around the fulcrum of the apparatus, around which the second arm rotates. The arm with the protractor is named the stationary arm; the second arm is called the moving arm. Protractor goniometers were first introduced in the Grand Palais Hospital in Paris by Camus and Amar in 1915 (Fox, 1917).

The **inclinometer** is based on the principle that a joint movement is recorded as an angular change against the vector of the gravity force.

In **hygrometers**, angular values are recorded by moving a bubble of air or a fluid level relative to an initial zero position, using the fact that the bubble will always seek the highest position within a small fluid container, or using the principle that a fluid level will always tend to remain in a horizontal position.

The **pendulum goniometer** uses the effect of the gravity force on the pointer (needle) of the goniometer, which is positioned in the centre of a protractor scale. The *Leighton Flexometer* (Leighton, 1966) contains a rotating circular dial marked off in degrees and a pointer counterbalanced to ensure it always points vertically. It is strapped on the appropriate body segment and the range of motion is determined in respect to this perpendicular. The length of limbs or segment does not influence this assessment, neither is the axis of the bone lever a disturbing factor. On the other hand, most movements must be made actively against gravity and the distinction between hip and back ROM measurement is questionable.

The **electrogoniometer** is a device like a protractor which is used to measure the joint angle at both extremes of the total range of movement. The essence of the apparatus is that the protractor has been replaced by a potentiometer which can modify a given voltage proportional to the angle of the joint. It is possible to assess the degree of flexibility exhibited during an actual physical action as opposed to more conventional measures of static flexibility (Adrian, 1973).

Other techniques include measurements of joint angles from arthographs (Wright and Johns, 1960), photographs (Hunebelle *et al.*, 1972) and radiography (Kottke and Mundale, 1959).

Unfortunately, the area of flexibility measurement is characterized by confusion in terminology and lack of standardization (e.g. the units, warming-up or not, starting position, active or passive motion, detailed description of procedures). During the past decade, renewed interest and efforts towards developing and/or improving measurement procedures are noticeable (Ekstrand *et al.*, 1982; Borms *et al.*, 1987).

6.3 PRACTICAL: FLEXIBILITY MEASUREMENTS WITH GONIOMETRY

6.3.1 DEFINITIONS

(a) Goniometry

From a clinical point of view goniometry can be described as a technique for measuring human joint flexibility by expressing in degrees the range of motion, according to a given degree of freedom. Traditionally, degrees of freedom are assigned in relation to an anatomical reference frame. Hence, joint motion is an expression of functional anatomy. Clinical goniometry in most cases is restricted to the angular changes of peripheral pathways of limb segments, measured in a two-dimensional way. Although goniometry emphasizes relative angular changes between bony or body segments in joint motion, it should be mentioned that small amounts of translations simultaneously occur, and are therefore an essential part of the arthrokinematic mechanisms.

(b) Goniometers

A goniometer measures the angle between two bony segments. When a maximal amplitude of a movement is reached, this maximal amplitude is then read and recorded. Figure 6.1 shows the *international standard goniometer*.

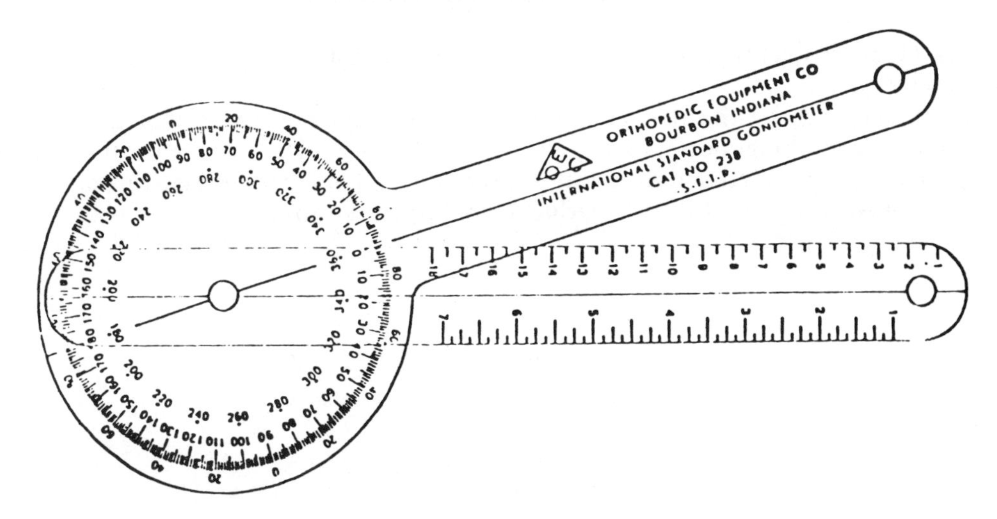

Figure 6.1 The international standard goniometer.

The *goniometer of Labrique* (1977) is a pendulum goniometer with a needle, constructed within the protractor and which maintains a vertical direction under the influence of gravity. This needle permits a rapid evaluation of the ROM of a joint, in relation to the vertical or the horizontal if the scale on the reverse side of the apparatus is used (Figure 6.2).

The *VUB-goniometer* was developed at the Vrije Universiteit Brussel (VUB) (Van Roy *et al.*, 1985) and was applied in several projects studying the optimal duration of static stretching exercises (Borms *et al.*, 1987) and the maintenance of coxo-femoral flexibility (Van Roy *et al.*, 1987). This goniometer differs from traditional protractor goniometers in that the graduation scale, the goniometer fulcrum and the moving arm are mounted on a carriage which slides along the stationary arm of the goniometer (Figure 6.3). This construction allows an easy orientation of the transparent 55 cm long arms of the goniometer along the longitudinal axes of the body segments. Joint range can then be measured without centring the fulcrum of the goniometer on the joint axis. A previous study (Van Roy, 1981)

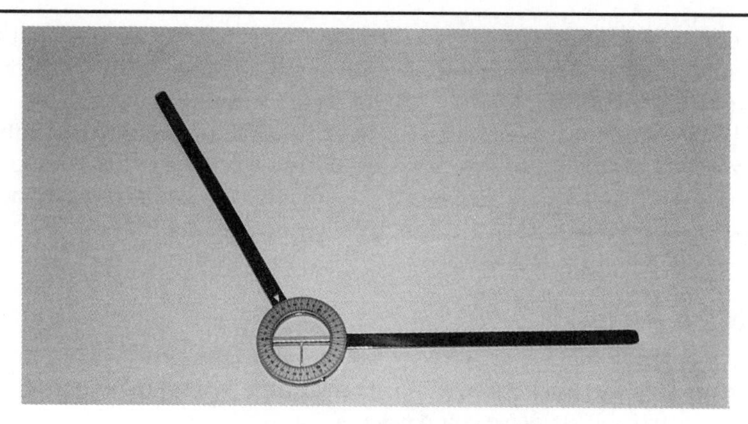

Figure 6.2 The Labrique goniometer.

indicated that considering fixed joint axes as reference points introduces systematic errors in goniometry.

The rationale behind the development of such a goniometer was that goniometric measurements of hip motion (flexion) are not valid unless they account for the angular change between the pelvis and the femur (Clayson *et al.*, 1966). Straight leg raising indeed includes a posterior pelvic tilt and a reduction of lumbar lordosis.

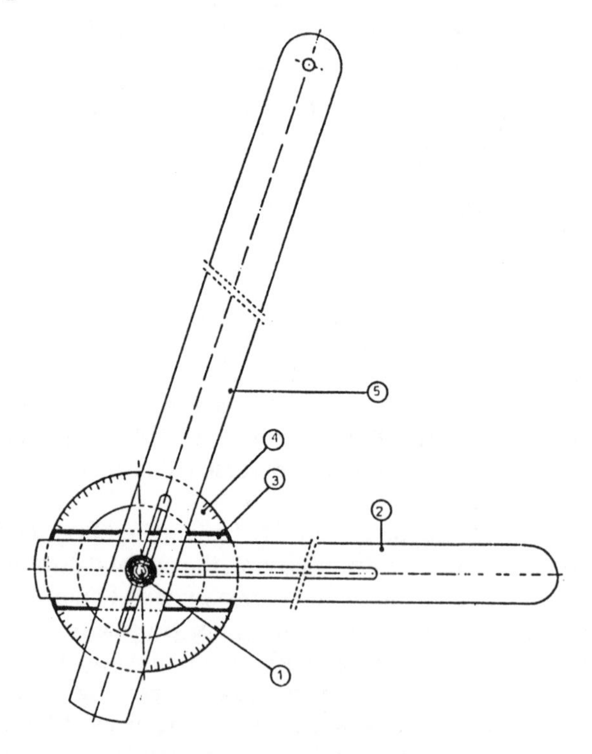

Figure 6.3 The VUB-goniometer. Patent no. 899964 (Belgium). 1. fulcrum; 2. stationary arm; 3. sliding carriage; 4. protractor scale; 5. moving arm.

(c) Possible interpretations of a range of motion

In Figure 6.4 OA always represents the segment which moves from point 1 to point 2 over an angle of 50°. As OA rotates around a point O, it changes the angular position in relation to OB, the stationary segment. This motion over an angle of 50° can be measured in four different ways (after Rocher and Rigaud, 1964):

1. The *true angle* between the skeletal segments in the end position of the motion: angle BOA_2 ($BOA_2 = BOA_1 - 50°$) (Figure 6.4a).
2. The *complementary angle* A_2Ox (Figure 6.4b).
3. The *supplementary angle* A_2Oy (Figure 6.4c)
4. The *range of motion angle* A_2OA_1 (Figure 6.4d).

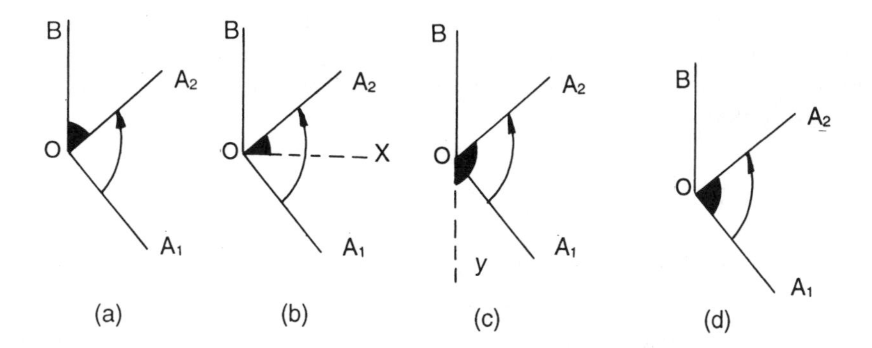

Figure 6.4 Four different ways to evaluate the angle in a joint (after Rocher and Rigaud, 1964). (a) true angle; (b) complementary angle; (c) supplementary angle; (d) ROM.

From the above, it is clear that confusion can arise in the interpretation of the measurements obtained. If the measurement of the ROM is of interest, then it should also be specified from which reference point the range of motion has been measured. An important attempt to standardize goniometric techniques has been worked out by the American Academy of Orthopaedic Surgeons (1965). The standardization generalizes the 'Neutral Zero Method' of Cave and Roberts (1936). Herein the ROM is measured from a specific reference position which for every joint is defined as the *zero starting position*. In this international convention, increasing ROM is always characterized by increasing angular values (which is not obvious in all manuals on goniometry). Moreover, rather than the anatomical position, an upright position with feet together, arms hanging alongside the body, thumbs forwards, is the basis of a reference position for measurement.

6.3.2 ADAPTATION OF THE GONIOMETRIC TECHNIQUES TO RECENT KNOWLEDGE OF SYNOVIAL JOINTS' FLEXIBILITY

(a) Limitation of the validity of goniometry

Realizing that real joint motion includes several angular components and small components of translation relative to different degrees of freedom, it is clear that two-dimensional goniometry is only a two-dimensional criterion to estimate the real flexibility, which in fact occurs tridimensionally (Van Roy, 1981). Although the reliability and the objectivity of two-dimensional goniometry in standardized situations can be very high, the content validity therefore always remains restrained.

(b) Measurement without positioning of the goniometer's axis relative to the joint's axis

From the knowledge that motion does not occur around axes which remain constant, it is clear that attempts to let the goniometer's axis coincide with the axis of the motion are not only useless, but also generate a systematic measurement error (Van Roy, 1981). Therefore, the goniometer has to be positioned in such a way that the arms coincide with the longitudinal axes of the moving segments in the end position of the motion. When the angular position at that moment is measured with respect to the zero position, the relative ROM can be evaluated.

6.3.3 GENERAL GUIDELINES FOR GONIOMETRY

(a) Knowledge of anatomy of the motion apparatus

Measurements have to be carried out on the nude skin, whereby the examiner palpates two specific anthropometric reference points for each segment. These 'landmarks' can shift considerably under the skin as motion occurs. Therefore, all reference points should be marked in the end position of the segment.

(b) Knowledge of internal factors influencing flexibility

Understanding is required, as well as kinesiological knowledge, of the compensation movements which are to be expected in joints situated proximal and distal of the joint to be measured. It is therefore important that the starting position is described precisely and that compensatory movements are controlled. Lateroflexion of the spine can compensate lack of arm abduction. On the other hand, a particular degree of hip abduction should theoretically represent pure coxofemoral abduction, but in most cases hip abduction results from a combination between pure coxofemoral abduction and lateral bending of the pelvis. One should differentiate between *osteokinematic* and *arthrokinematic* readings of flexibility, the former being an expression of angular changes in space in relation to an anatomical reference system, the latter being an expression of angular changes within a particular joint (starting from a zero position which of course can also be expressed in terms of an anatomical reference frame).

It is also very important to determine if the motion had been carried out actively or passively. A special point is the type of warm-up used (see discussion).

(c) Knowledge of external factors influencing flexibility

Some external factors influencing flexibility are temperature, exercise, gender, age, race, professional flexibility needs, sports flexibility needs and pathology.

(d) Scientific rigour and precision in the choice and use of the goniometer. The following recommendations are made:

1. The goniometer needs to have long arms sufficient to reach two reference points;
2. The goniometer needs to have a protractor with a precision of one degree;
3. Esch and Lepley (1974) have pointed out the danger of creating parallax errors; therefore readings should be made at eye level;
4. The presence of a thin indicator line on the goniometer's arms can be helpful for increasing its precision;
5. No loose articulation in the goniometer should be allowed;
6. Readings should be made prior to removing the goniometer from the segments;
7. The measurements should be recorded with three figures. If a recorder assists the examiner, the values should be dictated by the examiner as, for example, one-five-three rather than one hundred and fifty three. This should then be repeated and recorded on a proforma by the recorder;
8. The proforma (Figure 6.5) should contain personal details of the subject being measured (e.g. age, gender, profession, sport activities, daily habitual activity) as well as technical information regarding the measurements (starting position, room temperature).

(e) Replication of measurements

From experience, we know that data from a very large number of consecutive measurements are normally distributed around a value which very likely approaches the true amplitude. Thus, a difference of, for example, 5° with a later measurement is not necessarily an increase of amplitude but rather the result of a summation of small systematic errors and the absolute measurement error. Therefore, it is recommended to perform triple measurements with the median or the average of the two closest results as central value.

6.3.4 THE MEASUREMENTS

Considering the limitation of space in this book, only a selection of possible measurements is presented in the following pages. Special emphasis is given to a technique for measuring straight leg raising as a measurement of coxofemoral flexibility.

(a) Shoulder flexion

The international or modified goniometer is recommended. The subject lies supine on a table, legs bent, thorax fixed on the table with velcro straps. The subject executes a bilateral

PROFORMA FOR GONIOMETRIC MEASUREMENTS

01. Subject .... □□□□

(Last name) (First name)

02. Identity Sex F=2 M=1 □

03. Date of observations year □□ mo □□ day □□ □□□□□

04. Date of birth year □□ mo □□ day □□ □□□□□

05. Room t° □□□

---

06. Body Mass (kg) □□□□

07. Stature (stretched/cm) □□□□ □□□□ □□□□ □□□□

---

08. Shoulder flexion	□□□	□□□	□□□	□□□
09. Shoulder extension	□□□	□□□	□□□	□□□
10. Shoulder lateral rotation	□□□	□□□	□□□	□□□
11. Shoulder medial rotation	□□□	□□□	□□□	□□□
12. Shoulder abduction	□□□	□□□	□□□	□□□
13. Shoulder horizontal adduction	□□□	□□□	□□□	□□□
14. Elbow flexion	□□□	□□□	□□□	□□□
15. Elbow extension	□□□	□□□	□□□	□□□
16. Forearm pronation	□□□	□□□	□□□	□□□
17. Forearm supination	□□□	□□□	□□□	□□□
18. Wrist flexion	□□□	□□□	□□□	□□□
19. Wrist extension	□□□	□□□	□□□	□□□
20. Wrist radial deviation	□□□	□□□	□□□	□□□
21. Wrist ulnar deviation	□□□	□□□	□□□	□□□
22. Hip flexion (bent leg)	□□□	□□□	□□□	□□□
23. Hip flexion (straight leg)	□□□	□□□	□□□	□□□
24. Hip extension	□□□	□□□	□□□	□□□
25. Hip abduction	□□□	□□□	□□□	□□□
26. Hip adduction	□□□	□□□	□□□	□□□
27. Hip medial rotation	□□□	□□□	□□□	□□□
28. Hip lateral rotation	□□□	□□□	□□□	□□□
29. Knee flexion	□□□	□□□	□□□	□□□
30. Knee extension	□□□	□□□	□□□	□□□
31. Knee medial rotation	□□□	□□□	□□□	□□□
32. Knee lateral rotation	□□□	□□□	□□□	□□□
33. Ankle dorsiflexion	□□□	□□□	□□□	□□□
34. Ankle plantarflexion	□□□	□□□	□□□	□□□

WARM-UP : YES ☐ NO ☐

IF YES : HOW LONG, WHAT KIND ?

....

....

SPORT :

....

DAILY PHYSICAL ACTIVITY :

....

BODY TYPE :

....

INJURIES :

....

TESTING : Passive ☐ Active ☐

Figure 6.5 Proforma for goniometric measurements.

shoulder flexion in a pure sagittal plane, hand palms turned towards each other, elbows extended (Figure 6.6). Landmarks are made at the middle of the lateral side of the upper arm at the level of the deltoid tuberosity and of the lateral epicondyle of the humerus.

The stationary arm of the goniometer is positioned along the thorax parallel to the board of the table, while the moving arm is in line with the longitudinal axis of the upper arm, oriented on both landmarks.

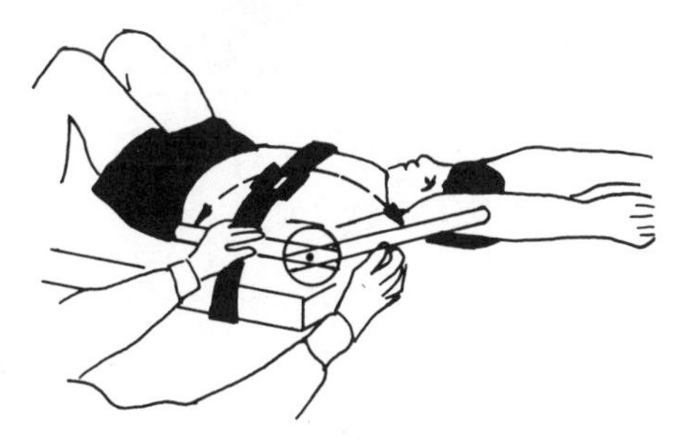

Figure 6.6 Measurement of shoulder flexion.

(b) Shoulder extension

We recommend the international or modified goniometer. The subject lies prone on a table, head in neutral position (if possible), small pillow under abdomen to avoid hyperlordosis. A bilateral shoulder extension is executed in a sagittal plane, elbows extended, hand palms in the prolongation of the forearms turned towards each other (Figure 6.7). The landmarks are: the middle of the lateral side of the upper arm at the level of the deltoid tuberosity and the lateral epicondyle of the humerus. The stationary arm of the goniometer is positioned along the thorax parallel to the board of the table and the moving arm is in line with the longitudinal axis of the upper arm, oriented on both landmarks.

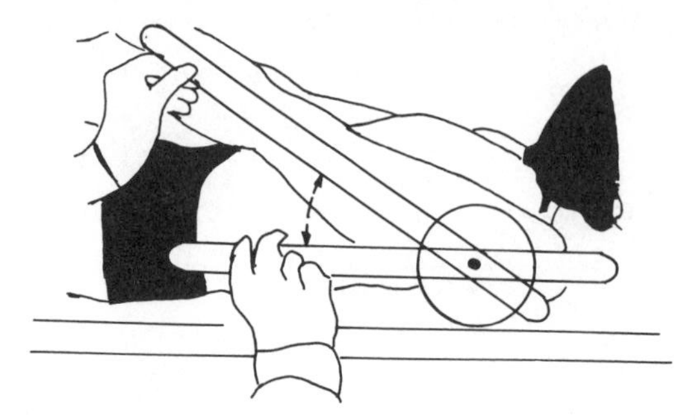

Figure 6.7 Measurement of shoulder extension.

(c) Shoulder lateral (external) rotation

We recommend the Labrique goniometer and the use of its blue scale. The subject lies prone on a table, shoulder in 90° abduction, elbow flexed 90°, wrist in neutral position (hand in prolongation of forearm, palm towards end of table, thumb directed towards the medial axis of the body), upper arm resting on table, elbow free. The subject performs a maximal lateral rotation, fixing humerus in the same abduction angle on the table, shoulder in contact with table, head in neutral position (if possible) (Figure 6.8). The landmarks are the tip of the olecranon and the tip of the ulnar styloid process (this side is facing end of table). The goniometer is positioned in line with the longitudinal axis of the forearm, oriented on both landmarks.

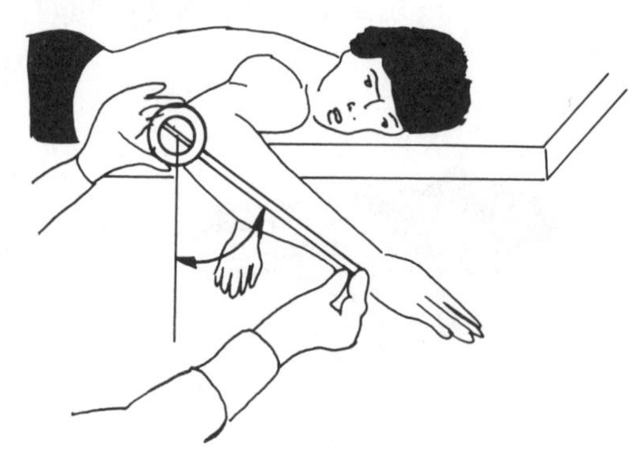

Figure 6.8 Measurement of shoulder lateral rotation.

(d) Shoulder medial (internal) rotation

We recommend the Labrique goniometer and the use of its blue scale. The subject lies prone on a table, shoulder in 90° abduction, elbow flexed 90°, wrist in neutral position (hand in prolongation of forearm), palm towards end of table, thumb directed towards the medial axis of the body, upper arm resting on table, elbow free. The subject performs a maximal medial rotation, fixing humerus in the same abduction angle on the table, shoulder in contact with table, head in neutral position (Figure 6.9). The landmarks are the tip of the olecranon and the tip of the ulnar styloid process (this side is facing the end of table). The goniometer is positioned in line with the longitudinal axis of the forearm, oriented on both landmarks.

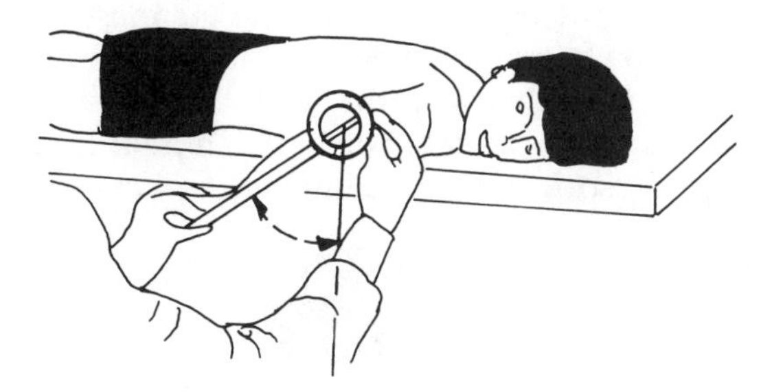

Figure 6.9 Measurement of shoulder medial rotation.

(e) Shoulder abduction

The international goniometer is recommended for this measurement. The subject sits on a chair, feet on the floor, hips and knees flexed 90°. The abduction is performed bilaterally in order to avoid compensatory movements within the spine (Figure 6.10). The palms are kept in a pure sagittal plane, thumbs directed forwards, elbows extended, wrists in neutral position (palms in prolongation of forearms). Landmarks are indicated, when maximal abduction is reached, on the middle of the superior part of the upper arm and on the lateral epicondyle of the humerus. The angulus acromii, the deltoid tuberosity can be helpful in determining the middle of the upper part of the humerus. The stationary arm of the goniometer is positioned parallel with the spine, the moving arm is in line with the longitudinal axis of the humerus, oriented on both landmarks.

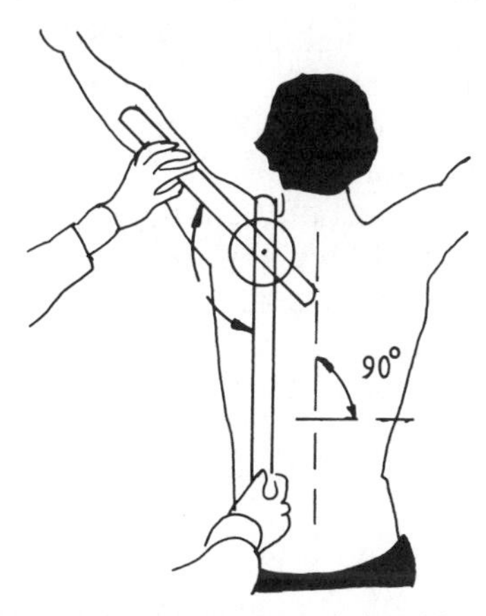

Figure 6.10 Measurement of shoulder abduction.

(f) Shoulder horizontal adduction

The international goniometer is recommended for this measurement. The subject sits on a chair, feet on the floor, hips and knees flexed 90°, back against a wall; the extended arm is kept 90° horizontally forwards and the hand is in the prolongation of the forearm, palm facing the medial axis of the body. A maximal adduction of the arm is performed in a horizontal plane, while both shoulder blades remain in contact with the wall (Figure 6.11). When maximal horizontal adduction is reached, landmarks are indicated on the middle of the upper and the lower part of the humerus. The deltoid tuberosity and the most ventral aspect of the lateral epicondyle of the humerus can be helpful in determining these landmarks.

The stationary arm is kept parallel with the wall, the moving arm is parallel with the longitudinal axis of the upper arm, oriented on both landmarks. It is important to read the ROM on the external (green) scale of the goniometer.

Figure 6.11 Measurement of shoulder horizontal adduction.

(g) Elbow flexion

The international goniometer is recommended for this measurement. The subject lies supine on a table, knees flexed, feet on the table.

The arm to be measured is held in a sagittal plane. The forearm is in a neutral position (palm directed toward the thigh). The subject performs a complete flexion of the elbow (Figure 6.12). The hand remains extended, in the prolongation of the forearm.

The stationary arm is positioned parallel with the longitudinal axis of the humerus. The deltoid tuberosity and the ventral aspect of the lateral epicondyle of the humerus under the extensor carpi radialis longus and brevis muscles can be helpful in determining the midline of the humerus. The moving arm is aligned parallel with the longitudinal axis of the forearm. The middle of the radial head under the extensor carpi radialis longus and brevis muscle, and the styloid process of the radius can be helpful in determining the reference points for the forearm.

(h) Elbow extension

The international goniometer is recommended for this measurement. The subject lies supine on a table, knees flexed, feet on the table. The arm to be measured is situated in a

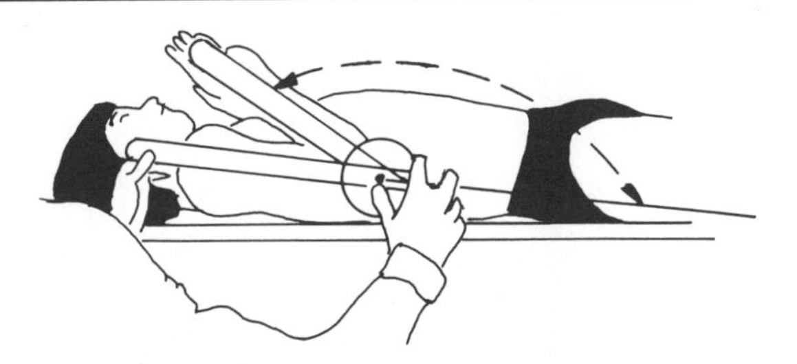

Figure 6.12 Measurement of elbow flexion.

sagittal plane, the elbow is flexed and the forearm is in a position between pronation and supination.

For the measurement of elbow hyperextension, the subject sits on a chair with the arm and forearm in the same base position as above. The subject extends (or eventually hyperextends) the elbow (Figure 6.13). The hand remains extended in the prolongation of the forearm. The thumb and fingers are kept together. Landmarks are indicated, at maximal ROM, on the acromiale, the tip of the lateral epicondyle of the humerus and on the head of the capitatum bone. The stationary arm is positioned parallel with the longitudinal axis of the humerus. The deltoid tuberosity and the ventral aspect of the lateral epicondyle of the humerus under the extensor carpi radialis longus and brevis muscles can be helpful in determining the midline of the humerus. The moving arm is aligned parallel with the longitudinal axis of the forearm. The middle of the radial head under the extensor carpi radialis longus and brevis muscle, and the styloid process of the radius can be helpful in determining the reference points for the forearm.

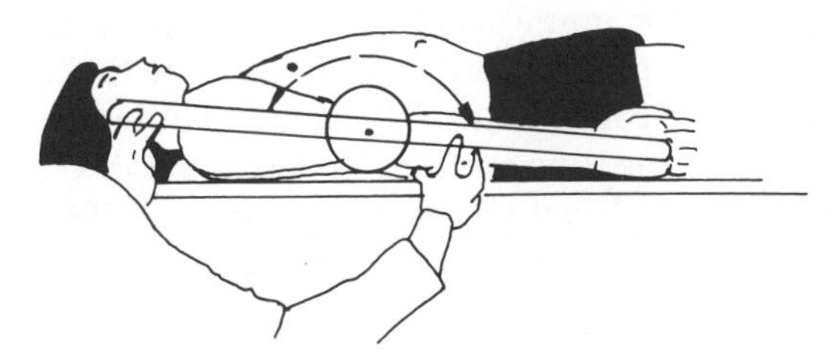

Figure 6.13 Measurement of elbow extension.

(i) Forearm pronation

The goniometer of Labrique used in its holder is recommended. The subject sits on a chair. The upper arm of the side to be measured is held in a neutral position, the elbow is flexed 90°, and the forearm is kept in a neutral position between pronation and supination.

The hand is extended, in the prolongation of the forearm with the fingers extended and kept together. The subject performs a complete pronation (Figure 6.14), taking care that the humerus remains in a pure vertical position and that no compensatory motion occurs in the shoulder girdle and/or the spine (should this occur, bilateral pronations should be carried out). Eventually, landmarks could be indicated on the dorsal side of the head of the ulna and on the distal epiphysis of the radius. The flat side of the goniometer holder is

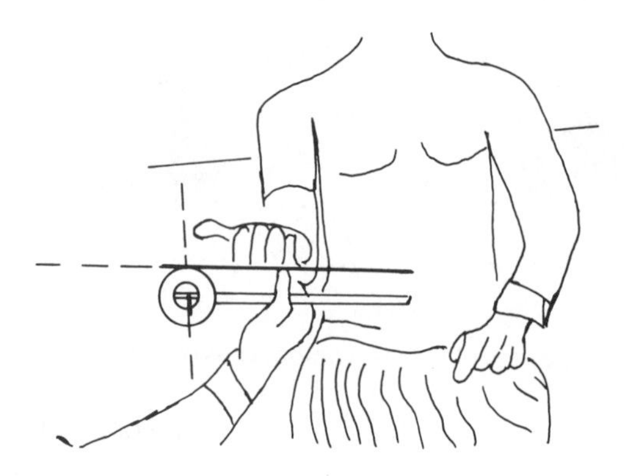

Figure 6.14 Measurement of forearm pronation.

placed against the dorsal side of the most distal part of the forearm, while the red scale is kept upwards and the pointer indicates zero degrees before pronation is performed.

(j) Forearm supination

The goniometer of Labrique used in its holder is recommended for this technique. The subject sits on a chair. The upper arm of the side to be measured is held in a neutral position, the elbow is flexed 90°, and the forearm is kept in a neutral position between pronation and supination. The hand is extended, in the prolongation of the forearm with the fingers extended and kept together. The subject performs a complete supination (Figure 6.15), taking care that the humerus remains in a pure vertical position and that no compensatory motion occurs in the shoulder girdle and/or the spine (should this occur bilateral supinations should be carried out). Eventually, landmarks could be indicated on the dorsal side of the head of the ulna and on the distal epiphysis of the radius. The flat side of the goniometer holder is placed against the dorsal side of the most distal part of the forearm, while the blue scale is kept upwards and the pointer indicates zero degrees before supination is performed.

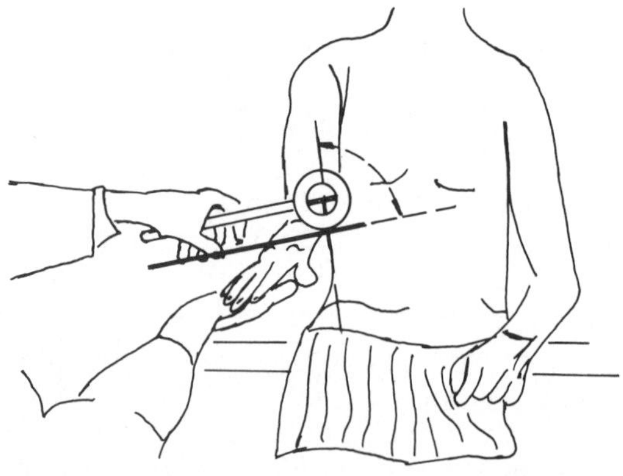

Figure 6.15 Measurement of forearm supination.

(k) Wrist flexion

The international goniometer is recommended. The subject sits on a chair, upper arm along the trunk, elbow flexed 90°, forearm in pronation, not in support, hand and fingers are aligned with the forearm. A maximal wrist flexion is executed, metacarpals and phalanges of fingers are kept in one line, thumb kept in neutral position (Figure 6.16). A first line reflecting the longitudinal axis of the third metacarpal bone, between the base and the head of this metacarpal at the dorsal side functions as one landmark; a second line reflecting the longitudinal axis of the forearm which, for this purpose, can be drawn between the lateral epicondyle of the humerus and the tip of the styloid process of the ulna serves as the other landmark.

The stationary arm of the goniometer is positioned parallel with the longitudinal axis of the forearm, oriented on both landmarks. The moving arm is in line with the longitudinal axis of the third metacarpal bone, observed at the dorsal side.

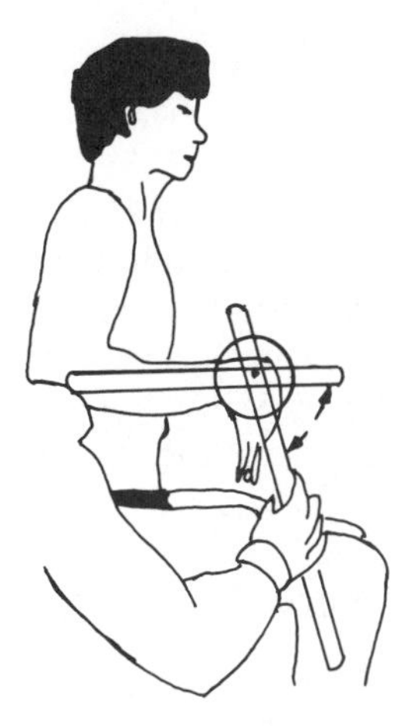

Figure 6.16 Measurement of wrist flexion.

(l) Wrist extension

The international goniometer is recommended. The subject sits on a chair, upper arm along the trunk, elbow flexed 90°, forearm in pronation, not in support, hand and fingers are aligned with the forearm. A maximal wrist extension is executed, fingers flexed to avoid passive insufficiency of the finger flexors, thumb fixed inside the closed fist (Figure 6.17). A first line reflecting the longitudinal axis of the third metacarpal bone, between the base and the head of this metacarpal at the dorsal side functions as one landmark; a second line reflecting the longitudinal axis of the forearm which, for this purpose, can be drawn between the lateral epicondyle of the humerus and the tip of the styloid process of the ulna serves as the other landmark. The stationary arm of the goniometer is positioned parallel with the longitudinal axis of the forearm, oriented on both landmarks. The moving arm is in line with the longitudinal axis of the third metacarpal bone, observed at the dorsal side.

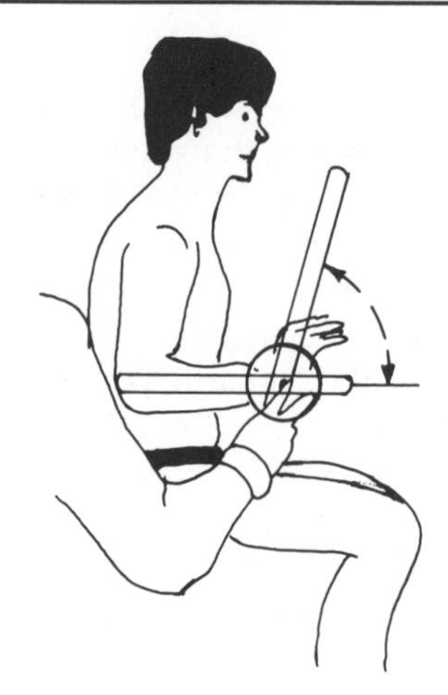

Figure 6.17 Measurement of wrist extension.

(m) Wrist radial deviation

The international goniometer is recommended for this measurement which is alternatively indicated in the literature as radial abduction or radial inclination.

The subject sits on a chair with upper arms kept along the body. The elbow at the side to be measured is flexed 90°, the forearm is in pronation and in support on the table. The hand and fingers are in the prolongation of the forearm.

The subject performs a radial deviation in the wrist (Figure 6.18) while the palm of the hand remains continuously in contact with the table. The fingers and thumbs are kept together. The humerus should not move.

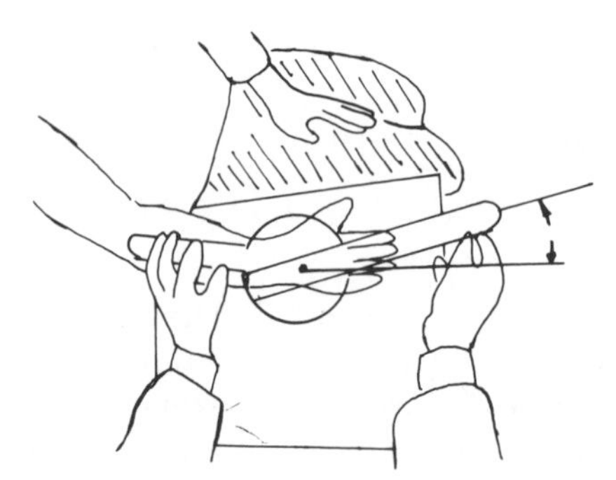

Figure 6.18 Measurement of wrist radial deviation.

Landmarks are indicated at maximal radial deviation. The stationary arm of the goniometer is parallel with the longitudinal axis of the forearm, held in pronation. To identify this line, it can be helpful to situate the middle of the upper part of the forearm between the brachioradialis muscle and the extensor carpi radialis muscle, and to localize the middle of the connection between the radial and the ulnar styloid processes in the lower part of the forearm.

The moving arm is held parallel with the longitudinal axis of the third metacarpal, situated between the middle of the dorsal aspect of the basis and the middle of the dorsal aspect of the head of this metacarpal bone.

(n) Wrist ulnar deviation

The international goniometer is recommended for this measurement which is alternatively indicated in the literature as ulnar abduction or ulnar inclination.

The subject sits on a chair with upper arms kept along the body. The elbow at the side to be measured is flexed 90°, the forearm is in pronation and in support on the table. The hand and fingers are in the prolongation of the forearm.

The subject performs ulnar deviation in the wrist (Figure 6.19) while the palm of the hand remains continuously in contact with the table. The fingers and thumbs are kept together. The humerus should not move.

Figure 6.19 Measurement of wrist ulnar deviation.

Landmarks are indicated at maximal ulnar deviation. The stationary arm of the goniometer is parallel with the longitudinal axis of the forearm, held in pronation. To identify this line, it can be helpful to situate the middle of the upper part of the forearm between the brachioradialis muscle and the extensor carpi radialis muscle, and to localize the middle of the connection between the radial and the ulnar styloid processes in the lower part of the forearm.

The moving arm is held parallel with the longitudinal axis of the third metacarpal, situated between the middle of the dorsal aspect of the basis and the middle of the dorsal aspect of the head of this metacarpal bone.

(o) Hip flexion (bent leg)

We recommend the Labrique goniometer and use of its red scale. The subject lies supine on a table and carries out, in a pure sagittal plane, a complete flexion in the hip, bent knee to avoid passive insufficiency of the hamstrings (Figure 6.20). When the opposite leg is beginning to lose contact with the table, a reading of the amplitude should be made, as this is a sign that the movement is continued in the spine. Therefore it is recommended to use a velcro strap at the distal end of the opposite thigh or to call for assistance. The landmarks are the tip of the greater trochanter and the lateral femoral epicondyle. The goniometer is kept with the red scale left of the examiner (the needle is then at zero degrees at the start of the motion), in line with the longitudinal axis of the thigh oriented on both landmarks.

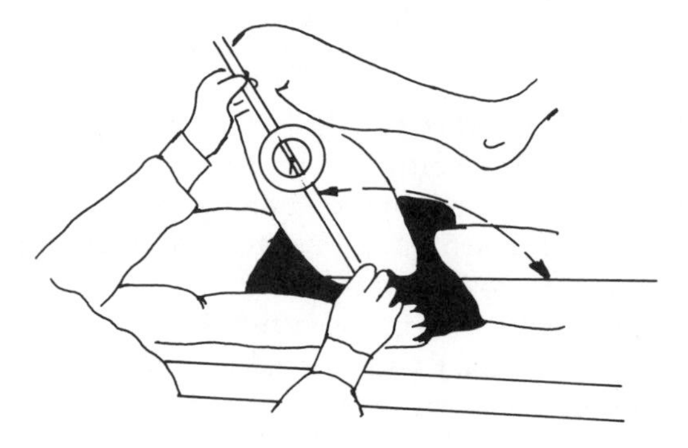

Figure 6.20 Measurement of hip flexion (bent leg).

(p) Straight leg raising as a measurement of coxofemoral flexibility

When the effect of hamstring stretches on coxofemoral flexibility (hip flexion with a straight leg) is measured by goniometry, the examiner should take into account the angular change between the pelvis and the femur (Clayson *et al.*, 1966). Straight leg raising indeed includes a posterior pelvic tilt and a reduction of lumbar lordosis.

First a transverse line for the pelvis should be considered, connecting the anterior superior iliac spine with the posterior superior iliac spine (line AB in Figure 6.21). A line CD drawn perpendicular to this line in the direction of the most superior point of the greater trochanter serves as the longitudinal axis for the pelvis, and a line DE from the most superior point of the greater trochanter to the lateral epicondyle of the femur serves as the

Figure 6.21 Reference lines for the measurementof hip extension described by Mundale *et al.* (1956).

longitudinal axis of the femur. Between the lines CD and DE, an angle, α, can be measured in the resting position. An angle, β, is obtained between these reference lines in maximal flexion (Figure 6.22). Hence, in order to obtain the result of an isolated coxofemoral flexion, the value of α must be subtracted from that of β. We recommend the VUB-goniometer with a second carriage (Figure 6.23) which can slide along one of the arms and through which a very flexible piece of plastic can be inserted (based on previous work by Clayson *et al.*, 1966). The subject lies sideways with the trunk aligned with the posterior

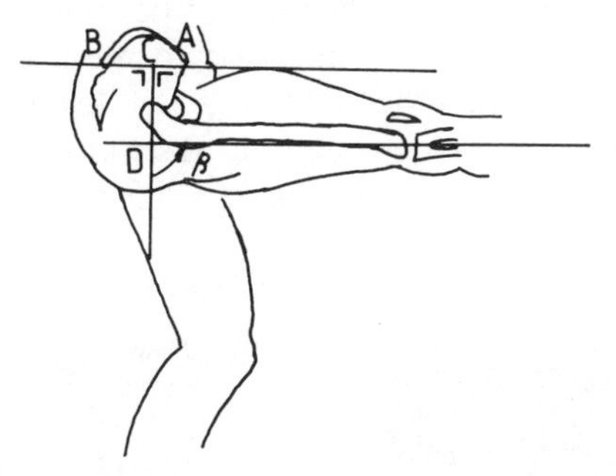

Figure 6.22 Angle β between the reference lines considered in the position of maximal hip flexion with the straight leg.

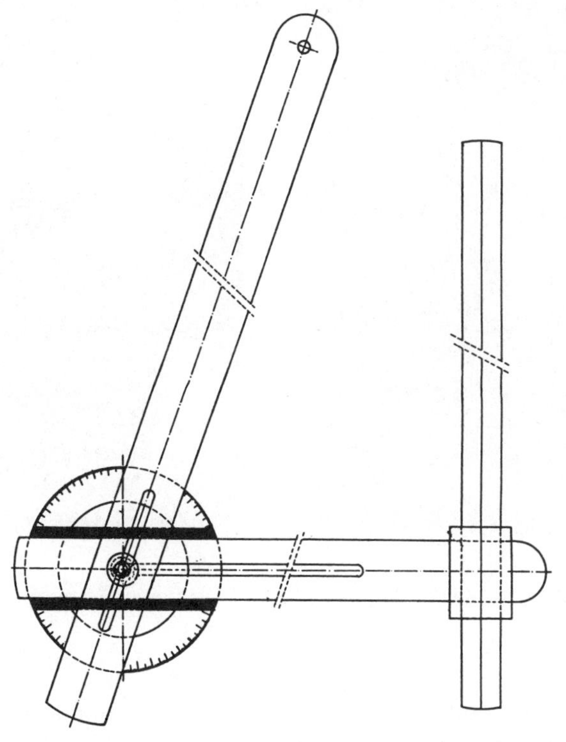

Figure 6.23 VUB-goniometer with second carriage.

edge of the table (Figure 6.24 a, b). For reasons of stability the supporting leg is slightly bent in hip and knee joint, with the sole of the foot parallel with the posterior edge of the table. Before starting the measurements, care must be taken to ensure that the acromiale, the superior point of the greater trochanter and the lateral epicondyle of the femur are well aligned. This position offers several advantages. The reference points on the pelvis and femur can be more easily reached. It also offers stability of the subject's body while moving, and hip flexion against gravity is avoided. In one study (Van Roy *et al.*, 1987) a significant difference was obtained between the measurements of angle α in lying side-ways and those of angle α in the normal standing position. Once angle α is determined, maximal hip flexion without bending the knee is performed. Abduction of the subject's leg can be eliminated by an assistant who supports the leg during the movement. This assistant should not push the leg into passive hip flexion and should instruct the subject not to perform movements of hip rotations, knee flexions or movements of the ankle joint during hamstring stretching.

The angle β is determined. The final score is obtained by subtracting angle α from angle β.

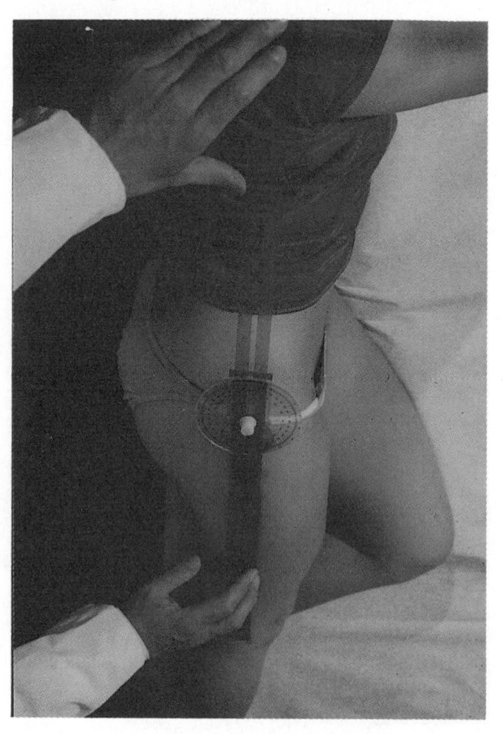

(a)

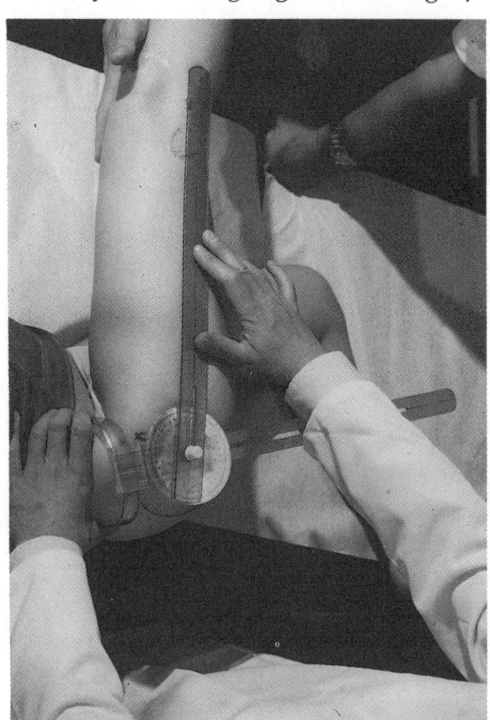

(b)

Figure 6.24 (a+b) Measurement of hip flexion (straight leg).

(q) Hip extension

The Labrique goniometer and its blue scale are used, or another inclinometer with long arm(s) is recommended. The subject lies prone at the end of table, legs outside the table, feet on ground, a small pillow under the abdomen; opposite leg in greatest possible flexion in the hip, hands fixing sides of table. A maximal extension in the hip is performed while the opposite leg is kept bent (Figure 6.25). The landmarks are the tip of the greater trochanter and the lateral femoral condyle. The goniometer is kept with the blue scale left of the examiner (the needle is then at zero degrees at the start of the motion), in line with the longitudinal axis of the thigh oriented on both landmarks.

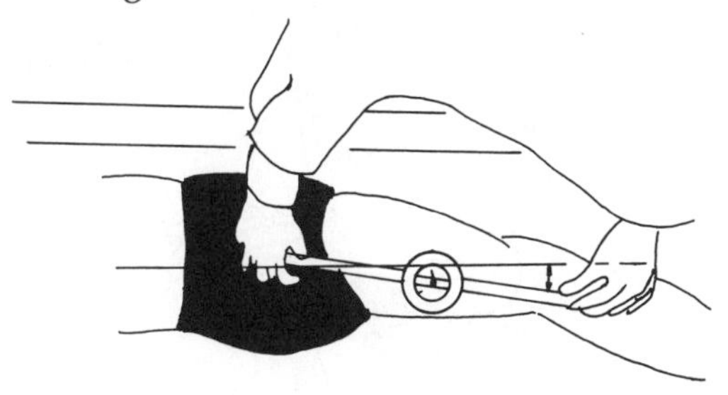

Figure 6.25 Measurement of hip extension.

(r) Hip abduction

An international (with long arms) or modified goniometer is recommended. The subject lies supine on a table with the opposite hip in slight abduction in order to allow the lower leg of the opposite leg to hang outside the table so that the hips can be stabilized. A maximal abduction is performed with straight leg in the plane of the table, without lateral rotation of foot point at the end of the movement (Figure 6.26). The landmarks are the left and right superior anterior iliac spines and the lateral board of the quadriceps tendon. The stationary arm of the goniometer is positioned on the line between both spines; the moving arm is in line with the longitudinal axis of the thigh, oriented on the spine of the side to be measured and the lateral board of the quadriceps tendon.

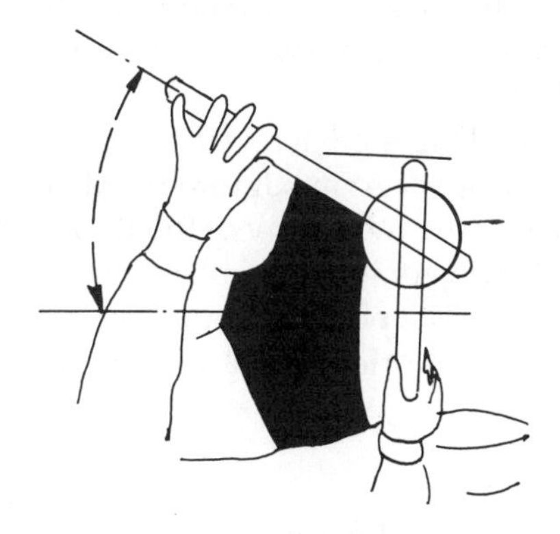

Figure 6.26 Measurement of hip abduction.

(s) Hip adduction

An international goniometer (with long arms) is recommended. The subject lies supine on a table. A maximal adduction is performed with slightly elevated thigh (about 40° hip flexion), and extended knee, without rotation in the hip (Figure 6.27). The landmarks are the left and right superior anterior iliac spines and lateral board of the quadriceps tendon.

The stationary arm of the goniometer is positioned on the line between both spines; the moving arm is in line with the longitudinal axis of the thigh, oriented on the spine of the side to be measured and the lateral board of the quadriceps tendon.

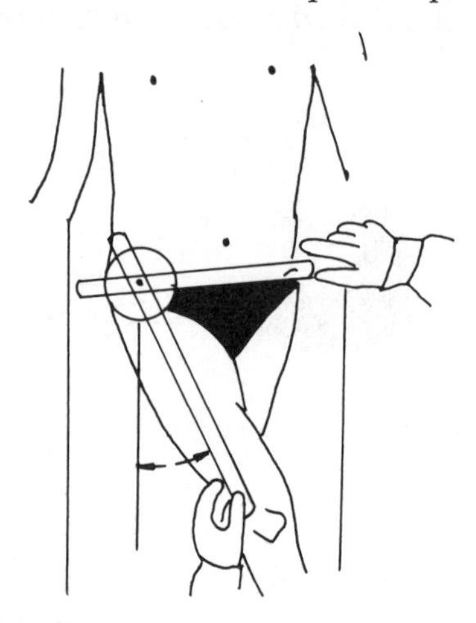

Figure 6.27 Measurement of hip adduction.

(t) Hip medial rotation

The goniometer of Labrique with its blue scale is recommended for this measurement which is alternatively indicated in the literature as hip internal rotation. The subject lies supine on a table with heterolateral leg bent in knee and hip and with heel in support on the table. The hip at the side to be measured is in neutral position relative to the trunk, the knee is flexed 90° and the lower leg hangs outside and at the end of the table. The pelvis is fixed on the table with a velcro strap.

The subject performs a maximal hip medial rotation (Figure 6.28). Compensatory motion such as pelvis tilting must be avoided. At maximum ROM, landmarks are indicated on the ventral margin of the tibia below the tuberosity of the tibia and on a point located about 5 cm above the tibiotarsal joint. The goniometer is kept so that the blue scale is positioned at the upper part of the tibia bone. The pointer now indicates zero degrees at the beginning of the movement. The goniometer is oriented on the landmarks.

(u) Hip lateral rotation

The goniometer of Labrique with its blue scale is recommended for this measurement which is alternatively indicated in the literature as hip external rotation. The subject lies supine on a table with heterolateral leg bent in knee and hip and with heel in support on the table. The hip at the side to be measured is in neutral position relative to the trunk, the knee is flexed 90° and the lower leg hangs outside and at the end of the table. The pelvis is fixed on the table with a velcro strap.

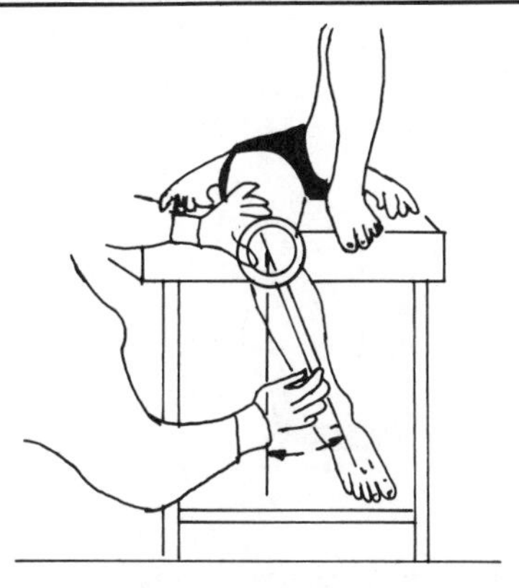

Figure 6.28 Measurement of hip medial rotation.

The subject performs a maximal hip lateral rotation (Figure 6.29). Compensatory motion such as pelvis tilt must be avoided. At maximum ROM, landmarks are indicated on the ventral margin of the tibia below the tuberosity of the tibia and on a point located about 5 cm above the tibiotarsal joint. The goniometer is kept so that the blue scale is positioned at the upper part of the tibia bone. The pointer now indicates zero degrees at the beginning of the movement. The goniometer is oriented on the landmarks.

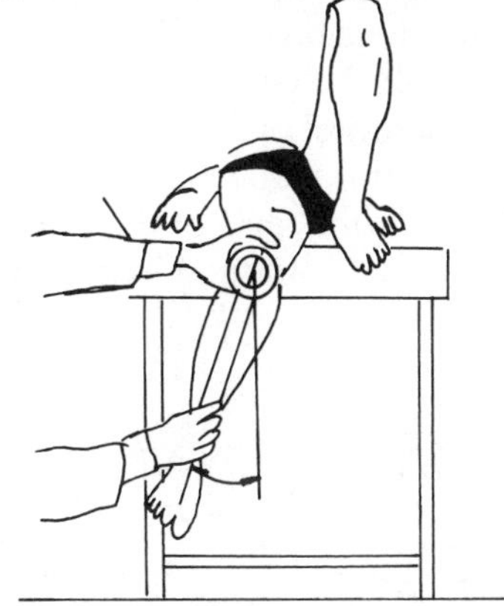

Figure 6.29 Measurement of hip lateral rotation.

(v) Knee flexion

An international goniometer (with long arms) is recommended. The subject lies supine on a table. A maximal flexion of the knee is performed, footsole gliding over the table in the direction of the heel (Figure 6.30). The landmarks are the tip of the greater trochanter, the lateral femoral epicondyle, the tip of the fibular head and the middle of the inferior side of the lateral malleolus. The stationary arm of the goniometer is positioned in line with the longitudinal axis of the thigh, oriented on the tip of the greater trochanter and the lateral

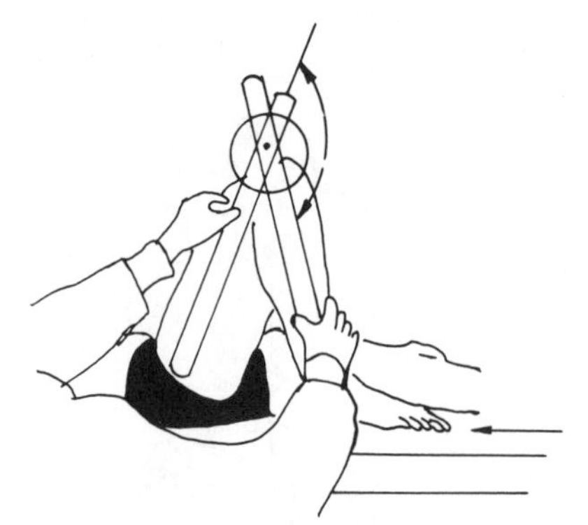

Figure 6.30 Measurement of knee flexion.

femoral epicondyle. The moving arm is in line with the longitudinal axis of the lower leg, oriented on both landmarks.

(w) Knee extension

An international (with long arms) goniometer is recommended. The subject lies supine on a table, leg to be measured flexed, foot supported on the table, the opposite leg extended, arms alongside body. A maximal extension of the knee is performed, footsole gliding over the table in the direction of the end of the table (Figure 6.31). The landmarks are the tip of the greater trochanter, the lateral femoral epicondyle, the tip of the fibular head and the middle of the inferior side of the lateral malleolus. The stationary arm of the goniometer is positioned in line with the longitudinal axis of the thigh, oriented on both landmarks. The moving arm is in line with the longitudinal axis of the lower leg, oriented on both landmarks.

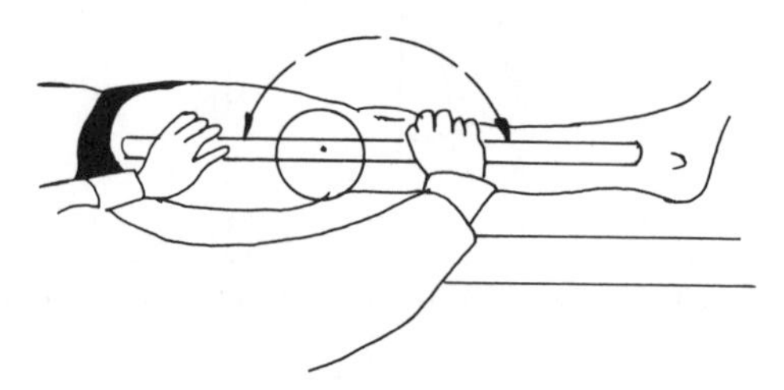

Figure 6.31 Measurement of knee extension.

(x) Knee medial rotation

The international goniometer is recommended. The subject sits on a chair with hip and knee at the side to be measured flexed 90°. The foot is flat on a paper (size about 30 × 50 cm), fixed on the floor. The heterolateral knee is a little more extended in order not to disturb the execution of the movement. The subject grasps with both hands the front side of the chair close to the knee to fix the lower limb. A maximal knee medial rotation is performed (Figure 6.32) without compensatory hip motion and knee flexion or extension. Landmarks are indicated on the projection of the middle of the calcaneus tuberosity at the bottom side of the heel and at the longitudinal axis of the second metatarsal bone. The landmarks must be localized on the paper when the foot is in neutral position (AA′); the same landmarks must then be indicated when the knee medial rotation is performed (BB′). Two lines A–A′ and B–B′ should be drawn and continued until the junction. The angle between the two lines on the paper is subsequently read with the goniometer.

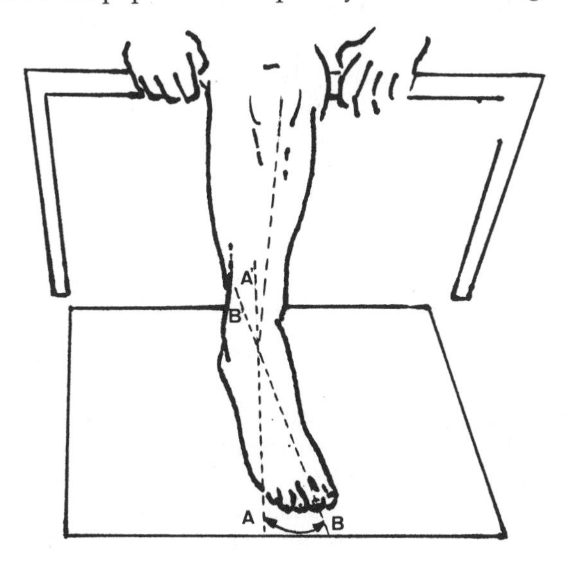

Figure 6.32 Measurement of knee medial rotation.

(y) Knee lateral rotation

The international goniometer is recommended. The subject sits on a chair with hip and knee at the side to be measured flexed 90°. The foot is flat on a paper (size about 30 × 50), fixed on the floor. The heterolateral knee is a little more extended in order not to disturb the execution of the movement. The subject grasps with both hands the front side of the chair close to the knee to fix the lower limb. A maximal knee lateral rotation is performed (Figure 6.33) without compensatory hip motion and knee flexion or extension. Landmarks are indicated on the projection of the middle of the calcaneus tuberosity at the bottom side of the heel and at the longitudinal axis of the second metatarsal bone. The landmarks must be localized on the paper when the foot is in neutral position (AA′); the same landmarks must then be indicated when the knee lateral rotation is performed (BB′). Two lines A–A′ and B–B′ should be drawn and continued until the junction. The angle between the two lines on the paper is subsequently read with the goniometer.

(z) Ankle dorsiflexion

We recommend a modified or international goniometer with an extended stationary arm. The subject lies supine on a table, lower legs hanging outside table, knees flexed 90° (to

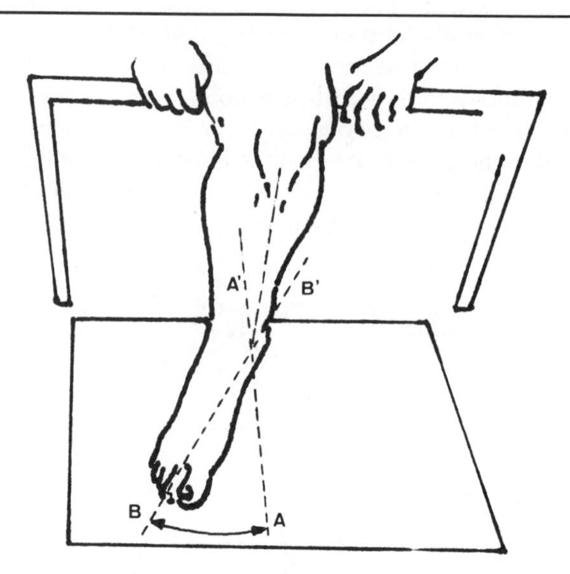

Figure 6.33 Measurement of knee lateral rotation.

eliminate passive insufficiency of the gastrocnemius muscle). A maximal dorsiflexion is executed at the talocrural joint, making sure that the knee remains at 90° flexion (Figure 6.34). The landmarks are the tip of the fibular head at the lateral side of the lower leg; the middle of the inferior side of the lateral malleolus; a line parallel to the footsole is drawn starting from the middle of the lateral side of the head of the fifth metatarsal. The stationary arm of the goniometer is in line with the longitudinal axis of the lower leg, oriented on both landmarks. The moving arm is in line with the longitudinal axis of the foot, oriented on the constructed reference line.

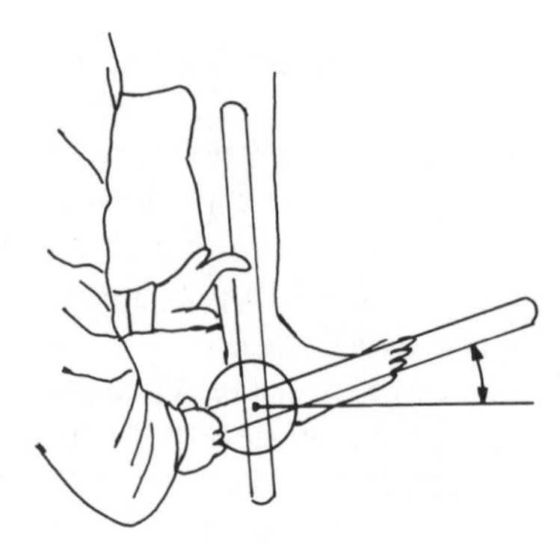

Figure 6.34 Measurement of ankle dorsiflexion.

(aa) Ankle plantarflexion

We recommend a modified or international goniometer with an extended stationary arm. The subject lies supine on a table, lower legs hanging outside table, knees flexed 90°. A maximal plantarflexion is executed at the talocrural joint, making sure that the knee remains at 90° flexion. A flexion of the toes is normal with this movement (Figure 6.35). The landmarks are the tip of the fibular head at the lateral side of the lower leg; the middle of the inferior side of the lateral malleolus; a line parallel to the footsole is drawn starting from the middle of the lateral side of the head of the fifth metatarsal. The stationary arm of the goniometer is in line with the longitudinal axis of the lower leg, oriented on both landmarks. The moving arm is in line with the longitudinal axis of the foot, oriented on the constructed reference line.

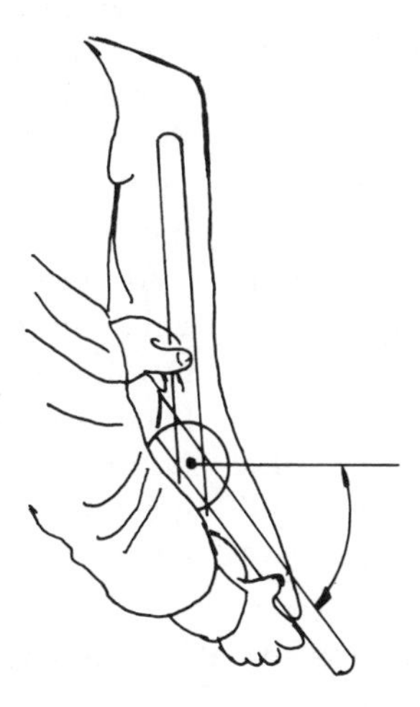

Figure 6.35 Measurement of ankle plantarflexion.

6.4 GENERAL DISCUSSION

From the detailed descriptions of the measurements above, it should be clear that goniometry requires a good knowledge of anatomy and anthropometry. The goniometer is a reliable instrument when used by experienced individuals who follow carefully the standardized protocol.

When bony landmarks are visible or easy to determine, the goniometer usually provides an accurate and convenient clinical method of measuring joint motion. However, when the bony landmarks are not easy to locate, for whatever reasons, the goniometer may not give accurate information and satisfaction.

Measurement precision will also improve when the examiner is assisted by a second examiner, checks and calibrates the equipment, explains the test procedures to the subject, adheres to triple measurements and notes on the proforma those factors that may affect the test results such as age, gender, body type, certain pathologies or injuries, daily physical activities, room temperature and previous warm-up. Although most of these variables and their eventual causal relationship with flexibility have been reviewed elsewhere (Borms, 1984; Hubley-Kozey, 1991), it is nonetheless important to mention two factors, namely, temperature and warm-up.

Although Wright (1973) demonstrated that stiffness increases with decreased temperature and vice-versa and thus found a means of explaining the circadian variation in joint stiffness with lowest levels in the morning and late evening, others (Grobaker and Stull, 1975, Lakie *et al.*, 1979) could not entirely confirm these findings.

Research tends to indicate positive effects of warm-up (Skubic and Hodgkins, 1957; Atha and Wheatly, 1976). Most coaches and athletes believe that warm-up is essential to prevent injuries, but there is very little direct research evidence to support their beliefs. Even though the scientific basis for recommending warm-up exercises is not conclusive, we advise a general warm-up prior to the main activity and prior to flexibility testing. A 5–10 minutes moderate intensity warm-up is suggested before testing, but should be standardized.

The interpretation of results can be done in different ways: pre- and post-comparisons (athletic season, before and after treatment and so on), carry-over effect, left–right comparisons and finally comparison with norms. The latter is difficult as few normative data exist for 'normal' populations (per age and gender) or for athletic groups. 'Normal' ROMs for athletes from different sports are not so well documented in the literature. Tables 6.1 and 6.2 give norms based on the measurements described in this chapter for a population of over 100 physical education and physiotherapy students (mixed sample), male and female (as separate groups). They were all tested in the period 1984–90. A typical proforma, used by us, is displayed in Figure 6.5.

In general, there has been little appreciation that flexibility is more complex than one might think. Thus measurement procedures have remained relatively simple.

Although two-dimensional goniometry is very common in the daily practice of rehabilitation medicine and physiotherapy, it becomes clear that many shortcomings of two-dimensional joint motion analysis in general hamper its content validity. With an increasing interest in the different rotation

Table 6.1 Flexibility norms for men (physical education and physiotherapy students 20 years of age)

	Range	P_{25}	P_{50}	P_{75}
Shoulder flexion	154–195	170	177	188
Shoulder extension	25–80	43	49	59
Shoulder lateral rotation	43–93	56	72	79
Shoulder medial rotation	16–92	47	64	75
Shoulder abduction	110–199	143	156	181
Shoulder horizontal adduction	17–60	30	35	46
Elbow flexion	130–156	139	144	151
Elbow extension	168–191	175	179	181
Forearm pronation	40–98	78	85	91
Forearm supination	56–98	80	90	92
Wrist flexion	60–94	65	69	79
Wrist extension	45–88	58	67	75
Wrist radial deviation	12–38	20	27	30
Wrist ulnar deviation	19–59	33	44	50
Hip flexion (bent leg)	105–155	120	128	133
Hip flexion (straight leg)	–	–	–	–
Hip extension	9–29	18	21	26
Hip abduction	–	–	–	–
Hip adduction	9–68	16	29	31
Hip medial rotation	26–50	30	33	38
Hip lateral rotation	26–70	32	36	42
Knee flexion	130–155	136	142	146
Knee extension	160–187	175	178	181
Knee medial rotation	21–60	27	37	46
Knee lateral rotation	20–53	25	28	37
Ankle dorsiflexion	4–37	6	13	22
Ankle plantarflexion	18–78	47	57	70

Table 6.2 Flexibility norms for women (physical education and physiotherapy students 20 years of age)

	Range	P_{25}	P_{50}	P_{75}
Shoulder flexion	154–197	172	177	183
Shoulder extension	20–86	46	54	59
Shoulder lateral rotation	13–89	51	65	77
Shoulder medial rotation	24–89	52	66	74
Shoulder abduction	105–203	125	147	179
Shoulder horizontal adduction	11–55	27	36	40
Elbow flexion	128–161	136	144	151
Elbow extension	170–190	178	181	185
Forearm pronation	40–99	79	88	94
Forearm supination	51–99	80	88	91
Wrist flexion	62–95	68	70	79
Wrist extension	30–89	62	69	75
Wrist radial deviation	12–49	22	29	33
Wrist ulnar deviation	19–58	39	45	50
Hip flexion (bent leg)	103–155	115	126	130
Hip flexion (straight leg)	–	–	–	–
Hip extension	8–29	10	18	24
Hip abduction	–	–	–	–
Hip adduction	20–69	21	33	40
Hip medial rotation	24–65	29	32	37
Hip lateral rotation	23–62	27	30	35
Knee flexion	131–160	139	145	152
Knee extension	165–190	177	181	184
Knee medial rotation	20–69	38	48	56
Knee lateral rotation	22–54	26	34	43
Ankle dorsiflexion	1–31	12	14	20
Ankle plantarflexion	26–90	53	70	84

and translation components of joint motion, many biomechanical studies on three-dimensional aspects of the joints of the extremities and the spine have been presented during the past decades.

In the search for standardization, attempts should be made to link the biomechanical methodology and the biomechanical language to the clinical needs and the traditional language of functional anatomy. This would help to reduce the gap between fundamental research and applied technology in this field (Van Roy, 1988). In this respect, the present decade calls for appropriate but simple real time three-dimensional measuring techniques for use in clinical practice. Other practical considerations deal with further study on the so-called neutral zero position of the joints and the clinical implications of alterations of the helical axes of joint motion.

REFERENCES

AAHPERD (1984) *Technical Manual, Health Related Physical Fitness*, AAHPERD, Reston, VA.

Adrian, M. J. (1973) Cinematographic, electromyographic and electrogoniometric technique for analyzing human movements, in *Exercise and Sport Sciences Reviews*, Vol. 1. (ed. J. Wilmore), Academic Press, New York.

American Academy of Orthopaedic Surgeons (1965) Joint motion. *Method of Measuring and Recording*. Churchill Livingstone, Edinburgh, London and New York.

Atha, J. and Wheatly, D. W. (1976) The mobilising effects of repeated measurement of hip flexion. *British Journal of Sports Medicine*, **10**, 22–5.

Borms, J. (1984) Importance of flexibility in overall physical fitness. *International Journal of Physical Education*, **XXI**, 15–26.

Borms, J., Van Roy, P., Santens, J. P. and Haentjens, A. (1987) Optimal duration of static stretching exercises for improvement of coxo-femoral flexibility. *Journal of Sports Sciences*, **5**, 39–47.

Broer, M. H. and Galles, N. R. G. (1958) Importance of relationship between body measurements in performance of toe-touch test. *Research Quarterly*, **29**, 253–63.

Cave, E. F. and Roberts, S. M. (1936) A method of measuring and recording joint function. *Journal of Bone and Joint Surgery*, **18**, 455–65.

Clayson, S., Mundale, M. and Kottke, F. (1966) Goniometer adaptation for measuring hip extension. *Archives of Physical Medicine and Rehabilitation*, **47**, 255–61.

Council of Europe, Committee for the Development of Sport, Eurofit (1988) *Handbook for the Eurofit Tests of Physical Fitness*, Committee of the Development of Sport within the Council of Europe, Rome, 72 pp.

Cureton, T. K. (1941) Flexibility as an aspect of physical fitness. *Research Quarterly*, **12**, 381–90.

Ekstrand, J., Wiktorsson, M., Oberg, B. and Gillquist, J. (1982) Lower extremity goniometric measurements: a study to determine their reliability. *Archives of Physical Medicine and Rehabilitation*, **63**, 171–5.

Esch, D. and Lepley, M. (1974) *Evaluation of Joint Motion; Methods of Measurement and Recording*, University of Minnesota Press, Minneapolis, p. 33.

Fox, R. F. (1917) Demonstration of the mensuration apparatus in use at the Red Cross Clinic for the physical treatment of Officer. *Proceedings of the Royal Society of Medicine*, **10**, 63–9.

Grobaker, M. R. and Stull, G. A. (1975) Thermal applications as a determiner of joint flexibility. *American Corrective Therapy Journal*, **25**, 3–8.

Hubley-Kozey, C. L. (1991) Testing flexibility, Chapter 7. *Physiological Testing of the High-Performance Athlete* (eds J. D. MacDougall, H. A. Wenger and H. J. Green), Human Kinetics, Champaign, Il, pp. 309–59.

Hunebelle, G., Marechal, J. P. and Falize, J. (1972) Relationships between amplitude of hip movements and jumping performances, in *Training: Scientific Basis and Application* (ed. A. W. Taylor), C. C. Thomas, Springfield.

Kottke, F. J. and Mundale, M. O. (1959) Range of mobility of the cervical spine. *Archives of Physical Medicine and Rehabilitation*, **47**, 379–82.

Kraus, H. and Hirschland, R. P. (1954) Minimum muscular fitness tests in school children. *Research Quarterly*, **25**, 178–88.

Labrique, Ph. (1977) *Le Goniomètre de Labrique*, Prodim, Brussels.

Lakie, M. I, Walsh, E. G. and Wright, G. W. (1979) Cooling and wrist compliance. *Journal of Physiology*, **296**, 47–8.

Larson, L. A. (ed.) (1974) *Fitness, Health and Work Capacity: International Standards for Assessment*, Macmillan, New York.

Leighton, J. R. (1966) The Leighton flexometer and flexibility test. *Journal of the Association for Physical and Mental Rehabilitation*, **20**, 86–93.

Mundale, M. O., Hislop, H. J., Rabideau, R. J. and Kottke, F. J. (1956) Evaluation of extension of the hip. *Archives of Physical Medicine*, **37**, 75–80.

Rocher, C. and Rigaud, A. (1964) Fonctions et bilans articulaires, *Kinésitherapie et Rééducation*, Masson, Paris.

Scott, M. G. and French, E. (1950) *Evaluation in Physical Education*, C. V. Mosby, St Louis.

Skubic, V. and Hodgkins, J. (1957) Effect of warm-up activities on speed, strength and accuracy. *Research Quarterly*, **28**, 147–52.

Van Roy, P. (1981) Investigation on the validity of goniometry as measuring technique to assess wrist flexibility (in Dutch). Unpublished Licentiate thesis, Vrije Universiteit Brussel.

Van Roy, P. (1988) Magnetic resonance imaging of the knee joint, with a special application: 3-D arthrokinematic investigation of the screw-home movement of the knee (in Dutch). Unpublished PhD thesis, Vrije Universiteit Brussel.

Van Roy, P., Hebbelinck, M. and Borms, J. (1985) Introduction d'un goniomètre standard modifié avec la graduation et la branche pivotante montées sur un chariot déplacable. *Annales de Kinésitherapie*, **12**, 255–9.

Van Roy, P., Borms, J. and Haentjens, A. (1987) Goniometric study of the maintenance of hip flexibility resulting from hamstring stretches. *Physiotherapy Practice*, **3**, 52–9.

Wells, K. F. and Dillon, E. K. (1952) The sit and reach, a test of back and leg flexibility. *Research Quarterly*, **23**, 115–18.

Wright, V. (1973) Stiffness: a review of its measurement and physiological importance. *Physiotherapy*, **59**, 107–11.

Wright, V. and Johns, R. J. (1960) Physical factors concerned with the stiffness of normal and diseases joints. *Johns Hopkins Hospital Bulletin*, **106**, 215–31.

PART THREE

AEROBIC AND ANAEROBIC CONSIDERATIONS

LUNG FUNCTION 7

R. G. Eston

7.1 INTRODUCTION

7.1.1 PULMONARY VENTILATION AT REST AND DURING EXERCISE

Pulmonary ventilation refers to the mass movement of gas in and out of the lungs. It is regulated to provide the gaseous exchange necessary for aerobic energy metabolism. Inhaled volumes and exhaled volumes are usually not equal, since the volume of inspired oxygen is usually greater than the volume of expired carbon dioxide. Inspiratory volumes are therefore usually larger than expiratory volumes. **Pulmonary ventilation** means the volume of air that is exhaled per minute. It is dependent on the rate (frequency) and depth of ventilation per breath (tidal volume). Under normal resting conditions, pulmonary ventilation varies between 4 and 15 litres per minute. Naturally, this varies with body size and is smaller in women than in men. At rest, typical values for tidal volume and frequency are 400–600 ml and 10–20 breaths per minute, respectively.

7.1.2 FACTORS AFFECTING PULMONARY VENTILATION

Pulmonary ventilation varies with exercise intensity not only within the same individual, but also between individuals because of other factors. These factors mainly relate to body size, age and sex. Peak values for pulmonary ventilation are reached at about 15 years of age for females and 25 years of age for males. It then decreases with age when it declines to less than half the peak value (Figure 7.1).

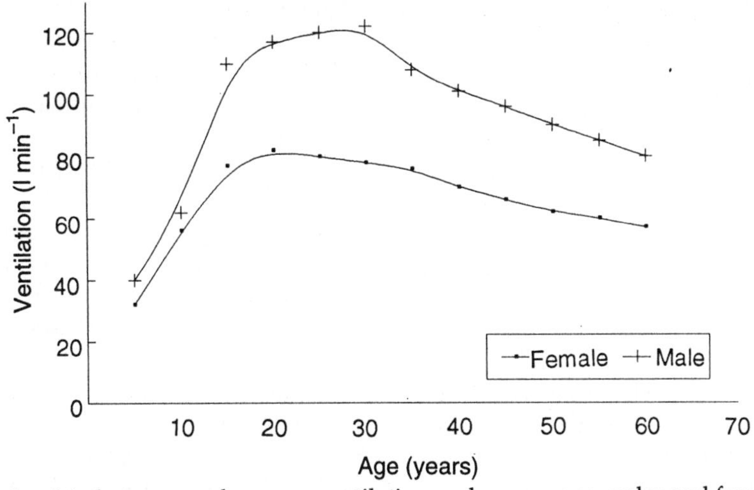

Figure 7.1 Relationship between pulmonary ventilation and age among males and females. (Data from Åstrand, 1952.)

Kinanthropometry and Exercise Physiology Laboratory Manual: Tests, procedures and data Edited by Roger Eston and Thomas Reilly. Published in 1996 by E & FN Spon. ISBN 0 419 17880 5

Increases in ventilation from young age to adulthood are primarily caused by physical maturation. As children grow in weight and particularly in height, total lung capacity and pulmonary ventilation increase accordingly. However, adults over 25 years of age who have reached full physical growth, experience reduced ventilation even though body size remains the same or increases. The decline after young adulthood is due to a decrease in the inspiratory volumes and expiratory volumes as a consequence of physical inactivity and by a reduction of the elastic components in the wall of the thoracic cage. The greater pulmonary ventilation in males compared to females after the age of about 14 years is primarily the result of body size. When the male hormone testosterone is secreted in larger quantities, the skeleton and muscle mass of males increases rapidly. As the rib cage enlarges, the thoracic cavity can accommodate larger quantities of air, which increases pulmonary ventilation.

7.1.3 ALVEOLAR VENTILATION AND DEAD SPACE

Only part of the inspired tidal volume (V_T) of air reaches the alveoli where gaseous exchange takes place. This is known as **alveolar ventilation** (V_A). The air that remains in the respiratory passages that do not participate in gaseous exchange is referred to as the **dead space volume** (V_D). The average resting value of the dead space volume is about 150 and 100 ml in men and women, respectively, although this depends on body size. The total expired gas is therefore a mixture of dead space and alveolar gas, or

$$V_T = V_A + V_D$$

If, at a ventilation of 6.0 lmin, the respiratory frequency is 10, and the dead space is 0.15 l, the alveolar ventilation is

$$60 - (10 \times 0.15) = 4.5\,\mathrm{l\,min^{-1}}$$

However, if the respiratory rate is 20, and the gross ventilation dead space is unchanged, the alveolar ventilation becomes

$$6.0 - (20 \times 0.15) = 3.0\,\mathrm{l\,min^{-1}}$$

During exercise, dilation of the respiratory passages may cause anatomical dead space to double, but since the tidal volume also increases, an adequate alveolar ventilation, and therefore gas exchange, is maintained. When submerged in water, breathing through a snorkel presents a considerable challenge to gaseous exchange. The snorkel represents an extension of the respiratory dead space, and the tidal volume has to be increased by an amount equal to the volume of the tube if alveolar ventilation is to be maintained and unchanged. Although it is not possible to measure the dead space exactly, it is possible to estimate the dead space volume with the aid of Bohr's formula, which is explained in Practical 1 of this chapter.

7.2 EVALUATION OF PULMONARY VENTILATION DURING EXERCISE

In light to moderate exercise, ventilation increases linearly with oxygen consumption ($\dot{V}O_2$), with a relatively greater increase at the heavier exercise intensities (Figure 7.2). It is notable from this relationship that pulmonary ventilation does not limit the maximal oxygen uptake. Maximal ventilation can reach values as high as $180\,\mathrm{l\,min^{-1}}$ and $130\,\mathrm{l\,min^{-1}}$ for male and female athletes, respectively. When pulmonary ventilation is expressed in relation to the magnitude of oxygen uptake, it is termed the **ventilatory equivalent** ($\dot{V}_E/\dot{V}O_2$). It is maintained at about 20–25 litres of air breathed per litre of oxygen consumed. However, in non-steady-rate exercise, ventilation increases disproportionately with increases in oxygen consumption, and $\dot{V}_E/\dot{V}O_2$ may reach 35–40. In children under 10 years of age, the values are about 30 during light exercise and up to 40 during maximal exercise (Åstrand and Rodahl, 1986). When the partial pressure of ambient oxygen is reduced, such as during exposure to high altitude, the ventilation equivalent increases to compensate for the hypoxic conditions (Figure 7.3).

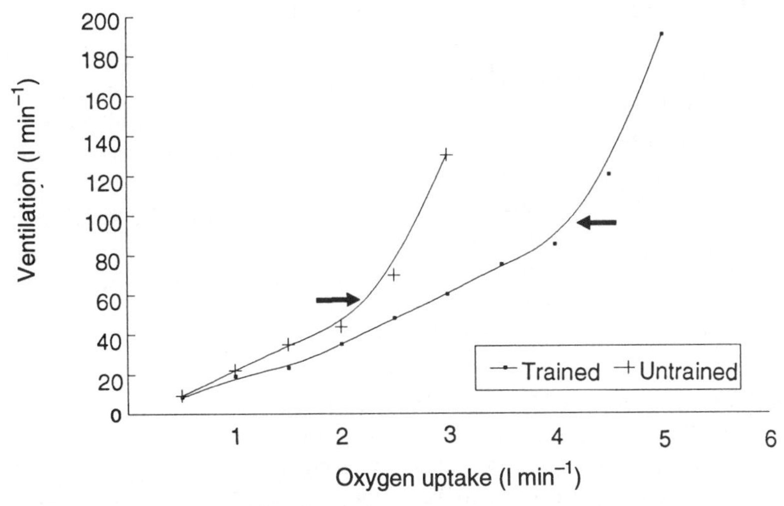

Figure 7.2 Relationship between pulmonary ventilation and maximal oxygen consumption in trained and untrained individuals. (Data from Saltin and Åstrand, 1967.)

During exercise of low intensity, it is primarily the tidal volume rather than the breathing frequency that is increased. In many types of exercise, this may amount to approximately 50% of the vital capacity when the rate of exercise is moderately heavy or heavy. Children about 5 years of age may have a respiratory frequency of about 70 breaths min^{-1} at maximal exercise, 12-year-old children about 55 breaths min^{-1}, and 25-year-old individuals 40–45 breaths min^{-1}. In well trained athletes with high aerobic power, respiratory frequencies of about 60 breaths min^{-1} are usual (Åstrand and Rodahl, 1986).

7.2.1 THE VENTILATORY THRESHOLD

As exercise intensity increases, the $\dot{V}O_2$ increases linearly, but the blood lactate level

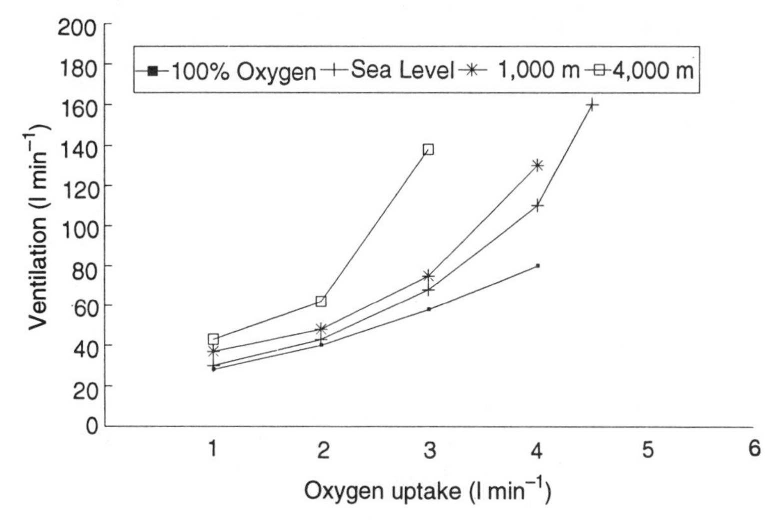

Figure 7.3 Pulmonary ventilation (BTPS) in relation to oxygen uptake at different altitudes. (Modified from Åstrand, 1954.)

changes only slightly until about 60–70% of $\dot{V}O_{2\,max}$ is reached. After this, the blood lactate increases more rapidly (Figure 7.4). Because blood acidity is one of the factors that increases V_E it has been hypothesized that an abrupt increase in V_E during exercise could be used to indicate the inflection point in the blood lactate curve. This has been termed the **'anaerobic threshold'** and procedures for its derivation are explained in detail by Wasserman *et al.* (1987). The concept is considered to be a misnomer by some experts as the physiological reasons for the rapid increase in V_E beyond the inflection point are not necessarily due to metabolic acidosis. Consequently, the disportionate rise in $\dot{V}_E$ with increasing $\dot{V}O_2$ is preferably referred to as the **'ventilatory threshold'**.

One of the most pertinent refutations of the 'anaerobic threshold' was the study by Hagberg *et al.* (1982) on patients with McArdle's syndrome. Victims of this disease lack the enzyme phosphorylase, which renders them incapable of catabolizing glycogen and forming lactate. Hagberg *et al.* (1982) showed that these patients possess ventilation thresholds despite the fact that there is no change in blood lactate concentrations (Figures 7.4 and 7.5).

7.2.2 PULMONARY VENTILATION AND TRAINING

Endurance training reduces total ventilation volumes at given exercise intensities in adolescents and young and old men and women (Jirka and Adamus, 1965; Tzankoff *et al.*, 1972; Fringer and Stull, 1974; Rasmussen *et al.*, 1975). In general, the tidal volume becomes larger and the breathing frequency is reduced with endurance training. Consequently, air remains in the lungs for a longer period of time between breaths. This results in an increase in the amount of oxygen extracted from the inspired air. The exhaled air of trained individuals often contains only 14–15% oxygen during submaximal exercise, whereas the expired air of untrained persons may contain 18% oxygen at the same workload (McArdle *et al.*, 1991). The untrained person must therefore ventilate proportionately more air to achieve the same oxygen uptake (Figure 7.2). This is important for performing prolonged vigorous exercise because the lower breathing rate reduces the fatiguing effects of exercise on the ventilatory musculature and allows the extra oxygen available to be used by the exercising muscles.

Aerobic training also brings about changes in pulmonary ventilation during maximal

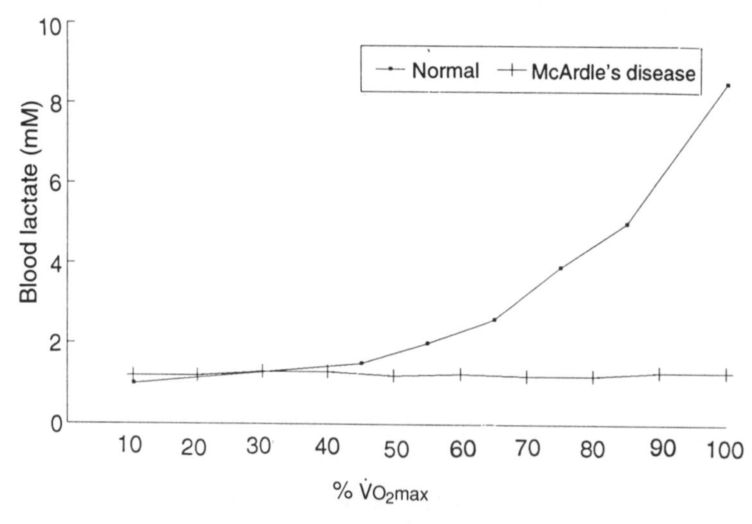

Figure 7.4 Blood lactate response in normal controls and in victims of McArdle's disease during continuous, progressive exercise on a cycle ergometer.

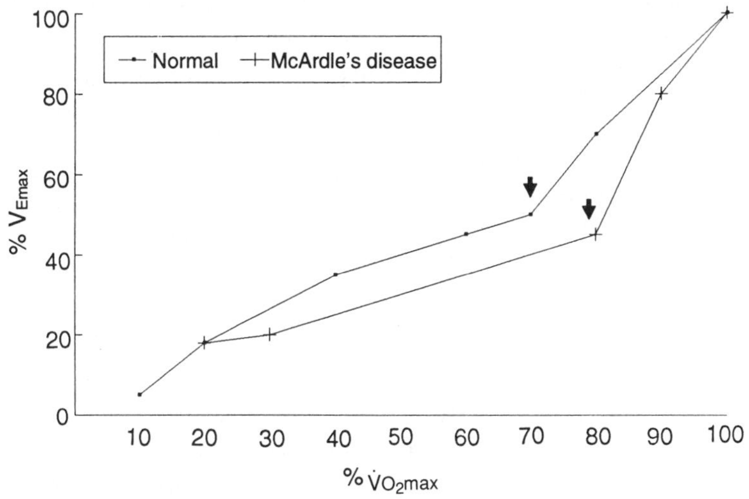

Figure 7.5 Both groups display a ventilatory threshold (arrow), despite the fact that there is no corresponding lactate threshold in the McArdle's patients. (Modified from Hagberg *et al.*, 1982.)

exercise. Maximal ventilatory capacity increases with improvements in maximal oxygen uptake. This is an expected response, since an increase in maximal oxygen uptake results in a larger oxygen requirement and a correspondingly larger production of carbon dioxide that must be eliminated through increased alveolar ventilation (McArdle *et al.*, 1991).

7.2.3 ACUTE AND CHRONIC VENTILATORY ADAPTATIONS TO ARM AND LEG EXERCISE

Ventilatory adaptations appear to be specific to the type of exercise performed. The ventilatory equivalent is greater during arm exercise than during leg work (Rasmussen *et al.*, 1975; Eston and Brodie, 1986). In the latter study, breathing frequency and tidal volume were also higher for arm work compared to leg work (Figure 7.6). During more exhaustive arm exercise the increase in ventilation was attributed largely to the disproportionate increase in breathing frequency. As arm exercise elicits higher lactate levels for any given work rate (Stenberg *et al.*, 1967) it is likely that this factor, in conjunction with the higher sympathetic outflow for arm work (Davies *et al.*, 1974) is the most likely reason for the higher ventilation during arm exercise. Bevegard *et al.* (1966) have suggested that the higher ventilation rate during arm exercise could be an important factor in maintaining ventricular filling pressures and stroke volume in the absence of the mechanical effect of the leg muscle pump. Additional factors which influence minute ventilation during arm exercise may include (a) a mechanical limitation of tidal volume by static contrac-

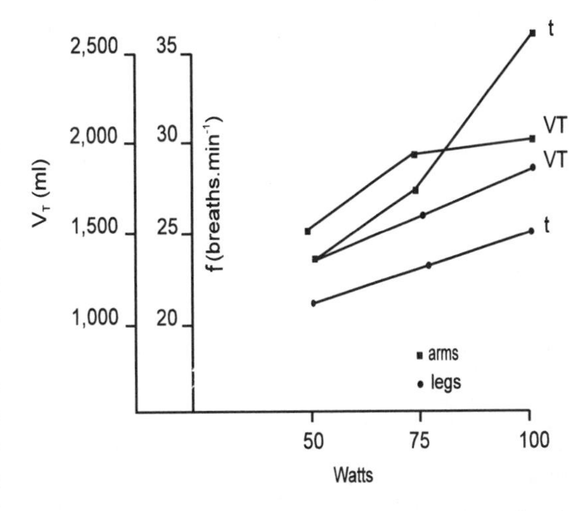

Figure 7.6 Comparison of the rate and depth of ventilation for arm and leg ergometry. (Data from Eston and Brodie (1986), reproduced by permission of the publishers Butterworth Heinemann Ltd.)

tions of the pectoralis and abdominal musculature and (b) a metering or synchronization of respiratory rate caused by the rhythmic movement of the arms (Mangum, 1984).

The reduction in ventilatory equivalent which occurs through training is also dependent on the specificity of training. Rasmussen *et al.* (1975) observed that reductions in ventilatory equivalent occurred only when the mode of exercise training matched the activity. In a comparison of groups trained either by arm ergometry or leg ergometry, the ventilatory equivalent was reduced only in arm exercise for the arm-trained group (from 30 to 25) and only in leg exercise for the leg-trained group (from 26 to 23). Arm training did not reduce the ventilatory equivalent during leg exercise and vice versa.

7.3 POST-EXERCISE CHANGES IN LUNG FUNCTION

Changes in lung volumes and function occur *after* acute exercise. After all-out exercise, some people, particularly oarsmen (Rasmussen *et al.*, 1988) experience coughing with expectation and dyspnoea. The cough may persist for several days. A decrease in the forced vital capacity immediately following exercise (Miles *et al.*, 1991), reductions in peak expiratory flow rate (Rasmussen *et al.*, 1988) and increases in residual volume have been reported (Buono *et al.*, 1981). Shifts in central blood volume, changes in lung mechanics, respiratory muscle fatigue and the development of subclinical extravascular pulmonary fluid retention have all been suggested as contributing factors for the observed transitory changes in lung volume following exercise.

Table 7.1 Predicted values for FEV_1 and FVC from selected regression equations for non-smoking Caucasian men and women (modified from American Thoracic Society (1991))

			FEV_1				*FVC*			
Source	*Age*	*Number studied*	*FEV_1 for Ht and age*[a]	*Regression coefficient*		*SEE*	*FVC for Ht and age*[a]	*Regression coefficient*		*SEE*
				Ht	*Age*			*Ht*	*Age*	
Men										
Morris *et al.* (1971)	20–84	517	3.63	3.62	−0.032	0.55	4.84	5.83	−0.025	0.74
Knudson *et al.* (1983)	25–84	86	3.81	6.65	−0.029	0.52	4.64	8.44	−0.030	0.64
Crapo *et al.* (1981)	15–91	125	3.96	4.14	−0.024	0.49	4.89	6.00	−0.021	0.64
Women										
Morris *et al.* (1971)	20–84	471	2.72	3.50	−0.025	0.47	3.54	4.53	−0.024	0.52
Knudson *et al.* (1983)	20–87	204	2.79	3.09	−0.020	0.39	3.36	4.27	−0.017	0.49
Crapo *et al.* (1981)	15–84	126	2.92	3.42	−0.026	0.33	3.54	4.91	−0.022	0.39

Format of Equation

Men

Predicted FEV_1 or FVC = Predicted value[a] for: Ht 1.75 m, Age 45
+ {Ht Coefficient × (Ht − 1.75)} + {Age Coefficient × (Age − 45)}

Women

Predicted FEV_1 or FVC = Predicted value[a] for: Ht 1.65 m, Age 45
+ {Ht Coefficient × (Ht − 1.65)} + {Age Coefficient × (Age − 45)}

7.4 ASSESSMENT OF RESTING LUNG FUNCTION

Lung function tests are widely employed to assess respiratory status. In addition to their use in clinical case management, they are routinely used in health examinations in respiratory, occupational and sports medicine, and for public health screening. Assessment of lung function, particularly in the clinical and occupational health settings, is mostly concerned with the testing of lung volumes and capacities observed in the resting state. It is common practice for the results of lung function tests to be interpreted in relation to reference values, and in terms of whether or not they are considered to be within the 'normal' range of values. Many published reference values and prediction equations are available for this purpose. The American Thoracic Society (1991) has summarized the most common equations for use with black and white adults. Some of these equations are shown in Tables 7.1–7.3. Equations for children and adolescents have also been provided by Cotes (1979) and Polgar and Promadhat (1971) (Table 7.4).

It is appropriate here to describe and distinguish the various volumes, capacities and peak flow rate classifications which are frequently measured. The lung volumes can be classified as either *'static'* – referring to the quantity of air with no relation to time, or *'dynamic'* – which are measured in relation to time.

7.4.1 STATIC LUNG VOLUMES

Lung volumes are measured by a spirometer (Figure 7.7). The bell of the spirometer falls and rises as air is inhaled and exhaled from it. This provides a record of the ventilatory volume and breathing frequency (spirogram), as depicted in Figure 7.8. As the bell moves up and down the movement is recorded on a rotating drum (kymograph) by a stylus or pen. The capacity of the spirometer is usually 9 litres, but may be up to 100 litres (Tissot). It should have a wide-bore connection (diameter > 3.2 cm) and timing which is accurate to 2% (Cotes, 1979: 22). In addition, if it is to form part of a closed-circuit system, it should include a soda-lime canister to absorb carbon dioxide.

The volume of air moved during a normal breath is the **tidal volume** (V_T). At rest V_T usually ranges between 0.4 and 1.0 litre per breath. During exercise it increases linearly with the ventilatory requirement of the subject up to a limiting value, which is about 50% of the vital capacity (Cotes, 1979). The reserve ability for inhalation beyond the tidal volume is termed the **inspiratory reserve volume** (IRV). This is the amount of air that can be inspired maximally at the end of a normal inspiration. At rest it is normally about 2.5–3.5 litres. The volume of air that can be expired maximally after normal expiration is the **expiratory reserve volume** (ERV), which ranges from 1.0 to 1.5 litres for the average sized man. The IRV and ERV show big variations with posture on account of changes in the **functional residual capacity** (FRC). This is defined as the volume of air in the chest at the end of a normal expiration when the elastic recoil of the lung and the thoracic cage are equal and opposite. In normal subjects the FRC is affected by posture. This affects the position of the chest wall and reduces FRC by about 25% in the supine position compared to the upright position. In the upright position, in healthy adults, FRC is in the range 0.8–5.5 and 0.7–4.9 litres for men and women, respectively. The FRC is increased in the presence of emphysema (a condition which causes an increase in the size of air spaces distal to the terminal bronchioles) when this is accompanied by a reduction in the elastic recoil of the chest wall. It is reduced when V_T is increased, such as during exercise, or by breathing a gas mixture of carbon dioxide in air. The **total lung capacity** (TLC) is defined as the volume of gas in the thorax at the end of a full inspiration. In healthy adults, depending on size, the TLC is in the range 3.6–9.4 and 3.0–7.3 litres for males and females, respectively. The TLC is reduced if there is a decrease in the

Table 7.2 Predicted values for FEV_1 and FVC from selected regression equations for black men and women (modified from American Thoracic Society (1991))

Source	Age	Number studied	FEV_1: FEV_1 for Ht and age[a]	FEV_1: Regression coefficient Ht	FEV_1: Regression coefficient Age	FEV_1: SEE	FVC: FVC for Ht and age[a]	FVC: Regression coefficient Ht	FVC: Regression coefficient Age	FVC: SEE
Men										
Lapp *et al.* (1974)	34.9 ± 11.9	79	3.53	3.54	−0.025	0.23	4.11	3.94	−0.021	0.32
Cookson *et al.* (1976)	43.6 ± 15.1	141	3.12	2.20	−0.024	0.50	3.74	3.90	−0.017	0.65
Women										
Johannsen and Erasmus (1968)	20–50	100	2.25	2.18	−0.013	0.34	2.74	2.51	−0.015	0.35
Cookson *et al.* (1976)	36.7 ± 11.6	102	2.35	2.35	−0.028	0.41	2.86	3.00	−0.019	0.42

Format of equation

Men

Predicted FEV_1 or FVC = Predicted value[a] for: Ht 1.75 m, Age 45 + {Ht Coefficient × (Ht − 1.75)} + {Age Coefficient × (Age − 45)}

Women

Predicted FEV_1 or FVC = Predicted value[a] for: Ht 1.65 m, Age 45 + {Ht Coefficient × (Ht − 1.65)} + {Age Coefficient × (Age − 45)}

Table 7.3 Predicted values for total lung capacity (TLC) and residual volume (RV) from selected regression equations for men and women (modified from American Thoracic Society (1991))

Source	Age	Number studied	TLC: TLC for Ht and age[a]	TLC: Regression coefficient Ht	TLC: Regression coefficient Age	TLC: SEE	RV: RV for Ht and age[a]	RV: Regression coefficient Ht	RV: Regression coefficient Age	RV: SEE
Men										
Boren *et al.* (1966)	20–62	422	6.35	7.80	–	0.87	1.62	1.90	0.012	0.53
Crapo *et al.* (1982)	15–91	123	6.72	7.95	0.003	0.79	1.87	2.16	0.021	0.37
Women										
Hall *et al.* (1979)	27–74	113	5.30	7.46	−0.013	0.51	1.80	2.80	0.016	0.31
Crapo *et al.* (1982)	17–84	122	5.20	5.90	–	0.54	1.73	1.97	0.020	0.38

Format of Equation

Men

Predicted TLC or RV = Predicted value[a] for: Ht 1.75 m, Age 45 + {Ht Coefficient × (Ht − 1.75)} + {Age Coefficient × (Age − 45)}

Women

Predicted TLC or RV = Predicted value[a] for: Ht 1.65 m, Age 45 + {Ht Coefficient × (Ht − 1.65)} + {Age Coefficient × (Age − 45)}

Table 7.4 Regression relationships for the prediction of indices of lung function from height and sitting height in healthy boys and girls of European descent (modified from Cotes (1979))

		Height (H)		*Sitting height (SH)*	
Index	*Sex*	*Relationship*	*SD%*	*Relationship*	*SD%*
Cotes (1979)					
TLC (l)	M	$1.227\ H^{2.80}$	9	$7.242\ SH^{2.90}$	11
	F	$1.189\ H^{2.64}$	10	$6.554\ SH^{2.90}$	
VC (l)	M	$1.004\ H^{2.72}$	11	$5.641\ SH^{2.80}$	11
	F	$0.946\ H^{2.61}$	10	$5.053\ SH^{2.80}$	
FEV_1 (l)	M	$0.812\ H^{2.67}$	11	$4.807\ SH^{2.93}$	12
	F	$0.788\ H^{2.73}$	10	$4.527\ SH^{2.93}$	
RV (l)	M + F	$0.237\ H^{2.77}$	27	$1.448\ SH^{3.12}$	31
PEFR ($l\ s^{-1}$)	M + F	$7.59\ H^{-5.53}$	13	$15.94\ SH^{-6.87}$	13
Polgar and Promadhat (1971)					
TLC (l)	M	$1.226\ H^{2.67}$	11.6		
	F	$1.153\ H^{2.73}$			
VC (l)	M	$0.963\ H^{2.67}$	13.0		
	F	$0.909\ H^{2.72}$			
FEV_1 (l)	M + F	$0.796\ H^{2.80}$	9.0		
RV (l)	M + F	$0.291\ H^{2.41}$	22.8		

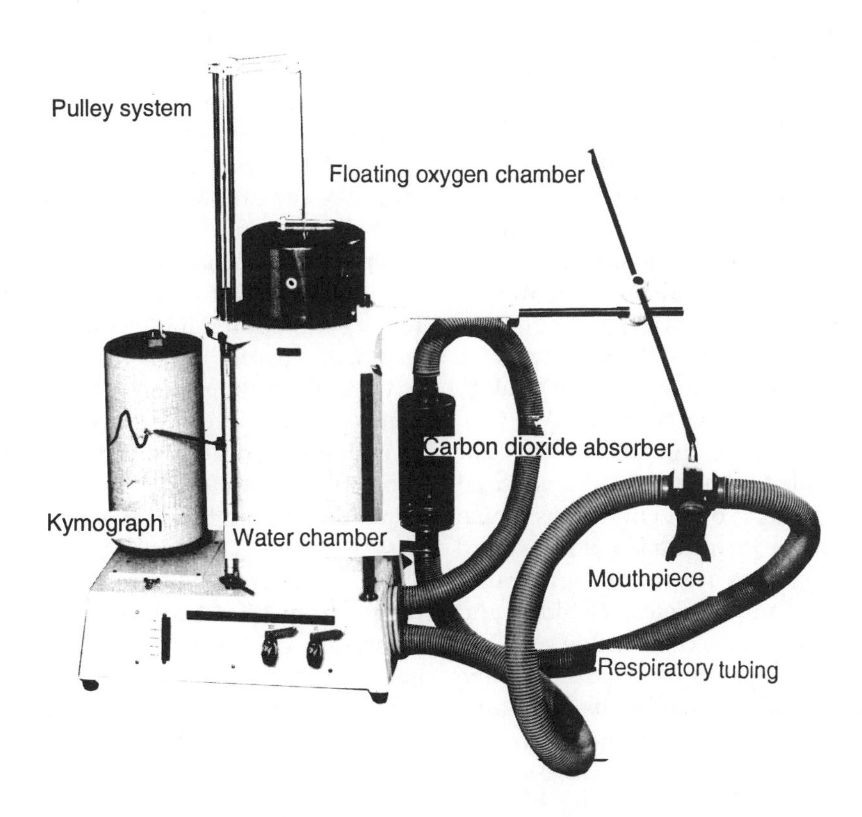

Figure 7.7 *Harvard* 9 Litre Spirometer.

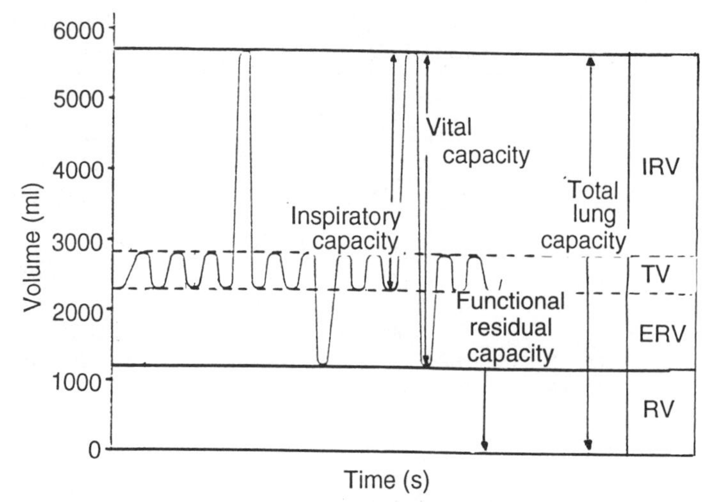

Figure 7.8 Spirogram showing the various lung volumes and capacities. IRV, inspiratory reserve volume; ERV, expiratory reserve volume; RV, residual volume; TV, tidal volume.

strength of the respiratory muscles, as in diseases such as interstitial fibrosis or muscular dystrophy. It is enlarged when the compliance of the lung is increased by emphysema or as a result of physical training. Hanson (1973) observed TLC values ranging from 7.0 to 9.8 litres in seven international cross-country skiers. During exercise, the IRV particularly and the ERV are reduced which is a natural consequence of an increase in V_T.

The total volume of air that can be moved voluntarily from the lung from full inspiration to full expiration is the **vital capacity** (VC). It is the sum of V_T, IRV and ERV. In healthy adults, depending on age and size, VC is in the range 2.0–6.6 litres and 1.4–5.6 litres for males and females, respectively. It is reduced in emphysema and in other conditions which cause an increase in residual volume. Vital capacities of 6–7 litres are not uncommon for tall individuals and athletes. Ekblom and Hermansen (1968) observed a value of 7.7 litres in a champion male athlete. Although the size of the lung is influenced by the same anthropometric factors which may also predispose an individual to athletic success, vital capacity can be increased by training, but this is only in certain circumstances and with special types of training. Cotes (1979) reported that training of the muscles of the shoulder girdle probably leads to an increase in VC by virtue of the increased strength of the accessory muscles of inspiration. This is a feature of oarsmen, weightlifters and participants in archery and other sports in which these muscles are employed. When differences for body size and age are taken into account, middle distance runners, cyclists and swimmers tend to have a higher than normal vital capacity. A larger lung leads to the V_T contributing more to the ventilation minute volume than in subjects with smaller lungs. The increased VC is not usually accompanied by a corresponding increase in the forced expiratory volume and thus, the proportion of the VC which these subjects can expire in 1 second tends to be relatively low. In this respect, Hanson (1973) observed $FVC_{1.0\%}$ values ranging from 61 to 85% in male cross-country skiers whose VCs ranged from 4.8 to 7.3 litres. In swimmers, the increase in VC due to muscle training is superimposed on that associated with a long trunk length which probably also confers a competitive advantage (Cotes, 1979). Vital capacity is reduced by about 7% when the subject lies down. This change is due to the displacement of gas by blood which enters the thorax from the lower parts of the body.

The volume of air that cannot be exhaled after a maximal expiration is the **residual volume** (RV). Functionally, this makes sound physiological sense or there would be complete collapse (closure) of all airways as well as cessation of all gaseous exchange at the lung. In healthy adults, depending on size and age, the RV is in the range of 0.5–3.5 and 0.4–3.0 for males and females, respectively. The RV tends to increase with age, whereas the IRV and ERV become proportionately smaller. The loss in breathing reserve and the concomitant increase in RV with age are generally attributed to the loss of elasticity in the lung tissue (Turner *et al.*, 1968), although there is evidence to suggest that the effects of ageing on lung function can be altered with training (Hagberg *et al.*, 1988). As indicated previously, various studies have shown that RV is temporarily increased during and after recovery from acute bouts of exercise of both short- and long-term duration. The precise reason for an increase in RV with exercise is unknown, although it has been postulated that it is partially attributed to an accumulation of pulmonary extravascular fluid with exercise, which prevents a person from achieving a maximal exhalation (McArdle *et al.*, 1991).

7.4.2 DYNAMIC LUNG VOLUMES (INDICES OF MAXIMAL FLOW)

An important consideration is the individual's ability to *sustain* high levels of flow. This depends on the speed at which the volumes can be moved and the amount that can be moved in one breathing cycle. This can be considered in terms of either a short period of hyperventilation or a single maximal respiratory effort. The term usually given to the former is maximal voluntary ventilation (MVV), which involves rapid and deep breathing for 15 seconds. The exact procedure for this is explained in Practical 1. The MVV in adults, depending on age and size, is in the range of 47–253 and 55–139 l min^{-1} in males and females, respectively. The MVV is usually about 25% higher than the ventilation volume observed during maximal exercise ($\dot{V}_{E\,max}$). This is because the ventilatory system is **not** stressed maximally in exercise. Figure 7.2 clearly shows that the rate of ventilation ($\dot{V}_E$) is not the limiting factor for maximal oxygen uptake, as $\dot{V}_E$ continues to increase when maximal oxygen uptake is reached. McArdle *et al.* (1991) have reported values of 140–180 and 80–120 l min^{-1} in college-aged males and females, respectively. Hanson (1973) reported average values of 192 l min^{-1} for the men's US Ski Team with the highest value being 239 l min^{-1}. Figure 7.9 shows one of the Movement Science students at Liverpool University performing the MVV test. This student, a former amateur boxer, had an abnormally high MVV, which was measured at 294 l min^{-1} (BTPS). Patients with obstructive lung disease can achieve only about 40% of the MVV predicted for their age and size (Levison and Cherniack, 1968).

Figure 7.9 Procedure for measuring maximal voluntary ventilation (MVV). The student photographed here (ht 1.97 m, mass 97 kg, age 24) had an abnormally high MVV of 294 litres (BTPS).

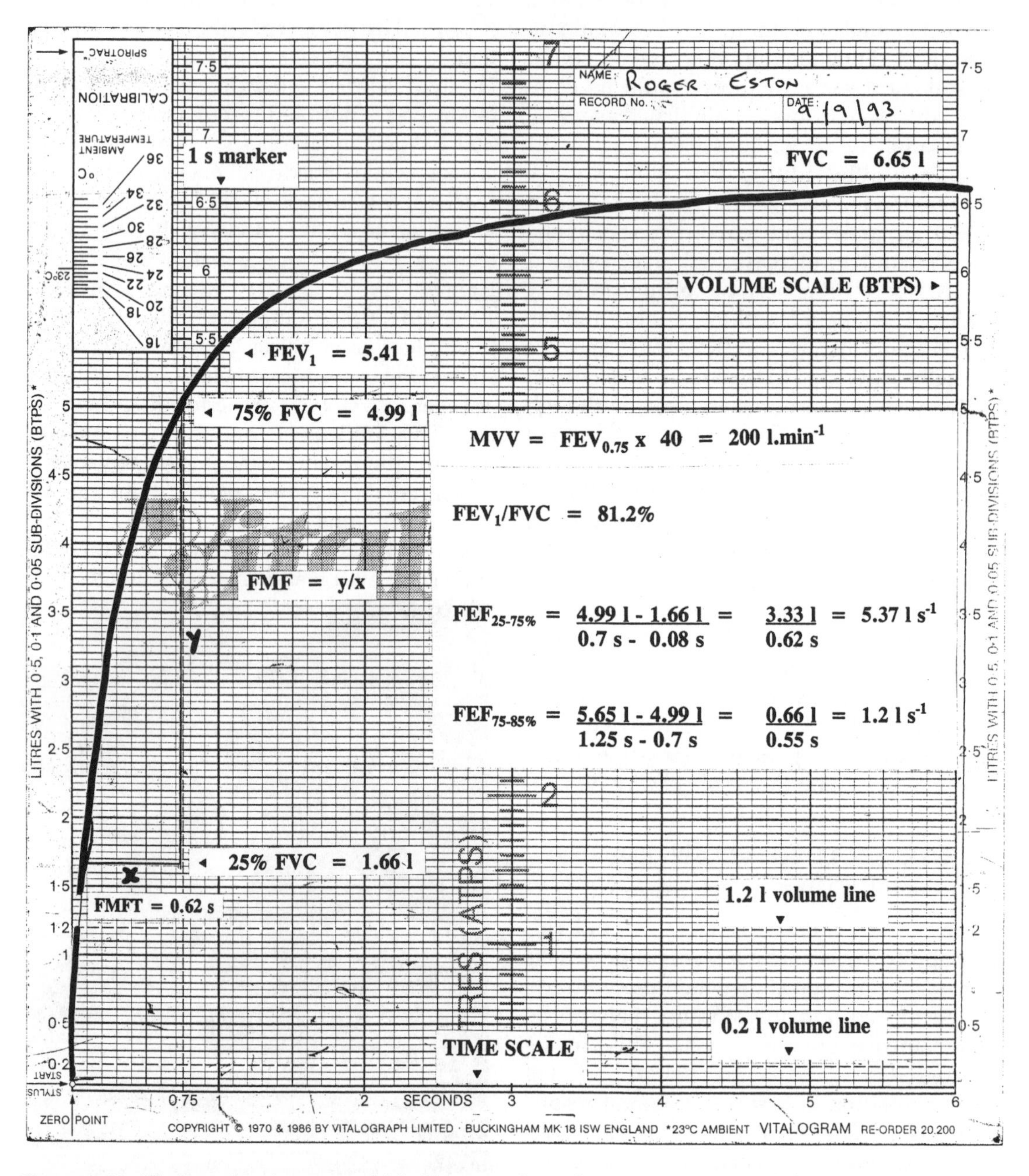

Figure 7.10 *Vitalograph* spirogram which illustrates how the various static and dynamic lung function parameters can be calculated. (Reproduced with permission of Vitalograph Ltd, Buckingham, UK.)

The MVV can be increased by exercises that increase the strength of the respiratory muscles. This applies to both normal subjects and to pulmonary patients (Sonne and Davis, 1982; Akabas *et al.*, 1989).

When the ventilatory capacity is considered in terms of a single forced expiration or inspiration, it is expressed as either the maximal flow rate at a defined point in the respiratory cycle (for example, $FEV_{1.0}$, see below), the average over part of the breath, or portion of the vital capacity. This is usually the middle half (for example, $FEF_{25-75\%}$, see below).

The peak expiratory flow rate (PEFR) is the maximum flow rate that can be sustained for a period of 10 ms. The PEFR in healthy adults, depending on age and size, is in the range of 6–15 l s^{-1} and 2.8–10.1 l s^{-1} in males and females, respectively.

The amount of air expired over a specific time period of a forced expiration is termed the forced expiratory volume qualified by the time over which the measurement is made, for example, $FEV_{1.0}$, $FEV_{3.0}$. In healthy adults, depending on age and size, the $FEV_{1.0}$ is in the range of 1.2–5.7 l and 0.8–4.2 l in males and females, respectively.

The forced mid-expiratory flow (FMF) is the average flow rate over the middle half of the FVC. It is also called the forced expiratory flow (FEF) for the appropriate segment of the FVC, for example, $FEF_{25-75\%}$. Graphic analysis involves location of 25% and 75% volume points on the spirogram. The two points are then connected by a straight line and protracted to intersect the two time lines that are one second apart. The number of litres per second is then measured between the points of the intersection. Alternatively, the FMF can be calculated by dividing the change in volume by the time period between FEV at 25% FVC ($FVC_{25\%}$) and $FVC_{75\%}$. Another conventional flow rate is $FEF_{75-85\%}$, which is calculated in a similar manner. The average flow for one litre of gas starting at 200 ml after the beginning of a forced expiration is also used as an index ($FEF_{200-1200}$).

A frequently used ratio is the forced expiratory volume in a second ($FEV_{1.0}$) expressed as a proportion of the vital capacity ($FEV_{1.0\%} = (FEV_{1.0}/FVC) \times 100$). This value provides an indication of the respiratory power and the resistance to air flow. The ratio in healthy adults, depending on age and size, is 51–97% and 59–93% in males and females, respectively. Normally, the demarcation point for airway obstruction is the point at which less than 70% of the FVC can be expired in 1 second. Figure 7.10 is a typical spirogram of a healthy, active 38-year-old male as measured by the Vitalograph^{TM} spirometer to illustrate some of the above parameters and how they are calculated.

7.5 PULMONARY DIFFUSING CAPACITY

The pulmonary diffusing capacity (D_L) is an indication of the rate of diffusion from the alveoli membrane to the pulmonary vascular bed. As greater volumes of air are brought into the alveoli during exercise, this is matched by a greater volume of pulmonary blood flow (ventilation : perfusion ratio). The rate of gaseous exchange is therefore increased considerably. The D_L therefore provides an indication of the available surface area interface of the alveolar and capillary membrane at any given point in time. It is theoretically dependent upon (a) the surface area of the pulmonary capillaries in contact with alveolar gas, (b) the thickness of the pulmonary membrane and (c) the specific resistance to gas diffusion of the tissue making up the membrane (Ogilvie *et al.*, 1957). It is commonly measured by a single-breath hold of a gaseous mixture of 0.03% CO, 10.0% He, 21% O_2 balanced with N_2. The technique is abbreviated as DL_{COsb}. A practical example of the method is described in more detail in Practical 3.

The measurement of D_L at rest provides an additional clinical measure which may be used in the diagnosis of disease, which may not be apparent from the normal FVC, $FEV_{1.0}$ and $FEV_{1.0\%}$ measurements. In normal subjects, values at rest range from about 20 to 30 mlCO min^{-1} $mmHg^{-1}$ but this is dependent on body size and sex, since oxygen consumption increases with body size. Ogilvie *et al.* (1957) observed that D_L was directly related to surface area and could be calculated by the equation:

$$D_L = \text{surface area (m}^2) \times 18.55 - 6.8 \; (r = 0.81, \; SEE = 3.92 \text{ ml min}^{-1} \text{ mmHg}^{-1})$$

This equation was derived on subjects in the sitting position, since D_L, like residual volume, increases progressively as the person assumes a change in position from standing erect to supine. The increase in D_L is ascribed to a large pulmonary capillary blood volume and a more uniform balance between ventilation and perfusion in the supine position (Turino *et al.*, 1963).

Below normal values are observed in patients who have suffered from such ailments as chronic obstructive emphysema, asthma, pulmonary arterial disease, pulmonary carcinoma, kyphoscoliosis and in patients who have suffered chemical burns or who have been exposed to asbestos dust (refer to Ogilvie *et al.*, 1957 for specific examples).

7.5.1 EFFECTS OF EXERCISE ON PULMONARY DIFFUSING CAPACITY

An increase in D_L with exercise was first reported by Krogh (1915). Using the DL_{COsb} technique, the pulmonary diffusing capacity increases to about 55–70 ml min^{-1} mmHg^{-1} (Turino *et al.*, 1963; Turcotte *et al.*, 1992), depending on the intensity of the exercise. Turino *et al.* compared the diffusing capacity of the lung during exercise in the upright and supine positions. Although they observed differences at rest, they showed that during exercise the body position has less of an effect on the determinants of D_L. They observed that D_L continued to increase as the intensity of the exercise increased and concluded that it was unlikely that D_L limited maximum oxygen uptake. This conclusion is consistent with the proposition that circulatory performance, rather than pulmonary diffusing capacity, sets the ceiling for physical exertion. There is also evidence to suggest that pulmonary diffusing capacity increases with training (Newman *et al.*, 1962).

7.6 SOURCES OF VARIATION IN LUNG FUNCTION TESTING

Measurements of pulmonary function are subject to a number of sources of variation. This can be attributed to technical factors, such as instrumentation, procedure, observer error and so on. The variation could also be attributed to dysfunction, or disease, or as a result of biological variation. The major focus here is on biological sources of variation within individuals and between individuals. For a more detailed discussion of all sources of variation in lung function testing the reader is guided to the position statement of the American Thoracic Society (1991).

7.6.1 WITHIN-SUBJECT VARIATION

The main sources of within-subject variation in ventilatory parameters both at rest and during exercise that are not related to disease, environment, drugs or subject compliance, are body position, head position and the degree of effort exerted during the test. There is also a circadian rhythm.

The FVC is 7–8% lower in the supine compared to the standing position and 1–2% lower in the sitting compared to the standing position (Townsend, 1984; Allen *et al.*, 1985). The standing position is also preferable for obese subjects. Systematic increases in maximal expiratory flows have been documented during neck hyperextension. This may be due to elongation and stiffening of the trachea. Conversely, neck flexion may decrease peak expiratory flow rate and increase airway resistance (Melissinos and Mead, 1977). The $FEV_{1.0}$ may be 100–200 ml lower when the effort is maximal compared to submaximal because the airway is narrower in relation to the exhaled volume (Krowka *et al.*, 1987). In some subjects, repeated maximal efforts may trigger bronchospasm, resulting in a progressive decrease in FVC and $FEV_{1.0}$ (Gimeno *et al.*, 1972). Residual volume also increases by about 20% on changing from a standing to a sitting position and by about 30% on changing from a sitting to a supine position (Blair and Hickam, 1955).

Another source of intrasubject variation is the time of day due to circadian rhythms. For maximal expiratory flows, the lowest values are usually seen in the morning (04:00 to 06:00 hours) and the largest values usually occur around midday (Hetzel, 1981). Guberan *et al.* (1969) observed significant increases in $FEV_{1.0}$ of 150 ml in the morning which decreased by 50 ml in the afternoon in shift workers. In addition, Hetzel and Clark (1980) have reported that PEFR peak-to-trough amplitude of the circadian rhythm is about 8%. A rhythm in $\dot{V}_E$ is also evident during submaximal exercise, the rhythm in $\dot{V}_E$ being closely related to the circadian curve in body temperature (Reilly, 1990).

7.6.2 BETWEEN-SUBJECT VARIATION

The main anthropometric factors responsible for intersubject variation in lung function are sex, body size and ageing. These alone account for 30, 22 and 8%, respectively, of the variation in adults (Becklake, 1986). Other factors are race and past and present health.

Although sitting height explains less of the variability in lung function than standing height (Ferris and Stoudt, 1971; Cotes, 1979), it may be a useful predictor when dealing with mixed ethnic origins due to the fact that blacks have a lower trunk to leg ratio than whites (Van de Wal *et al.*, 1971). It is also used to predict lung function in children, particularly during periods of rapid growth. Arm span measurements provide a practical substitute for standing height in subjects unable to stand or those with a skeletal deformity such as kyphoscoliosis (Hibbert *et al.*, 1988). Measurements of chest circumference may also slightly improve the prediction of lung function (Damon, 1966). After correcting for body size, girls appear to have higher expiratory flows than boys, but men have larger volumes and flows than women (Schwartz *et al.*, 1988). With regard to *age*, after adult height is attained, there is either an increase (usually in young men) or little or no decrease in function (usually in young women) after which lung function decreases at an accelerating rate with increasing age (American Thoracic Society, 1991). *Race* is an important determinant of lung function (American Thoracic Society, 1991). Caucasians of European descent have greater static and dynamic lung volumes and greater forced expiratory flow rates but similar or lower FEV_1/FVC ratios. In this respect, regression equations derived from white populations using standing height as the measure of size usually overpredict values measured in blacks by about 12% for TLC, FEV_1 and FVC and by about 7% for FRC and RV (Cotes, 1979). Differences have been attributed to body build differences and frame size (Jacobs *et al.*, 1992). It has already been noted that blacks have a lower trunk : leg ratio than whites.

A factor related to the size of the lung is *growth in standing height*, as this affects lung function measurements in childhood and adolescence. Growth in standing height is not in phase with lung growth during the adolescent growth spurt (DeGroodt *et al.*, 1986) and growth in chest dimensions lags behind that of the legs (DeGroodt *et al.*, 1988). In males, standing height and VC are often not maximal by the age of 17 years. The VC continues to increase after increases in height cease and may not be maximal until about 25 years of age. Girls, however, attain their maximal values around the age of 16 years (DeGroodt *et al.*, 1986).

The ratio of FEV_1/FVC and the ratio of maximal expiratory flow (derived from flow–volume curves) to the FVC are almost constant from childhood to adulthood. Girls have larger expiratory flows than boys of the same age and stature (DeGroodt *et al.*, 1986). This is partly due to the fact that girls have a smaller VC for the same TLC than boys. It may also reflect the smaller muscle mass and the smaller number of alveoli found in girls

(Thurlbeck, 1982). The American Thoracic Society (1991) has recommended that such sex differences warrant the use of different prediction equations for boys and girls at all ages. Ideally, developmental rather than chronological age should be included in prediction equations for children and adolescents, although such equations are neither available nor practical.

The size of the lung determines the total lung capacity, its subdivisions and the indices which are dependent on lung size, for example, forced expiratory flow rates. In children up to the age of puberty, these indices are related to stature, usually in a curvilinear manner; the relationship is linear when height is raised to the power of about 2.6 (Cotes, 1979; Table 7.4).

After stature has been taken into account, the indices are independent of age and usually independent of body weight and sitting height. During the adolescent growth spurt, the rate of growth of the trunk and its contents, including the lungs, is relatively greater than that of the legs. It is therefore useful to use sitting height as an alternative reference variable during this stage of growth (Cotes, 1979; Cotes *et al.*, 1979). Equations to predict lung function, which use stature and sitting height in children are shown in Table 7.4. Relative to stature, boys and girls have similar values for residual volume, peak expiratory flow rate and flow rate at 50% of vital capacity. The ERV is slightly larger and the inspiratory capacity is about 12% larger for boys than for girls. Thus, boys have larger values for the functional residual capacity, the vital capacity and the total lung capacity. As a consequence of these differences in lung size, boys also have larger values for FEV_1.

7.7 LUNG FUNCTION IN SPECIAL POPULATIONS

7.7.1 HIGH-ALTITUDE NATIVES

Like the acclimatized visitor, the high-altitude native hyperventilates relative to a normal sea-level person. This increases alveolar ventilation and limits the fall in the partial pressure of oxygen in the alveoli which lessens the reduction in the oxygen pressure gradient across the alveolar membrane. At any given altitude, the ventilation of the acclimatized visitor is greater by about 20% than that of the native highlander (Minors, 1985). Thus, the high-altitude native seems to have lost some respiratory sensitivity to hypoxia.

Native highlanders developed certain anthropometric differences which enable them to tolerate the hypobaric conditions experienced at high altitude. They have a smaller stature than lowlanders of the same age. Although the difference in height varies by about 10%, the chest circumference of native highlanders is about 5% greater (Frisancho, 1975). This is accompanied by a larger vital capacity, larger lung volume and residual lung volume than sea-level subjects. In addition, morphometric measurements of the lungs of high-altitude natives resident at 4000 m have shown alveoli which are larger and greater in number than those in lowland natives of the same body size. The increased alveolar surface area in contact with functioning pulmonary capillaries, in combination with an increased pulmonary capillary blood volume, leads to an increased pulmonary diffusing capacity in the high-altitude native lung. The combination of increased alveolar ventilation and pulmonary diffusing capacity increases the total alveolar gas exchange in the highlander.

7.7.2 LUNG FUNCTION IN DIVERS

Certain physical adaptations to long-term diving have been noted in in US Navy Escape Training Tank Instructors (Carey *et al.*, 1956) and to a lesser extent in male recreational divers (Hong *et al.*, 1970). These changes include an increase in VC, a decrease in RV and a lowered RV/TLC ratio.

Differences have also been observed in the Korean diving women known as the *ama*. Before each dive an ama hyperventilates then dives between 5–18 metres for 20–40 s in repeated dives for approximately 3 h per day. Song *et al.* (1963) observed VC and MVV maximal volumes to be 125% and 128%, respectively, of predicted values. They also observed a higher inspiratory capacity, but no difference in ERV between the ama and a group of controls. The RV, expressed as a proportion of total lung capacity, was also lower in the ama.

The reason for the increased VC was attributed to the increased inspiratory capacity of the ama. The reason for this difference was attributed to better developed inspiratory muscles. This was thought to be an adaptation to the constant hydrostatic pressure which the ama must overcome on inspiration before a dive. The lower RV/TLC ratio was considered to be important since it determines the maximal depth of diving.

7.8 PREDICTION OF LUNG FUNCTION

Reference equations provide a context for evaluating pulmonary function in comparison to the distribution of measurements in a reference population. Linear regression is the most common, but not the only model used to describe pulmonary function data in adults. These types of equations perform less well at the edges of the data distribution. Further, estimates are likely to be misleading if they go beyond the range of the independent variables used to create the equation. The most commonly reported measures of how well regression equations fit the data they describe are the square of the correlation coefficient (r^2) and the standard error of the estimate (SEE). The proportion of variation in the observed data explained by the independent variables is measured by r^2. The SEE is the average standard deviation of the data around the regression line. This will decrease and r^2 will increase as regression methods reduce the differences between predicted and observed values in the reference population. When the same equations are used to describe a different population, SEE will invariably be larger, and r^2 will be smaller.

Tables 7.1–7.4 contain a listing of various regression equations which predict the various lung function indices in black and white adults and children. The American Thoracic Society (1991) has recommended that, ideally, publications which describe reference populations should also include a means of defining the lower limits of the regression equations. Nevertheless, it is possible to estimate lower limits of normal from a regression model.

7.8.1 ESTIMATION OF *LOWER* LIMITS OF NORMAL

Values below the 5th percentile are conventionally taken as below the expected range and those above the 5th percentile are taken as within the expected range (American Thoracic Society, 1991). It is possible to calculate percentiles if there are sufficient measurements within each category. The value of the 5th percentile can be roughly estimated as:

$$\text{Lower limit of normal} = \text{Predicted value} - 1.645 \times \text{SEE}$$

For example, the predicted value of FVC for a 45-year-old male, height 1.75 m (Table 7.1) is 5.83 l according to the prediction equation of Morris *et al.* (1971). The standard error of estimate is 0.74 l for this equation. Thus, the lower limit of normal (i.e. the lower 5% of the population) for a man of this age and height would be 4.63 litres ($5.83 - (1.645 \times 0.74)$).

Defining a fixed FEV_1/FVC ratio as a lower limit of normal (e.g. 80%) is not recommended in adults because FEV_1/FVC is inversely related to age and height (American Thoracic Society, 1991). The use of a fixed ratio will therefore result in an apparent increase in dysfunction associated with ageing. In addition, some athletes have values for FVC that are relatively larger than those for FEV_1, which results in a lower FEV_1/FVC ratio. Thus, the definition of the lowest 5% of the reference population is also the preferred method to predict abnormality in this parameter.

7.9 DEFINITION OF OBSTRUCTIVE AND RESTRICTIVE VENTILATORY DEFECTS

7.9.1 OBSTRUCTIVE DEFECT

An obstructive ventilatory defect is defined as a disproportionate reduction in maximal airflow from the lung with respect to the maximal volume (vital capacity) that can be displaced from the lung (American Thoracic Society, 1991). It implies narrowing of the airway during expiration.

Indications of an obstructive defect can be seen in the latter stages of the flow–volume curve. The slowing is reflected in a reduction in the instantaneous flow after 75% of the FVC has been exhaled ($FEF_{75-85\%}$) or in the $FEF_{25-75\%}$. As airway disease becomes more advanced, the FEV_1 becomes reduced out of proportion to the reduction in VC.

7.9.2 RESTRICTIVE DEFECT

One may infer the presence of a restrictive ventilatory defect when VC is reduced and FEV_1/FVC is normal or increased. A reduction in VC may occur because airflow is so slow that the subject cannot continue to exhale long enough to complete emptying or because airways collapse.

7.9.3 INTERPRETATION OF LUNG FUNCTION TESTS

The basic parameters used to interpret spirometry are the VC, FEV_1 and FEV_1/FVC ratio (American Thoracic Society, 1991). Although FVC is often used instead of VC, it is preferable to use the largest VC, whether obtained on inspiration (IVC), slow expiration (EVC) or forced expiration (FVC) for clinical testing. The FVC is usually reduced more than IVC or EVC in airflow obstruction.

The FEV_1/FVC ratio is the most important measurement for distinguishing an obstructive impairment. According to the American Thoracic Society (1991), expiratory flow measurements other than the FEV_1 and FEV_1/FVC should be considered only after determining the presence and clinical severity of obstructive impairment using the basic parameters measured above. When FEV_1 and the FEV_1/VC ratio are within the normal range, abnormalities in flow occurring late in the maximal expiratory flow–volume curve should not be graded as to severity and, if mentioned, interpreted cautiously. When there is a borderline value of FEV_1/FVC, these values may help to confirm the presence of airway obstruction. The same is true for average flows such as $FEF_{25-75\%}$. It is important to note that there is wide variability of these measurements in healthy subjects and this must therefore be taken into account in the final interpretation.

7.10 PRACTICAL EXERCISES

In the following section three laboratory practicals are suggested to determine lung function in the resting state (Practical 1) and during exercise (Practical 2). Practical 3 describes a procedure for measuring D_L with examples of values and calculations. Each practical contains actual data to exemplify the relationships between variables and provide examples and applications of the various formulae for assessing lung function.

7.11 PRACTICAL 1: ASSESSMENT OF RESTING LUNG VOLUMES

7.11.1 PURPOSE

The purpose of this practical is to measure static and dynamic lung volumes in the resting state, to determine relationships between lung function and anthropometric variables and to assess the effects of changes in posture on lung function. Some data are presented in Table 7.5 to exemplify some of these measurements.

Table 7.5 Assessment of resting lung volumes: Example of lung volumes at rest in a 38-year-old active male

Descriptive Data

Name	RGE	Age	38
Height (m)	1.78	Mass (kg)	86
Sitting Height (m)	0.91	Arm span (m)	1.84

Ambient conditions

Laboratory temperature (°C)	20	P_{Bar} (mmHg)	760

(a) Resting measurements (dry spirometer)[a]

FVC (l)	*$FEV_{1.0}$ (l)*	*$FEV_{1.0\%}$*	*$FEF_{25-75\%}$ (ls^{-1})*	*$FEF_{75-85\%}$ (ls^{-1})*	*$FEF_{0.2-1.2}$ (ls^{-1})*	*FMFT (s)*	*MVV (l min^{-1})*
Standing							
6.65	5.41	81.2	5.37	1.2	13.0	0.62	230
Supine							
6.32	5.1	80.6	5.21	1.1	11.0	0.81	190
Predicted Values							
5.02	4.04	80.0	4.60	1.27	9.00	0.73	200

(b) Resting measurements (wet spirometer)[a]

V_T (l)	*IRV (l)*	*ERV (l)*	*FVC (l)*	*RV (l)*	*FRC (l)*	*TLC (l)*
Measured						
0.60	3.20	1.65	6.65	1.80	3.45	8.45
Predicted Values						
0.60	2.91	1.39	5.02	1.90	2.70	6.80

(c) Resting measurements (Douglas bag)[a]

$\dot{V}_E$ (l min^{-1})	*f (breaths min^{-1})*	*V_T (l)*	*V_T as %FVC*	*MVV (l min^{-1})*
7.0	10.0	0.70	10.0	210.0

[a] All values should be recorded at BTPS

7.11.2 PROCEDURE

All data should be recorded on the data sheet for this laboratory.

1. Record subject age, height, weight, physical activity/training status.
2. Record ambient conditions (temperature, barometric pressure).
3. Record sitting height, arm span and chest circumference.
4. Measurement of inspired and expired volumes using a wet spirometer with kymograph.
   (a) Sanitize all equipment and mouthpiece.
   (b) Subject puts on a nose clip.
   (c) Procedure:
      (i) Breathe normally into and out of the spirometer to allow measurement of *tidal volume* (V_T) and breathing frequency (f).
      (ii) At the end of a normal inspiration, inhale as deeply as possible to measure *inspiratory reserve volume* (IRV) and return to normal breathing.

(iii) At the end of a normal expiration, expire as much as possible to determine the *expiratory reserve volume* (ERV) and return to normal breathing.
(iv) The subject is then requested to inhale as deeply as possible and exhale as forcefully as possible to measure the *forced vital capacity* (FVC).
(v) *Residual volume* can be predicted from the relevant equation in Table 7.3 or it can be measured by the method explained in the laboratory practical described in Chapter 1. This will allow *total lung capacity* (TLC) and *functional residual capacity* (FRC) to be calculated.

5. Measurement of FVC, FEV_1, $FEV_{1\%}$, FMF ($FEF_{25-75\%}$), $FEF_{75-85\%}$, PEFR, $FEF_{0.2-1.2}$, FMFT.
   (a) Set the spirometer to zero.
   (b) From the standing position, inhale as deeply as possible, place the spirometer mouthpiece into the mouth, and exhale as forcefully as possible over a period of 4–5 s. Record the best of three readings.
   (c) Calculate the various lung function parameters as indicated in Figure 7.10.
   (d) Compare individual scores with predicted scores using one of the appropriate regression equations listed in Tables 7.1–7.4 and record all data.
   (e) Repeat the above procedures whilst in the supine position.

6. Measurement of maximal voluntary ventilation (MVV) (Figure 7.9).
   (a) Predict MVV using the formula:

$$MVV = FEV_{0.75} \times 40 \text{ (Cotes, 1979)}$$

$$\text{where: } FEV_{0.75} = 0.92 \times FEV_{1.0} - 0.07 \text{ (95\% limits} \pm 8\%)$$

   (b) Insert respiratory valve and attach the noseclip.
   (c) Breathe as deeply and rapidly as possible for 15 s into either a Douglas bag or directly into a dry gas spirometer. Convert the values into litres per minute (BTPS).
   (d) Record values on data sheet.

7. Measurement of V_T, f and pulmonary ventilation ($\dot{V}_E$) at rest.
Sit quietly for 5 min. Expired air is collected into a Douglas bag in the final minute. The respiratory frequency can be counted by rise and fall of the chest wall or by movement of the respiratory valves. Tidal volume can be calculated from the following:

$$V_T = \dot{V}_{BTPS}\, \text{l min}^{-1}/f$$

8. Computation of dead space.
The volume of dead space can be calculated with the aid of Bohr's formula, which is based on the fact that the expired volume of oxygen at each respiration ($V_T \times FEO_2$) is equal to the sum of the volume of oxygen contained in the dead space compartment ($V_D \times FIO_2$) and the volume of oxygen coming from the alveolar air $V_A \times FAO_2$. We therefore arrive at the following formula:

$$V_T \times FEO_2 = (V_D \times FIO) + (V_A \times FAO_2)$$

Since $V_A = V_T - V_D$, the formula may be simplified as follows:

$$V_D = V_T \times \frac{FEO_2 - FAO_2}{FIO_2 - FAO_2}$$

If the oxygen content of the inspired air is 21%, the oxygen content of the expired air is 16%, the oxygen content of the alveolar air is 14%, and the depth of the respiration (V_T) is 500 ml, the dead space volume (V_D) is:

$$V_D = 500 \times \frac{16-14}{21-14} = 143 \text{ ml}$$

7.11.3 ASSIGNMENTS

1. Examine the spirogram from the wet spirometry practical. Comment on the relative magnitude of the various volumes, e.g. compare IRV with ERV.
2. Comment on the relationship between height, sitting height, weight, chest circumference, arm span and the lung function measurements (FEV_1, FVC).
3. Compare the accuracy of the prediction of MVV by the FEV_1 method with the 15 s Douglas bag method.
4. Compare the measured values with the predicted values in Tables 7.1–7.4.
5. Compare the spirometry values in the standing and supine position.
6. Compare the resting $\dot{V}_E$, V_T and f measurements with expected values. Consider the effects of body size on these measurements.
7. Calculate the relative size of each breath as a proportion of the vital capacity in the standing and supine positions (%FVC = (V_T/FVC) × 100).
8. Compare male and female values.
9. Is there any relationship between the level of physical training and lung function values?

7.12 PRACTICAL 2: ASSESSMENT OF LUNG VOLUMES DURING EXERCISE

7.12.1 PURPOSE

To assess the influence of arm and leg exercise on pulmonary ventilation, alveolar ventilation, breathing frequency, tidal volume and the ventilatory equivalent. Some data are presented in Table 7.6 to exemplify these measurements.

Table 7.6 Assessment of lung volumes during exercise: Example of lung volumes at rest and during different modes of exercise in a 38-year-old active male

Descriptive Data

Name	*RGE*	*Age*	38
Height (m)	1.78	Mass (kg)	86
Sitting Height (m)	0.91	Arm span (m)	1.84

Ambient conditions

Laboratory temperature (°C)	20	P_{Bar} (mmHg)	760

(a) Resting values

V_E l min^{-1} (BTPS)	*V_T (l)*	*V_T as %FVC*	*f*	*%O_2*	*%CO_2*	*$\dot{V}O_2$ (l min^{-1})*	*V_{Eeq}*	*V_D(ml)[a]*
9.1	0.70	10.0	13	15.7	4.00	0.36	25.0	172.0

Table 7.6 (continued)

(b) Arm exercise

Watts	V_E *l min*$^{-1}$ *(BTPS)*	V_T *(l)*	V_T *as %FVC*	*f*	*%*O_2	*%*CO_2	$\dot{V}O_2$ *(l min*$^{-1}$*)*	V_{Eeq}
25	21.6	1.20	18.0	18	16.4	4.1	0.82	26.3
50	32.2	1.40	21.0	23	16.2	4.3	1.29	25.0
75	50.4	1.80	27.0	28	16.4	4.3	1.91	26.3
100	70.5	2.13	32.0	33	16.4	4.5	2.63	26.6
125	95.5	2.45	37.0	39	17.0	4.5	2.97	32.1
150	118.4	2.80	42.0	42	17.2	4.5	3.43	34.4

(c) Leg exercise

Watts	V_E *l min*$^{-1}$ *(BTPS)*	V_T *(l)*	V_T *as %FVC*	*f*	*%*O_2	*%*CO_2	$\dot{V}O_2$ *(l min*$^{-1}$*)*	V_{Eeq}
25	16.0	1.0	15.0	16	16.3	4.0	0.63	25.4
50	24.3	1.43	21.4	17	16.0	4.0	1.03	23.6
75	29.4	1.47	22.1	20	16.0	4.1	1.24	23.7
100	38.6	1.68	25.2	23	16.3	4.2	1.51	25.7
125	47.1	1.96	29.5	24	16.5	3.9	1.80	26.2
150	53.3	2.05	30.8	26	16.4	4.0	2.05	26.0
200	69.1	2.03	30.5	30	16.6	4.4	2.44	28.3
250	96.3	2.91	43.8	33	16.8	4.6	3.18	30.2
300	130.0	3.51	52.8	37	17.0	4.6	4.02	32.3

Formulae:

$$V_T = V_{EBTPS}/f$$

$$V_T \text{ as \%FVC} = (V_T/\text{FVC}) \times 100$$

$$\dot{V}O_2 = \dot{V}_{ESTPD} \times (\{(1 - (FEO_2 + FECO_2)) \times 0.265\} - FEO_2$$

$$\dot{V}O_2 = \dot{V}_E \times 0.04$$

$$\dot{V}_E = \dot{V}O_2 \times 20 - 25$$

$$V_{Tmax} = 0.74\,\text{FVC} \times 1.11$$

$$V_{Eeq} = \dot{V}_{EBTPS}/\dot{V}O_{2\,STPD}$$

$$V_D = V_T \times \frac{FEO_2 - FAO_2}{FIO_2 \quad FAO_2}$$

$$FEO_2 = \%O_2/100$$

7.12.2 PROCEDURE

All data should be recorded on the data sheet for this laboratory.

1. Record subject age, height, weight, physical activity/training status.
2. Record ambient conditions (temperature, barometric pressure).
3. Assessment of resting pulmonary values

The subject rests and breathes normally for 5 min. Expired air is collected in the final minute in a Douglas bag. Record the respiratory frequency and compute tidal volume as described in Practical 1.

4. Determine the oxygen and carbon dioxide fraction.
5. Measure volume at BTPS in a Douglas bag.
6. Incremental exercise test: the subject exercises at 25 W on the arm ergometer with increments of 25 W every 3 min until maximal volitional exhaustion (or 150 W). Expired air is directed into a Douglas bag to obtain the oxygen and carbon dioxide fractions. Respiratory frequency is measured. The volume of expired air is then determined through the dry gas meter.
7. The subject rests for 10–15 min.
8. Repeat the procedure described in step 6 on a cycle ergometer at identical work rates (for comparison of arm and leg values). Work rates are then increased by 50 W every 3 min until maximal volitional exhaustion. Collect expired air over the final minute of each increment.
9. The subject rests for 5 min.
10. Perform FVC test to obtain spirogram for analysis of post-exercise static and dynamic volumes.

7.12.3 ASSIGNMENTS

1. Determine V_T and the relative size of each breath in relation to the FVC for arm and leg work (%FVC = $(V_T/FVC) \times 100$).
2. Determine the ventilatory equivalent (V_{Eeq}) at rest, and during submaximal and maximal work intensities for arm and leg ergometry.

$$V_{Eeq} = \dot{V}_{EBTPS} / \dot{V}O_{2STPD}$$

3. What do you notice about the pulmonary ventilation for arm ergometry at submaximal and maximal work rates?
4. Are there any differences in the $\dot{V}_E$ and V_{Eeq} responses for trained and untrained individuals?
5. Compare the post-exercise spirogram results with those taken at rest. What do you notice about the static and dynamic lung volumes and flow rates?
6. How accurate are the following equations for predicting $\dot{V}_E$, $\dot{V}O_2$ and $\dot{V}T_{max}$?

$$\dot{V}_E = \dot{V}O_2\,(\text{l min}^{-1}) \times 20 - 25$$

$$\dot{V}O_2 = \dot{V}_E\,(\text{l min}^{-1}) \times 0.04 \text{ (Datta and Ramanathan, 1969)}$$

$$VT_{max} = 0.74\,\text{FVC} - 1.11 \text{ (Jones, 1984)}$$

7. How does the relationship between $\dot{V}_E$ and $\dot{V}O_2$ compare to previously observed values from the literature? Does $\dot{V}_E$ limit $\dot{V}O_{2max}$?
8. Compare the MVV obtained from the 15 s test to the maximum $\dot{V}_E$ obtained in the exercise test. Why is MVV greater than $\dot{V}E_{max}$?

7.13 PRACTICAL 3: MEASUREMENT OF PULMONARY DIFFUSING CAPACITY

7.13.1 PURPOSE

Pulmonary diffusing capacity (D_L) is commonly measured by the single-breath method. This technique requires the subject to inspire a mixture of 0.3% carbon monoxide (CO), 10% helium (He), 21% oxygen (O_2) and a balance of nitrogen (N_2). Specifically, the technique measures the rate of diffusion of CO from the alveoli to the pulmonary vascular bed in a single full 10 s breath-hold of the gas mixture and is hence abbreviated DL_{SOsb}. The rationale for its measurement was described in section 7.5.

7.13.2 PROCEDURE

The method is described in detail by Ferris (1978) and is summarized here for ease of reference.

7.13.3 APPARATUS (FIGURE 7.11)

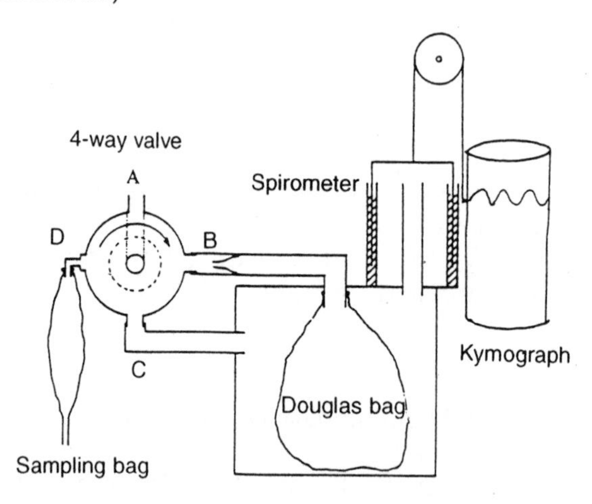

Figure 7.11 Conventional manual system for DL_{COsb}. (Modified from Ferris, 1978.)

1. A 30 litre Douglas bag is flushed several times with the He–CO mixture.
2. Just before the test, the inspiratory tubing and valve section is also flushed with the He–CO mixture.
3. The subject is seated, fitted with a noseclip, and breathes ambient air (valve directed to A).
4. With the valve directed to A (ambient air), the subject is instructed to (1) exhale maximally to residual volume, signal by hand, and on instruction (2) inhale rapidly and maximally from the Douglas bag and hold the breath for 10 s. On a signal, the subject then exhales rapidly. The four-way valve is adjusted by the investigator to enable the subject to breathe normal air and exhale maximally to normal air (A), inspire from the bag (B), expire to space surrounding the bag (C, 1 litre wash-out) and to ensure 1 litre collection of alveolar air in the sampling bag (D).
5. The following values are recorded: (1) breath-hold time from mid-inspiration to beginning of the alveolar sampling (Figure 7.12), (2) the inspired volume (ATPS), (3) the final

He concentration in the sampling bag and (4) the final CO concentration in the sampling bag.

It is important to note that a number of factors affect the calculation of DL_{COsb} such as the Valsalva manoeuvre, the method of measuring the breath-hold time, the actual breath-hold time and other factors. For more detail of these factors refer to the American Thoracic Society Epidemiology Standardization Project compiled by Ferris (1978). It is possible to reduce the breath-hold time to as low as 3 s with a minimum loss of accuracy during strenuous exercise (Turcotte *et al.*, 1992).

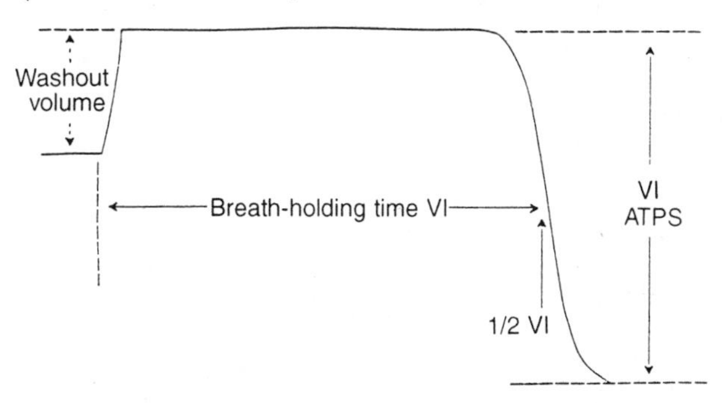

Figure 7.12 Standardized measurements from the spirographic tracing obtained during the single breath diffusing capacity maneouvre. The inspired volume (VI_{ATPS}) is measured from the maximal expiration to the fullest inspiration. The breath-holding time is measured from the time when one-half of the inspiration is made to the time when washout has been completed and collection of alveolar gas has begun.

7.13.4 GAS ANALYSIS

The analysers for CO and He are connected in series, preceded by an H_2O absorber (e.g. drierite), CO_2 absorber, dust filter and a flow meter. A small pump should draw air through at a rate of 400 ml min^{-1} and a stable reading for CO and He is obtained in 30–40 s.

Example calculation of DL_{COsb}

Equation:

$$DL_{COsb} = V_{A(STPD)} \times \frac{60}{\text{breath holding time}} \times \frac{1}{P_B - 47} \times \frac{CO_A}{CO_E}$$

where:

DL_{COsb} = single breath diffusing capacity for CO
P_B = barometric pressure
CO_A = initial concentration of CO
CO_E = expired concentration of CO
V_A = alveolar volume (STPD) at which the breath was held
$V_A = V_I(\text{ATPS}) \times (He_I / He_E) \times 1.05 \times$ STPD correction factor
where: V_I = inspired volume (ATPS)
He_I = inspired He
He_E = expired He

$$CO_A = CO_I \times \frac{He_E}{He_I}$$

Sample data

$P_B = 754$ mmHG $\quad He_E = 12.0\%$

$CO_I = 0.3\ \% \quad T = 21^{\circ}$

$He_I = 10.0\ \% \quad$ STPD cf = 0.895

V_I(ATPS) = 5000 ml $\quad CO_E = 0.2\ \%$

Breath-hold time = 10 s

Stage 1 (Solve for $VA_{(STPD)}$)

$$V_{ASTPD} = 5000\ \text{ml} \times \frac{0.10}{0.12} \times 1.05 \times 0.895$$

$$V_{ASTPD} = 3915\ \text{ml}$$

Stage 2 (Solve for CO_A)

$$CO_A = 0.003 \times \frac{0.12}{0.10} = 0.0036$$

Stage 3 (Solve for DL_{COsb})

$$DL_{COsb} = 3915\ \text{ml} \times \frac{60\text{s}}{10\text{s}} \times \frac{1}{754 - 47} \times \frac{0.0036}{0.0020}$$

$$DL_{COsb} = 33.8\ \text{ml CO min}^{-1}\ \text{mmHg}^{-1}$$

REFERENCES

Akabas, S. R., Bazzyar, A., Dimauro, S. and Haddad, G. G. (1989) Metabolic and functional adaptation of the diaphragm to training with resistive loads. *Journal of Applied Physiology*, **66**, 529–35.

Allen, S. M., Hunt, B. and Green, M. (1985) Fall in vital capacity with posture. *British Journal of Diseases of the Chest*, **79**, 267–71.

American Thoracic Society (1991) Lung function testing: selection of reference values and interpretation strategies. *American Review of Respiratory Disease*, **144**, 1202–18.

Åstrand, P. O. (1952) *Experimental Studies of Physical Work Capacity in Relation to Sex and Age.* E. Munksgard, Copenhagen.

Åstrand, P. O. (1954) The respiratory activity in man exposed to prolonged hypoxia. *Acta Physiologica Scandinavica*, **30**, 343–68.

Åstrand, P. O., and Rodahl, K. (1986) *Textbook of Work Physiology*, McGraw Hill, New York.

Becklake, M. R. (1986) Concepts of normality applied to the measurement of lung function. *American Journal of Medicine*, **80**, 1158–64.

Bevegard, S., Freyschuss, U. and Strandell, T. (1966) Circulatory adaptation to arm and leg exercise in supine and sitting position. *Journal of Applied Physiology*, **21**, 37–46.

Blair, E. and Hickam, J. B. (1955) The effect of change in body position on lung volume and intrapulmonary gas mixing in normal subjects. *Journal of Clinical Investigations*, **34**, 383–9.

Boren, H. G., Kory, R. C. and Syner, J. C. (1966) The Veterans Administration Army cooperative study of pulmonary function. *American Journal of Medicine*, **41**, 96–114.

Buono, M. J., Constable, S. A., Morton, A. R. *et al.* (1981) The effect of an acute bout of exercise on selected pulmonary function measurements. *Medicine and Science in Sports and Exercise*, **13**, 290–3.

Carey, C. R., Schaefer, K. E. and Alvis, H. J. (1956) Effect of skin diving on lung volume. *Journal of Applied Physiology*, **8**, 519–23.

Cookson, J. B., Blake, G. T. W. and Faranisi, C. (1976) Normal values for ventilatory function in Rhodesian Africans. *British Journal of Diseases of the Chest*, **70**, 107–111.

Cotes, J. E. (1979) *Lung Function: Assessment and Application in Medicine*, Blackwell Scientific, Oxford.

Cotes, J. E., Dabbs, J. M., Hall, A. M. *et al.* (1979) Sitting height, fat-free mass and body fat as reference variables for lung function in healthy British children: comparison with stature. *Annals of Human Biology*, **6**, 307–14.

Crapo, R. O., Morris, A. H. and Gardner, R. M. (1981) Reference spirometric values using techniques and equipment that meet ATS recommendations. *American Review of Respiratory Disease*, **123**, 659–64.

Crapo, R. O., Morris, A. H., Clayton, P. D. and Nixon, C. R. (1982) Lung volumes in healthy non-smoking adults. *Bulletin European de Physiopathologie Respiratoire*, **18**, 419–25.

Damon, A. (1966) Negro–white differences in pulmonary function (vital capacity, timed vital capacity and expiratory flow rate). *Human Biology*, **38**, 381–93.

Datta, S. R. and Ramanathan, N. L. (1969) Energy expenditure in work predicted from heart rate and pulmonary ventilation. *Journal of Applied Physiology*, **26**, 297–302.

Davies, C. T., Few, J., Foster, K. G. and Sargeant, T. (1974) Plasma catecholamine concentration during dynamic exercise involving different muscle groups. *European Journal of Applied Physiology*, **32**, 195–206.

DeGroodt, E. G., Quanjer, P. H., Wise, J. E. and Van Zomeren, B. C. (1986) Changing relationships between stature and lung volumes during puberty. *Respiration Physiology*, **65**, 139–53.

DeGroodt, E. G., van Pelt, W., Quanjer, P. H. *et al.* (1988) Growth of lung and thorax dimensions during the pubertal growth spurt. *European Respiratory Journal*, **1**, 102–8.

Ekblom, B. and Hermansen, L. (1968) Cardiac output in athletes. *Journal of Applied Physiology*, **25**, 619–25.

Eston, R. G. and Brodie, D. A. (1986) Responses to arm and leg ergometry. *British Journal of Sports Medicine*, **20**, 4–7.

Ferris, A. (1978) Epidemiology standardization project. (Part III) *American Review of Respiratory Disease*, **118**, 55–89.

Ferris, B. G. and Stoudt, H. E. (1971) Correlation of anthropometry and simple tests of pulmonary function. *Archives of Environmental Health*, **22**, 672–6.

Fringer, M. N. and Stull, G. A. (1974) Changes in cardiorespiratory parameters during periods of training and detraining in young adult females. *Medicine and Science in Sports*, **6**, 20–5.

Frisancho, A. R. (1975) Functional adaptation to high-altitude hypoxia. *Science*, **187**, 313–19.

Gimeno, F., Berg, W. C., Sluiter, H. J. and Tammeling, G. J. (1972) Spirometry-induced bronchial obstruction. *American Review of Respiratory Disease*, **105**, 68–74.

Guberan, E., Williams, M. K., Walford, J. and Smith, M. M. (1969) Circadian variation of FEV in shift workers. *British Journal of Industrial Medicine*, **26**, 121–5.

Hagberg, J. M., Coyle, E. F., Carroll, J. E. *et al.* (1982) Exercise hyperventilation in patients with McArdle's disease. *Journal of Applied Physiology*, **52**, 991–4.

Hagberg, J. M., Yerg, J. E. and Seals, D. R. (1988) Pulmonary function in young and older athletes and untrained men. *Journal of Applied Physiology*, **65**, 101–5.

Hall, A. M., Heywood, C., and Cotes, J. E. (1979) Lung function in healthy British women. *Thorax*, **34**, 359–65.

Hanson, J. S. (1973) Maximal exercise performance in members of the US Nordic Ski Team. *Journal of Applied Physiology*, **35**, 592–5.

Hetzel, M. R. (1981) The pulmonary clock. *Thorax*, **36**, 481–6.

Hetzel, M. R. and Clark, T. J. H. (1980) Comparison of normal and asthmatic circadian rhythms in peak expiratory flow rate. *Thorax*, **35**, 732–8.

Hibbert, M. E., Lanigan, A., Raven, J. and Phelan, P. D. (1988) Relation of armspan to height and the prediction of lung function. *Thorax*, **43**, 657–9.

Hong, S. K., Moore, T. O., Seto, G. *et al.* (1970) Lung volumes and apneic bradycardia in divers. *Journal of Applied Physiology*, **29**, 172–6.

Jacobs, D. R., Nelson, E. T., Dontas, A. S. *et al.* (1992) Are race and sex differences in lung function explained by frame size? *American Review of Respiratory Disease*, **146**, 644–9.

Jones, N. L. (1984) Dyspnea in exercise. *Medicine and Science in Sports and Exercise*, **16**, 14–19.

Jirka, Z. and Adamus, M. (1965) Changes of ventilation equivalents in young people in the course of three years of training. *Journal of Sports Medicine and Physical Fitness*, **5**, 1–6.

Johannsen, Z. M. and Erasmus, L. D. (1968) Clinical spirometry in normal Bantu. *American Review of Respiratory Disease*, **97**, 585–97.

Knudson, R. J., Lebowitz, M. D., Holberg, C. J. and Burrows, B. (1983) Changes in normal maximal expiratory flow–volume curve with growth and aging. *American Review of Respiratory Disease*, **127**, 725–34.

Krogh, M. (1915) Diffusion of gases through the lungs of man. *Journal of Physiology*, **49**, 271–300.

Krowka, M. J., Enright, P. L., Rodarte, J. R. and Hyatt, R. E. (1987) Effect of effort on forced expiratory effort in one second. *American Review of Respiratory Disease*, **136**, 829–33.

Lapp, N. L., Amandus, H. E., Hall, R. and Morgan, W. K. C. (1974) Lung volumes and flow rates in black and white subjects. *Thorax*, **29**, 185–8.

Levison, H. and Cherniack, R. M. (1968) Ventilatory cost of exercise in chronic obstructive pulmonary disease. *Journal of Applied Physiology*, **25**, 21–7.

Mangum, M. (1984) Research methods: application to arm crank ergometry. *Journal of Sports Sciences*, **2**, 257–63.

McArdle, W., Katch, F. I. and Katch, V. L. (1991) *Exercise Physiology: Energy, Nutrition and Human Performance*, Lea and Febiger, Philadelphia.

Melissinos, C. G. and Mead, J. (1977) Maximum expiratory flow changes induced by longitudinal tension on trachea in normal subjects. *Journal of Applied Physiology*, **43**, 537–44.

Miles, D. S., Cox, M. H., Bomze, J. P. and Gotshall, R. W. (1991) Acute recovery profile of lung volumes and function after running 5 miles. *Journal of Sports Medicine and Physical Fitness*, **31**, 243–8.

Minors, D. S. (1985) Abnormal pressure, in *Variations in Human Physiology* (ed. R. M. Case), Manchester University Press, Manchester, pp. 78–110.

Morris, J. F., Koski, A. and Johnson, L. C. (1971) Spirometric standards for healthy non-smoking adults. *American Review of Respiratory Disease*, **103**, 57–67.

Newman, F., Smalley, B. F. and Thomson, M. L. (1962) Effect of exercise, body and lung size on CO diffusing capacity in athletes and non-athletes. *Journal of Applied Physiology*, **17**, 649–55.

Ogilvie, C. M., Forster, R. E., Blakemore, W. S. and Morton, J. W. (1957) A standardized breath holding technique for the clinical measurement of the diffusing capacity of the lung for carbon monoxide. *Journal of Clinical Investigations*, **36**, 1–17.

Polgar, G. and Promadhat, V. (1971) *Pulmonary Function Testing in Children: Techniques and Standards*, WB Saunders, Philadelphia, p. 272.

Rasmussen, B., Klausen, K., Clausen, J. P. and Trap-Jensen, J. (1975) Pulmonary ventilation, blood gases and pH after training of the arms and legs. *Journal of Applied Physiology*, **38**, 250–6.

Rasmussen, R. S., Elkjaer, P. and Juhl, B. (1988) Impaired pulmonary and cardiac function after maximal exercise. *Journal of Sports Sciences*, **6**, 219–28.

Reilly, T. (1990) Human circadian rhythms and exercise. *Critical Reviews in Biomedical Engineering*, **18**, 165–80.

Saltin, B. and Åstrand P. O. (1967) Maximal oxygen uptake in athletes. *Journal of Applied Physiology*, **23**, 353–8.

Schwartz, J. D., Katz, S. A., Fegley, R. W. and Tockman, M. S. (1988) Analysis of spirometric data from a national sample of healthy 6–24 year olds (NHANES II). *American Review of Respiratory Disease*, **138**, 1405–14.

Song, S. H., Kang, D. H., Kang, B. S. and Hong, S. K. (1963) Lung volumes and ventilatory responses to high CO_2 and low O_2 in the ama. *Journal of Applied Physiology*, **18**, 466–70.

Sonne, L. J. and Davis, J. A. (1982) Increased exercise performance in patients with severe COPD following inspiratory resistive training. *Chest*, **81**, 436–9.

Stenberg, J., Åstrand, P. O., Ekblom, B. *et al.* (1967) Hemodynamic response to work with different muscle groups, sitting and supine. *Journal of Applied Physiology*, **22**, 61–70.

Thurlbeck, W. M. (1982) Postnatal human lung growth. *Thorax*, **37**, 564–71.

Townsend, M.C. (1984) Spirometric forced expiratory volumes measured in the standing versus the sitting posture. *American Review of Respiratory Disease*, **130**, 123–4.

Turcotte, R. A., Perrault, H., Marcotte, J. E. and Beland, M. (1992) A test for the measurement of pulmonary diffusing capacity during high intensity exercise. *Journal of Sports Sciences*, **10**, 229–35.

Turino, G. M., Bergofsky, E. H., Goldring, R. M. and Fishman A. P. (1963) Effect of exercise on pulmonary diffusing capacity. *Journal of Applied Physiology*, **18**, 447–56.

Turner, J. M., Mead, J. and Wohl, M. E. (1968) Elasticity of human lungs in relation to age. *Journal of Applied Physiology*, **25**, 664–71.

Tzankoff, S. P., Robinson, S., Pyke, F. S. and Brown, C. A. (1972) Physiological adjustments to work in older men as affected by physical training. *Journal of Applied Physiology*, **33**, 346–50.

Van de Wal, B. W., Erasmus, L. D. and Hechter, R. (1971) Sitting and standing heights in Bantu and white South Africans – The significance in relation to pulmonary function values. *South African Medical Journal*, **45** (Suppl.), 568–70.

Wasserman, K., Hansen, J. E., Sue, D. Y. and Whipp, B. J. (1987) *Principles of Exercise Testing and Interpretation*, Lea and Febiger, Philadelphia, pp. 33–6.

METABOLIC RATE AND ENERGY BALANCE

8

C. B. Cooke

8.1 BASAL METABOLIC RATE (BMR)

The main component of daily energy expenditure in the average subject is the energy expenditure for maintenance processes, usually called basal metabolic rate (BMR). The BMR is the energy expended for the ongoing processes in the body in the resting state, when no food is digested and no energy is needed for temperature regulation. The BMR reflects the body's heat production and can be determined indirectly by measuring oxygen uptake under strict laboratory conditions. No food is eaten for at least 12 h prior to the measurement so there will be no increase in the energy required for the digestion and absorption of foods in the digestive system. This fast ensures that measurement of BMR occurs with the subject in the postabsorptive state. In addition, no undue muscular exertion should have occurred for at least 12 h prior to the measurement of BMR.

Normally, a good time to make a measurement of BMR is after waking from a night's sleep, and in a hospital situation BMR is typically measured at this time. In laboratory practicals and exercise physiology experiments involving volunteer subjects, it is often impossible to obtain the correct conditions for a true measure of BMR. It is likely that in a laboratory practical the subject will have eaten a meal in the preceding 12 h, which will increase metabolism in certain tissues and organs such as the liver. This is known as the specific dynamic effect. Any measurement not made under the strict laboratory conditions already described is referred to as resting metabolic rate (RMR). However, if the subject has only eaten a light meal some 3–4 h prior to the experiment, and is allowed to rest in a supine position for at least 30 min, then the measurement of RMR will only be slightly elevated above the true BMR value. A description of the procedures for the measurement of RMR using the Douglas bag technique is given in section 8.7. Although the Systeme International (SI) unit for rate of energy expenditure is the Watt (W), RMR and BMR values are typically quoted in kcal min^{-1}. A calorie is defined as the amount of heat necessary to raise the temperature of 1 kg of water 1°C, from 14.5 to 15.5°C. The calorie is therefore typically referred to as the kilocalorie (kcal). To convert kcal into kilojoules (kJ) (the Joule (J) is the SI unit of energy), multiply the kcal value by 4.2. To convert kcal min^{-1} into kilowatts (kW) multiply the kcal min^{-1} by 0.07. (See the Appendix for a full list of conversion factors between different units of measurement.)

Estimates of BMR values can be used to establish an energy baseline for constructing programmes for weight control by means of diet, exercise, or the more effective and healthier option of combining both diet and exercise prescriptions. The measurement of BMR on subjects drawn from a variety of

Kinanthropometry and Exercise Physiology Laboratory Manual: Tests, procedures and data Edited by Roger Eston and Thomas Reilly. Published in 1996 by E & FN Spon. ISBN 0 419 17880 5

populations provides a basis for studying the relationships between metabolic rate and body size, sex and age.

8.1.1 BODY SIZE, SEX AND AGE EFFECTS ON BMR AND RMR

Since the time of Galileo scientists have believed that BMR and RMR are related to body surface area. Rubner (1883) showed that the rate of heat production divided by body surface area was more or less constant in dogs which varied in size. He offered the explanation that metabolically produced heat was limited by ability to lose heat, and was therefore related to body surface area. This relationship between body surface area and basal and resting metabolic rate has since been verified for animals ranging in size from the mouse up to the elephant (Kleiber, 1975; McMahon, 1984; Schmidt-Nielson, 1984) and is an important consideration when comparing children and adults. The 'surface area law' therefore states that metabolic rates of animals of different size can be made similar when BMR or RMR is expressed per unit of body surface area.

Table 8.1 shows that, related to body surface area, BMR is at its greatest in early childhood and declines thereafter (Altman and Dittmer, 1968; Knoebel, 1963). When RMR is based on oxygen uptake values the differences between a 10-year-old boy and a middle-aged man are of the order of 1–2 ml kg^{-1} min^{-1}, which amounts to a 25–35% greater metabolic rate in the child (MacDougall *et al.*, 1979). As can be seen from Table 8.1, BMR values are about 5% lower in women than in men. This does not reflect a true sex difference in the metabolic rate of specific tissues, but is largely due to the differences in Body composition (McArdle *et al.*, 1991). Women generally have a higher percentage of body fat than men of a similar size, and stored fat is essentially metabolically inert.

If the BMR values are expressed per unit of lean body mass (or fat-free mass) then the sex differences are essentially eliminated. Differences in body composition also largely explain the 2% decrease in BMR per decade observed through adulthood.

8.1.2 ESTIMATION OF BODY SURFACE AREA AND RESTING METABOLIC RATE

Using the mean BMR values (kJ m^{-2} h^{-1}) for age and sex from Altman and Dittmer (1968) shown in Table 8.1 it is possible to predict an individual's BMR value using an estimate of body surface area. The procedure is outlined in section 8.3.

Table 8.1 Basal metabolic rate as a function of age and sex (data from Altman and Dittmer, 1968)

Age (years)	*Females*	*Males*
5	196.7	205.1
10	178	183.3
15	163.2	177.9
20	152.4	165.8
25	151.5	162.0
30	151.1	157.4
35	151.1	155.7
40	151.1	156.1
45	150.3	155.3
50	146.5	154.5
55	142.7	152.4
60	139.4	149.4
65	136.9	146.5
70	135.6	144.0
75	134.8	141.5
80	133.5	139.0

8.2 MEASUREMENT OF ENERGY EXPENDITURE

Energy expenditure can be measured using either direct or indirect calorimetry. Both methods depend on the principle that all the energy used by the body is ultimately degraded into heat. Therefore the measurement of heat produced by the body is also a measure of energy expenditure (direct calorimetry). Direct measures of energy expenditure are made when a subject remains inside a chamber with walls specifically designed to absorb and measure the heat produced. This method is both technically difficult and costly. Since the energy provided from food can only be used as a result of oxidations using oxygen obtained from air, measurement of steady-state oxygen uptake by the body is also used as a measurement of energy expenditure (indirect calorimetry). Detailed procedures for the measurement of oxygen uptake using the Douglas bag technique are given in section 8.5.

8.3 PRACTICAL 1: ESTIMATION OF BODY SURFACE AREA AND RESTING METABOLIC RATE

With the mean BMR values (kJ $m^{-2}\,h^{-1}$) for age and sex from Altman and Dittmer (1968) shown in Table 8.1, it is possible to predict an individual's BMR value using an estimate of body surface area. The most commonly used formula is that of DuBois and DuBois (1916) which only requires measures of height and body mass.

Subjects should remove their shoes for both the height and body mass measures. Height is measured to the nearest mm using a stadiometer. The subject should stand up as tall as he or she can keeping the heels on the floor and maintaining the head position in the Frankfort plane (i.e. the straight line through the lower bony orbital margin and the external auditory meatus should be horizontal).

Mass should be measured on calibrated weighing scales to the nearest 0.1 kg. The subject should be wearing minimal clothing.

The formula for estimation of body surface area according to DuBois and DuBois (1916) is:

$$BSA = M^{0.425} \times H^{0.725} \times 71.84 \times 10^{-4}$$

where: BSA is body surface area in m^2, M is body mass in kg and H is height in cm.

For example, a subject with a mass of 70 kg and height of 177 cm will have a body surface area of

$$\begin{aligned} BSA &= 70^{0.425} \times 177^{0.725} \times 71.84 \times 10^{-4} \\ &= 6.0837 \times 42.6364 \times 71.84 \times 10^{-4} \\ &= 1.86\ m^2 \end{aligned}$$

If the subject is male aged 20 then according to the average values of BMR (kJ $m^{-2}\,h^{-1}$) of Altman and Dittmer (1968) (Table 8.1) he would have an approximate BMR value of 165.8 kJ $m^{-2}\,h^{-1}$ (± 10%). This would compute to a resting energy expenditure of 165.8 kJ $m^{-2}\,h^{-1} \times 1.86\ m^2 = 308.4$ kJ h^{-1}. Over a 24 h period this would result in an estimated resting energy expenditure of 308.4 kJ $h^{-1} \times 24\ h = 7401$ kJ (1768 kcal).

Other sex specific formulae based on weight, height and age have also been widely used for the estimation of BMR:

- Harris and Benedict (1919)

103 lean females BMR = 655 + 9.6(M) + 1.85(Ht) – 4.68(age)

136 lean males BMR = 66 + 13.8(M) + 5.0(Ht) − 6.8(age)

- Owen *et al.* (1986)

32 non-athletic females RMR = 795 + 7.2(M)

- Owen *et al.* (1987)

60 lean to obese males RMR = 879 + 10.2(M)

- Mifflin *et al.* (1990)

247 lean to obese females RMR = − 161 + 10(M) + 6.25(Ht) − 5(age)
247 lean to obese males RMR = 5 + 10(M) + 6.25(Ht) − 5(age)

where: M = body mass (kg), Ht = height (cm), age = age (years), RMR and BMR are expressed in kcal day^{-1}.

Mifflin *et al.* (1990) provided the most general equations for age and weight. The equations of Harris and Benedict (1919) are shown to predict within 5% of RMR values, with the equations of Owen *et al.* (1986, 1987) performing even better (Cunningham, 1991).

8.4 PRACTICAL 2: ESTIMATION OF RESTING METABOLIC RATE FROM FAT-FREE MASS

The resting metabolic rate (RMR) can be estimated from fat-free mass (FFM) according to the following regression equation from Cunningham (1991):

$$RMR = 370 + 21.6 \times FFM$$

This equation was derived from a review by Cunningham (1991) where all studies measured FFM according to the whole body potassium K^{40} method and RMR, BMR and resting energy expenditure (REE) were considered to be physiologically equivalent. An equation was also presented for FFM estimated from triceps skinfold thickness:

$$RMR = 261 + 22.6 \times FFM$$

Number of subjects = 77 and variance accounted for (r^2) = 0.65.

Unfortunately, no reference to the specific source of the estimation of FFM from triceps skinfold thickness was given. However, values of fat-free mass from a variety of methods can be used in the estimation of RMR.

8.5 PRACTICAL 3: MEASUREMENT OF OXYGEN UPTAKE USING THE DOUGLAS BAG TECHNIQUE

Oxygen uptake can be measured using the open circuit Douglas bag technique. With this method the subject breathes from normal air into a Douglas bag, while wearing a nose clip. (All valve boxes, valves, tubing and Douglas bags should be routinely checked for wear and tear and leaks.) If subjects are exercising it is preferable to use a lightweight, low resistance, low dead space valve box such as that described by Jakeman and Davies (1979). This is attached to lightweight tubing which is at least 30 mm internal diameter (e.g. Falconia tubing), as these provide for some movement of the head and do not require fixed support, or the wearing of a headset. During gas collection the subject must also wear a nose clip (Figure 8.1).

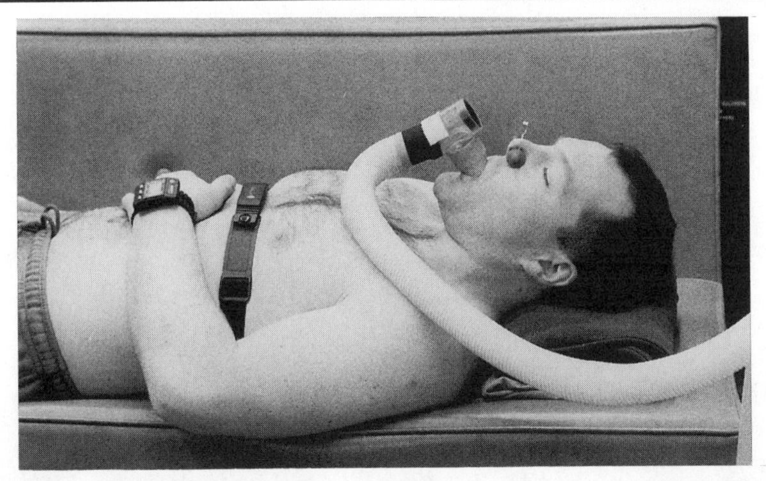

Figure 8.1 Photograph of a subject lying in a supine position showing expired air collection through a mouth piece attached to a Salford valve and light weight tubing, which is connected to a Douglas bag. The subject is wearing a nose clip and heart rate data are being recorded by a Polar Sport Tester.

Mouth pieces, valve boxes and tubing should be sterilized and dried prior to use by the next subject. Douglas bags must be completely empty before a collection of expired air is made. Ideally, they should be flushed out with a sample of the subject's expired air prior to data collection. For ease of data collection and long life the Douglas bags should be hung on suitable racks and evacuated by means of vacuum cleaners, rather than rolling them out.

Naïve subjects need habituating to breathing through a mouth piece prior to data collection. This should be done firstly at rest, and then included in the habituation to ergometry prior to any exercise testing. For steady-state protocols, with three or four minute stages, the subject need only exercise with the mouthpiece in for 15–20 s before gas collection, as this gives ample time to clear any dead space in the tubing. In ramp protocols and in maximal testing during the latter stages it is necessary to keep the mouth piece in all the time (Figure 8.2).

Prior to any measurements of gas concentration or volume of expired air the O_2 and CO_2 analysers should be calibrated and the dry gas meters checked. Gas meters should be calibrated with a minimum of a three-point calibration. This is most conveniently achieved by using 100% nitrogen to set the zero for both analysers, and two known concentrations of O_2 and CO_2 which span the working range. If Haldane or Micro-Scholander apparatus is available then this can be used to check new standard gases before they are used for routine calibration purposes. Room air can be used as a span gas for setting oxygen to 20.93%, but caution should be used in the site of collection of room air. Gas meters can be checked with a suitable calibration syringe or with a Tissot Spirometer.

8.5.1 SIMPLIFIED ESTIMATION OF OXYGEN UPTAKE

The most straightforward estimation of oxygen uptake ($\dot{V}O_2$) only requires the following measures to be made:

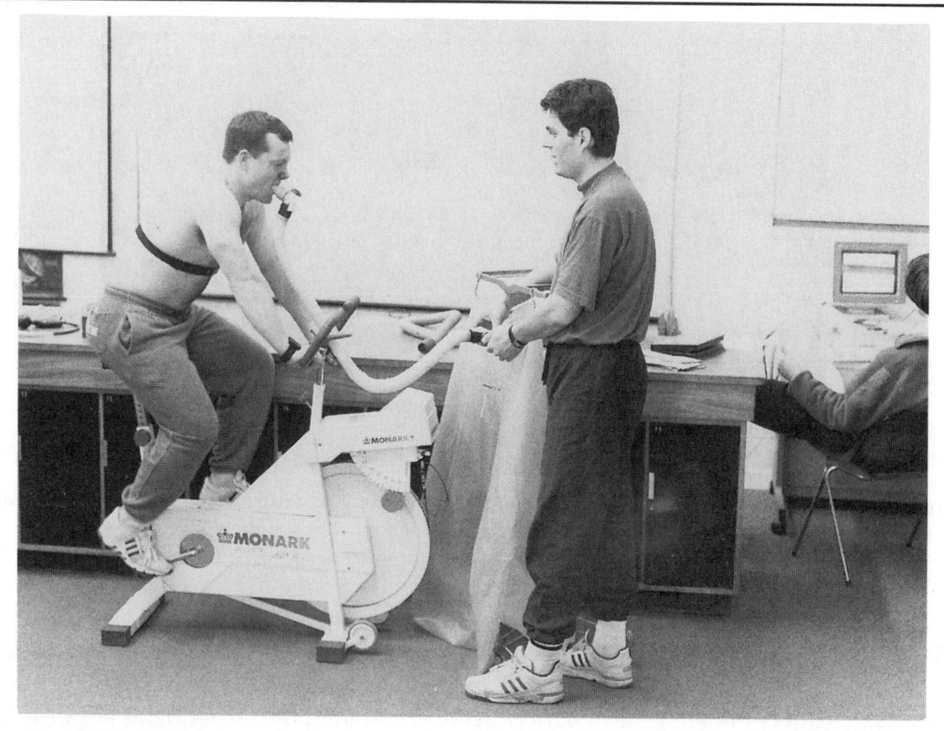

Figure 8.2 Photograph showing a subject on a standard Monark cycle ergometer, with expired air collection to a Douglas bag, and heart rate monitored by a radio telemeter (Polar Sport Tester).

- Volume of expired air collected in the Douglas bag = V_E (litres)
- Temperature of air as volume is measured (°C)
- Barometric pressure (mmHg)
- Fraction of oxygen in expired air (F_EO_2 or $\%O_{2E}$)
- Time taken for collection of expired air in Douglas bag (s)

Oxygen uptake ($\dot{V}O_2$) is the volume of oxygen inspired minus the volume of oxygen expired, i.e.:

$$\dot{V}O_2 = [(\dot{V}_I \times F_IO_2) - (\dot{V}_E \times F_EO_2)]$$

where: $\dot{V}O_2$ = oxygen uptake ($l\ min^{-1}$)
$\dot{V}_I$ = volume of air inspired ($l\ min^{-1}$)
F_IO_2 = fraction of oxygen in inspired air = constant value of 0.2093 (i.e. 20.93%)
$\dot{V}_E$ = volume of air expired ($l\ min^{-1}$)
F_EO_2 = fraction of oxygen in expired air

8.5.2 TIMING GAS COLLECTIONS AND CORRECTION OF GAS VOLUMES

It should be noted that V stands for volume, whereas $\dot{V}$ stands for volume per unit of time, usually per minute.

$$V_E = \text{volume of air expired in the Douglas bag.}$$

$\dot{V}_E$ = volume of expired air per minute (l min^{-1})

$\dot{V}O_2$ = volume of oxygen consumed per minute (l min^{-1})

Expired air collections should always be timed accurately over a complete number of respiratory cycles, from end expiration to end expiration. Collection times are therefore rarely equal to 30 s or 1 min, but can be easily converted into minute ventilation values by the following general calculation:

$$\dot{V}_E\,(\text{l min}^{-1}) = \frac{\text{Volume of expired air collection}}{\text{time of collection (s)}} \times 60$$

End expiration can be judged by the following.

1. Watching for the closure of the expiratory valve in the valve box.
2. Feeling the air flow stop at the tap before turning it to fill the Douglas bag.
3. In strenuous exercise, listening for each breath of expired air rushing down the tubing into the Douglas bag.

A stop-watch should be used to time collections.

Gas volumes obtained in laboratory experiments are typically expressed in one of three ways.

ATPS = ambient temperature, pressure and saturated
STPD = standard temperature, pressure and dry
BTPS = body temperature, ambient pressure and saturated

The conditions at the time of the measurement of the volume of expired air in the Douglas bag are reflected in ATPS. It should be noted that the volume of gas varies with temperature and pressure, and its water content, even though the number of molecules in the gas does not change. More specifically, as the temperature of gas increases the volume increases proportionately and vice versa (i.e. if the pressure is constant then a doubling of the temperature will result in a doubling of the volume). This is known as Charles' Law. However, gas volumes vary inversely with pressure. Thus, an increase in pressure causes a proportionate decrease in volume, and vice versa (i.e. if temperature is constant then a doubling of pressure will cause a halving of volume). This is known as Boyle's Law. Finally, the volume of a gas increases with the amount of water content.

To compare measures of volume taken under different environmental conditions, there is a need for a standard set of conditions which are defined by STPD and BTPS.

Standard temperature and pressure dry (STPD) refers to a gas volume expressed under *S*tandard *T*emperature (273 K or 0 °C), *P*ressure (760 mmHg) and *D*ry (no water vapour). Volumes corrected to STPD conditions therefore allow comparison between values collected at different temperatures, altitudes and degrees of saturation. Values of $\dot{V}_E$, $\dot{V}O_2$, and $\dot{V}CO_2$ are always expressed at STPD.

The formula for conversion of a volume of moist gas to STPD such as V_E is:

$$\dot{V}_{ESTPD} = \dot{V}_{EATPS}\,\frac{(273)}{273 + T\,^{\circ}C} \times \frac{(P_B - P_{H_2O})}{760}$$

Where T °C is the temperature of the expired air; P_B is barometric pressure; and P_{H_2O} is the water vapour pressure of the sample at the time volume is measured. P_{H_2O} is not measured directly because conversion factors are tabulated for the normal range of temperatures of moist gas samples.

Furthermore, none of the correction factors for volumes need to be calculated since tables for converting moist gas volumes into STPD conditions are readily available for the range of values of temperature and pressure normally experienced in most laboratories (Carpenter, 1964; McArdle *et al.*, 1991).

Body temperature and pressure saturated (BTPS) refers to a gas volume expressed at *B*ody *T*emperature (273 K + 37 K), *A*mbient pressure and *S*aturated with water vapour with a partial pressure of 47 mmHg at 37°C. This is the conventional standard used by respiratory physiologists for lung function volumes.

As with correction from ATPS to STPD, corrections from BTPS to STPD can be achieved by use of tabulated values of correction factors for a broad range of temperatures.

When using the simplified estimation of $\dot{V}O_2$ the composition of inspired air remains relatively constant ($F_IO_2 = 0.2093$, $\%O_{2I} = 20.93\%$; $F_ICO_2 = 0.0003$, $\%CO_{2I} = 0.03\%$ and $F_IN_2 = 0.7904$, $\%N_{2I} = 79.04\%$).

Substituting the value for the fraction of O_2 in inspired air of F_IO_2 the expression becomes:

$$\dot{V}O_2\ \text{STPD}\ (\text{l min}^{-1}) = V_E\ \text{STPD}\ (0.2093 - F_EO_2)$$

For example, given $\dot{V}_E$ ATPS = 60 l min^{-1} (volume measured in Douglas bag), barometric pressure = 754 mmHg (measured by barometer), temperature of gas = 22 °C (measured by thermometer as volume is measured), $F_EO_2 = 0.1675$ (measured by oxygen analyser), then

$$\dot{V}_{E\,STPD} = \dot{V}_{E\,ATPS} \times 0.891 \text{ (correction factor taken from Table 8.2)}$$

$$\dot{V}_{E\,STPD} = 60 \times 0.891$$

$$\dot{V}_{E\,STPD} = 53.46\ \text{l min}^{-1}$$

$$\dot{V}O_{2\,STPD}\ (\text{l min}^{-1}) = 53.46\ (0.2093 - 0.1675)$$

$$\dot{V}O_2\ (\text{l min}^{-1}) = 2.23\ \text{l min}^{-1}$$

In summary, there are two steps to the calculation.

1. Correct the V_E value from ATPS to STPD by multiplying by the appropriate correction factor from the appropriate table of values (Table 8.2).
2. Calculate the difference between the concentration of O_2 in inspired and expired air. Then all variables on the right of the equation are known and VO_2 can be calculated.

8.5.3 CALCULATION OF OXYGEN UPTAKE ($\dot{V}O_2$) USING THE HALDANE TRANSFORMATION

In addition to the measurements required for the simplified calculation of $\dot{V}O_2$ a value for the fraction of carbon dioxide in expired air is also required (F_ECO_2).

Although the concentrations of oxygen (O_2), carbon dioxide (CO_2) and nitrogen (N_2) are constant for inspired air, the values recorded for expired air fractions will vary. The value for F_EO_2 will be less than F_IO_2 as some of the O_2 is extracted from the lungs into the blood capillaries. The F_EO_2 will therefore range between approximately 0.15 and 0.185. The

Table 8.2 Conversion of gas volumes from ATPS to STPD (data from Carpenter,1964; McArdle *et al.,* 1991)

Baro-metric reading	*Temperature (°C)*																	
	15	16	17	18	19	20	21	22	23	24	25	26	27	28	29	30	31	32
700	0.855	851	847	842	838	834	829	825	821	816	812	807	802	797	793	788	783	778
702	857	853	849	845	840	836	832	827	823	818	814	809	805	800	795	790	785	780
704	860	856	852	847	843	839	834	830	825	821	816	812	807	802	797	792	787	783
706	862	858	854	850	845	841	837	832	828	823	819	814	810	804	800	795	790	785
708	865	861	856	852	848	843	839	834	830	825	821	816	812	807	802	797	792	787
710	867	863	859	855	850	846	842	837	833	828	824	819	814	809	804	799	795	790
712	870	866	861	857	853	848	844	839	836	830	826	821	817	812	807	802	797	792
714	872	868	864	859	855	851	846	842	837	833	828	824	819	814	809	804	799	794
716	875	871	866	862	858	853	849	844	840	835	831	826	822	816	812	807	802	797
718	877	873	869	864	860	856	851	847	842	838	833	828	824	819	814	809	804	799
720	880	876	871	867	863	858	854	849	845	840	836	831	826	821	816	812	807	802
722	882	878	874	869	865	861	856	852	847	843	838	833	829	824	819	814	809	804
724	885	880	876	872	867	863	858	854	849	845	840	835	831	826	821	816	811	806
726	887	883	879	874	870	866	861	856	852	847	843	838	833	829	824	818	813	808
728	890	886	881	877	872	868	863	859	854	850	845	840	836	831	826	821	816	811
730	892	888	884	879	875	871	866	861	857	852	847	843	838	833	828	823	818	813
732	895	890	886	882	877	873	868	864	859	854	850	845	840	836	831	825	820	815
734	897	893	889	884	880	875	871	866	862	857	852	847	843	838	833	828	823	818
736	900	895	891	887	882	878	873	869	864	859	855	850	845	840	835	830	825	820
738	902	898	894	889	885	880	876	871	866	862	857	852	848	843	838	833	828	822
740	905	900	896	892	887	883	878	874	869	864	860	855	850	845	840	835	830	825
742	907	903	898	894	890	885	881	876	871	867	862	857	852	847	842	837	832	827
744	910	906	901	897	892	888	883	878	874	869	864	859	855	850	845	840	834	829
746	912	908	903	899	895	890	886	881	876	872	867	862	857	852	847	842	837	832
748	915	910	906	901	897	892	888	883	879	874	869	864	860	854	850	845	839	834
750	917	913	908	904	900	895	890	886	881	876	872	867	862	857	852	847	842	837
752	920	915	911	906	902	897	893	888	883	879	874	869	864	859	854	849	844	839
754	922	918	913	909	904	900	895	891	886	881	876	872	867	862	857	852	846	841
756	925	920	916	911	907	902	898	893	888	883	879	874	869	864	859	854	849	844
758	927	923	918	914	909	905	900	896	891	886	881	876	872	866	861	856	851	846
760	930	925	921	916	912	907	902	898	893	888	883	879	874	869	864	859	854	848
762	932	928	923	919	914	910	905	900	896	891	886	881	876	871	866	861	856	851
764	936	930	926	921	916	912	907	903	898	893	888	884	879	874	869	864	858	853
766	937	933	928	924	919	915	910	905	900	896	891	886	881	876	871	886	861	855
768	940	935	931	926	922	917	912	908	903	898	893	888	883	878	873	868	863	858
770	942	938	933	928	924	919	915	910	905	901	896	891	886	881	876	871	865	860

F_ECO_2 will increase in expired air since the body excretes CO_2 with the lungs from the blood by gas exchange. The F_ECO_2 will range from approximately 0.025 to 0.05. Although nitrogen is inert, that is the same number of molecules of N_2 exist in both the inspired and expired air, they will change in concentration if the number of O_2 molecules removed from inspired air is not equal to the number of CO_2 molecules excreted in expired air. In simple terms, when the molecules of O_2 removed do not equal the molecules of CO_2 added then the volume of inspired air (V_I) will not equal the volume of air expired (V_E), and the constant number of N_2 molecules will represent a different fraction or percentage of the inspired and expired volumes.

For example: inspired air constant fractions:

$$F_IO_2 = 0.2093, \text{ or } \%O_{2I} = 20.93\%; F_ICO_2 = 0.0003, \text{ or } \%CO_{2I} = 0.03\%;$$

$$\text{and } F_IN_2 = 0.7904, \text{ or } \%N_{2I} = 79.04\%$$

$$\%O_{2I} + \%CO_{2I} + \%N_{2I} = 100\%; (20.93 + 0.03 + 79.04 = 100)$$

Given expired air measured values from experiment:

$$\%O_{2E} = 16.75\%; \%CO_{2E} = 3.55\%$$

$$\%O_{2E} + \%CO_{2E} + \%N_{2E} = 100$$

$$\%N_{2E} = 100 - (\%O_{2E} + \%CO_{2E})$$

$$\%N_{2E} = 100 - (16.75 + 3.55)$$

$$\%N_{2E} = 79.7\%$$

Here the fraction of oxygen in inspired air has decreased from a value of 0.2093 to 0.1675 in expired air, whereas the concentration of carbon dioxide in inspired air has increased from a value of 0.0003 to 0.0355 in expired air. The decrease in oxygen concentration is therefore greater than the increase in carbon dioxide concentration in expired air. Therefore the fraction of nitrogen in inspired air ($F_IN_2 = 0.7904$) rises to a value of 0.7970 in expired air (the same number of molecules but increased in concentration).

The constant number of N_2 molecules representing a different percentage or concentration of inspired and expired volumes can be used to calculate V_I from V_E or vice versa. This is possible because the change in volume from inspired to expired is directly proportional to the change in nitrogen concentration:

$$\text{Mass of } N_2 \text{ inspired} = \text{Mass of } N_2 \text{ expired}$$

$$\text{As concentration} = \frac{\text{Mass}}{\text{Volume}}$$

$$\%N_{2I} = \frac{\text{Mass of } N_2}{V_I} \quad \text{and} \quad \%N_{2E} = \frac{\text{Mass of } N_2}{V_E}$$

$$\therefore \text{Mass of } N_2 = \%N_{2I} \times V_I = \%N_{2E} \times V_E$$

$$\dot{V}_{I\,STPD} = \frac{\dot{V}_{E\,STPD} \times \%N_{2E}}{\%N_{2I}}$$

Given the same values as for the simplified calculation, i.e. $V_{E\,ATPS} = 60\,l\,min^{-1}$ temperature = 22 °C, barometric pressure = 754 mmHg, correction factor from ATPS to STPD = 0.891, then $\dot{V}_{E\,STPD}$ will also be the same: $\dot{V}_{E\,STPD} = 53.46\,l\,min^{-1}$

Given that $\%N_{2E}$ was calculated from expired $\%O_{2E}$ and $\%CO_{2E}$ as 79.7% and $\%N_{2I}$ is constant at 79.04%, all the values on the right of the equation are known and can be used to calculate $\dot{V}O_{2\,STPD}$.

Oxygen uptake ($\dot{V}O_2$, $l\,min^{-1}$) can now be calculated as the volume of oxygen removed from expired air per minute:

$$\dot{V}O_2 = [(V_I \times \%O_{2I}) - (V_E \times \%O_{2E})] \div 100$$

Substituting using the Haldane transformation $\dot{V}_I = \dot{V}_E \times \frac{\%\,N_{2E}}{\%N_I}$ we can replace $\dot{V}_I$ by our known expression $\dot{V}_E \times \frac{\%\,N_{2I}}{\%N_I}$

$$\dot{V}O_2 = \frac{[(\dot{V}_E \times \%N_{2E} \times \%O_{2I}) - (\dot{V}_E \times \%O_{2E})]}{\%N_{2I}} \div 100$$

Substituting in constants for inspired air and simplifying the expression:

$$\dot{V}O_2 = \frac{[\dot{V}_E\,(\%N_{2E} \times 20.93\% - \%O_{2E})]}{79.04\%} \div 100$$

With the most simple form of the equation for computation being:

$$\dot{V}O_2 = \dot{V}_E \times [(\%N_{2E} \times 0.265) - \%O_{2E}] \div 100$$

where $\dot{V}_E$ is measured under ATPS conditions and corrected to STPD conditions before substitution into this equation, $\%O_{2E}$ is measured from O_2 analyser and $\%N_{2E} = 100 - \%O_{2E} - \%CO_{2E}$ ($\%CO_{2E}$ is measured from CO_2 gas analyser).

Inserting the example values into the simplified equation gives:

$$\dot{V}O_2\,(l\,min^{-1}) = 53.46[(79.7 \times 0.265) - 16.75\%] \div 100$$

$$\dot{V}O_2\,(l\,min^{-1}) = 53.46\,[4.3705] \div 100$$

$$\dot{V}O_2 = 2.34\,l\,min^{-1}$$

8.5.4 CALCULATION OF CARBON DIOXIDE PRODUCTION ($\dot{V}CO_2$)

The volume of carbon dioxide produced is calculated according to the following equation:

$$\dot{V}CO_2 = [\dot{V}_E\,(\%CO_{2E} - \%CO_{2I})] \div 100$$

Where $\dot{V}_E$ is measured and corrected to STPD conditions, $\%CO_{2I} = 0.03\%$ (constant for inspired air) and $\%CO_{2E}$ is measured from CO_2 gas analyser.

Since the fraction of CO_2 in inspired air is negligible, the Haldane transformation is unimportant in the calculation of $\dot{V}CO_2$. In many cases the fraction of CO_2 in inspired air is often ignored altogether.

Using the data from the example calculation of $\dot{V}O_2$.

$$\dot{V}CO_2\ (\mathrm{l\ min^{-1}}) = [53.46\ (3.55 - 0.03)] \div 100$$

$$\dot{V}CO_2 = 1.88\ (\mathrm{l\ min^{-1}})$$

8.6 PRACTICAL 4: THE RESPIRATORY QUOTIENT

The respiratory quotient (RQ) is calculated as the ratio of metabolic gas exchange:

$$RQ = \frac{\dot{V}CO_2}{\dot{V}O_2}\ \frac{\text{(Volume of carbon dioxide produced)}}{\text{(Volume of oxygen consumed)}}$$

The RQ gives an indication of what combination of carbohydrates, fats and proteins are metabolized in steady-state submaximal exercise or at rest. The specific equation associated with the RQ for oxidation of pure carbohydrates, fats and proteins is as follows:

(a) RQ for carbohydrates (glucose)

$$C_6H_{12}O_6 + 6O_2 = 6CO_2 + 6H_2O$$

Therefore during the oxidation of a glucose molecule six molecules of oxygen are consumed and six molecules of carbon dioxide are produced, therefore:

$$RQ = \frac{6CO_2}{6O_2} = 1$$

The RQ value for carbohydrate is therefore 1.

(b) RQ for fat (palmitic acid)

$$C_{16}H_{32}O_2 = 16CO_2 + 16H_2O$$

$$RQ = \frac{16CO_2}{23O_2} = 0.696$$

Generally, the RQ value for fat is taken to be 0.7.

(c) RQ for protein

The process is more complex for protein to provide energy as proteins are not simply oxidized to carbon dioxide and water, during energy metabolism. Generally, the RQ value for protein is taken to be 0.82.

McLean and Tobin (1987) published equations for the calculation of calorific factors from elemental composition, which included the following equation for respiratory quotient (RQ):

$$RQ = 1/(1 + 2.9789\, f_H/f_C - 0.3754\, f_O/f_c)$$

where 1 g of a substance contains f_C, f_H and f_O g of carbon, hydrogen and oxygen respectively.

Given the formula for the chemical composition of carbohydrate, fat or protein, together with the atomic weights for carbon, hydrogen and oxygen ($a_C = 12.011$, $a_H = 1.008$ and $a_O = 15.999$) it is then possible to calculate f_C, f_H and f_O and solve the equation for RQ.

If we use the example of glucose ($C_6H_{12}O_6$):

$$C_6 \text{ gives } a_C \times 6 = 72.1$$

$$H_{12} \text{ gives } a_H \times 12 = 12.1$$

$$O_6 \text{ gives } a_O \times 6 = 96.0$$

The total is therefore 180.2, which gives fractions for each of 0.4, 0.067 and 0.533 for carbon, hydrogen and oxygen respectively. Substitution of these values in the equation above gives an RQ of 1 as previously derived.

As previously stated the RQ calculated as the ratio of $V\text{CO}_2$ and $V\text{O}_2$ will reflect a combination of carbohydrates, fats and proteins currently being metabolized to provide energy. However, the precise contribution of each of the nutrients can be obtained from the calculation of the non-protein RQ.

(d) Non-protein RQ

This calculation of the non-protein RQ is based upon McArdle *et al.* (1991), where the procedures are discussed in more detail.

Although this is typical of the approach in most text books, Durnin and Passmore (1967) described the non-protein RQ as 'an abstraction which has no physiological meaning, as protein metabolism is never zero'. Durnin and Passmore (1967) preferred the four equations set out by Consolazio *et al.* (1961) which are used to define the metabolic mixture and calculate energy expenditure. The four equations are also based on oxidation of carbohydrates, fats and proteins and require the measurement of $\dot{V}\text{CO}_2$, $\dot{V}\text{O}_2$ and urinary nitrogen. Furthermore, they give the same answer as the classical method using non- protein RQ.

Approximately 1 g of nitrogen is excreted in the urine for every 6.25 g of protein metabolized for energy. Each gram of excreted nitrogen represents a carbon dioxide production of approximately 4.8 litres and an oxygen consumption of about 6.8 litres.

Example calculation:

A subject consumes 3.8 litres of oxygen and produces 3.1 litres of carbon dioxide during 15 min of rest, during which 0.11 g of nitrogen are excreted into the urine.

1. CO_2 produced in the catabolism of protein is given by 4.8 l CO_2 $g^{-1} \times 0.11$ g = 0.53 l of CO_2
2. O_2 consumed in the catabolism of protein is given by 6.0 l O_2 g^{-1} protein $\times 0.11$ g = 0.66 l of O_2

3. Non-protein CO_2 produced = 3.1 − 0.53 = 2.57 l CO_2
4. Non-protein O_2 consumed = 3.8 − 0.66 = 3.14 l of O_2
5. Non-protein RQ = 2.57/3.14 = 0.818

Table 8.3 shows the energy equivalents per litre of oxygen consumed for the range of non-protein RQ values and the percentage of fat and carbohydrates utilized for energy. As Table 8.3 shows 20.20 kJ per litre of oxygen are liberated for a non-protein RQ of 0.82 as calculated above. Thus, 59.7% of the energy is derived from carbohydrate and 40.3% from fat. The non-protein energy production from carbohydrate and fat for the 15 min period is 63.42 kJ (20.20 $kj^{-1} \times 3.14$ l O_2), whereas the energy derived from protein is 12.71 kJ (19.26 kJ $l^{-1} \times 0.66$ l O_2). Therefore, the total energy for the 15 min period is 76.13 kJ (63.42 kJ non-protein + 12.71 kJ protein).

Table 8.3 Thermal equivalent of O_2 for non-protein respiratory quotient, including percentage energy and grams derived from carbohydrate and fat

Non-protein RQ	*Energy (kJ) per litre oxygen used*	*Percentage energy derived from*		*Grams per litre O_2 consumed*	
		Carbohydrate	*Fat*	*Carbohydrate*	*Fat*
0.707	19.62	0	100	0.000	0.496
0.71	19.63	1.10	98.9	0.012	0.491
0.72	19.68	4.76	95.2	0.051	0.476
0.73	19.73	8.40	91.6	0.090	0.460
0.74	19.79	12.0	88.0	0.130	0.444
0.75	19.84	15.6	84.4	0.170	0.428
0.76	19.89	19.2	80.8	0.211	0.412
0.77	19.94	22.8	77.2	0.250	0.396
0.78	19.99	26.3	73.7	0.290	0.380
0.79	20.04	29.9	70.1	0.330	0.363
0.80	20.10	33.4	66.6	0.371	0.347
0.81	20.15	36.9	63.1	0.413	0.330
0.82	20.20	40.3	59.7	0.454	0.313
0.83	20.25	43.8	56.2	0.496	0.297
0.84	20.30	47.2	52.8	0.537	0.280
0.85	20.35	50.7	49.3	0.579	0.263
0.86	20.41	54.1	45.9	0.621	0.247
0.87	20.46	57.5	42.5	0.663	0.230
0.88	20.51	60.8	39.2	0.705	0.213
0.89	20.57	64.2	35.8	0.749	0.195
0.90	20.61	67.5	32.5	0.791	0.178
0.91	20.66	70.8	29.2	0.834	0.160
0.92	20.71	74.1	25.9	0.875	0.143
0.93	20.77	77.4	22.6	0.921	0.125
0.94	20.82	80.7	19.3	0.981	0.108
0.95	20.87	84.0	16.0	1.008	0.080
0.96	20.92	87.2	12.8	1.052	0.072
0.97	20.97	90.4	9.58	1.097	0.054
0.98	21.02	93.6	6.37	1.142	0.036
0.99	21.08	96.8	3.18	1.186	0.018
1.00	21.13	100.0	0	1.231	0.000

In terms of carbohydrate and fat metabolism, for the non-protein RQ of 0.818, 0.454 g of carbohydrate and 0.313 g of fat were metabolized per litre of O_2 respectively (Table 8.3). This amounts to 1.43 g of carbohydrate (3.141 $O_2 \times 0.455$) and 0.98 g of fat (3.141 $O_2 \times 0.313$) in the 15 min rest period.

During rest or steady-state exercise such as walking or running slowly, the RQ does not reflect the oxidation of pure carbohydrate or fat, but a mixture of the two, producing RQ values which range between 0.7 and 1.00. As shown by the sample calculation of non-protein RQ, protein contributes only a minor amount of the total energy expenditure. For this reason the specific contribution of protein is often ignored, avoiding the monitoring of N_2 excretion together with the more complex and lengthy calculations. In most instances an RQ of 0.82 can be assumed (40% carbohydrate and 60% fat) and the energy equivalent of 23.24 kJ (4.825 kcal) per litre of oxygen can be used in energy expenditure calculations. The maximum error associated with this simplification in estimating energy expenditure from $\dot{V}O_2$ is only of the order of 4% (McArdle *et al.*, 1991).

Durnin and Passmore (1967) stated that in most studies of energy expenditure there is no need to find out how much carbohydrate, fat or protein is used. Furthermore, they advocated the use of Weir's (1949) formula for estimation of energy expenditure which negates the need for CO_2 measurement.

$$\text{Energy (kcal min}^{-1}) = \frac{4.92}{100}\,\dot{V}_{E\,STPD}\,(20.93 - \%O_{2E})$$

The advice of Durnin and Passmore (1967) is worth serious consideration, given the possible sources of error associated with the Douglas bag technique, gas analysis and volume measurement in unskilled hands.

8.6.1 RESPIRATORY QUOTIENT (RQ) AND RESPIRATORY EXCHANGE RATIO (RER)

Under steady-state conditions of exercise, the assumption that gas exchange at the lungs reflects gas exchange from metabolism in the cells is reasonably valid. When conditions are other than steady state, such as in severe exercise, or with hyperventilation, the assumption is no longer valid. Under such conditions the ratio of carbon dioxide production to oxygen consumption is known as RER even though it is calculated in exactly the same way.

8.7 PRACTICAL 5: ESTIMATION OF RMR USING THE DOUGLAS BAG TECHNIQUE

Under ideal conditions RMR should be estimated as soon as the person wakes up from an overnight sleep. This is not possible in most practical situations, but provided that the subject can rest in a supine position for a reasonable period of time a good estimate of RMR can be obtained. During the test the subject lies quietly in a supine position (Figure 8.3), preferably in a temperature-controlled room, thus ensuring a thermoneutral environment. After 30–60 min, the subject's oxygen uptake is measured for a minimum of 6–10 min, preferably 15 min. If O_2 and CO_2 concentrations are measured in expired air then the RQ, energy expenditure, and substrate utilization can be estimated according to the procedures outlined above. Values for oxygen uptake used as an estimate of BMR range between 160 and 290 ml min^{-1} (3.85–6.89 kJ min^{-1}), depending upon a variety of factors, but particularly on body size (McArdle *et al.*, 1991).

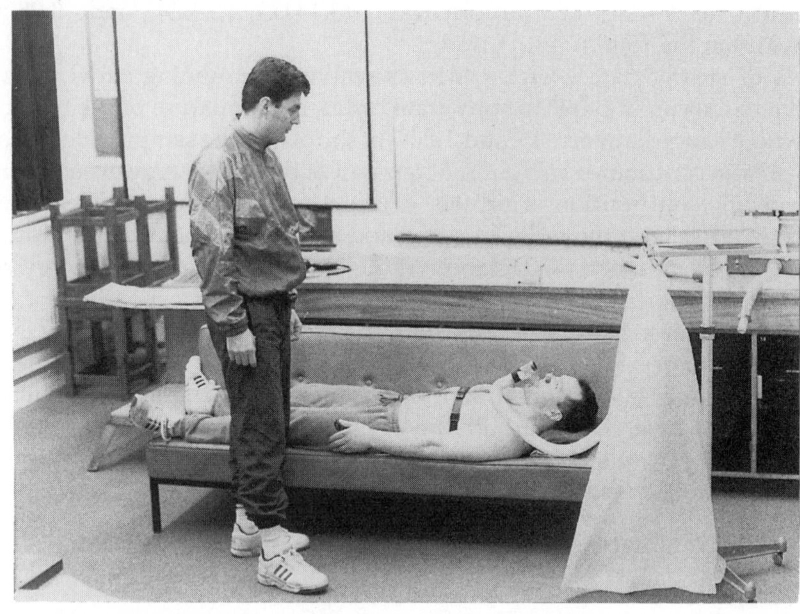

Figure 8.3 A subject lying in a supine position in a laboratory practical for the estimation of resting metabolic rate (RMR) with expired air collection to a Douglas bag, together with heart rate monitoring via a short-range radio telemeter (Polar Sport Tester).

8.8 PRACTICAL 6: ENERGY BALANCE

This practical introduces the procedures for the measurement of energy balance, incorporating a simplified assessment of energy expenditure and food intake. In simple terms, if the total energy intake is repeatedly greater than the daily energy expenditure, the excess energy is stored as fat. In contrast, if daily energy expenditure is greater than energy intake the subject will lose weight. The aim of the laboratory practical is to calculate the energy expenditure and energy intake for a typical day. An understanding of key concepts in energy expenditure and intake is important for several areas of exercise physiology, such as the use of diet and exercise to alter body composition, thermoregulation and mechanical efficiency. Energy expenditure is calculated by a combination of measurements, using the Douglas bag technique, and estimations using generalized predictive equations and tables for a range of activities. The estimation of energy intake is based on the energy value of food using standard reference tables. The subject should keep a diary of activities (duration and intensity) and food consumed (quantity and preparation) for a 24 h period. Energy intake and expenditure can then be calculated from standard tables and from direct measures of energy expenditure completed in the laboratory.

8.8.1 ENERGY EXPENDITURE

It is possible to measure oxygen uptake for a range of everyday activities, which should be ordered such that the least demanding are completed first. Oxygen uptake should be measured for RMR, and compared with RMR from the predictive formulae in section 8.3. Oxygen uptake values can then be obtained for sitting, standing, self-paced walking, stair climbing and an appropriate form of exercise for the subject, such as running or cycling. If time permits, duplicate gas collections should be made. Most of the measurements can be made in the laboratory, but some may necessitate access to other buildings, such as stair climbing and descending, and self-paced walking. In such cases, the Douglas bag should be supported in some way. All gas collections should be made under steady-state conditions for an appropriate length of time to analyse the expired air accurately (minimum of 10 min for RMR, dropping to 1 min for the most strenuous exercise to ensure an accurately quantifiable volume).

Energy expenditure can than be calculated using the $\dot{V}O_2$, $\dot{V}CO_2$ and RQ values and their energy equivalents shown in Table 8.3 or Weir's formula presented in section 8.6. A comparison of the two forms of calculation will indicate whether the extra precision associated with the measurement of carbon dioxide concentration and the calculation of RQ is warranted if the aim is to calculate energy expenditure.

The directly measured energy expenditure values can then be used in the calculation of the daily energy expenditure from the information recorded in the diary of activities. Where direct measurement was not possible values for energy expenditure must be taken from mean values of energy expenditure published in the literature (e.g. Durnin and Passmore, 1967; Bannister and Brown, 1968; McArdle *et al.*, 1991; Ainsworth *et al.*, 1993). (Table 8.4 gives some examples of common activities.) The disadvantage of using mean values of energy expenditure taken from the literature is that they will not be specific to the individual, in terms of efficiency, and often are not very sensitive to the intensity of the activity.

Ainsworth *et al.* (1993) have presented a comprehensive compendium of physical acti-

Table 8.4 Energy expenditure values for selected activities

Activity	*kcal kg^{-1} min^{-1}*[a]	*METS*[b]
Badminton	0.097	4.5 (general)
		7.0 (competitive)
Basketball	0.138	6.0 (general)
		8.0 (competitive)
Cycling	0.100 (15 km h^{-1})	6.0 (16–19 km h^{-1})
	0.169 (racing)	16.0 (racing > 32 km h^{-1})
Dancing (aerobics)	0.135 (intense)	7.0 (high impact)
		5.0 (low impact)
		6.0 (general)
Home (cleaning general)	0.060	3.5 (general)
Home (play with child)		5.0 (run/walk – vig)
		2.5 (sitting)
Home (inactivity – quiet)	0.022 (lying)	1.0 (sitting)
Running	0.163 (cross-country)	9.0 (cross-country)
	0.193 (10.4 km h^{-1})	10.0 (9.6 km h^{-1})
	0.252 (16.0 km h^{-1})	16.0 (16 km h^{-1})
Squash	0.212	12.0
Swimming (crawl)	0.156 (fast)	11.0 (fast)
	0.128 (slow)	8.0 (slow)
Volleyball	0.050	4.0 (competitive)
		3.0 (non-competitive)

Table 8.4 (continued)

Activity	*kcal* kg^{-1} min^{-1}[a]	*METS*[b]
Walking	0.080 (normal pace)	3.5 (4.8 km h^{-1}) 4.5 (6.4 km h^{-1}) 6.0 (backpacking) 3.0 (downstairs) 8.0 (upstairs)

[a] Values in kcal kg^{-1} min^{-1} are from McArdle *et al.* (1991).
[b] Values in METS are from Ainsworth *et al.* (1993).

vities classified in terms of intensity according to the number of METS of energy required. A MET is defined as the energy requirement for RMR. The most accurate way to compute the energy expenditure values for a given individual using their compendium is to measure the RMR and multiply it by the MET value associated with the physical activity of interest. For example, if the oxygen uptake measured as an estimate of RMR for a person of mass 70 kg was 270 ml min^{-1} with an RQ of 0.87 this would equate to an RMR value of 0.27 × 20.46 kJ l^{-1}, which equals 5.52 kJ min^{-1} (331 kJ h^{-1} or 7954 kJ day^{-1}) (1900 kcal day^{-1}). This value of RMR would represent one MET and could be multiplied by the appropriate MET value for a given physical activity. According to Ainsworth *et al.* (1993), fencing requires an energy expenditure equivalent to 6 METS. For the 70 kg individual this equates with an energy expenditure value of 6 × 5.52 kJ min^{-1}, which equals 33.1 kJ min^{-1} (7.91 kcal min^{-1}).

In the absence of a measure or prediction of RMR diaries of self-reported physical activity can be conveniently assessed for energy expenditure based on a mean estimate of RMR of 1 kcal kg^{-1} h^{-1}. For a body mass of 70 kg this value would produce an energy expenditure value of (6 METS × 70 kg × 1 kcal kg^{-1} h^{-1}/60 min = 7.00 kcal min^{-1} (29.3 kJ min^{-1})) for fencing. This value represents 88% of the value calculated from the measured RMR value.

The diary of physical activities for the day should be broken down into periods of the order of 10–15 min, with high intensity activities of a short duration, such as stair climbing, also recorded as these events can have a significant cumulative effect on the total energy expenditure for the day. Table 8.5 shows a proforma for such a diary which has been completed by a young female (age 24 years; mass 57 kg) who has a sedentary desk job. The data indicate that this person spends much of her time sitting, but walks to work, walks the children home from school, and attends an aerobics class in the evening. Using the appropriate MET values from Ainsworth *et al.* (1993), the daily energy expenditure can be estimated using a mean estimated RMR of l kcal kg^{-1} h^{-1}. For a body mass of 57 kg, this value would produce the following estimates of energy expenditure for Table 8.5:

Sleep = (57 kg × 0.9 MET × 1 kcal kg^{-1} h^{-1} × 38 (15 min periods))/4	= 487 kcal
Walking = (57 × 3.5 × 1 × 11)/4	= 548 kcal
Typing = (57 × 1.5 × 1 × 20)/4	= 428 kcal
Sitting = (57 × 1 × 1 × 11)/4	= 157 kcal
Play = (57 × 5 × 1 × 2)/4	= 143 kcal
Eating = (57 × 1.5 × 1 × 5)/4	= 107 kcal
Cooking = (57 × 2.5 × 1 × 2)/4	= 71 kcal
Cleaning = (57 × 3.5 × 1 × 2)/4	= 100 kcal
Aerobics = (57 × 6 × 1 × 4)/4	= 342 kcal
Total	= 2383 kcal (9975 kJ)

Table 8.5 Proforma for recording activity over a 24-hour period.

	15-MINUTE TIME PERIODS			
HOUR	1	2	3	4
1	SLEEP	SLEEP	SLEEP	SLEEP
2	SLEEP	SLEEP	SLEEP	SLEEP
3	SLEEP	SLEEP	SLEEP	SLEEP
4	SLEEP	SLEEP	SLEEP	SLEEP
5	SLEEP	SLEEP	SLEEP	SLEEP
6	SLEEP	SLEEP	SLEEP	SLEEP
7	SLEEP	SLEEP	SITTING	EATING
8	WALKING	WALKING	WALKING	TYPING
9	TYPING	TYPING	TYPING	TYPING
10	SITTING	MEETING	MEETING	MEETING
11	TYPING	TYPING	TYPING	TYPING
12	TYPING	TYPING	TYPING	TYPING
13	WALKING	EATING	EATING	TYPING
14	TYPING	TYPING	TYPING	TYPING
15	TYPING	TYPING	WALKING	WALKING
16	WALKING	SITTING	PLAY CHILD	PLAY CHILD
17	COOKING	COOKING	CLEANING	CLEANING
18	EATING	SITTING	WALKING	SITTING
19	AEROBICS (GENERAL)	AEROBICS	AEROBICS	AEROBICS
20	WALKING	SITTING	EATING	SITTING
21	SITTING	SITTING	SITTING	SITTING
22	SLEEP	SLEEP	SLEEP	SLEEP
23	SLEEP	SLEEP	SLEEP	SLEEP
24	SLEEP	SLEEP	SLEEP	SLEEP

(SHORT INTENSIVE ACTIVITY SHOULD BE NOTED SEPARATELY)

This fictitious young female subject therefore expends 2383 kcal of energy on this particular day. Table 8.6 shows an example of an alternative data collection form for recording physical activity (Ainsworth *et al.*, 1993).

Table 8.6 Example of recording form for physical activities (Ainsworth *et al.*,1993)

	Type of activity	*Reason for activity*	*Subjective intensity level*	*Duration hours: min*	*Code or MET level (for clinic use only)*
1					
2					
3					

8.8.2 MEASURING ENERGY INTAKE

A set of calibrated kitchen weighing scales should be used to weigh all food that is consumed in the 24 h period under examination. The weight of the food, its form of preparation (e.g. fried, boiled) and the amount and type of fluid drinks should be recorded in the 24 h food diary. An example of a 24 h diet for the young female subject for whom a 24 h activity diary was analysed is shown in Table 8.7. The diet can then be analysed for energy intake using standard tables for common foods (e.g. McArdle *et al.*, 1991; Holland *et al.*, 1992). For the example shown in Table 8.7, using COMPEAT software, the total energy intake is calculated to be 8346 kJ (1994 kcal). This means that for this particular day the young female subject would be in negative energy balance, expending 1629 kJ (389 kcal) more energy than she consumes. The dietary analysis can easily be extended to a seven day weighed food intake, with a more accurate dietary analysis of nutrients and percentages of recommended daily allowances of fat, carbohydrate and protein which can be performed using commercially available software (e.g. COMPEAT, based on Holland *et al.*, 1992).

Table 8.7 Example of a 24-hour diet record sheet

Food description	*Mass (g)*
Special K	50.0
Skimmed milk	150.0
Water	1700.0
Indian tea	520.0
Meat paste	30.0
Wholemeal bread	76.0
Tomatoes (raw)	65.0
Eating apples (Cox's Pippin)	100.0
Crisps	25.0
Chocolate digestive biscuits	51.0
Cheese and tomato pizza	365.0
Hot cross bun	50.0
Ribena (undiluted)	30.0

8.9 SUMMARY

This chapter has set out a small selection of laboratory practicals which will give an introduction to the measurement of metabolic rate and energy balance. These procedures form the basis of many aspects of experimental work in a variety of areas of study, such as kinanthropometry, nutrition and exercise physiology, and can easily be adapted to the specific requirements of a large number of experiments using different items of equipment.

REFERENCES

Ainsworth, B. E., Haskell, W. L., Leon, A. S. *et al.* (1993) Compendium of physical activities: classification of energy costs of human physical activities. *Medicine and Science in Sports and Exercise*, **25**, 71–80.

Altman, P. L. and Dittmer, D. S. (1968) *Metabolism*, FASBEB, Bethesda, MD.

Åstrand, P. O. and Rodahl, K. (1986) *Textbook of Work Physiology, Physiological Bases of Exercise*, 3rd edn, McGraw Hill, New York.

Bannister, E. W. and Brown, S. R. (1968) The relative energy requirements of physical activity, in *Exercise Physiology* (ed. H. B. Falls), Academic Press, New York.

British Association of Sports Sciences (1992) *Position Statement on the Physiological Assessment of the Elite Athlete*, British Association of Sports Sciences (Physiology Section)

Carpenter, T. M. (1964) *Tables, Functions, and Formulas for Computing Respiratory Exchange and Biological Transformation of Energy*, 4th edn, Carnegie Institution of Washington Publication 303C, Washington, DC.

Consolazio, C. F., Johnson, R. E. and Pecora, L. J. (1963) *Physiological Measurements of Metabolic Functions in Man*, McGraw-Hill, New York.

Cunningham, J. J. (1991) Body composition as a determinant of energy expenditure: a synthetic review and a proposed general prediction equation. *American Journal of Clinical Nutrition*, **54**, 963–9.

DuBois, D. and DuBois, E. F. (1916) Clinical calorimetry. A formula to estimate the approximate surface area if height and weight are known. *Archives of Internal Medicine*, **17**, 863–71.

Durnin, J. V. G. A. and Passmore, R. (1967) *Energy, Work and Leisure*, Heinemann, London.

Harris, J. and Benedict, F. (1919) *A Biometric Study of Basal Metabolism in Man*. Carnegie Institution, Publication 279, Washington, DC.

Holland, B., Welch, A. A., Unwin, I. D. *et al.* (1992) *McCance and Widdowson's The Composition of Foods*, 5th edn, The Royal Society of Chemistry and Ministry of Agriculture, Fisheries and Food, Richard Clay Ltd, UK.

Jakeman, P. and Davies, B. (1979) The characteristics of a low resistance breathing valve designed for measurement of high aerobic capacity. *British Journal of Sports Medicine*, **13**, 81–3.

Kleiber, M. (1975) *The Fire of Life. An Introduction to Animal Energetics*, Kreiger, New York.

Knoebel, L. K. (1963) Energy metabolism, in Physiology (ed. E. E. Selkurt), Little, Brown, Boston, pp. 564–79.

MacDougall, J. D., Roche, P. D., Bar-Or, O. and Moroz, J. R. (1979) Oxygen cost of running in children of different ages; maximal aerobic power of Canadian school children. *Canadian Journal of Applied Sports Sciences*, **4**, 237–41.

McArdle, W. D., Katch, F. I. and Katch, V. L. (1991) *Exercise Physiology, Energy Nutrition and Human Performance*, 3rd edn, Lea and Febiger, Malvern, Philadelphia.

McLean, J. A. and Tobin, G. (1987) *Animal and Human Calorimetry*. Cambridge University Press, Cambridge.

McMahon, T. A. (1984) *Muscles, Reflexes and Locomotion*, Princeton University Press, Princeton, NJ.

Mifflin, M. D., St Jeor, S. T., Hill, L. A. *et al.* (1990) A new predictive equation for resting energy expenditure in healthy individuals. *American Journal of Clinical Nutrition*, **51**, 241–7.

Owen, O. E., Kavle, E. and Owen, R. S. (1986) A re-appraisal of the caloric requirements in healthy women. *American Journal of Clinical Nutrition*, **44**, 1–19.

Owen, O. E., Holup, J. L. and D'Allessio, D. A. (1987) A re-appraisal of the caloric requirements of healthy men. *American Journal of Clinical Nutrition*, **46**, 875–85.

Rubner, M. (1883) Uber den Einfluss der korpergrosse auf Stoff- und Kraftwechsel. *Z. Biology. Munich*, **19**, 535–62.

Schmidt-Nielsen, K. (1984) *Scaling: Why is Animal Size so Important*? Cambridge University Press, Cambridge.

Weir, J. B. De. V. (1949) New methods for calculating metabolic rate with special reference to protein metabolism. *Journal of Physiology*, **109**, 1–9.

MAXIMAL OXYGEN UPTAKE, ECONOMY AND EFFICIENCY 9

C. B. Cooke

9.1 INTRODUCTION

Measurements of maximal oxygen uptake, economy and efficiency of different forms of exercise are important in gaining an understanding of the differences between groups of athletes, and the requirements of sporting, recreational and occupational activities. They also serve to help highlight effects of sex, age and size differences.

Maximal oxygen uptake and economy are commonly measured in studies in which the aerobic performances of different individuals or groups of athletes are compared. Defining the current training status of an elite runner, or comparing the physiological profiles of different standards of athlete are examples. Efficiency measures, other than average values for estimating oxygen uptake from external work done, are less often quoted in the literature due to problems of measurement which are often exacerbated by the use and abuse of different definitions (Cavanagh and Kram, 1985).

9.2 DIRECT DETERMINATION OF MAXIMAL OXYGEN UPTAKE

9.2.1 RELEVANCE

There is an upper limit to the oxygen that is consumed during exercise requiring maximal effort. This upper limit is defined as maximal oxygen uptake ($\dot{V}O_{2\,max}$), which is the maximum rate at which an individual can take up and utilize oxygen while breathing air at sea level (Åstrand and Rodahl, 1986). It has traditionally been used as the 'gold standard' criterion of cardiorespiratory fitness, as it is considered to be the single physiological variable which best defines the functional capacity of the cardiovascular and respiratory systems. However, it is more accurate to consider it as an indicator of both potential for endurance performance and, to a lesser extent, training status.

At any given time the $\dot{V}O_{2\,max}$ of an individual is fixed and specific for a given task, e.g. running, cycling, rowing and so on. The $\dot{V}O_{2\,max}$ can be increased with training or decreased with a period of enforced inactivity, such as bed rest. Indeed, changes of up to 100% in $\dot{V}O_{2\,max}$ have been reported after a period of training following prolonged bed rest (Saltin *et al.*, 1968). Pollock (1973) published a review in which the effect of endurance training is reported to have produced changes in $\dot{V}O_{2\,max}$ which ranged from 0 to 93%. The initial level of fitness (a reflection of an individual combination of endowment and habitual activity), intensity, frequency and duration of training are factors which will influence the effects of endurance training on $\dot{V}O_{2\,max}$. The age and sex of the individual are relevant considerations also. It is, therefore, not surprising that training studies carried out on habitually

Kinanthropometry and Exercise Physiology Laboratory Manual: Tests, procedures and data Edited by Roger Eston and Thomas Reilly. Published in 1996 by E & FN Spon. ISBN 0 419 17880 5

active endurance athletes have produced non-significant changes in $\dot{V}O_{2\,max}$, of the order of only 2–3%, whereas endurance performance has dramatically increased. Training programmes carried out on previously sedentary subjects can produce significant changes in $\dot{V}O_{2\,max}$ values, usually of the order of 20–30%.

Measurements of $\dot{V}O_{2\,max}$ indicate aerobic potential and to a lesser extent, training status. The sensitivity of $\dot{V}O_{2\,max}$ to changes in training or the establishment of regular habitual physical activity is strongly related to the degree of development in the $\dot{V}O_{2\,max}$ that may be ultimately realized, which reflects a combination of endowment and habitual physical activity. Although it is generally agreed that genetic factors play an important role in defining the potential for development of physiological variables such as $\dot{V}O_{2\,max}$, the extent to which $\dot{V}O_{2\,max}$ is determined by endowment has been adjusted downwards in more recent studies from 90% to something of the order of 40–70% (Bouchard and Malina, 1983).

The maximal oxygen uptake ($\dot{V}O_{2\,max}$) is also important as a baseline measure to be used with other measures of endurance performance, such as fractional utilization (%$\dot{V}O_{2\,max}$ that can be sustained for prolonged periods), onset of blood lactate accumulation (OBLA) and running economy. A high $\dot{V}O_{2\,max}$ may be considered to be a prerequisite for elite performance in endurance sport, but does not guarantee achievement at the highest level of sport. Technique, state of training and psychological factors also have positive and negative modifying effects on performance. It is for these reasons that measures of $\dot{V}O_{2\,max}$ do not allow an accurate prediction of an individual's performance potential in aerobic power events. Shephard (1984) reviewed 37 studies reporting correlation coefficients between all-out running performance and measured $\dot{V}O_{2\,max}$ and found coefficients ranging from 0.04 to 0.90.

(a) Age, sex and $\dot{V}O_{2\,max}$

A combination of cross-sectional and longitudinal studies provides a reasonably clear picture of the development of $\dot{V}O_{2\,max}$ during childhood and adolescence and its decline during adulthood (Bar-Or, 1983; Krahenbuhl *et al.*, 1985; Åstrand and Rodahl, 1986; Allied Dunbar National Fitness Survey, 1992). Absolute $\dot{V}O_{2\,max}$ values increase steadily prior to puberty with the growth of the pulmonary, cardiovascular and musculoskeletal systems. At the onset of puberty the curves relating age and $\dot{V}O_{2\,max}$ values for males and females begin to diverge and continue to do so during adolescence. After the acceleration of $\dot{V}O_{2\,max}$ values in males at puberty which reflects the increased muscle mass, and given that $\dot{V}O_{2\,max}$ in females remains virtually unchanged after early teens, females' $\dot{V}O_{2\,max}$ values are on average 65–75% of those of males.

In both sexes there is a peak in $\dot{V}O_{2\,max}$ values at 18–20 years of age followed by a gradual decline with increasing age. The results of the Allied Dunbar National Fitness Survey (1992), where $\dot{V}O_{2\,max}$ was estimated for over 1700 men and women, produced average values for the age category 16–24 years which were of the order of 55 ml kg^{-1} min^{-1} and 40 ml kg^{-1} min^{-1} for men and women, respectively. Then $\dot{V}O_{2\,max}$ declined steadily with increasing age, resulting in average values for the age category 65–74 years which were of the order of 30 ml kg^{-1} min^{-1} and 25 ml kg^{-1} min^{-1} for men and women, respectively. In contrast, $\dot{V}O_{2\,max}$ values for elite endurance athletes may exceed 80 ml kg^{-1} min^{-1}. Data from a variety of population studies indicate that at the age of 65 the average $\dot{V}O_{2\,max}$ value is approximately 70% of that of a 25 year old of the same sex.

(b) Body size and $\dot{V}O_{2\,max}$

Comparisons of physiological measurements between subjects of different size are commonplace, especially in the case of children versus adults. These comparisons are made in both cross-sectional and longitudinal studies, which in the latter case include comparisons of the same subjects during the growing years.

In the case of $\dot{V}O_{2\,max}$ there is a strong positive relationship between body size and absolute $\dot{V}O_{2\,max}$ ($l\,min^{-1}$). Generally speaking, the larger the subject the larger the $\dot{V}O_{2\,max}$ in absolute terms ($l\,min^{-1}$). In an attempt to overcome the effects of differences in body mass when comparing $\dot{V}O_{2\,max}$ values, the latter are often divided by body mass prior to comparison. The $\dot{V}O_{2\,max}$ ($ml\,kg^{-1}\,min^{-1}$) is therefore considered to be a weight-adjusted expression of $\dot{V}O_{2\,max}$ where the effects of differences in body mass have been factored out.

However, $\dot{V}O_{2\,max}$ expressed in $ml\,kg^{-1}\,min^{-1}$ correlates negatively with body mass. Far from eliminating the effect of body mass, this form of expression converts a positive relationship between $\dot{V}O_{2\,max}$ ($l\,min^{-1}$) and body mass into a negative one between $\dot{V}O_{2\,max}$ ($ml\,kg^{-1}\,min^{-1}$) and body mass. Therefore, this common form of weight correction does not eliminate the effects of body mass or weight at all.

Nevertheless, $\dot{V}O_{2\,max}$ has probably continued to be related to body mass in the form $ml\,kg^{-1}\,min^{-1}$ because body mass is easily obtained. It also correlates well with most measures of cardiorespiratory function. There is also a strong positive relationship with performance in weight-bearing activities such as running, so expressing the power output per kilogram of body mass would seem appropriate where the body mass has to be carried in the activity.

If dividing $\dot{V}O_{2\,max}$ by body mass does not factor out the effects of body mass on ($\dot{V}O_{2\,max}\,l\,min^{-1}$), then the question arises as to what form of expression of $\dot{V}O_{2\,max}$ is independent of body mass and can therefore allow meaningful comparisons among individuals differing in body size?

Theoretically, since maximal force in muscle is dependent on cross-sectional area, muscle force will be proportional to length^2 (l^2), the squared function representing an area. Similarly, work or energy is based on force $\times$ distance, therefore work done or energy expended is proportional to $F \times L$ or L^3 (on a cubic function). As $\dot{V}O_{2\,max}$ is an expression of energy expenditure per unit of time or power output, which is $(F \times L)/t$, and time is proportional to L then $\dot{V}O_{2\,max}$ ($l\,min^{-1}$) is proportional to $L^3\,L^{-1}$ or L^2.

Since mass (M) is proportional to volume which is proportional to L^3 then $\dot{V}O_{2\,max}$ ($l\,min^{-1}$) should be proportional to $M^{2/3}$ (since M is proportional to L^3, $\dot{V}O_{2\,max}$ is proportional to L^2 and $M^{2/3} = L^2$). A more detailed discussion of the scaling effects of body size and dimensional analysis can be found in Schmidt-Nielson (1984), McMahon (1984) and Åstrand and Rodahl (1986).

The theoretical expectation that $\dot{V}O_{2\,max}$ ($l\,min^{-1}$) should be proportional to L^2 or $M^{2/3}$ is true for well-trained adult athletes (Åstrand and Rodahl, 1986) and recreationally active adult males and females (Nevill *et al.*, 1992). However, in children longitudinal studies of $\dot{V}O_{2\,max}$ ($l\,min^{-1}$) have identified exponents of L which range from 1.51 to 3.21 (or M from 0.503 to 1.07) (Bar-Or, 1983).

In the case of active adults and athletes, expressing $\dot{V}O_{2\,max}$ in $ml\,kg^{-2/3}\,min^{-1}$ would appear to eliminate the confounding effects of body mass on $\dot{V}O_{2\,max}$ ($l\,min^{-1}$). It, therefore, provides a more meaningful index than the more conventional expression of $\dot{V}O_{2\,max}$ in $ml\,kg^{-1}\,min^{-1}$, which disadvantages heavier individuals.

Besides demonstrating the superiority of the expression of $\dot{V}O_{2\,max}$ in $ml\,kg^{-2/3}\,min^{-1}$, in adjusting for differences in body mass, Nevill *et al.* (1992) also showed that the more conventional expression of $\dot{V}O_{2\,max}$ in $ml\,kg^{-1}\,min^{-1}$ held true in terms of predicting ability to run 5 km expressed as a function of average running speed. This supports the use of the conventional expression of $\dot{V}O_{2\,max}$ in $ml\,kg^{-1}\,min^{-1}$ for weight-bearing activities which are highly dependent on body size. It is therefore important to be clear on the aim of comparing different forms of expression, since performance and physiological function do not always use the same criteria.

9.2.2 PROTOCOLS

There is a large number of protocols reported in the literature for the direct determination of $\dot{V}O_{2\,max}$. These range from short single-load experiments performed at so-called 'supra-maximal' workloads lasting no longer than 6 minutes, to relatively long discontinuous protocols where the subject exercises for anything from 3 to 6 minutes at each workload and then rests for about 3 minutes between each workload (Åstrand and Rodahl, 1986).

One of the general recommendations for the assessment of $\dot{V}O_{2\,max}$ is that subjects should perform rhythmic exercise which requires a large muscle mass. This ensures that the cardiorespiratory system is taxed and the test is not limited by local muscular endurance of only a small percentage of total muscle mass. The muscle mass engaged explains why simulated cross-country skiing produces the highest $\dot{V}O_{2\,max}$ values, followed by graded treadmill running, flat treadmill running and cycle ergometry. The specificity of the activity of the subject undergoing assessment should take precedence if the aim is to produce meaningful values for interpretation of aerobic potential or current training status. For example, canoeists should be tested on a canoe ergometer, but will generally produce lower $\dot{V}O_{2\,max}$ values than if they were running on a treadmill. It has been known, in exceptional cases, for a subject only used to strenuous exercise in canoeing to produce a higher $\dot{V}O_{2\,max}$ value than when running on a treadmill.

Given the plethora of protocols for the direct determination of $\dot{V}O_{2\,max}$, it is worthwhile to consider attempts at standardization through guidelines such as those published by the British Association of Sports Sciences (1992) in its 'Position Statement on the Physiological Assessment of the Elite Competitor'. These guidelines give tables for establishing the appropriate exercise intensities for the direct determination of $\dot{V}O_{2\,max}$ using leg and arm cycling and graded treadmill running (Tables 9.1 and 9.2). There is also a list of criteria for consideration when establishing maximal oxygen uptake in adult subjects.

Table 9.1 Guidelines for establishing exercise intensity for the determination of maximum oxygen uptake during leg or arm cycling

	Warm up (W)	*Initial work rate (W)*	*Work rate increment (W)*
Leg cycling (pedal frequency 60 min^{-1})			
Male	120	180–240	30
Female	60	150–200	30
Arm cycling (pedal frequency 60 min^{-1})	60	90	30
Elite cyclists (pedal frequency 90 min^{-1})			
Male	150	200–250	35
Female	100	150	35

Table 9.2 Guidelines for establishing exercise intensity for the determination of maximum oxygen uptake during treadmill running

	Warm up speed (ms^{-1})	*Test speed (ms^{-1})*	*Initial grade %*	*Grade increment*
Endurance athletes				
Male	3.13	4.47	0	2.5
Female	2.68	4.02	0	2.5
Games players				
Male	3.13	3.58	0	2.5
Female	2.68	3.13	0	2.5

(British Association of Sports Sciences, Physiology Section, Position statement on the physiological assessment of the elite athlete, 1992).

1. A plateau in the oxygen uptake–exercise intensity relationship. This has been defined as an increase in oxygen uptake of less than 2 ml kg^{-1} min^{-1} or 5% with an increase in exercise intensity. If this plateau is not achieved, then the term peak $\dot{V}O_2$ is preferred.

2. A final respiratory exchange ratio of 1.15 or above.
3. A final heart rate of within 10 beats min^{-1} of the predicted age-related maximum. (Maximum heart rate can be estimated from the formula: Maximal Heart Rate = 220 – age (years) if the maximum value is unknown.)
4. A post-exercise (4–5 min) blood lactate concentration of 8 mmol l^{-1} or more.

(a) Example treadmill protocol (continuous protocol)

The protocol in Table 9.2 is based on that of Taylor *et al.* (1955) and is suitable for the habitually active and sports participants. The recommended exercise intensities should produce volitional exhaustion in 9–15 min of continuous exercise, following a 5 min warm up.

(b) Example cycle ergometer protocol (discontinuous protocol).

A detailed description of such a protocol and associated procedures is given in section 9.6.

9.2.3 RESULTS

Table 9.3 shows a completed proforma for the discontinuous cycle ergometer protocol. It can be used for most protocols involving expired air collection and analysis using the Douglas bag technique, but is easily adapted for variations in data collection or experimental protocols. Figure 9.1 shows the results from a $\dot{V}O_{2\,max}$ test performed on the treadmill by a trained male runner aged 21. Data for the treadmill test were collected using an Oxycon 5 automated gas analysis system (Mjnhardt, Netherlands). The test was continuous until volitional exhaustion, after which the subject attempted two further workloads to demonstrate a plateau in oxygen uptake.

9.3 PREDICTION OF MAXIMAL OXYGEN UPTAKE

Although a direct determination of maximal oxygen uptake is feasible with well-conditioned and highly motivated individuals, provided there is access to appropriate laboratory facilities, it is often only possible to con-

Table 9.3 Douglas bag data collection during an intermittent cycle ergometer protocol

Subject: J. Bloggs	*Date:* 30-9-1993	*Time:* 2.00	*Mass (kg):* 81
Age: 21	*DoB:* 7.12.71	P_B *(mmHg):* 753.5	*Ht (cms):* 180
Temp. (°C): 21	*Humidity* (%) 65	*Protocol: Discontinuous*	*Ergometer:* Cycle (3 *min work, 3 min rest)*

Bag No.	*1*	*2*	*3*	*4*	*5*
Work rate (W)	200	250	300	350	400
Exercise time (min)	2–3	5–6	8–9	11–12	14–15
Collection time (s)	60	60	60	60	60
Temperature expired air (°C)	24.0	24.0	23.8	24.0	24.0
Volume (l) (ATPS)	68.60	93.75	125.5	162.1	170.3
Volume CO_2 sample (l)					
Volume O_2 sample (l)	2.0	2.0	2.0	2.0	2.0
V_E (L) ATPS	70.60	95.75	127.5	164.1	172.3
V_E STPD (l min^{-1})	62.44	84.68	113.1	145.1	152.4
F_EO_2 (%)	16.13	17.03	17.37	17.71	17.82
F_ECO_2 (%)	4.30	3.46	3.34	3.25	3.22
VO_2 (l min^{-1})	3.09	3.41	4.10	4.69	4.73
VCO_2 (l min^{-1})	2.66	2.91	3.74	4.69	4.86
RER	0.863	0.852	0.913	1.00	1.03
Borg RPE	13	15	16	19	20
Heart rate (beats min^{-1})	154	168	183	197	198

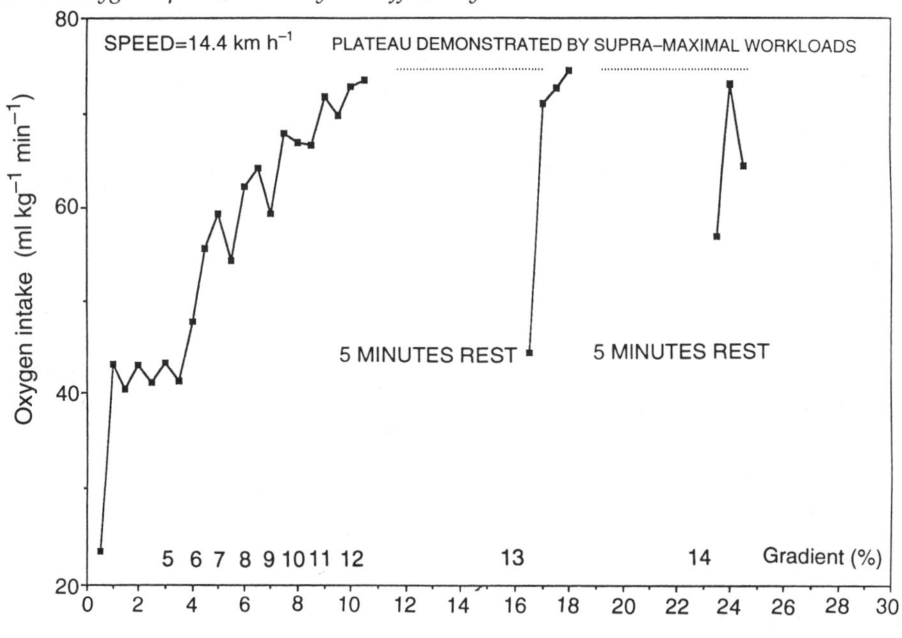

Figure 9.1 Results of a $\dot{V}O_{2\,max}$ test performed by a 21-year-old male runner on a motorized treadmill.

duct either a submaximal exercise test, or a maximum performance test in the field. The results from many such tests are then used to estimate maximal oxygen uptake (Åstrand and Rhyming, 1954; Siconolfi *et al.*, 1982; Åstrand and Rodahl, 1986).

Probably the most widely used procedure for predicting maximal oxygen uptake is the Åstrand–Rhyming (1954) nomogram. Use of the nomogram in submaximal field tests is based on measuring the heart rate response to a quantifiable form of external work for which the mechanical efficiency is known. Thus, the oxygen uptake elicited by the external work can be estimated (i.e. cycle ergometry, treadmill walking and running, stepping). The nomogram consists of scales for work rate in cycle ergometry, and steps of 33 cm and 40 cm in height, which are located alongside a scale for oxygen uptake. Therefore, if the appropriate step height or cycle ergometry is used, then a prediction of maximal oxygen uptake can be obtained from the measured heart rate response. The value can then be age-adjusted based on empirically derived age-correction factors. Shephard (1970) produced an algorithm for a computer solution of the Åstrand–Rhyming nomogram which is easily programmed in most languages.

Åstrand and Rodahl (1986) described a simple submaximal cycle ergometer test which when used in conjunction with the nomogram will provide an estimate of maximal oxygen uptake. For women a work rate of 75–100 W has been suggested, and for men 100–150 W. If the heart rate exceeds 130 beats min^{-1} the test is stopped after 6 min. If the heart rate is lower than 130 beats min^{-1} after a couple of minutes of exercise, the work rate should be increased by 50 W. The steady-state heart rate response, taken as the mean of the value at 5 and 6 min, together with the work rate can then be used to predict the maximal oxygen uptake. There is error associated with the prediction of $\dot{V}O_{2\,max}$ using the Åstrand–Rhyming nomogram and associated submaximal test procedures. Some of the reasons for this are: assumptions of linearity in the heart rate oxygen uptake relationship for all subjects, decline and variation in maximum heart rate with increasing age and variations in mechanical efficiency. In addition, there are factors which affect the heart rate response to a given exercise intensity, but not maximal oxygen uptake, such as anxiety, dehydration, prolonged heavy exercise, exercise with a small muscle mass and exercise after consumption of alcohol.

The standard error for predicting maximal oxygen uptake from the studies used to validate the nomogram is 10% in relatively well-trained individuals of the same age as the original sample, but up to 15% in moderately trained individuals of different ages when the age correction factors are used. Values for untrained subjects are often underestimated, whereas elite athletes are often overestimated (Åstrand and Rodahl, 1986). This limitation in accuracy for estimation of maximal oxygen uptake is an important consideration, especially when dealing with repeated measures of subjects participating in a training study. The authors concluded that, 'this drawback (in accuracy) holds true for any submaximal cardiopulmonary test'.

Another common form of submaximal test using a step or a cycle ergometer is to exercise the subject at four different work intensities and measure the heart rate and oxygen uptake at each work rate (Wyndham *et al.*, 1966; Harrison *et al.*, 1980). Using linear regression the heart rate oxygen uptake relationship is extrapolated to a predicted maximum heart rate value (e.g. maximum heart rate = 220 – age in years) to obtain an estimate of maximal oxygen uptake.

The Physical Work Capacity (PWC) test is also a popular form of submaximal exercise test, and was adopted as the cycle ergometer test for use with children in the Eurofit initiative (Council of Europe, 1988). The relationship between heart rate and work rate is established using three or four submaximal work rates and the PWC is calculated by extrapolation to a specific heart rate, which is most commonly 170 beats min^{-1}; hence the score is called a PWC_{170}. However, if the oxygen uptake can be measured directly, then it is preferable to do so as the PWC procedure takes no account of individual variations in mechanical efficiency.

There is also a large number of field tests which include an equation for the prediction of maximal oxygen uptake, such as a one mile walk test (Kline *et al.*, 1987), a 20 m multistage shuttle test (Leger and Lambert, 1982; Paliczka *et al.*, 1987; Boreham *et al.*, 1990), and Cooper's 12 minute walk/run test (Cooper, 1968). All these tests are maximal in that the subjects have to go as fast as possible in the walk and run tests, and for as long as possible in the multistage shuttle test. They are therefore dependent on subjects being well motivated and used to strenuous exercise. However, they are acceptable as indicators of current training status as they are all performance tests, irrespective of their accuracy in the prediction of maximal oxygen uptake. The reliability and validity of run–walk tests have been reviewed by Eston and Brodie (1985).

In conclusion, whatever form of submaximal test is adopted, whether it is based on either the work rate–heart rate relationship or the oxygen uptake–heart rate relationship, extreme caution should be used in the interpretation of predicted maximal oxygen uptake scores.

9.4 RUNNING ECONOMY

9.4.1 INTRODUCTION

Economy of energy expenditure is important in any endurance event which makes demands on aerobic energy supply. If a lower oxygen uptake can be achieved through the optimization of skill and technique for a given exercise intensity, be it cross-country skiing, kayaking or running, then, all other things being equal, performance can be maintained for a longer period of time at a given exercise intensity, or at a slightly increased exercise intensity for the same period of time. Although the measurement of economy of energy expenditure described here is that of running economy, similar principles, procedures and protocols also apply to other activities.

Running economy can be defined as the metabolic cost, measured as oxygen uptake per kilogram per minute for a given treadmill speed and slope. A lower oxygen uptake for a given running speed is therefore interpreted as a better running economy.

There is a strong correlation between $\dot{V}O_{2\,max}$ and distance running performance in studies based on a wide range of running capabilities (Cooper, 1968; Costill *et al.*, 1973). This relationship is not evident in a homogeneous sample of elite runners (Conley and Krahenbuhl, 1980). However, running economy is correlated significantly with distance running performance (Costill, 1972; Costill *et al.*, 1973; Conley and Krahenbuhl, 1980) and therefore may, in part, account for why $\dot{V}O_{2\,max}$ is not a good predictor.

9.4.2 METHODOLOGY

Running economy is measured by means of establishing the oxygen cost to running speed (or speed and gradient) relationship. Many of the studies in the literature have entailed comparisons of measures of running economy for a single running speed (e.g. equivalent to race pace and/or training pace). Nevertheless, there is value in measuring oxygen uptake over a range of running speeds, especially if comparing the performance of children and adults.

In order to obtain a 'true' measure of running economy at a range of running speeds the oxygen uptake must be measured under steady-state conditions. The subject should be exercising in the aerobic range (i.e. no significant contribution to metabolic energy from anaerobic sources). Åstrand and Rodahl (1986) defined a number of $\dot{V}O_{2\,max}$ protocols, but suggested that those based on work rates where a steady state of oxygen uptake is achieved have the advantage of simultaneously establishing relationships between submaximal oxygen cost and running speed, in the case of treadmill tests. Similarly, measures of running economy can be made at the same time as the establishment of blood lactate responses. These are used for the determination of the exercise intensity corresponding to the 'onset of blood lactate accumulation' (OBLA).

The $\dot{V}O_{2\,max}$ of the subject may be known. In this case it is common practice to select four running speeds which are predicted to elicit 60%, 70%, 80% and 90% of $\dot{V}O_{2\,max}$.

(a) Protocol

A protocol for measurement of running economy is described in section 9.7. This protocol and associated procedures can easily be adapted for other forms of ergometry.

9.4.3 RESULTS

Figure 9.2 shows the relationships between oxygen cost and running speed for three groups of adult male runners: 10 elite, 10 club and 10 recreational runners. There was a significant linear increase (ANOVA; $P < 0.001$) in the oxygen cost of running over the range of speeds analysed (2.67–4.00 m s^{-1}) in all three groups. Linear regression equations for the three groups are:

Elite $\dot{V}O_2(\text{ml kg}^{-1}\text{min}^{-1}) = 8.07 \times \text{SPEED}(\text{m s}^{-1}) + 8.87$ ($r = 0.99$; $r^2 = 0.98$ (variance accounted for))

Club $\dot{V}O_2(\text{ml kg}^{-1}\text{min}^{-1}) = 8.27 \times \text{SPEED}(\text{m s}^{-1}) + 13.27$ ($r = 0.99$; $r^2 = 0.98$ (variance accounted for))

Rec $\dot{V}O_2(\text{ml kg}^{-1}\text{min}^{-1}) = 7.80 \times \text{SPEED}(\text{m s}^{-1}) + 14.35$ ($r = 0.99$; $r^2 = 0.98$ (variance accounted for))

There was a significant difference in the oxygen cost of running in the three groups (ANOVA; $P < 0.001$). The elite group required significantly lower (Scheffé; $P < 0.001$) oxygen

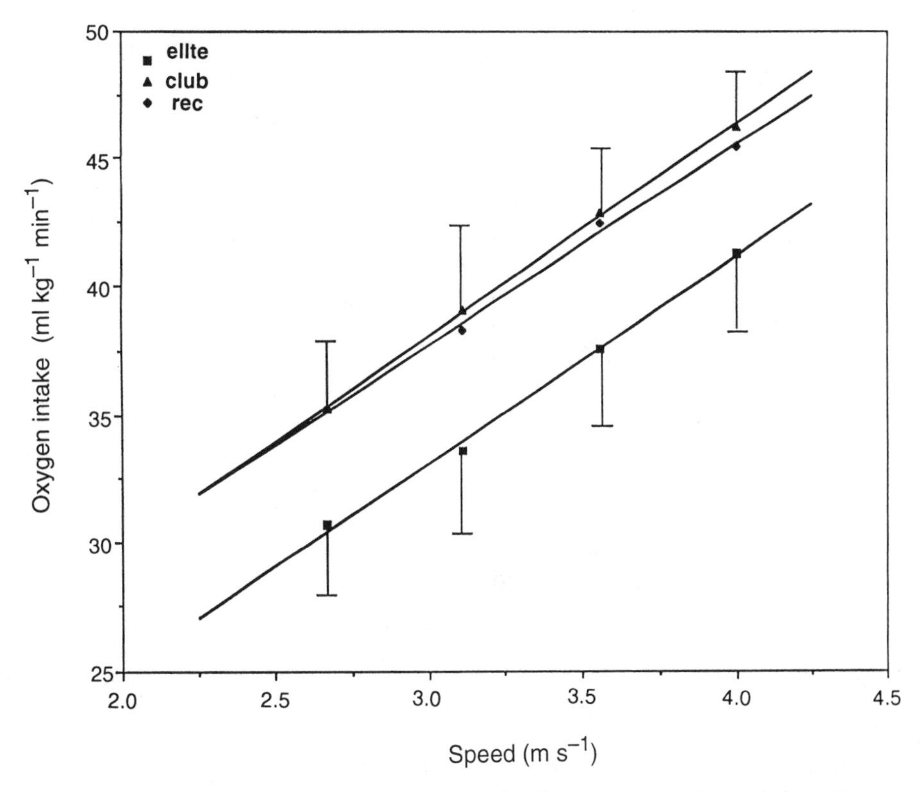

Figure 9.2 Oxygen cost to running speed relationship for three groups of ten adult male runners: elite, club and recreational.

uptakes than either the club or recreational runners (mean difference of 4.7 ml kg^{-1} min^{-1}; 11.5%). The recreational runners appeared to have slightly better running economy at the higher running speeds than the club runners (Figure 9.2). Blood lactate values revealed that not all the recreational runners were meeting the energy requirements by aerobic sources alone, which would account for the less steep slope of their regression line. It is therefore important to ensure that comparisons of running economy are made on subjects who are exercising aerobically so that steady state oxygen uptake values reflect the energy requirements of the exercise.

Figure 9.3 shows the relationships between oxygen cost and running speed for two groups of male runners: adults aged 21.3 ± 2.3 years and children aged 11.9 ± 1.0 years (Cooke *et al.*, 1991). A significant linear increase (ANOVA, $P < 0.001$) is evident in the oxygen cost of running over the range of speeds studied (2.67, 3.11, 3.56 and 4.0 m s^{-1}) in both the children and adults. The children required a significantly greater (ANCOVA; $P < 0.001$) $\dot{V}O_2$, on average 7 ml kg^{-1} min^{-1} (18.5%), for any given running speed. The divergence of the two regression lines shows the significant difference (ANCOVA; $P < 0.05$) in the $\dot{V}O_2$ response of the children and the adults over the range of speeds. Slopes of 10.87 for the children and 9.05 for the adults equate to a difference of 5.8 ml kg^{-1} min^{-1} at 2.67 m s^{-1} and 8.55 ml kg^{-1} min^{-1} at 4.0 m s^{-1}.

As the correlation between oxygen uptake and body mass is non-significant when oxygen uptake is expressed in ml kg$^{-0.75}$ min^{-1} (Kleiber, 1975), the ANCOVA was

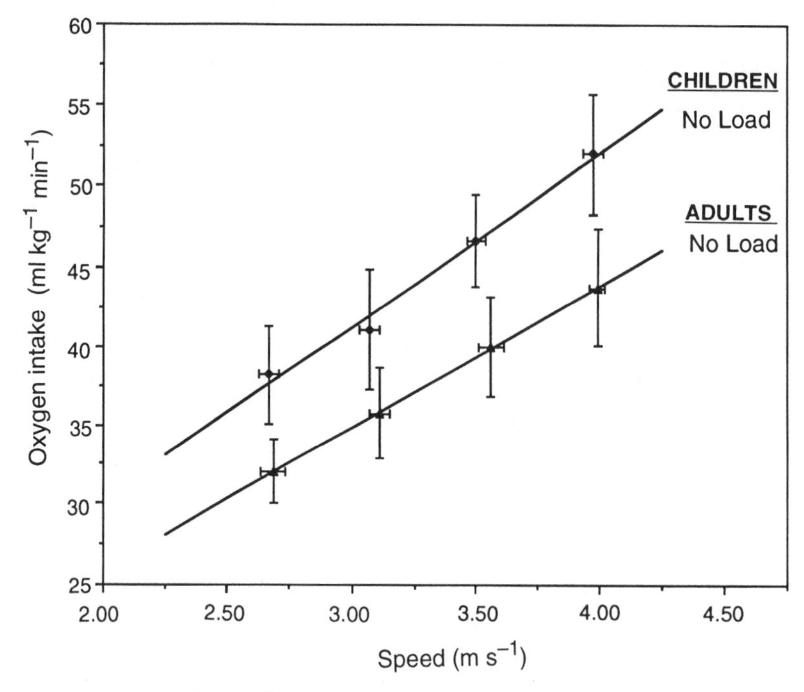

Figure 9.3 Oxygen cost (ml kg^{-1} min^{-1}) to running speed relationship for two groups of well trained male runners: 8 boys and 8 men (Cooke *et al.*, 1991).

repeated with $\dot{V}O_2$ expressed in ml kg$^{-0.75}$ min^{-1} to establish whether the group differences in the oxygen cost of unloaded running could be accounted for by differences in body mass. Figure 9.4 shows that there was no significant difference between the groups, as the regression lines became similar. For an explanation of the analysis of covariance procedure and its application, see Chapter 15 in this text.

9.4.4 DISCUSSION

(a) Adult running economy values

The running economy results for the three groups of adult male runners reflect that elite runners have trained themselves in the technique of running, optimizing their running style to produce significantly lower oxygen uptake values for any given running speed. This finding is in agreement with other cross-sectional studies which have reported that highly trained distance runners have better running economy than runners of club and recreational standard (Costill and Fox, 1969; Costill, 1972; Pollock, 1973; Bransford and Howley, 1977; Conley and Krahenbuhl, 1980). Longitudinal studies have also shown that running economy can improve with training (Conley *et al.*, 1981).

One criticism of comparing weight-corrected oxygen uptake values between individuals or groups is that oxygen uptake per kilogram body mass is not itself independent of body mass. Since the elite subjects had a lower mean body mass, the differences between the elite, club and recreational runners would be increased only slightly if oxygen uptake was expressed in ml kg$^{-0.75}$ min^{-1}.

(b) Child and adult running economy values

The mass-specific equations relating oxygen uptake to running speed for both children and adults shown in Figure 9.3 are similar to

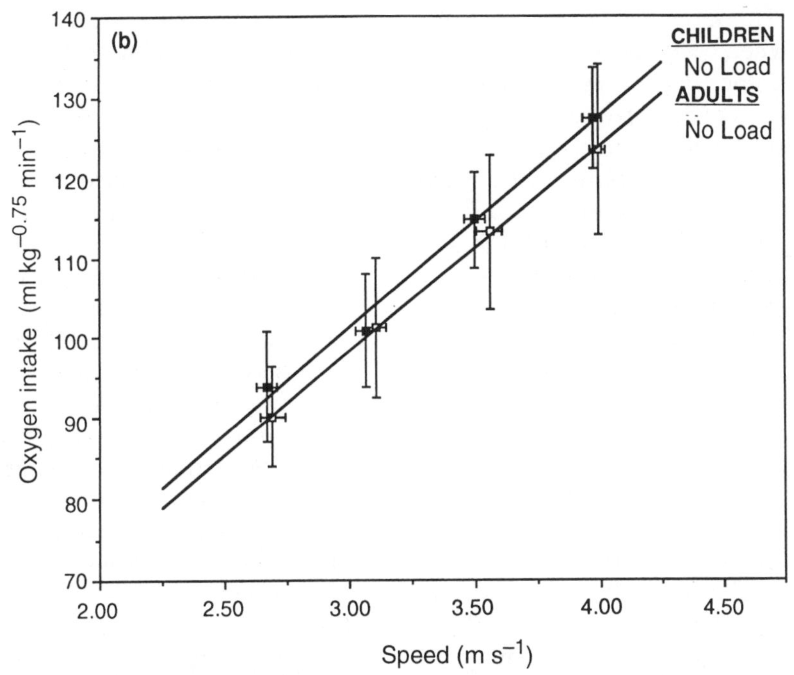

Figure 9.4 Oxygen cost (ml kg$^{-0.75}$ min^{-1}) to running speed relationships for two groups of well trained male runners: 8 boys and 8 men (Cooke *et al.*, 1991).

others reported in the literature (Åstrand, 1952; Margaria *et al.*, 1963; Davies, 1980). Some variation in equations due to population bias, treadmill type, and measurement techniques is to be expected. However, the mean difference between children and adults of 8 ml kg^{-1} min^{-1} in oxygen uptake is similar to that of other studies.

Smaller animals are metabolically more active than larger ones. This difference is also apparent in a comparison of mass-specific resting metabolic rates of children and adults. If the estimated resting metabolic rate is subtracted from the gross oxygen cost of running shown in Figure 9.3 then the difference between the regression lines decreases by 1.8 ml kg^{-1} min^{-1} (25%). Resting metabolic rate was estimated from the data of Altman and Dittmer (1968) using the formula of DuBois and DuBois (1916) for estimating body surface area.

The correlation between metabolic rate per unit of body size and body mass is non-significant when metabolic rate is divided by body mass to the power of 0.75 (Kleiber, 1975). The data for boys and men shown in Figure 9.4 are consistent with this established comparative measure of metabolic body size.

The data also agree closely with a power function developed to predict the mass-specific oxygen cost of running from body mass and running speed in over 50 animal species (Taylor *et al.*, 1982). The power function was indicated by:

$$\frac{\dot{V}O_2}{M} = 0.533 \times M^{-0.316} \times V + 0.300 \times M^{-0.303}$$

where $\frac{\dot{V}O_2}{M}$ = oxygen cost (ml kg^{-1} s^{-1})

V = velocity (m s^{-1})

M = body mass (kg)

The analogy between animals of different mass (from the flying squirrel with a mass of 0.063 kg to the Zebu cattle with a mass of 254 kg) would appear to suggest that differences in the relationship between oxygen cost and running speed in children and adults might be expected. However, Eston *et al.* (1993) showed that when body mass was used as a covariate (i.e. the dependent variable of oxygen uptake was linearly adjusted such that comparisons were made as if all subjects had the same body mass) differences between the oxygen uptake of boys and men running at the same speeds were non-significant. The use of scaling techniques to partition out the effects of size is currently an area of renewed interest and investigation.

Several factors have been suggested as possibly contributing to the differences between running economy in children and adults. Rowland (1990) described six such factors.

1. Ratio of surface area to mass: as discussed previously, differences in BMR may account for something of the order of 25% of the greater oxygen cost of running in children compared with adults. This difference in BMR is based on the surface area law as described in Chapter 8.
2. Stride frequency: the higher oxygen uptake for a given running speed in children may be partly explained by the necessarily higher stride frequency, resulting in the more frequent braking and acceleration of the centre of mass of the body, and the increased metabolic cost of producing more muscle contractions (Unnithan and Eston, 1990).
3. Immature running mechanics: the running styles of children are different from those of adults, with changes occurring through the growing years to adulthood (Wickstrom, 1983). However, the extent to which variations in running style with age might explain the differences between adults and children in the realtionship between oxygen uptake and running speed are as yet unknown.
4. Speed–mass mismatch: the speed at which a muscle contracts is inversely related to the force generated. Thus, as muscles contract more quickly they produce less force (Hill, 1939). Davies (1980) suggested that an imbalance of these two factors might help to explain the differences between children and adults in running economy. This suggestion was based on observations that when children were loaded with a weight jacket their oxygen uptake per kilogram total mass decreased, and approached adult values. However, similar experiments have revealed different results, suggesting that children and adults may be equally efficient at running with different forms of loading (Thorstensson, 1986; Cooke *et al.*, 1991).
5. Differences in anaerobic energy: it is well known that children are unable to produce anaerobic energy as effectively as adults. It is therefore important that subjects are exercising aerobically to prevent any inflation of child–adult differences in running economy values due to anaerobic energy contributions in the adult subjects.
6. Less efficient ventilation: children need to ventilate more than adults for each litre of oxygen consumed (i.e. $\dot{V}_E/\dot{V}O_2$, the ventilatory equivalent for oxygen is greater in children). These differences in ventilation patterns in children and adults may contribute to the differences in economy, since during maximal exercise the oxygen cost of ventilation may reach 14–19% of total oxygen uptake.

9.5 EFFICIENCY

9.5.1 INTRODUCTION

Efficiency is defined as:

$$\%\ \text{Efficiency} = \frac{\text{Output}}{\text{Input}} \times 100$$

In order to produce an efficiency ratio, both the numerator and the denominator have to be measured. With regard to activities such as walking, running and load carriage, there are several definitions of efficiency which are based on different forms of numerator and denominator in the efficiency equation (Whipp and Wasserman, 1969; Gaesser and Brooks, 1975). However, the numerator is always based on some measure of work done (either internal, external or both) and the denominator is based on some measure of metabolic rate (oxygen uptake).

These efficiency ratios are defined as:

Gross efficiency

$$\%\text{Efficiency} = \frac{\text{Work accomplished} \times 100}{\text{Energy expended}}$$

$$= \frac{W \times 100}{E}$$

Net efficiency

$$\%\text{Efficiency} = \frac{\text{Work accomplished} \times 100}{\text{Energy expended above that at rest}}$$

$$= \frac{W \times 100}{E - e}$$

Apparent or work efficiency

$$\%\text{Efficiency} = \frac{\text{Work accomplished} \times 100}{\text{Energy expened above unloaded}}$$

$$= \frac{W \times 100}{EL - EU}$$

Delta efficiency

$$\%\text{Efficiency} = \frac{\text{Delta work accomplished}}{\text{Delta energy expended}}$$

$$= \frac{DW \times 100}{DE}$$

where: W = caloric equivalent of mechanical work done
E = gross caloric output
e = resting caloric output
EL = caloric output loaded condition
EU = caloric output unloaded condition
DW = caloric equivalent of increment in work performed above previous work rate
DE = increement in caloric output above that at previous work rate

These definitions of efficiency are not a complete set and have received criticism by several authors (e.g. Stainsby *et al.*, 1980; Cavanagh and Kram, 1985).

Muscle efficiency is the efficiency of the conversion of chemical energy into mechanical energy at the cross-bridges and is based on phosphorylative coupling and contraction coupling, which are essentially linked in series. Phosphorylative coupling efficiency, which is defined as:

$$\frac{\text{Free energy conserved as ATP}}{\text{Free energy of oxidized food}} \times 100$$

has been estimated to be between 40 and 60% (Krebs and Kornberg, 1957). Contraction coupling, the conversion of energy stored as phosphates into tension in the muscle is of the order of 50% efficient, giving an overall theoretical maximum muscle efficiency of 30% (Whipp and Wasserman, 1969; Wilkie, 1974; Gaesser and Brooks, 1975). Given a maximum value of only 30% for muscle efficiency, it is of interest to examine why gross efficiency values quoted in the literature for activities such as running are often considerably higher, and can even exceed 100% using certain forms of calculation in the estimation of mechanical work done (Norman *et al.*, 1976).

Measures of whole-body efficiency or implied changes based on the different $\dot{V}O_2$ responses of children and adults to unloaded running (Davies, 1980) do not indicate the efficiency of muscle. The different definitions of efficiency quoted above are therefore important when trying to compare values from various sources.

The efficiency experiment which will be described in detail is that originally proposed by Lloyd and Zacks (1972). It was designed to measure the mechanical efficiency of running against a horizontal impeding force.

9.5.2 METHODOLOGY

The problem of accurately measuring external work in horizontal running was overcome, to a large extent, by Lloyd and Zacks (1972) who reported an experimental procedure in which they used a quantifiable external workload in the form of a horizontal impeding force, on adult subjects running on the treadmill. Loaded running efficiency (LRE) was then calculated for a given running speed from the linear relationship between metabolic rate (oxygen uptake) and external work rate. The value of LRE is therefore consistent with apparent or work efficiency as defined by Whipp and Wasserman (1969). This method was also used by Cooke *et al.* (1991) to test the hypothesis that there are differences in LRE between children and adults.

(a) Protocol

The protocol and procedures for the LRE experiment are described in detail in section 9.8.

9.5.3 RESULTS

The results presented here are from a comparison of LRE values between a group of well-trained boys and men (Cooke *et al.*, 1991). Figure 9.5 shows that no significant differences were found between the two groups in terms of LRE and the effects of speed. The mean LRE was 43.8% for the boys and 42.9% for the men.

9.5.4 DISCUSSION

The major finding from the horizontal impeding force experiment on boys and men is that there is no significant difference between the LRE values. The mean LRE values quoted in the results fall between the small number of values published in the literature (36%, Lloyd and Zacks, 1972; 39.1%, Zacks, 1973; 53.8%, Asmussen and Bonde-Peterson, 1974). These data support the hypothesis that there is no significant difference in efficiency

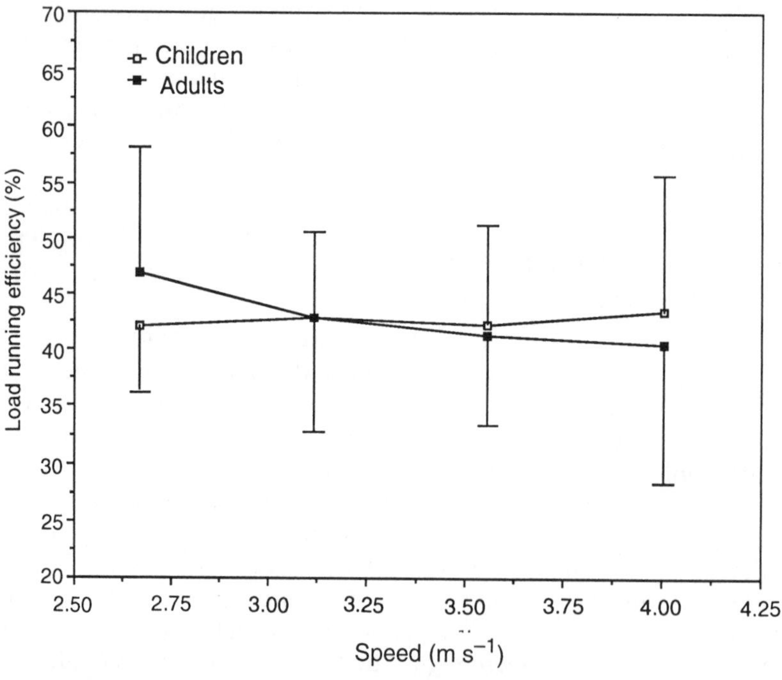

Figure 9.5 Loaded running efficiency values (means ± SD) for two groups of well trained male runners: 8 boys and 8 men (Cooke *et al.*, 1991).

between children and adults in the performance of external work.

Measures of mechanical efficiency for other forms of ergometry such as the cycle or the step are necessary for the estimation of energy expenditure from mechanical work done when $\dot{V}O_2$ is not measured. For example, such values form the basis of the Åstrand–Rhyming (1954) nomogram, when only the mechanical work done is known. Oxygen uptake is estimated from the work performed in stepping or cycling, which together with the heart rate response can be used to estimate $\dot{V}O_{2\,max}$. A description of how to measure mechanical efficiency in both stepping and cycle ergometry is given in section 9.9.

9.6 PRACTICAL 1: DIRECT DETERMINATION OF $\dot{V}O_{2\,max}$ USING A DISCONTINUOUS CYCLE ERGOMETER PROTOCOL

9.6.1 PROTOCOL

1. Warm-up: cycle for 3 min at 50 W for females or 100 W for males.
2. Rest: 2 min
3. Initial work rate: 50–150 W for females, 100–200 W for males, depending on type of subject, e.g. lighter less active subjects would be set lower work rates (heart rate response during warm up is a good guide to selection of appropriate work rate). Record heart rate every 30 s. Collect expired air for last 30 s of work rate.
4. Rest: 3 min (during which time team members can analyse expired air).
5. Increase workload by 50 W and repeat stages 3 and 4 of the protocol.
6. At higher workloads increments of 25 W may be used. If the subject cannot complete a 3 min workload then a gas collection can be made on a signal from the subject (minimum 30 s, preferably 1 min).
7. Recovery: at the end of the test the subject should continue to pedal gently at a low work rate of the order of 25–50 W.

The subject should be closely monitored at all times, both during the test and recovery, since the probability of some sort of cardiac episode occurring is higher at exercise intensities above 80% of age-related maximum heart rate and during the 20 min or so following the cessation of the test. The subject may need verbal encouragement to complete the latter stages of the test in order to attain a maximal oxygen consumption.

Although heart rate can be monitored effectively by telemetry, it is preferable to use chest electrodes linked to an oscilloscope and/or chart recorder. This enables the shape of the electrocardiogram (ECG) to be observed. In the event of a gross abnormality or arrhythmia occurring, the test can be stopped and the hard copy of the ECG examined by a qualified person. Clearly the more sophisticated the ECG equipment used, the more objective will be the ECG analysis. It is possible to see arrhythmias such as ventricular ectopics with a simple three lead system, which is available in most laboratories.

9.6.2 PROCEDURES

The procedures for the cycle ergometer protocol are as described, but they can be generalized in most cases to any direct determination of $\dot{V}O_{2\,max}$ using the Douglas bag technique.

1. The procedures and protocol should be explained to the subject, and should include a statement that he or she can stop the test at any time.

2. The subject should sign an informed consent form.
3. The name, age and sex of the subject should be recorded.
4. The height (m) and body mass (kg) of the subject should be measured.
5. The heart rate measuring device or ECG electrodes should be attached and a check made that a good signal is being recorded or displayed.
6. The handlebar and saddle positions should be adjusted to suit the size of the subject, especially as subjects can become uncomfortable during the latter stages of the test, resulting in the premature cessation of the test. If the saddle is too low, the subject may experience undue fatigue in the quadriceps muscles and possibly pain in the knee joint. If the saddle is too high, the subject will have to raise and lower his/her left and right hips repeatedly in order to maintain effective contact with the pedals. The recommended position is obtained by placing the middle of the foot on the pedal at the bottom of its travel. If the saddle height is correct the leg will be very slightly flexed. More sophisticated guidelines are available in the literature, but the simple procedure described here works well in most cases. Competitive cyclists will have their own measures for obtaining an optimal saddle height and handlebar position. They also prefer their own bicycles mounted on turbo-trainers. More sophisticated examples, such as the King Cycle™ have gained wider acceptance in exercise physiology laboratories.
7. The respiratory value and mouthpiece should be connected to allow room air to be inspired and then expired into the Douglas bag.
8. The nose clip should be placed on the subject's nose so that all the expired air passes into the Douglas bag.
9. The warm-up and the test proper should be completed according to the protocol described above.

With respect to the control of cycle ergometers, the following points should be considered.

1. All cycle ergometers should be calibrated regularly according to the manufacturers' instructions.
2. Recommended pedalling frequencies for mechanically braked cycle ergometers are traditionally of the order of 50–60 rev min^{-1}. Although a frequency of 60 rev min^{-1} is comfortable and efficient for low workloads, it is recommended that the pedal frequency be increased above workloads of the order of 200 W to 70–80 rev min^{-1}. This will decrease the force required per pedal revolution, thus decreasing the strength component of the pedalling action and the probability of cessation of the test due to quadriceps fatigue.
3. It is always important to inform the subject in advance of alterations in work rate in continuous protocols. This is especially important in the use of electronically braked cycle ergometers, which automatically alter the resistance at the pedals to accommodate changes in pedalling frequency, thus keeping the power output constant. A tired subject pedalling at 200 W with an unexpected increase of 50 W who is already pedalling at the lower end of the pedalling frequency range (approximately 50 rev min^{-1}) may well let the cadence drop still further with the increase in load. This will result in a further increase in resistance offered at the pedals. The result could then be that the subject terminates the test, so a warning of pending

increases in workload should always be given, together with encouragement to pedal faster to accommodate the increase in workload on an electronically braked cycle ergometer.

4. Mechanically braked cycle ergometers of the type used in most laboratories require the subject to pedal at a constant frequency in order to maintain a constant power output. To help maintain a constant pedalling frequency the subject may pedal in time to a metronome and/or use a digital display of pedalling frequency, which is now fitted to most new cycle ergometers. Another alternative is to mount small mechanical cams or opto-electric devices on the flywheel to count the number of revolutions during each workload. Use of these suggestions should help ensure that quantification of external power output is as objective as possible.

9.6.3 CALCULATIONS

Gas analysis, volume measurement, $\dot{V}O_2$, $\dot{V}CO_2$ and RER calculations should be performed in accordance with the procedures outlined in Chapter 8.

9.6.4 RESULTS

Table 9.3 shows a completed proforma for the discontinuous cycle ergometer test described above.

9.7 PRACTICAL 2: MEASUREMENT OF RUNNING ECONOMY

9.7.1 PROTOCOL

The protocol outlined here is recommended by The British Association of Sport and Exercise Sciences. Where the $\dot{V}O_{2\,max}$ of the subject is known, an appropriate generalized equation relating $\dot{V}O_2$ to running speed can be used to predict the running speeds that should elicit 50–90% of $\dot{V}O_{2\,max}$. For example, PE Students (British Association of Sport Sciences, 1992):

$$\text{Males } n = 58 \qquad Y = 11.6\,X + 0.72$$

$$\text{Females } n = 44 \qquad Y = 10.7\,X + 3.30$$

where: $Y = \dot{V}O_2$ (ml kg^{-1} min^{-1}) and X = running speed (m s^{-1})
or those cited in section 9.4.3. However, the selection of the running speeds should take into account the state of training of the subjects since only well-conditioned athletes can cope with running speeds that elicit 90% of $VO_{2\,max}$.

1. Warm-up: no warm up other than gentle jogging and stretching is required since the first workload represents a running speed approximately equivalent to 60% $\dot{V}O_{2\,max}$. Ideally, naïve subjects should be habituated to treadmill running on a previous occasion so $\dot{V}O_2$ values will be a true reflection of running economy.
2. Test: the protocol consists of 16 min of running on a level treadmill during which running speed is increased every 4 min. For children aged between 11 and 15 years a 3 min interval is recommended.

3. Expired air should be collected for the 4th, 8th 12th and 16th minute for adults, and for the 3rd, 6th, 9th and 12th minute for children.

9.7.2 DATA COLLECTION, GAS ANALYSIS AND CALCULATIONS

Follow the procedures outlined in Chapter 8 for the collection and analysis of expired air using the Douglas bag technique, and the calculation of oxygen uptake.

9.7.3 RESULTS

The results from the experiment should be plotted with oxygen uptake on the *y* axis and running speed on the *x* axis. The method of least squares can then be used to establish the extent to which the data conform to the expected linear relationship, with the production of a linear regression equation, correlation coefficient (r) and coefficient of determination (r^2 = variance accounted for) (see Chapter 14). Group data can then be compared using appropriate statistical techniques such as ANOVA or ANCOVA. Examples of group comparisons for both equations and graphs appear in sections 9.4.3 and 9.4.4.

9.8 PRACTICAL 3: MEASUREMENT OF LOADED RUNNING EFFICIENCY (LRE)

9.8.1 PROTOCOL

For each running speed the subject should run unloaded for 3 min. A horizontal impeding force is then exerted via weights attached to the subject by a cord running over a pulley (Figure 9.6). A total of three increasing loads can then be added to the system, one every 3 min (a total of 12 min continuous running including the 3 min unloaded), followed by 5 min rest. Weights should be individually selected such that the maximum external load applied to the system does not elicit a $\dot{V}O_2$ greater than 85% of $\dot{V}O_{2\,max}$ in well-trained subjects (this value would have to be adjusted down for less active individuals as it is important that the energy expenditure is derived from aerobic metabolism and therefore reflected in the measured $\dot{V}O_2$ values). Even increments in $\dot{V}O_2$ can be achieved by predicting the increase in $\dot{V}O_2$ per kilogram of mass added to the pulley, on the basis of a mean LRE value from the literature of approximately 40%. Running speeds and weight increments can then be individually tailored to the subject in terms of $\dot{V}O_{2\,max}$ and running economy. However, where subjects represent a homogeneous sample it is better in terms of experimental design to have all subjects run at the same speeds with the same increments. Typical values for weights to be added to the pulley would be 1, 2 and 3 kg for adults and 0.5, 1 and 1.5 kg for children.

9.8.2 PROCEDURES

Collection and analysis of expired air can be performed either according to the procedures outlined for the Douglas bag technique in Chapter 8, or using an automated gas analysis system. The data presented and discussed on p. 210 were collected using an Oxycon 4 system (Mijnhardt, Netherlands). A full description of the experimental procedures can be found in Cooke *et al.* (1991).

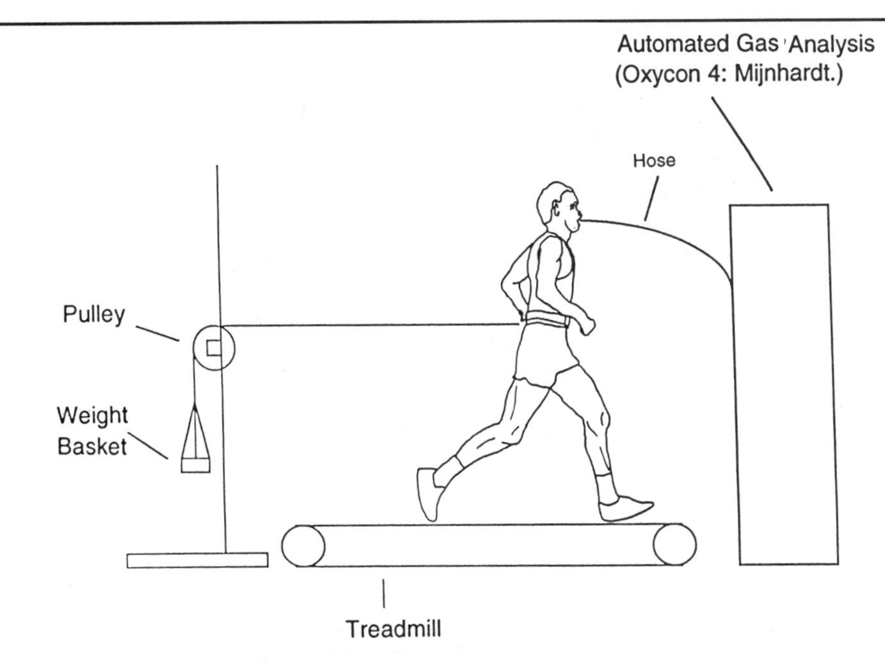

Figure 9.6 A diagram of the horizontal impeding force experiment used to calculate loaded running efficiency (Lloyd and Zacks, 1972).

9.8.3 CALCULATION OF LRE

Metabolic work rate is calculated from steady-state $\dot{V}O_2$ for each load condition. A value of 20.9 kJ (5.0 kcal min^{-1}, 348.8 W) can be used as the energy equivalent for one litre of oxygen since this will cause no more than a 4% variation based on observed respiratory exchange ratios.

External work rate is calculated by the product of the force exerted by the weight over the pulley and the distance moved per unit of time by the treadmill belt. A linear regression equation is then fitted to the data, with metabolic rate as the dependent variable and external work rate as the independent variable. Apparent efficiency of running against a horizontal load, or LRE is then calculated for each speed of running by taking the inverse of the slope of the regression equation, as shown in Figure 9.7.

For example, given the raw data which form the basis for Figure 9.7, the calculations are as follows.

Running speed constant at 11.2 km h^{-1} ($11.2 \times 1000/600/60 = 3.11$ m s^{-1})

The calculation of metabolic work rate (MWR) in watts is given by:

$$\text{MWR (W)}\ \dot{V}O_2\ (\text{l min}^{-1}) \times 348.8$$

where: $\dot{V}O_2$ = measured oxygen uptake for each load condition
= 20.9 kJ = 348.8 W = 5 kcal min^{-1} = 1 litre of oxygen

The calculation of external work rate (EWR) in watts is given by:

$$\text{EWR (W)} = M\ (\text{kg}) \times g\ (\text{m s}^{-2}) \times D\ (\text{m s}^{-1})$$

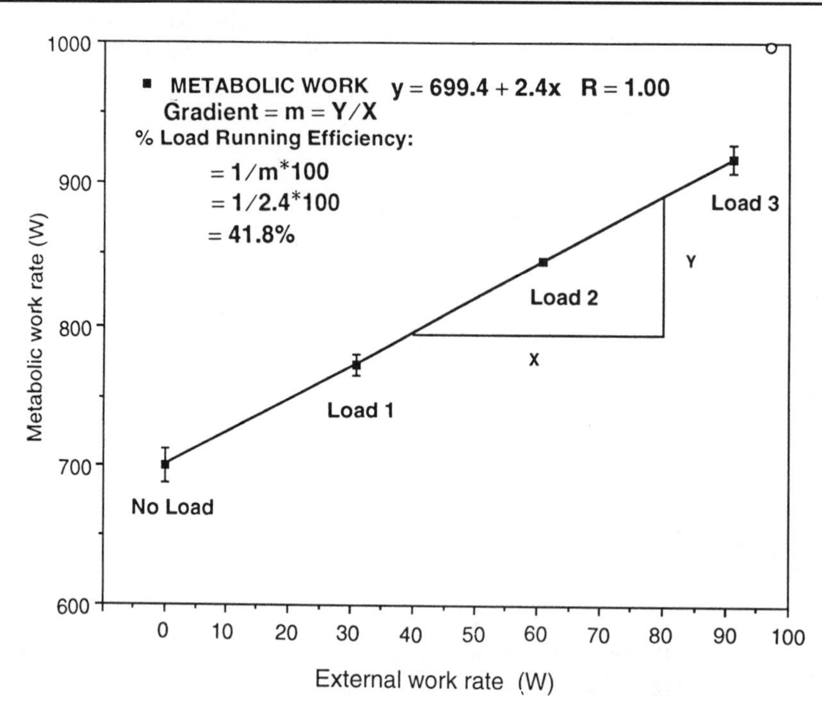

Figure 9.7 Calculation of loaded running efficiency (LRE) in the horizontal impeding force experiment for a subject running at 11.2 km h^{-1}. Values are means ± SD for data collected in two experiments completed by the same subject on different days (Cooke *et al.*, 1991).

where: M is mass applied to runner acting over pulley, g is acceleration due to gravity, D is distance moved by treadmill belt in 1 s = velocity of treadmill (m s^{-1})

Given the following oxygen uptake values for each of four external loads measured as mass applied to the pulley the metabolic work rate and external work rate can be calculated according to the formulae above:

Mass on pulley (kg)	EWR (W)	$\dot{V}O_2$ (l min^{-1})	MWR (W)
0	0	2.01	699.4
1	30.51	2.22	772.6
2	61.02	2.43	845.8
3	91.53	2.63	919.1

The EWR and MWR values are plotted in Figure 9.7, which also shows the linear regression equation fitted by the method of least squares. Given that EWR is the independent variable it has to be plotted on the x axis, and the dependent variable, MWR, is plotted on the y axis. Loaded running efficiency expressed as a percentage is therefore given by the reciprocal of the gradient of the linear regression equation multiplied by 100:

$$\% \text{ Loaded running efficiency} = 1/2.4 \times 100 = 41.8\%$$

9.8.4 RESULTS

The results can be reported in terms of individual LRE values for each speed of running, and combined in a variety of ways depending on the aim of the experiment (e.g. either to investigate the effects of running speed on LRE or to compare the apparent efficiency of horizontal treadmill running against other forms of ergometry).

9.9 PRACTICAL 4: MEASUREMENT OF THE EFFICIENCY OF CYCLING AND STEPPING

9.9.1 CYCLE ERGOMETRY

In mechanical cycle ergometry the external power output (W) or mechanical work rate is quantified as the product of the frictional force (N) or resistance applied to the flywheel and the distance travelled (m) by one point on the circumference of the flywheel, which gives the work done (J), divided by the time to do the work (s):

$$\text{External power output (W)} = \frac{\text{Force (N)} \times \text{Distance (m)}}{\text{Time (s)}}$$

Most cycle ergometers allow the work rate to be set in watts, whether they are mechanically or electronically braked.

As with the LRE experiment metabolic work rate is calculated from steady state $\dot{V}O_2$:

$$\text{Metabolic work rate (W)} = (\dot{V}O_2 \text{ l min}^{-1}) \times 348.8$$

A gross measure of efficiency can then be calculated by dividing the external power output by the metabolic power output:

$$\%\text{Gross efficiency} = \frac{[(\text{Force} \times \text{Distance}) \text{ Time}]}{\dot{V}O_2 \text{ l min}^{-1} \times 348.8} \times 100$$

Net efficiency can be calculated by dividing the external power output by net metabolic power, the latter being obtained by subtracting an estimate of resting $\dot{V}O_2$ (see Chapter 8) from the gross measured value. Provided that both the numerator and denominator are in the same units (Watts kJ min^{-1} or kcal min^{-1}) the correct ratio will be calculated and when multiplied by 100 will give percentage net efficiency.

9.9.2 STEPPING

For stepping, the external work rate (W) is calculated as a function of the vertical height that the centre of mass of the body is raised (m). This is estimated by multiplying the step height (m) by the number of complete step cycles performed. The total vertical height is then multiplied by the force (body weight (N)), and divided by the duration (s) of the stepping exercise:

$$\text{External power output (W)} = \frac{\text{Step height (m)} \times \text{No. steps} \times \text{Weight (N)}}{\text{Time (s)}}$$

The gross and net efficiency ratios can then be calculated using the external work rate and metabolic work rate as for cycle ergometry.

The net efficiency of stepping is of the order of 16% (Shephard *et al.*, 1968).

9.9.3 EXPERIMENTAL PROCEDURES AND PROTOCOLS

Gross and net efficiency ratios can be calculated over the submaximal range of exercise intensities, provided that the energy demands of the exercise are matched by a steady state of oxygen uptake. Efficiency values calculated for high intensity exercise, where anaerobic sources make a significant contribution to the energy demands, will be higher than expected since under such conditions oxygen uptake will not reflect the energy demands of the exercise.

For stepping on a double 'nine-inch' step (total vertical height 45 cm) the oxygen uptake can be estimated to be:

$$\dot{V}O_2\ (\text{ml kg}^{-1}\ \text{min}^{-1}) = 1.34 \times n$$

where n = number of step cycles per minute.

For example stepping on a double step requires a six beat cadence, therefore stepping to a metronome set at 120 beats per minute would result in the completion of 20 step cycles per minute, giving an estimated oxygen uptake of 26.8 ml kg^{-1} min^{-1}.

A suitable submaximal range of workrates for the above step would consist of four by three minute workrates with metronome cadences set at 60, 90, 120 and 150 beats min^{-1}. Expired air can be collected during the third minute of each workload and analysed according to the methods described in Chapter 8.

Although stepping is considered to be a simple inexpensive form of ergometry, every effort must be made to ensure that the subject keeps in time with the metronome and that he/she stand up straight on a flat foot with full knee extension.

For cycle ergometry a suitable range of submaximal exercise intensities would consist of 50–150 W depending on the age, sex and condition of the subjects. As a guide, heart rate response should not exceed 85% of age-related maximum heart rate during a submaximal test. Traditionally a pedal frequency of 50 rev min^{-1} has been used in submaximal exercise tests using mechanically braked cycle ergometers. However, 60 rev min^{-1} is often a more comfortable pedalling frequency.

Shephard (1968) showed that over a range of submaximal loads the mean net mechanical efficiency for stepping and cycle ergometry were 16% and 23% respectively.

9.9.4 DISCUSSION

The values quoted from Shephard (1968) represent group means for subjects performing repeated experiments in both stepping and cycling to a randomized design. There was more variability in stepping (coefficient of variation approximately 10%) than cycling (coefficient of variation approximately 7%). There was also some variation in mechanical efficiency values associated with loading.

Individual values for mechanical efficiency can be used as calibration factors for estimating oxygen uptake from work done, rather than having to use estimates from the literature. There are several experiments that can be conducted with either stepping or cycle ergometry to investigate variations in mechanical efficiency values. For example, the effects of pedalling frequency, stepping frequency, work rate, saddle height, single or double step, step height and leg length in relation to step height can all be investigated.

REFERENCES

Allied Dunbar National Fitness Survey (1992) *Main Findings*. Sports Council and Health Education Authority.

Altman, P. L. and Dittmer, D. S. (1968) *Metabolism*, FASBEB, Bethesda, MD.

Asmussen, E. and Bonde-Peterson, F. (1974) Apparent efficiency and storage of elastic energy in human muscles during exercise. *Acta Physiologica Scandanavica*, **92**, 537–45.

Åstrand, P. O. (1952) *Experimental Studies of Physical Working Capacity in Relation to Sex and Age, Munksgaard, Copenhagen*.

Åstrand, P. O. and Rhyming, I. (1954) A nomogram for the calculation of aerobic capacity (physical fitness) from pulse rate during submaximal work. *Journal of Applied Physiology*, **7**, 218.

Åstrand, P. O. and Rodahl, K. (1986) *Textbook of Work Physiology, Physiological Bases of Exercise*, 3rd edn, McGraw Hill, New York.

Bar-Or, O. (1983) Pediatric sports medicine for the practitioner, in *Physiological Principles to Clinical Application*. Springer, New York.

Boreham, C. A. G., Paliczka, V. J. and Nichols, A. K. (1990) A comparison of PWC_{170} and 20-MST tests of aerobic fitness in adolescent schoolchildren. *Journal of Sports Medicine and Physical Fitness*, **30**, 19–23.

Bouchard, C. (1986) Genetics of aerobic power and capacity, in *Sport and Human Genetics* (eds R. M. and C. Bouchard), Human Kinetics, Champaign, IL, pp. 58–88.

Bouchard, C. and Malina, R. M. (1983) Genetics of physiological fitness and and motor performance. *Exercise and Sport Sciences Reviews*, **11**, 306–39.

Bransford, D. R. and Howley, E. T. (1977) Oxygen cost of running in trained and untrained men and women. *Medicine and Science in Sports and Exercise*, **9**, 41–4.

British Association of Sports Sciences (1992) *Position Statement on the Physiological Assessment of the Elite Athlete, British Association of Sports Sciences (Physiology Section)*.

Cavanagh, P. R. and Kram, R. (1985) The efficiency of human movement – a statement of the problem. *Medicine and Science in Sports and Exercise*, **17**, 304–8.

Conley, D. L. and Krahenbuhl, G. (1980) Running economy and distance running performance of highly trained athlete. *Medicine and Science in Sports and Exercise*, **12**, 357–60.

Conley, D. L., Krahenbuhl, G. and Burkett, L. (1981) Training for aerobic capacity and running economy. *Physician and Sportsmedicine*, **9** (4), 107–15.

Cooke, C. B., McDonagh, M. J. N., Nevill, A. M. and Davies, C. T. M. (1991) Effects of load on oxygen intake in trained boys and men during treadmill running. *Journal of Applied Physiology*, **71**, 1237–44.

Cooper, K. H. (1968) A means of assessing maximal oxygen intake, correlation between field and treadmill testing. *Journal of American Medical Association*, **203**, 201–4.

Costill, D. L. (1972) Physiology of marathon running. *Journal of the American Medical Association*, **221**, 1024–9.

Costill, D. L. and Fox, E. L. (1969) Energetics of marathon running. *Medicine and Science in Sports*, **1**, 81–6.

Costill, D. L., Thomson, H. and Roberts, E. (1973) Fractional utilisation of the aerobic capacity during distance running. *Medicine and Science in Sports and Exercise*, **5**, 248–52.

Council of Europe (1988) *Testing Physical Fitness*, Eurofit, Strasbourg.

Davies, C. T. M. (1980) Metabolic cost of exercise and physical performance in children with some observations on external loading. *European Journal of Applied Physiology*, **45**, 95–102.

DuBois, D. and DuBois, E. F. (1916) Clinical calorimetry. A formula to estimate the approximate surface area if height and weight are known. *Archives of Internal Medicine*, **17**, 863–71.

Eston, R. E. and Brodie, D. A. (1985) The assessment of maximal oxygen uptake from running tests. *Physical Education Review*, 28–36.

Eston, R. G., Robson, S. and Winter, E. (1993) A comparison of oxygen uptake during running in children and adults, in *Kinanthropometry IV* (eds W. Duquet and J. A. P. Day), E & FN Spon, London, pp. 236–41.

Gaesser, G. A. and Brooks, G. A. (1975) Muscular efficiency during steady-rate exercise: effects of speed and work rate. *Journal of Applied Physiology*, **38**, 1132–9.

Harrison, M. H., Bruce, D. L., Brown, G. A. and Cochrane, L. A. (1980) A comparison of some indirect methods of predicting maximal oxygen uptake. *Aviation Space and Environmental Medicine*, **51**, 1128.

Hill, A. V. (1939) The mechanical efficiency of frog's muscle. *Proceedings of the Royal Society of London*, **127**, 434–51.

Kleiber, M. (1975) *The Fire of Life. An Introduction to Animal Energetics*, Kreiger, New York.

Kline, G. M., Porcari, J. P., Hintermeister, R. *et al.* (1987) Estimation of $\dot{V}O_{2\,max}$ from a one-mile track walk, gender, age, and body weight. *Medicine and Science in Sports and Exercise*, **19**, 253–9.

Krahenbuhl, G. S., Skinner, J. S. and Kohrt, W. M. (1985) Developmental aspects of maximal aerobic power in children. *Exercise and Sport Sciences Reviews*, **13**, 503–38.

Krebs, H. A. and Kornberg, H. L. (1957) *Energy Transformations in Living Matter*, Springer, Berlin.

Leger, L. and Lambert, J. (1982) A maximal multistage 20 m shuttle run test to predict $\dot{V}O_{2\,max}$. *European Journal of Applied Physiology*, **49**, 1–12.

Lloyd, B. B. and Zacks, R. M. (1972) The mechanical efficiency of treadmill running against a horizontal impeding force. *Journal of Physiology (London)*, **223**, 355–63.

Margaria, R., Cerretelli, P., Aghemo, P. and Sassi, G. (1963) Energy cost of running. *Journal of Applied Physiology*, **18**, 367–70.

McMahon, T. A. (1984) *Muscles, Reflexes and Locomotion*, Princeton University Press, Princeton, N. J.

Nevill, A. M., Ramsbottom, R. and Williams, C. (1992) Scaling physiological measurements for individuals of different body size. *European Journal of Applied Physiology*, **65**, 110–17.

Norman, R., Sharrat, M., Pezzack, J. and Noble, E. (1976) Re-examination of the mechanical efficiency of horizontal treadmill running. *Biomechanics*, **7**, 87–98.

Paliczka, V. J., Nichols, A. K. and Boreham, C. A. G. (1987) A multi-stage shuttle run test as a predictor of running performance and maximal oxygen uptake in adults. *British Journal of Sports Medicine*, **21**, 163–5.

Pollock, M. L. (1973) The quantification of endurance training programmes, in *Exercise and Sport Sciences Reviews* (ed. J. H. Wilmore), Academic Press, New York, pp. 155–88.

Rowland, T. W. (1990) *Exercise and Childrens Health*, Human Kinetics Books, Champaign, IL.

Saltin, B., Blomquist, G., Mitchell, J. H. *et al.* (1968) Response to exercise after bed rest and after training. *Circulation*, **38** (suppl. 7), 1–78.

Schmidt-Nielsen, K. (1984) *Scaling: Why is Animal Size so Important?* Cambridge University Press, Cambridge.

Shephard, R. J. (1970) Computer programs for solution of the Åstrand nomogram and calculation of body surface area. *Journal of Sports Medicine and Physical Fitness*, **10**, 206–12.

Shephard, R. J. (1984) Tests of maximum oxygen intake: a critical review. *Sports Medicine*, **1**, 99–124.

Shephard, R. J., Allen, C., Benade, A. J. S. *et al.* (1968) Standardization of submaximal exercise tests. *Bulletin of the World Health Organization*, **38**, 765–75.

Siconolfi, J. F., Cullinane, E. M., Carleton, R. A. and Thompson, P. D. (1982) Assessing $\dot{V}O_{2\,max}$ in epidemiologic studies: modifications of the Åstrand–Rhyming test. *Medicine and Science in Sports and Exercise*, **14**, 335–8.

Stainsby, W. N., Gladden, L. B., Barclay, J. K. and Wilson, B. A. (1980) Exercise efficiency: validity of baseline subtractions. *Journal of Applied Physiology*, **48**, 518–22.

Taylor, C. R., Heglund, N. C. and Maloiy, G. M. O. (1982) Energetics and mechanics of terrestrial locomotion I. Metabolic energy consumption as a function of speed and body size in birds and mammals. *Journal of Experimental Biology*, **97**, 1–22.

Taylor, H. L., Buskirk, E. and Henschel, A. (1955) Maximal oxygen uptake as an objective measure of cardiorespiratory performance. *Journal of Applied Physiology*, **8**, 73–7.

Thorstensson, A. (1986) Effects of moderate external loading on the aerobic demand of submaximal running in men and 10 year old boys. *European Journal of Applied Physiology and Occupational Physiology*, **55**, 569–74.

Unnithan, V. B. and Eston, R. G. (1990) Stride frequency and submaximal treadmill running economy in adults and children. *Pediatric Exercise Science*, **2**, 149–55.

Whipp, B. J. and Wasserman, K. (1969) Efficiency of muscular work. *Journal of Applied Physiology*, **26**, 644–8.

Wickstrom, R. L. (1983) *Fundamental Motor Patterns*, Lea and Febiger, Philadelphia.

Wilkie, D. R. (1974) The efficiency of muscular contraction. *Journal of Mechanochemistry and Cell Motility*, **2**, 257–67.

Wyndham, C. H., Strydom, N. B., Leary, W. P. and Williams, C. G. (1966) Studies of the maximum capacity of men for physical effort. *Internationale Zeitschrift fur Angewandte Physiologie*, **22**, 285–95.

Zacks, R. M. (1973) The mechanical efficiencies of running and bicycling against a horizontal impeding force. *Internationale Zeitschrift für Angewandte Physiologie*, **31**, 249–58.

EXERCISE INTENSITY REGULATION 10

J. G. Williams and R. G. Eston

10.1 INTRODUCTION

People participate in physical exercise for a variety of reasons. These include the desire to improve general health, to improve performance-related fitness for a particular sport, and as recreation and relaxation. Improved fitness results from adaptations in central cardiovascular haemodynamics and local responses in the muscle groups engaged. Such modifications are commonly referred to as 'training effect'. The nature and magnitude of this effect are influenced by the frequency, duration, and intensity with which exercise is undertaken. It is widely accepted that the key variable is intensity. The process of determining and gauging an appropriate level of exercise intensity is a challenging problem which has implications related both to physiological changes and to individual compliance within an exercise programme.

In this chapter crucial considerations for the determination and control of exercise intensity are examined. The reader is introduced to essential physiological and psychological background material related to participation in vigorous physical exercise. This is followed by a series of practical tasks designed to increase understanding of determining exercise intensity. The final section comprises a summary of the main points.

10.2 METHODS OF DETERMINING EXERCISE INTENSITY

An important principle to be assimilated at the outset is that intensity is interpreted by the person doing the exercise. Thus, no matter how sophisticated the physiological measurements, the psychological interpretations of cardiorespiratory and musculoskeletal functions will play a major role in this process. This has been recognized by exercise scientists working in both laboratory-based and clinical research who now routinely collect information about how hard people perceive the physical work to be. This is used to augment the usual measures of physiological response (see, for example, recommendations provided by the American College of Sports Medicine, 1991 pp. 69–71 and 97–102; also, Borg and Ottoson, 1986).

Whatever the personal judgements of exercise intensity, accurate determination will be enhanced by assessment of individual functional capacity and adequate monitoring to ensure that optimal intensity is not exceeded. The acquisition of much of these data is only possible in a fully equipped exercise physiology laboratory using trained personnel. Plainly, this requirement invokes considerable practical limitations for many categories of participant. The American College of Sports Medicine (ACSM, 1991) and British Association of Sport and Exercise Sciences (1988) have provided concise guidelines for the conduct of such assessments. The main physiological criteria are discussed next.

10.2.1 PHYSIOLOGICAL INFORMATION

Various measurements for use in gauging exercise intensity for exercise modalities such

Kinanthropometry and Exercise Physiology Laboratory Manual: Tests, procedures and data Edited by Roger Eston and Thomas Reilly. Published in 1996 by E & FN Spon. ISBN 0 419 17880 5

as running, cycling, swimming, rowing and the like have been devised and applied. These include proportion of maximum oxygen consumption (%$\dot{V}O_{2\,max}$), proportion of maximum heart rate (HR_{max}), proportion of maximum heart rate reserve (HRR_{max}), and blood lactate (La) indices.

(a) Oxygen consumption

Exercising at a high (or moderate) intensity for a sustained period of time requires the ability to deliver oxygen to the active muscles. The most frequently cited criterion measure is the maximal capacity for doing this, i.e., the maximal oxygen uptake ($\dot{V}O_{2\,max}$). Acquisition of this information requires appropriately equipped facilities and expert personnel as well as a high degree of compliance on the part of the person involved. The method is explained in Chapter 9. Ideally, this index is used to specify exercise intensity levels. The recommended intensity range arrived at in this manner can be anywhere between 40 and 85% of functional capacity depending on the health and training status of the individual (ACSM, 1991).

(b) Prediction of oxygen consumption levels using a multistage test

Although the measurement of $\dot{V}O_{2\,max}$ is preferred, it is possible to predict $\dot{V}O_{2\,max}$ with acceptable levels of accuracy using the equations suggested by the ACSM (1991) for both cycle and treadmill ergometry. Oxygen uptake can be predicted for any speed of walking and running on the level and uphill, as well as for cycling at specific work rates. In this way, the predicted oxygen uptake values can be compared against the subject's heart rate and extrapolated to the maximal heart rate to predict $\dot{V}O_{2\,max}$. With knowledge of the subject's $\dot{V}O_{2\,max}$, it is then possible to prescribe speeds/work rates which correspond to a given exercise intensity (%$\dot{V}O_{2\,max}$ values), using the ACSM formulae. The formula used to predict $\dot{V}O_2$ at any given speed and gradient is:

$$\dot{V}O_2\ (\text{ml kg}^{-1}\ \text{min}^{-1}) = \text{horizontal component} + \text{vertical component} + \text{resting component}$$

For running

$$\dot{V}O_2\ (\text{ml kg}^{-1}\ \text{min}^{-1}) = (\text{Speed (ml min}^{-1}) \times 0.2\ \text{ml kg}^{-1}\ \text{min}^{-1}) + \text{gradient} \times \text{m min}^{-1} \times 1.8\ \text{ml kg}^{-1}\ \text{min}^{-1} \times 0.5) + 3.5\ \text{ml kg}^{-1}\ \text{min}^{-1}$$

For cycling

$$\dot{V}O_2\ (\text{ml}) = (\text{Work rate(kg m min}^{-1}) \times 2\ \text{ml kgm}^{-1}\ \text{min}^{-1}) + (\text{Mass} \times 3.5\ \text{ml kg}^{-1}\ \text{min}^{-1})$$

(Note: 1 W = 6.118 kgm min^{-1})

In a multistage test the subject runs or cycles at two levels. When two submaximal $\dot{V}O_2$ values are calculated, the slope of the HR:$\dot{V}O_2$ regression line is calculated and this is used to predict the $\dot{V}O_{2\,max}$ by extrapolation of one of the multistage $\dot{V}O_2$:HR values.

Calculation of the 'slope' of the $\dot{V}O_2$:HR relationship is determined by:

Slope (b) =
$$(\dot{V}O_{2\,stage\,2} - \dot{V}O_{2\,stage\,1})/(HR_{stage\,2} - HR_{stage\,1})$$

$$\dot{V}O_{2\,max} = \dot{V}O_{2\,stage\,2} + b\,((220 - \text{age}) - HR_{stage\,2})$$

What follows is an example of the method used to predict $\dot{V}O_{2\,max}$ using actual data based on one of the authors (RGE age 38, mass 86 kg). An important point to note is that the HR values must be at steady state. The subject must therefore exercise for at least 3 minutes. If the HR is not at steady state (i.e. it is still increasing) it will predict an unrealistic overestimation of the $\dot{V}O_{2\,max}$ and be inaccurate for prescription of subsequent exercise intensity.

(i) Prediction of $\dot{V}O_{2\,max}$ (treadmill protocol)

Treadmill data

	Stage 1	Stage 2
Speed (mph)	6	8
Gradient (%)	4	8
HR	134	172

Calculation of submaximal $\dot{V}O_2$

Stage 1

$\dot{V}O_2$ (ml kg^{-1}min^{-1}) = (160.8 m min^{-1} × 0.2 ml kg^{-1} min^{-1} + (0.04 × 160.8 m min^{-1} × 1.8 ml kg^{-1}min^{-1} × 0.5) + 3.5 ml kg^{-1} min^{-1}

= 41.4 ml kg^{-1} min^{-1}

Stage 2

$\dot{V}O_2$ (ml kg^{-}1min^{-1}) = (214.4 m min^{-1} × 0.2 ml kg^{-1} min^{-1}) + (0.08 × 214.4 m min^{-1} × 1.8 ml kg^{-1} min^{-1} × 0.5) + 3.5 ml kg^{-1} min^{-1}

= 61.8 ml kg^{-1} min^{-1}

(*Note:* 1 mph = 26.8 m min^{-1})

Calculation of slope (*b*)

$$b = (61.8 - 41.4)/(172 - 134) = 0.54$$

Calculation of $\dot{V}O_{2\,max}$

$\dot{V}O_{2\,max}$ (ml kg^{-1} min^{-1}) = 61.8 + 0.54 ((220 − 38) − 172)

$\dot{V}O_{2\,max}$ (ml kg^{-1} min^{-1}) = 67.2

(ii) Prediction of $\dot{V}O_{2\,max}$ (cycle ergometry protocol)

Cycle ergometry data

	Stage 1	**Stage 2**
Work rate (kgm min^{-1})	900 (150 W)	1200 (200 W)
Heart rate	124	138

Calculation of submaximal $\dot{V}O_2$

Stage 1

$\dot{V}O_2$ (ml) = (900 kgm min^{-1} × 2 ml kgm^{-1} min^{-1}) + (86 kg × 3.5 ml kg^{-1} min^{-1})

$\dot{V}O_2$(ml) = 2101

$\dot{V}O_2$ (ml kg^{-1} min^{-1}) = 2101 ml/86 kg = 24.4

$\dot{V}O_2$ (ml kg^{-1} min^{-1}) = 24.4

Stage 2

$\dot{V}O_2$ (ml) = (1200 kgm min^{-1} × 2 ml kgm^{-1}min^{-1}) + (86 kg × 3.5 ml kg^{-1} min^{-1})

$\dot{V}O_2$ (ml) = 2701

$\dot{V}O_2$ (ml kg^{-1} min^{-1}) = 2701 ml/86 kg = 31.4

$\dot{V}O_2$ (ml kg^{-1} min^{-1}) = 31.4

Calculation of slope (*b*)

$$b = (31.4 - 24.4)/(138 - 124) = 0.50$$

Calculation of $\dot{V}O_{2\,max}$ for cycle ergometry

$\dot{V}O_{2\,max}$ (ml kg^{-1}min^{-1}) = 31.4 + 0.50 ((220 − 38) − 138)

$\dot{V}O_{2\,max}$ (ml kg^{-1} min^{-1}) = 53.4

10.2.2 DETERMINING THE EXERCISE PRESCRIPTION

Once a maximal aerobic capacity has been determined, it is possible to prescribe a running speed/work rate that corresponds to a given exercise intensity. In the following example, the exercise intensity corresponding to 70% $\dot{V}O_{2\,max}$ is determined, for running and for cycling for RGE.

(i) For running

In the above example the $\dot{V}O_{2\,max}$ was determined to be 67 ml kg^{-1} min^{-1}; 70% of this is 46.9 ml kg^{-1} min^{-1}

By substitution into the formula:

$\dot{V}O_2$ = (m min^{-1} × 0.2 ml m^{-1} min^{-1}) + 3.5

The running speed (m min^{-1})

= ($\dot{V}O_2$ − 3.5)/ 0.2

= (46.9 − 3.5)/0.2

= 217 m min^{-1} (3.61 m s^{-1})

This equates to a running speed of 8.1 mph or a running pace of 7 min 24 s per mile (60 min/8.1 mph).

(ii) For cycling

In the above example the $\dot{V}O_{2\,max}$ was determined to be 53.4 ml kg^{-1} min^{-1}; 70% of the this is 37.4 ml kg^{-1} min^{-1}.
This value is multiplied by mass (86 kg) to give an absolute $\dot{V}O_2 = 3216.4$ ml
By substitution into the formula

$$\dot{V}O_2\,(\text{ml}) = (\text{kgm min}^{-1} \times 2\ \text{ml kgm}^{-1}) + (3.5\ \text{ml kg}^{-1}\ \text{min}^{-1} \times \text{Mass})$$

The work rate (kgm min^{-1})

$$= (\dot{V}O_2 - (3.5 \times \text{Mass}))/2$$
$$= (3216.4 - (3.5 \times 86))/2$$
$$= 1457.7\ \text{kgm min}^{-1}\ (238\ \text{W})$$

The next thing to decide is the preferred cycling frequency. Obviously, the higher the pedal frequency the lower the load. If we assume that one pedal revolution is equal to a forward motion of 6 m, the loading can be calculated by the formula:

$$\text{Load (kg)} = (\text{kgm min}^{-1})/(6\ \text{m} \times \text{rev min}^{-1})$$

Thus, for a pedal frequency of 50 rev min^{-1} the loading will be 4.86 kg and for a pedal frequency of 70 rev min^{-1} it would be 3.47 kg, and so on.

10.2.3 DETERMINATION OF ENERGY EXPENDITURE

The total energy expenditure can be calculated on the basis that 1 MET (3.5 ml kg^{-1} min^{-1}) is equivalent to an energy expenditure of approximately 4.2 kJ kg h^{-1} (1 kcal kg^{-1} h^{-1}). Thus, an 86 kg person would expend approximately 361 kJ min^{-1} (86 kcal min^{-1}) at rest. In the above example, to run at a pace which corresponds to 70% $\dot{V}O_{2\,max}$, the metabolic equivalent is about 13.4 METs. Thus, the energy expenditure per hour is 86 kg × 13.4 kcal kg^{-1} h^{-1} = 1154 kcal h^{-1} (4831 kJ h^{-1}). If the person runs for 30 min, the theoretical energy expenditure at this level can be calculated by the appropriate time proportion, i.e. 30/60 = 577 kcal (2415 kJ).

10.2.4 USING HEART RATE TO PRESCRIBE EXERCISE INTENSITY

The advent of non-encumbering telemetry methods has made the accurate measurement of heart rate a relatively straightforward process. Since heart rate and oxygen uptake share a positive, linear relationship regardless of age and sex, target heart rate ranges may be selected to correspond with $\dot{V}O_{2\,max}$ values (Karvonen and Vuorimaa, 1988). This method is used in a variety of field tests and exercise protocols to approximate and monitor exercise intensity.

As a general rule, maximal aerobic power improves if exercise is sufficiently intense to increase heart rate to about 70% of maximum. This is equivalent to about 50–55% of $\dot{V}O_{2\,max}$. This is a level of intensity which is said to be the minimal stimulus required to produce a training effect (Gaesser and Rich, 1984). Estimation of $\dot{V}O_{2\,max}$ from percentage HR is subject to error in all populations because of the need for a true heart rate maximum value. McArdle *et al.* (1991) asserted that this could be attained from 2–4 minutes of 'all-out' exercise in the activity of interest. Such a procedure demands sound health coupled with a high level of commitment from an individual and is only really appropriate for competitive athletes. For this reason, maximum heart rate is usually arrived at by subtracting the individual's age from a theoretical maximum of 220 beats min^{-1} regardless of sex and age.

Although all people of the same age (or sex) do not possess the same maximum heart rate, the loss in accuracy for individual variation of approximately ±10 beats min^{-1} as one standard deviation at any age-predicted heart rate is usually considered to be of small significance in establishing an effective exercise programme for healthy individuals. Nevertheless, caution is required with the predictive procedure because, within normal variation, only 68% of 20-year-olds will have a heart rate maximum between 190 and 210 beats min^{-1} (i.e. 220–20 ± 10 beats min^{-1}). This formula is also inappropriate for certain types of activity such as swimming because flotation in the supine position and the cooling effect of water reduce maximum heart rate values to an average of about 10–13 beats min^{-1} lower than in running. The intensity assessment for swimming should therefore be at least 10 beats min^{-1} lower than the age-predicted maximum heart rate (McArdle *et al.*, 1991).

A preferred method to prescribe exercise intensity is the percentage maximal heart rate reserve method (%HRR_{max}) as described by Karvonen and Vuorimaa (1988). This method uses the percentage difference between resting and maximal heart rate added to the resting heart rate. When compared to the %HR_{max} method, %HRR_{max} yields at least a 10 beat higher training heart rate when calculated for exercise intensities between 60 and 85% $\dot{V}O_{2\,max}$. This method equates more closely with given submaximal $\dot{V}O_{2\,max}$ values in both healthy adults and cardiac patients (Pollock *et al.*, 1982).

The procedure for calculating %HRR_{max} values to determine exercise heart rates and the method of calculating %HRR_{max} from exercise heart rates is shown below.

RHR = Resting heart rate
HRR = Heart rate reserve
%HRR_{max} = Percentage maximal heart rate reserve
HR_{max} = 220 – age (e.g. at age 25 the predicted HR_{max} = 195 beats min^{-1})
HRR = HR_{max} – RHR (e.g. if RHR = 60 then HRR = 195 – 60 = 135 beats min^{-1})
%HRR_{max} = (Training intensity (% of maximum) × HRR) + RHR

The training intensity at 70% of HRR_{max} is therefore ((0.7 × 135) + 60) = 154 beats min^{-1}.

To calculate %HRR_{max} from an exercising heart rate the following formula is used:

$$\%HRR_{max} = \frac{\text{Exercise HR} - \text{RHR}}{HR_{max} - \text{RHR}}$$

$$\text{e.g. } \frac{154 - 60}{195 - 60} = 70\%HRR_{max}$$

Table 10.1 provides results from our laboratory in support of the %HRR_{max} method. The data represent actual $\dot{V}O_2$ and HR data collected on one of the authors (RGE) during a progressive exercise test to maximum on the treadmill. It can be seen that the %HRR_{max} values correspond very closely to the %$\dot{V}O_{2\,max}$ values, and may be used to prescribe exercise intensity at a given %$\dot{V}O_{2\,max}$.

Table 10.1 A comparison of %$\dot{V}O_{2\,max}$ at equivalent %HRR_{max} and %HR_{max} levels for RGE March 1994

%HR level	*HR at % HR_{max}*	*$\dot{V}O_2$ (ml kg^{-1} min^{-1})*	*% $\dot{V}O_{2\,max}$*	*HR at % HRR_{max}*	*$\dot{V}O_2$ (ml kg^{-1} min^{-1})*	*% $\dot{V}O_{2\,max}$*
40	73	8	13	105	26	41
50	91	21	33	118	33	52
60	109	28	44	131	38	60
70	127	37	59	144	46	73
80	140	43	68	157	52	82
90	164	56	89	169	58	92
100	182	63	100	182	63	100

10.2.5 BLOOD LACTATE INFORMATION

From a physiological standpoint the ability to sustain a given exercise intensity is a function of the supply of oxygen to the working muscles and the biochemical processes of muscular contraction. If the supply of oxygen is insufficient, there is a build-up of lactic acid. Technological advance has made the efficient assay of blood lactate concentration almost routine. This has spawned research interest in the relationship between oxygen uptake and lactate concentration profiles for endurance activities such as running, cycling, rowing, and so on. The general findings indicate that maximal oxygen uptake, formerly considered to be the best determinant of endurance capacity, is now only recognized as a valid predictive criterion for short-term endurance efforts; defined as reaching exhaustion in 3–10 min (Heck *et al.*, 1985). Evidence for this comes from studies in which there is improvement in endurance performance without improvement in $\dot{V}O_{2\,max}$.

In adults, exercise intensities at a reference value of whole blood lactate of 4 mM are used as an indication of endurance performance (Jacobs, 1986). However, it has been observed that a predetermined level of exercise intensity derived from this figure is sometimes too strenuous even for trained individuals (Stegmann and Kindermann, 1982). In addition, it is well documented that exercise at any given relative intensity is accompanied by a lower blood lactate response in children. Children are able to exercise at intensities close to peak $\dot{V}O_2$ before the reference value of 4 mM is reached (Williams and Armstrong, 1991a). It has therefore been suggested that a 2.5 mM criterion might be more appropriate for children (Williams and Armstrong, 1991b). Plainly, the determination of exercise intensity is an individual matter.

10.3 PSYCHOLOGICAL INFORMATION

The realization that physical performance emanates from a complex interaction of both perceptual, cognitive and metabolic processes occurred a long time ago (see discussion by Borg, 1962). Perceived exertion is now recognized to play an important role in regulating the exercise intensity. Use of the Rating of Perceived Exertion Scale was first adopted as a principle in the professional guidelines of the ACSM in 1986 (ACSM, 1986). Since then more detail has been added on the use of this important tool (ACSM, 1991).

The reasoning behind the use of what appears to be 'cardboard technology' is that humans possess a well-developed system for sensing the strain involved in physical effort. This system is in constant use. All of us have experienced vigorous physical work and have sensed whether we are able to continue or have to stop. Furthermore, during a bout of work, we are able to report both current, overall feelings of exertion and the locus of particular strain (say, in the chest or arms). With some experience of various levels of exercise most people would have little difficulty in numerically scaling or at least ordering samples of exercise to which they have been subjected.

Attempts have been made to establish a basis for interpreting bodily sensations during exercise. By applying established psychophysics principles (Stevens, 1957; Ekman, 1961) to gross motor action, Borg introduced and developed two rating scales, the *Category Scale* (Borg, 1970) and the *Category-Ratio Scale* (Borg, 1982). The most commonly used device is the 6 to 20 Category Scale (Table 10.2). With this scale, the RPE increases linearly as exercise intensity increases. It is most closely correlated with physiological responses that also increase linearly, for example, heart rate and oxygen consumption. For physiological variables which increase as a curvilinear function of power output, such as blood lactate, ventilatory equivalent for oxygen and hormonal responses, Borg (1982) proposed the 0 to 10 Category-Ratio Scale (Table 10.3). In both scales, numbers are anchored to verbal expressions. However, in the Category-Ratio Scale the numerical values have a fixed relation to one another. For example, an intensity judgement of 5 would be gauged to be half that of 10. However, it is important to note that a rating of 10 is not truly maximal. If the subjective intensity rises above a rating of 10, the person is free to choose any number in proportion to 10 which describes the proportionate growth in the sensation of effort. For example if the exercise intensity feels 50% harder than at the rating of 10, the RPE would be 15. More detailed information on the rationale and use of perceived exertion scales is provided by Borg (1985, 1986). It should be noted that when working with young children the developmentally adjusted Children's Effort Rating Table (CERT) is more appropriate (Eston *et al.*, 1994; Williams *et al.*, 1994). This is shown in Table 10.4.

Table 10.2 The Borg 6 to 20 rating of perceived exertion scale (Borg, 1986)

6	No exertion at all
7	Extremely light
8	
9	Very light
10	
11	Light
12	
13	Somewhat hard
14	
15	Hard (heavy)
16	
17	Very hard
18	
19	Extremely hard
20	Maximal exertion

Table 10.3 The Borg 0 to 10 rating of perceived exertion scale (Borg, 1982)

0	Nothing at all
0.5	Extremely weak
1	Very weak
2	Weak (light)
3	Moderate
4	Somewhat strong
5	Strong (heavy)
6	
7	Very strong
8	
9	
10	Extremely strong (almost maximal)
•	Maximal

Table 10.4 Children's Effort Rating Table (CERT) (Williams *et al.*, 1994)

1	Very, very easy
2	Very easy
3	Easy
4	Just feeling a strain
5	Starting to get hard
6	Getting quite hard
7	Hard
8	Very hard
9	Very, very hard
10	So hard I am going to stop

Investigators who have examined the relationship between perceived exertion ratings and the indices of relative intensity discussed above (%$\dot{V}O_{2\,max}$, %HR_{max} etc.), for graded exercise testing have generally reported high and positive correlation values ($r = 0.85$ plus). Also, perceived exertion, HR, and La for cycling, running, walking and arm ergometry are related in a consistent manner in that the incremental curve for perceived exertion can be predicted from a simple combination of HR and La (Borg *et al.*, 1987). Furthermore, criterion group differences (such as trained versus untrained, lean versus obese) observed at equivalent absolute workloads diminish at the same %$\dot{V}O_{2\,max}$. These results apply to both intermittent and continuous protocols.

Pollock *et al.* (1982) compared the validity of the RPE scale for prescribing exercise intensity with the two HR methods in young adult, old adult and cardiac patients. They observed that the %HRR_{max} method coupled with RPE was a much better indicator of exercise intensity and that the differences in RPE were greatly diminished at equivalent %HRR_{max} levels.

The weight of empirical evidence which supports the notion that the regulation of exercise intensity is a psychophysiological process has led to the assertion that perceived exertion alone may be a sufficient basis for gauging exercise intensity. Ratings of 12 to 13 on the Borg 6 to 20 scale correspond to about 60–80% of $\dot{V}O_{2\,max}$ in most individuals and 16 to 17 is approximately 90% $\dot{V}O_{2max}$ for treadmill running (Eston *et al.*, 1987). However, for cycle ergometry ratings of 13 and 17 correspond to exercise intensities of 58% and 80% $\dot{V}O_{2\,max}$, respectively (Parfitt *et al.*, 1995). Stemming from these findings, a worthwhile practical application would be to use the rating scale as a frame of reference for regulating various intensities of exercise (Eston and Williams, 1988). Such an approach is clearly applicable to endurance training in various sports, but also applies to the attainment of general fitness and rehabilitation. As a rule it seems sensible to encourage people to 'tune' to their effort sense and develop sufficient awareness for determining an appropriate exercise intensity without recourse to external devices.

Several studies have confirmed the validity of self-regulation guided by the 6–20 rating scale. In other words, the RPE can be used to regulate exercise intensities by enabling a subject to repeat a given physiological measure or exercise level from trial to trial. This has been done for treadmill running with young adults (Eston *et al.*, 1987; Dunbar *et al.*, 1992; Glass *et al.*, 1992), cycling (Eston and Williams, 1988; Dunbar *et al.*, 1992), wheelchair exercise in children (Ward *et al.*, 1995) and cycling in children (Williams *et al.*, 1991). In the latter study, it was noted that there were problems involved in the interpretation of the 6–20 category scale by the children and that a more *developmentally appropriate* scale could be more accurate. Since then a 1–10 scale has been suggested (Williams *et al.*, 1994) (Table 10.4) and its initial usefulness ascertained during a stepping task (Williams *et al.*, 1993) and during cycling (Eston *et al.*, 1994).

An important consideration of the plausibility of determining exercise intensity through perceived exertion is that much of the research in this area has been undertaken in controlled laboratory conditions. The implication of this approach is that physical sensations cause the percepts of exertion. It should be noted, however, that if exercise prescription is to be based on RPE, then the exercise mode must be specified because the source of the effort percept varies and influences the magnitude of the rating (Pandolf, 1983). When work of different modes is performed, the RPE is greater for work involving small muscle groups (Berry *et al.*, 1989). The classic study by Ekblom and Goldbarg (1971) which differentiated between *local* and *central* effort percepts showed that the RPE for a given submaximal oxygen uptake or heart rate was higher for cycling compared to running. Eston and Williams (1988) also showed that RPE was higher for a given $\%\dot{V}O_{2\,max}$ value for cycling compared to running, when RPE was used to *self-regulate* exercise intensity. Recent data by Parfitt *et al.* (1995) would also seem to support this observation. Similarly, Pivarnik *et al.* (1988) observed that at similar arm and leg exercise power outputs, the RPE was higher for arm work despite similar energy expenditure levels. In addition, local and central factors are influenced by pedalling rate on a cycle ergometer (Robertson *et al.*, 1979). Higher RPE values were reported for pedalling rates of 40 rev min^{-1} compared to 80 rev min^{-1}.

The timing of the measurement of RPE is also important. Parfitt and Eston (1995) observed that RPEs measured during cycle ergometry were significantly higher in the final 20 s of a 4 min exercise bout, compared to 2 min into the exercise bout for men and women.

Dunbar *et al.* (1992) observed that there was greater test–retest reliability when RPE was estimated during cycle ergometry compared to treadmill running. This was attributed to the greater localization of muscle fatigue during cycle ergometry, allowing for a more accurate assessment of the intensity of the peripheral signal. They reported that a comparatively greater attentional focus on these intense regionalized perceptual signals might sharpen input to the perceptual cognitive framework. It follows that the production of a target RPE on the cycle would be facilitated. This has been shown in adults (Eston and Williams, 1988) and in children using the CERT (Eston *et al.*, 1994). Another possible explanation suggested by Dunbar *et al.* (1992) involves the more stable position of the subject during cycle ergometry. They postulated that the task of maintaining balance on a moving belt may distract the individual from the quantity and intensity of the perceptual signals. Although the process is not the same, the role of *dissociation*, as a method of alleviating the discomfort associated with exercise-induced fatigue has been the subject of interest for some time (Benson *et al.*, 1978). It has been shown to be a useful coping mechanism (Morgan *et al.*, 1983), although Rejeski (1985) has reported that theoretical explanations of why and how it works are often lacking. He suggested that dissociative strategies provide a relief from fatigue by occupying limited channel capacity that is critical to bringing a percept into focal awareness. In addition, the subject is faced with the task of regulating speed and gradient of the treadmill and it is likely that the perception of speed is fundamentally different from the perception of exertion for whole-body exercise.

Sex-role orientation also influences RPE. Hochstetler *et al.* (1985) recorded more negative pre-task measures of affect in a sample of feminine-typed women prior to running on a treadmill at 70% $\dot{V}O_{2\,max}$, compared to masculine or androgynous-typed women. Also, the feminine-typed women reported significantly higher RPEs than the other women. These observations have been repeated by Rejeski *et al.* (1987) who demonstrated that feminine-typed males reported significantly more negative affect and higher RPEs than androgynous or masculine typed males whilst working at 85% $\dot{V}O_{2\,max}$.

Those involved in assessing and giving advice on exercise prescription should be aware of the numerous factors which can influence this process. Apart from obvious differences such as sex and age, contrasting styles of sensory processing may predispose individuals to modulate intensity (Robertson *et al.*, 1977). Furthermore, perceptual reactance mediated by sensory processing probably interacts with personality traits (characteristic ways of behaving). Whereas such variables may well be randomized out in general perceived exertion research these are vital considerations for individual exercise prescription. Reference should be made to Morgan (1981), Williams and Eston (1989), Cioffi (1991) and Watt and Grove (1993) for discussions of these variables. Cioffi (1991) examined the viability of a cognitive-perceptual model contrasted with a biomedical model of somatic interpretation. The contents of Cioffi's paper have far-reaching implications for exercise intensity setting and regulation in 'real world' settings.

The next stage for the reader is to gain practical experience of exercise intensity determination which involves perceived exertion. Two practical exercises, an *effort estimation* and an *effort production* protocol, are described. It is recommended that the tasks are undertaken in succession with students working as a small group within a regular exercise science practical schedule. It is assumed that adequate facilities and resources are available and that students have already developed some competence in the measurement of basic physiological parameters. The data shown in Tables 10.5, 10.6 and 10.7 were taken on one of the authors (RGE) over three consecutive days.

10.4 PRACTICAL: USE OF RATINGS OF PERCEIVED EXERTION TO DETERMINE AND CONTROL THE INTENSITY OF CYCLING EXERCISE

10.4.1 ESTIMATION PROTOCOL

(a) Purpose

To determine the relationships between heart rate (HR), rating of perceived exertion (RPE), and power output for cycle ergometry.

(b) Procedure

The subject is prepared for exercise with a heart rate monitoring device and informed that consecutive bouts of exercise will be performed on a cycle ergometer for 4 min. In the last 15 s of each 2 min period the HR is recorded and the subject is requested to provide a rating of how effortful the exercise feels. After the 4 min period the resistance is increased by 25 W and the procedure repeated. The subject continues exercising in this way until

85% of the predicted maximal heart rate (220 minus age) is reached. At this point the resistance is removed and the subject is allowed a 5 minute warm-down period. All data are recorded as in Table 10.5.

Table 10.5 RPE estimation protocol

Name Roger Eston *Age* 38 *HT* 1.78 m
Body mass 83 kg *Date* 21st Sept '94 *Rest HR* 45

Power (W)	*Time (min)*	*HR*	*RPE*	*%HR$_{max}$*	*%HRR$_{max}$*
50	2	67	6	37	16
	4	73	7	40	20
75	2	81	7	44	26
	4	82	7	45	27
100	2	86	9	47	30
	4	92	10	50	34
125	2	96	10	53	37
	4	97	10	53	38
150	2	117	11	64	53
	4	122	12	67	56
175	2	135	12	74	66
	4	140	13	77	69
200	2	148	14	81	75
	4	153	15	84	79
225	2	157	15	86	82
	4	160	16	88	84
250	2	163	16	90	86
	4	165	17	91	88

Immediately prior to exercising, each subject is introduced to the Borg 6 to 20 Rating of Perceived Exertion Scale. It is essential that the subjects clearly understand that an accurate interpretation of the overall feeling of exertion brought about by the exercise is required when requested by the investigator. To do this, the subject uses the verbal expressions on the scale to provide a numerical rating of effort during exercise. It is recommended that standardized instructions are used to introduce the scale. Also, that complete comprehension of the process is checked during a brief warm-up period. Customized instructions may be needed for special applications of RPE, but the following is currently recommended for graded exercise testing by the ACSM (1991):

> During the graded exercise tests we want you to pay close attention to how hard you feel the work rate is. This feeling should be your total amount of exertion and fatigue, combining all sensations and feelings of physical stress, effort and fatigue. Don't concern yourself with any one factor such as leg pain, shortness of breath or exercise intensity, but try to concentrate on your total, inner feeling of exertion. Don't underestimate or overestimate, just be as accurate as you can.

10.4.2 PRODUCTION PROTOCOL

(a) Purpose

To use heart rate and a given perceived exertion rating to produce exercise intensity levels on a cycle ergometer.

(b) Procedure

The subjects, apparatus, exercise mode and general organization remain the same as in task 1. However, in this task the approach is quite different. Two protocols are followed. Both are representative of procedures used in the determination of exercise intensity. The investigator should register the results into a record as shown in Tables 10.6 and 10.7 which also serves as a guide to each step in the process.

Table 10.6 Using heart rate to control exercise intensity

HR	*Power output*(W)	*RPE*	$\%HRR_{max}$
110	159	11	47
130	188	12	62
150	223	14	77
170	260	18	91

Table 10.7 Using RPE to control exercise intensity

RPE	*Power output*(W)	*HR*	$\%HRR_{max}$
11	105	107	45
13	182	135	66
15	217	150	77
17	253	165	88

(c) Protocol A: Use of heart rate to produce selected levels of exercise intensity (Table 10.6)

The subject is allowed a brief period to habituate and warm-up for exercise. Following this the investigator increases power output in a randomized manner to elicit steady heart rate levels of 110, 130, 150 and 170 beats min^{-1} for between 3 and 4 min. The RPE (Category Scale) is applied in the final 15 s of the exercise period.

(d) Protocol B: Use of RPE to produce selected levels of exercise intensity (Table 10.7)

The subject uses the Borg 6 to 20 category scale as a frame of reference to determine selected levels of exercise intensity using only his or her bodily sensations arising from the exercise. All visual (except pedalling frequency which is constant) and auditory information feedback is removed. The subject exercises and self-adjusts power output until steady-state levels of RPE 11, 13, 15 and 17 are established and maintained for between 3 and 4 min. The investigator records power output at steady state and heart rate in the final 15 s of exercise, when the subject is confident that he or she is exercising at a constant RPE.

10.4.3 BRIEF ANALYSIS OF THE EFFORT ESTIMATION AND PRODUCTION TEST DATA SHOWN IN TABLES 10.5–10.7

Table 10.5 contains an example of data collected during an 'estimation test' on one of the authors (RGE). It is possible to determine relationships between power output, heart rate and the rating of perceived exertion. It is evident from these data that there is a strong correlation between HR, RPE and power output (PO) with correlations around 0.98. The importance of allowing sufficient time to adapt to the work rate is also evident. A related *t* test indicated a significantly lower HR and RPE at minute 2 compared to minute 4 $P < 0.01$.

The data from the estimation test can be compared to data derived from the production test. As already indicated above, the high correlations between HR, PO and RPE allow predictions of PO and RPE to be made from HR in Protocol A (Table 10.6) and predictions of HR and PO from RPE in the effort production test (Protocol B, Table 10.7). The following section provides an example of such calculations. Note that only steady-state values have been used.

The regression equation for HR and PO is: PO = 1.9(HR) − 79 ($r = 0.99$, SEE = 20 W). Thus, with prescribed heart rates of 110, 130, 150 and 170 beat min^{-1} the predicted PO values are 130, 168, 206 and 244 W respectively. A similar analysis reveals that the predicted RPEs at these heart rates are 10.8, 12.9, 14.9 and 17 (RPE = 0.102(HR) − 0.4; $r = 0.98$, SEE = 1.2). The reliability of predicted POs and RPEs versus actual POs and RPEs obtained in Protocol A is 0.94 for PO and 0.98 for RPE. A related *t* test reveals no significant difference between the means.

To compare the efficacy of RPE in the effort production protocol (Protocol B), it is necessary to recompute the linear regression equation for RPE: PO and RPE: HR, with RPE as the predictor variable. The regression equation for RPE and HR is: HR = 9.47 (RPE) + 7.82 ($r = 0.98$, SEE = 11 beats min^{-1}). Thus, for an RPE 11, 13, 15 and 17, the predicted HRs are 112, 131, 150 and 169. Compare these heart rates against the obtained HRs in Table 10.7. A similar analysis reveals that the predicted PO at these RPEs is 134 W, 171 W, 208 W and 244 W, respectively. The regression equation for this prediction is: PO = 18.4 (RPE) − 68.4 ($r = 0.99$, SEE = 22W). The reliability of the predicted versus actual HR and PO values at the prescribed RPEs is 0.99 and 0.98, respectively. Related *t* tests revealed no significant difference between the means.

For this subject, therefore, the exercise test provided useful data which enabled him to regulate subsequent exercise intensities using both RPE and HR information obtained in the estimation test. One should remember, however, that the subject was an experienced user of the RPE scale and that practice improves the reliability of RPE for prescribing exercise intensities.

10.5 SUMMARY

1. Beneficial effects of exercise accrue when individuals engage in activity with appropriate frequency, duration, and intensity. The interplay of all three dimensions is important, but the determination of appropriate intensity requires careful consideration because of the impact of numerous variables.
2. One approach to determining intensity is to base judgements on physiological information. The usual method is to recommend intensity levels relative to actual or predicted maximal capacity based on measures of heart rate response, oxygen utilization, ventilation and blood lactate.
3. A comprehensive approach to setting exercise intensity is desirable. This requires the coupling of indices of bodily response during exercise with information on how hard the individual perceives the exercise to be. The most commonly used perceived exertion device used in this process has been the Borg 6 to 20 Category Scale. For young children, the Children's Effort Rating Table (CERT) is recommended.

4. Perceived exertion ratings have been mainly used in two ways, namely the response or estimation method and the production method. In the former, the subject provides a rating for a power output selected by the investigator. In the latter, the subject is requested to produce a power output which is judged to correspond with a given RPE.
5. Whilst the correlation between physiological information and perceived exertion ratings measured in an exercise physiology laboratory for both *response* and *production* methods are usually high, 25% of the variance in the relationship between the two methods remains unaccounted for. The remnant is probably due to individual differences which predispose people to modulate their interpretation of intensity. Thus, the fine-tuning of exercise intensity within an exercise programme comes down to individual decision-making emanating from effort sense. The exercise scientist's role is to arrive at balanced judgements from a psychophysiological perspective by taking into account the variables discussed.

The purpose of this chapter has been to introduce the reader to the concept of exercise intensity determination as a multifaceted process which requires consideration of both physiological and psychological information about the individual relative to specific activities. Through reading the introductory material, following up some of the primary reference material and undertaking the practical tasks which were suggested, a sound knowledge base for decision-making in this area should have been acquired.

REFERENCES

American College of Sports Medicine (1986) *Guidelines for Exercise Testing and Prescription*, 3rd edn, Lea & Febiger, Philadelphia.

American College of Sports Medicine (1991) *Guidelines for Exercise Testing and Prescription*, 4th edn, Lea & Febiger, Philadelphia.

Åstrand, P. O. and Rodahl, K. (1986) *Textbook of Work Physiology*, McGraw-Hill, New York.

Benson, H., Dryer, T. and Hartley, H. (1978) Decreased $\dot{V}O_2$ consumption during exercise with elicitation of the relaxation response. *Journal of Human Stress*, **4**, 38–42.

Berry, M. J., Weyrich, A. S., Robergs, R. A. *et al.* (1989) Ratings of perceived exertion in individuals with varying fitness levels during walking and running. *European Journal of Applied Physiology*, **58**, 494–9.

Borg, G. A. V. (1962) *Physical Performance and Perceived Exertion*, Gleerup, Lund.

Borg, G. (1970) Perceived exertion as an indicator of somatic stress. *Scandinavian Journal of Rehabilitation Medicine*, **2**, 92–98.

Borg, G. (1982) Psychophysical basis of perceived exertion. *Medicine and Science in Sports and Exercise*, **14**, 377–81.

Borg, G. (1985) *An Introduction to Borg's RPE-Scale*. Mouvement Publications, Ithaca, NY.

Borg, G. (1986) Psychophysical studies of effort and exertion: some historical, theoretical, and empirical aspects, in *The Perception of Exertion in Physical Work* (eds G. Borg and D. Ottoson), Macmillan, London, pp. 3–14.

Borg, G. and Ottoson, D. (eds) (1986) *The Perception of Exertion in Physical Work*, Macmillan, London.

Borg, G., Van de Burg, M., Hassmen, P. *et al.* (1987) Relationships between perceived exertion, HR, and La in cycling, running, and walking. *Scandinavian Journal of Sports Science*, **9**, 69–77.

British Association of Sports Sciences (1988) *Physiological Assessment of the Elite Athlete: Position Statement*, White Line Press, Leeds.

Cioffi, D. (1991) Beyond attentional strategies: a cognitive-perceptual model of somatic interpretation. *Psychological Bulletin*, **109**, 25–41.

Dunbar, C., Robertson, R., Baun, R. *et al.* (1992) The validity of regulating exercise intensity by ratings of perceived exertion. *Medicine and Science in Sports and Exercise*, **24**, 94–9.

Ekblom, B. and Goldbarg, A. N. (1971) The influence of physical training and other factors in the subjective rating of perceived exertion. *Acta Physiologica Scandinavica*, **83**, 399–406.

Ekman, G. (1961) A simple method for fitting psychophysical power functions. *Journal of Psychology*, **51**, 343–50.

Eston, R. and Williams, J. G. (1988) Reliability of ratings of perceived effort for the regulation of exercise intensity. *British Journal of Sports Medicine*, **22**, 153–4.

Eston, R., Davies, B. and Williams, J. G. (1987) Use of perceived effort ratings to control exercise intensity in young, healthy adults. *European Journal of Applied Physiology*, **56**, 222–4.

Eston, R., Lamb, K. L., Bain, A. *et al.* (1994) Validity of CERT: a perceived exertion scale for children: a pilot study. *Perceptual and Motor Skills*, **78**, 691–7.

Gaesser, G. A. and Rich, E. G. (1984) Effects of high performance and low intensity training on aerobic capacity and blood lipids. *Medicine and Science in Sports and Exercise*, **16**, 269–74.

Glass, S., Knowlton, R. and Becque, M. D. (1992) Accuracy of RPE from graded exercise to establish exercise training intensity. *Medicine and Science in Sports and Exercise*, **24**, 1303–7.

Heck, H., Mader, A., Hess, G. *et al.* (1985) Justification of the 4 mmol/l lactate threshold. *International Journal of Sports Medicine*, **6**, 117–30.

Hochstetler, S., Rejeski, W. J. and Best, D. (1985) The influence of sex-role orientation on rating of perceived exertion. *Sex Roles*, **12**, 825–35.

Jacobs, I. (1986) Blood lactate: implications for training and sports performance. *Sports Medicine*, 3, 10–25.

Karvonen, J. & Vuorimaa, T. (1988). Heart rate and exercise intensity during sports activities. *Sports Medicine* **5**, 303–12.

McArdle, W. D., Katch, F. and Katch, V. L. (1991) *Exercise Physiology: Energy, Nutrition and Human Performance*, Lea & Febiger, Philadephia.

Morgan, W. (1981) Psychophysiology of self-awareness during vigorous physical activity. *Research Quarterly for Exercise and Sport*, **52**, 385–427.

Morgan, W. P., Horstman, D. J., Cymerman, A. and Stokes, J. (1983) Facilitation of physical performance by means of a cognitive strategy. *Cognitive Therapy and Research*, **7**, 251–64.

Pandolf, K. D. (1983) Advances in the study and application of perceived exertion, in *Exercise and Sport Sciences Reviews* (ed. R. L. Terjung), Franklin Institute Press, Philadelphia, pp. 118–58.

Parfitt, G. and Eston, R. G. (1995) Changes in ratings of perceived exertion and psychological affect in the early stages of exercise. *Perceptual and Motor Skills*, **80**, 259–66.

Parfitt, G., Eston, R. and Connolly, D. (1995) Psychological affect at different ratings of perceived exertion in high- and low-active women: implications for exercise promotion. *Journal of Sports Sciences* (in press).

Pivarnik, J., Grafner, T. R. and Elkins, E. S. (1988) Metabolic, thermoregulatory and psychophysical responses during arm and leg exercise. *Medicine and Science in Sports and Exercise*, **20**, 1–5.

Pollock, M. L., Foster, C., Rod, J. L. and Wible, G. (1982) Comparison of methods of determing exercise training intensity for cardiac patients and healthy adults, in *Comprehensive Cardiac Rehabilitation* (ed. J. J. Kellermann), S Karger, Basel, pp. 129–33.

Rejeski, W. J. (1985) Perceived exertion: an active or a passive process. *Journal of Sport Psychology*, **7**, 371–8.

Rejeski, W. J., Best, D., Griffith, P. and Kenny, E. (1987) Sex-role orientation and the responses of men to exercise stress. *Research Quarterly for Exercise and Sport*, **58**, 260–4.

Robertson, R. J., Gillespie, R. L., Hiatt, E. and Rose, K. D. (1977) Perceived exertion and stimulus intensity modulation. *Perceptual and Motor Skills*, **45**, 211–18.

Robertson, R. J., Gillespie, R. L., McArthy, J. and Rose, K. D. (1979) Differentiated perceptions of exertion: Part 1: mode of integration and regional signals. *Perceptual and Motor Skills*, **49**, 683–9.

Stegmann, H. and Kindermann, W. (1982) Comparison of prolonged exercise tests at the individual anaerobic threshold and the fixed anaerobic threshold of 4 mmol l^{-1} lactate. *International Journal of Sports Medicine*, **3**, 105–9.

Stevens, S. S. (1957) On the psychophysical law. *Psychological Review*, **64**, 153–81.

Ward, D. S. Bar-Or, O. Longmuir, P. and Smith, K. (1995) Use of RPE to control exercise intensity in wheelchair-bound children and adults. *Pediatric Exercise Science*, **7**, 94–102.

Watt, B. and Grove, R. (1993) Perceived exertion: antecedents and applications. *Sports Medicine*, **15**, 225–42.

Williams, J. R. and Armstrong, N. (1991a) The influence of age and sexual maturation on children: blood lactate responses to exercise. *Pediatric Exercise Science*, **3**, 111–20.

Williams, J. R. and Armstrong, N. (1991b) The maximal lactate steady state and its relationship to performance at fixed blood lactate reference values in children. *Pediatric Exercise Science*, **17**, 333–41.

Williams, J. G. and Eston, R. (1989) Determination of the intensity dimension in vigorous exercise programmes with particular reference to the use of the Rating of Perceived Exertion. *Sports Medicine*, **8**, 177–89.

Williams, J.G., Eston, R. and Stretch, C. (1991) Use of the Rating of Perceived Exertion to control exercise intensity in children. *Pediatric Exercise Science*, **3**, 21–7.

Williams, J. G., Furlong, B., Mackintosh, C. and Hockley, T. J. (1993) Rating and regulation of exercise intensity in young children. *Medicine and Science in Sports and Exercise*, Suppl. 25, 5, S8.

Williams, J. G. Eston, R. and Furlong, B.A.F. (1994) CERT: a perceived exertion scale for young children. *Perceptual and Motor Skills*, **79**, 1451–8.

MAXIMAL INTENSITY EXERCISE 11

E. M. Winter

11.1 INTRODUCTION

Maximal intensity exercise (MIE) is exercise that is performed 'all-out'. This should not be confused with intensities of exercise which elicit a maximal physiological response. For instance, maximal oxygen uptake ($\dot{V}O_{2\,max}$) can be produced by intensities of exercise that are only a third or quarter of MIE (Williams, 1987). This type of exercise is linked directly to kinanthropometry because performance measures can be related to total body size or anthropometric characteristics of body segments.

Movement does not always occur during maximal efforts. The scrum in rugby and maintenance of the crucifix and balance in gymnastics are examples where maximal force production occurs during isometric muscle activity. Furthermore, use of the term *supramaximal exercise* should be avoided where possible; logically one cannot exercise at an intensity greater than one's maximum capability. Durations of exercise are short and range from approximately 1 to 2 s in discrete activities like the shot putt and golf swing to 20–45 s of sprinting during running and cycling. Even in these latter activities, there is probably an element of pacing rather than genuinely all-out effort. Also, associated mechanisms of energy release are predominantly anaerobic but it should be recognized that they are not exclusively so. During 30 s of flat-out cycling for example, 13–29% of energy provision could be provided from aerobic sources (Inbar *et al.*, 1976; Bar-Or, 1987).

The purpose of this section is to outline current developments in assessments of MIE. Special attention is given to those that use cycle ergometry, and investigations into accompanying metabolism.

11.2 TERMINOLOGY

Maximal intensity exercise (MIE) can be assessed in different ways and care should be taken to ensure that descriptions of performance adhere to principles of mechanics. These descriptions can be categorized into one of three broad groups. First and the most basic, are scalar quantities such as time (t), distance (s) and speed ($m\ s^{-1}$). Time is probably the most widely used field measure and is employed to assess performance in activities such as running, swimming and cycling; distance is used to assess performance in activities which involve throwing and jumping, either for height or distance; and speed can be used to assess performance when both time taken and distance moved are known.

Next are vector quantities such as force (F), impulse (Ns) and momentum (mv) which are assessments that tend to be *laboratory* rather than *field* based. Thirdly there are measures of energy which also tend to be laboratory based and concern either energy expended (J) or mechanical power output (W). Clearly, power output is only one measure of MIE, yet there is a tendency to assume that MIE and

Kinanthropometry and Exercise Physiology Laboratory Manual: Tests, procedures and data Edited by Roger Eston and Thomas Reilly. Published in 1996 by E & FN Spon. ISBN 0 419 17880 5

power output are synonymous. Adamson and Whitney (1971) and Smith (1972) addressed this point in detail and suggested that in explosive activities such as jumping, the use of power is meaningless and unjustified. Horizontal velocity in sprinting and vertical velocity in jumping are determined by impulse. Consequently, it is the impulse generating capability of muscle, not its power producing capability that is the determinant of effective performance.

Unless the units of performance are watts, performance cannot be described as power. Even when these units are used and the description appears to be sound, underlying theoretical bases might not be sustainable. These considerations are important because they influence the purpose of assessments. Performance *per se* could be the focus in studies which investigate the effects of training. However, an assessment could also be used to investigate changes in metabolism brought about, say, by training or growth; the integrity of the procedure has to be sound, otherwise the insight into underlying mechanisms could be obscured. An understanding of principles of mechanics is a prerequisite of effective test selection and subsequent description of measures.

11.3 HISTORICAL BACKGROUND

Concerted interest in MIE has a long history which can be traced back to 1885 when Marey and Demeney introduced a force platform to investigate mechanisms which underpinned jumping (Cavagna, 1975). Investigations into how muscle functions were based on studies of isolated mammalian and amphibian tissue (Hill, 1913). Attention turned to humans and investigations into $\dot{V}O_2$ at running speeds which were in excess of those that could be maintained at steady state (Hill and Lupton, 1922; Sargent, 1926; Furusawa *et al.*, 1927). There were also attempts to determine mechanical efficiency and equations to describe motion during MIE (Lupton, 1923; Best and Partridge, 1928, 1929).

In 1921 D. A. Sargent introduced a jump test which is still used today. In 1924 L. W. Sargent suggested that the test could be used as a measure of power. More recently, the Lewis nomogram (Fox *et al.*, 1988) has been suggested as a means to estimate power output from vertical jump data in spite of the forcible objections stated earlier by Adamson and Whitney (1971) and Smith (1972).

Investigations into the mechanics of bicycle pedalling during high intensity exercise also have a long history (Dickinson, 1928; Fenn, 1932; Hill, 1934), as have attempts to increase the sensitivity of assessment in this type of exercise. Kelso and Hellebrandt (1932) introduced an ergometer that used a direct current generator to apply resistive force and Tuttle and Wendler (1945) modified the design so that alternating current could be used. It was not until Fleisch (1950) and von Döbeln (1954) introduced the forerunners that inexpensive friction-braked devices became available commercially. It was a further twenty or so years later before these types of ergometer had a marked impact on studies into MIE when microprocessor-based data logging systems (McClenaghan and Literowitch, 1987) presented new opportunities.

In 1938 Hill published one of the most influential papers on muscle function ever written which described the relationship between the force a muscle can exert and the accompanying speed with which it can shorten. This has become known as the *force–velocity relationship of muscle*. Hill was remarkably modest about this work and claimed later that he 'stumbled upon it' (Hill, 1970, p. 3) and that Fenn and Marsh (1935) had already outlined a similar relationship. A major point to be emphasized here is that peak power output is produced by an optimum load; if the load is either greater or lower, a muscle or group of muscles will not exert peak power output. This presents major implications for meaningful assessments of peak power output during MIE.

11.4 SCREENING

Tests of maximal intensity exercise entail strenuous efforts which might produce feelings of nausea or giddiness. It is important that potential subjects are screened carefully before they are recruited.

11.5 CYCLE ERGOMETER BASED TESTS

Cycle ergometer tests can be categorized into one of four groups:

1. Wingate-type procedures
2. Optimization procedures
3. Correction procedures
4. Isokinetic procedures

The first three of these use friction braked devices whereas the last group uses more elaborate control systems which restrain pedalling to constant velocity. Details of laboratory procedures for the first three types now follow.

11.6 PRACTICAL 1: WINGATE-TYPE PROCEDURES

11.6.1 INTRODUCTION

The Wingate Anaerobic Test (WAnT), so named because it was developed at the Wingate Institute in Israel, was introduced as a prototype in 1974 by Ayalon *et al*. Since then it has been refined and a comprehensive description was published by Bar-Or (1981) and subsequently reviewed (Bar-Or, 1987). Its use has become widespread. Subjects have to pedal flat-out for 30 s on a cycle ergometer against an external resistive load which is usually equivalent to 7.5% of body weight for Monark type ergometers and 4% on Fleisch systems. The aim of the practical proposed here is twofold: first, to describe external power output characteristics during WAnT and second, to examine changes in blood lactate concentration.

11.6.2 EQUIPMENT

A Monark 814E basket-type cycle ergometer with microprocessor linked data logging facilities is used to record movements of either the flywheel or pedals; a separate ergometer can be used during the warm-up. Figure 11.1 shows the general arrangement for the test and Figures 11.2 and 11.3 illustrate detection systems for logging data from movements of the flywheel and pedals, respectively.

11.6.3 METHODS

1. Take a finger prick blood sample at rest. Collect the blood in duplicate i.e. in two microcapillary tubes. One tube is labelled *a* the other *b*. (See Hale *et al*. (1988) for a code of practice on blood sampling.)
2. Subjects should be dressed in shorts and a 'T' shirt. Loose-fitting tracksuit trousers and boot type footwear should be avoided because they can interfere with data logging systems based on the pedal crank.
3. Subjects have a 5 min warm up at 100 W with a flat-out sprint for 5 s at 3 min, followed by 5 min rest.
4. During this time subjects transfer to the test machine. Seat height is adjusted for comfort (Hamley and Thomas, 1967; Nordeen-Snyder, 1977), toe clips are secured (La Voie *et al*., 1984), the resistive load is positioned and a restraining harness should be fixed to ensure that the subject cannot rise from the saddle.

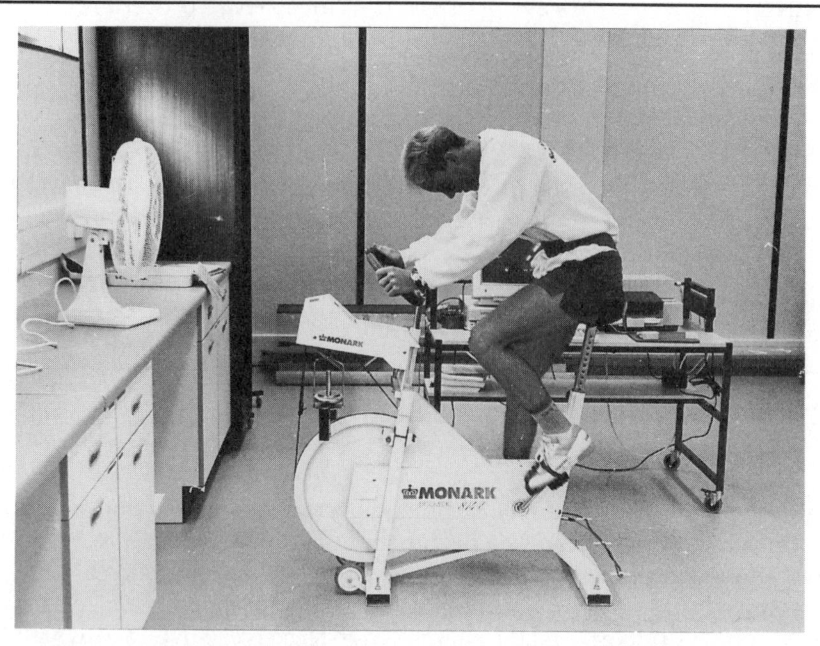

Figure 11.1 General layout of the equipment used in the Wingate Anaerobic Test. The cycle ergometer is bolted to the floor and has a modified load hanger. Note also the use of toe clips and a restraining belt.

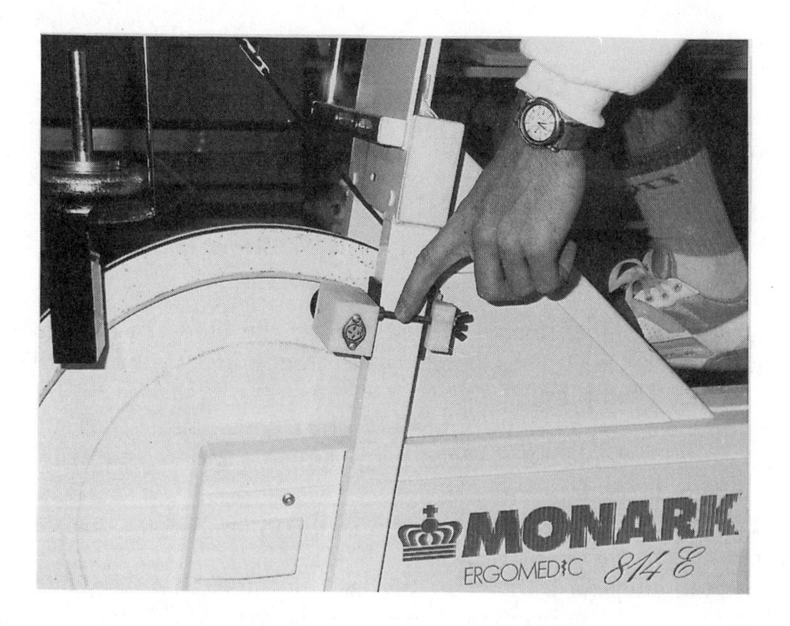

Figure 11.2 Data logging from the flywheel by means of a precision DC motor (Lakomy, 1986).

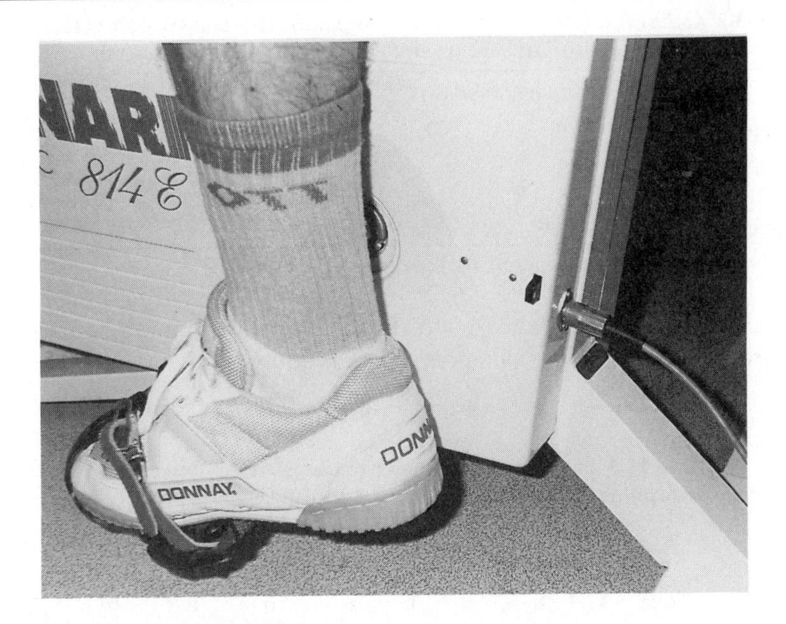

Figure 11.3 Data logging from the passage of the left pedal by means of a photo-optic sensor housed in the chain guard (Winter *et al.*, 1991).

5. Subjects pedal at 50–60 rev min^{-1} with the external load supported. Upon the command, '3, 2, 1, go!' the load is applied abruptly, subjects begin to pedal flat-out and data logging is started.
6. Subjects pedal for 30 s.
7. At the end of the test subjects undertake a suitable warm down, e.g. 2 min of cycling at 100 W.

Table 11.1 Raw data for WAnT on a small sample of 20-year-old male college students

Subject	*Time to peak power (s)*	*Mean power (W)*	*Decay (W)*
1	4.50	635	456
2	2.87	806	538
3	3.45	745	426
4	5.34	813	562
5	3.83	830	446
Mean	4.00	765.8	485.6
SD	0.96	79.8	60.4

8. Take blood samples as in 1. immediately at the end of exercise, 7.5 min and 12.5 min later and determine blood lactate concentration (HLa). This can be done by means of fast response analysers but this practical uses Maughan's (1982) fluorimetric technique which has greater control over the precision of measurement.
9. Complete the results sections (Tables 11.1–11.4).

Table 11.2 Calibration data for blood lactate (HLa). This is a six point calibration, i.e. a blank and five standards are used. Each is analysed in duplicate.

		Standards(mmol l^{-1})				
Tube	*Blank*	*2.5*	*5.0*	*7.5*	*10.5*	*12.5*
1	0	18	35	53	70	91
2	0	18	37	54	72	90
Mean	0	18.0	36.0	53.5	71.0	90.5

Plot the calibration curve including the regression analysis.

The regression equation for the above, which minimizes the sum of squares of residuals about the regression line in a *horizontal* direction, is equal to:

$$x = 0.015 + 0.139y$$

Table 11.3 Samples (fluorimeter reading); note how each of the capillary tubes is analysed in duplicate

	Rest		*0*		*7.5 min PE*		*12.5 min PE*	
Tube	a	b	a	b	a	b	a	b
1	5	6	64	66	75	75	68	61
2	5	6	62	64	76	75	70	62

Table 11.4 Blood lactate values in mmol l^{-1}. Use the regression data from Table 11.2 to convert the instrument readings in Table 11.3. Note how each blood sample is analysed in quadruplicate

	Rest		*0*		*7.5 min*		*12.5 min*	
Tube	a	b	a	b	a	b	a	b
1	0.71	0.85	8.92	9.19	10.45	10.45	9.47	8.50
2	0.71	0.85	8.64	8.92	10.58	10.45	9.75	8.64
Mean	0.71	0.85	8.78	9.06	10.52	10.45	9.61	8.57
Mean	0.78		8.92		10.49		9.09	

11.6.4 SAMPLE RESULTS (TABLES 11.5 AND 11.6)

Mean power output ranges from 400 to 900 W although differences in body size account for some of the difference. Time to peak power output is in the approximate range of 2–6 s, very early in the test, and decay, the difference between the highest value of peak power output and the subsequent lowest value is approximately 40–60% of the mean value. Blood lactate concentrations tend to peak approximately 7–8 min after exercise has ended.

Table 11.5 Sample results for WAnT.

	Mean	*SD*	*Range*
Time to peak power (s)	3.6	1.2	2–6
Mean power (W)	650	80	400–900
Decay (W)	300	50	150–500

Table 11.6 Sample results for blood lactate following performance of the Wingate Anaerobic Test (values are mean, SD)

	Blood lactate ($mmol\ l^{-1}$)
Rest	0.70, 0.15
Immediately post-execise	9.6, 2.1
7.5 min post-execise	12.5, 2.4
12.5 min post-execise	11.0, 2.1

11.6.5 DISCUSSION

In the original WAnT, three measures of performance were recorded: peak power output, mean power output and power decay. For the purposes of recording, the test was subdivided into six 5 s blocks and peak power output invariably occurred in the first 5 s. Although mean power output was demonstrated to be a robust measure and could withstand variations above and below the proposed optimum (Dotan and Bar-Or, 1983), reservations were expressed about the integrity of peak power output. Sargeant *et al.* (1981) suggested that the fixed load of 7.5% of body weight was unlikely to satisfy Hill's force–velocity relationships so casting doubt on this particular measure. Later, Bar-Or (1987) acknowledged that this might be the case and confirmation was provided by Winter *et al.* (1987, 1989). Consequently, it is advisable to omit this measure from data summaries.

Time to peak power can be of interest although the importance placed on this particular measure depends to a large extent on the timing system that is used. With rolling starts, the precise beginning of the test is difficult to identify. Although a stationary start would resolve this issue, it is difficult to set the system in motion from standstill.

After the highest value of power output is produced and although maximal effort is continued, performance begins to deteriorate. This inability to maintain the level of performance is interpreted as 'fatigue'. Traditionally it was thought that mechanisms of adenosine triphosphate (ATP) synthesis are being demonstrated and that performance could be partitioned into *alactic* and *lactacid* phases. Studies that have used muscle biopsy techniques have demonstrated clearly that lactic acid is produced from the moment all-out exercise begins, not when phosphocreatine stores are depleted (Boobis, 1987). Consequently, use of the terms alactacid and lactacid are best avoided.

Blood lactate provides some insights into underlying metabolism, although there are some points of caution that have to be considered. Peak HLa occurs some minutes after exercise has ended and coincidentally, tends to correspond with feelings of nausea. Efflux of lactic acid from muscle cells into interstitial fluid and then into blood takes time and not all of the lactic acid that is produced enters the circulation. Some is used by muscle cells as substrate (Brooks, 1986). Furthermore, some is removed from the circulation before subsequent sampling occurs. This is a timely reminder that although blood lactate can be a useful indicator of metabolism, when non-steady state exercise is under examination, it might well provide a less than clear window through which mechanisms can be viewed.

Differences in performance are partly attributable to differences in body size between subjects so ways to partition out size have to be introduced. This scaling, as it is called, is currently an area of renewed interest (Nevill *et al.*, 1992; Winter, 1992) although early considerations date back more than 40 years (Tanner, 1949). It is now appreciated that the construction of straightforward ratio standards in which a performance variable is simply divided by an anthropometric characteristic such as body mass, probably misleads by distorting the data under investigation. Comparisons between subjects, especially when there are marked differences in size say between men and women or adults and children, should be based on *power function ratios* (Nevill *et al.*, 1992; Welsman *et al.*, 1993; Winter *et al.*, 1993) that are obtained from the allometric relationship between performance and anthropometric variables (Schmidt-Nielsen, 1984). This issue is discussed in more detail in Chapter 15.

Another feature that may be deceptive arises from the expression of fatigue profiles. One might expect that after training, the difference between peak power output and the succeeding lowest value should decrease, but this is not necessarily the case (Hale *et al.*, 1988). Training can produce a higher peak power value so that fatigue actually appears to increase, but this is most likely an artefact of the computation.

11.6.6 CONCLUSIONS

- The Wingate Anaerobic Test is a useful laboratory procedure to demonstrate how fatigue occurs.
- The fixed external resistive force might not satisfy muscle force–velocity relationships so values of peak power output are probably affected adversely.
- Blood lactate does not necessarily provide a full insight into the underlying metabolism.
- Fatigue profiles are ambiguous.
- Differences in the size of subjects should be scaled out using allometry (see Chapter 15).

11.7 PRACTICAL 2: OPTIMIZATION PROCEDURES

11.7.1 INTRODUCTION

Anxieties about the potential inability of fixed external loads to satisfy muscle force–velocity relationships lead to the development of alternative procedures which do provide theoretically sound indications of peak power output. The concern here is not simply with a single isolated muscle, but groups of muscles *in vivo* whose leverage characteristics undergo constant change throughout a complete mechanical cycle.

The availability of 'drop-loading' basket ergometers has played a key role, but the origins of developments date back almost 70 years to when Dickinson (1929) identified an inverse linear relationship between peak pedalling rate and applied load. Vandewalle *et al.* (1985) and Nakamura *et al.* (1985) used the principle to calculate optimized peak power output (OPP) on the basis of data derived from missing flywheel velocity. Acknowledging the reservations about the use of instantaneous values of power output expressed by Adamson and Whitney (1971) and Smith (1972), Winter *et al.* (1991) modified the protocol and recorded movements of the pedals.

The relationship between peak pedalling rate in rev min $^{-1}$ (R) and applied load (L) is in the form:

$$R = a + bL$$

Where: a = intercept of the line of best fit; b = slope of the line of 'best fit.'

On Monark ergometers, one revolution of the pedal crank moves a point on the flywheel a distance of 6 m. Consequently, an expression for power output (W) can be produced: As

$$1\,W = 1\,J\,s^{-1} = 1\,Nm\,s^{-1} \text{ then } W = \frac{R}{60} \times 6\,m \times L \text{ (Newtons)}$$

(R is in rev min^{-1} so has to be divided by 60 to convert it into rev s^{-1})

$$\therefore W = \frac{(a + bL)}{60} \times 6m \times L \text{ (Newtons)}$$

$$\therefore W = \frac{aL}{10} + \frac{bL^2}{10}$$

We can use differential calculus to help us interpret the relationship. By differentiating the power/load expression, which is a quadratic relationship, the gradient at any point on the curve can be identified:

$$\frac{dW}{dL} = a + 2bL$$

At the top of the curve, the gradient is zero:

$$\therefore 0 = a + 2bL$$

$$\therefore L = \frac{-a}{2b}$$

Substituting this value of L in the original equation yields the optimized peak power output i.e.:

$$\text{Optimized peak power output} = \frac{a\left(\frac{-a}{2b}\right)}{10} + \frac{b\left(\frac{-a}{2b}\right)^2}{10}$$

$$= \frac{-0.025\,a^2}{b}$$

Thus, three key measures of performance can be identified:

- Optimized peak power output
- The load corresponding to the optimized peak power output.
- The pedalling rate corresponding to optimized peak power output.

Consider a worked example. Table 11.7 gives peak pedalling rate and applied load data for a female sports studies student.

Table 11.7 Sample results for peak pedalling rate and applied load

Load (N)	*Peak pedalling rate (rev min^{-1})*
44.1	128
34.3	144
53.9	105
24.5	164

Pearson's product moment correlation coefficient and regression data are as follows:

$$r = -0.998$$

$$R = 212.5 - 1.969L$$

$$\text{i.e. } a = 212.5$$

$$b = -1.97$$

Substituting these values of a and b:

Optimized peak power output = 573 W
Optimized load = 53.9 N (5.49 kg)
Optimized pedalling rate = 106.2 rev min^{-1}

The purposes of this practical are to (a) assess these three measures (b) compare them with Wingate derived data and (c) establish the extent to which muscle force–velocity relationships are not satisfied by the Wingate Anaeobic Test (WAnT).

11.7.2 EQUIPMENT

The same as for the WAnT.

11.7.3 METHODS

1. Dress, warm-up and screening procedures are the same as for WAnT.
2. Subjects perform four bouts of all-out exercise against randomly assigned loads as indicated in Figure 11.4. Each bout lasts 10 s and is followed by 1 min of warm down. A period of rest is allowed such that each exercise bout is separated in total by 5 min. Each bout is started in the same way as for WAnT.
3. Loads are assigned according to body mass and guidelines are given in Table 11.8.
4. The order for applying the loads is: Wingate (i.e. 7.5% of body weight), load 2, load 4 and finally load 1.
5. Record peak pedalling rate for each load and calculate the optimized peak power output, optimized load and optimized pedalling rate (Table 11.9).
6. Compare the Wingate derived values of peak power output and peak pedalling rate with the optimized values.

11.7.4 SAMPLE RESULTS

Figure 11.5 illustrates the relationship between peak pedalling rate, power output and applied load. The quadratic relationship between power output and applied load is easily seen.

Tables 11.10 and 11.11 illustrate some typical results. The calculation of the optimized peak power output, load and pedalling rate depends on the linearity of the relationship between peak pedalling rate and applied load. In this example, r was -0.996 ± 0.005 for the men and -0.996 ± 0.006 for the women so the required linearity is clearly illustrated. Values of peak power output derived from the Wingate Anaerobic Test were only ~ 88% of the optimized peak power output (OPP) in men and ~ 90% in women. In addition, the reductions were not consistent. Although values of r were significant ($P < 0.001$), ~20% of the variance of OPP in men and ~16% in women is not accounted for by the relationship with Wingate-derived peak power output values.

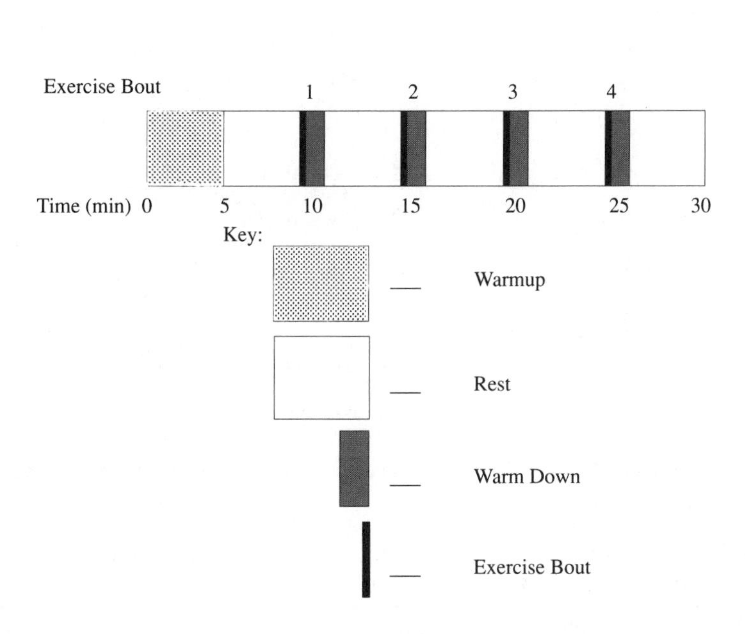

Figure 11.4 Schematic illustration of the protocol for determining optimized peak power output (OPP).

Table 11.8 Suggested loads in newtons for the optimization procedure according to body mass

	Body mass (kg)					
Load	< 50	50–59.95	60–69.95	70–79.95	80–89.95	> 90
1	20.0	25.0	25.0	25.0	30.0	30.0
2	30.0	35.0	37.5	40.0	45.0	47.5
3	Wingate	Wingate	Wingate	Wingate	Wingate	Wingate
4	50.0	55.0	62.5	70.0	75.0	82.5

(9.81 N ≡ 1 kg)

Table 11.9 Peak pedalling rate, load and power output data

Body mass: . . . . . . (kg) Braking forces: 1 . . . . . . kg/ . . . . . . N

2 . . . . . . kg/ . . . . . . N
3 . . . . . . kg/ . . . . . . N
4 . . . . . . kg/ . . . . . . N

Complete the table:

Exercise bout	*Braking force (N)*	*Peak pedalling rate (rev min^{-1})*	*Peak power (W)*
1			
2			
3			
4			

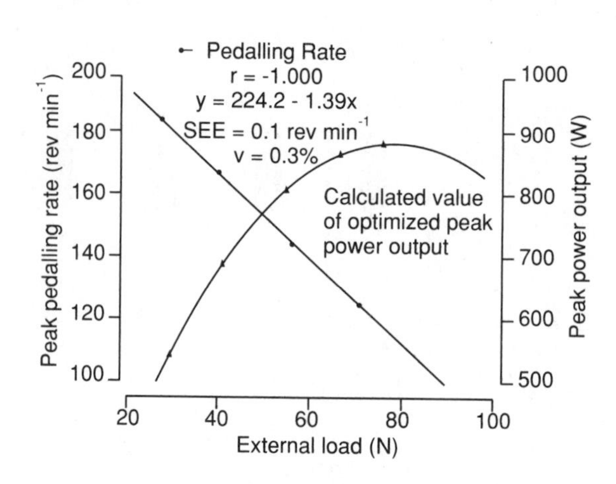

Figure 11.5 An example of the way in which peak pedalling rate and power output are related to the applied braking force.

Table 11.10 Sample results for optimized and WAnT-derived data in men, $n = 19$. Values are mean, SEM (Winter *et al.*, 1987)

	Optimum	*Wingate*	*r*	*t*	*V%*
Peak power (W)	1012, 30	883, 21	0.898[a]	−9.029[a]	5.8
Pedal rate	118.4, 1.8	155.9, 2.5	0.589[b]	−19.078[a]	5.4

[a] $P < 0.001$; [b]$P < 0.01$.

Table 11.11 Sample results for optimized and WAnT-derived data in women, $n = 28$. Values are mean, SEM (Winter *et al.*, 1987)

	Optimum	*Wingate*	*r*	*t*	*V%*
Peak power (W)	640, 20	579, 17	0.918[a]	9.22[a]	6.8
Pedal rate	103.8, 1.6	134.5, 1.7	0.582[b]	−22.571[a]	6.7

[a] $P < 0.001$; [b]$P < 0.01$.

11.7.5 DISCUSSION

The results demonstrate clearly that optimized peak power output (OPP) is greater than Wingate-derived peak power output (WPP) and that the pedalling rate which accompanied WPP is greater than the pedalling rate which accompanied OPP. Consequently, these data confirm the suggestion (Sargeant *et al.*, 1981) that the Wingate load of 7.5% of body weight does not necessarily satisfy muscle force–velocity relationships. Optimized pedalling rate is ~115 rev min^{-1} in men (Sargeant *et al.*, 1984; Nakamura *et al.*, 1985; Winter *et al.*, 1991) and ~ 105 rev min^{-1} in women (Sargeant *et al.*, 1984; Winter *et al.*, 1991). Pedalling rate at WPP is some 15–20% higher in each case. The higher pedalling rate is at the expense of effective force production and hence power output. This reduction in effectiveness is also illustrated by the optimized load which is ~ 11% of body weight in both men and women, and considerably higher than the Wingate value.

Seemingly, optimization procedures are useful and they increase the sensitivity with which maximal intensity exercise can be assessed. However, the protocols are considerably longer than WAnT, even if, as Nakamura *et al.* (1985) suggested, only three loads are used to establish the regression equation that provides the basis for calculating the optimized peak power output. Furthermore, while peak values are identified, the protocols do not assess fatigue profiles and this is a distinct limitation. Nevertheless, the protocols have one distinct advantage; because body weight is supported they isolate activity to the legs and remove potentially contaminating effects from the trunk, head and arms. Similarly, they could be applied to studies that investigate performance characteristics of the arms. Coupled with this is an especially useful anthropometric technique that can assess the total and lean volume of the leg (Jones and Pearson, 1969) and meaningful comparisons of performance capabilities between groups can be made.

Winter *et al.* (1991) compared MIE of men and women and found that there were distinct differences in performance that were independent of differences in the size of the leg. The study also demonstrated the importance of applying correct scaling procedures. Similarly, the techniques have been used to compare children and adults (Winter *et al.*, 1993) where it is suggested that traditional ratio standard measures overestimate children's MIE.

11.7.6 CONCLUSIONS

- Optimization procedures appear to satisfy muscle force–velocity relationships and produce theoretically sound assessments of peak power output.
- Useful studies can be performed when optimization is coupled with anthropometric procedures that assess limb volumes.
- Optimization procedures do not produce valid fatigue profiles.

11.8 PRACTICAL 3: CORRECTION PROCEDURES

11.8.1 INTRODUCTION

Optimization procedures are not the only tests that have been proposed for friction braked cycle ergometers. The completeness of calculations that are used to determine OPP have been questioned by Lakomy (1986) who pointed out that the external resistive load does not account for all the forces applied to the pedals and transmitted to an ergometer's flywheel. Clearly, as the flywheel is accelerated, a force greater than the resistive load is applied to the system and this extra force is ignored in traditional calculations of mechanical work done and hence power output.

Lakomy (1986) determined an 'acceleration balancing load' (EL) which was identified by plotting deceleration of the flywheel from 150 rev min^{-1} against the conventional resistive force. As a result, the effective load, i.e. the actual force applied, could be calculated as:

$$\text{Effective Load (F)} = \text{Resistive Load (RL)} + \text{Excess Load (EL)}$$

The value of F could then be multiplied by the velocity of the flywheel to provide an instantaneous value of power output. By introducing this correction, Lakomy (1985) demonstrated that the lightest loads produced peak power output. A commercially available kit (Concept II) which contains a generator mounted on the flywheel and related computer software can be used with Monark friction-braked ergometers. A similar system was developed by Bassett (1989).

By using the kit, simultaneously data can be logged from the flywheel to calculate corrected peak power output (PPcorr), and from the pedals to calculate OPP. The purpose of this practical is to make such a comparison.

11.8.2 METHODS

1. Warm-up procedures as for Practical 1.
2. Subjects perform the optimization procedure outlined previously.
3. During the 'Wingate Load' bout, i.e. bout one, data are also recorded using the Concept II system and PPcorr is calculated.
4. Record PPcorr, OPP and the pedalling rates for both.

11.8.3 SAMPLE RESULTS

Sample data are illustrated in Table 11.12. The important points to note are that PPcorr is greater than OPP and similarly, pedalling rate is higher for the corrected peak power values.

Table 11.12 Sample data for optimized and corrected peak power output in men, $n = 19$. Values are mean, SEM (Winter and Roberts, 1991)

	Optimized	*Corrected*	*r*	*t*	*V%*
Peak power (W)	915, 35	1005, 32	0.923^{a}	-6.79^{a}	5.4
Pedal rate	110.6, 1.2	127.9, 1.9	0.644^{b}	-11.77^{a}	5.1

^{a} $P < 0.001$; $^{b}P < 0.01$.

11.8.4 DISCUSSION

The value for PPcorr is ~ 10% greater than OPP although the relationship between the measures is strong, 85% of the variance in PPcorr being accounted for by its relationship with OPP. Similarly the pedalling rate for PPcorr is ~15% greater, but in this case only 41% of the variance in this value is accounted for by its relationship with the optimized equivalent. However, the coefficient of variation is smaller than for OPP and this is a good example of the caution that has to be taken when *r* is interpreted. The magnitude of *r* is influenced by the range in the data and it does not necessarily give a proper indication of the relationship between variables. This is a reminder of the care that has to be taken when using *r* (Sale, 1991).

Why should the procedures produce different results? The explanation could be technical in that it is associated with the precision of measurement, but the sensitivity of measurement procedures suggests that this is unlikely. The reason could still be technical because of the procedures for calculating power output which are, of course, distinctly different. The value for OPP is calculated at peak velocity for a complete mechanical cycle of activity whereas PPcorr is based on products of force and instantaneous velocity. This latter procedure has been questioned by Adamson and Whitney (1971) and Smith (1972). Although these products yield the units of power, the meaningfulness of using W is still not clear. Correction procedures are based on systems in which acceleration occurs and in section 11.2, it was pointed out that acceleration and hence change in momentum is attributable not to power but to preceding impulse. Hence, it is the impulse-generating capability of muscle that is manifest but it is described in terms of power. Although there is a difference between OPP and PPcorr, the difference is systematic and the association between the variables is particularly strong.

Clearly, this unresolved debate impacts directly on our understanding of how muscle functions and in particular, how it functions in concert with skeletal, neurophysiological and metabolic systems *in vivo*. Winter and Roberts (1991) have compared OPP and PPcorr but no studies have been undertaken to compare the way in which these values reflect changes in performance brought about by training. From a practical point of view, correction procedures are easier to administer than optimization tests because only one bout of exercise has to be performed. On the other hand optimization procedures satisfy muscle force–velocity relationships and appear to be sound theoretically. This area is still a rich field for further investigative work.

11.8.5 CONCLUSIONS

- Correction and optimization procedures produce different absolute results.
- The relationship between test results is high.

11.9 OTHER PROCEDURES

11.9.1 ISOKINETIC SYSTEMS

Before the advent of optimization and correction procedures, isokinetic systems were introduced to assess peak power output in a way that satisfied muscle force–velocity relationships. Sargeant *et al.* (1981) designed an ergometer in which the pedals were driven at constant angular velocity by an external electric motor and forces applied to the pedals were detected by strain gauges attached to the pedal cranks. By altering pedalling rate externally, force–velocity relationships were explored. McCartney *et al.* (1983) developed a similar system but in this case, the pedals of the ergometer are driven by the subject until an electric motor restricts any further acceleration of the system.

The acquisition of data from these systems is demanding. Data have to be transmitted from a rotating device via a slip ring; this can introduce noise into the signals which can be difficult to suppress. Also, previously questioned instantaneous values of power output are calculated from the products of force and velocity. Conversely, calibration is easier than in friction-braked systems. In the latter, frictional losses from the chain and bearing assemblies are not usually considered whereas in the former, especially with the motor driven version, these losses are irrelevant.

11.9.2 NON-MOTORIZED TREADMILLS

Although cycle ergometry has a number of key advantages, there is one major limitation; it is task specific and therefore does not necessarily reflect performance in running. Within the last decade attempts have been made to redress this problem by means of non-motorized treadmills in which the subject drives the belt of the treadmill. These systems can be used to assess power output while running horizontally (Lakomy, 1984). Subjects are tethered to the apparatus by a suitable harness which contains a force transducer fitted in series. Horizontal force and treadmill speed provide the basis for calculation.

It has been claimed that substantial periods of habituation are required before valid data can be obtained (Gamble *et al.*, 1988). Nevertheless, this type of assessment has been used successfully to examine mechanical characteristics of running (Brooks *et al.*, 1985; Cheetham and Williams, 1985; Cheetham *et al.*, 1986).

11.9.3 'MULTIPLE SPRINT' TYPE PROTOCOLS

Maximal intensity exercise might have to be performed in repeated bouts interspersed with periods of rest. This is typified in what have been termed multiple sprint sports (Williams, 1987) such as soccer, hockey and racket games and is probably the most common type of activity in sport. Common though it is, this type of activity is difficult to model but the challenge has been met by proposals of field-based and laboratory-based procedures.

Léger and Lambert (1982) devised a shuttle running type protocol in which subjects ran 20 m lengths in time to a metronome. Running speed increased progressively until volitional exhaustion occurred. Since then this system has been commercialized (Brewer *et al.*, 1988).

Wootton and Williams (1983) used cycle ergometry and subjects performed five bouts of exercise each of which lasted 6 s with a 30 s rest between each bout. Hale *et al.* (1988) suggested 10 × 6 s sprints and more recently non-motorized treadmills have been used (Hamilton *et al.*, 1991; Nevill *et al.*, 1993) in which up to 30 repeated sprints are required. It is likely that these types of assessment will be used increasingly as investigations into metabolism and mechanisms of fatigue continue.

11.9.4 METABOLISM

Clearly, considerable progress has been made in the development of procedures that can be used to assess MIE and both the sensitivity and integrity of measures have been improved. Although performance can be quantified and underlying metabolism demonstrated, quantification of this underlying metabolism is still a considerable challenge. By way of comparison, the reference measure or gold standard for aerobic exercise is maximum oxygen uptake $\dot{V}O_{2\,max}$ but as Williams (1990) stated (p. 29):

> ... there is not, as yet, an equivalent gold standard for anaerobic exercise which offers the same opportunities for standardization of exercise intensities ...

Why should this be so? The problem is to measure the contribution from anaerobic energy releasing mechanisms up to and including the maximum contribution, i.e. a person's *anaerobic capacity* (AnC). Immediately a dilemma is presented; anaerobic capacity could be expressed as an amount, but the concern is more likely to be with the rate at which energy can be released and the length of time for which this release can be sustained. Furthermore, it was alluded to in section 11.1 that even in a short duration test like WAnT, aerobic mechanisms account for ~20% of total energy provision. To add yet another twist, we have also already seen that previous suggestions that MIE could be partitioned into alactacid and lactacid phases are oversimplifications; energy release from high energy phosphagens and glycolysis occurs simultaneously, not sequentially.

In spite of these difficulties, techniques that attempt to assess anaerobic capacity have been devised and can be categorized into two broad groups (Saltin, 1990). The first uses measures of blood lactate and the second uses measures of excess post-exercise oxygen consumption (EPOC).

Margaria *et al.* (1963) made detailed estimates of the amount of energy released anaerobically based on blood lactate concentrations but the assumptions are bedevilled by confounding factors. Lactic acid produced by muscle cells might be taken up by adjacent fibres and used as substrate (Brooks, 1986) although Saltin (1990) suggested that the amount might be trivial. Furthermore, it is difficult to identify when muscle and blood lactate concentrations are at equilibrium and before an even distribution in the intervening interstitial spaces occurs, at least some lactate will have been metabolized. Lactate in blood does not necessarily reflect the total amount of lactate that is produced. Thus, although it is clear that blood lactate concentrations are an indication of anaerobic metabolism, it is far less clear how these concentrations lead to a precise quantification of anaerobiosis.

The second approach has been to measure the amount of oxygen consumed after exercise has ended. It takes approximately 2–4 min for oxygen uptake to meet the demands of submaximal intensities of exercise, a feature demonstrated more than 70 years ago by Krogh and Lindhard (1919). Contributions from endogenous ATP and CP stores, oxygen from myoglobin and haemoglobin, and glycolysis provide the energy until aerobic mechanisms equilibrate to the demands of exercise. This deficit is restored during recovery. When exercise cannot be performed at steady state, EPOC increases; recently, it has been used in renewed attempts to determine AnC. Medbø *et al.* (1988) measured EPOC in subjects who had performed exhausting exercise and used the term maximal accumulated oxygen deficit (MAOD) to describe EPOC.

The energy cost of exercise has to be known if the contribution from aerobic and anaerobic mechanisms is to be determined. When the exercise is exhausting, this becomes a problem because it is especially difficult to assess the efficiency with which the exercise is performed. Also, as Saltin (1990) stated (p. 391):

> . . . more energy is needed to use lactate as substrate for gluconeogenesis than when lactate is produced and an unknown quantity of lactate is oxidised, which will not then appear as 'extra' oxygen consumption.

Finally, values tend to be expressed as a simple ratio with body mass and so probably scale incorrectly. Nevertheless, in spite of these objections, this seems to be the only method which offers at least the potential to quantify AnC.

11.9.5 SUMMARY

- There has been considerable progress in assessments of MIE which involve brief single bouts of exercise.
- Similarly, successful field- and laboratory-based attempts have been made to model multiple sprint type sports.
- Unequivocal quantification of accompanying metabolism is a challenge that has yet to be met.

REFERENCES

Adamson, G. T. and Whitney, R. J. (1971) Critical appraisal of jumping as a measure of human power, in *Medicine and Sport 6, Biomechanics II* (eds J. Vredenbregt and J. Wartenweiler), S Karger, Basel, pp. 208–11.

Ayalon, A., Inbar, O. and Bar-Or, O. (1974) Relationships among measurements of explosive strength and anaerobic power, in *International Series on Sport Sciences* Vol. I, *Biomechanics IV* (eds R. C. Nelson and C. A. Morehouse), University Press, Baltimore, pp. 572–7.

Bar-Or, O. (1981) Le test Anaérobie de Wingate: caractéristiques et applications. *Symbioses*, **13**, 157–72.

Bar-Or, O. (1987) The Wingate Anaerobic Test: an update on methodology, reliability and validity. *Sports Medicine*, **4**, 381–94.

Bassett, D. R. (1989) Correcting the Wingate Test for changes in kinetic energy of the ergometer flywheel. *International Journal of Sports Medicine*, **10**, 446–9.

Best, C. H. and Partridge, R. C. (1928) The equation of motion of a runner exerting maximal effort. *Proceedings of the Royal Society of London Series B*, **103**, 218–25.

Best, C. H. and Partridge, R. C. (1929) Observations on Olympic athletes. *Proceedings of the Royal Society of London Series B*, **105**, 323–32.

Boobis, L. H. (1987) Metabolic aspects of fatigue during sprinting, in *Exercise: Benefits, Limitations and Adaptations* (eds D. Macleod, R. Maughan, M. Nimmo *et al.*), E & FN Spon, London, pp. 116–43.

Brewer, J., Ramsbottom, R. and Williams, C. (1988) *Multistage Fitness Test – a Progressive Shuttle-run Test for the Prediction of Maximum Oxygen Uptake.* National Coaching Foundation, Leeds.

Brooks, G. A. (1986) The lactate shuttle during exercise and recovery. *Medicine and Science in Sports and Exercise*, **18**, 355–64.

Brooks, S., Cheetham, M. E. and Williams, C. (1985) Endurance training and catecholamine response to maximal exercise. *Journal of Physiology*, **361**, 81P.

Cavagna, G. A. (1975) Force platforms as ergometers. *Journal of Applied Physiology*, **39**, 174–9.

Cheetham, M. E. and Williams, C. (1985) Blood pH and blood lactate concentrations following maximal treadmill sprinting in man. *Journal of Physiology*, **361**, 79P.

Cheetham, M. E., Boobis, L. H., Brooks, S. and Williams, C. (1986) Human muscle metabolism during sprint running in man. *Journal of Applied Physiology*, **61**, 54–60.

Dickinson, S. (1928) The dynamics of bicycle pedalling. *Proceedings of the Royal Society of London Series B*, **103**, 225–33.

Dickinson, S. (1929) The efficiency of bicycle pedalling as affected by speed and load. *Journal of Physiology*, **67**, 242–55.

Dotan, R. and Bar-Or, O. (1983) Load optimisation for the Wingate Anaerobic Test. *European Journal of Applied Physiology*, **51**, 409–17.

Fenn, W. O. (1932) Zür Mechanik des Radfahrens im Vergleich zu der des Laufens. *Pflügers Archiv für gesante Physiologie*, **229**, 354–66.

Fenn, W. O. and Marsh, B. S. (1935) Muscular force at different speeds of shortening. *Journal of Physiology*, **85**, 277–97.

Fleisch, A. (1950) Ergostat a puissances constantes et multiples. *Helvetica Medica Acta Series A*, **17**, 47–58.

Fox, M. L., Bowers, R. W. and Foss, M. L. (1988) *The Physiological Basis of Physical Education and Athletics*, 4th edn, Saunders, Philadelphia.

Furusawa, K., Hill, A. V. and Parkinson, J. L. (1927) The energy used in 'sprint' running. *Proceedings of the Royal Society of London Series B*, **102**, 43–50.

Gamble, D. J., Jakeman, P. M. and Bartlett, R. M. (1988) Force velocity characteristics during non-motorised treadmill sprinting. *Journal of Sports Sciences*, **6**, 156.

Hale, T., Armstrong, N., Hardman, A. *et al.* (1988) *Position Statement on the Physiological Testing of the Elite Competitor*, 2nd edn, British Association of Sports Sciences, Leeds.

Hamilton, A. L., Nevill, M. E., Brooks, S. and Williams, C. (1991) Physiological responses to maximal intermittent exercise: differences between endurance-trained runners and games players. *Journal of Sports Sciences*, **9**, 371–82.

Hamley, E. J. and Thomas, V. (1967) Physiological and postural factors in the calibration of the bicycle ergometer. *Journal of Physiology*, **193**, 55P–57P.

Hill, A. V. (1913) The absolute mechanical efficiency of the contraction of an isolated muscle. *Journal of Physiology*, **46**, 435–69.

Hill, A. V. (1934) The efficiency of bicycle pedalling. *Journal of Physiology*, **82**, 207–10.

Hill, A. V. and Lupton, H. (1922) The oxygen consumption during running. *Journal of Physiology*, **56**, xxxii–iii.

Hill, A. V. (1938) The heat of shortening and the dynamic constants of muscle. *Proceedings of the Royal Society of London Series B*, **126**, 136–95.

Hill, A. V. (1970) *First and Last Experiments in Muscle Mechanics*, Cambridge University Press, London.

Inbar, O., Dotan, R. and Bar-Or, O. (1976) Aerobic and anaerobic components of a thirty-second supramaximal cycling task. *Medicine and Science in Sports*, **8**, 51.

Jones, P. R. M. and Pearson, J. (1969) Anthropometric determination of leg fat and muscle plus bone volumes in young male and female adults. *Journal of Physiology*, **204**, 63P–66P.

Kelso, L. E. A. and Hellebrandt, F. A. (1932) The recording electrodynamic brake bicycle ergometer. *Journal of Clinical and Laboratory Medicine*, **19**, 1105–13.

Krogh, A. and Lindhard, J. (1919) The changes in respiration at the transition from work to rest. *Journal of Physiology*, **53**, 431–7.

Lakomy, H. K. A. (1984) An ergometer for measuring the power generated during sprinting. *Journal of Physiology*, **354**, 33P.

Lakomy, H. K. A. (1985) Effect of load on corrected peak power output generated on friction loaded cycle ergometers. *Journal of Sports Sciences*, **3**, 240.

Lakomy, H. K. A. (1986) Measurement of work and power output using friction loaded cycle ergometers. *Ergonomics*, **29**, 509–17.

La Voie, N., Dallaire, J., Brayne, S. and Barrett, D. (1984) Anaerobic testing using the Wingate and Evans–Quinney protocols with and without toe stirrups. *Canadian Journal of Applied Sport Sciences*, **9**, 1–5.

Léger, L. A. and Lambert, J. (1982) A maximal multistage 20 m shuttle run test to predict $VO_{2\,max}$. *European Journal of Applied Physiology*, **49**, 1–5.

Lupton, H. (1923) An analysis of the effects of speed on the mechanical efficiency of human muscular movement. *Journal of Physiology*, **57**, 337–53.

McCartney, N., Heigenhauser, G. J. F. Sargeant, A. J. and Jones, N. L. (1983) A constant-velocity cycle ergometer for the study of dynamic muscle function. *Journal of Applied Physiology: Respiratory, Environmental and Exercise Physiology*, **55**, 212–17.

McClenaghan, B. A. and Literowitch, W. (1987) Fundamentals of computerised data acquisition in the human performance laboratory. *Sports Medicine*, **4**, 425–45.

Margaria, R., Cerretelli, P., Di Pramprero, P. E. *et al.* (1963) Kinetics and mechanism of oxygen debt contraction in man. *Journal of Applied Physiology*, **18**, 371–7.

Maughan, R. J. (1982) A simple rapid method for the determination of glucose, lactate, pyruvate, alanine, β-hydroxybutyrate and acetoacetate on a single 20 µl blood sample. *Clinica Chimica Acta*, **122**, 231–40.

Medbø, J. I., Mohn, A., Tabata, I. *et al.* (1988) Anaerobic capacity determined by the maximal accumulated oxygen deficit. *Journal of Applied Physiology*, **64**, 50–60.

Nakamura, Y., Mutoh, Y. and Miyashita, M. (1985) Determination of the peak power output during maximal brief pedalling bouts. *Journal of Sports Sciences*, **3**, 181–7.

Nevill, A. M., Ramsbottom, R. and Williams, C. (1992) Scaling measurements in physiology and medicine for individuals of different size. *European Journal of Applied Physiology*, **65**, 110–17.

Nevill, M. E. Williams, C., Roper, D. *et al.* (1993) Effect of diet on performance during recovery from intermittent sprint exercise. *Journal of Sports Sciences*, **11**, 119–26.

Nordeen-Snyder, K. (1977) The effect of bicycle seat height variation upon oxygen consumption and lower limb kinematics. *Medicine and Science in Sports and Exercise*, **9**, 113–17.

Sale, D. G. (1991) Testing strength and power, in *Physiological Testing of the High-Performance Athlete*, 2nd edn (eds J. D. MacDougall, H. A. Wenger and H. A. Green). Human Kinetics, Champaign, IL, pp. 21–106.

Saltin, B. (1990) Anaerobic capacity: past, present and prospective, in *Biochemistry of Exercise VII* (eds A. W. Taylor, P. D. Gollnick, H. J. Green *et al.*), Human Kinetics, Champaign, IL, pp. 387–412.

Sargeant, A. J., Hoinville, E. and Young, A. (1981) Maximum leg force and power output during short term dynamic exercise. *Journal of Applied Physiology: Respiratory, Environmental and Exercise Physiology*, **53**, 1175–82.

Sargeant, A. J., Dolan, P. and Young, A. (1984) Optimal velocity for maximal short-term (anaerobic) power output in cycling. *International Journal of Sports Medicine*, **5**, 124–5.

Sargent, D. A. (1921) The physical test of a man. *American Physical Education Review*, **26**, 188–94.

Sargent, L. W. (1924) Some observations on the Sargent Test of Neuromuscular Efficiency. *American Physical Education Review*, **29**, 47–56.

Sargent, R. M. (1926) The relation between oxygen requirement and speed in running. *Proceedings of the Royal Society of London Series B*, **100**, 10–22.

Schmidt-Nielsen, K. (1984) *Scaling: Why is Animal Size so Important?* Cambridge University Press, Cambridge.

Smith, A. J. (1972) A study of the forces on the body in athletic activities, with particular reference to jumping. Unpublished Doctoral Thesis, University of Leeds.

Tanner, J. M. (1949) Fallacy of per-weight and per-surface area standards and their relation to spurious correlation. *Journal of Applied Physiology*, **2**, 1–15.

Tuttle, W. W. and Wendler, A. J. (1945) The construction, calibration and use of an alternating current electrodynamic brake bicycle ergometer. *Journal of Laboratory and Clinical Medicine*, **30**, 173–83.

Vandewalle, H., Pérès, G., Heller, J. and Monod, H. (1985) All out anaerobic capacity tests on cycle ergometers: a comparative study on men and women. *European Journal of Applied Physiology*, **54**, 222–9.

Von Döbeln, W. (1954) A simple bicycle ergometer. *Journal of Applied Physiology*, **7**, 222–4.

Welsman, J., Armstrong, N., Winter, E. and Kirby, B. J. (1993) The influence of various scaling techniques on the interpretation of developmental changes in peak VO_2. *Pediatric Exercise Science*, **5**, 485.

Williams, C. (1987) Short term activity, in *Exercise: Benefits, Limits and Adaptations* (eds D. Macleod, R. Maughan, M. Nimmo *et al.*), E & FN Spon, London, pp. 59–62.

Williams, C. (1990) Metabolic aspects of exercise, in *Physiology of Sports* (eds T. Reilly, N. Secher,

P. Snell and C. Williams), E & FN Spon, London, pp. 3–40.

Winter, E. M. (1992) Scaling: partitioning out differences in body size. *Pediatric Exercise Science*, **4**, 296–301.

Winter, E. M. and Roberts, N. K. A. (1991) Optimized and corrected peak power output during cycle ergometry in men. *Journal of Sports Sciences*, **9**, 436.

Winter, E. M., Brookes, F. B. C. and Hamley, E. J. (1987) A comparison of optimised and non-optimised peak power output in young, active men and women. *Journal of Sports Sciences*, **5**, 71.

Winter, E. M., Brookes, F. B. C. and Hamley, E. J. (1989) Optimised loads for external power output during brief, maximal cycling. *Journal of Sports Sciences*, **7**, 69–70.

Winter, E. M., Brookes, F. B. C. and Hamley, E. J. (1991) Maximal exercise performance and lean leg volume in men and women. *Journal of Sports Sciences*, **9**, 3–13.

Winter, E. M., Brookes, F. B. C. and Roberts, K. W. (1993) The effects of scaling on comparisons between maximal exercise performance in boys and men. *Pediatric Exercise Science*, **5**, 488.

Wootton, S. and Williams, C. (1983) The influence of recovery duration on repeated maximal sprints, in *Biochemistry of Exercise* (eds H. G. Knuttgen, J. A. Vogel and J. Poortmans), Human Kinetics, Champaign, IL, pp. 269–73.

PART FOUR

SPECIAL CONSIDERATIONS

THERMOREGULATION 12

T. Reilly and N. T. Cable

12.1 INTRODUCTION

The human is homeothermic, meaning that body temperature is maintained within narrow limits independently of fluctuations in environmental temperature. For thermoregulatory purposes the body can be regarded as consisting of a core within which the temperature is 37°C and an outer shell where the ideal temperature is 33°C, although this is largely dependent on environmental factors. The precise temperature gradient from core to skin depends on the body part, but generally speaking the size of the gradient that exists between the skin and the environment will determine the amount of heat that is lost or gained by the body.

12.2 PROCESSES OF HEAT LOSS/HEAT GAIN

Normally the body is maintained in thermoequilibrium or heat balance. Heat is produced by metabolism and the level of heat production can be increased dramatically by physical exercise. The processes of conduction, convection and radiation allow for either heat loss or heat gain (depending on environmental conditions) with evaporation being a major avenue of heat loss when body temperature is rising.

The heat of basal metabolism is about 1 kcal $kg^{-1} h^{-1}$. 'One kcal (4.186 kJ) is the energy required to raise 1 kg of water through 1°C. The specific heat of human tissue is less than this, 0.83 kcal of energy being needed to raise 1 kg of tissue through 1°C. Thus if there were no avenue of heat loss, the temperature of the body would rise by 1°C per hour in an individual with body mass of about 72 kg, and within 4–6 hours death from overheating would follow. The process would be accelerated during exercise when energy expenditure might approach 25 kcal min^{-1} (105 kJ min^{-1}). This value might include 1 kcal min^{-1} for basal metabolism and 6 kcal min^{-1} for producing muscular work. The remaining 18 kcal is dissipated as heat which builds up within the body. In this instance the theoretical rise in body temperature would be 20°C in just over one hour. Obviously maintaining life depends on the ability to exchange heat with the environment.

A number of factors contribute to heat production and heat loss (Figure 12.1). The maintenance of a relatively constant core

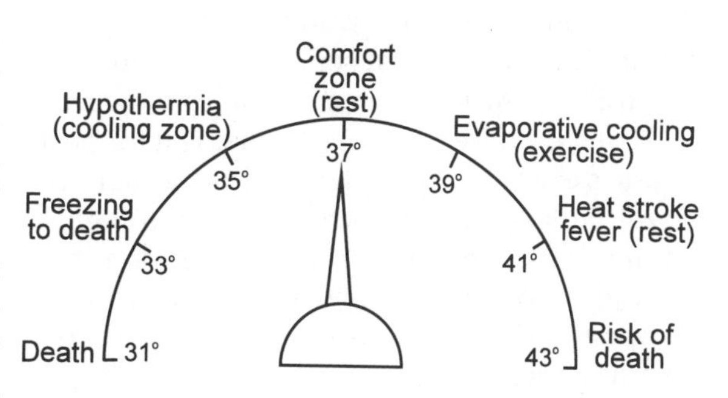

Figure 12.1 The body temperature range.

Kinanthropometry and Exercise Physiology Laboratory Manual: Tests, procedures and data Edited by Roger Eston and Thomas Reilly. Published in 1996 by E & FN Spon. ISBN 0 419 17880 5

temperature is frequently expressed in the form of a heat balance equation:

$$\text{Heat stored} = \text{Metabolic rate} - \text{Evaporation} \pm \text{Radiation} \pm \text{Convection} \pm \text{Conduction} - \text{Work done}$$

Heat may be gained from terrestrial sources of radiation or from solar radiation while the body radiates heat to its immediate environment. In physical terms the human body can be regarded as a black box, the body surface being a good absorber of radiant heat and also a good radiator. Convection refers to transfer of heat by movement of gas or fluid. The barriers to convective heat exchange include subcutaneous adipose tissue, clothing and films of stationary air or water in immediate contact with clothing. Conduction describes heat transfer from core through body fluids to the surface of the body and exchange with the environment by direct contact of the skin with objects, materials or surfaces.

Evaporative heat loss includes vaporization of water from moist mucous membrane of the upper respiratory tract with breathing, insensible perspiration through the skin and evaporation of sweat from the surface of the body. When water evaporates from any surface, that surface is cooled. When sweat droplets fall from the skin, no heat is exchanged. At rest in a room temperature of 21°C the heat lost by a nude man would be about 60% from radiation, 25% evaporation from lungs and skin, 12% by means of convective air currents and 3% by means of conduction from the feet. During exercise the main mechanism for heat loss is evaporation of sweat. This mechanism will be less effective when the air is highly humid, 100% relative humidity meaning that the air is totally saturated already with water vapour and can take up no more at the prevailing temperature.

The rate of evaporative heat loss is dependent on the vapour pressure gradient across the film of stationary air surrounding the skin and on the thickness of the stationary film. It is influenced also by air movement over the skin surface. Evaporative loss from the lungs depends on minute ventilation, dryness of the atmosphere and the barometric pressure. Consequently, dry nose and throat are experienced at altitude where the atmosphere pressure is lower than at sea level.

12.3 CONTROL OF BODY TEMPERATURE

Body temperature is regulated by temperature-sensitive neurons located in the anterior and posterior hypothalamus. These cells detect the temperature of the circulating blood, with those cells in the anterior hypothalamus responding to an increase in body temperature and those in the posterior portion triggering the effector response to a decrease. These areas also receive afferent input from peripheral warm and cold receptors located in the skin and therefore receive information about changes in the body's immediate environment. Warm receptors in the skin are stimulated in the temperature range of 28–45°C. Paradoxically, above this level the cold receptors begin to fire, particularly if the skin is subjected to a rapid increase. This is called paradoxical inhibition and gives the sensation of cold in very hot surroundings (e.g. shower).

During exposure to cold, or when body temperature decreases, the posterior hypothalamus initiates a number of responses. This activity will be neurally mediated via the sympathetic nervous system, and will result in a generalized vasoconstriction of the cutaneous circulation. Blood will be displaced centrally away from the peripheral circulation, promoting a fall in skin temperature which will ultimately increase the temperature gradient between the core and the skin. Importantly however, this reduction in skin temperature will decrease the gradient that exists between the skin and the environment, and therefore reduce the potential for heat loss from the body. Superficial veins are also affected such that blood returning from the limbs is diverted from them to the vena comitantes that overlie the main arteries. The result is that arterial blood is cooled by the venous return almost immediately it enters the limb by means of the countercurrent heat exchange mechanism.

The reduction in blood flow is not uniform throughout the body, its effects being most pronounced in the extremities. Severe cold may decrease blood flow to the fingers to 2.5% of its normal value whereas, in contrast, flow to the head remains unaltered. There are no vasoconstrictor fibres to the vessels of the scalp which seem to be slow in responding to the direct effect of cooling (Webb, 1982). As heat loss to the head can account for up to 25% of the total heat production, the importance of covering the head to protect against the cold is clear. This would apply equally to the underwater swimmer moving headfirst through the water and to the jogger or skier in winter weather. Froese and Burton (1957) showed that there is a linear relationship between heat loss through the head and ambient temperature within the range – 20° C to + 32°C, emphasizing the need to insulate the top of the head in extreme cold.

Paradoxically, if the environment is extremely cold, there may be a delayed vasodilation of the blood vessels in the skin which alternates with intense vasoconstriction in cycles of 15–30 min and leads to excessive heat loss. This has been described as a hunting reaction in the quest for an appropriate skin temperature to effect the best combination of gradients between core, shell and environment. The vasodilation may be the result of accumulated vasoactive metabolites arising from increased anaerobic metabolism in local tissues which is associated with the reduced blood flow. The explanation by Keatinge (1969) is that the smooth muscle in the walls of peripheral blood vessels are paralysed at temperatures of 10°C; as the muscles cannot then respond to noradrenaline released by vasoconstrictor nerves, the muscles relax to allow a return of blood flow through the vessels, thus completing the cycle. This alternation of high and low blood flow to local tissue produced by ice-pack application is exploited in the treatment of sports injuries by physiotherapists. The phenomenon is also well recognized by runners and cyclists if they train in cold conditions without wearing gloves; initially the fingers are white but become a ruddy colour as blood enters the digits in increased volumes. Blood flow to the skin may also be influenced by alcohol which has a vasodilator effect. Though alcohol can make the individual feel more comfortable when exposed to cold, it will increase heat loss and so may endanger the individual. Consequently, drinking alcohol is not recommended when staying outdoors overnight in inclement weather conditions and the customary hip-flask of whisky serves no useful protective function for recreational skiers or mountaineers.

Shivering represents a response of the autonomic nervous system to cold. It constitutes involuntary activity of skeletal muscles and the resultant heat production may be as large as three times the basal metabolic rate. Indeed, metabolic rates five times that at rest have been reported (Horvath, 1981), though such values are rare. Shivering tends to be intermittent and persists during exercise until the exercise intensity is sufficient on its own to maintain core temperature. The piloerection response to cold that is found in animals is less useful to the human who lacks the furry overcoat to the skin that cold-dwelling animals possess. Contraction of the small muscles attached to hair roots causes air to be trapped in the fur and this impedes heat loss. The pilomotor reflex in humans has little thermal impact but is reflected in the appearance of goose pimples. Paradoxically, the 'gooseflesh syndrome' is sometimes found in marathon runners during heat stress when heat loss mechanisms begin to fail, the condition being accompanied by a sensation of coldness (Pugh, 1972).

Elevation of basal heat production may be brought about by the neuroendocine system in conditions of long-term cold exposure. The hypothalamus stimulates the pituitary gland to release hormones that affect other target organs, notably the thyroid and adrenal glands. Thyroxine causes an increase in metabolic rate within 5–6 hours of cold exposure. This elevation will persist throughout a sojourn, the metabolic rate at rest being greater in cold than in temperate climates and elevated over that of tropical residents. Adrenaline and adrenocortical hormones may also cause a slight increase in metabolism, though the combined hormonal effects are still relatively modest. Brown fat, so-called because of its iron-containing cytochromes active in oxidative processes, is a potential source of thermogenesis. This form of fat is located primarily in and around the kidneys and adjacent to the great vessels, beneath the shoulder blades and along the spine. It is evident in abundance in infants but its stores decline during growth and development. Its high metabolic rate has been presented as an explanation of why some individuals fail to increase body weight despite appearing to overeat, though this point is highly contentious.

The anterior hypothalamus initiates vasodilation of the cutaneous circulation in response to an increase in body temperature. This results in an expansion of the core and ultimately increases the temperature gradient between the skin and the environment, allowing for greater heat exchange. Cutaneous vasodilation is initiated by a removal of vasoconstrictor tone in the skin, and enhanced by the release of vasodilator substances (bradykinin and vasoactive intestinal polypeptide) from the sweat glands following stimulation via sympathetic cholinergic fibres. These substances are thought to cause the smooth muscle of the cutaneous blood vessels to relax and allow total peripheral resistance to decrease and thereby increasing blood flow. Evidence for this response comes from individuals with a congenital lack of sweat glands, who are not able to increase skin blood flow when body temperature increases.

It is, therefore, evident that the process of thermoregulation is subserved by the cardiovascular system. That is to say, heat is gained or lost by changes in blood flow. Such changes in blood flow must obviously have ramifications for the control of blood pressure. If total peripheral resistance is increased (i.e. when body temperature falls and skin blood flow is restricted), blood pressure will increase. Conversely with peripheral vasodilation skin blood flow is enhanced and blood pressure may fall. Thus thermoregulatory responses can initiate changes in non-thermal control mechanisms. Examples of this include the increased diuresis seen in cold weather. As total peripheral resistance increases, antidiuretic hormone secretion is reduced and therefore less fluid is reabsorbed from the kidney; ultimately some blood volume is lost which returns blood pressure to normal. Conversely, the soldier that stands on parade for a number of hours in the heat will, following increases in skin blood flow, no longer be able to maintain blood pressure sufficiently to perfuse the cerebral circulation, and therefore may faint to allow blood flow to return to normal.

12.4 THERMOREGULATION AND OTHER CONTROL SYSTEMS

During exercise, particularly in the heat, sweating becomes the main mechanism for losing heat. Sweat is secreted by corkscrew-shaped glands within the skin and it contains a range of electrolytes as well as substances such as urea and lactic acid. Its concentration is less than in plasma and so sweat is described as hypotonic. Altogether there are about 2 million eccrine sweat glands in the human body, though the number varies between individuals; the other type, apocrine sweat glands are found mainly in the axilla and groin and are not important in thermoregulation in the human. While exercising hard in hot conditions, the amount of fluid lost in sweat may exceed $2\,l\,h^{-1}$ so athletes may lose 5–6% of body weight as water within 2 hours of heavy exercise. This would amount to over 8% of body water stores and represent a serious level of dehydration. The normal body water balance is illustrated in Table 12.1. As thermoregulatory needs tend to override the physiological controls over body water, sweat secretion will continue and exacerbate the effects of dehydration until heat injury is manifest. Costill (1981) demonstrated how losses are distributed among body water pools during prolonged exercise. Muscle biopsies were taken before, during and after exercise in active and non-active muscles and blood samples were also obtained. It was calculated that extracellular and intracellular and total body water values decreased by 9, 3 and 7.5%, respectively. The conclusion was that electrolyte losses in sweat did not alter the calculated membrane potential of active and inactive muscles sufficiently to be the cause of cramp suffered in such conditions.

Table 12.1 The 24-hour water balance in a sedentary individual

Intake (ml)		*Output (ml)*	
Solid and semi-solid food	1200	Skin	350
Water released in metabolism	300	Expired air	500
Drinks (water, tea, fruit juice, coffee, milk and so on)	1000	Urine	1500
Total	2500	Faeces	150
		Total	2500

Effects of dehydration are manifest at a water deficit of 1% of body weight in a sensation of thirst. This is due to a change in cellular osmolarity and to dryness in the mucous membrane of the mouth and throat. The sensation can be satisfied long before the fluid is replaced so that thirst is an imperfect indicator of the body's needs. As fluid may be lost at a greater rate than it can be absorbed, regular intakes of water, say 150 ml every 10–15 min, are recommended in events such as marathon running. This can halt the rise in heart rate and body temperature towards hyperthermic levels that might otherwise have resulted. Energy drinks have no added value for thermoregulatory purposes, though hypotonic solutions have marginal benefits in terms of the speed at which the ingested fluid is absorbed. Indeed it is a sound practice to start contests in hot conditions well stocked up with body water and then take small amounts of fluid frequently en route. However, in prolonged endurance events care must be taken not to over-hydrate as this can lead to the development of hyponatraemia or water toxicity, which if severe may need hospitalization. This condition usually only presents itself in avid water drinkers, but is becoming more common during events such as 'ironman' triathlons and 'ultra marathons'.

Boxers and wrestlers are known to use dehydrating practices to lose weight before their events and stay within the limit of their particular weight categories. In many cases the use of diuretics for the purpose of body water loss has been suspected. The practice is dangerous, especially if the impending contest is to be held in hot conditions and severe levels of dehydration have been induced prior to weighing-in. It was soundly condemned by a position statement of the American College of Sports Medicine in 1976 which was updated in 1984.

Effects of dehydration on performance vary with the amount of fluid lost and the nature of the activity being performed. These are compounded when accompanied by imminent hyperthermia due to a combination of high humidity and high ambient temperature. Throughout the history of sport there are many dramatic examples of competitors suffering from heat stress. Television audiences witnessing transmission of the first Women's Olympic Marathon in 1984 empathized with the struggle of the Swiss competitor to complete the course. The Irish boxer, Barry McGuigan, lost his world title in the heat of Las Vegas, having had difficulty in making the scheduled weight limit before the fight. Examples of less fortunate victims of heat stress were the deaths of the Danish cyclist at the Rome Olympics in 1960 and later that of the British professional cyclist, Tommy Simpson. In both cases the use of amphetamines was allegedly implicated, these having an enhanced effect on performance but a deleterious effect on thermoregulatory mechanisms.

The fact that body water content is variable should be taken into account when body composition is assessed from measurements of body water. This applies to chemical methods for measuring body water and predicting body fat values from the measurements. It applies also to the use of bioelectric impedance analysis (BIA) methods which record conductance or resistance of the whole body in response to a low voltage signal administered to the subjects. The resistance is dependent on water content and estimates of body fat will be affected by the state of the subject's hydration (Brodie *et al.*, 1991).

Women are often reputed to have inferior thermoregulatory functions to men during exercise in the heat. It seems that the early studies reporting women to be less tolerant of exercise in the heat ignored the low fitness levels of the women. Though women tend to have more body fat than men and so greater insulation properties, their larger surface area relative to mass gives them an advantage in losing heat. There appears to be no sex difference in acclimatization to heat and the frequency of heat illness in road races in the USA is approximately the same for each sex (Haymes, 1984).

There are, however, differences between the sexes that should be considered when body temperature is concerned. The greater subcutaneous tissue layers in females should provide them with better insulation against the cold. In females the set point is not fixed at 37°C but varies with the menstrual cycle. In mid-cycle there is a sharp rise of about 0.5°C which is due to the influence of progesterone and this elevation is indicative of ovulation.

There is also a circadian rhythm in body temperature which is independent of the environmental conditions. Core temperature is at a low point during sleep and is at its peak at about 18:00 hours (Figure 12.2). The peak to trough variation is about 0.6°C and this applies to both males and females. The amplitude is less than this in aged individuals. There is a wealth of evidence intimating that many types of sports performance follow a curve during the day that is closely linked to the rhythm in body temperature (Reilly, 1990).

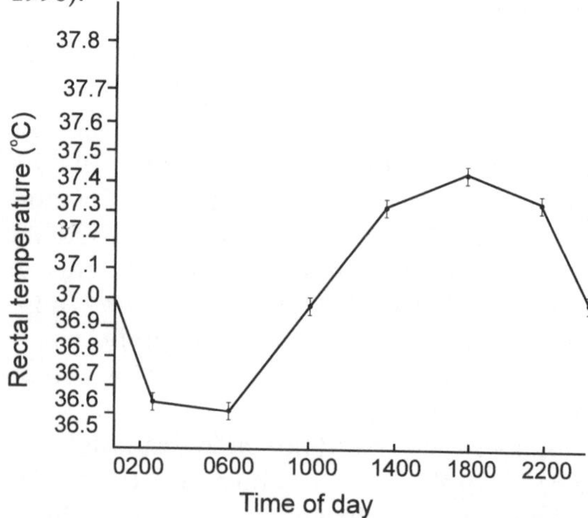

Figure 12.2 Circadian variation in core temperature.

12.5 MEASUREMENT OF BODY TEMPERATURE

Core temperature refers to the thermal state of essential internal organs such as heart, liver, viscera and brain. Although it is normally considered that core temperature is regulated about an internal temperature of 37°C, this value varies depending on the site of measurement. There are also rhythmic changes in the temperature set point which varies during exercise and in fever.

Rectal temperature is the most commonly used site for indicating core temperature in athletes. The probe should be inserted to a depth of

8 cm beyond the sphincter ani if reliable measures are to be obtained. Care is also necessary that probes are sterilized and treated with HIV risk in mind. Rectal temperature is not the best measure of core temperature in situations where temperature is changing rapidly. For this reason oesophageal temperature is preferred in some exercise experiments. This entails inserting a probe through the nose and threading it into the oesophagus.

An alternative is tympanic temperature where a sensor is placed adjacent to the tympanic membrane. Caution is necessary as it is easy to damage the membrane and also the ear must be completely insulated to avoid environmental influences. External auditory meatus temperatures can also be measured by inserting a probe 1 cm inside the ear canal and insulating the ear. However, with this measurement and those of rectal and oesophageal temperatures, it is best to represent data as a change from baseline since a temperature gradient exists down these tissues.

Oral or sublingual temperatures, typically measured with a mercury thermometer, are used in clinical rather than exercise contexts and give values about 0.4°C lower than rectal temperature. Oral temperature is of little use in swimmers, for example, whose mouths are affected by surrounding water and high ventilation rates. Similarly measurement of axilla or groin temperatures in athletic subjects gives a poor indication of their thermal status. A radiosensitive pill which can be swallowed and then monitored by radio-telemetry has been used in occupational contexts. Difficulties include the necessity for accurate calibration, differences in temperature between the internal organs adjacent to the passage of the pill, the influences of recently digested food on core temperature and the unsavoury task of its retrieval once the pill has traversed the full course of the digestive tract. A more acceptable alternative is to measure the temperature of mid-stream urine which gives a reasonable indication of internal body temperature.

Skin temperature has conventionally been measured by thermistor and thermocouples. Optoelectronic devices are now also available. The common method is to place thermistors over the surface of the skin and tape over them. From measurements of a number of designated skin sites, a mean skin temperature may be calculated. The formulae that require the least number of observations are;

$$\text{MST} = 0.5\,T_c + 0.36\,T_l + 0.14\,T_a$$

(Burton, 1935)

$$\text{MST} = 0.3\,T_c + 0.3\,T_a + 0.2\,T\,\text{thigh} + 0.2\,T_l$$

(Ramanathan, 1964)

where MST is mean skin temperature, T_c is temperature of the chest juxta nipple, T_l is leg temperature measured over the lateral side of the calf muscle, and T_a is lower arm temperature. Mean body temperature (MBT) may then be calculated by weighting rectal temperature T_r and MST in the ratio 4:1. In other words: $\text{MBT} = 0.8\,T_r + 0.2\,\text{MST}$.

12.6 THERMOREGULATORY RESPONSES TO EXERCISE

Exercise implies activity of skeletal muscle and this demands energy. Most of the energy utilized is dissipated as heat, a small amount contributing towards mechanical work. The muscular efficiency represents the work performed as a percentage of the total energy expenditure. For cycle ergometry this value is about 22% depending on whether or not the resting energy expenditure is taken into consideration. In swimming, this value is much lower; in weight-lifting, it has been calculated to be about 12% (Reilly, 1983). It is acknowledged that the mechanical efficiency is difficult to estimate in activities such as running.

During sustained exercise the cardiac output supplies oxygen to the active muscles but also distributes blood to the skin to cool the body. In cases where cardiac output is maximal, the exercise performance is impaired by thermoregulatory needs. Since the maximal cardiac output determines how well blood can be distributed for peripheral cooling, the heat load induced by exercise is a function of the percentage of maximal oxygen uptake rather than the absolute work rate engaged.

The body acts as a heat sink in the early minutes of exercise and blood is shunted from viscera and other organs to the exercising muscles. Blood flow to the brain remains intact although there seems to be differential distribution to areas within the brain. If exercise imparts a severe heat load, the sweat glands are activated and droplets appear on the skin surface after about 7 min. The extent to which body temperature rises then depends on the exercise intensity and the environmental conditions.

12.7 ENVIRONMENTAL FACTORS

Heat exchange with the environment is influenced by a number of environmental variables as well as individual characteristics. The clothing and equipment used also affect heat exchange. Thus some background is provided on relevant interactions with the environment in this section before progressing to anthropometric considerations in the next.

Athletic contests are sometimes held in conditions that challenge the body's thermoregulatory system. Cold is less of a problem than heat since athletes usually choose to avoid extremes of cold. Exceptions are winter sports such as mountaineering where it is imperative to protect the individuals against the cold. Outdoor games, such as American football, are also sometimes played in freezing conditions.

Experiments in cold air close to freezing have not consistently shown a significant effect on the maximal oxygen uptake. The effects are more marked in the periphery of the body where the drop in temperature of tissues is most pronounced. Normally the mean skin temperature is about 33°C and extreme discomfort is felt when this drops below 25°C. As skin temperature of the hand falls below 23°C, movements of the limb begin to get clumsy and finger dexterity is severely affected at skin temperatures between 13 and 16°C. This is especially critical in winter sport activities that require fine manipulative actions of the fingers which are impaired because of numbness in those digits. Tactile sensitivity in the fingers is also affected for the worse to the extent that an impact on the skin at 20°C has to be about six times greater than normal for usual sensations to be felt. The skeletal muscles function at an optimal internal temperature and when this drops to about 27°C, the muscle's contractile force is much impaired. This can be demonstrated by the progressive decline in grip strength with increased cooling of the arm. In sports such as downhill skiing, the performer could be cooled during the chair lift to the top of the ski-run and must therefore take steps to keep the limb muscles warm prior to skiing. Synovial fluid in the joints also becomes colder and more viscous, thus increasing the stiffness of the joints. The fatigue curve of muscle also deteriorates due to a combination of factors such as impaired strength, lower blood flow, increased resistance of connective tissue and increased discomfort.

One of the most important consequences of sports participation outdoors in the cold is the poorer neuromuscular co-ordination that may result. As temperature in nervous tissue falls, conduction velocity of nerve impulses is retarded and this slows reaction time. If the slide in temperature is not reversed, eventually complete neural block occurs. Co-ordination is also impaired by the effect of cold on the muscle spindles which, at 27°C, respond to only 50% of normal to a standardized stimulus. Consequently, the stumbling and poor locomotion of climbers in the cold may be due to impairments in peripheral nerves.

Frostbite is one of the risks of recreational activities in extreme cold. This can occur when the temperature in the fingers or toes falls below freezing and at – 1°C ice crystals are formed in those tissues. The results can be a gangrenous extremity often experienced by mountaineers in icy conditions when their gloves or boots fail to provide adequate thermal insulation. Recent clinical experience is that amputation of damaged tissue is not a necessary consequence of frostbite and prognosis tends to be more optimistic than thought in previous decades. Of more serious consequence is a fall in the body's core temperature. The cold stress is progressively manifested by an enlargement of the area of the shell while the area of the core becomes smaller until its temperature ultimately begins to fall dangerously. A core temperature of 34.5°C is usually taken as indicative of grave hypothermic risk, though there is no absolute consensus of a critical end point. Some researchers assume that a rectal temperature of 32–33°C is a critical end point, though the exact value of hypothalamic temperature for fatality is subject to controversy.

Scientists have used metaphorical models to predict survival time by extrapolating from initial rates of decline in core temperature to an arbitrary value of 30°C (Ross *et al.*, 1980). This avoids the need to take subjects too close to a risk of hypothermia. Researchers in Nazi concentration camps were not so considerate to their prisoners who were cooled to death at core temperatures of about 27°C. An example was given by Holdcroft (1980) of an alcoholic woman exposed overnight in Chicago to subfreezing temperatures and whose rectal temperature was reported to be 18°C when she was found in a stupor. In hindsight it is doubtful if this was representative of core temperature in these conditions. Happily, she survived after being re-warmed in a hospital room temperature of 20°C. Death usually occurs at a much higher core temperature than that reported for the fortunate Chicago woman, shivering being usually replaced by permanent muscle rigidity, then loss of consciousness at core temperatures of 32°C and heart failure may follow. The range of clinical symptoms associated with hypothermia is presented in texts such as Holdcroft (1980).

Behavioural strategies and proper clothing can safeguard individuals in cold environments. Enormous strides have been made in the provision of protective equipment against the cold for sportsmen and -women. Major advances have been made in clothing design and in the reliability and durability of tents. A similar systematic improvement is noted in the provision of first-aid and rescue services for most outdoor pursuits. The specially treated sheets of foil paper readily availed of by recreational marathon runners to safeguard against rapid heat loss on cessation of activity are an example.

Existence of good rescue facilities is no excuse for climbing parties to take risks in inclement weather. Early warning systems used by rangers on mountainsides must be heeded if they are to be effective and this inevitably means consumer education. Otherwise, the safety of the rescue team in addition to that of the climbing party may be jeopardized if weather conditions further deteriorate. Assessment of the risk involves some calculations of the magnitude of cold stress. On the mountainside the wind velocity may be the most influential factor in cooling the body so that the ambient temperature alone would grossly underestimate the prevailing risk. The wind-chill index designed by Siple and Passel (1945), and widely used by mountaineers and skiers, provides a method of comparing different combinations of temperature and wind speed. The values calculated correspond to a caloric scale for rate of heat loss per unit body surface area; they are then converted in to a sensation scale ranging from hot (about 80) through cool (400) to bitterly cold (1200) and on to a value where exposed flesh freezes within 60 s. The cooling effects of combinations of certain temperatures and wind speeds are expressed as 'temperature equivalents' and are estimated with a nomogram. Use of the wind-chill index enables sojourners to evaluate the magnitude of cold stress and take appropriate precautions. Wet conditions can exacerbate cold stress, especially if the clothing worn begins to lose its insulation. Attention to safety may be even more important in water sports since, apart from the risk of drowning, body heat is lost much more rapidly in water than in air.

The formula of Siple and Passel for calculating heat loss was:

$$K_O = (\sqrt{100\,V} + 10.5 - V)\,(33 - T)$$

where K_O = heat loss in kcal h^{-1}
V = wind velocity in m s^{-1}
T = environmental temperature in °C
10.5 = a constant
33 = assumed normal skin temperature in °C

Water has a much greater heat conduction capacity than air and so heat is readily exchanged with the environment when the human body is immersed. Though mean skin temperature is normally about 33°C, a bath at that temperature feels cold, yet if the water temperature is elevated by 2°C, the temperature of the body will begin to rise. This suggests that the human is poorly equipped for spending long spells in the water. Finding the appropriate water temperature is important for swimming pool managers who have to cater for different levels of ability. The preferred water temperature for inactive individuals is 33°C, for learners it is about 30°C, for active swimmers it is in the range of 25–27°C, whereas competitive swimmers are more content with temperatures between 20 and 25°C. Generally the water is regulated to suit the active user. Indeed, the whole environment of the swimming pool must be engineered for the comfort of users. Condensation in the arena may not be welcomed by spectators, but the high humidity in the swimming pool militates against heat loss when the swimmer is out of the water. Engineering may involve double glazing of the surround to avoid losing radiant heat outwards from the building as well as provision of supplementary radiant heating. Permissible indoor dew points can be calculated from temperature differences between outdoors and inside the pool to avoid high condensation risks, these being the points where moisture is deposited. Ventilation rates inside the building may reduce the moisture content of indoor areas to decrease the discomfort of spectators, but this will cool the bather and call for increased heating costs. A practical compromise is to have air temperatures in the region of 28–30°C, which are much warmer than normal office room temperatures.

In hot conditions, heat stroke is a major risk and should be classed as an emergency. It reflects failure of normal thermoregulatory mechanism. It is characterized by body temperature of 41°C or higher, cessation of sweating and total confusion. Once sweating stops, the body temperature will rise quickly and soon cause irreversible damage to liver, kidney and brain cells. In such an emergency immediate treatment is essential.

Calculating the risk of heat injury requires accurate assessment of environmental conditions. The main factors to consider are dry bulb temperature, relative humidity, radiant temperature, air velocity and cloud cover. Dry bulb temperature can be measured with a mercury glass thermometer whereas relative humidity can be calculated from data obtained from a wet bulb thermometer used in either a sling psychrometer or a Stevenson screen. The dew point temperature, the point at which the air becomes saturated, is a measure of absolute humidity and it can be measured with a whirling hygrometer. Radiant temperature is measured by a globe thermometer inserted into a hollow metal sphere coated with black matt paint. Air velocity can be measured by means of a vane anemometer or an alcohol thermometer coated with polished silver. Cloud cover will protect against solar radiation and may provide some intermittent relief to the athlete. More details of the measuring devices and their operations are contained in the classical publication by Bedford (1946).

A problem for the sports scientist is to find the proper combination of factors to reach an integrated assessment of the environmental heat load. Many equations have been derived for this purpose and three-quarters of a century of research to this end were reviewed by Lee (1980). Most of the formulae incorporate composites of the environmental measures whereas some, such as the predicted 4-hour sweat rate (P4SR), predict physiological responses from such measures. Probably the most widely used equation in industrial and military establishments has been the WBGT Index, WBGT standing for wet bulb and globe temperature. The US National Institute of Occupational Safety and Health recommended it as the standard heat stress index in 1972. The weightings underline the importance of considering relative humidity:

$$WBGT = 0.7\,WBT + 0.2\,GBT + 0.1\,DBT$$

where WB represents wet bulb
G indicates globe
DB represents dry bulb
T indicates temperature

A comprehensive selection of indices derived in the United Kingdom and the USA was given by Lee (1980). A later development is the Botsball which was validated by Beshir *et al.* (1982). It combines the effects of air temperature, humidity, wind speed and radiation into a single reading. It got its name from its designer, Botsford, and the WBGT can be reliably predicted from it if necessary.

Heat stress indices provide a framework for evaluating the risk of competing in hot conditions and for predicting the casualties. The American College of Sports Medicine (1984) has set down guidelines for distance races, recommending that events longer than 16 km should not be conducted when the WBGT Index exceeds 28°C. This value is often exceeded in distance races in Europe and in the USA during the summer months and in many marathon races in Asia and Africa. It is, however, imperative in all cases that the risks be understood and that symptoms of distress are recognized and promptly attended to. The plentiful provision of fluids en route and facilities for cooling participants are important precautionary steps.

12.8 ANTHROPOMETRY AND HEAT EXCHANGE

The exchange of heat between the human and the environment is affected by both body size and body composition. Age, sex and physique of the individual are relevant considerations also.

The exchange of heat is a function of the body surface area relative to body mass. The dimensional exponent for this relation is 0.67. The smaller the individual the easier it is to exchange heat with the environment. Consequently children gain and lose heat more quickly than do adults and marathon runners on average tend to be smaller than those specializing in shorter running events. It is important to recognize that children are more vulnerable than grown ups in extremes of environmental conditions.

It is thought that elderly people living alone prefer warmer environments than younger individuals due to their lower metabolic rate. This is countered by a decrease in insensible perspiration due to a change in the vapour diffusion resistance of the skin with age. There is a higher incidence of death from hypothermia in old people living alone in the European winter than in the general population. These deaths are more likely to be due to socioeconomic conditions and physical immobility than to thermoregulatory changes with age.

Physiological thermoregulatory responses, notably skin blood flow and sweat rates, to heat stress tend to diminish with increasing age. This is probably due to age-related changes in the skin. Nevertheless, changes in core temperature and heat storage often show only marginal age-related effect if healthy men and women preserve a high degree of aerobic fitness. The ability to exercise in hot conditions is more a function of the status of the oxygen transport system (especially maximal oxygen uptake and cardiac output) than of chronological age.

Differences between the sexes in heat exchange are largely explained by body composition, physique and surface to volume ratios. These predominate once differences in fitness levels are taken into account.

Adipose tissue layers beneath the skin act to insulate the body and are protective in cold conditions. The degree of muscularity or mesomorphy can add to this. Ross *et al.* (1980) demonstrated that prediction of survival time in accidental immersion in water should take both endomorphy and mesomorphy into consideration and the best prediction was when the entire somatotype was taken into account. Pugh and Edholm (1955) in their classical studies of English channel swimmers showed that the leaner individuals suffered from the cold much earlier than did those with high proportions of body adiposity. They compared responses of two ultra-distance swimmers in water of 15°C. The larger and fatter individual showed no decrease in rectal temperature for 7 h, after which his radial pulse was impalpable for 50 min. The lighter and leaner swimmer was taken from the water after half an hour when his rectal temperature had dropped from 37 to 34.5°C. In their studies in a swimming flume Holmer and Bergh (1974) found that oesophageal temperature was constant at a water temperature of 26°C in subjects operating at 50% $\dot{V}O_{2\,max}$, except for a decrease in those with low body fat. They would be at an even greater disadvantage in colder water.

Racial differences in thermoregulatory response to heat seem to reflect physiological adjustments to environmental conditions more than genetic factors. Acclimatization to heat occurs relatively rapidly, a good degree of adaptation being achieved within two weeks. Sweating capacity is increased, concentrations of electrolytes in sweat are reduced due to an influence of aldosterone and there is an expansion of plasma volume. The sensitivity of the sweat glands is altered so that more sweat is produced for a given rise in core temperature. It is less clear how genetic and acclimatization factors are separated for cold exposure, since diet, activity, living conditions and so on are confounding factors. Studies of the Ama, professional pearl divers of Korea and Japan, suggest a mild adjustment to chronic cold water exposure occurs (Rahn and Yokoyama, 1965). Thermal conductance in a given water temperature was found to be lower for diving than for non-diving women matched for skinfold thickness. These divers were also reported to have higher resting metabolic rates which would help them to preserve heat. A similar vasoconstriction to reduce thermal conductance of tissues was reported by Skreslet and Aarefjord (1968) in subjects diving with self-contained underwater breathing apparatus (SCUBA) in the Arctic for 45 days.

The elevation of metabolic rate is also found in Eskimos when their thermal values are compared to Europeans. To what extent this can be attributed to diet and the specific dynamic activity of food is not clear. Adaptive vasoconstriction is most pronounced in Aborigines sleeping semi-naked in near-freezing temperatures in the Australian 'outback'. By restricting peripheral circulation, they can tolerate cold conditions that would cause grave danger to sojourners similarly exposed. This circulatory adjustment occurs without an increase in metabolic rate.

12.9 PRACTICAL EXERCISES

It is easier to demonstrate thermoregulatory factors using single-case studies as examples. Experiments require controlled laboratory conditions and usually prolonged exercise is involved. In the absence of an environmental chamber, three different laboratory demonstrations are suggested.

12.10 PRACTICAL 1: MUSCULAR EFFICIENCY

This practical entails exercise under steady-rate conditions on a cycle ergometer with work rate being controlled and metabolic responses measured. From these measurements the muscular efficiency of exercise can be calculated.

12.10.1 AIM

To examine the efficiency of various cycling cadences.

12.10.2 EQUIPMENT

Electrically braked cycle ergometer.
Oxygen consumption (e.g. On-line system or Douglas bags and oxygen and carbon dioxide analysers).

12.10.3 PROTOCOL

An electrically braked ergometer maintains workload independent of changes in pedal cadence. In this instance the work rate chosen was 120 W. The subject has $\dot{V}O_2$ measured whilst sitting still, then commences exercise pedalling at a frequency of 50 rev min^{-1} for 20 min with $\dot{V}O_2$ measured during the last 2 min. This is followed by a 10 min rest period and then this regimen is performed twice more using exactly the same workload but with new pedalling frequencies of 70 and 100 rev min^{-1}.

12.10.4 CALCULATIONS

$$\text{Gross efficiency} = \frac{\text{Work done (kJ min}^{-1}\text{)}}{\text{Energy expended (kJ min}^{-1}\text{)}}$$

where 1 Watt = 0.06 kJ min^{-1}
Energy expended = $\dot{V}O_2$ (l min^{-1}) × Caloric equivalent (see Table 8.3).
Net efficiency; as above except that resting $\dot{V}O_2$ must be subtracted from the exercise value.
(Note: If an electrically braked cycle ergometer is not available, use a mechanically braked ergometer and exercise entailing a steady-state protocol.)

12.10.5 EXAMPLES OF CALCULATIONS

Efficiency

e.g. Work rate = 120 W
= 7.2 kJ min^{-1}

Resting $\dot{V}O_2$ = 0.25 l min^{-1}

Exercise $\dot{V}O_2$ = 2.0 l min^{-1}

RER = 0.85

Energy equivalent for 2.0 l min^{-1} at RER = 0.85 = 20.3 KJ min^{-1}.

$$\text{Therefore Gross efficiency} = \frac{7.2}{2.0 \times 20.3} \times 100$$

$$= 17.74\%$$

$$\text{Net efficiency} = \frac{7.2}{(2.0 - 0.25) \times 20.3} \times 100$$

$$= 20.3\%$$

12.11 PRACTICAL 2: THERMOREGULATORY RESPONSES TO EXERCISE

The laboratory exercise involves recordings of rectal and skin temperatures at regular intervals during sustained performance. This may be undertaken on either a motor-driven treadmill or a cycle ergometer. The purpose is to demonstrate physiological responses to exercise using thermoregulatory variables.

An example is shown in Figure 12.3. The exercise intensity was 210 W sustained for 60 min. Rectal temperature and skin temperatures were calculated. The rectal temperature rose by 2°C during the experiment.

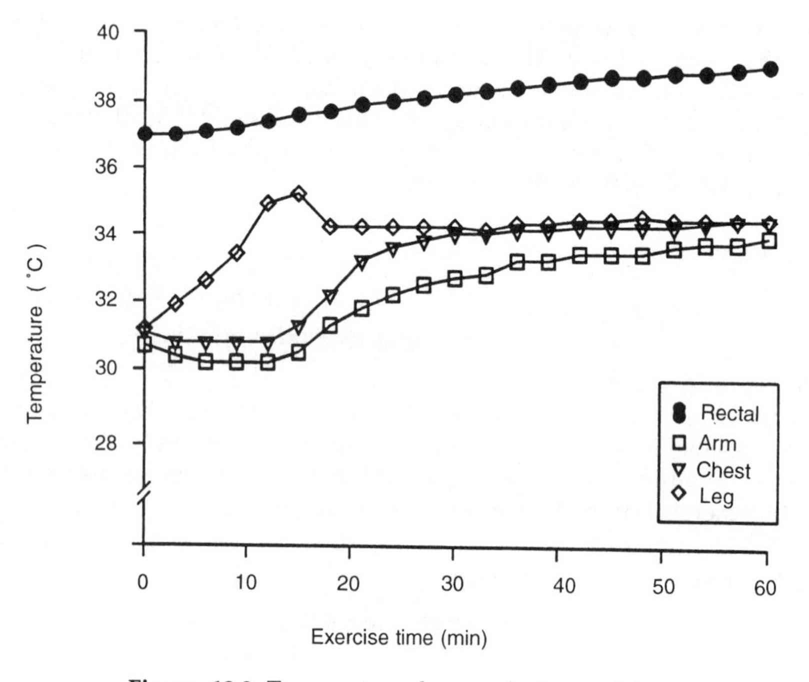

Figure 12.3 Temperature changes during exercise.

12.11.1 AIM

To investigate the thermoregulatory response to steady state and incremental exercise.

12.11.2 EQUIPMENT

- Cycle ergometer
- Weighing scales
- Rectal thermistor (e.g. Yellow Springs)
- Analogue or digital temperature monitor
- Electrocardiogram or short-range radio telemetry (e.g. Sport Tester)

12.11.3 PROTOCOL

The subjects should place the rectal thermistor 10 cm beyond the external anal sphincter and attach skin thermistors on the sternum, on the medial forearm midway between elbow and wrist, on the anterior surface of the thigh midway between hip and knee and on the lateral surface of the lower leg between knee and ankle. Measure the subject's mass immediately prior to exercise. One subject exercises at 70% maximum heart rate for 60 min with measurements of all variables taken at 5 min intervals. The other subject exercises at 60 W for 5 min with the workload increased by 30 W each subsequent 5 min until exhaustion. Variables should be measured every minute. At the completion of exercise subjects should be weighed immediately (without drying the skin) to obtain an index of sweat evaporation rate.

12.11.4 CLEANING OF PROBES

Rectal probes should be washed in warm soapy water and then immersed in a 1:20 concentrate of Milton solution (sterilization fluid) for at least 30 min. On removal from the solution, the probes should be left to dry completely in room air before further use. Skin probes can be washed and immersed in a 1:40 solution of Milton for 10 min and left to dry.

12.12 PRACTICAL 3: ESTIMATION OF PARTITIONAL HEAT EXCHANGE

12.12.1 AIM

To examine the effect of different environmental conditions on evaporative and partitional heat exchange during exercise.

12.12.2 EQUIPMENT

- Cycle ergometer
- Weighing scales
- Rectal thermistor (e.g. Yellow Springs)
- Four skin thermistors (e.g. Yellow Springs)
- Analogue or digital temperature monitor

12.12.3 PROTOCOL

The same subject exercises on two separate occasions, once in normal ambient conditions (21°C) and again in a hotter environment at the same workload. Immediately prior to exercise the individual is weighed (with all probes and clothes) and then completes 30–60 min of exercise followed by rapid reweighing. All temperatures are measured every 5 min and $\dot{V}O_2$ at 20 min intervals.

12.12.4 CALCULATIONS

Heat balance equation

$$HS = M \pm (R \pm C \pm C) - E - W$$

where

$$\text{Metabolism} = \frac{\dot{V}O_2\ (\text{l min}^{-1}) \times \text{caloric equivalent} \times 60}{\text{Body surface area (BSA)}}$$

$$\text{Evaporation} = \frac{(\text{pre-mass} - \text{post-mass})\ (\text{kg}) \times 2430\ (\text{kJ l}^{-1}\ \text{sweat loss})}{\text{Time of exercise (h)} \times \text{BSA}}$$

$$\text{Work} = \frac{\text{work rate (kJ min}^{-1} \times 60)}{\text{BSA}}$$

$$\text{Stored heat} = \frac{(\text{post } T_B - \text{pre } T_B) \times 3.47\ (\text{kJ kg}^{-1}\ \text{h}^{-1} \times \text{mass})}{\text{Time (h)} \times \text{BSA}}$$

All units are kJ m^{-2} h^{-1}.
Example of calculations using the following data:

$\dot{V}O_2$ = 2.0 l min^{-1}
RER = 0.85
pre-rectal temp = 36.5°C
post-rectal temp = 38.0°C
pre-skin temp = 33.0°C
post-skin temp = 33.9°C
pre-mass = 72.0 kg
post-mass = 71.5 kg
body surface area = 1.8 m^2
work rate = 120 W
duration of exercise = 60 min

$$\text{Metabolism} = \frac{\dot{V}O_2 \times \text{caloric equivalent} \times 60}{\text{BSA}}$$

$$= \frac{2.0 \times 20.3 \times 60}{1.8}$$

$$= 1353.33\ \text{kJ m}^{-2}\ \text{h}^{-1}$$

$$\text{Evaporation} = \frac{\text{Weight loss} \times 2430}{\text{Time} \times \text{BSA}}$$

$$= \frac{(72.0 - 71.5) \times 2430}{1 \times 1.8}$$

$$= 675 \text{ kJ m}^{-2} \text{h}^{-1}$$

$$\text{Work} = \frac{\text{Workload} \times 60}{\text{BSA}}$$

$$= \frac{7.2 \times 60}{1.8} \text{ i.e. } 7.2 \text{ kJ min}^{-1}$$

$$= 240 \text{ kJ m}^{-2} \text{h}^{-1}$$

$$\text{Stored heat (HS)} = \frac{(\text{post-}T_B - \text{pre-}T_B) \times 3.47 \times 72}{\text{Time} \times \text{BSA}}$$

where $T_B = (0.65 \text{ rectal}) + (0.35 \text{ skin})$

$$= \frac{(36.57 - 35.28) \times 3.47 \times 72}{1 \times 1.8}$$

$$= 179.1 \text{ kJ m}^{-2} \text{h}^{-1}$$

$$\text{Heat balance HS} = M - E \pm (R \pm C \pm C) - W$$

therefore rearranging

$$\text{partitional heat exchange} = HS - M + E + W$$

$$= 179.1 - 1353.3 + 675 + 240$$

$$= -259.2 \text{ kJ m}^{-2} \text{h}^{-1}$$

Therefore in the above example 259.2 kJ m^{-2} h^{-1} is lost from the body by the combined processes of radiation, conduction and convection.

REFERENCES

American College of Sports Medicine (1984) Position Statement. Prevention of thermal injuries during distance running. *Physician and Sportsmedicine*, **12** (7), 43–51.

Bedford, T. (1946) Environmental warmth and its measurement. *Medical Research Council War Memorandum no. 17*. HMSO London.

Beshir, M. Y., Ramsey, J. D. and Burford, C. L. (1982) Threshold values for the Botsball: a field study of occupational heat. *Ergonomics*, **25**, 247–54.

Brodie, D. A., Eston, R.G., Coxon, A. Y. (1991) Effect of changes of water and electrolytes on the validity of conventional methods of measuring fat-free mass. *Annals of Nutrition and Metabolism*, **35**, 89–97.

Burton, A. L. (1935) Human calorimetry. *Journal of Nutrition*, **9**, 261–79.

Costill, D. L. (1981) Muscle water and electrolyte distribution during prolonged exercise. *International Journal of Sports Medicine*, **2**, 130–4.

Froese, G. and Burton, A. C. (1957) Heat loss from the human head. *Journal of Applied Physiology*, **10**, 235–41.

Haymes, E. M. (1984) Physiological responses of female athletes to heat stress: a review. *Physician and Sportsmedicine*, **12**, no. 3, March.

Holdcroft, P. (1980) *Body Temperature Control*, Bailliere Tindall London.

Holmer, I. and Bergh, U. (1974) Metabolic and thermal responses to swimming in water at varying temperatures. *Journal of Applied Physiology*, **37**, 702–5.

Horvath, S. M. (1981) Exercise in a cold environment. *Exercise and Sport Science Reviews*, **9**, 221–63.

Keatinge, W. R. (1969) *Survival in Cold Water*, Blackwell, Oxford.

Lee, D. H. K. (1980) Seventy five years of searching for a heat index. *Environmental Research*, **22**, 331–56.

Pugh, G. (1972) The gooseflesh syndrome in long distance runners. *British Journal of Physical Education*, March, ix–xii.

Pugh, L. G. C. and Edholm, O. G. (1955) The physiology of channel swimmers. *Lancet*, **ii**, 761–8.

Rahn, H. and Yokoyama, T. (eds) (1965) *Physiology of Breathold Diving and the Ama of Japan*, National Academy of Sciences, Washington, DC.

Ramanathan, N. L. (1964) A new weighting system for mean temperature of the human body. *Journal of Applied Physiology*, **19**, 531–3.

Reilly, T. (1981) *Sports Fitness and Sports Injuries*, Faber and Faber, London.

Reilly, T. (1983) The energy cost and mechanical efficiency of circuit weight training. *Journal of Human Movement Studies*, **9**, 39–45.

Reilly, T. (1990) Human circadian rhythms and exercise. *Critical Reviews in Biomedical Engineering*, **18**, 165–80.

Ross, W. R., Drinkwater, D. T. Bailey, D. A. *et al.* (1980) Kinanthropometry; traditions and new perspectives, in *Kinanthropometry II* (eds M. Ostyn, G. Beunen and J. Simons), University Park Press, Baltimore, pp. 3–27.

Siple, P. A. and Passel, C. F. (1945) Measurement of dry atmospheric cooling in sub-freezing temperatures. *Proceeding of the American Philosophical Society*, **89**, 177–99.

Skreslet, S. and Aarefjord, F. (1968) Acclimatisation to cold in man induced by frequent scuba diving in cold water. *Journal of Applied Physiology*, **24**, 177–81.

Webb, P. (1982) Thermal problems in *The Physiology and Medicine of Diving* (eds O. G. Edholm and J. S. Weiner), Bailliere Tindall, London, pp. 297–318.

ASSESSING PERFORMANCE IN YOUNG CHILDREN 13

C. Boreham

13.1 INTRODUCTION

Physiological testing of children's performance may be undertaken for a number of reasons, including the following.

1. Performance enhancement – the regular monitoring of physiological function in young sportspersons may help in the identification of strengths and weaknesses, and as a motivation for training.
2. Educational – there is little doubt that fitness testing in the school setting is enjoyable and instructive for the vast majority of pupils, and can be used as an educational tool, particularly in relation to health-related aspects of exercise.
3. Research – there is a growing academic interest in paediatric exercise science, whether from the health, performance or growth viewpoints. The measurement of physiological fitness and various anthropometric factors may shed light on important issues such as the effect of intensive sport participation on growth, and the effect of growth on sport performance.
4. Clinical diagnosis and rehabilitation – as with adults, the diagnosis and treatment of certain clinical conditions in children may be helped by exercise testing. This topic has been comprehensively covered by Bar-Or (1983) and Rowland (1993).

The diversity of approaches outlined above is matched by the variety of methods used to measure performance in children. These vary from sophisticated laboratory-based techniques (e.g. for measuring aerobic power and capacity, isokinetic strength, anaerobic power and so on) to simple 'field' tests of fitness (e.g. sit ups, jumping tests, timed distance runs and grip strength). The latter have often been grouped into 'batteries' of tests, which purportedly measure a variety of fitness variables in children. Such batteries include the North American AAHPERD tests (1988) and the European EUROFIT tests (1988). The limitations of such test batteries may include the high skill factor involved in performing individual test items (and hence the possibility of improvement merely reflecting the learning process) and difficulties in validation. However, their usefulness, particularly in an educational setting or where large numbers of individuals need to be tested with limited resources, is often underestimated (Kemper, 1990).

Before examining specific areas of performance testing in children, it is important to review the processes of growth and maturation, and how these may influence test results. Without doubt, a basic understanding of the biological changes which occur throughout childhood, but most particularly at adolescence, is essential if test results are to be interpreted correctly.

Kinanthropometry and Exercise Physiology Laboratory Manual: Tests, procedures and data Edited by Roger Eston and Thomas Reilly. Published in 1996 by E & FN Spon. ISBN 0 419 17880 5

13.2 GROWTH, MATURATION AND PERFORMANCE

Postnatal growth may be divided into four phases: infancy (from birth to one year), early childhood (preschool), middle childhood (to adolescence) and adolescence (from 8–18 years for girls and 10–22 years for boys). As children younger than 8–9 years are seldom engaged in competitive sport, and may not possess the motor skills or the intellectual or emotional maturity required for successful fitness testing, the remainder of this chapter will deal primarily with the immediate pre-adolescent and adolescent phases of childhood. Important gender differences will be highlighted.

Generally speaking, sex differences which may influence performance are minimal before adolescence. However, girls begin their adolescent growth spurt on average, two years before boys (12 years and 14 years, respectively), which can confer a temporary advantage of height and weight for girls around this time (Figure 13.1). Boys eventually surpass girls in most dimensions during their adolescent growth spurt to attain, on average, a larger stature in adulthood. During the early part of the growth spurt, rapid growth in the lower extremities is evident, whereas an increased trunk length occurs later, and a greater muscle mass later still. There are also noticeable regional differences in growth during adolescence. Boys, for example have only a slightly greater increase in calf muscle mass than girls, but nearly twice the increase in muscle mass of the arm during the adolescent growth spurt (Malina and Bouchard, 1991).

Relatively minor somatic differences between boys and girls are magnified during

Figure 13.1 A group of 12-year-old schoolchildren illustrates typical variation in biological maturation at this age.

adolescence. Following the growth spurt, girls generally display a broader pelvis and hips, with a proportionately greater trunk: leg ratio. Body composition also changes from approximately 20% body fat to 25% body fat over this period. Boys, in contrast, may actually become slightly leaner (from 16% to 15% body fat) over the adolescent growth period – a change that is accompanied by a dramatic rise in lean body mass, shoulder width (the shoulder/hip ratio is 1.40 in prepubertal children, but 1.45 in postpubertal boys and 1.35 in mature girls), and leg length. Such differences between the sexes – the boys being generally leaner, more muscular, broader shouldered and narrower hipped with relatively straighter limbs and longer legs – have obvious implications for physical performance. Some examples of results from common field tests applied over the adolescent period illustrate these differences clearly (Figure 13.2a, b). It should be borne in mind when comparing physical performances of male and female adolescents, that other factors such as motivation and changes in social interests (Malina and Bouchard, 1991) and the documented fall-off in physical activity, particularly in girls (Boreham *et al.*, 1993) may also influence results.

There is no such individual as the 'average adolescent' performer and confusion can arise as a result of the enormous individual variation inherent in the processes of biological maturation and sexual differentiation. Although peak height velocity may, on average, be reached at 12 years for girls and 14 years for boys, there may be as much as five years difference in the timing of this phenomenon, and similar variation in the development of secondary sex characteristics, between any two individuals of the same sex. Thus, a child's chronological age may bear only a passing resemblance to its biological age – the latter being of greater significance to physical performance. This is illustrated in Figure 13.3 which shows that for most performance measures – the notable exception being maximal aerobic power – the early maturer is at a distinct advantage. This is particularly so for tasks requiring strength and power, possibly reflecting the tendency for early maturers to be more mesomorphic than late developers. Such biological variation may be exacerbated by differences in chronological age. Within a single year group, a given child may be up to 11 months older than his or her peer. In the rapidly growing adolescent age group, this age difference may confer considerable physical advantages to the older child. A

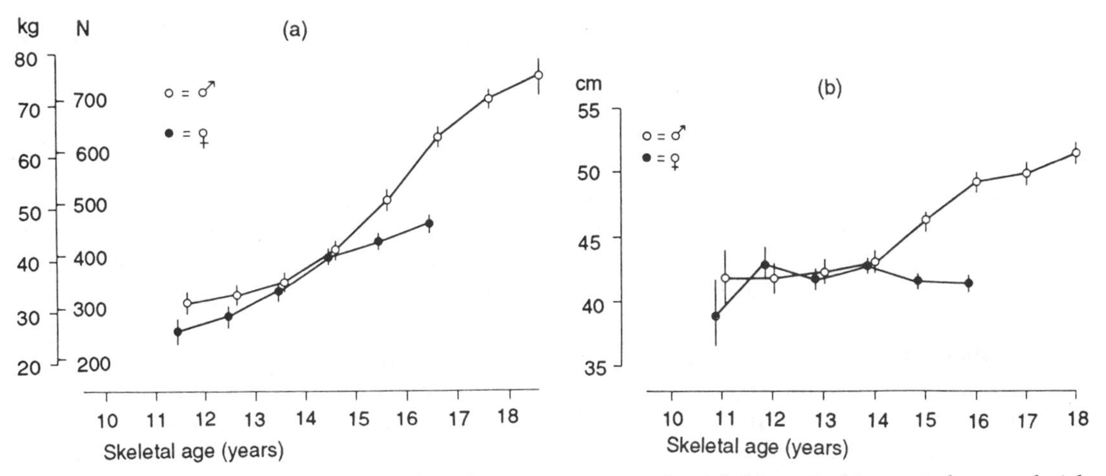

Figure 13.2 Mean and standard error for (a) static arm strength, and (b) vertical jump, in boys and girls versus skeletal age. (Reproduced from Kemper (1985) with the permission of S Karger AG, Basel.)

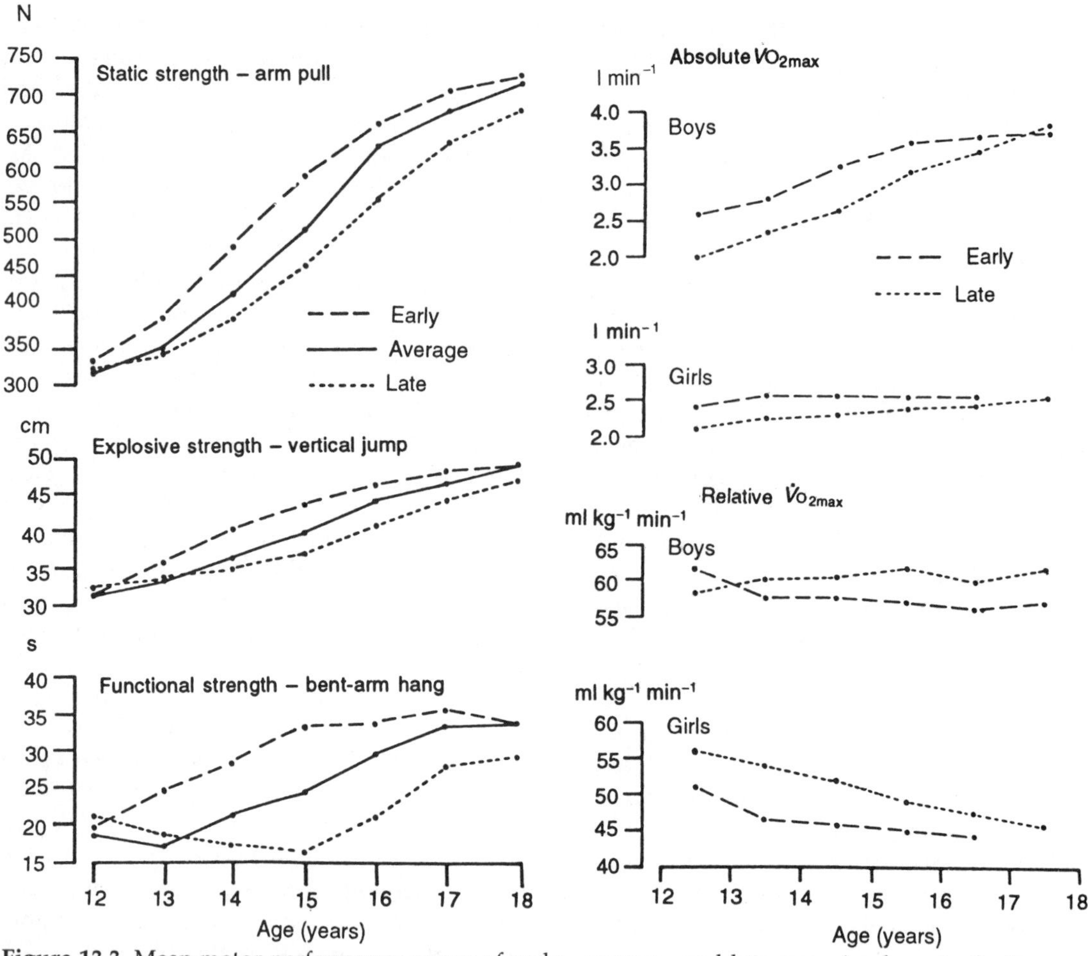

Figure 13.3 Mean motor performance scores of early-, average- and late-maturing boys in the Leuven Growth study of Belgian Boys. (Modified from *Growth, Maturation and Physical Activity* (p. 296) by R. M. Malina and C. Bouchard, 1991, Champaign, IL, Human Kinetics. Copyright 1991 by Robert M. Malina and Claude Bouchard. Reprinted by permission.)

good example of this was provided by Brewer *et al.* (1992) who studied 59 members of the Swedish under-17 soccer squad. They reported that the majority of the players were born in the first three months of the year, probably resulting in a slightly more advanced biological development. It is noteworthy that, possibly as a result of the relationship between adiposity and early maturity in girls, many of the physical advantages apparent in early maturing boys are absent in females (Malina and Bouchard, 1991). Given the rapid rate of growth during the adolescent growth spurt (peak height velocity of 7–9 cm per year), it is perhaps not surprising that there is a common perception of 'adolescent awkwardness' during this period. The temporary disruption of motor function during the growth spurt, particularly relating to balance, may be due to a segmental disproportion arising from the period early in the growth spurt, when leg length increases in proportion to trunk length. Boys in particular may be affected, but only 10–30% of the adolescent male population (Beunen and Malina, 1988). Furthermore, the effects are temporary, lasting approximately six months, and disappear by early adulthood. The above summary of events associated with growth and development, particularly over the period of adolescence highlights the complexity of interpreting fitness test scores correctly in children of this age group. A 'poor' score may simply reflect a state of maturity, whereas an 'improved' score may reflect a change in maturity, irrespective of other factors such as training status.

13.3 PERFORMANCE TESTING OF CHILDREN

Although many of the protocols used for assessing performance in children are similar to those used with adults, there are several unique aspects which the investigator should be aware of. In brief these include the following.

- Although the risks associated with maximal testing of healthy children are low, the tester should take every reasonable precaution to ensure safety of the child. This may include a carefully worded explanation of the test, adequate familiarization beforehand, extra testing staff (e.g. one standing behind a treadmill during testing) and a simple questionnaire relating to clinical contraindications, recent or current viral infections, asthma, and so on.
- Children will be less anxious if the right environment for testing is created. If groups of children are brought to the laboratory, some bright pictures, comics and even a video will help occupy those who are not involved. Children recover very quickly from maximal effort, and should always be generously rewarded – at least verbally.
- Be aware of the sensitivities of children, particularly in the group situation. It is wise to underplay both extremes of performance.
- Approval for testing children must be sought from the appropriate authorities. For field testing in the school, it is normally sufficient to obtain the principal's consent as well as that of the children themselves, and to liaise closely with the physical education staff. For laboratory testing, it would be normal practice to obtain consent from parents, children and an appropriate peer-review Ethics Committee. Children should be told that they are free to withdraw at any time from the test procedures.

13.4 ANTHROPOMETRIC TESTS (BODY COMPOSITION)

Techniques for the anthropometric measurements of stature commonly used with children are somewhat specialized, and are dealt with at length elsewhere (e.g. Chapter 4 in Malina and Bouchard, 1991) and by Beunen (Chapter 3) in this text. However, it is worth examining measures that may be used to gauge the body composition of children in some detail.

Possibly the simplest measure of assessing body composition in adults is the Body Mass Index (BMI $kg\,m^{-2}$), or Quetelet's Index ($weight/height^2$). In growing children, particularly boys, the use of this index as a measure of relative obesity may be misleading, as a large proportion of weight gain during adolescence is lean rather than adipose tissue. Thus, the BMI may increase from 17.8 to 21.3 in 11- and 16-year-old boys, respectively, whereas the sum of four skinfolds falls from 33.7 mm to 31.5 mm over the same period. The increase in BMI in girls from 11 to 16 years (from 18.6 to 21.5) may be a better indicator of increased adipose tissue (sum of four skinfolds rises from 37.2 to 43.1 mm; Riddoch *et al.*, 1991).

By far the most common methods of measuring body composition in children rely on the use of skinfold thicknesses (Figure 13.4). At least three options are open to the investigators.

1. The classic method published by Durnin and Rahaman (1967), in which the sum of four skinfold thicknesses (from the biceps, triceps, subscapular and suprailiac sites)

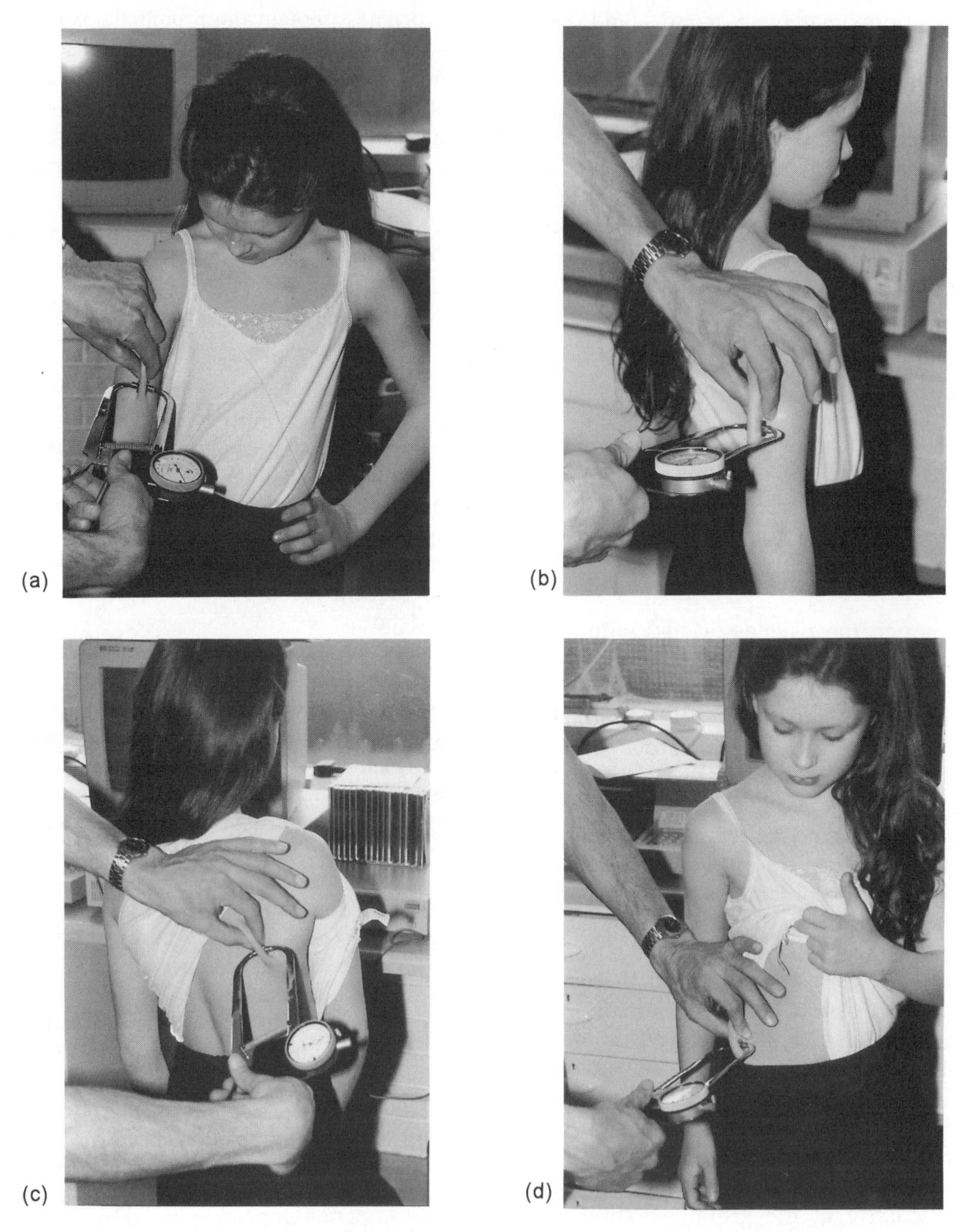

Figure 13.4 Skinfold thicknesses may be measured from (a) biceps, (b) triceps, (c) subscapula and (d) suprailiac sites.

measured with precision skinfold calipers, are transformed into a measure of body fat percentage using the equation of Siri (1956). This method is open to criticism,

due to the relatively small number of boys and girls measured for the original study, and the potential error arising out of the changing body density of growing children (the water content of a child's fat free mass decreases from 75.2% in a 10-year-old boy, to 73.6% at 18 years; Haschke, 1983).
2. Because of the above reservations, some investigators choose simply to sum the four skinfold thicknesses for use as a comparator.
3. The third option is to utilize more recently developed child-specific equations for two skinfolds only (Lohman, 1992). These are shown in Table 13.1.

Table 13.1 Prediction equations of percentage fat from triceps and subscapular skinfolds in children and youth for males and females[a]

Triceps and subscapular skinfolds > 35mm
%Fat = 0.783 Σ SF + I Males
%Fat = 0.546 Σ SF + 9.7 Females

Triceps and subscapular skinfolds (< 35 mm)[b]
%Fat = 1.21 (Σ SF) – 0.008 (Σ SF)^2 + I Males
%Fat = 1.33 (Σ SF) – 0.013 (Σ SF)^2 + 2.5 Females (2.0 blacks, 3.0 whites)
I = Intercept varies with maturation level and racial group for males as follows

Age	*Black*	*White*
Prepubescent	–3.5	–1.7
Pubescent	–5.2	–3.4
Postpubescent	–6.8	–5.5
Adult	–6.8	–5.5

[a] From *Advances in Body Composition Assessment* (p. 74) by T.G. Lohman (1992), Champaign, IL: Human Kinetics. Copyright 1992 by Timothy G. Lohman. Reprinted by permission.
Calculations were derived using the equation of Slaughter *et al.* (1988).
[b] Thus for a white pubescent male with a triceps of 15 mm and a subscapular of 12 mm, the % fat would be:
%Fat = 1.21 (27) – 0.008 (27)^2 – 3.4
= 23.4%

13.5 AEROBIC ENDURANCE PERFORMANCE

If endurance performance is examined in children, a characteristic pattern emerges whereby boys improve continuously until late adolescence, but girls do not, and may even display a drop in performance in their late teens. Figure 13.5 shows the number of 20 metre 'laps' completed on a multi-stage shuttle run test, plotted against age. What factors may account for these changes in performance?

It is generally accepted (Sjödin and Svedenhag, 1985) that endurance performance is governed by three factors: (1) aerobic power, or maximum

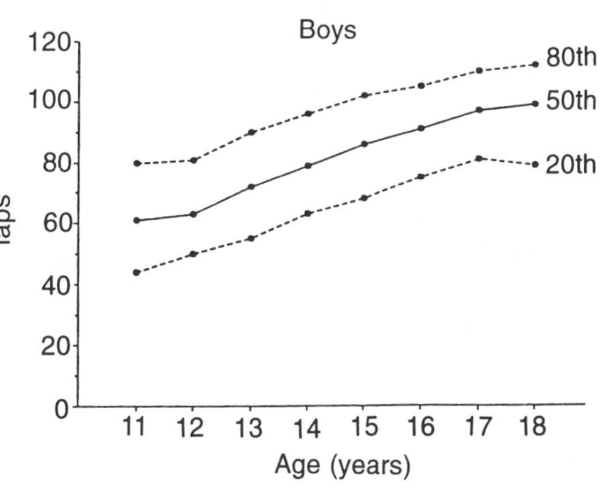

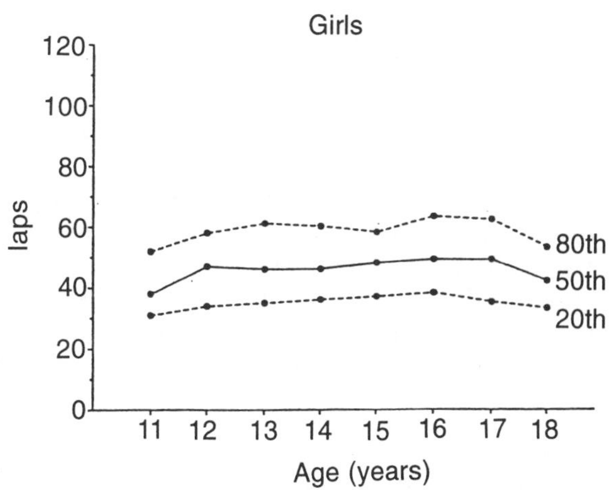

Figure 13.5 Endurance running ability, measured by 'laps' completed in the 20 m endurance shuttle run. Mean scores and 20th and 80th percentiles are shown. (Reproduced from the Northern Ireland Fitness Survey, 1990.)

oxygen uptake ($\dot{V}O_{2\,max}$); (2) aerobic capacity (or sustainable aerobic power), which is largely governed by the individual's 'anaerobic threshold', and (3) movement economy.

13.5.1 $\dot{V}O_{2\,max}$ IN CHILDREN

During growth, $\dot{V}O_{2\,max}$ (expressed in litres of oxygen consumed per minute) increases steadily in boys and remains stable or increases only slightly in girls (Figure 13.6a). Such changes are thought to reflect proportional growth during childhood of the relevant structures involved in the transportation and utilization of oxygen during exercise (lungs, heart, muscle and mitochondrial mass). The notable exception is a disproportionate increase in haemoglobin concentration in boys (from 13 g 100 ml^{-1} blood to 16 g 100 ml^{-1} during adolescence) compared with girls (from 13 to 14 g 100 ml^{-1}).

However, $\dot{V}O_{2\,max}$ has been traditionally expressed (at least for ambulatory movement) relative to body weight. When viewed in this manner (Figure 13.6b) the $\dot{V}O_{2\,max}$ of boys remains relatively stable, whereas that of girls declines over the adolescent period (the latter largely as a result of changes in fat

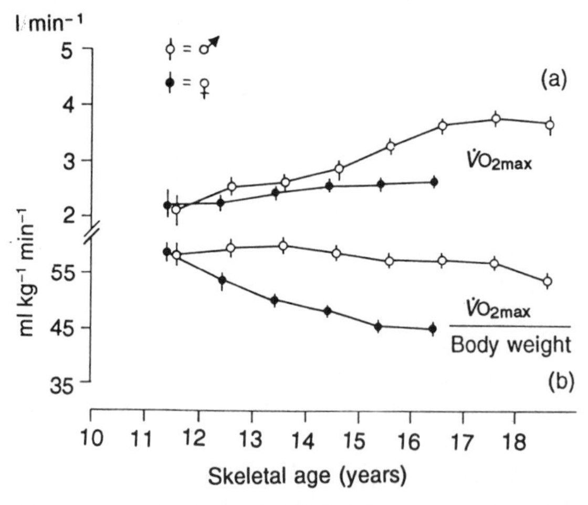

Figure 13.6 Mean and standard error of (a) absolute (l min^{-1}) and (b) relative (ml kg^{-1} min^{-1}) $\dot{V}O_{2\,max}$ of boys and girls. (Reproduced from Kemper (1985) with the permission of S Karger AG, Basel.)

mass). Although some argue convincingly that these changes in relative $\dot{V}O_{2\,max}$ may be influenced by the scaling method used (Nevill *et al.*, 1992; Winter, 1992) it seems, for the present, that changes in relative $\dot{V}O_{2\,max}$ cannot account for the observed development of endurance performance over childhood (Figure 13.5).

13.5.2 ANAEROBIC THRESHOLD IN CHILDREN

It is now well established that the skeletal muscle of children is metabolically geared more to aerobic energy metabolism than to anaerobic energy metabolism (Table 13.2). This results in a reduced ability to produce lactic acid during exercise in younger children (Figure 13.7) and a consequent need to adjust the traditional concepts of the 'anaerobic threshold'. For example, the 4.0 mmol l^{-1} blood lactate concentration (Heck *et al.*, 1985) which has often been used as a marker of running capacity, may occur at over 90% of $\dot{V}O_{2\,max}$ in 13–14-year-old children, compared with 77% of $\dot{V}O_{2\,max}$ in adults (Williams and Armstrong, 1991). Thus, these authors have suggested the use of 2.5 mmol l^{-1} in children as a guide to running capacity, rather than 4.0 mmol l^{-1}. Improvements over the adolescent period in the child's ability to produce energy anaerobically (Figure 13.7) may influence maximal running performance, particularly in boys.

Table 13.2 Biochemical characteristics of m. vastus lateralis in 11–15-year-old boys and adults (Eriksson, 1972; Saltin and Gollnick, 1983)

Characteristic	*Boys*	*Adults*
Substrate concentration (mmol kg^{-1} ww)		
ATP	4.3	5.0
CP	14.5	10.7
Glycogen (glucose units)	54.0	83.8
Enzyme activity (μ mol g^{-1} min^{-1})		
Phosphofructokinase	8.4	25.2–25.3
Succinate dehydrogenase	4.7–5.8	3.6–4.4

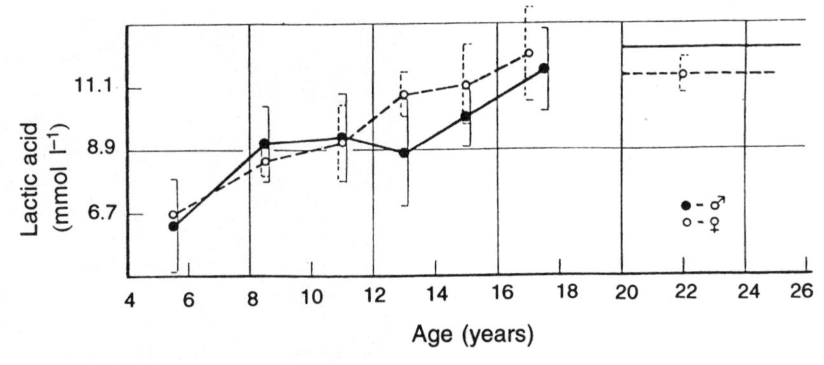

Figure 13.7 Maximal exercise blood lactate concentration in relation to age. (Reproduced from Åstrand (1952), with permission of Munksgaard International Publishers Ltd, Copenhagen.)

13.5.3 MOVEMENT ECONOMY IN CHILDREN

Economy may be defined as the metabolic cost, measured by oxygen consumption, of exercising at a given submaximal workload. It is clear from Figure 13.8 that for running, prepubertal children are 10–15% less efficient than adults, and that as they mature, they become progressively more economical in their movements. Such differences in efficiency are less apparent in cycle ergometry, leading to the conclusion that biomechanical rather than biochemical factors may be responsible. Although various biomechanical differences between children and adults (gait, stretch–shortening cycle, and so on) have been postulated, it may be that the simple observation of a relatively higher stride frequency at a given speed in children accounts for a large proportion of the observed differences in running efficiency (Unnithan and Eston, 1990). However, Eston *et al.* (1993) showed that when body mass was used as a covariate (i.e. the dependent variable of oxygen uptake was linearly adjusted such that comparisons were made as if all subjects had the same body mass) differences between the oxygen uptake of boys and men running at the same speeds were non-significant. This is discussed in greater detail in Chapter 9.

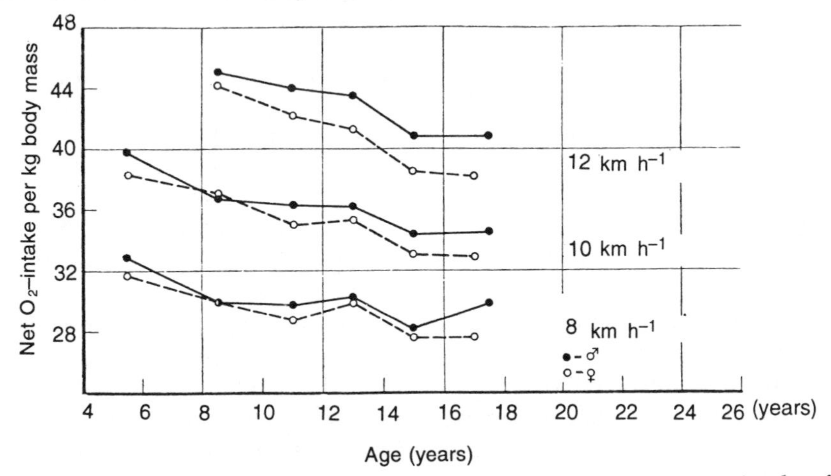

Figure 13.8 Changes in running efficiency with age. Values are mean net oxygen intakes for boys and girls while running at three different speeds. (Reproduced from Åstrand (1952) with permission of Munksgaard International Publishers Ltd, Copenhagen.)

From the above observations, it would appear that the improvement in running performance of growing children – particularly boys – observed in Figure 13.5, is more likely to be due to changes in 'anaerobic threshold' and running economy, than to improvements in maximal oxygen uptake. Although girls also appear to improve their 'anaerobic threshold' and running efficiency over the period of adolescence, these improvements may be counterbalanced by a decline in relative $\dot{V}O_{2\,max}$.

13.6 AEROBIC ENDURANCE TESTING IN CHILDREN

Aerobic endurance is often measured in children, as it is in adults, using a progressive, incremental exercise test of some sort, during which oxygen uptake ($\dot{V}O_2$) is measured. Although the recent development of sophisticated miniaturized gas analysers may permit measurement of $\dot{V}O_2$ in 'free-living' exercise conditions (Figure 13.9a), the bulk of such testing in children takes place using standard laboratory equipment (Figure 13.9b).

13.6.1 EQUIPMENT

Exercise tests are normally carried out using either a treadmill or cycle ergometer. In general, the treadmill is the preferred instrument with children who may find pedalling difficult, particularly if asked to maintain a set cadence on a mechanically braked cycle. In addition cycle ergometry may create local muscular fatigue in the legs of children at higher submaximal intensities, and specially built paediatric cycle ergometers may be required for exercise testing of very small children. Poorly motivated children may also respond better to treadmill exercise. On the other hand, the use of a treadmill can hinder procedures such as blood sampling and sphygmomanometry during exercise.

(a)

Figure 13.9 The measurement of oxygen uptake during exercise may be carried out using portable gas analysers such as the Cosmed K-2 (a), or more usually, in the laboratory setting (b *next page*).

If a cycle ergometer is to be used, the seat height should be adjusted so that the extended leg is almost completely straight at the bottom of the pedal revolution (with the foot in the horizontal position). If a mechanically braked cycle is used, a metronome can provide an audible signal to guide the child's pedalling cadence. A familiarization period should always precede the test, and children should be instructed not to grip the handlebars too tightly.

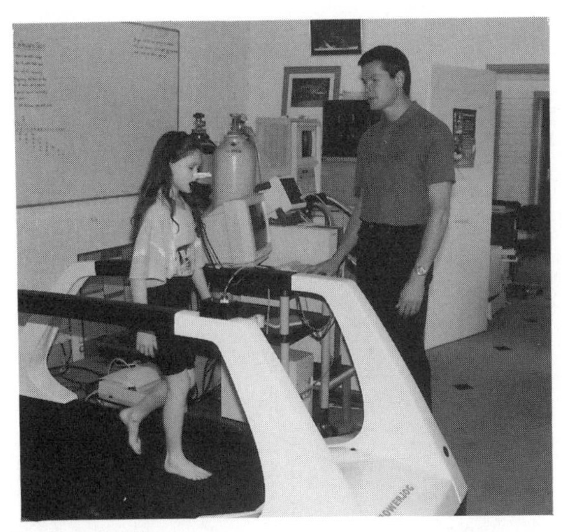

Figure 13.9(b)

If the treadmill is used, it may be advisable for the child to wear a safety harness, and for padding to be provided at the rear of the treadmill. Front and side rails may also need adjusting for small children. Before testing, the child should be familiarized with the sensation of walking and running on a moving belt, and with how to mount and dismount the treadmill. Non-verbal signals for stopping should be confirmed.

During the test, the investigator should communicate in a positive, friendly manner continuously, and should avoid enquiring as to whether the child feels tired – invariably the answer will be 'yes'! Instead, signs of fatigue (both selective and objective) should be noted, and a heightened state of vigilance maintained towards the end of a test. Above intensities of approximately 85% of $\dot{V}O_{2\,max}$, children may suddenly stop exercising without prior warning (Rowland, 1993). Anticipation of such an event by the investigator may be helped by the use of a developmentally appropriate perceived exertion rating scale during the exercise test. The Children's Effort Rating Table is discussed in Chapter 10.

After the test, a cool down at walking speed of at least 5 minutes is recommended, to avoid peripheral venous pooling and syncope. The mouthpiece and noseclip should be removed as soon as possible, and a drink of water, or preferably juice, offered. In the unlikely event of prolonged or repeated exercise testing of prepubertal children, in whom thermoregulatory responses may not be fully developed (Sharp, 1991), frequent drinking by the subject should be encouraged if possible.

13.6.2 CRITERIA FOR $\dot{V}O_{2\,max}$

Theoretically, the most objective criterion for determining whether a subject has reached $\dot{V}O_{2max}$ is a plateau in oxygen consumption despite an increase in workload. Most investigators, however, have found difficulty in identifying such a levelling-off in children (Zwiren, 1989). Thus, the term 'peak $\dot{V}O_2$' rather than 'maximum $\dot{V}O_2$' may be more appropriate for children, and the following criteria used to confirm attainment of peak $\dot{V}O_2$ during a test.

1. Heart rate that is 95% of age-related predicted maximum
2. Respiratory exchange ratio (RER) greater than 1.0
3. Extreme forced ventilation, or subjective signs of exhaustion

In practice, it is often subjective exhaustion that terminates a paediatric exercise test. As mentioned above, the onset of this exhaustion may be rapid in the exercising child.

13.6.3 PROTOCOLS FOR MAXIMAL EXERCISE TESTING

Treadmill protocols for children generally involve either the Balke protocol, in which treadmill speed (usually 4.5–5.5 km h^{-1}) is held constant, while the slope is increased every minute by 2% (Rowland, 1993) or, more commonly, a modified Bruce protocol (Table 13.3). An appropriate cycle ergometer protocol is that of McMaster (Table 13.4). For further details, the reader is referred to Bar-Or (1983).

Table 13.3 The Bruce treadmill protocol

Stage	*Speed ($km\,h^{-1}$)*	*Grade (%)*	*Duration (min)*
1	2.7	10	3
2	4.0	12	3
3	5.5	14	3
4	6.8	16	3
5	8.0	18	3
6	8.8	20	3
7	9.7	22	3

Table 13.4 The McMaster continuous cycling protocol

Body height (cm)	*Initial load (Watts)*	*Increments (Watts)*	*Duration of each load (min)*
≤ 119.9	12.5	12.5	2
120–139.9	12.5	25	2
140–159.9	25	25	2
≥ 160	25	♀ 25 ♂ 50	2

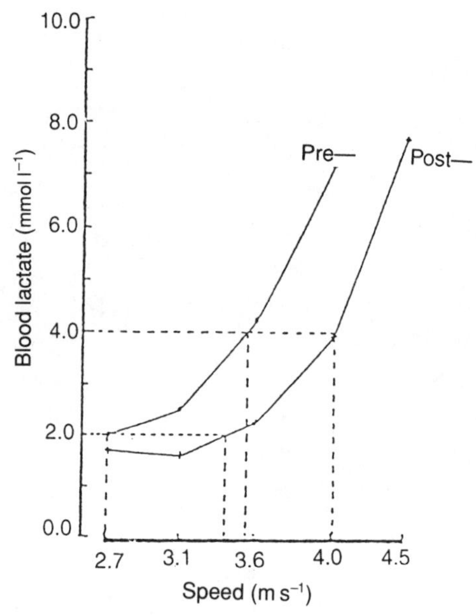

Figure 13.10 Blood lactate concentration during an incremental running test, pre and post one year's endurance training in an individual. (Reproduced with permission from the British Association of Sports Science Position Statement on the Physiological Assessment of the Elite Competitor (1988).)

13.7 DETERMINATION OF THE ANAEROBIC THRESHOLD

Although there is some controversy over terminology, largely arising out of methodological differences, the term 'anaerobic threshold' (AT) is still widely used to describe the intensity of exercise at which the oxygen supply becomes insufficient to meet the energy demands of the active muscles. It is generally determined in one of three ways. The first is by blood sampling at various steady-state points of the incremental exercise test, and the determination of blood lactate concentrations in those samples. Lactate concentration may then be plotted against variables such as running speed or $\dot{V}O_2$, to denote the sudden changes in slope referred to as the 'lactate threshold'. Alternatively, fixed blood concentrations of lactate (usually 2.0 and 4.0 mmol l^{-1} in adults) may be used as reference points against which exercise intensity may be compared. This latter approach may be less prone to observer error, and is extremely useful for comparing states of training (Figure 13.10) or maturation. Care should be taken in specifying sampling sites and assay media in the interpretation of blood lactate concentrations (Williams *et al.*, 1992). Second is the so-called ventilatory anaerobic threshold (T_{vent}). This non-invasive method may be particularly relevant to paediatric exercise testing, and relies on the identification of an increased ventilatory drive (arising from increased CO_2 production associated with elevated blood lactate concentrations) during exercise. The point at which ventilation $\dot{V}_E$ rises out of proportion to $\dot{V}O_2$ is known as the ventilatory threshold (T_{vent}). This threshold has also been identified by non-linear increases in CO_2 production (Wasserman, 1984), and abrupt increases in the respiratory exchange ratio (Smith and O'Donnell, 1984), although a comparison of methods (Ciozzo *et al.*, 1982) favoured the use of $\dot{V}_E/\dot{V}O_2$. The third method uses the heart-rate deflection point, proposed by Conconi *et al.* (1982). If heart rate is plotted against a progressive workload, a downward deflection can be identified, which has been claimed to coincide with the lactate threshold (Gaisl and Wiesspeiner, 1990) or T_{vent} (Mahon and Vaccaro, 1991). Much debate surrounds the use of the heart-rate deflection point to determine 'anaerobic threshold', and to date, relatively little research has been carried out on this topic with children.

13.8 FIELD TESTS OF AEROBIC ENDURANCE

Not all tests of aerobic endurance require laboratory facilities, and several field tests have been developed to cater for larger groups of children, or where time and equipment may be limited. Most of these tests, such as the 20 m multistage shuttle run (20-MST), and the timed one-mile run/walk, may involve maximal effort, whereas the cycle ergometer test of physical work capacity PWC_{170} does not, requiring only approximately 85% of maximum heart rate to be achieved. The PWC_{170} is, in effect, a compromise between laboratory and field, being restricted to one child at a time, and requiring some equipment (cycle ergometer, metronome, stopwatch) and expertise on behalf of the tester. For full details of the test protocol, the EUROFIT handbook should be consulted (EUROFIT, 1988).

The 20-MST and one mile run/walk tests have been employed extensively by European and North American investigators, respectively. Both have shown variable but generally moderate correlations against laboratory-measured $\dot{V}O_{2\,max}$ (van Mechelen *et al.*, 1986; Boreham *et al.*, 1990; Safrit, 1990) but this is not surprising given that endurance running performance is governed by other factors such as anaerobic threshold and running efficiency as well as $\dot{V}O_{2\,max}$ (see above).

The one mile run/walk test has been incorporated into both the AAHPERD (1988) and FITNESSGRAM (1987) test batteries, and criterion-referenced standards for health developed. The standards adopted for AAHPERD are somewhat more stringent (Table 13.5).

Table 13.5 Criterion referenced health standards for the one mile run/walk test (min)

Age	*FITNESSGRAM*	*AAHPERD*
9	12.00	10.00
10	11.00	9.30
11	11.00	9.00
12	10.00	9.00
13	9.30	8.00
14	8.30	7.45
15	8.30	7.30
16	8.30	7.30

The 20-MST, unlike the one mile run/walk test, does not require a large, marked running area, and can conveniently be carried out indoors, providing that a hall at least 20 m long is available. Originally developed by Léger and Lambert (1982), the test consists of running to and fro between two lines, 20 m apart, in time with a prerecorded audio signal from a cassette tape (Figure 13.11). Starting at a pace of 8.5 km h^{-1}, the speed progressively increases each minute until the child can no longer keep up with the required pace. A lap scoring protocol has been developed (Queen's University, Belfast) which may be particularly useful for testing children. Full details of the 20-MST are available in the EUROFIT manual (1988), and norms are also available (see Table 13.8).

13.9 STRENGTH AND POWER

Strength is the ability of muscle to generate force, and is determined both by myogenic factors (mainly muscle cross-sectional area) and neurogenic factors (e.g. skill, muscle fibre 'recruitment'; Sharp, 1991). Typical isometric strength gains during adolescence for boys and girls are illustrated in Figure 13.2(a), and it is thought that the sudden increase in strength of boys in late adolescence is primarily due to the increases in muscle size. Thus, whereas girls may be 90% as strong as boys at age 11–12 years, this drops to 85% by 13–14 years and 75% by 15–16 years (Israel, 1992). Strength may be measured in the laboratory,

Figure 13.11 The 20 metre endurance shuttle run test (20-MST).

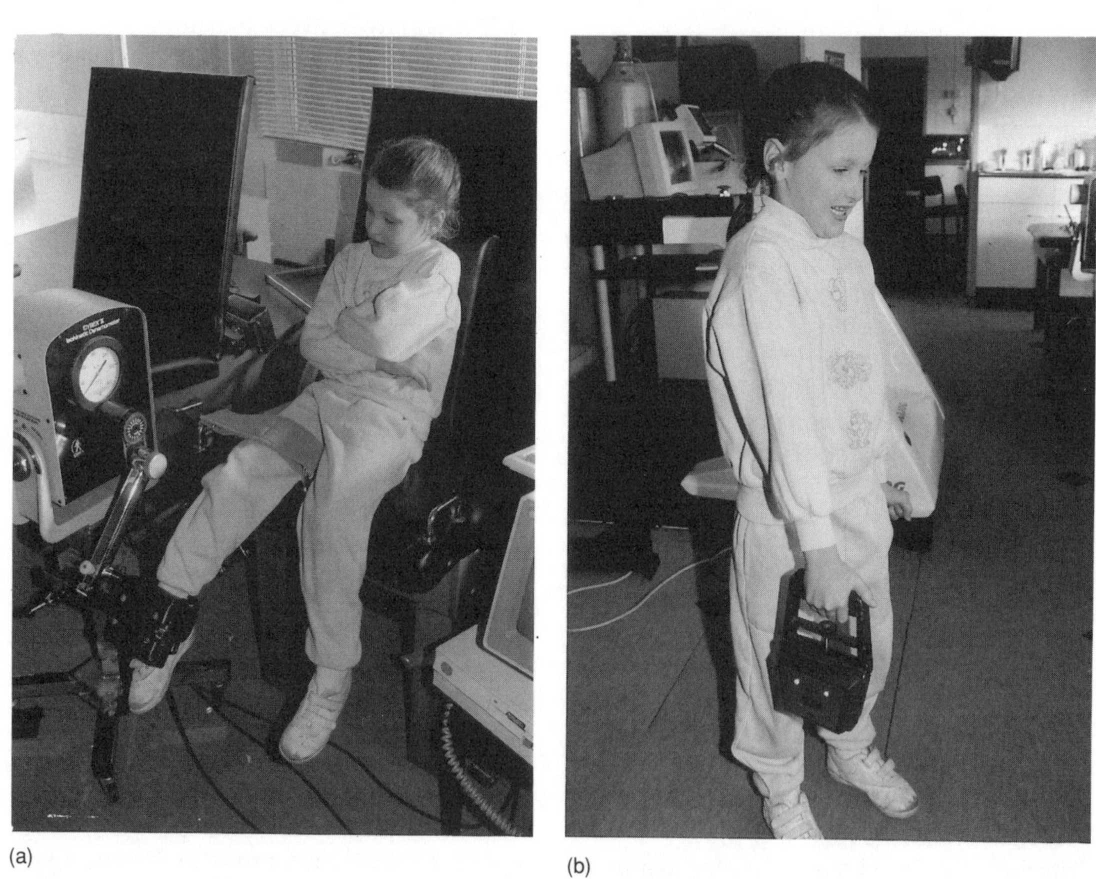

(a) (b)

Figure 13.12 Strength may be tested (a) in the laboratory, using isokinetic apparatus, or (b) using a simple isometric hand dynamometer.

Table 13.6 Optimal resistance for the Wingate anaerobic test, by body-weight groups, using the Monark Cycle Ergometer

Body mass (kg)	Resistance (kp^a)	
	Legs	Arms
20–24.9	1.75	1.25
25–29.9	2.13	1.50
30–34.9	2.50	1.75
35–39.9	2.83	2.00
40–44.9	3.25	2.25
45–49.9	3.63	2.50
50–54.9	4.00	2.75
55–59.9	4.50	3.00
60–64.9	5.00	3.35
65–69.9	5.50	3.70

(Reproduced from Bar-Or (1983) with the permission of Springer-Verlag.)

[a] 1 kp is the force acting on the mass of 1 kg at normal acceleration of gravity: 1 kp = 9.8066 N or approximately 10 N.

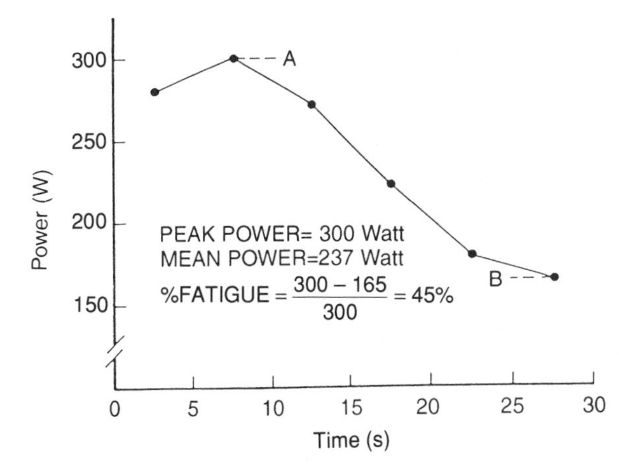

Figure 13.13 The Wingate anaerobic test. Peak power (A) and lowest power (B) may be used to calculate % fatigue. (Reproduced from Bar-Or (1983) with permission of Springer-Verlag, Heidelberg.)

using sophisticated isokinetic dynamometers (Figure 13.12a), or more usually with simple portable or hand-held dynamometers (Figure 13.12b). The protocols are essentially the same for both adult and child subjects (McDougall *et al.*, 1982).

Tests of muscular power (force/speed) may involve instantaneous, explosive movements, such as the standing vertical jump (Figure 13.2b), or a more prolonged series of supramaximal movements lasting several seconds. The best known example of the latter type of performance test is the Wingate Anaerobic Cycling Test (Bar-Or, 1983). In this test, the child pedals or arm-cranks a cycle ergometer at maximal speed against a high constant resistance, normally for 30 s. Table 13.6 indicates optimal resistances for children according to body weight. Power output is therefore a function of pedalling velocity, whereas mechanical work is a function of the total number of revolutions during the time period. A typical performance curve is shown in Figure 13.13.

13.10 FIELD TEST BATTERIES FOR CHILDREN

The use of laboratory tests to determine performance in children is not always appropriate or feasible, and several batteries of field tests have been proposed mainly to cater for large-scale population studies and/or the educational testing environment. Such test batteries include the American Alliance for Health, Physical Education, Recreation and Dance (AAHPERD) 'Physical Best' programme (1988) and the more comprehensive Council of Europe's 'EUROFIT' test battery (Tables 13.7 and 13.8). Although the purpose (Pate, 1989), validity, reliability (Safrit, 1990) and interpretation (Plowman, 1992) of such tests have been the subject of intense debate, their expanding use, particularly in an educational setting, continues. It is likely that much of this debate is generated by an inability to (a) appreciate the limitations of the tests as scientific tools, (b) understand the underlying biological processes during growth which may contribute to a child's score on a particular test item, and (c) reach a consensus regarding criterion-referenced norms, particularly for health-related tests such as body composition and aerobic endurance.

Table 13.7 EUROFIT tests of physical fitness (EUROFIT, 1988)

Dimension	*Factor*	*EUROFIT test*
Cardiorespiratory endurance	Cardiorespiratory endurance	Endurance shuttle run (ESR) Cycle ergometer test (PWC_{170})
Strength	Static strength Explosive power	Hand grip (HGR) Standing broad jump (SBJ)
Muscular endurance	Functional strength Trunk strength	Bent arm hang (BAH) Sit-ups (SUP)
Speed	Running speed – agility Speed of limb movement	Shuttle run: 10 × 5 metres (SHR) Plate tapping (PLT)
Flexibility Balance	Flexibility Total body balance	Sit and reach (SAR) Flamingo balance (FLB)
Anthropometric measures	Height (cm): Body mass (kg): Skinfold thicknesses (5 skinfolds)	 biceps, triceps, subscapular, suprailiac, calf
Identification data	Age (years, months): Sex:	

Table 13.8 Normscales for British children: selected EUROFIT test battery items (adapted from N. Ireland Fitness Survey, 1990)

Percentile	*Age 11*	*12*	*13*	*14*	*15*	*16*	*17*
Height (mm)							
Boys 80	1502	1573	1630	1686	1744	1800	1817
50	1441	1496	1560	1628	1690	1732	1756
20	1389	1436	1498	1558	1642	1668	1703
Mean	1449	1503	1566	1621	1689	1734	1760
SD	69	76	82	84	68	70	67
Girls 80	1534	1573	1617	1642	1647	1670	1679
50	1470	1510	1562	1595	1601	1617	1626
20	1408	1443	1511	1546	1555	1566	1574
Mean	1471	1511	1563	1594	1602	1620	1626
SD	75	77	67	60	60	59	63
Body mass (kg)							
Boys 80	43.7	48.7	54.5	59.3	64.4	72.0	74.2
50	36.3	41.1	44.7	50.4	57.1	63.5	66.0
20	31.8	34.1	38.4	43.2	50.9	56.4	58.5
Mean	37.7	42.1	46.5	51.7	58.0	64.2	66.5
SD	7.2	8.8	9.9	10.1	9.5	9.6	9.0
Girls 80	47.7	50.3	54.9	59.1	60.1	61.9	62.6
50	39.2	41.5	47.9	52.2	53.4	55.7	55.9
20	32.9	36.3	41.2	46.8	48.2	49.8	50.6
Mean	40.6	43.1	48.7	52.9	54.0	56.5	56.6
SD	8.9	8.8	9.3	7.9	7.4	7.7	6.9
Skinfolds (sum of four sites)							
Boys 80	41.9	45.9	41.4	39.0	36.7	38.8	35.7
50	29.4	30.1	26.6	27.7	26.9	28.3	27.4

Percentile	*Age 11*	*12*	*13*	*14*	*15*	*16*	*17*
20	22.8	23.3	21.2	21.9	22.7	22.8	22.8
Mean	33.7	35.6	32.3	31.9	31.6	31.5	30.0
SD	14.6	16.0	14.9	13.1	13.0	11.4	10.5
Girls 80	48.8	45.5	49.0	53.2	51.6	53.7	49.4
50	33.1	33.5	34.6	40.2	40.3	41.5	40.1
20	23.8	26.4	27.7	29.9	31.3	32.3	31.7
Mean	37.2	36.6	39.2	42.1	42.4	43.1	43.3
SD	17.0	13.0	14.4	13.8	12.7	12.5	11.7
20 Metre shuttle run (laps)							
Boys 80	80	81	90	96	102	105	110
50	61	63	72	79	86	91	97
20	44	50	55	63	68	75	81
Mean	61	65	72	79	86	90	96
SD	19	17	19	20	20	18	18
Girls 80	52	58	61	60	58	63	62
50	38	47	46	46	48	49	49
20	31	34	35	36	37	38	35
Mean	41	47	48	49	49	50	50
SD	13	14	15	16	14	15	16
Sit and reach (cm)							
Boys 80	21.5	21.0	22.5	22.5	26.5	28.0	30.5
50	16.0	15.0	16.0	17.0	20.0	22.0	24.0
20	11.5	9.5	10.0	11.5	13.5	15.0	17.0
Mean	16.5	15.0	16.0	17.0	19.5	22.0	23.5
SD	6.0	6.5	7.0	6.5	7.5	7.5	8.5
Girls 80	26.5	25.5	27.0	30.5	31.0	31.0	33.0
50	21.0	21.0	22.0	25.0	25.5	25.5	26.5
20	15.5	15.5	16.0	19.0	19.5	18.5	20.5
Mean	20.5	20.5	21.5	24.5	25.0	25.0	26.0
SD	6.5	6.0	6.5	6.5	6.5	7.0	7.5
Standing broad jump (cm)							
Boys 80	162	166	180	188	204	214	218
50	146	150	161	170	184	194	201
20	129	133	138	149	162	173	183
Mean	145	150	161	169	183	195	200
SD	19	20	23	25	24	24	24
Girls 80	146	153	158	165	163	168	169
50	130	136	138	143	143	147	148
20	117	121	122	126	128	128	133
Mean	131	136	140	144	459	147	151
SD	19	19	21	22	21	22	22
Sit-ups in 30 s (number completed)							
Boys 80	25	25	27	28	29	29	29
50	22	23	24	25	25	26	26
20	19	20	21	21	22	22	22
Mean	22	23	24	25	25	26	26
SD	4	4	4	4	4	4	4
Girls 80	22	23	23	23	23	23	23
50	19	20	19	20	20	20	20
20	16	17	16	17	17	17	16
Mean	19	20	19	20	20	20	19
SD	4	4	4	4	4	4	4

Table 13.8 (Continued)

Percentile	*Age 11*	*12*	*13*	*14*	*15*	*16*	*17*
Handgrip strength (N)							
Boys 80	230	260	300	370	440	480	520
50	190	220	260	290	370	420	460
20	170	190	220	240	310	360	400
Mean	200	230	260	300	370	420	460
SD	40	50	60	70	80	70	70
Girls 80	220	240	270	300	310	320	320
50	190	200	240	260	270	280	290
20	150	160	200	230	240	240	250
Mean	190	200	230	260	270	280	290
SD	40	40	40	40	40	50	50
10 × 5 m shuttle sprint (s)							
Boys 80	23.3	23.2	21.9	21.5	20.9	20.3	20.0
50	21.7	21.4	20.6	20.1	19.8	19.1	18.7
20	20.4	20.1	19.4	18.9	18.6	17.9	17.6
Mean	21.9	21.6	20.8	20.3	19.8	19.1	18.9
SD	1.9	1.8	1.6	1.6	1.5	1.4	1.4
Girls 80	25.0	24.1	23.9	23.9	23.6	23.5	23.8
50	23.3	22.5	22.5	22.4	22.1	21.9	21.9
20	22.1	21.1	21.3	20.8	20.8	20.4	20.3
Mean	23.5	22.6	22.7	22.4	22.1	22.0	22.0
SD	1.8	2.0	1.7	1.9	2.2	1.9	2.0

REFERENCES

AAHPERD Physical Best Program (1988) American Alliance for Health, Physical Education, Recreation and Dance. Reston, VA.

Åstrand, P. O. (1952) *Experimental Studies of Physical Working Capacity in Relation to Sex and Age*, Munksgaard, Copenhagen.

Bar-Or, O. (1983) *Pediatric Sports Medicine for the Practitioner: from Physiologic Principles to Clinical Applications*, Springer-Verlag, New York.

Beunen, G. and Malina, R. M. (1988) Growth and physical performance relative to the timing of the adolescent spurt. *Exercise and Sports Sciences Reviews*, **16**, 503–46.

Boreham, C. A. G., Paliczka, V. J. and Nichols, A. K. (1990) A comparison of the PWC_{170} and 20-MST tests of aerobic fitness in adolescent schoolchildren. *Journal of Sports Medicine and Physical Fitness*, **30**, 19–23.

Boreham, C. A. G., Savage, J. M., Primrose, D. *et al.* (1993) Coronary risk in schoolchildren. *Archives of Disease in Childhood*, **68**, 182–6.

Brewer, J., Balsom, P. D., Davis, J. A. and Ekblom, B. (1992) The influence of birth date and physical development on the selection of a male junior international soccer squad. *Journal of Sports Sciences*, **10**, 561–2.

British Association of Sports Sciences (1988) *Position Statement on the Physiological Assessment of the Elite Competitor*. British Association of Sports Sciences, Leeds.

Ciozzo, V. J., David, J., Ellis, J. F. *et al.* (1982) A comparison of gas exchange indices used to detect the anaerobic threshold. *Journal of Applied Physiology*, **53**, 1184–9.

Conconi, F., Ferrari, M., Ziglio, P. G. *et al.* (1982) Determination of the anerobic threshold by a non-invasive field test in runners. *Journal of Applied Physiology*, **52**, 869–73.

Durnin, J. V. G. A. and Rahaman, M. M. (1967) The assessment of the amount of fat in the human body from measurements of skinfold thickness. *British Journal of Nutrition*, **21**, 681–9.

Eriksson, B. O. (1972) Physical training, oxygen supply and muscle metabolism in 11- to 15-year-old boys. *Acta Physiologica Scandinavica, Suppl.*, **384**, 1–48.

Eston, R. G., Robson, S. and Winter, E. (1993) A comparison of oxygen uptake during running in children and adults, in *Kinanthroponetry IV* (eds

W. Duquet and J. A. P. Day) E & FN Spon, London, pp. 236–41.

EUROFIT (European Test of Physical Fitness) (1988) Council of Europe, Committee for the Development of Sport (CDDS), Rome.

FITNESSGRAM Users Manual (1987) Institute for Aerobics Research, Dallas, TX.

Gaisl, G. and Wiesspeiner, G. (1990) A non-invasive method of determining the anaerobic threshold in children. *Pediatric Exercise Science*, **2**, 29–36.

Haschke, F. (1983) Body composition of adolescent males. Part 2. Body composition of male reference adolescents. *Acta Paediatrica Scandinavica*, **307** (Suppl), 1–12.

Heck, H., Mader, A., Hess, G. *et al.* (1985) Justification of the 4-mmol/lactate threshold. *International Journal of Sports Medicine*, **6**, 117–30.

Israel, S. (1992) Age-related changes in strength and special groups, *Strength and Power in Sport* (ed. P. V. Komi), Blackwell Scientific Publications, Oxford, pp. 319–28.

Kemper, H. C. G. (ed.), (1985) *Medicine and Sports Science*, vol. 20, *Growth, Health and Fitness of Teenagers*. Karger, Basel.

Kemper, H. C. G. (1990) Physical fitness testing in children: is it a worthwhile activity? *Proceedings of the European EUROFIT Research Seminar*, Ismir. Council of Europe, pp. 7–27.

Léger, L. and Lambert, J. (1982) A maximal 20 metre shuttle run test to predict $\dot{V}O_{2\,max}$. *European Journal of Applied Physiology*, **49**, 1–12.

Lohman, T. (1992) Advances in body composition assessment. *Current Issues in Exercise Science Series* (Monograph Number 3). Human Kinetics, Champaign, IL.

Mahon, A. D. and Vaccaro, P. (1991) Can the point of deflection from linearity of heart rate determine ventilatory threshold in children? *Pediatric Exercise Science*, **3**, 256–62.

Malina, R. M. and Bouchard, C. (1991) *Growth, Maturation and Physical Activity*, Human Kinetics, Champaign, IL.

McDougall, J. D., Wenger, H. A. and Green, H. J. (1982) *Physiological Testing of the Elite Athlete*, Canadian Association of Sports Sciences, in collaboration with the Sports Medicine Council of Canada. Mutual Press.

N. Ireland Fitness Survey (1990) *The Fitness, Physical Activity, Attitudes and Lifestyles of N. Ireland Post-primary Schoolchildren*. Division of Physical and Health Education, The Queen's University of Belfast.

Nevill, A. M., Ramsbottom, R. and Williams, C. (1992) Scaling measurements in physiology and medicine for individuals of different size. *European Journal of Applied Physiology*, **65**, 110–17.

Pate, R. R. (1989) The case for large-scale physical fitness testing in American youth. *Pediatric Exercise Science*, **1**, 290–4.

Plowman, S. A. (1992) Criterion – referenced standards for neuromuscular physical fitness tests: an analysis. *Pediatric Exercise Science*, **4**, 10–19.

Riddoch, C., Savage, J. M., Murphy, N. *et al.* (1991) Long term health implications of fitness and physical activity patterns. *Archives of Disease in Childhood*, **66**, 1426–33.

Rowland, T. W. (ed.) (1993) *Pediatric Laboratory Exercise Testing: Clinical Guidelines*. Human Kinetics, Champaign, IL.

Safrit, M. J. (1990) The validity and reliability of fitness tests for children: a review. *Pediatric Exercise Science*, **2**, 9–28.

Saltin, B. and Gollnick, P. D. (1983) Skeletal muscle adaptability: significance for metabolism and performance, in *Handbook of Physiology; Skeletal Muscle*, section 10 (eds Peachey *et al.*). Americal Physiological Society, Williams and Wilkins, Baltimore, pp. 555–631.

Sharp, N. C. C. (1991) The exercise physiology of children, in *Children and Sport* (ed. V. Grisogono), W. H. Murray, London, pp. 32–71.

Siri, W. E. (1956) The gross composition of the body. *Advances in Biological and Medical Physics*, **4**, 239–80.

Sjödin, B. and Svedenhag, J. (1985) Applied physiology of marathon running. *Sports Medicine*, **2**, 83–99.

Slaughter, M. H., Lohman, T. G., Boileau, R. A. *et al.* (1988) Skinfold equations for estimation of body fatness in children and youth. *Human Biology*, **60**, 709–23.

Smith, D. A. and O'Donnell, T. V. (1984) The time course during 36 weeks endurance training of changes in $\dot{V}O_{2\,max}$ and anaerobic threshold as determined with a new computerised method. *Clinical Science*, **67**, 229–36.

Unnithan, V. B. and Eston, R. G. (1990) Stride frequency and submaximal treadmill running economy in adults and children. *Pediatric Exercise Science*, **2**, 149–55.

van Mechelen, W., Hlobil, H. and Kemper, H. C. G. (1986) Validation of two running tests as estimates of maximal aerobic power in children. *European Journal of Applied Physiology*, **55**, 503–6.

Washington, R. L. (1989) Anaerobic threshold in children. *Pediatric Exercise Science*, **1**, 244–56.

Wasserman, K. (1984) The anaerobic threshold measurement to evaluate exercise performance.

American Review of Respiration Disease, **129**, S35–40.

Williams, J. R. and Armstrong, N. (1991) Relationship of maximal lactate steady state to performance at fixed blood lactate reference values in children. *Pediatric Exercise Science*, **3**, 333–41.

Williams, J. R., Armstrong, N. and Kirby, B. J. (1992) The influence of the site of sampling and assay medium upon the measurement and interpretation of blood lactate responses to exercise. *Journal of Sports Sciences*, **10**, 95–107.

Winter, E. M. (1992) Scaling: partitioning out differences in size. *Pediatric Exercise Science*, **4**, 296–301.

Zwiren L. D. (1989) Anaerobic and aerobic capacities of children. *Pediatric Exercise Science*, **1**, 31–44.

STATISTICAL METHODS IN KINANTHROPOMETRY AND EXERCISE PHYSIOLOGY

14

A. M. Nevill

14.1 INTRODUCTION

This chapter outlines the statistical methods most commonly used to describe the results of laboratory-based experiments in exercise physiology and kinanthropometry. All sections are illustrated with examples from exercise physiology and kinanthropometry and, due to the easy access to personal computers and statistical software, the appropriate commands to carry out the same analyses, using the statistical software package MINITAB (1989), are listed at the end of each section.

14.2 ORGANIZING AND DESCRIBING DATA IN KINANTHROPOMETRY AND EXERCISE PHYSIOLOGY

Kinanthropometry is a relatively new branch of science that is concerned with measuring the physical characteristics of human beings and the movements they perform. In our attempt to further our understanding of 'the human in motion', there is a clear need for laboratory-based tests or experiments that will frequently involve the collection of one or more measurements or variables on a group(s) of subjects.

14.2.1 VARIABLES IN KINANTHROPOMETRY AND EXERCISE PHYSIOLOGY

A variable is any characteristic or measurement that can take on different values. When planning or designing a laboratory-based experiment, the researcher will be able to identify those measurements that can be regarded as either independent or dependent variables. A variable that is under the control of the researcher is referred to as the independent variable. The resulting measurements that are recorded on each subject as a response to the independent variable are known as the dependent variable. For example, in an experiment investigating the oxygen cost of treadmill running, the independent variable would be the different running speeds, set by the researcher, and the recorded oxygen cost would be the resulting dependent variable.

(a) Classifying measurements in kinanthropometry and exercise physiology

Measurements in kinanthropometry and exercise physiology can be classified as either categorical or numerical data.

(i) Categorical data

The simplest type of measurement is called the nominal scale where observations are allocated to one of various categories. Examples of nominal data with only two categories (binary) are; male/female, winners/losers or presence/absence of a disease. Examples of

Kinanthropometry and Exercise Physiology Laboratory Manual: Tests, procedures and data Edited by Roger Eston and Thomas Reilly. Published in 1996 by E & FN Spon. ISBN 0 419 17880 5

nominal data with more than two unordered categories are: country of birth, favourite sport, team supported and most popular equipment manufacturer. As long as the categories are exhaustive (include all cases) and non-overlapping or mutually exclusive (no case is more than one category), we have the minimal conditions necessary for the application of statistical procedures on observations catagorized on a nominal scale.

Suppose that we retain the idea of grouping from the nominal scale and add the restriction that the variable that we are measuring has an underlying continuum so that we may speak of a person having 'more than' or 'less than' another person of the variable in question. This would be an ordinal scale or rank order scale of measurement. Socioeconomic class is a good example, i.e. 'upper', 'middle' and 'lower' classes. Level of achievement at a particular sport would be another example, i.e. beginner, recreational participant, club standard, county representative, national or international standard.

(ii) Numerical data

Numerical data, often referred to as either interval or ratio scales of measurement, are the highest level of measurement. The distinction between interval and ratio scales (the latter has a fixed zero, the former does not) is not very useful, since most data collected in kinanthropometry and exercise physiology are measured using the ratio scale, e.g. one of the few examples of an interval scale of measurement in kinanthropometry would be the results from a sit- and-reach flexibility test. An interval or ratio scale variable can be either a discrete count or a 'continuous' variable. A discrete count can only take on specific values. The number of heart beats per minute and the number of people in a team are examples of discrete variables. A 'continuous' variable may take any value within a defined range of values. Height, weight and time are examples of continuous variables. Quotation marks are used around 'continuous' because all such variables are in practice measured to a finite precision, so they are actually discrete variables with a large number of numerical values. For example, height may be measured to the nearest centimetre and the time to run 100 m to the nearest 0.01 s.

14.2.2 FREQUENCY TABLES OR DISTRIBUTIONS

The first step necessary to investigate and understand the results of experiments is to discover how the experimental results vary over the range of responses. Are the scores evenly spread over the entire range of responses or do they tend to be more frequent in a particular section of the range, i.e. are the scores symmetric over the range or are they skewed with one or two atypical results or outliers? The scores, often referred to as the raw data, need to be arranged in the form of a frequency table to discover the distribution of measurements over the range of subjects' responses. Consider the following maximum oxygen uptake $\dot{V}O_{2\,max}$ results given in Table 14.1 (Nevill *et al.* 1992a).

Table 14.1 The maximal oxygen uptake $\dot{V}O_{2\,max}$ results of 30 recreationally active male subjects (Nevill *et al.*, 1992a)

$\dot{V}O_{2\,max}$ (ml kg^{-1} min^{-1})					
60.9	59.3	59.2	58.9	58.3	58.1
55.7	53.4	53.0	51.8	50.6	54.4
63.0	60.3	59.5	57.3	57.1	57.0
56.1	55.1	55.0	54.4	54.0	53.0
52.9	52.8	52.4	51.2	48.5	53.6

The first step in calculating a frequency table is to obtain the range of scores, i.e.

$$\text{Range} = \text{highest score} - \text{lowest score}$$
$$= 63.0 - 48.5 = 14.5\ (\text{ml kg}^{-1}\ \text{min}^{-1})$$

The next step is to divide the range into a convenient number of class intervals of equal size. Since the number of intervals should lie between 5 and 15 depending on the number of observations, we can obtain a rough estimate of the interval size. In this example, a reasonable number of intervals would be about 8 or 9 that would require an interval size of 2 (ml kg^{-1} min^{-1}). Hence Table 14.2 might result.

Table 14.2 Frequency table for the maximal oxygen uptake results in Table 14.1

Class intervals	*Mid-points* (M_i)	*Tally*	*Frequency* (f_i)
47.0–48.9	47.95	I	1
49.0–50.9	49.95	I	1
51.0–52.9	51.95	IIIII	5
53.0–54.9	53.95	II IIIII	7
55.0–56.9	55.95	IIII	4
57.0–58.9	57.95	I IIIII	6
59.0–60.9	59.95	IIIII	5
61.0–62.9	61.95		0
63.0–64.9	63.95	I	1

Note: the class intervals do not overlap (there are no points in common), and do not exclude scores in the gaps between class intervals.

14.2.3 HISTOGRAMS AND FREQUENCY POLYGONS

A histogram or frequency polygon is a graphical representation of a frequency table. A histogram is a set of adjacent rectangles with the class intervals forming the base of the rectangles and the areas proportional to the class frequencies. If the class intervals are all of equal size, it is usual to take the height of the rectangles as the class frequencies. However, if the class intervals are not of equal size, the height of the rectangles must be adjusted accordingly, e.g. if one of the class intervals is twice the size of all the other intervals, then the height of this rectangle should be the frequency score divided by 2. The histogram describing the maximum oxygen uptake (ml kg^{-1} min^{-1}) results from Table 14.2 is given in Figure 14.1

A frequency polygon is a broken-line graph of frequencies plotted against their class intervals. It can be obtained by simply joining the mid-points of the rectangles in the histogram. In order to preserve the area representation of the frequencies, the end points of the polygon have been positioned on the base line at the mid-points of the intervals on either side of the two extreme intervals (Figure 14.1). If the class intervals are made smaller and smaller and at the same time the number of measurements or counts further increase, the frequency polygon may approach a smooth curve, called a frequency distribution. An important example of a frequency distribution that is symmetrical and bell shaped is the normal distribution. The results of tests and experiments in kinanthropometry and exercise physiology are often found to take on the form of a normal distribution. However, the normal distribution is not the only type of frequency distribution obtained when results of such tests and experiments come to be investigated. Other asymmetric or skewed frequency distributions are also obtained. An asymmetric or skewed frequency distribution has a longer tail to one side of the central maximum than the other. If the longer tail is found to the right hand side of the distribution, the data are

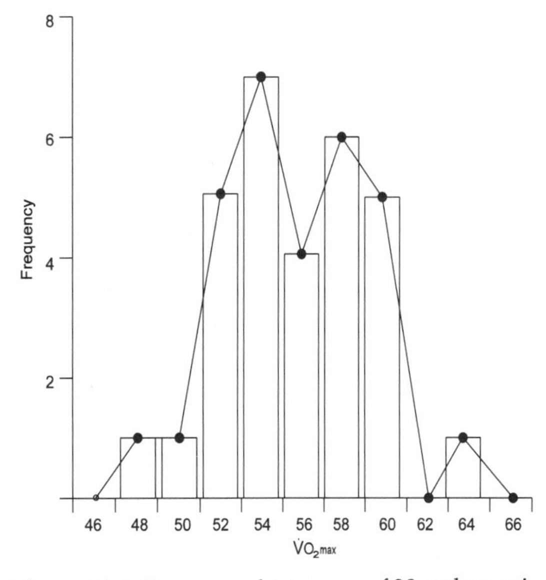

Figure 14.1 Frequency histogram of 30 male maximal oxygen uptake results (ml kg^{-1} min^{-1}). (From Nevill *et al.*, 1992a.)

described as positively skewed, whereas if the longer tail is found on the left side of the distribution, the data are described as negatively skewed. Certain transformations can be used to overcome the problems of skewed data that correct the asymmetry in the frequency distribution, e.g. a log transformation will frequently correct positively skewed data such as body mass (kg) or maximal oxygen uptake ($l\ min^{-1}$) that have a 'log-normal' distribution.

14.2.4 MEASURES OF LOCATION OR CENTRAL TENDENCY (AVERAGES)

(a) Arithmetic mean

The arithmetic mean of a set of measurements is defined as the sum of all the scores divided by the total number of measurements. When using the raw data such as the maximum oxygen uptake ($ml\ kg^{-1}\ min^{-1}$) measurements from Table 14.1, we need to calculate

$$\bar{X} = \Sigma X_i/n = (X_1 + X_2 + X_3 + \ldots + X_n)/n$$
$$= (60.9 + 59.3 + 59.2 + \ldots + 48.5 + 53.6)/30$$
$$= 1666.8/30$$
$$= 55.56$$

where X_i refers to the individual scores and Σ is the usual 'sigma' summation notation.

If the data are available only in the form of a frequency table (secondary data), an estimate of the arithmetic mean can be obtained by assuming all the scores of each class interval are approximated by its mid-point M_i. The estimated arithmetic mean for the maximum oxygen uptake ($ml\ kg^{-1}\ min^{-1}$) results given in Table 14.2 is given by,

$$\bar{X} = \Sigma (f_i M_i)/n = (f_1 M_1 + f_2 M_2 + \ldots + f_k M_k)/n$$
$$= (1 \times 47.95 + 1 \times 49.95 + 5 \times 52.95 + \ldots$$
$$+ 1 \times 63.95)/30$$
$$= 1670.5/30$$
$$= 55.68$$

where k equals the number of class intervals and M_i and f_i are the mid-point and frequency of the ith class interval respectively.

(b) Median

The median is the middle score of the ranked data. If there is an odd number of scores, the median is unique. However, if the number of scores is even, we simply take the arithmetic mean of the two middle values. To obtain the median of maximal oxygen uptake ($ml\ kg^{-1}\ min^{-1}$) results of Table 14.1 we need to arrange the scores in order of magnitude as follows:

48.5 50.6 51.2 51.8 52.4 52.8 52.9 53.0 53.0 53.4 53.6 54.0 54.4 54.4 55.0 55.1 55.7 56.1 57.0 57.1

57.3 58.1 58.3 58.9 59.2 59.3 59.5 60.3 60.9 63.0

Hence, the median (M) becomes

$$M = (55.0 + 55.1)/2 = 55.05$$

(c) Mode

The mode is the most frequent observation. In small data sets, the mode is not always unique. In the case of grouped or secondary data where a frequency table has been constructed, the mode can be obtained as follows;

$$\text{Mode} = L_1 + c(d_1/(d_1 + d_2))$$

where L_1 = lower class boundary of the modal class (i.e. the most frequent class interval)
c = size of the modal class interval
d_1 = excess of the modal frequency over frequency of the next lower class
d_2 = excess of the modal frequency over frequency of the next higher class

The mode for the maximum oxygen uptake results taken from Table 14.2 becomes

$$\text{Mode} = L_1 + c(d_1/(d_1 + d_2))$$
$$= 52.9 + 2(2/(2+3))$$
$$= 52.9 + 4/5 = 52.9 + 0.8$$
$$= 53.7$$

In summary, if the data are numerical (interval and ratio scales) and symmetric, the mean, median, and mode will all tend to coincide at the centre of the frequency distribution. As such, the arithmetic mean provides the simplest and best measure of central tendency. If, however, the numerical data have a skewed frequency distribution, the arithmetic mean will be distorted towards the longer tail of the distribution and the median would become a more representative average. If the observed information on a group of subjects is categorical, the calculation of the arithmetic mean is impossible. When the observed data are recorded as an ordered categorical (ordinal) scale, the median and mode are available as measures of central tendency. However, if the observed information on a group of subjects is simply a normal scale, the mode is the only measure of central tendency that remains available, e.g. the most popular sports footwear manufacturer.

14.2.5 MEASURES OF VARIATION OR DISPERSION

Although the arithmetic mean provides a satisfactory measure of location or central tendency, it fails to indicate the way the data are spread about this central point. Are all the observed measurements very similar, demonstrating little variation among the scores, or are the measurements spread over a wide range of observations? The degree to which the numerical data are spread out is called the variation or dispersion in the data. A number of measures of variation or dispersion is available, the most common being the range, mean deviation, the variance and the standard deviation (the standard deviation = $\sqrt{\text{variance}}$).

(a) Range

The range = highest score – lowest score (section 14.2.1), is the simplest measure of variation and has the advantage of being quick and simple to calculate. Its limitation is that it fails to represent the variation in all the data since it is obtained from just the two extreme scores.

(b) Mean deviation

The mean deviation is the sum of the deviations of a set of scores from their mean,

$$\text{Mean deviation} = \text{MD} = \Sigma \mid X_i - \overline{X} \mid / n$$

where the notation $\mid X_i - \overline{X} \mid$ denotes the absolute value of $(X_i - \overline{X})$, without regard to its sign. The mean deviation of the maximum oxygen uptake (ml kg^{-1} min^{-1}) results from Table 14.1 becomes,

$$\text{MD} = (\mid 160.9 - 55.56 \mid + \mid 59.3 - 55.56 \mid + \ldots$$
$$+ \mid 48.5 - 55.56 \mid + \mid 53.6 - 55.56 \mid)/30$$
$$= (5.34 + 3.74 + \ldots + 7.06 + 1.96)/30$$
$$= 85.71/30$$
$$= 2.857 \text{ (ml kg}^{-1}\text{ min}^{-1})$$

The advantages of the mean deviation are that it includes all the scores, it is easy to define, and it is easy to compute. Its disadvantage is its unsuitability for algebraic manipulations, since signs must be adjusted (ignored) in its definition, e.g. if the mean and mean deviations of two sets of scores are known, there is no formula allowing the calculations of the mean deviations of the combined set without going back to the original data.

(c) Variance

The variance of a set of data, denoted by s^2, is defined as the average of the squared deviations from the mean.

$$s^2 = \sum (X_i - \overline{X})^2/n$$

The variance overcomes the problem of converting positive and negative deviations into quantities that are all positive by the process of squaring. Unfortunately, whatever the units of the original data, the variance has to be described in these units 'squared'. For this reason the standard deviation = $\sqrt{\text{variance}}$, is more frequently reported. An alternative method of defining the variance is to divide the sum of squared deviations by $n-1$ rather than n. When we divide the sum of square deviations by n, the variance will show a systematic tendency to underestimate the variance of the entire population of scores, denoted by the Greek letter sigma (σ^2). When we divide the sum of squared deviations by $n-1$, however, we obtain an unbiased estimate of σ^2. Hence, the unbiased estimate of σ^2 is $s^2 = \Sigma(X_i - \overline{X})^2/(n-1)$ where the variance of estimate, s^2, has $n-1$ 'degrees of freedom', i.e. the maximum number of variates that can be freely assigned before the rest of the variates are completely determined.

(d) Standard deviation

The standard deviation, denoted by s, is the square root of the variance.

$$s = \sqrt{(\textstyle\sum_i (X_i - \overline{X})^2/n)}$$

The standard deviation of the maximal oxygen uptake (ml kg^{-1} min^{-1}) results from Table 14.1 can be found as follows,

$$s = \sqrt{[(60.9 - 55.56)^2 + (59.3 - 55.56)^2 + \ldots}$$
$$\sqrt{+ (48.5 - 55.56)^2 + (53.6 - 55.56)^2)/30]}$$
$$= \sqrt{[(28.52 + 13.99 + \ldots + 49.84 + 3.84)/30]}$$
$$= \sqrt{(341.53/30)}$$
$$= \sqrt{11.38}$$
$$= 3.373$$

The calculation above employs more computation than necessary and for many reasons it is more convenient to calculate the standard deviation using the alternative 'short method' formula:

$$s = \sqrt{[\Sigma X^2/n - (\Sigma X/n)^2]}$$
$$= \sqrt{(2949/30 - (1666.8/30)^2)}$$
$$= \sqrt{[3098.3 - (55.56)^2]}$$
$$= \sqrt{(3098.3 - 3086.9)}$$
$$= \sqrt{11.4}$$
$$= 3.376$$

The variance and standard deviation have a number of advantages over the mean deviation. In particular, they are more suitable for algebraic manipulation as demonstrated by the more convenient 'short method' formula given above.

14.2.6 RELATIVE MEASURE OF PERFORMANCE OR THE 'Z' STANDARD SCORE

A 'z' standard score is the difference between a particular score X_i and the mean X, relative to the standard deviation s, i.e.

$$z_i = (X_i - \overline{X})/s$$

An important characteristic of a standard score is that it provides a meaningful way of comparing scores from different distributions that have different means and standard deviations. To illustrate the value of standard scores, suppose we wished to compare a decathlete's performance in two events relative to the other competitors, e.g. 1500 and 100 metre run times, at a certain competition. Suppose the athlete ran the 1500 m in 4 min 20 s and the 100 m in 10.2 s. Clearly, a direct comparison of the two performances is impossible. However, if the mean performance (and standard deviation) of all the competing athletes at the two events were 4 min 30 s (10 s) and 10.5 s (0.2 s), respectively, the decathlete's standard scores at each event, recorded in seconds, are given by,

z(1500 metres) = (260 – 270)/10 = –10/10 = – 1.0

z(100metres) = (10.2 – 10.5)/0.2 = – 0.3/0.2

= – 1.5.

Clearly, the greater standard score, $z = -1.5$, indicates that the athlete performed better at the 100 metres than the 1500 metres relative to the other competitors. Note that standard scores also play an essential role when carrying out parametric tests of significance, discussed in section 14.4.

14.2.7 THE MINITAB COMMANDS TO ILLUSTRATE THE METHODS OF SECTION 14.2

Data in MINITAB are stored in columns. To enter the data we can use either the READ or SET command, e.g. the maximum oxygen uptake data in Table 14.1 could be entered or SET into column 1 (C1) by

```
MTB > SET C1
DATA > 60.9 59. 3 59 .2 5 8.9 58.3 58.1  55.7
         53.4 53.0 51.8
DATA > 50.6 54.4 63.0 60.3 59.5 57.3  57.1 57.0
         56.1 55.1
DATA > 55.0 54.4 54.0 53.0 52.9 52.8  52.4 51.2
         48.5 53.6
DATA > END
```

To help identification, the data in column C1 can now be named as follows:

```
MTB > NAME C1 'VO2 MAX'
```

The frequency table and distribution can be displayed with the histogram command, i.e.

```
MTB > HISTOGRAM C1
HISTOGRAM OF VO2 MAX N = 30
MID POINT COUNT
  48  1  *
  50  1  *
  52  5  *****
  54  7  *******
  56  4  ****
  58  6  ******
  62  0
  64  1  *
```

Note that when using the MINITAB histogram command, observations falling on a class boundary are put into the interval with the larger midpoint. Hence, in the above example, a score of 49 would be put into the class interval with midpoint 50. In reality, this decision rule will result in precisely the same frequency table and distribution given in Table 14.2 derived in section 14.2.1.

The simplest method to obtain most of the descriptive statistics given in sections 14.2.4 and 14.2.5 is to use the DESCRIBE command as follows:

```
MTB > DESCRIBE C1
              N  MEAN   MEDIAN  TRMEAN
VO2 MAX  30 55.60    55.050     55.531
            STDEV  SEMEAN
            3.432     0.627
               MIN      MAX   Q1     Q3
VO2 MAX  48.500 63.000 52.975 58.540
```

The term TRMEAN represents a trimmed mean, averaged from the middle 90% of the data, where 5% of the smallest and largest values are ignored. The standard error of the mean, SEMEAN, is defined as $s/\sqrt{n}$. The first and third quartiles are denoted by Q1 and Q3. Quartiles are obtained by ranking the data from the smallest to the largest scores. As described in section 14.2.3, the median or second quartile (Q2), is the middle score or the 50th percentile and Q1 and Q3 are the 25th and 75th percentiles, respectively. Note that the STDEV is calculated using the unbiased definition for the population variance σ^2, i.e. by dividing the sum of squared deviations by $n - 1$.

14.3 INVESTIGATING RELATIONSHIPS IN KINANTHROPOMETRY AND EXERCISE PHYSIOLOGY

14.3.1 CORRELATION

The first and most important step when investigating relationships between variables in kinanthropometry and exercise physiology is to plot the data in the form of a scatter diagram. The eye can still identify patterns or relationships in data better than any statistical tests. If X and Y denote the independent and dependent variables respectively of our experiment, a scatter diagram describes the location of points (X, Y) on rectangular co-ordinate system. The term correlation is used to describe the degree of relationship that exists between the dependent and independent variables.

(a) Positive correlation

Example 1: An example of a positive correlation is seen in Figure 14.2 between the mean power output (W) of 16 subjects, recorded on a non-motorized treadmill, and their body mass (kg) (Nevill *et al.*, 1992b). The scatter diagram demonstrates a positive correlation since the subjects with a greater body mass (X) are able to record a higher mean power output (Y), i.e. as X increases, Y also increases.

(b) Negative correlation

Example 2: In contrast, an example of a negative correlation is seen in Figure 14.3 between maximum oxygen uptake (ml kg^{-1} min^{-1}) and 10 mile run times (min) of 16 male subjects, representing a wide range of distance running abilities (adapted from Costill *et al.*, 1973). Figure 14.3 describes a negative correlation because the subjects with a lower 10 mile (16.1 km) run times (X) are found to have recorded higher maximum oxygen uptake measurements (Y), i.e. as X increases Y is found to decrease. If a scatter diagram indicates no obvious pattern or relationship between the two variables, then the variables are said to have no correlation, i.e. they are uncorrelated.

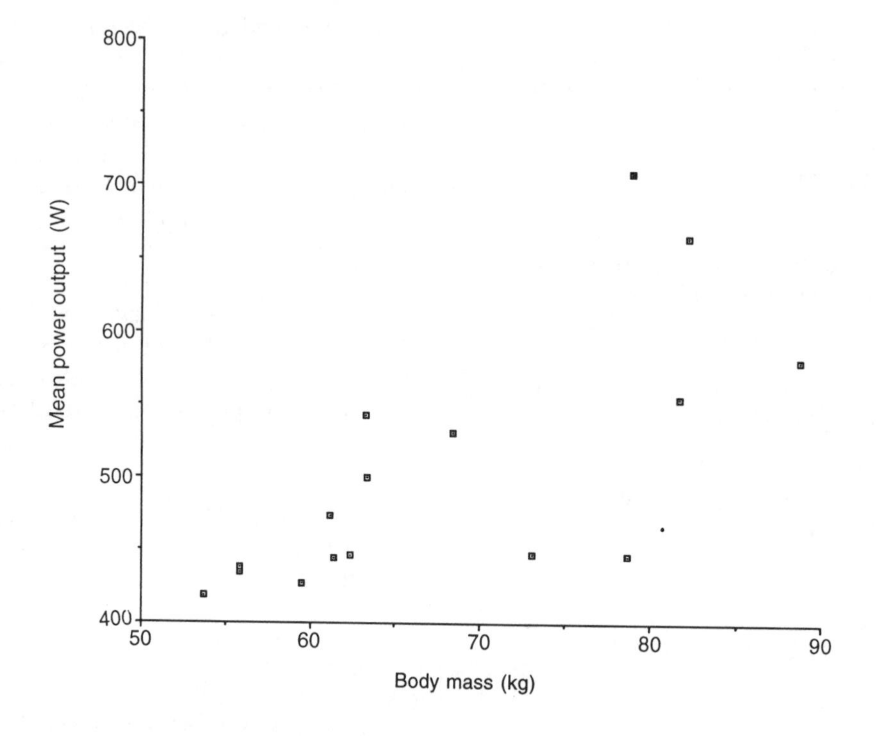

Figure 14.2 Mean power output (W) versus body mass (kg) of 16 male subjects, recorded on a non-motorized treadmill (Nevill *et al.*, 1992b).

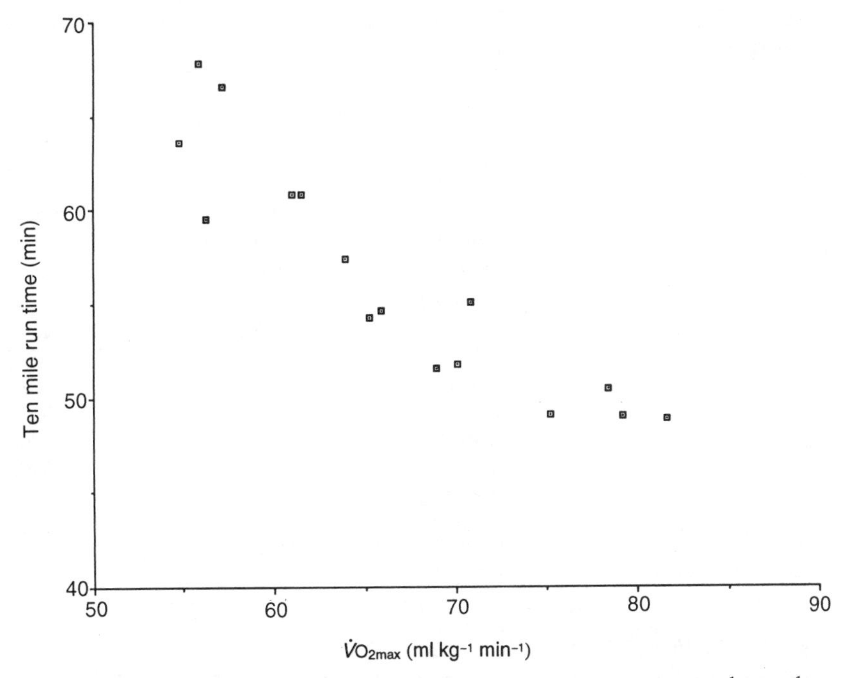

Figure 14.3 Ten mile run times (min) versus maximal oxygen uptake (ml kg^{-1} min^{-1}) of 16 male subjects (Costill *et al.*, 1973).

14.3.2 MEASURES OF CORRELATION

Although a scatter diagram gives a clear indication of the degree of relationship between two variables, a single numerical statistic or correlation coefficient would summarize the relationship and facilitate the comparison of several different correlations.

(a) Pearson's product–moment correlation coefficient

The most appropriate correlation coefficient for numerical variables was introduced by Karl Pearson and hence is often referred to as the Pearson's product–moment correlation coefficient. The definition of the product–moment correlation coefficient requires a new measure of variation similar to the variance introduced in section 14.2.3, known as the covariance, i.e.

$$s_{xy} = \Sigma (X_i - \overline{X}) (Y_i - \overline{Y}) / n$$

The covariance is a measure of the joint variation in X and Y, but its magnitude will depend on the variation in both variables. Hence, the product–moment correlation coefficient is defined as the ratio of the covariance to the product of the standard deviations of X and Y, given by

$$r = \frac{\Sigma(X_i - \overline{X})(Y_i - \overline{Y})}{\sqrt{[\Sigma (X_i - \overline{X})^2] [\Sigma (Y_i - \overline{Y})^2]}} \quad (14.1)$$

Note that the divisor (n) cancels in both the numerator and denominator terms in the ratio.

A more convenient formula to calculate the product–moment correlation coefficient (14.1) is given by

$$r = \frac{n \Sigma X_i Y_i - (\Sigma X)(\Sigma Y)}{\sqrt{[n \Sigma X_i^2 - (\Sigma X)^2] [n \Sigma Y_i^2 - (\Sigma Y)^2]}} \quad (14.2)$$

The correlation coefficient in section 14.3.1(a), from Nevill *et al.* (1992b), between mean power output (W) and body mass (kg)

Table 14.3 Data required to calculate the correlation coefficient between mean power output (W) and body mas (kg) for example 1 (Nevill *et al.*, 1992b)

Mean power (Y)	*Body mass (X)*	(Y^2)	(X^2)	(YX)
499.6	63.4	249600.2	4019.56	31674.6
473.7	61.2	224391.7	3745.44	28990.4
444.5	61.4	197580.2	3769.96	27292.3
438.0	55.8	191844.0	3113.64	24440.4
446.2	78.7	199094.5	6193.69	35115.9
665.8	82.1	443289.7	6740.41	54662.2
709.2	78.8	502964.7	6209.44	55885.0
542.5	63.3	294306.3	4006.89	34340.2
581.0	88.7	337561.0	7867.69	51534.7
434.1	55.8	188442.8	3113.64	24222.8
554.7	81.7	307692.1	6674.89	45319.0
418.3	53.7	174974.9	2883.69	22462.7
530.8	68.4	281748.6	4678.56	36306.7
446.8	62.4	199630.2	3893.76	27880.3
447.4	73.1	200166.8	5343.61	32704.9
426.6	59.5	181987.6	3540.25	25382.7
Total 8059.2	1088.0	4175275.3	75795.12	558214.8

can be obtained as follows. From the two columns 'mean power (Y)' and 'body mass (X)', three further columns are required, i.e. Y^2, X^2 and YX, given in Table 14.3.

The only additional information required to calculate the correlation coefficient, given by equation (14.2), is the number of subjects, $n = 16$. Hence, the correlation coefficient becomes

$$r = \frac{16\,(558214.8) - (1088.0)(8059.2)}{\sqrt{[16(75795.12) - (1088)^2]\,[16(4175275.3) - (8059.2)^2]}}$$

$$= \frac{8931436.8 - 8768409.6}{\sqrt{[1212721.9 - 1183744]\,[66804405 - 64950705]}}$$

$$= \frac{163027.2}{\sqrt{[28977.9]\,[1853699.8]}}$$

$$= \frac{163027.2}{231767.8}$$

$$= 0.703$$

The obtained value of + 0.703 indicates that for this group of subjects, there was a high positive correlation between the two variables. The correlation coefficient can take any value between + 1.00 and − 1.00, with values of r close to zero indicating no linear relationship between the two variables. The above calculations are somewhat complex due to the size or scale of the variables X and Y. However, the correlation coefficient is unaffected by adding or subtracting a constant value to or from either column. Hence, in example 2 (Costill *et al.*, 1973), by subtracting convenient constants, say 40 from the Y column, i.e. $y = (Y - 40)$ and 50 from the X column, i.e. $x = (X - 50)$ in the data in Table 14.4, an alternative 'short method' of calculating the correlation coefficient, between 10 mile run times (min) and maximal oxygen uptake or $\dot{V}O_{2\,max}$ (ml kg^{-1} min^{-1}) can be used to simplify the arithmetic.

Hence, the correlation coefficient between 10 mile run times (min) and maximum oxygen uptake or $\dot{V}O_{2\,max}$ (ml kg^{-1} min^{-1}) becomes

$$r = \frac{16\,(3593.1) - (261.4)(265.9)}{\sqrt{[16\,(4858.4) - (261.4)^2]\,[16\,(5566.3) - (265.9)^2]}}$$

$$= \frac{57489.6 - 69506.26}{\sqrt{[77734.4 - 68329.96]\,[89060.8 - 70702.8]}}$$

$$= \frac{-120116.7}{\sqrt{[9404.4]\,[18358]}}$$

$$= \frac{-12016.7}{13139.48}$$

$$= -0.9145$$

Table 14.4 Data required to calculate the correlation coefficient between 10 mile run time (min) and maximal oxygen uptake (ml kg^{-1} min^{-1}) for example 2 (Costill *et al.*, 1973)

Run time (*Y*)	$\dot{V}O_{2\,max}(X)$	$y = (Y - 40)$	$x = (X - 50)$	x^2	y^2	xy
48.9	81.6	8.9	31.6	79.21	998.56	281.24
49.0	79.2	9.0	29.2	81.00	852.64	262.80
49.1	75.2	9.1	25.2	82.81	635.04	229.32
50.5	78.4	10.5	28.4	110.25	806.56	298.20
51.6	68.9	11.6	18.9	134.56	357.21	219.24
51.8	70.1	11.8	20.1	139.24	404.01	237.18
54.3	65.2	14.3	15.2	204.49	231.04	217.36
54.6	65.9	14.6	15.9	213.16	252.81	232.14
55.1	70.8	15.1	20.8	228.01	432.64	314.08
57.4	63.9	17.4	13.9	302.76	193.21	241.86
59.5	56.3	19.5	6.3	380.25	39.69	122.85
60.8	61.0	20.8	11.0	432.64	121.00	228.80
60.8	61.5	20.8	11.5	432.64	132.25	239.20
63.6	54.8	23.6	4.8	556.96	23.04	113.28
66.6	57.2	26.6	7.2	707.56	51.84	191.52
67.8	55.9	27.8	5.9	772.84	34.81	164.02
Total 901.4	1065.9	261.4	265.9	4858.4	5566.3	3593.1

In this example, the value of $r = -0.91$ indicates that for this group of subjects, there was a high negative correlation between the two variables. Pearson's product–moment correlation coefficient is an appropriate statistic to describe the relationship between two variables provided the data are approximately linear and numerical (interval or ratio scales of measurement). However, Pearson's correlation coefficient is not the only method of measuring the relationship between two variables.

Table 14.5 Six gymnasts ranked on performance by two independent judges

	Ranks given by			
Gymnast	*Judge1* (R_1)	*Judge2* (R_2)	$D = R_1 - R_2$	D^2
1	5	6	−1	1
2	2	5	−3	9
3	1	1	0	0
4	6	3	3	9
5	3	4	−1	1
6	4	2	2	4
Totals			0	$\Sigma D^2 = 24$

(b) Spearman's rank correlation coefficient

The ranks given by two independent judges to a group of six gymnasts are given in Table 14.5. Are the two judges in agreement?

The most frequently used statistic to describe the relationship between ranks is Spearman's rank correlation coefficient r_s, given by

$$r_s = 1 - \frac{6.\sum D^2}{N(N^2 - 1)}$$

where D is the difference between paired ranks and N is the number of pairs. For the ranks given in Table 14.5, the Spearman's rank correlation becomes,

$$r_s = 1 - \frac{6.24}{6(6^2 - 1)}$$

$$= 1 - 24/35$$

$$= 0.313$$

As with the Pearson's correlation coefficient, the value of r_s lies between $+1.0$ and -1.0. Suppose Judge 1 decided that gymnast 2 and gymnast 3 were equally good in their performances and should share first place. This can be incorporated into the calculation by averaging the two shared ranks in question. In this example the two gymnasts were sharing ranks 1 and 2, so the average 1.5 would be given to both performers. Note that the next best gymnast would receive the rank of 3.

14.3.3 PREDICTION AND LINEAR REGRESSION

Suppose we wish to predict a male endurance athlete's 10 mile (16.1 km) run time having previously recorded his maximal oxygen uptake. If we assume that our athlete is of a similar standard as the subjects used by Costill *et al.* (1973), we could use these data to predict the 10 mile run time of such an athlete. Nevill *et al.* (1990) were able to show that since maximal oxygen uptake was a rate of using oxygen per minute, i.e. (ml kg^{-1} min^{-1}), running performance was also better recorded as a rate, e.g. average run speed in metres per second (m s^{-1}). Hence, when the 10 mile run times of Costill *et al.* (1973) were recalculated as average run speeds m s^{-1} and correlated with their maximal oxygen uptake results, the relationship appeared more linear, Figure 14.4, and correlation increased from $r = -0.91$ to $r = 0.935$.

Let us assume that we wish to predict the average running speed (Y) of an athlete from the maximal oxygen uptake (X). The predicted variable Y, is often described as the dependent variable whereas the variable X that provides the information on which the predictions are based, is referred to as the independent variable. If it is accepted that the relationship in Figure 14.4 between running speed and maximal oxygen uptake is a straight line, the equation of a line can be written as follows:

$$Y = a + bX$$

where a, the Y-intercept, and b, the slope of the line, are both constants.

The simplest method of estimating the constants a and b is to use 'the method of least squares'. If we denote the predicted or estimated value of the dependent variable Y as $Y_e = a + bX$, the 'method of least squares' is the method that minimizes the squared differences $d^2 = \Sigma(Y - Y_e)^2$. The equation of the line, often referred to as the 'least squares regression line of Y on X', fitted to n points (X, Y) by the method of least squares is given by,

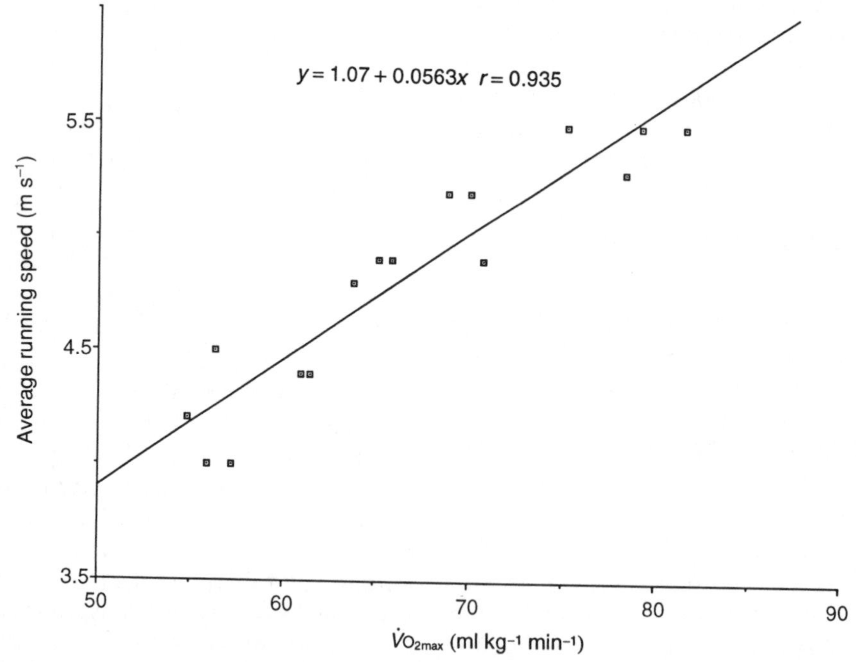

Figure 14.4 Ten mile run times, recalculated as average run speeds (m s^{-1}), versus maximal oxygen uptake results (ml kg^{-1} min^{-1}) (Costill *et al.*, 1973).

$$Y_e = a + bX$$

$$\text{where } b = \frac{n\,\Sigma X_i Y_i - (\Sigma X)(\Sigma Y),}{n\,\Sigma X_i^2 - (\Sigma X)^2} \qquad (14.3)$$

and

$$a = \Sigma Y_i/n - b\,\Sigma X_i/n \qquad (14.4)$$

The regression line to predict the average 10 mile run speed from an athlete's maximal oxygen uptake measurements can be obtained from the quantities in Table 14.6. Using equation (14.3), the slope of the line becomes,

$$b = \frac{16.5200.87 - (1065.9)(77.1)}{16.72156.35 - (1065.9)^2}$$

$$= \frac{(83213.92 - 82180.89)}{1154501.6 - 1136142.8}$$

$$= 1033.03/18358.8$$

$$= 0.05627$$

and the intercept a becomes,

$$a = \Sigma Y_i/n - b\,\Sigma X_i/n$$

$$= 77.1/16 - 0.05627.\,1065.9/16$$

$$= 4.82 - 3.75$$

$$= 1.07$$

Table 14.6 Data required to calculate the regression line between average 10 mile (16.1 km) run speed ($m\,s^{-1}$) and maximal oxygen uptake ($ml\,kg^{-1}\,min^{-1}$) for example 2 (Costill *et al.*, 1973)

$\dot{V}O_{2\,max}$ (X)	*Speed* (Y)	X^2	Y^2	XY
81.6	5.5	6658.56	30.25	448.80
79.2	5.5	6272.64	30.25	435.60
75.2	5.5	5655.04	30.25	413.60
78.4	5.3	6146.56	28.09	415.52
68.9	5.2	4747.21	27.04	358.28
70.1	5.2	4914.01	27.04	364.52
65.2	4.9	4251.04	24.01	319.48
65.9	4.9	4342.81	24.01	322.91
70.8	4.9	5012.64	24.01	346.92
63.9	4.7	4083.21	22.09	300.33
56.3	4.5	3169.69	20.25	253.35
61.0	4.4	3721.00	19.36	268.40
61.5	4.4	3782.25	19.36	270.60
54.8	4.2	3003.04	17.64	230.16
57.2	4.0	3271.84	16.00	228.80
55.9	4.0	3124.81	16.00	223.60
Totals 1065.9	77.1	72156.35	375.65	5200.87

Hence, the least squares regression line, required to predict the average 10 mile run speed from maximal oxygen uptake, is given by

$$Y_e = a + bX$$

$$Y_e = 1.07 + 0.05627\,X$$

An athlete who recorded a maximal oxygen uptake of 80 ($ml\,kg^{-1}\,min^{-1}$) would expect to run 10 miles (16 km) at an average speed of $1.07 + 0.05627.(80) = 5.57$ ($m\,s^{-1}$), i.e., he would expect to complete the 10 mile distance in 48.14 (min).

14.3.4 THE MINITAB COMMANDS TO ILLUSTRATE THE METHODS OF SECTION 14.3

One of the most important and useful statistical tools used to explore relationships is the scatter diagram. This can be easily obtained using the MINITAB 'PLOT' command as follows (Figure 14.5):

```
MTB > PLOT C1 C2
```

The Pearson product–moment correlation coefficient can be obtained using the MINITAB 'CORRELATION' command as follows:

```
MTB > CORRELATION C1 C2

CORRELATION OF POWER AND MASS
= 0.703
```

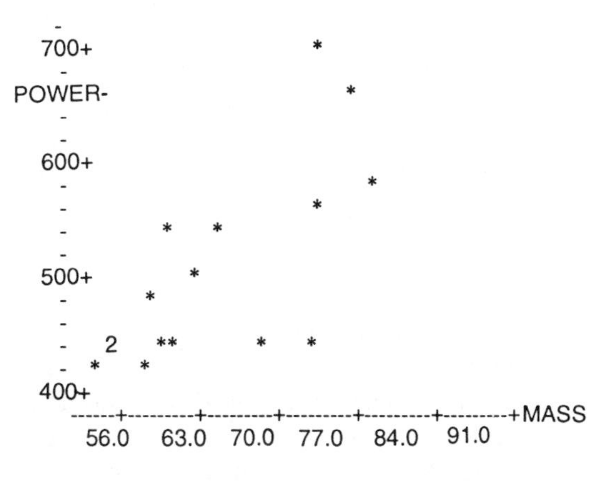

Figure 14.5 Example of MINITAB scatterplot.

Similarly, the correlation between the 10 mile run times and maximal oxygen uptake can be obtained as,

MTB CORRELATION C3 C4

CORRELATION OF RUNTIME AND VO2MAX = – 0.915

However, when the 10 mile run times were recalculated as an average speed (m s^{-1}) using the 'LET' command, as follows (there are 1609.35 metres in a mile),

MTB > LET C5 = 10*1609.35/(C3*60)

MTB > NAME C5 'SPEED'

MTB > CORRELATION C5 C4

CORRELATION OF SPEED AND VO2MAX = 0.935

The least squares linear regression line to predict average 10 mile run speed from maximal oxygen uptake, can be obtained as follows,

MTB REGRESSION C5 1 C4

THE REGRESSION EQUATION IS

SPEED = 1.07 + 0.0563 VO2MAX

PREDICTOR	COEF	STDEV	T-RATIO	P
CONSTANT	1.0702	0.3714	2.88	0.012
VO2MAX	0.056269	0.005531	10.17	0.000

s = 0.1874 R–SQ = 88.1% R–SQ(ADJ) = 87.2%

ANALYSIS OF VARIANCE

SOURCE	DF	SS	MS	F	P
REGRESSION	1	3.6330	3.6330	103.50	0.000
ERROR	14	0.4914	0.0351		
TOTAL	15	4.1244			

The first table in the above output gives the estimated values of the coefficients, the intercept *a* (CONSTANT) and the slope *b* ($\dot{V}$O2MAX), along with their standard deviations, *t*-values for testing if the coefficients are 0, and the *P*-value for this test. Below this table, the estimated standard deviation about the regression line, $s = 0.1874$ is given. This is followed by the coefficient of determination, $R^2 = 88.1$ and the R^2(adj.) = 87.2, adjusted for the degrees of freedom.

Finally, the Analysis of Variance table contains the component sums of squares. The total variation of the dependent variable (SPEED) is partitioned into that explained by the regression line (REGRESSION) and the remaining unexplained variation (ERROR). Note that the estimated variance about the regression line MS ERROR $= s^2 = (0.1874)^2 = 0.0351$.

14.4 COMPARING EXPERIMENTAL DATA IN KINANTHROPOMETRY

Laboratory-based experiments are not conducted simply to describe the results of the experiment as outlined in sections 14.2 and 14.3. The researcher will often wish to 'test' whether the experimental results (dependent variable) have been affected by different experimental conditions (the independent variable). This important step is the function of inferential statistics. For further reading in the methods of inferential statistics, see Snedecor and Cochran (1989).

14.4.1 DRAWING INFERENCES FROM EXPERIMENTAL DATA: INDEPENDENT SUBJECTS

The simplest experiment to design involves a group of subjects that require to be divided into two groups on a random basis. The two most frequently used tests that adopt this design are:

1. The *t*-test for independent samples.
2. The Mann–Whitney test for independent samples.

These tests will be introduced together with some general points about inferential statistics with examples from kinanthropometry and exercise physiology.

(a) The *t*-test for independent samples

Example 3: A group of 13 male subjects was divided into two groups at random. One group of six subjects was given an exercise training programme for 6 months whereas the remaining seven subjects acted as a control group. The blood lactate concentrations m mol l^{-1} of seven untrained and six trained male subjects were taken while running at 70% of $\dot{V}O_{2\,max}$ and are given in Table 14.7.

The requirements of the independent *t*-test are that: (1) the samples are drawn from a normal population with equal variance, and (2) the variable is measured in the interval scale.

Clearly the blood lactate measurements can take any value within a certain range of observations and hence, we can assume the measurements are recorded on an interval scale. Also by simply producing a frequency table, the two sets of data can be checked to demonstrate an approximate normal distribution, i.e. symmetric and bell shaped. All these characteristics are described in section 14.2.

Table 14.7 Blood lactate concentrations recorded at 70% of $\dot{V}O_{2\,max}$

Lactate conc. (mmol l^{-1})	
Untrained subjects	Trained subjects
2.5	1.8
2.9	2.6
1.9	2.4
3.6	1.5
2.9	2.4
3.7	2.0
2.6	

The steps required to implement the *t*-test for independent samples are as follows.

1. Calculate the mean, standard deviation and variance for both samples.

	Untrained subjects ($n_1 = 7$)	Trained subjects ($n_2 = 6$)
Mean	$\overline{X}_1 = 2.87$	$\overline{X}_2 = 2.12$
Standard deviation	$s_1 = 0.63$	$s_2 = 0.42$
Variance	$(s_1)^2 = 0.3969$	$(s_2)^2 = 0.1764$

2. The assumption of equal variances can be confirmed using the *F* ratio test. For this test we need to calculate the ratio of variances, taking care to put the largest variance on top, i.e.

$$F = (s_1)^2/(s_2)^2 = 0.3969/0.1764 = 2.25$$

The value of the *F* ratio has two 'degrees of freedom' parameters. The degrees of freedom associated with the numerator variance is $n_1 - 1 = 6$, whereas the degrees of freedom associated with the denominator variance is $n_2 - 1 = 5$.

If the two variances are similar, the value of *F* would be expected to be near unity. If a very large value of *F* (a small *F* ratio, less than unity, has been precluded by always requiring the largest variance to be the numerator term) is obtained, the assumption of equal variances should be rejected. From the *F* tables (Table 14.A.2) we find that the critical value of *F* is given by $F_{0.025}$. Hence, we conclude that the two variances are not significantly different (5% level of significance).

3. Since the population variances are assumed to be the same, the variances of the two samples can now be combined to produce a single (pooled) estimate for the population variance σ^2. As in our example the sample sizes are not equal. Hence, a weighted average must be used to obtain the pooled estimate of the variance s^2, i.e.

$$s^2 = \frac{(n_1 - 1)\,(s_1)^2 + (n_2 - 1)\,(s_2)^2}{(n_1 + n_2 - 2)}$$

$$s^2 = \frac{(6)\,(0.3969) + (5)\,(0.1764)}{(7 + 6 - 2)}$$

$$s^2 = \frac{2.38 + 0.882}{(11)}$$

$$s^2 = 3.262/11 = 0.297$$

4. We can now proceed to test for differences between the sample means. Provided the population means are normally distributed with a common variance, the

distribution of differences between means is known as the t distribution. Under the assumption that no difference exists between the two population mean (commonly referred to as the Null hypothesis), the standard score t value (and therefore a probability value) can be found for any difference, as follows:

$$t = \frac{\overline{X}_1 - \overline{X}_2}{\sqrt{(s^2/n_1 + s^2/n_2)}}$$

$$t = \frac{2.87 - 2.12}{\sqrt{(0.297/7 + 0.297/6)}}$$

$$t = \frac{0.75}{\sqrt{(0.0424 + 0.0494)}}$$

$$t = \frac{0.75}{\sqrt{(0.0918)}}$$

$$t = 0.75/0.303 = 2.48$$

The degrees of freedom associated with this value of t is determined from the estimate of the population variance in step 3 above, i.e. $df = n_1 + n_2 - 2 = 11$. If the two sample means are similar, the value of t would be expected to be near zero. If a large value of t is obtained, the assumption of equal means should be rejected. From t tables (Table 14.A.1) we find that the critical value of t is given by $t_{0.025}(11) = 2.201$. Hence, we conclude that the two means are significantly different (5% level of significance), i.e., there is evidence to suggest that there is a significant difference in blood lactate concentrations between trained and untrained subjects whilst running at 70% of $\dot{V}O_{2\,max}$.

The above t test is called a two-tailed test of significance. The assumption of equal means would have been rejected if the t value was either greater than the critical $t_{0.025}$ value or less than $t_{0.025}$. On the other hand, if we suspect that a difference between the mean blood concentrations does exist, the trained subjects would have lower scores than the untrained subjects, a one-tailed test can be used. For this one-tailed test, the critical value of t is given by $t_{0.05}(11) = 1.796$, allowing the 5% level of significance to remain in one tail of the t distribution. In our example, the observed t value of 2.48 still exceeds this critical value of 1.796 and the conclusion remains the same.

(b) The Mann–Whitney test for independent samples

If any of the requirements of the independent t-test are not satisfied, the Mann–Whitney test will provide a similar test but make no assumptions about the level of measurement nor the shape and size of the population distributions.

Example 4: The calf muscle's time-to-peak tension (TPT) values of eight male sprint trained athletes and eight male endurance trained athletes are given in Table 14.8. (A muscle's time-to- peak tension is thought to be an indicator of its fibre type.)

The steps required to implement the Mann–Whitney test for independent samples are as follows.

1. Let n_1 be the size of the smaller group of scores, and n_2 be the size of the larger group. In our example, the sample sizes are equal. Hence, either group can be arbitrarily assigned as the group with n_1 scores.
2. Rank the combined set of $n_1 + n_2$ results. Use rank 1 for the lowest, 2 for the next

Table 14.8 The calf muscle's time-to-peak tension recorded in milliseconds (ms) and corresponding ranks

	Sprint trained athletes ($n_1 = 8$)		*Endurance trained athletes* ($n_2 = 8$)	
	TPT	Rank	TPT	Rank
	110	4	118	12.5
	117	10	109	3
	111	5	122	15
	112	6	114	8
	117	10	117	10
	113	7	120	14
	106	1	124	16
	108	2	118	12.5
Total		45		91

lowest, and so on (if two or more scores have the value, give each score the arithmetic mean of the shared ranks).

3. Sum the ranks of the group with n_1 scores. Let this sum be called R_1. For our example, the sprint trained athletes ranks sum to $R_1 = 45$.
4. Calculate the Mann–Whitney U statistic as follows

$$U = n_1 n_2 + n_1(n_1 + 1)/2 - R_1$$

$$= 8.8 + 8\,(8 + 1)/2 - 45$$

$$= 64 + 36 - 45 = 55$$

5. Calculate U′ statistic, given by

$$U' = n_1 n_2 - U$$

$$= 64 - 55 = 9$$

6. From the tables for the Mann–Whitney U statistic (Table 14.A.4) and assuming a two-tailed test (5% level of significance), we find the critical value is 13. If the observed value of U or U′ (whichever is the smaller) is less than or equal to the critical value of U, the assumption that the two samples have identical distributions can be rejected.

In our example, U′ = 9 (the smaller of 55 and 9) is less than the critical value 13. Hence, there is a significant difference between the sprint-trained and endurance-trained athletes in time-to-peak tension of their calf muscles.

14.4.2 DRAWING INFERENCES FROM EXPERIMENTAL DATA: CORRELATED SAMPLES

In the previous section, we considered experiments that use independent groups of subjects. The problem with this type of design is that subjects can vary dramatically in their response to the task, i.e. the differences between subjects tend to obscure the experimental effect. Fortunately 'correlated samples' experimental designs will overcome these problems of large variations between subjects. This can be done using a repeated measures design, where the same subject performs both experimental conditions. Alternatively, subjects can be paired off on the basis of relevant characteristics andthe subjects from each pair are then allocated at random to one or the other experimental condition. This type of experimental design in known as the paired subjects design.

Two of the most frequently used tests to investigate correlated sample experimental designs are:

1. The t-test for correlated samples.
2. The Wilcoxon test for correlated samples.

As in section 14.4.1, these tests will be introduced using examples from kinanthropometry and exercise physiology.

(a) The t-test for correlated samples

Example 5: Ten subjects were randomly selected to take part in an experiment to determine if isometric training can increase leg strength. The results are given in Table 14.9

The requirements of the correlated t-test are that (a) the differences between each pair of scores are drawn from a normal population and (b) these differences are measured in the interval scale.

Clearly, the differences in the strength measurements can take any value within a continuous range, confirming an interval scale. A simple frequency table can be used to

Table 14.9 Leg strength in newtons (N) before and after isometric training

Before training (X_i)	*After training* (Y_i)	*Differences* ($D_i = Y_i - X_i$)
480	484	4
669	676	7
351	355	4
450	447	−3
373	372	−1
320	322	2
612	625	13
510	517	7
480	485	5
492	502	10

check the differences have an approximate normal distribution, i.e. symmetric and bell shaped (in particular, no obvious outliers). Again, all these characteristics are described in section 14.2.

The steps required to implement the t-test for correlated samples are as follows.

1. Calculate the differences between each pair of scores, i.e., $D_i = X_i - Y_i$. Care should be taken to subtract consistently, recording any negative differences.
2. Calculate the mean and standard deviation of the differences D_i using the unbiased estimate for the population standard deviation, i.e. $s = \sqrt{[\Sigma (X_i - \bar{X})^2/(n-1)]}$. In the present example the mean and standard deviation were $\bar{D} = 4.8$ and $s = 4.8$.
3. Calculate the t standard score given by

$$t = \bar{D}/(s/\sqrt{n})$$
$$= 4.8/(4.8/\sqrt{10})$$
$$= 4.8/(4.8/3.16) = 4.8/1.52$$
$$= 3.16$$

4. The degrees of freedom associated with this value of t is determined from the estimate of the population variance in step 3 above, i.e. $df = n - 1 = 9$. If the two experimental conditions produce a similar response to the given task, the differences D_i will be relatively small and the value of t would be expected to be near zero. If a large value of t is obtained, the assumption of equal differences should be rejected. From the t tables (Table 14.A.1) we find that the critical value of t is given by $t_{0.025}(9) = 2.262$. Hence, we conclude that the two experimental conditions are significantly different (5% level of significance), i.e., it would appear that leg strength measurements before and after isometric training are significantly different. Clearly, by observing the differences in Table 14.9, the leg strength had improved, on average, by 4.8 N.

As with the tests for independent samples, if we assume that isometric training will improve leg strength, a one-tailed test can be used. For this one-tailed test, the critical value of t is given by $t_{0.05}(9) = 1.833$, allowing the 5% level of significance to remain in one tail of the t distribution. In this case, the observed t value of 3.16 still exceeds this critical value of 1.833 and our conclusion remains the same.

(b) The Wilcoxon test for correlated samples

If some of the requirements of the correlated t-test were not satisfied, the Wilcoxon matched-pairs sign-ranks test will provide the same function as the correlated t-test but would make no assumptions about the shape of the population distributions.

Example 6: A study was designed to investigate the effects of an aerobics class on reducing percentage body fat. The percentage body fat measurements of ten subjects, before and after the aerobics course, are given in Table 14.10.

The steps required to implement the Wilcoxon test for correlated samples are as follows.

1. Calculate the differences between each pair of scores, i.e., $D_i = X_i - Y_i$. As with the correlated t-test, care should be taken to subtract consistently, recording any negative differences.
2. Ignoring the sign, rank the differences using rank 1 for the lowest, 2 for the next lowest, and so on (if two or more differen-

Table 14.10 The percentage body fat, before and after an aerobics course, and the corresponding differences and ranked differences (ignoring signs)

Subject	*Before* (X_i)	*After* (Y_i)	*Differences* $(D_i = Y_i - X_i)$	*Ranks*
1	34.4	33.5	−0.9	4
2	37.9	34.7	−3.2	10
3	35.2	35.3	0.1	1
4	37.2	34.2	−3.0	9
5	45.1	43.9	−1.2	5
6	34.1	35.7	1.6	6
7	36.0	34.2	−1.8	7
8	38.9	36.2	−2.7	8
9	36.1	35.9	−0.2	2
10	28.3	27.8	−0.5	3

ces have the value, give each score the arithmetic mean of the shared ranks. Any pairs with differences equal to zero are eliminated from the test).

3. Sum the ranks of the less frequent sign and call this sum *T*. For our example, the positive ranks are less frequent and give $T = 1 + 6 = 7$.
4. Using the critical tables for the Wilcoxon T statistic (Table 14.A.5), assuming a two-tailed test (5% level of significance), we find the critical value ($n = 10$). If the observed value of T is less than or equal to the critical value of *T*, the assumption that the experimental conditions are the same can be rejected.

In our example, the observed $T = 7$ value is less than the critical value 8. Hence, there is a significant reduction in percentage body fat during the aerobics course.

14.4.3 THE MINITAB COMMANDS TO ILLUSTRATE THE METHODS OF SECTION 14.4

The *t*-test for independent samples is obtained in MINITAB as follows. First, the two groups of data are SET into two separate columns C1 and C2. Then by typing the command TWO-SAMPLE C1 C2, we get the following output.

MTB > TWO SAMPLE C1 C2;
SUBC > POOLED.

TWO SAMPLE T FOR UNTRAIN VS TRAINED

	N	MEAN	STDEV	SE MEAN
UNTRAIN	7	2.871	0.629	0.24
TRAINED	6	2.117	0.422	0.17

95 PCT CI FOR MU UNTRAIN - MU TRAINED: (0.09, 1.42)

TTEST MU UNTRAIN = MU TRAINED (VS NE): T = 2.49 P = 0.030 DF = 11

POOLED STDEV = 0.545

The subcommand POOLED will provide the solution that assumes the two populations have equal variances. By default, the 95% confidence interval is given, followed by the two sample (independent) *t*-test. A two-tailed test is provided automatically with the standard score t value, associated probability and appropriate degrees of freedom. If a one-tailed t-test is required, the subcommand ALTERNATIVE = +1 or – 1 gives the alternative test C1 > C2 or C1 < C2 respectively.

The MINITAB command to implement the MANN-WHITNEY test for independent samples, stored in C3 (SPRINT) and C4 (ENDURE), is given as follows;

MTB MANN-WHITNEY C3 C4

MANN-WHITNEY CONFIDENCE INTERVAL AND TEST

SPRIT N = 8 MEDIAN = 111.50
ENDURE N = 8 MEDIAN = 118.00

POINT ESTIMATE FOR ETA1-ETA2 IS – 6.50
95.0 PCT C.1. FOR ETA1 – ETA 2 is (– 11.00, – 1.00) W= 45
TEST OF ETA1 = ETA2 VS. ETA1 N.E. ETA2 IS SIGNIFICANT AT 0.0181

THE TEST IS SIGNIFICANT AT 0.0177 (ADJUSTED FOR TIES)

The median values are given for both samples followed by the 95% confidence intervals for the difference between population medians ETA1 – ETA2. Note that the confidence interval does not contain the value zero. Next the sum of ranks W (R_1 in our notation) is given followed by the Mann–Whitney (two-tailed) test of significance. As with the two sample independent *t*-test, if a one-tailed Mann–Whitney test is required, the subcommand ALTERNATIVE $= +1$ *or* -1 gives the alternative test C3 > C4 or C3 < C4, respectively.

The MINITAB commands to implement the *t*-test for correlated samples, stored in columns C5 (AFTER1) and C6 (BEFORE1), are as follows. First, the differences between the leg strength before and after training need to be calculated. This is achieved using the LET command.

MTB > LET C7 = C5 – C6
MTB > NAME C7 'DIFF1'

The *t*-test for correlated samples is obtained using the TTEST command.

MTB > TTEST C7

TEST OF MU = 0.00 VS MU N.E 0.00

	N	MEAN	STDEV	SE MEAN	T	P VALUE
DIFF1	10	4.80	4.80	1.52	3.16	0.012

The resulting table provides the mean differences, the standard deviation (using the unbiased estimate for the population mean $s = \sqrt{[\Sigma (X_i - \overline{X})^2/(n-1)]}$, the standard error of the mean $s/\sqrt{n}$, followed by the *t* standard score and its associated probability.

The MINITAB commands for the WILCOXON test are similar to the *t*-test for correlated samples. Once again, the differences between the percentage body fat measurements before and after the aerobics course, in C8 (AFTER2) and C9 (BEFORE2), need to be calculated. This is achieved using the LET command.

MTB > LET C10 = C8 – C9

MTB > NAME C10 'DIFF2'

The Wilcoxon test for correlated samples is obtained using the WTEST command.

MTB WTEST C10

TEST OF MEDIAN = 0.00 VERSUS MEDIAN N.E. 0.00

	N	N FOR TEST	WILCOXON STATISTIC	P-VALUE	ESTIMATED MEDIAN
DIFF2	10	10	7.0	0.041	-1.200

The test conducts a Wilcoxon signed-rank test assuming the median value of the differences is zero, using a two-tailed test. The number of differences is stated. This is followed by the sum of ranks corresponding to the positive differences together with its associated probability. Finally, the estimated median is provided, indicating the nature of the differences. In our example, the majority of differences were negative. Hence, the estimated median was also negative, confirming the findings of the Wilcoxon test, i.e., the aerobics course resulted in a significant reduction in the participants' percentage body fat.

APPENDIX A: CRITICAL VALUES

Table 14.A.1 The critical values of the *t*-distribution

	Level of significance for one-tailed test					
	0.10	*0.05*	*0.025*	*0.01*	*0.005*	*0.0005*
df	*Level of significance for two-tailed test*					
	0.20	*0.10*	*0.05*	*0.02*	*0.01*	*0.001*
1	3.078	6.314	12.706	31.821	63.657	636.619
2	1.886	2.920	4.303	6.965	9.925	31.598
3	1.638	2.353	3.182	4.541	5.841	12.941
4	1.533	2.132	2.776	3.747	4.604	8.610
5	1.476	2.015	2.571	3.365	4.032	6.859
6	1.440	1.943	2.447	3.143	3.707	5.959
7	1.415	1.895	2.365	2.998	3.499	5.405
8	1.397	1.860	2.306	2.896	3.355	5.041
9	1.383	1.833	2.262	2.821	3.250	4.781
10	1.372	1.812	2.228	2.764	3.169	4.587
11	1.363	1.796	2.201	2.718	3.106	4.437
12	1.356	1.782	2.179	2.681	3.055	4.318
13	1.350	1.771	2.160	2.650	3.012	4.221
14	1.345	1.761	2.145	2.624	2.977	4.140
15	1.341	1.753	2.131	2.602	2.947	4.073
16	1.337	1.746	2.120	2.583	2.921	4.015
17	1.333	1.740	2.110	2.567	2.898	3.965
18	1.330	1.734	2.101	2.552	2.878	3.922
19	1.328	1.729	2.093	2.539	2.861	3.883
20	1.325	1.725	2.086	2.528	2.845	3.850
21	1.323	1.721	2.080	2.518	2.831	3.819
22	1.321	1.717	2.074	2.508	2.819	3.792
23	1.319	1.714	2.069	2.500	2.807	3.767
24	1.318	1.711	2.064	2.492	2.797	3.745
25	1.316	1.708	2.060	2.485	2.787	3.725
26	1.315	1.706	2.056	2.479	2.779	3.707
27	1.314	1.703	2.052	2.473	2.771	3.690
28	1.313	1.701	2.048	2.467	2.763	3.674
29	1.311	1.699	2.045	2.462	2.756	3.659
30	1.310	1.697	2.042	2.457	2.750	3.646
40	1.303	1.684	2.021	2.423	2.704	3.551
60	1.296	1.671	2.000	2.390	2.660	3.460
120	1.289	1.658	1.980	2.358	2.617	3.373
∞	1.282	1.645	1.960	2.326	2.576	3.291

Adapted from Table III of R.A. Fisher and F. Yates, *Statistical Tables for Biological, Agricultural and Medical Research* (1948 ed.), Oliver and Boyd, Edinburgh and London, by permission of the authors and publishers.

Table 14.A.2 The critical values of the F-distribution at the 5% level of significance (one-tailed)

df [a]	*Degrees of freedom for numerator*																		
	1	*2*	*3*	*4*	*5*	*6*	*7*	*8*	*9*	*10*	*12*	*15*	*20*	*24*	*30*	*40*	*60*	*120*	*∞*
1	161	200	216	225	230	234	237	239	241	242	244	246	248	249	250	251	252	253	254
2	18.5	19.0	19.2	19.3	19.3	19.4	19.4	19.4	19.4	19.4	19.4	19.4	19.4	19.5	19.5	19.5	19.5	19.5	19.5
3	10.1	9.55	9.28	9.12	9.01	8.94	8.89	8.85	8.81	8.79	8.74	8.70	8.66	8.64	8.62	8.59	8.57	8.55	8.53
4	7.71	6.94	6.59	6.39	6.26	6.16	6.09	6.04	6.00	5.96	5.91	5.86	5.80	5.77	5.75	5.72	5.69	5.66	5.63
5	6.61	5.79	5.41	5.19	5.05	4.95	4.88	4.82	4.77	4.74	4.68	4.62	4.56	4.53	4.50	4.46	4.43	4.40	4.37
6	5.99	5.14	4.76	4.53	4.39	4.28	4.21	4.15	4.10	4.06	4.00	3.94	3.87	3.84	3.81	3.77	3.74	3.70	3.67
7	5.59	4.74	4.35	4.12	3.97	3.87	3.79	3.73	3.68	3.64	3.57	3.51	3.44	3.41	3.38	3.34	3.30	3.27	3.23
8	5.32	4.46	4.07	3.84	3.69	3.58	3.50	3.44	3.39	3.35	3.28	3.22	3.15	3.12	3.08	3.04	3.01	2.97	2.93
9	5.12	4.26	3.86	3.63	3.48	3.37	3.29	3.23	3.18	3.14	3.07	3.01	2.94	2.90	2.86	2.83	2.79	2.75	2.71
10	4.96	4.10	3.71	3.48	3.33	3.22	3.14	3.07	3.02	2.98	2.91	2.85	2.77	2.74	2.70	2.66	2.62	2.58	2.54
11	4.84	3.98	3.59	3.36	3.20	3.09	3.01	2.95	2.90	2.85	2.79	2.72	2.65	2.61	2.57	2.53	2.49	2.45	2.40
12	4.75	3.89	3.49	3.26	3.11	3.00	2.91	2.85	2.80	2.75	2.69	2.62	2.54	2.51	2.47	2.43	2.38	2.34	2.30
13	4.67	3.81	3.41	3.18	3.03	2.92	2.83	2.77	2.71	2.67	2.60	2.53	2.46	2.42	2.38	2.34	2.30	2.25	2.21
14	4.60	3.74	3.34	3.11	2.96	2.85	2.76	2.70	2.65	2.60	2.53	2.46	2.39	2.35	2.31	2.27	2.22	2.18	2.13
15	4.54	3.68	3.29	3.06	2.90	2.79	2.71	2.64	2.59	2.54	2.48	2.40	2.33	2.29	2.25	2.20	2.16	2.11	2.07
16	4.49	3.63	3.24	3.01	2.85	2.74	2.66	2.59	2.54	2.49	2.42	2.35	2.28	2.24	2.19	2.15	2.11	2.06	2.01
17	4.45	3.59	3.20	2.96	2.81	2.70	2.61	2.55	2.49	2.45	2.38	2.31	2.23	2.19	2.15	2.10	2.06	2.01	1.96
18	4.41	3.55	3.16	2.93	2.77	2.66	2.58	2.51	2.46	2.41	2.34	2.27	2.19	2.15	2.11	2.06	2.02	1.97	1.92
19	4.38	3.52	3.13	2.90	2.74	2.63	2.54	2.48	2.42	2.38	2.31	2.23	2.16	2.11	2.07	2.03	1.98	1.93	1.88
20	4.35	3.49	3.10	2.87	2.71	2.60	2.51	2.45	2.39	2.35	2.28	2.20	2.12	2.08	2.04	1.99	1.95	1.90	1.84
21	4.32	3.47	3.07	2.84	2.68	2.57	2.49	2.42	2.37	2.32	2.25	2.18	2.10	2.05	2.01	1.96	1.92	1.87	1.81
22	4.30	3.44	3.05	2.82	2.66	2.55	2.46	2.40	2.34	2.30	2.23	2.15	2.07	2.03	1.98	1.94	1.89	1.84	1.78
23	4.28	3.42	3.03	2.80	2.64	2.53	2.44	2.37	2.32	2.27	2.20	2.13	2.05	2.01	1.96	1.91	1.86	1.81	1.76
24	4.26	3.40	3.01	2.78	2.62	2.51	2.42	2.36	2.30	2.25	2.18	2.11	2.03	1.98	1.94	1.89	1.84	1.79	1.73
25	4.24	3.39	2.99	2.76	2.60	2.49	2.40	2.34	2.28	2.24	2.16	2.09	2.01	1.96	1.92	1.87	1.82	1.77	1.71
30	4.17	3.32	2.92	2.69	2.53	2.42	2.33	2.27	2.21	2.16	2.09	2.01	1.93	1.89	1.84	1.79	1.74	1.68	1.62
40	4.08	3.23	2.84	2.61	2.45	2.34	2.25	2.18	2.12	2.08	2.00	1.92	1.84	1.79	1.74	1.69	1.64	1.58	1.51
60	4.00	3.15	2.76	2.53	2.37	2.25	2.17	2.10	2.04	1.99	1.92	1.84	1.75	1.70	1.65	1.59	1.53	1.47	1.39
120	3.92	3.07	2.68	2.45	2.29	2.18	2.09	2.02	1.96	1.91	1.83	1.75	1.66	1.61	1.55	1.50	1.43	1.35	1.25
∞	3.84	3.00	2.60	2.37	2.21	2.10	2.01	1.94	1.88	1.83	1.75	1.67	1.57	1.52	1.46	1.39	1.32	1.22	1.00

Adapted from Table V of R. A. Fisher and F. Yates, *Statistical Tables for Biological, Agricultural and Medical Research* (1948), Oliver and Boyd, Edinburgh and London, by permission of the authors and publishers.

[a] Degrees of freedom for denominator

Table 14.A.3 The critical values of the F-distribution at the 2.5% level of significance (one tailed) or 5% level of significance for a two-tailed test

df[a]	*Degrees of freedom for numerator*																		
	1	2	3	4	5	6	7	8	9	10	12	15	20	24	30	40	60	120	∞
1	648	800	864	900	922	937	948	957	963	969	977	985	993	997	1,001	1,006	1,010	1,014	1,018
2	38.5	39.0	39.2	39.2	39.3	39.3	39.4	39.4	39.4	39.4	39.4	39.4	39.4	39.5	39.5	39.5	39.5	39.5	39.5
3	17.4	16.0	15.4	15.1	14.9	14.7	14.6	14.5	14.5	14.4	14.3	14.3	14.2	14.1	14.1	14.0	14.0	13.9	13.9
4	12.2	10.6	9.98	9.60	9.36	9.20	9.07	8.98	8.90	8.84	8.75	8.66	8.56	8.51	8.46	8.41	8.36	8.31	8.26
5	10.0	8.43	7.76	7.39	7.15	6.98	6.85	6.76	6.68	6.62	6.52	6.43	6.33	6.28	6.23	6.18	6.12	6.07	6.02
6	8.81	7.26	6.60	6.23	5.99	5.82	5.70	5.60	5.52	5.46	5.37	5.27	5.17	5.12	5.07	5.01	4.96	4.90	4.85
7	8.07	6.54	5.89	5.52	5.29	5.12	4.99	4.90	4.82	4.76	4.67	4.57	4.47	4.42	4.36	4.31	4.25	4.20	4.14
8	7.57	6.06	5.42	5.05	4.82	4.65	4.53	4.43	4.36	4.30	4.20	4.10	4.00	3.95	3.89	3.84	3.78	3.73	3.67
9	7.21	5.71	5.08	4.72	4.48	4.32	4.20	4.10	4.03	3.96	3.87	3.77	3.67	3.61	3.56	3.51	3.45	3.39	3.33
10	6.94	5.46	4.83	4.47	4.24	4.07	3.95	3.85	3.78	3.72	3.62	3.52	3.42	3.37	3.31	3.26	3.20	3.14	3.08
11	6.72	5.26	4.63	4.28	4.04	3.88	3.76	3.66	3.59	3.53	3.43	3.33	3.23	3.17	3.12	3.06	3.00	2.94	2.88
12	6.55	5.10	4.47	4.12	3.89	3.73	3.61	3.51	3.44	3.37	3.28	3.18	3.07	3.02	2.96	2.91	2.85	2.79	2.72
13	6.41	4.97	4.35	4.00	3.77	3.60	3.48	3.39	3.31	3.25	3.15	3.05	2.95	2.89	2.84	2.78	2.72	2.66	2.60
14	6.30	4.86	4.24	3.89	3.66	3.50	3.38	3.28	3.21	3.15	3.05	2.95	2.84	2.79	2.73	2.67	2.61	2.55	2.49
15	6.20	4.77	4.15	3.80	3.58	3.41	3.29	3.20	3.12	3.06	2.96	2.86	2.76	2.70	2.64	2.59	2.52	2.46	2.40
16	6.12	4.69	4.08	3.73	3.50	3.34	3.22	3.12	3.05	2.99	2.89	2.79	2.68	2.63	2.57	2.51	2.45	2.38	2.32
17	6.04	4.62	4.01	3.66	3.44	3.28	3.16	3.06	2.98	2.92	2.82	2.72	2.62	2.56	2.50	2.44	2.38	2.32	2.25
18	5.98	4.56	3.95	3.61	3.38	3.22	3.10	3.01	2.93	2.87	2.77	2.67	2.56	2.50	2.44	2.38	2.32	2.26	2.19
19	5.92	4.51	3.90	3.56	3.33	3.17	3.05	2.96	2.88	2.82	2.72	2.62	2.51	2.45	2.39	2.33	2.27	2.20	2.13
20	5.87	4.46	3.86	3.51	3.29	3.13	3.01	2.91	2.84	2.77	2.68	2.57	2.46	2.41	2.35	2.29	2.22	2.16	2.09
21	5.83	4.42	3.82	3.48	3.25	3.09	2.97	2.87	2.80	2.73	2.64	2.53	2.42	2.37	2.31	2.25	2.18	2.11	2.04
22	5.79	4.38	3.78	3.44	3.22	3.05	2.93	2.84	2.76	2.70	2.60	2.50	2.39	2.33	2.27	2.21	2.14	2.08	2.00
23	5.75	4.35	3.75	3.41	3.18	3.02	2.90	2.81	2.73	2.67	2.57	2.47	2.36	2.30	2.24	2.18	2.11	2.04	1.97
24	5.72	4.32	3.72	3.38	3.15	2.99	2.87	2.78	2.70	2.64	2.54	2.44	2.33	2.27	2.21	2.15	2.08	2.01	1.94
25	5.69	4.29	3.69	3.35	3.13	2.97	2.85	2.75	2.68	2.61	2.51	2.41	2.30	2.24	2.18	2.12	2.05	1.98	1.91
30	5.57	4.18	3.59	3.25	3.03	2.87	2.75	2.65	2.57	2.51	2.41	2.31	2.20	2.14	2.07	2.01	1.94	1.87	1.79
40	5.42	4.05	3.46	3.13	2.90	2.74	2.62	2.53	2.45	2.39	2.29	2.18	2.07	2.01	1.94	1.88	1.80	1.72	1.64
60	5.29	3.93	3.34	3.01	2.79	2.63	2.51	2.41	2.33	2.27	2.17	2.06	1.94	1.88	1.82	1.74	1.67	1.58	1.48
120	5.15	3.80	3.23	2.89	2.67	2.52	2.39	2.30	2.22	2.16	2.05	1.95	1.82	1.76	1.69	1.61	1.53	1.43	1.31
∞	5.02	3.69	3.12	2.79	2.57	2.41	2.29	2.19	2.11	2.05	1.94	1.83	1.71	1.64	1.57	1.48	1.39	1.27	1.00

Adapted from Table V of R. A. Fisher and F. Yates, *Statistical Tables for Biological, Agricultural and Medical Research* (1948 ed.), Oliver and Boyd, Edinburgh and London, by permission of the authors and publishers.

[a] Degrees of freedom for denominator

Table 14.A.4 The critical values of the Mann–Whitney U statistic at the 5% level of significance (two tailed)

	N_2															
N_s	5	6	7	8	9	10	11	12	13	14	15	16	17	18	19	20
5	2	3	5	6	7	8	9	11	12	13	14	15	17	18	19	20
6		5	6	8	10	11	13	14	16	17	19	21	22	24	25	27
7			8	10	12	14	16	18	20	22	24	26	28	30	32	34
8				13	15	17	19	22	24	26	29	31	34	36	38	41
9					17	20	23	26	28	31	34	37	39	42	45	48
10						23	26	29	33	36	39	42	45	48	52	55
11							30	33	37	40	44	47	51	55	58	62
12								37	41	45	49	53	57	61	65	69
13									45	50	54	59	63	67	72	76
14										55	59	64	67	74	78	83
15											64	70	75	80	85	90
16												75	81	86	92	98
17													87	93	99	105
18														99	106	112
19															113	119
20																127

Adapted from Table 5.3 of H. R. Neave (1978) *Statistical Tables*, George Allen and Unwin, London, by permission of the authors and publishers.

Table 14.A.5 The critical values of the Wilcoxon T statistic for correlated samples (two tailed)

	Level of significance		
	0.05	0.02	0.01
6	0	—	—
7	2	0	—
8	4	2	0
9	6	3	2
10	8	5	3
11	11	7	5
12	14	10	7
13	17	13	10
14	21	16	13
15	25	20	16
16	30	24	20
17	35	28	23
18	40	33	28
19	46	38	32
20	52	43	38
21	59	49	43
22	66	56	49
23	73	62	55
24	81	69	61
25	89	77	68

Adapted from Table I of F. Wilcoxon (1949) *Some Rapid Approximate Statistical Procedures*, The American Cyanamid Company, New York, by permission of the authors and publishers.

REFERENCES

Costill, D. L., Thomason, H. and Roberts, E. (1973) Fractional utilization of the aerobic capacity during distance running. *Medicine and Science in Sports*, **5**, 248–52.

MINITAB (1989) *Reference manual*, Minitab Inc., 3081 Enterprise Drive, State College, PA 16801, USA.

Nevill, A. M., Ramsbottom, R. and Williams, C. (1990) The relationship between athletic performance and maximal oxygen uptake. *Journal of Sports Sciences*, **8**, 290–2.

Nevill, A. M., Cooke, C. B., Holder, R. L. *et al.* (1992a) Modelling linear relationships between two variables when repeated measurements are made on more than one subject. *European Journal of Applied Physiology*, **64**, 419–25.

Nevill, A. M., Ramsbottom, R. and Williams, C. (1992b) Scaling physiological measurements for individuals of different body size. *European Journal of Applied Physiology*, **65**, 110–17.

Snedecor, G. W. and Cochran, W. G. (1989) *Statistical Methods*, 8th edn, Iowa State University Press, Ames, Iowa.

SCALING: ADJUSTING FOR DIFFERENCES IN BODY SIZE 15

E. M. Winter and A. M. Nevill

15.1 INTRODUCTION

Physiological and performance variables are frequently influenced by body size. For instance, the performance capabilities of children are less than those of adults. Similarly, there are track and field events such as hammer, discus and shot in which high values of body mass are especially influential. Furthermore, oxygen uptake ($\dot{V}O_2$) during a particular task in a large person will probably be greater than in a small person. These observations give rise to a simple question: to what extent are performance differences attributable to differences in size or to differences in qualitative characteristics of the body's tissues and structures?

To help answer this question, differences in body size have to be partitioned out. This partitioning is called *scaling* (Schmidt-Nielsen, 1984) and is a key issue in kinanthropometry. It has also become a subject of renewed interest (Nevill *et al.*, 1992a; Jakeman *et al.*, 1994; Nevill, 1994; Nevill and Holder, 1994) although it is an area of study that has been established for some time (Sholl, 1948; Tanner, 1949, 1964). There are four main uses (Winter, 1992):

1. to compare an individual against standards for the purpose of assessment
2. to compare groups
3. in longitudinal studies which investigate the effects of growth or training
4. to explore possible relationships between physiological characteristics and performance.

In this section, the first two of these applications will receive particular consideration.

15.2 THE RATIO STANDARD – THE TRADITIONAL METHOD

The most commonly used scaling technique is termed a *ratio standard* (Tanner, 1949) in which a performance or physiological variable is divided by an anthropometric characteristic such as body mass. A well-known ratio standard is $\dot{V}O_2$ expressed in ml kg^{-1} min^{-1}. This is used to compare groups using *t*-tests or analysis of variance as appropriate, to explore relationships between aerobic capabilities and performance and to evaluate the physiological status of subjects.

More than 40 years ago, Tanner (1949) warned against the use of these standards for evaluative purposes and demonstrated that they were '... theoretically fallacious and, unless in exceptional circumstances, misleading' (p. 1). Furthermore, he later stated (Tanner, 1964) that comparisons of groups based on mean values of ratio standards were also misleading because they '... involve some statistical difficulties and are neither as simple nor as informative as they seem' (p. 65). What is the problem?

A ratio standard is only valid when:

$$\frac{\upsilon_x}{\upsilon_y} = r$$

Kinanthropometry and Exercise Physiology Laboratory Manual: Tests, procedures and data Edited by Roger Eston and Thomas Reilly. Published in 1996 by E & FN Spon. ISBN 0 419 17880 5

where: υ_x = coefficient of variation of x i.e. $(SDx/\bar{x}) \times 100$
υ_y = coefficient of variation of y i.e. $(SDy/\bar{y}) \times 100$
r = Pearson's product–moment correlation coefficient

This expression is Tanner's (1949) 'exceptional circumstance' and is equivalent to the regression standard with an intercept of 0 and a slope the same as the ratio standard. If it is not satisfied, a distortion is introduced. Figure 15.1 illustrates the principle. The solid line represents the ratio standard whereas the other lines represent regression lines of $\dot{V}O_2$ on body mass for various values of r. The only point through which all the lines pass – the intersection point – is where the mean values for x and y occur. As r increases, the ratio standard and regression line get closer but they will be coincident only when the special circumstance is satisfied. Rarely, if ever, is this test made and arguably rarer still is it actually fulfilled. In fact there are numerous instances where it simply cannot be satisfied. As the value of r reduces, the regression line rotates clockwise. The further data points are from the intersection, the more the ratio standard distorts the 'true' relationship.

If the ratio standard is used for evaluative purposes, those with body mass values below the mean will be ascribed high aerobic capability whereas those whose body mass is greater than the mean will tend to be ascribed low aerobic capability. In other words, little people receive an artefactual arithmetic advantage whereas large people are similarly disadvantaged. The greater the distance of the point from the mean, the greater the distortion will be.

For this reason, Tanner (1964) suggested that *regression standards* should be used for evaluation and that groups should be

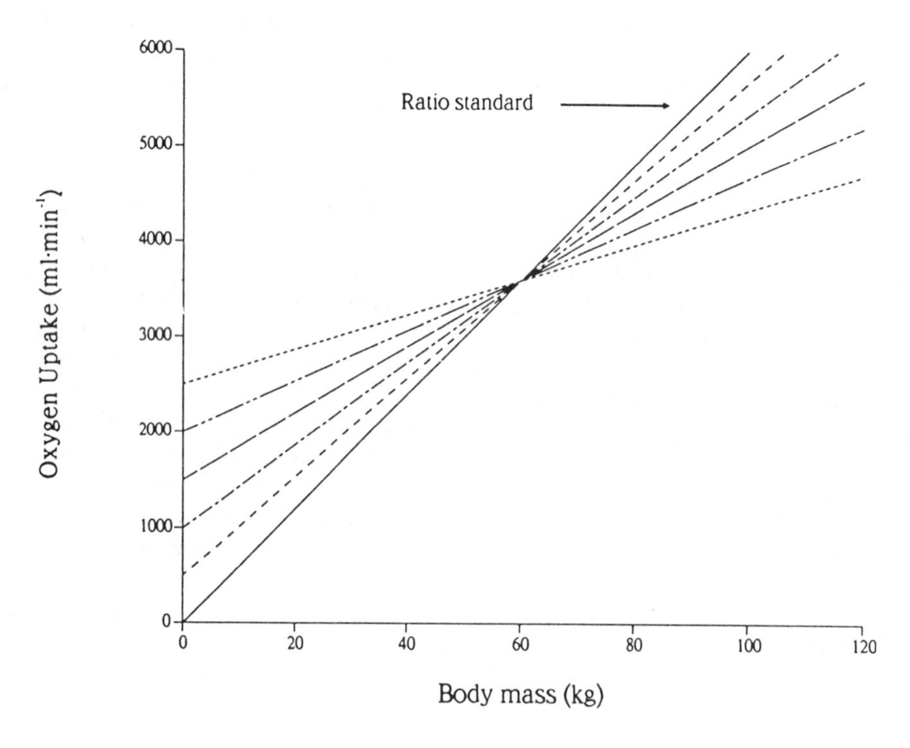

Figure 15.1 The effect of departures from Tanner's (1949) 'special circumstance' on the difference between regression standards and the ratio standard.

compared via the comparison of regression lines through the statistical technique *analysis of covariance* (ANCOVA) (Snedecor and Cochran, 1980).

15.3 REGRESSION STANDARDS AND ANCOVA

For the purposes of evaluation, a regression standard is straightforward. If an individual is above the regression line, he or she is above average, if below the line, he or she is below average. Norms can be established on the basis of how far above and how far below particular values lie. Comparisons of regression lines by means of ANCOVA so as to compare groups is more involved although the principles are actually simple. Computer packages such as MINITAB (1989) and SPSS (Norusis, 1992) can be used and texts such as Snedecor and Cochran (1980) and Tabachnick and Fidell (1989) provide a useful theoretical background.

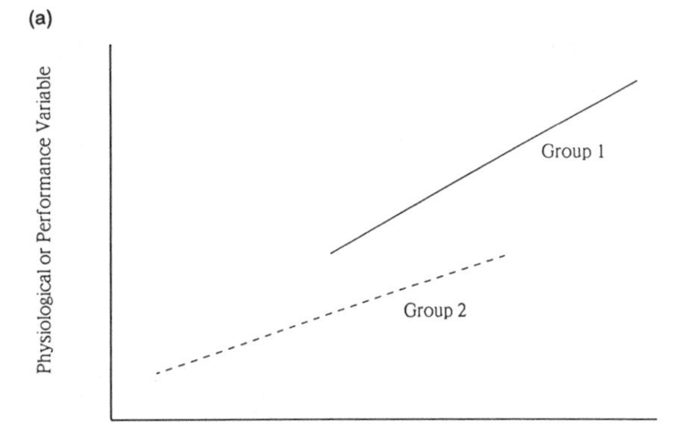

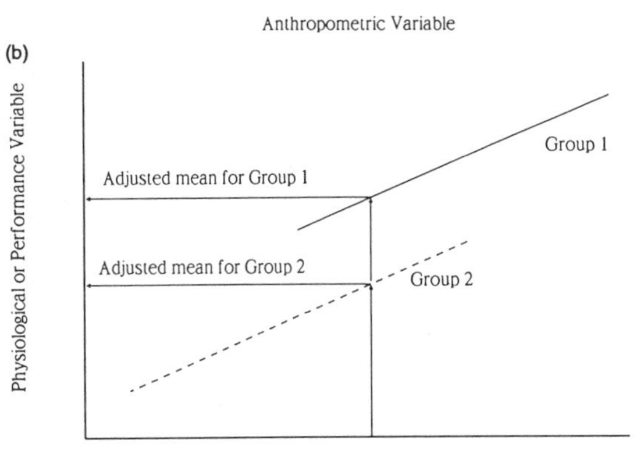

Figure 15.2 (a and b) The identification of 'adjusted means'. Actual slopes and slopes constrained to be parallel.

Figure 15.2 illustrates the basis for comparing two groups, 1 and 2. Regression lines for each group identify the linear relationship between variables. The x variable – the independent variable – is called a *covariate* because as x increases, so too does y – the dependent variable. The effect of x is partitioned out and what are called *adjusted means* are calculated. In the comparison of regression lines, three tests are made:

1. variance about regression
2. equality of slopes
3. comparison of elevations of the lines

Ideally there should be *homogeneity* of variance about regression, i.e. the variance about regression should be the same in both (or all) groups. (*Heterogeneity* means that the variances are not the same.) If this test is satisfied, the slopes are compared. If there is no statistical difference between the slopes, the lines are recast and constrained to be parallel. If the slopes of the lines are different, the analysis stops; the groups are qualitatively different. The parallel slopes are used to calculate the adjusted means (Figure 15.2a). For the overall mean value of x, equivalent values of y for each group are calculated. The error term for each group is the standard error of the estimate (SEE).

15.3.1 ANCOVA: A WORKED EXAMPLE

Table 15.1 contains data for lean leg volume and peak power output in men and women (Winter *et al.*, 1991). Figure 15.3 illustrates the regression lines and raw data plots for the two groups. Comparison of the ratio standards peak power output/lean leg volume showed that there was no difference between the groups ($136 \pm 3\ W\ l^{-1}$ *vs* $131 \pm 3\ W\ l^{-1}$ in men and women, respectively (mean, SEM) $P > 0.05$). This suggests that there is no difference between the qualitative characteristics of the groups. In marked contrast,

Table 15.1 Absolute and natural logarithm values (ln) for lean leg volume (LLV) and optimized peak power output (OPP) in men and women

Men				*Women*			
LLV (l)	*lnLLV (lnl)*	*OPP (W)*	*lnOPP (lnW)*	LLV *(l)*	*lnLLV (lnl)*	*OPP (W)*	*lnOPP (lnW)*
7.03	1.950	928	6.833	4.79	1.567	658	6.489
7.47	2.011	825	6.715	4.55	1.515	490	6.194
8.80	2.175	1113	7.015	4.94	1.597	596	6.390
7.44	2.007	950	6.856	5.26	1.660	491	6.196
7.16	1.969	1231	7.116	5.54	1.712	717	6.575
7.69	2.040	942	6.848	4.95	1.599	467	6.146
7.50	2.015	889	6.790	4.50	1.504	534	6.280
6.43	1.861	904	6.807	7.32	1.991	769	6.645
8.41	2.129	1235	7.119	5.09	1.627	644	6.468
7.73	2.045	889	6.790	3.57	1.273	427	6.057
6.70	1.902	917	6.821	4.63	1.533	664	6.498
6.72	1.905	850	6.745	4.93	1.595	624	6.436
6.41	1.858	997	6.905	4.33	1.466	573	6.351
8.26	2.111	1003	6.911	7.89	2.066	821	6.711
7.97	2.076	1205	7.094	6.82	1.920	733	6.597
8.46	2.135	1211	7.099	5.46	1.697	800	6.685
8.47	2.137	978	6.886	4.54	1.513	672	6.510
6.91	1.933	1087	6.991	5.85	1.766	590	6.380
8.50	2.140	1082	6.987	5.38	1.683	679	6.521
7.82	2.057	1026	6.933	5.68	1.737	607	6.409
7.45	2.008	970	6.877	5.09	1.627	714	6.571
7.74	2.046	1131	7.031	4.66	1.539	755	6.627
6.83	1.921	902	6.805	5.97	1.787	755	6.627
7.72	2.044	1129	7.029	4.95	1.599	561	6.330
6.04	1.798	832	6.724	5.10	1.629	518	6.250
8.29	2.115	1242	7.124	5.91	1.777	680	6.522
6.08	1.805	938	6.844	4.19	1.433	634	6.452
6.36	1.850	856	6.752	5.00	1.609	734	6.599
7.43	2.006	939	6.845	4.35	1.470	784	6.664
5.83	1.763	801	6.686	4.62	1.530	632	6.449
6.64	1.893	919	6.823	5.76	1.751	709	6.564
8.87	2.183	1091	6.995	5.35	1.677	712	6.568
7.46	2.010	977	6.884	4.75	1.558	639	6.460
7.48	2.012	1248	7.129	5.58	1.719	726	6.588
				5.60	1.723	815	6.703
				5.70	1.740	847	6.742
				5.45	1.696	701	6.553
				3.92	1.366	653	6.482
				4.09	1.409	550	6.310
				5.22	1.653	835	6.727
				4.89	1.587	893	6.795
				5.13	1.635	760	6.633
				4.40	1.482	564	6.335
				5.70	1.740	758	6.631
				4.60	1.526	630	6.446
				4.90	1.589	657	6.488
				7.06	1.954	841	6.735

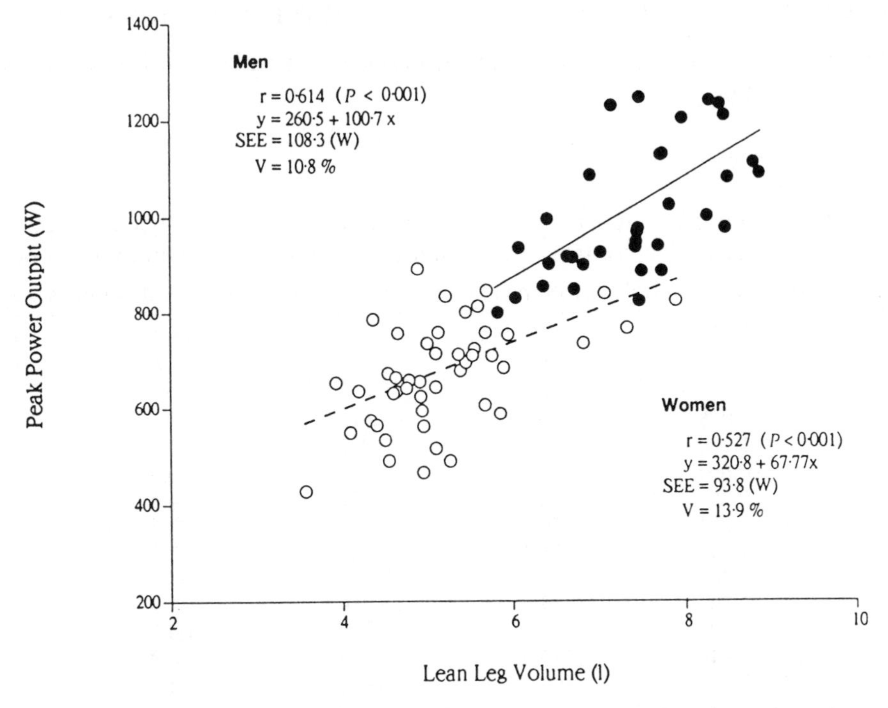

Figure 15.3 The relationship between optimized peak power output and lean leg volume in men (•— —) and women (O — — —) (Winter *et al.*, 1991).

ANCOVA produced adjusted means of 903 ± 108 W in men and 748 ± 94 W in women (mean, SEE) $P < 0.001$. The outcome of this analysis suggests that there are qualitative differences between men and women. The technique has also been applied to study strength and cross-sectional area of muscle (Winter and Maughan, 1991) with the same outcome. (See Appendix A to carry out the appropriate analysis using MINITAB.)

15.4 ALLOMETRY AND POWER FUNCTION STANDARDS

It would appear that ANCOVA on regression lines solves the problems associated with scaling. This is not the case. Nevill *et al.* (1992a) identified two major weaknesses in the use of linear modelling techniques on raw data:

1. data are not necessarily related linearly
2. error about regression is not necessarily additive, it might be multiplicative

Non-linear relationships between variables are well known to biologists (Schmidt-Nielsen, 1984) and curiously, although they receive attention in a notable text (Åstrand and Rodahl, 1986), have not been used widely by sport and exercise scientists.

Growth and development in humans and other living things is accompanied by differential changes in the size and configuration of the body's segments (Tanner, 1989). These changes are said to be *allometric* (Schmidt-Nielsen, 1984) a word derived from the Greek *allios* which means to change. Physiological variables y are scaled in relation to an index of body size x according to allometric equations. These are of the general form:

$$y = ax^b$$

where: a = constant multiplier
b = exponent

15.5 PRACTICAL 1: THE IDENTIFICATION OF ALLOMETRIC RELATIONSHIPS

The principles can be illustrated by using spheres as examples and Table 15.2 contains relevant data. In spheres:

$$\text{Area} = 4\,\pi r^2 \qquad \text{Volume} = \frac{4\,\pi r^3}{3}$$

where: r = radius

For area, the numerical value of a, the constant multiplier, is 12.566 i.e 4π, and the exponent is 2. Similarly, for volume, the constant multiplier is 4.189 and the exponent is 3.

Table 15.2 Absolute and natural logarithm values (ln) of radii, surface areas and volumes in spheres

Radius (cm)	*In Radius (ln cm)*	*Area (cm^2)*	*ln Area (ln cm^2)*	*Volume (cm^3)*	*ln Volume (ln cm^3)*
0		0	0	0	
0.125	−2.079	0.2	−1.628	0	−4.806
0.25	−1.386	0.8	−0.242	0.1	−2.726
0.5	−0.693	3.1	1.145	0.5	−0.647
1	0	12.6	2.531	4.2	1.433
2	0.693	50.3	3.917	33.5	3.512
3	1.099	113.1	4.728	113.1	4.728
4	1.386	201.0	5.303	268.1	5.591
5	1.609	314.1	5.750	523.7	6.261
6	1.792	452.3	6.114	904.9	6.808
7	1.946	615.6	6.423	1436.9	7.270
8	2.079	804.1	6.690	2144.9	7.671

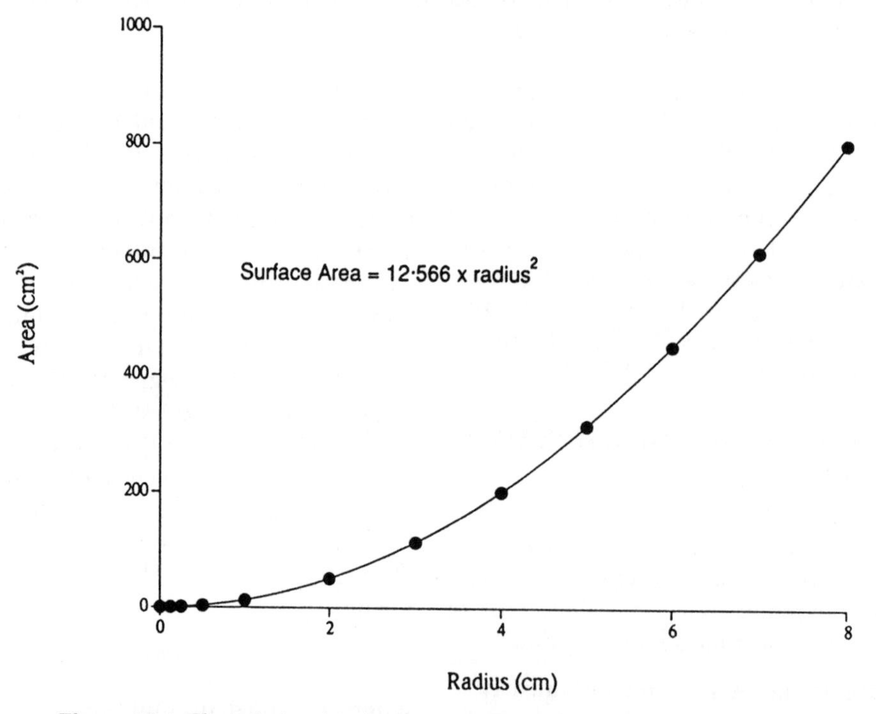

Figure 15.4 The relationship between surface area and radius in spheres.

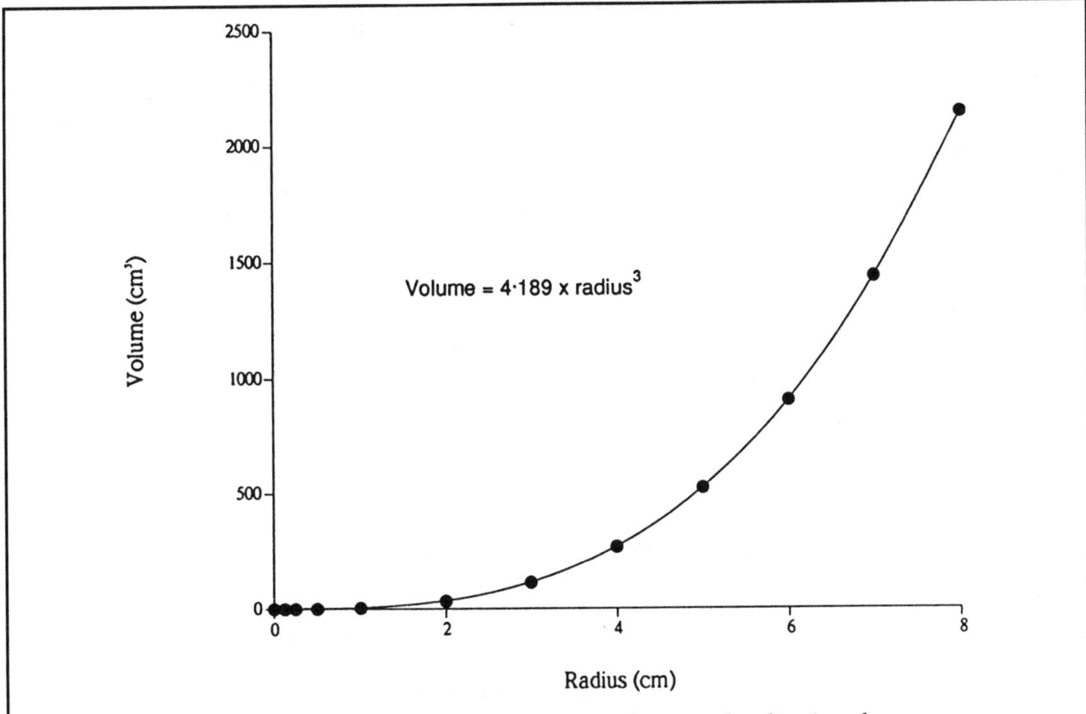

Figure 15.5 The relationship between volume and radius in spheres.

1. With radius on the abscissa, draw two graphs: one for surface area and one for volume. You should have something like Figures 15.4 and 15.5. How can these relationships be identified? The answer is simple. The raw variables are converted in to natural logarithms and ln y is regressed on ln x. This linearizes the otherwise non-linear relationship and produces an expression which is of the form:

$$\ln y = \ln \mathrm{a} + \mathrm{b} \ln x$$

   The antilog of ln a identifies the constant multiplier in the allometric equation and the slope of the line is the numerical value of the exponent.
2. Using the values in Table 15.2, with ln radius on the abscissa, plot two graphs: one for surface area and one for volume.
3. Calculate the regression equations for each graph. You should have something like Figures 15.6 and 15.7. For the graph of ln surface area regressed on ln radius, a (the constant multiplier in the allometric equation which relates the raw variables) is the antilog of 2.531. This value is 12.566. Similarly, the exponent is given by the slope of the log-log regression equation, i.e. 2. In the same way, the constant multiplier in the volume–radius relationship is the antilog of 1.432– 4.189 – and the exponent is 3.

   From these known relationships, we can explore an unknown one; the relationship between surface area and volume.
4. Again using the data in Table 15.2, identify the allometric relationship between surface area and volume. Make surface area the dependent variable. You should have something like Figures 15.8 and 15.9.

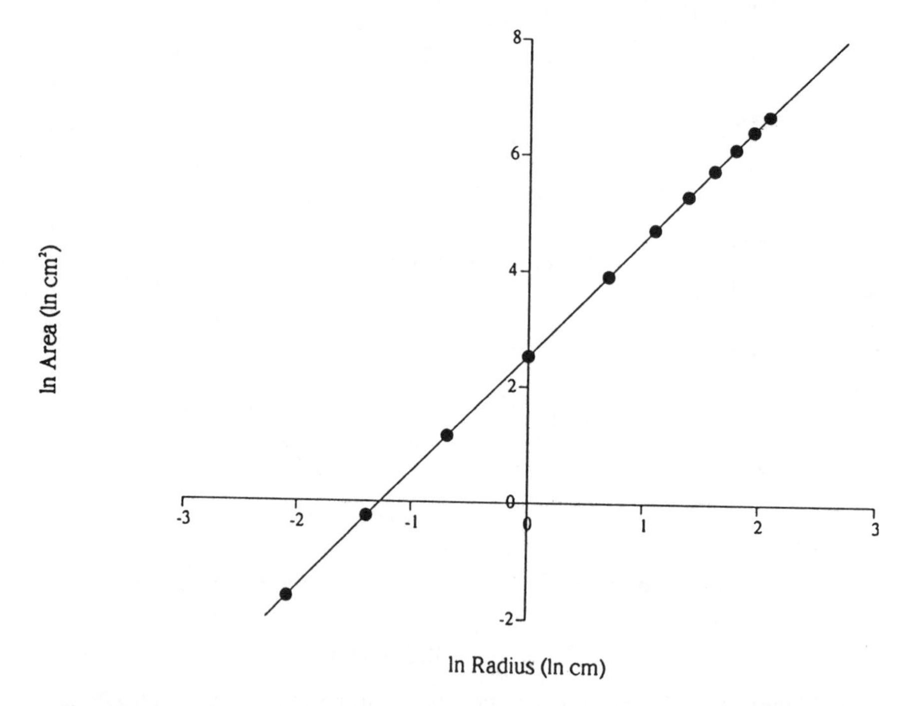

Figure 15.6 The relationship between ln surface area and ln radius in spheres.

15.6 POWER FUNCTION RATIO STANDARDS

The relationship in Figure 15.9 illustrates an important principle which is known as the *surface law* (Schmidt-Nielsen, 1984); the surface area of a body is related to its volume raised to the power 0.67. In other words, as the volume of a body increases, its surface area actually reduces in proportion. Nevill *et al.* (1992a) and Nevill and Holder (1994) have provided compelling evidence that measures such as $\dot{V}O_2$ are related to body mass raised to the power 0.67. In order to carry out scaling correctly, an independent variable should be raised to a power which is identified from log-log transformations. This value is called a *power function*. The power function can then be divided into the dependent variable to produce a *power function ratio standard*.

Another important point about allometric relationships concerns the error term. In linear models, error about the regression line is assumed to be constant. Such error is said to be additive or *homoscedastic*. Allometric models do not make this assumption, error is assumed to be multiplicative or *heteroscedastic*. In this case, error increases as the independent variable increases. This is what tends to happen with living things (Nevill and Holder, 1994).

Groups can be compared by using power function ratios and *t*-tests or analysis of variance as appropriate. They can also be compared using ANCOVA on the log-log transformations. These transformations constrain error to be additive and so allow the use of ANCOVA.

There is an interesting recognition of power functions in literature. In Jonathon Swift's *Gulliver's Travel* written in 1726, Lilliputian mathematicians were faced with challenge of calculating Gulliver's food requirements. Gulliver was twelve times taller than Lilliputians so the mathematicians claimed that the ship wreck victim would need 1728 times as much food as his diminutive counterpart, i.e. 12^3.

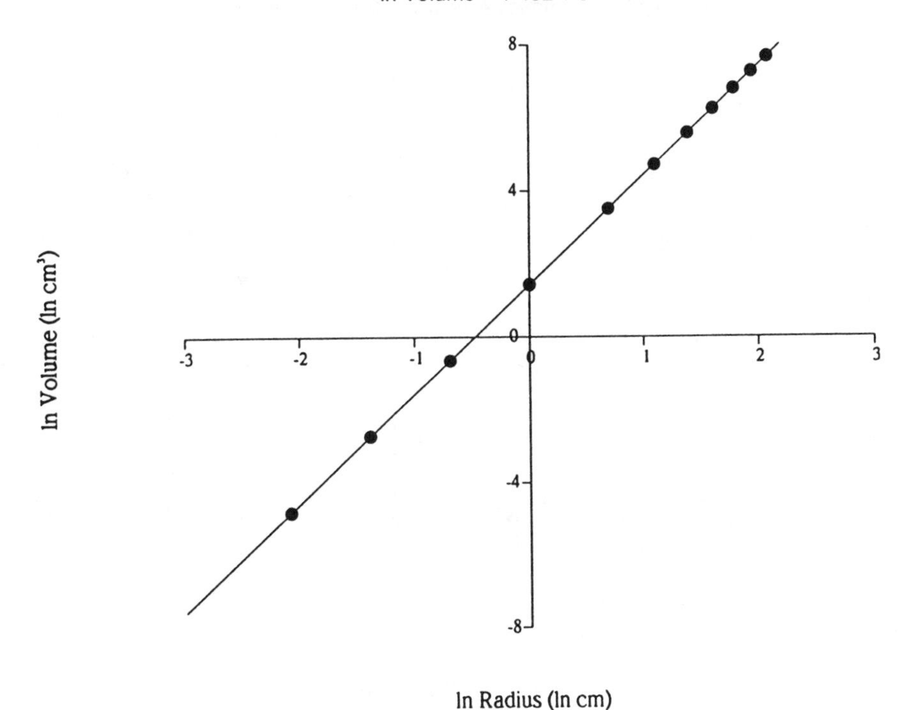

Figure 15.7 The relationship between ln volume and ln radius in spheres.

15.7 PRACTICAL 2: A WORKED EXAMPLE

The data in Table 15.1 can be revisited. The natural logarithms of lean leg volume and peak power output can now be used to compare performance in men and women. This is the analysis reported by Nevill *et al.* (1992b).

1. With ln lean leg volume on the abscissa, plot a graph with ln peak power output for men and women. Calculate the regression equations. You should have something like Figure 15.10.
2. Use of ANCOVA on these data (Nevill, 1994) confirms that for a given lean leg volume, peak power output in men is greater than in women ($P < 0.001$). (See Appendix B to implement ANCOVA using MINITAB.)
3. Plot the allometric relationships for men and women. You should have something like Figure 15.11.
4. Use of ANCOVA also demonstrates that the slopes of the log/log transformations (0.737 in men vs 0.584 in women) are not significantly different ($P > 0.05$). A common slope of 0.625 can be used for both groups. Note that this approximates to a theoretical value of 0.67 suggested by the surface law.
5. Produce power function ratio standards ($W\,l^{-0.625}$ for men and women and compare the groups. This should give means and SEM of 286 5 $W\,l^{-0.625}$ and 239 5 $W\,l^{-0.625}$, respectively ($P < 0.001$).

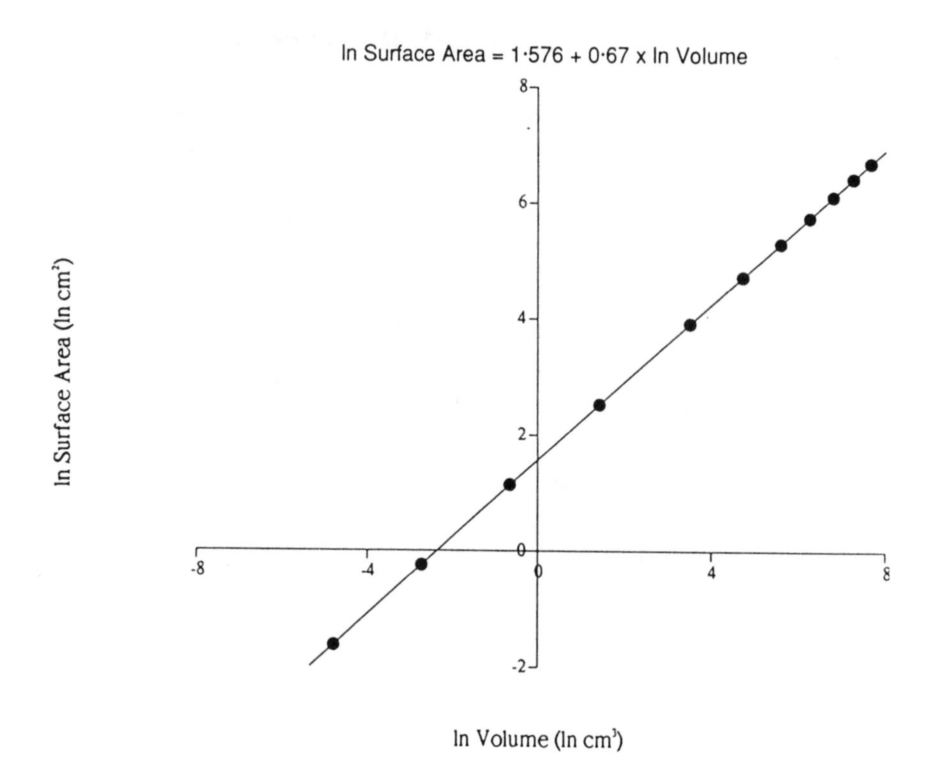

Figure 15.8 The relationship between ln surface area and ln volume in spheres.

15.8 SUMMARY

Two simple points can be stated about techniques which partition out differences in body size.

1. The *a priori* use of ratio standards is incorrect. These standards should only be used when Tanner's (1949) special circumstance is satisfied.
2. Allometric modelling should be used to partial out differences in body size.

APPENDIX A

When using MINITAB to carry-out the analyses described in section 15.3.1, the first step is to enter the peak power output and lean leg volume results, given in Table 15.1, into separate columns for both the male and female subjects. This can be done using either the 'data editor' or the READ or SET commands, i.e. by putting the male peak power output (OPPM) in C1, the male lean leg volume (LLVM) in C2, the female peak power output (OPPF) in C3 and finally the female lean leg volume (LLVF) in C4. The column names and counts (N) can be confirmed using the INFORMATION command as follows:

```
MTB > INFORMATION C1-C4
COLUMN    NAME    COUNT
C1        OPPM    34
C2        LLVM    34
C3        OPPF    47
C4        LLVF    47
```

Next we can calculate the ratio standards using the LET command as follows:

```
MTB > LET C5 = C1/C2
MTB > LET C6 = C3/C4
```

The most convenient method to compare the male and female results is to stack the data

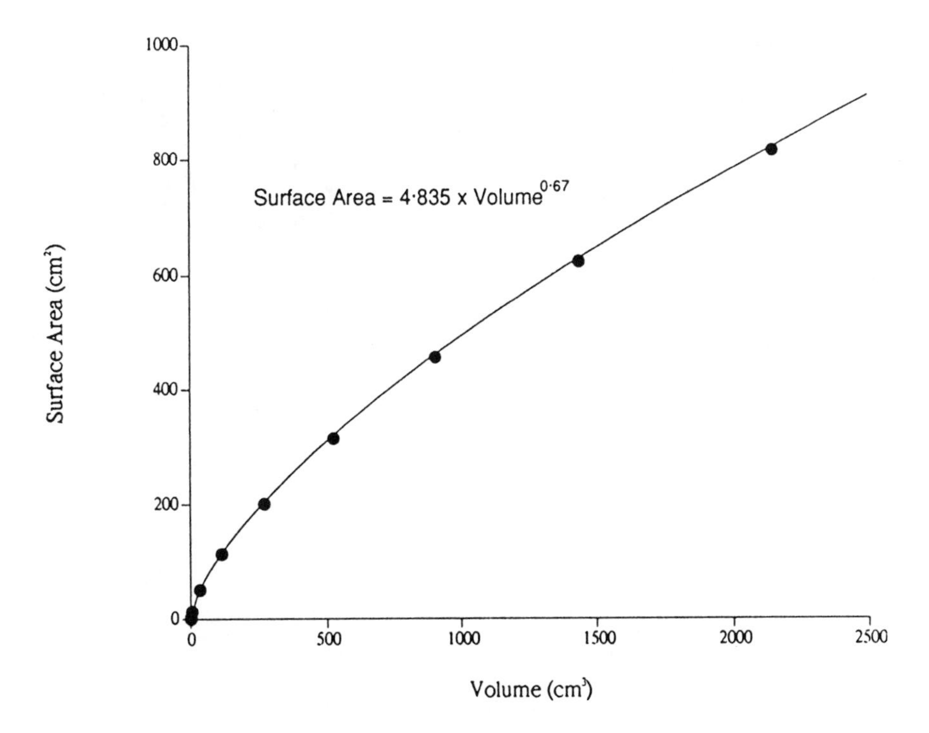

Figure 15.9 The relationship between surface area and volume in spheres.

into three 'combined' columns C11 (peak power output), C12 (lean leg volume) and C13 (peak power output, adjusted for lean leg volume), using the STACK command as follows:

```
MTB > STACK (C1 C2 C5) (C3 C4 C6)
(C11 C12 C13)
MTB > NAME C11 'OPP' C12 'LLV'
C13 'OPP/L'
```

The male and female subjects can now be identified by creating a 'SEX' variable in column C10 using the SET command, where the number (1) represents the male subjects (N=34) and the number (2) represents the female subjects (N = 47):

```
MTB > SET C10
DATA > (1)34 (2)47
DATA > END
```

A one-way analysis of variance, to compare the male and female ratio standards (OPP/LLV), can be performed using the ONEWAY command as follows:

```
MTB > ONEWAY C13 C10
ANALYSIS OF VARIANCE ON OPP/LLV
SOURCE   DF   SS      MS     F     P
SEX       1     547   547    1.63  0.206
ERROR    79   26589   337
TOTAL    80   27136
LEVEL    N    MEAN    STDEV
1        34   136.24  14.73
2        47   130.97  20.55
POOLED STDEV = 18.35
```

As mentioned in section 15.3, we need to test whether there is a significant difference between the slopes of the male and female covariates (LLV). To do this, we need to separate the sex variable into two 'indicator' variables. This will create two dummy columns for male (C8) and female (C9) subjects, where C8 will take the values one (1) for the male subjects and zero (0) for female subjects.

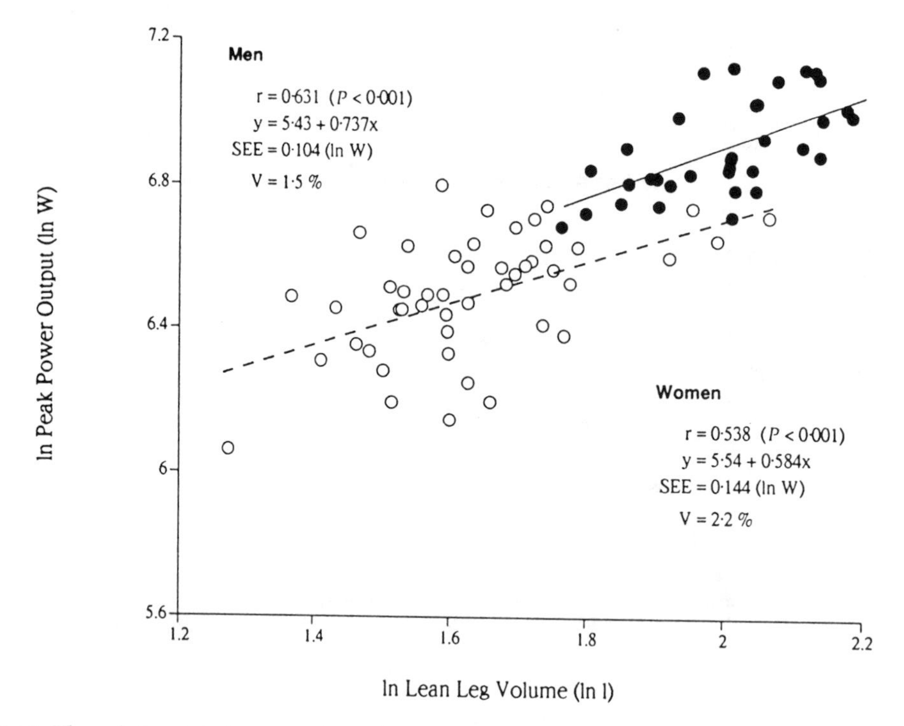

Figure 15.10 The relationship between ln peak power output and ln lean leg volume in men (● ——) and women (O — — —) (Nevill *et al.*, 1992b).

Conversely, the dummy column C9 will take the values one (1) for female subjects but zero (0) for male subjects, i.e.

MTB > INDICATOR C10 C8 C9
MTB > NAME C10 'SEX' C8 'SEX(M)' C9 'SEX(F)'

To test for differences in the slopes between the male and female covariates, we need to calculate the interaction between sex and the covariate (LLV) using the LET command as follows:

MTB > LET C14 = C8 × C12
MTB > NAME C14 'M × LLV'

To test for a significant difference between the male and female slopes, we use the REGRESSION command:

MTB > REGRESSION C11 3 C8 C12 C14 THE REGRESSION EQUATION IS OPP = 321 – 60 SEX(M) + 67.8 LLV + 32.9 M × LV

PREDICTOR	COEF	STDEV	T-RATIO	P
CONSTANT	320.84	91.31	3.51	0.001
SEX(M)	–60.4	182.1	–0.33	0.741
LLV	67.77	17.37	3.90	0.000
M × LLV	32.91	27.35	1.20	0.233

As can be seen from the above table, the interaction term, M × LLV, makes a non significant contribution to the regression equation and, hence, the need for separate slopes for the male and female covariates (LLV) can be rejected. Fitting a common slope can be achieved as follows:

MTB > REGRESSION C11 2 C8 C12
THE REGRESSION EQUATION IS
OPP = 252 + 154 SEX(M) + 81.0 LLV

PREDICTOR	COEF	STDEV	T-RATIO	P
CONSTANT	251.97	71.35	3.53	0.001
SEX(M)	154.12	37.50	4.11	0.000
LLV	81.04	13.45	6.02	0.000

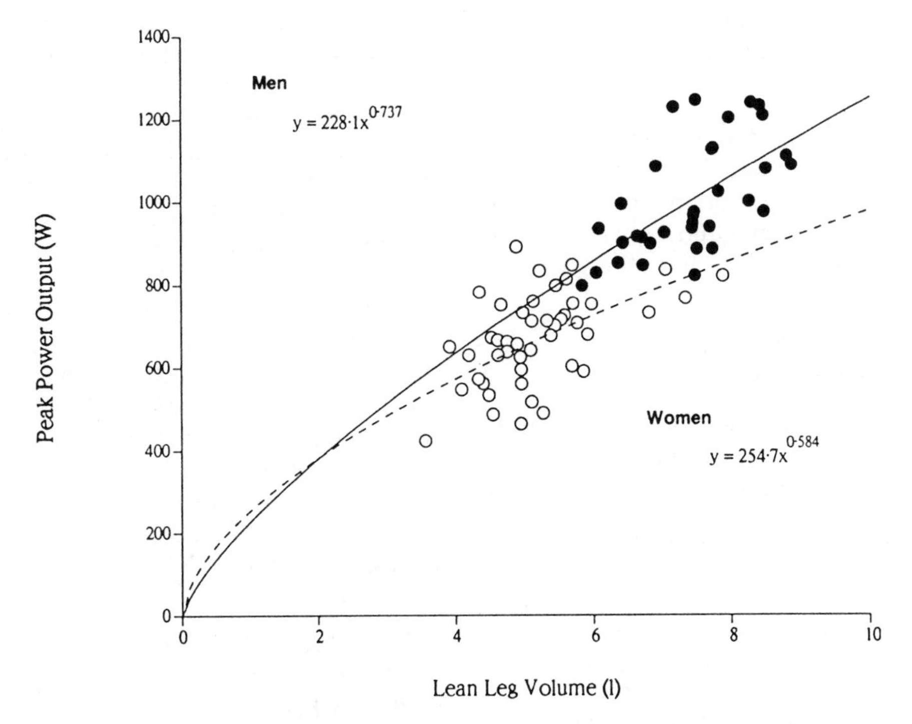

Figure 15.11 The allometric relationship between peak power output and lean leg volume in men (● ——) and women (O — — —) (Nevill *et al.*, 1992b).

The regression analysis given above is, in effect, an analysis of covariance, that identifies both the covariate LLV and the SEX(M) main effect as highly significant ($P < 0.001$). This result can be confirmed using the MINITAB ANCOVA command as follows:

MTB > ANCOVA C11=C10;
SUBC > COVARIATE C12;
SUBC > MEANS C10.

FACTOR	LEVELS	VALUES	
SEX	2	0	1

ANALYSIS OF COVARIANCE FOR OPP

SOURCE	DF	ADJSS	MS	F	P
CO-VARIATES	1	365449	365449	36.28	0.000
SEX	1	170173	170173	16.89	0.000
ERROR	78	785659	10073		
TOTAL	80	3356591			

COVARIATE	COEFF	STDEV	T-VALUE	P
LLV	81.04	13.5	6.023	0.000

ADJUSTED MEANS

SEX	N	OPP
1	47	748.27
2	34	902.39

Note that the difference between the adjusted means, given above, is precisely the same as the difference between the male and female intercept parameter, SEX(M) = 154.12, given in the regression analysis.

APPENDIX B

As described in section 15.4.3, when using allometric modelling to adjust for differences in body size, the first step is to take natural logarithms of the dependent variable, (PPOPT), and the covariate independent variable, (LLV). Once again, this can be done in MINITAB using the LET command, i.e.

```
MTB > LET C21 = LOG(C11)
MTB > LET C22 = LOG(C12)
MTB > NAME C21 'LN(OPP)' C22 'LN(LLV)
```

Again, we will need to confirm a common slope for the male and female subjects' log-transformed lean leg volume measurements, by creating the interaction between the sex indicator variable C8 and the covariate LN(LLV), i.e.

```
MTB > LET C24 = C8 × C22
MTB > NAME C24 'M × LN(L)'
```

To discover whether there is a significant difference between the male and female slopes, we use the REGRESSION command as before

```
MTB > REGR C21 3 C8 C22 C24
THE REGRESSION EQUATION IS
LN(PPOPT) = 5.54 - 0.108 SEX(M)
+ 0.584 LN(LLV) + 0.153 M × LN(L)
```

PREDICTOR	COEF	STDEV	T-RATIO	P
CONSTANT	5.5431	0.2001	27.70	0.000
SEX(M)	-0.1081	0.4453	-0.24	0.809
LN(LLV)	0.5839	0.1219	4.79	0.000
M × LN(L)	0.1527	0.2332	0.65	0.515

Once again, the interaction term M × LN(L) makes a non significant contribution to the regression equation and, hence, the assumption of separate male and female slopes can be rejected, i.e. we can adopt a common slope for LN(LLV). This can be fitted as follows;

```
MTB > REGR C21 2 C8 C22
THE REGRESSION EQUATION IS
LN(PPOPT) = 5.47 + 0.182 SEX(M)
            + 0.626 LN(LLV)
```

PREDICTOR	COEF	STDEV	T-RATIO	P
CONSTANT	5.4750	0.1703	32.15	0.000
SEX(M)	0.18167	0.04742	3.83	0.000
LN(LLV)	0.6256	0.1035	6.04	0.000

As before, the above regression analysis is equivalent to an analysis of covariance, with both the covariate LN(LLV) and the SEX(M) main effect, highly significant ($P < 0.001$). Using the above regression analysis, we can also identify the allometric models to describe the relationship between PPOPT and LLV for both the male and female subjects. By taking anti-logs of the constant (5.475) and the constant plus the SEX(M) indicator variable parameter (5.475 + 0.182 = 5.657), we obtain the 'a' constant multipliers for the female (238.6) and male (286.2) subjects, in the allometric model $PPOPT = a.LLV^{b}$. These constant multipliers (238.6) and (286.2) are also the mean power function ratio standards ($W\, l^{-0.6256}$) for the female and male subjects respectively. Note that b = 0.6256 is common to both sexes but also approximates the surface law discussed in section 15.4.2.

The above regression analysis can be confirmed using the MINITAB ANCOVA command as follows;

```
MTB > ANCOVA C21 = C10
SUBC > COVARIATE C22;
SUBC > MEANS C10.
```

FACTOR	LEVELS	VALUES	
SEX	2	0	1

ANALYSIS OF COVARIANCE FOR LN(PPOPT)

SOURCE	DF	ADJSS	MS	F	P
COVARIATES	1	0.6032	0.6032	36.50	0.000
SEX	1	0.2426	0.2426	14.68	0.000
ERROR	78	1.2890	0.0165		
TOTAL	80	5.1859			

COVARIATE	COEFF	STDEV	T-VALUE	P
LN(LLV)	0.6256	0.104	6.042	0.000

ADJUSTED MEANS

SEX	N	LN(PPOPT)
1	47	6.5928
2	34	6.7745

Simply be taking the anti-logarithms of the two adjusted means above, the difference between the female (730) and male (875) peak power output results are obtained (adjusted for differences in lean leg volume). Note that if we divide these two adjusted means by the mean lean leg volume for all 81 subjects, given by 5.97 (1), raised to the power b = 0.6256, i.e. $5.97^{0.6256} = 3.058$ we obtain the mean power function ratio standards for the female, 239 (W $l^{-0.6256}$), and male subjects, 286 (W $l^{-0.6256}$), as derived earlier.

REFERENCES

Åstrand, P. O. and Rodahl, K. (1986) *Textbook of Work Physiology*, 3rd edn, McGraw-Hill, New York.

Jakeman, P. M., Winter, E. M. and Doust, J. (1994) A review of research in sports physiology. *Journal of Sports Sciences*, **12**, 33–60.

Minitab Inc. (1989) *MINITAB Reference Manual*, Minitab, Philadelphia.

Nevill, A. M. (1994) The need to scale for differences in body size and mass: an explanation of Kleiber's 0.75 exponent. *Journal of Applied Physiology*, **77**, 2870–3.

Nevill, A. M. and Holder, R. L. (1994) Modelling maximum oxygen uptake – a case-study in non-linear regression model formulation and comparison. *Applied Statistics*, **43**, 653–66.

Nevill, A. M., Ramsbottom, R. and Williams, C. (1992a) Scaling physiological measurements for individuals of different body size. *European Journal of Applied Physiology*, **65**, 110–17.

Nevill, A. M., Ramsbottom, R., Williams, C. and Winter, E. M. (1992b) Scaling individuals of different body size. *Journal of Sports Sciences*, **9**, 427–8.

Norusis, M. J. (1992) *SPSS for Windows Advanced Statistics Release 5*, SPSS, Chicago.

Schmidt-Nielsen, K. (1984) *Scaling: Why is Animal Size so Important?* Cambridge University Press, Cambridge.

Sholl, D. (1948) The quantitative investigation of the vertebrate brain and the applicability of allometric formulae to its study. *Proceedings of the Royal Society Series B*, **35**, 243–57.

Snedecor, G. W. and Cochran, W. G. (1980) *Statistical Methods*, 7th edn, Iowa State Press, Ames.

Tabachnick, B. G. and Fidell, L. S. (1989) *Using Multivariate Statistics*, HarperCollins, New York.

Tanner, J. M. (1949) Fallacy of per-weight and per-surface area standards and their relation to spurious correlation. *Journal of Applied Physiology*, **2** 1–15.

Tanner, J. M. (1964) *The Physique of the Olympic Athlete*. George, Allen and Unwin, London.

Tanner, J.M. (1989) *Foetus into Man*, 2nd edn, Castlemead Publications, Ware.

Winter, E. M. (1992) Scaling: partitioning out differences in size. *Pediatric Exercise Science*, **4** 296–301.

Winter, E. M. and Maughan, R. J. (1991) Strength and cross-sectional area of the quadriceps in men and women. *Journal of Physiology*, **43S**, 175P.

Winter, E. M., Brookes, F. B. C. and Hamley, E. J. (1991) Maximal exercise performance and lean leg volume in men and women. *Journal of Sports Sciences*, **9**, 3–13.

APPENDIX: RELATIONSHIPS BETWEEN UNITS OF ENERGY, WORK, POWER AND SPEED

Table A.1 Energy and work units

1 joule[a] (J)	=	1 Newton-metre (Nm)
1 kilojoule (kJ)	=	1000 J
	=	0.23889 kcal
1 megajoule (MJ)	=	1000 kJ
1 kilocalorie (kcal)	=	4.186 kJ = 426.8 kg-m

[a]The joule is the SI unit for work and represents the application of a force of 1 newton (N) through a distance of 1 metre. A newton is the force producing an acceleration of 1 metre per second every second ($1\ m\ s^{-2}$) when it acts on 1 kg.

Table A.2 Relationships between various power units

	W	$kcal\ min^{-1}$	$kJ\ min^{-1}$	$kgm\ min^{-1}$
1 watt (W)[a]	1.0	0.014	0.060	6.118
1 kcal min^{-1}	69.77	1.0	4.186	426.78
1 kJ min^{-1}	16.667	0.2389	1.0	101.97
1 kgm min^{-1}	0.1634	0.00234	0.00981	1.0

[a] The watt is the SI unit for power and is equivalent to $1\ J\ s^{-1}$.

Table A.3 Conversion table for units of speed

$km\ h^{-1}$	$m\ s^{-1}$	mph
1	0.28	0.62
2	0.56	1.24
3	0.83	1.87
4	1.11	2.49
5	1.39	3.11
6	1.67	3.73
7	1.94	4.35
8	2.22	4.98
9	2.50	5.60
10	2.78	6.22

Index

Abdominal skinfold 23
Aerobic capacity, *see* Maximal oxygen uptake
Age, *see* Maturation
Allometric relationships, *see* Scaling
Alveolar ventilation
  computation 166
  definition and relationship to dead space 148, 166–7
Anaerobic capacity, *see* Maximal intensity exercise
Anaerobic threshold
  in children 284
  determination 288–9
  in McArdle's disease 150
  and ventilatory threshold 150
Ankle range of motion
  dorsiflexion 139–40
  plantarflexion 140–1
Anthropometer 99
Archimedes Principle 8
Arm girth
  upper arm girth 29
    for somatotype 38
Astrand–Rhyming test 202–3
Axilla skinfold 22

Balance
  at adolescent growth spurt 280
  as a component of physical fitness 53, 64, 66
Basal metabolic rate, *see* Metabolic rate
Biceps skinfold 24
Biepicondylar humerus breadth 30, 38
Biepicondylar femur breadth 31, 38
Bimalleolar breadth 31
Bioelectrical impedance analysis
  basic principles 10–11
  equations for predicting fat-free mass 28
  error in predicting fat-free mass 12
  recommended procedures 12–13, 27–8
  resistance index 12
  and total body water 264
Bistyloideus breadth 31
Blood lactate
  and anaerobic threshold 288–9
  after maximal intensity exercise 242–3
  calibration of Fluorimeter readings 242
  in children 284
  and exercise intensity prescription 225–6
  interpretation of Wingate Test data 243
  in McArdle's patients 150
  as a measure of anaerobic metabolism 252–3
  and relationship to running economy 205
  and ventilatory threshold 150–1
Body composition analysis 5–33
  in children 281–3
  definition and levels of organization 5–8
  evidence from cadaver studies 8
  validity of techniques 8
Body density
  measurement by hydrodensitometry 8–10
  method of hydrodensitometry 16–19
Body mass index
  in children 281
  historical development and interpretation 13–14
  method of determination 25–6
  relationship with lean and fat components 13
Bohr's formula, for computation of dead space 166–7
Bone
  assessment of bone mass 15–16
  density for body composition analysis 9
Bruce treadmill protocol 288

Calf girth 29, 38
Calf skinfold
  medial 30
  posterior 25
Carbon dioxide production 185–6
Cervical lordosis 96
Cheek skinfold 21, 22
Chin skinfold 21–2
Convection in thermoregulation 260
Core temperature, description and measurement sites 264–5

Dehydration and overhydration, effects on performance 263–4
Dead space volume
  definition 148
  effects of exercise 148
  effects of snorkelling 148
  practical assessment 166–7
Densitometry
  assumptions 9
  density of fat-free mass, bone tissue and fat 9–10
  error of estimation of percentage body fat 9–10
  method 16–19
  principles of assessing body composition 8–10
Douglas Bag technique 178–85
  for measurement of resting metabolic rate 189–90

Economy of running
  in elite versus recreational runners 205–8
  general principles of assessment 204
  practical measurement of 213–14
  relationship with oxygen uptake 204
  significance 203–4
Efficiency
  of cycling 217, 271–2
  general definitions 208–9
  gross, net, apparent and delta efficiency 209
  and heat loss 265–66
  of loaded running 209–11, 214–17
  of muscle 209
  of stepping 217–18
  of whole body 209
Elbow extension range of motion 126–7
Elbow flexion range of motion 126–7

Electromyography 107–8
Energy expenditure
  calculation for exercise prescription 224
  daily assessment of 192–3
  measurement of 190–1
  proforma for recording activities 193
  of selected activities 191–2
Energy intake 193–4
  example of 24 hour record sheet 194
Eurofit Test
  British norms 292–4
  components 64–6
  development of 53
  interpretation of results 66–8
  proforma for recording data 67
  reference values for 14 year old 65–6
Evaporative heat loss in thermoregulation 260
Exercise intensity prescription 221–6
  from blood lactate 225–6
  conceptual framework 221–2
  determination for running and cycling 223–4
  from heart rate 224–5
  and preferred pedalling rate 224
Expiratory reserve volume 153, 165

Fat-free mass
  see also Body composition assessment 6
Fat patterning 11
Flexibility
  as a component of health-related fitness 64
  and development of the sit and reach test 116
  measurement instruments 116–18
  see also Joint range of motion 115–44
Forced expiratory volume
  and body position 161
  and circadian variation 161
  definition 158
  effects of age, sex and race 161–2
  prediction equations for 153–5
  as a proportion of forced vital capacity 158–9
  on a Vitalograph spirometer 159
Forced mid-expiratory flow
  rate 158
  time 159
Forearm girth 29
Forearm pronation range of motion 127–8
Forearm skinfold 30
Forearm supination range of motion 128
Frankfort plane 25–6
Functional residual capacity 153
  factors influencing 156

Gas volume conversion from ambient to standard conditions 181–2
Goniometry
  general guidelines 120–1
  instrumentation 107, 116–18, 133
  for joint range of motion measurement 116–19
  for posture assessment 101–2
Growth
  and adolescent growth spurt 280
  applications of growth data 53–4
  confidence intervals 54
  data curve fitting techniques 55
  definition 51
  evaluation and interpretation 56–8
  and gender differences 278–9
  and lung function 147–8, 162
  reference values for height 54–8
  sampling techniques 54–5
  use of parental height 57–8

Haldane transformation
  see also Douglas Bag technique 181–5
Hamstring range of motion 132–4
Health-related physical fitness, *see* Physical fitness testing
Height, *see* Stature
Hip abduction measurement 135
Hip adduction measurement 135–6
Hip extension measurement 134–5
Hip flexion measurement 131, 134
Hip girth measurement 27
Hip lateral rotation measurement 136–7
Hip medial rotation measurement 136–7
Hip range of motion 131–7

Iliocristal skinfold 23
Inspiratory reserve volume 153, 165
Isokinetic dynamometry
  assessment of muscle function 83–8
  general principles and applications 80
  passive and active systems 80
  and peak power output 251
  reciprocal muscle group ratios 81
  for testing strength in children 290
  velocity-specific adaptations 81

Joint range of motion
  data proforma 122–3
  factors influencing 120, 141–3
  measurement procedures 121–41
  measurement techniques, *see* individual joints
  possible interpretation of angles 119
  standards for men and women 142–3

Knee extension range of motion 138
Knee flexion range of motion 137–8
Knee lateral rotation 139
Knee medial rotation 138–9
Kyphometer, for posture assessment 100–2

Lactic acid, *see* Blood lactate
Lean body mass
  definition 6
  as a predictor of basal metabolic rate 178
  see also Body composition analysis
Leg length
  and balance considerations in children 280
  measurement for posture assessment 111–12
  in relation to lung function 161
  to trunk ratio 161
Load optimization procedures, for Wingate Test
  historical perspective 244
  comparison to Wingate data 246–8
  and pedalling rate 244–6
  practical description 244–9
  suggested loads relative to body mass 247
Logarithmic transformation of data, *see* Scaling
Lumbar lordosis 96
Lung function 147–74
  at altitude 149, 162–3
  in arm and leg exercise 151–2
  in divers 163
  post exercise changes in 152
  pulmonary ventilation 147–50
  resting flow rates and volumes 152–67
Lung volumes
  and circadian variation 161
  and effect of anthropometric factors 161–2

effects of body position 161
measurement during exercise 167–9
measurement during rest 152–60, 164–7
prediction equations 153–5
typical spirometer reading 156

Maturation
age at menarche 58–9
dental age 59
gender differences 278–9
levels and methods of assessment 58–63
morphological age 59
percentage of predicted height 59
skeletal age 59–62
see also Growth
Maximal heart rate, measurement and prediction 224
Maximal intensity exercise
and anaerobic metabolism 252–3
conceptual framework 237–8
historical development 238
and isokinetic systems 251
and multiple sprints 252
and non-motorized treadmill 251–2
and the Wingate Test 239–51
see also Wingate Test
Maximal oxygen uptake
adjusting for differences in size 199–200
assessment in children 283–4, 286–8
criteria for reaching 200–2
definition and relevance 197–8
direct method 211–13
effects of age, sex and size 198–200
expression per unit mass, height 199
in relation to skeletal age 284
submaximal methods 201–3
test protocol guidelines 201–2
Maximal voluntary ventilation
description 157–8
training adaptations 157–8
measurement and prediction of 165–6
at rest and during exercise 157
McArdle's syndrome, *see* Ventilatory threshold
Mean skin temperature 265
Metabolic equivalent (MET)
to calculate energy expenditure 192, 224
definition 224
Metabolic rate
definition and conditions 175
effect of thyroxine 262
effects of age, sex and size 176
in heat balance equation 260
measurement by Douglas bag 189–90
prediction of 176–8
specific dynamic effect 175
Motor unit, innervation, classification and activation 75–6
Movement analysis systems 106–8
Muscle fibre type 75–6
Muscle cross-sectional area
and relationship to strength 15, 82–3
and strength in men and women 82–3
Muscle function
basic structure 75
concentric, eccentric, isometric 76–7
effects of sex and age 82–3
force–length relationship 77–8, 238
force–velocity relationship 77–8
functional components 77
moment and joint velocity 79–81
pennation angle 77
training adaptation 75–6
Muscle mass estimation
anthropometric procedures 28–30
basic principles and derivation 14–15
geometric assumptions 15
prediction equations 28–9
by urinary creatinine excretion 83
Muscular force measurements
by isokinetic dynamometry 81–8
by isometric dynamometry 83
and maximum isometric moment 88–90
and measurement of moment arm 83–4
and moment arm 79–81
relevance of joint position 83, 88–90

Obesity, definition by percentage body fat 19
Obstructive ventilatory defect 164–5
Oxygen uptake
in children versus adults 206–8
during loaded running 215–16
mass specific oxygen cost 207
measurement by Douglas bag 178–85
prediction equations 222–3
prediction from ventilatory volume 168–9
versus age in children 280
weight corrected oxygen uptake 205–6
see also Maximal oxygen uptake

Patella skinfold 24
Peak expiratory flow rates
and circadian variation 161
definition 158
prediction in children 155
Pectoral skinfold 21–2
Percentage maximal heart rate reserve method 225, 230, 231
Performance related fitness, *see* Physical fitness testing
Physical fitness, conceptual framework and components of 52–3
Physical fitness testing
components of test batteries 53, 64–5
Eurofit test norms 293–5
health-and performance-related 64
methodological considerations 63
reasons for testing in children 277
Physical work capacity at heart rate 170 test 203
Ponderal index 13, 40–1
Posture 95–112
Posture measurement
angle of trunk inclination 101, 103
and angles of kyphosis and lordosis 100–1
data proforma 111–12
of leg length 111
by photographic techniques 102–6
proclive and declive angles 101, 102–3
of sitting position 110
of spinal length curvature and shrinkage 99, 110–11
of standing position 109–10
of vertebral shape 101, 103
Pulmonary diffusing capacity
definition of 159
determinants of 160
effects of exercise and body position 160
at high altitude 163
measurement of 170–2
prediction from surface area 160
Pulmonary ventilation
for calculating oxygen consumption 181–2

Pulmonary ventilation (*cont.*)
  definition 147
  during arm and leg exercise 151–2
  effects of age, sex and size 147–8
  effects of training 150–1
  measurement of 167–9
  relationship with oxygen uptake 148–50

Quetelet Index 13, 52, 81

Radiation, in thermoregulation 260
Rating of Perceived Exertion
  analysis of estimation and production data 231–2
  in children 228, 287
  development of the measurement scales 226–7
  measurement during a production protocol 230–1
  measurement during an estimation protocol 229–30
  to quantify and regulate exercise intensity 227–8
  reliability and timing of measurement 228
  and specificity of exercise 227–8
Ratio standard
  for body composition analysis 13–14
  problems with 321–2
  use and underlying assumptions of 84–5
  see also Scaling
Rectal temperature, *see* Core temperature
Regression, linear equations
  in body composition assessment 20–1
  to calculate exercise intensity 232
  to calculate loaded running efficiency 216
  to convert fluorimeter readings to lactate 242–3
  for estimation of metabolic rate 177–8
  for estimation of oxygen uptake 204, 222–3
  general principles and method 308–10
  in lung function assessment 153–5, 163–4
Residual volume
  definition 156, 157
  effects of age, body position 157, 161
  measurement by nitrogen dilution 9, 17–18
  post exercise changes in 157
  prediction equations in adults 18, 154
  prediction in children 155
Respiratory exchange ratio, *see* Respiratory quotient 189
Respiratory frequency
  in adults and children 149–50
  in arm versus leg exercise 151–2
  response to endurance training 151
Respiratory quotient
  for carbohydrate, fat and protein 186–7
  and energy equivalents per litre oxygen 188–9
  for non-protion 187
Resting metabolic rate, *see* Metabolic rate
Restrictive ventilatory defect 164–5

Scaling techniques 321–35
  with allometric techniques 325–8
  with analysis of covariance 323–5
  oxygen uptake in children and adults 205–8
  with power function ratio standards 328–34
  power output for differences in size 243–4
  rationale for 321
Scoliometer 101
Scoliosis 103–4
Shoulder abduction range of motion 125
Shoulder extension range of motion 123–4
Shoulder flexion range of motion 121–3
Shoulder horizontal adduction 126
Shoulder lateral rotation range of motion 124
Shoulder medial rotation range of motion 124–5
Shuttle run test, to estimate maximal oxygen uptake 203, 252, 283, 289
Sit and reach test 64, 116–17
Sitting height, for lung function prediction 155, 162
Skeletal age
  and maximal oxygen uptake 284
  and relationship to strength and power 279–80
Skeletal age assessment
  principles and techniques 59–60
  by wrist and hand radiography (TWII system) 60–2, 68
Skeletal mass estimation 15–16, 30–1
Skinfold measurements
  in children 20–1, 281–3
  limitations and assumptions 10–11
  sites 21–5
  techniques and equations 19–21
  see also individual sites
Somatotyping 35–50
  the 13 categories 43–6
  anthropometric and photoscopic measurements 37–8
  conceptual framework and components 35–6
  equations 42
  Heath Carter Somatotype Rating Form 40
  manual calculation of 39–42
  methods of comparison 43–9
  migratory distance 37
  relevance of 38–9
  Somatochart 37, 45–6
  Somatotype Attitudinal Distance (SAD) 37, 47–8
Spinal length
  and diurnal variation 108
  and intervertebral fluid dynamics 108–9
Spirometer, characteristics 153, 155–6
Standard error of estimate
  for bioelectrical impedance analysis 12
  in lung function 153–5, 163–4
  for predicting maximal oxygen uptake 203
  for predicting muscle mass 14
Statistical methods
  classification of variables and data 297–8
  correlation techniques 303–8
  F distribution table 317
  F table 318
  frequency tables 298–9
  histograms and frequency polygons 299–300
  independent t-test 311–12
  linear regression 308–10
  Mann-Whitney Test 312–13
  Mann-Whitney U table 319
  mean, median, mode 300–1
  normal versus skewed distribution 299–300
  one and two tailed tests 312
  Pearson's Product Moment Correlation 305–7
  range, mean, deviation, variance, standard deviation 301–2
  related *t*-test 313–14
  Spearman's Rank Correlation 307–8

t-table 316
Wilcoxon T table 319
Wilcoxon test 314–15
z-scores 302–3
see also Scaling
Stature
methods of measurement 25–6
reference values for growth assessment 54–7
standards for British boys 56
standards for British girls 57
see also Growth
Strength
as a component of physical fitness 64
effects of sex and age 83
and muscle cross-sectional area 15, 82–3
versus chronological and skeletal age in children 279–80, 289–90
Subscapular skinfold 23
Suprailiac skinfold 23
Suprailium skinfold 23
Surface area
estimation of 176–7
relationship with BMR 176
and surface law 328
Sweating
and dehydration 262–3
and electrolyte loss 263
and weight loss 263

Temperature
and circadian variation 264
common sites for measurement 264–5
control in the body 260–2
core and skin measurement 264–5
effects of cold environment 266–8
effects of cold water immersion 268
and heat stroke 268
and the menstrual cycle 264
ranges in the body 259
see also Thermoregulation
Thermoregulation 259–76
effects of extreme cold 261
heat balance equation 260, 274–5
heat loss through the head 261
physiological mechanisms 260–2
and pilomotor reflex 261
and shivering 261
and specific heat and human tissue 259
see also Temperature
Thigh girth 29
Thigh skinfold 24
Thoracic Kyphosis 96
Tidal volume 149, 153
in arm versus leg exercise 151–2
effects of endurance training 150
maximal tidal volume 168
practical assessment 165–6
Total lung capacity
definition 156
in diseased and trained adults 156
prediction equation for 154
Triceps skinfold 24

Ventilatory equivalent
at altitude 148
in arm versus leg exercise 151–2
definition 148
practical assessment 167–9
specification of training response 151–2
values in adults and children 148
Ventilatory threshold
and anaerobic threshold 288–9
and blood lactate 150
in McArdle's disease 150–1
and percentage maximal oxygen uptake 150–1
Vertebral angles
angle of thoracic Kyphosis 100
angle of thoraco lumbar junction 102
angle of trunk inclination 101, 103
proclive and declive angles 101, 102, 103
Vertebral column
curvature of 96–7
distribution of loading 96–7
mobility of regions of 96–7
pain and injury 97
and relationship to upright posture 95–6
sexual dimorphism of 98
Vital capacity
definition 156
effects of body position 157, 161
effects of training 156–7
post exercise changes in 152
prediction equations for 153–5
see also Forced vital capacity

Waist girth measurement 26
Waist to hip ratio 14
methods and interpretation 26–7
recommended values for men and women 14
Wingate test
in children 290–1
correction procedures 249–51
data logging for flywheel 240–1
interpretation of data 243–4
layout of equipment 240
load optimization 244–9
post exercise blood lactate 242–3
power function ratios 244
practical assessment 239–44
Wrist extension assessment 130–1
Wrist flexion assessment 129
Wrist radial deviation 130
Wrist ulnar deviation 131